TRIBES AND CASTES OF ASSAM

TRIBES AND CASTES OF ASSAM

Anthropology and Sociology

Sipra Sen

GYAN PUBLISHING HOUSE
NEW DELHI-110002

Tribes and Caste of Assam
(Anthropology and Sociology)

ISBN: 978-81-212-0572-6

Price: ` 1500

Reprinted 2015 in India by
Gyan Publishing House
23, Main Ansari Road, Daryaganj,
New Delhi - 110002
Phones : 23282060, 23261060
Fax : (011) 23285914
E-mail: books@gyanbooks.com
Website: gyanbooks.com

Printed at: G. Print Process, Delhi

DEDICATED WITH LOVE AND TEARS TO THE MEMORY OF
MY BROTHER LATE SRI DILIP RANJAN SEN, INSTRUCTOR,
PVTC SAKTI ASHRAM, KOKRAJHAR, ASSAM
WHO LEFT FOR HIS HEAVENLY ABODE WHILE
IN SERVICE ON 9TH APRIL, 1997 WHOSE HONESTY,
HUMANITY AND IDEALISM INSPIRED ME

Contents

PART-III

Appendices

Key to Bibliography

All the references have been alphabetically arranged in chronological order with reference to each author.

For books, the author's name is followed by year, title of reference, place of publication and publisher's name with total number of pages.

For journals, the author's name is followed by year, title of the article and name of the journal in which it was published, volume, number, month and page numbers.

In the case of newspapers, the author's name or the newspaper's name is followed by year, title of the article, name of the newspaper and date of publication, page number and column number.

Most of the references are in English but Assamese, Bodo, Hindi, Bengali and other publications have also been included in this bibliography. Publications other than those in English are mentioned in brackets (in *A.*), (in *Bodo*), (in *Karbi*), (in *G*), (in *F*), (in *Hajong*), (in *Tai-Ahom*), (in *H.),* (in *B.),* etc. Here "*A*" means Assamese, *Bodo* means Bodo language, *Karbi* means Karbi language, "*G*" means German language, "*F*" means French language, *Hajong* means Hajong language, *Tai-Ahom* means Tai-Ahom language, "*H*" means Hindi, "*B*" means Bengali language and so on. After completion of each serial number of references a short theme or keynote is inserted within brackets ( ).

For books, journals, etc., I have marked against a few serial numbers as "n.p.", i.e. "not published." Similarly "n.d." indicates "no date," i.e. date of publication is not available in the book, journal, etc. The question mark "?" means "doubtful" about author, date of publication, etc., of the reference. "Sr" means Senior and "Jr" means Junior. "*Ed.*" means Editor, "*Jt*" means joint and "*Jr*" means "journal."

List of Illustrations

List of Tables

Preface

The literature on Assam and its tribes and castes are scattered in several monographs, journals, edited books, reports, proceedings, newspapers, weeklies, etc. There is an urgent need to bring together all the references of main publication works of this State and its people to provide a base for future research work. This book will facilitate macro-and micro-level researches on tribes and castes of Assam.

From this book, one can get an idea about the region and people regarding geography, flora, fauna, climate, religion, history, districts, ethnology of people of Assam and almost all the references of published and unpublished research materials which have been done so far on Assam and its people. This bibliographical book will indicate the gaps of work in the field of research and hopes that it will assist to fill the gaps and select future research projects on Assam and its people in various disciplines.

It covers all aspects of—Sociology, Ethnology, Archaeology, Linguistics, Folklore, Arts, Culture, Social Literature, Social History, Social Psychology, Women's Studies, Customary Laws, Religion, Demography, Medical Sciences, Public Health, etc. It describes Assam's twenty-three districts. Thus, this presents a multidimensional picture of the land, its people and their aspirations. To avoid making the size too unwieldy, I shall bring out some more volumes in the near future on different disciplines of Social Sciences about this State. For that, some selective publications other than Sociology and Anthropology have not been inserted here. Readers may get those in my forthcoming volumes on Assam.

As per Lila Gogoi (1986: 40-41) *Brahmi* words were used in the earlier days of Assamese language. In thirteenth century it was separated to form an independent Assamese vocabulary. However, we found written notice on Ahom pillars of Sadiya, old written documents of seventh century on Sanchi bark and copper-plate inscriptions. A few *Sanchi* bark manuscripts of *Bhagavat Purana, Gita Govinda,* etc., and manuscripts of paintings are found today in museums. Manuscripts of Sri Sri Sankardeva and his disciple Madhavdeva about history and culture of 15th and 16th centuries are available in original in *Barpeta Namghar*. The *Bible* was first translated into Assamese language in printing form by using Bengali words in 1813 by the missionaries of Srirampur.

Until some years ago, the whole North-East India was referred to as Assam. It is now divided into seven States and popularly known as *seven sisters* of North-East India. Till 1962, Meghalaya, Nagaland and Mizoram were districts of Assam. The Nagaland State was born in 1963, Meghalaya in 1972 and Mizoram was separated from Assam and became a Union Territory on 21st January, 1972 and it became a State on 20th February, 1987. Arunachal Pradesh which was earlier called *NEFA* (North-East Frontier Agency) was made a Union Territory and named Arunachal Pradesh on 21st January, 1972 and got its statehood on 20th February, 1987. Manipur and Tripura, former Princely States, were Union Territories until they got full-fledged status of States on 21st January, 1972.

The Assamese live in Assam, Meghalaya, Mizoram, Arunachal Pradesh, Nagaland and some parts of Manipur, Tripura and West Bengal. The Bengalis of Assam mainly live in Barak valley of Assam. Some of them live in Brahmaputra valley, West Bengal, Manipur, Meghalaya, Tripura, Arunachal Pradesh and Mizoram. The separation of Burma from India in 1935 and the partition of India in 1947 had badly affected and created a significant change in geographical boundary which caused economical, political and social changes in the life and culture of the people of North-East India.

In the initial stage, the systematic studies on Assam and its people were undertaken in English, mainly by the British administrators, surveyors, defence personnel, Christian missionaries, scientists and travellers. Britishers like G.E. Westmacott (1835), S.F. Hannay (1838), W. Robinson (1841), B.H. Hodson (1847), H. Brian (1849), E.T. Dalton (1851, 1872, 1895), R. Stewart (1855), H.M. Elliet (1869), J. Lubbock (1867), H. Beverley (1872), S.E. Peal (1872, 1879), C. Brownlow (1874), G.H. Damant (1875), W.W. Hunter (1879), H.W. Rowney (1882), W. Plowden (1883), E. Stack (1883), S. Endle (1884), C.A. Soppit (1885), J. Avery (1887), E.C.S. Baker (1892), J.D. Anderson (1895), W.B. Brown (1895), H. Balfour (1897) and many others published their reports, tour diaries, notes and accounts, articles, etc. on Assam and its people in the shape of handbooks, census reports, district gazetteers, proceedings, journals, and so on before these, there was a Persian book by Mohammed Cazim which was translated into English in 1792 by H. Vansittart. It seems that, from the Britishers we have got some earlier recorded systematic documents on Assam from the year 1792 and before that, there were no recorded English documents on Assam and its people. In 19th century probably no Indian scholars published any document in English on Assam and its people except S.C. Mitra (1846), Anandaram Dhekial Phukan (1854, 1955), Jagaram Barua (1875), Jogesh Chandra Dutta (1891), Mahendra Nath Ghose (1896), etc.

There are, however, a few Assamese and Bengali manuscripts of 19th century written by Haliram Dhekial Phukan (1829), Gunabhiram Barua (1876, 1880, 1855), Indibar Barua (1889), Ram Kumar Vidyaratna (1880), etc. The formation of Kamarupa Anusandhan Samity in April, 1912 helped to promote scientific reasearch. *Orunodoi*, an Assamese magazine, came out in 1846 and was in circulation for some years.

Before Independence several ethnographic works had been attempted by a good number of British scholars, specially L.A. Waddell (1901), P.R.T. Gurdon (1904, 1913), B.C. Allen (1902, 1905, 1906, 1908), E.A. Gait (1906), E. Stack (1908), C.J. Lyall (1908), S. Endle (1911), J. Shakespear (1911), L.W. Shakespear (1914), J.C. Brown (1914), H.G. Denneby (1927), J.C. Mill (1929), J.H. Hutton (1946), etc. In pre-Independence period a few Indian scholars had published books on Assam and its people. They are R.C. Roy (1902), Harmohan Sinha (1903), Benudhar Rajkhowa (1905), Padmanath Gohain Barua (1907), Hemchandra Goswami (1907), Kalipada Mitra (1928), K.L. Barua (1938), B.K. Barua (1941, 1942), etc. All their works are excellent and helpful.

After Independence several works have been written on Assam and its people by Praphulladatta Goswami, P.C. Choudhury, Pramod Chandra Bhattacharya, Banikanta Kakati, Hem Barua, Lila Gogoi, Birendranath Datta, S. Barkataki, Maheswar Neog, M.C. Goswami, A.C. Bhagabati, B.M. Das, P.B. Das, M.N. Phookan, T.C. Sharma, R.K. Kar, K.C. Mahanta, B.N. Bordoloi, G.C. Sharma Thakur, P.C. Saikia, P.D. Saikia, Dipali Ghosh Danda, Birinchi Kr. Barua and many others. But very few insider tribals of Assam have carried out the work. Though they are now gradually publishing their works on Assam, the major basic works have come out from the pens of Britishers, Assamese and Bengalese.

There are, however, four excellent books entitled *History of Assam* by E.A. Gait (1906), *The Background of Assamese Culture* by R.M. Nath (1948), *The History of Civilization of the People of Assam to the Twelfth Century A.D.* by P.C. Choudhury (1959) and *Kacharer Itibritta* (in Bengali) by Upendra Ch. Guha (*c.* 1921, reprinted in 1971) where some detailed accounts on Assam are inserted and all these systematic original information are rather rare to come by now. One can use these authentic books as a dependable basic source-books to know the past history of Assam and its people. Some other books entitled *Descriptive Ethnology of Bengal* by E.T. Dalton (1872), *The Tribes of the Brahmaputra Valley* by L.A. Waddell (1901), *A Statistical Account of Assam, Vol. I and II* by W.W. Hunter (1879), Provincial Gazetteer: Eastern Bengal and Assam by B.C. Allen *et al* (*c.* 1908), *The Red River and the Blue Hills* by Hem Barua (1962), *Assamiya Biswakosh, 1st Part (in Assamese)* edited by Rajanikanta Dev Sharma (1987), etc., have thrown sufficient light on many important aspects of Assam and its people. The following publications namely *The*

Mikirs by C.J. Lyall (1908), *The Kacharis* by S. Endle (1911), *The Rabhas* by B.M. Das (1960), *The Dimasa* by Dipali Ghosh Danda (1978), *The Lalungs* by N.K. Syamchaudhuri and M.M. Das (1973), *The Mishing (Miris) of Assam* by Jatin Mipin (1992), *The Mishings of Brahmaputra Valley* by J.S. Bhandari (1992), *The Tai Ahom Religion and Custom* by Padmeswar Gogoi (1976), *The Mataks and their kingdom* by S. Dutta (1985), *Semsa* by Dipali Ghosh Danda and Sanchita Ghatak (1985), *Social Relations in an Ahom Village* by Indira Barua (1978), *A Glimpse of the Scheduled Castes and their Socio-economic Development in Assam* by Bhakta Das (1986), *Cosmogony of Caste and Social Mobility in Assam* by B.J. Dev and D.K. Lahiri (1984), *The Assamese* by A. Cantlie (1984), *The Valley in Blossom* by M. Narimattam (1988), *Assam Muslims* by B.J. Dev and D.K. Lahiri (1985), *Microevolution* by B.M. Das(1981), *Children of North-East India* edited by B.M. Das (1985), *Demographic Profile of North-East India* by S.C. Srivastava (1987), *Archaeology of the Brahmaputra Valley of Assam* by R. Dev Choudhuri (1985), *Kirata-Jana-Kriti* by S.K. Chatterjee (1951), and such others are obviously dependable books about Assam and its people. There are some more books in Assamese language, which are also excellent and very much helpful. These are: *Asamar Janajati* edited by P.C. Bhattacharya (1962), *Asamar Loka Sanskriti* by B.K. Barua (1961), *Tiwa-Samaj* by Maneswar Deuri (1983), *Tiwa Sampradayar Parichaya* compiled by AATYCS (1975), *Deuri-Chutia* by Paban Ch. Saikia (1974), *Karbi Samaj Aru Sanskritir Echerenga* by Nirmal Prava Bordoloi (1982), *Karbi Sahitya Sanskritir Ebhumuki* by Rong Bong Terang (1982), *Singpho Janagoshthi* by S. Rajkumar (1982), *Chah Bagichar Jati Janajati* by Dewram Tasa (1986), *Chah Banuar Adi Katha Aru Chamu Itihas* by N. Bora (1980), *Chah Bagichar Asamiya Sampradaya* by Sushil Kurmi (1983), *Boro Kacharir Samaj Aru Sanskriti* by Bhabendra Narzi (1966), *Asamar Manuha* edited by B.M. Das (1986), *Asamiya Nepali Samaj Aru Sanskritir Ruprekha* by Manbahadur Chetri (1983) and so on.

This book is a multidisciplinary one on Anthropology and Sociology. It covers in its bibliography almost all the important writings on tribes and castes of Assam in the pre and post-Independence period about their Culture, Acculturation, Material Culture, Agriculture, Primitive Art, Kinship, Family, Marriage, Ritual and Belief, Custom and Manner, Demonology, Superstition, Religion, Festival, Women Studies, Caste System, Folklore, Ethnography, Prehistoric Archaeology, Urban and Rural Studies, Slums, Social Hygiene and Health, Human Biology, Genetics, Human Ecology, P.T.C., Dermatoglyphics, Anthropometry, Somatology, Nutrition, Food Habit, Growth and Development, Fertility and Mortality, etc. A detailed study of this bibliography will reveal the important gaps in our knowledge about them. A large number of publications listed in this book are articles published in journals and presented in various seminars and conferences.

It is observed that ethnographic monographs are now gradually being published after Independence by young scholars. Some other types of monographic books are also published on Assam about its History, Religion, Politics, Economics, Folklore, Linguistics, Insurgency, etc. It is also observed that there are a vast number of articles and monographs published in the last three decades specially from 1980 to 1996 on ethnographical, political, historical and religious aspects by several scholars and they have had their articles published in many journals and also in edited books.

This bibliographical work indicates that a large number of studies have been done on the Bodos, Rabhas, Mishings (Miri), Kachari, Karbi, Tiwa (Lalung), Dimasa, Ahom, Matak, Koch-Rajbansi, Deori, etc. But not much work has been done on the Mech, Barman, Sonowal, Hojai, Hajong, Tai, Phakial, Aitonia, Duonia, Turung, Khamyang, Chutia, Borahi, Choudang and a few other caste groups like the Kayastha, Hira, Koch, Sarania, Madahi, Patni, Sutradhar, Jalo/Malo, Bhuimali, Jugi (Nath), Madak, Barui and many other people of this State.

The main purpose of compiling this bibliography is, however, to assist the scholars and researchers so that the anthropologists, sociologists, ethnologists, archaeologists, historians, geographers, economists, politicians, psychologists, linguists, botanists, zoologists, geologists as well as librarians may get quick and ready references about the reference-queries without wastage of their precious time. Moreover, an individual researcher may select his own research theme from this bibliography.

In this book all the maps and sketches have been drawn by myself. Several old and new records, periodicals, books, newspapers, proceedings, dissertations, etc., were consulted by me from the year 1792 onwards. I have not found it necessary to annotate the references, because, a serious scholar must read all the relevant materials by himself and cryptic annotations are rarely of much use to him. I have, however, mentioned in a nutshell the keynote or themes of some articles and books within brackets ( ) after completion of each serial numbers of references of this book. Further, I have access here to a few unpublished research reports, articles of proceedings, seminars, symposia and even dissertations, etc., along with almost all the selective published references. The preparation of bibliography is an ongoing process. I have to decide compulsorily at some point of time to stop adding entries. As a result of this, there may be some omissions of publications which have been brought out after May, 1996. In spite of my best effort a few references are incomplete as these were collected from secondary sources and could not be procured for verification. The choice before me was either to reject or to include them in this book. I chose the latter because some information is better than none. Now, if this book can be of some help to the scholars to make the tribes and castes of Assam better known and understood and in any way assist the researchers, it will give me great and real satisfaction for my hard and painstaking efforts.

I shall welcome and be grateful to the scholars if they kindly send their comments, suggestions or additional information, directly to me to improve this study in the near future. And, as far as possible, I shall acknowledge them. I do not claim that all the statements in this book are proved. I have gathered information from different sources as well as what I have seen and thought. Further, I like to mention *Swamy Handbook's* Rule No. 4(4), page 6 of 1990 about the publication. Statements made, views expressed or conclusions drawn in this book are by me alone in my own personal capacity only and do not represent the views of anybody else. In spite of my great care, if any mistake, like grammatical errors, etc., are there, I solicit the indulgence of learned scholars for the lapses.

I like to acknowledge my debt to Sri N. Kalita, TIO, Guwahati; Sri A.K. Roy, Deputy Director, E & S, Silchar; Deputy Director, E & S, Haflong; Sri K.K. Sen, Deputy Director, E & S, Tezpur; Sri. K.R. Laskar, SDSO, Marigaon; Sri Bhabananda Buragohain, SDSO, Dhemaji; Sri P.D. Gogoi, T.O., Tinsukia; Sri K.C. Chakravorty, Deputy Director, E & S, Nalbari; E & S, Dibrugarh and Mrs. A. Banerjee, Assistant Librarian of National Library, Calcutta. I am very much grateful to them for their kind cooperation and esteemed help extended to me.

In the end, I must express my deep sense of gratitude to the National Library, Calcutta; Gauhati University Library, Guwahati; and Anthropological Survey of India Library, Shillong. I like to record my debt to my brother Dr. Salil Ranjan Sen who helped me to get the entire manuscript typed and for the photographs which I have used here. Finally, I must express my respectful regards to my mother Mrs. Malati Sen for her kind help and constant encouragement at every step to complete this work. Her immense inspiration has been of untold value. Had it not been for the active inspiration, sympathetic interest and help of my mother, the work would not have accelerated to its present tempo.

Rehabari, Guwahati **Sipra Sen**

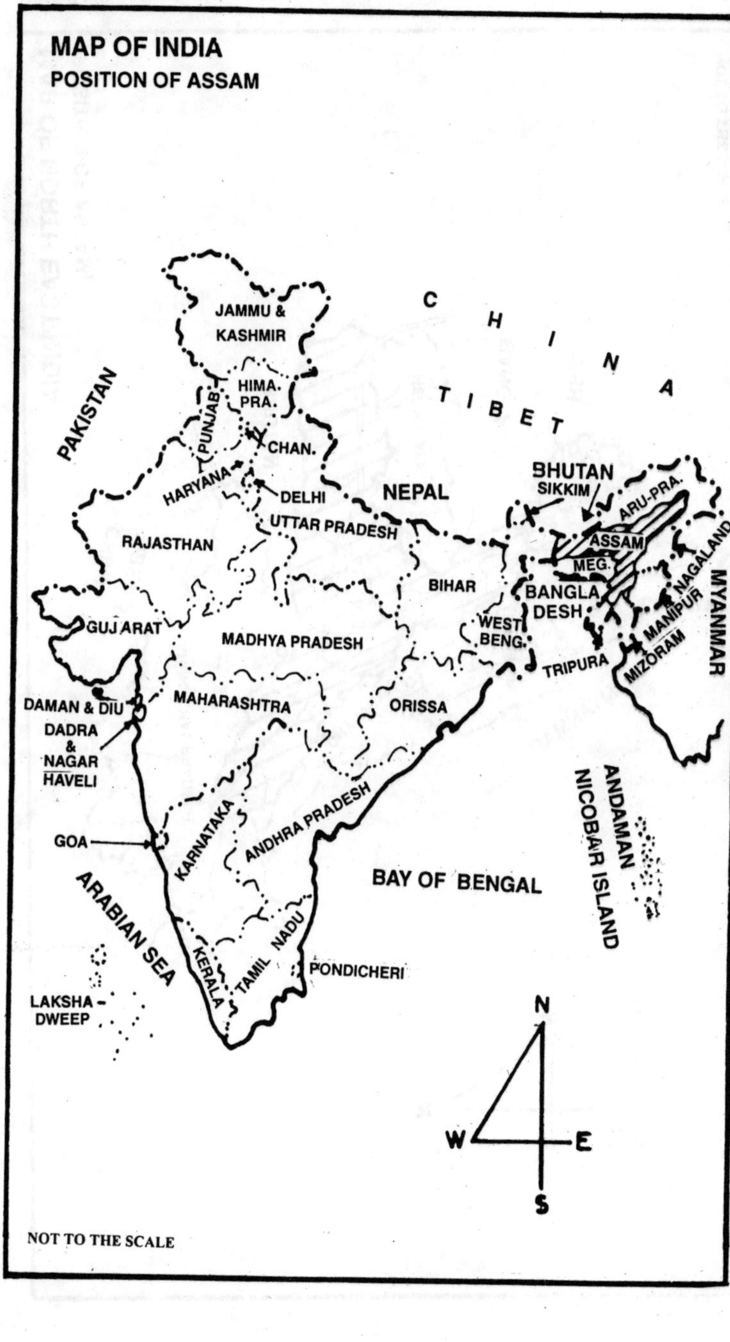
MAP OF INDIA
POSITION OF ASSAM
JAMMU & KASHMIR
HIMA. PRA.
PUNJAB
CHAN.
HARYANA
DELHI
PAKISTAN
CHINA
TIBET
NEPAL
BHUTAN
SIKKIM
ARU-PRA.
ASSAM
MEG.
NAGALAND
MANIPUR
MIZORAM
MYANMAR
BANGLA DESH
TRIPURA
WEST BENG.
BIHAR
UTTAR PRADESH
RAJASTHAN
GUJ ARAT
MADHYA PRADESH
MAHARASHTRA
ORISSA
DAMAN & DIU
DADRA & NAGAR HAVELI
GOA
KARNATAKA
ANDHRA PRADESH
TAMIL NADU
KERALA
PONDICHERI
ARABIAN SEA
BAY OF BENGAL
ANDAMAN NICOBAR ISLAND
LAKSHA-DWEEP
N
W
E
S
NOT TO THE SCALE

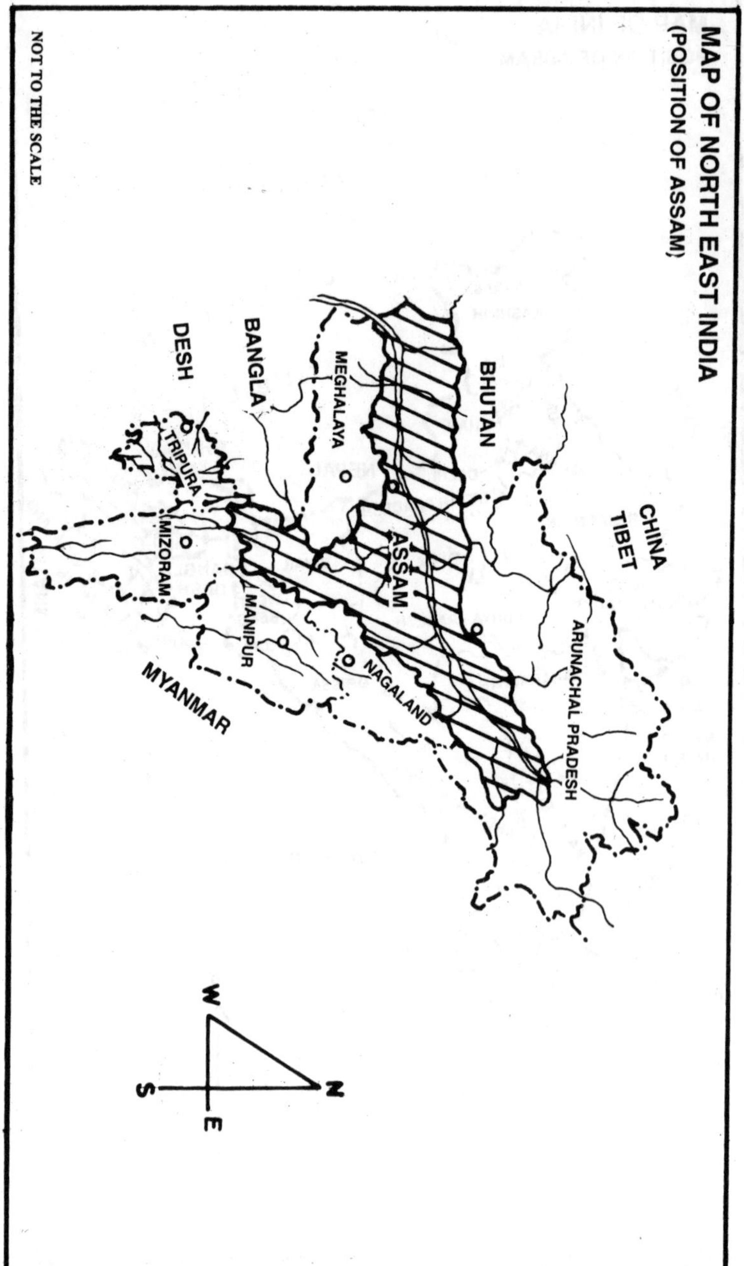
MAP OF NORTH EAST INDIA
(POSITION OF ASSAM)
CHINA
TIBET
BHUTAN
ARUNACHAL PRADESH
ASSAM
MEGHALAYA
BANGLA
DESH
TRIPURA
MIZORAM
MANIPUR
NAGALAND
MYANMAR
W
N
S
E
NOT TO THE SCALE

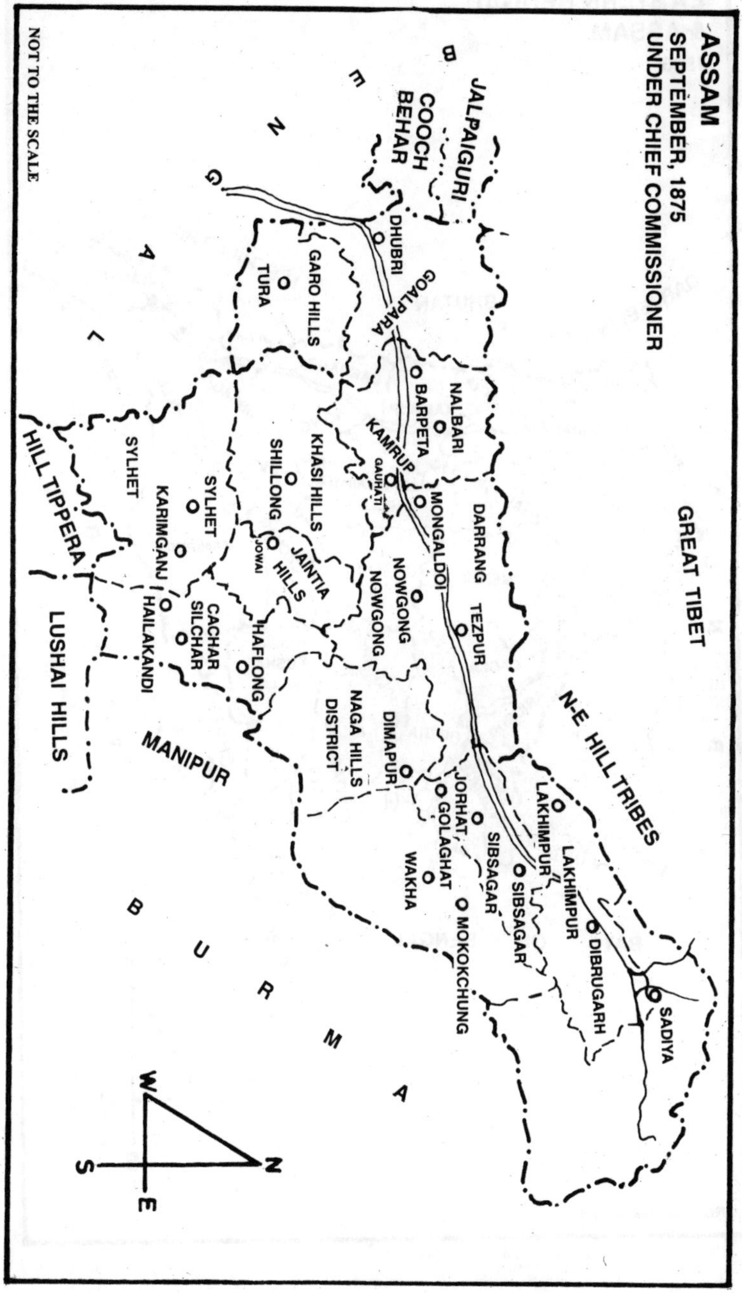
ASSAM
SEPTEMBER, 1875
UNDER CHIEF COMMISSIONER
GREAT TIBET
N-E HILL TRIBES
JALPAIGURI
COOCH BEHAR
B E N G A L
DHUBRI
GOALPARA
GARO HILLS
TURA
NALBARI
BARPETA
KAMRUP
GAUHATI
KHASI HILLS
SHILLONG
DARRANG
MONGALDOI
TEZPUR
NOWGONG
JAINTIA HILLS
JOWAI
SYLHET
KARIMGANJ
HAILAKANDI
CACHAR
SILCHAR
HAFLONG
HILL TIPPERA
LUSHAI HILLS
MANIPUR
NAGA HILLS DISTRICT
DIMAPUR
JORHAT
GOLAGHAT
WAKHA
SIBSAGAR
MOKOKCHUNG
LAKHIMPUR
DIBRUGARH
SADIYA
B U R M A
N
S
E
W
NOT TO THE SCALE

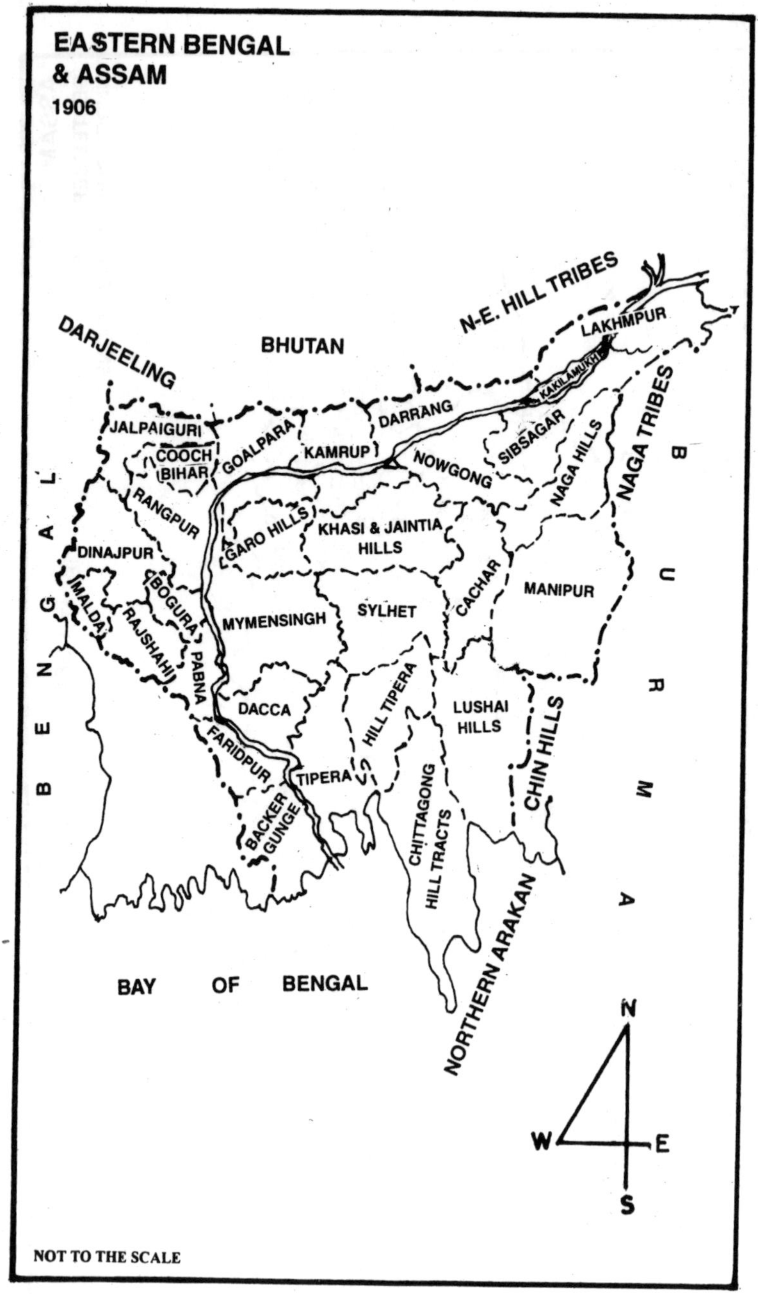
EASTERN BENGAL
& ASSAM
1906
DARJEELING
BHUTAN
N-E. HILL TRIBES
LAKHMPUR
KAKILAMUKH
DARRANG
SIBSAGAR
NAGA HILLS
NAGA TRIBES
JALPAIGURI
COOCH BIHAR
GOALPARA
KAMRUP
NOWGONG
RANGPUR
GARO HILLS
KHASI & JAINTIA HILLS
DINAJPUR
MALDA
BOGURA
RAJSHAHI
PABNA
MYMENSINGH
SYLHET
CACHAR
MANIPUR
DACCA
HILL TIPERA
LUSHAI HILLS
CHIN HILLS
FARIDPUR
TIPERA
BACKER GUNGE
CHITTAGONG HILL TRACTS
NORTHERN ARAKAN
BENGAL
BURMA
BAY OF BENGAL
N
W
E
S
NOT TO THE SCALE

1

Introduction

LAND AND PEOPLE OF ASSAM

Assam is the nerve-centre of North-Eastern Region of India. It is a paradisaical state to study Anthropology and Sociology for its colourful tribal population like Karbi, Bodo, Kachari, Chutiya, Dimasa, Mishing, Tiwa (Lalung), Rabha, Khamiyang, Phake, Turung, and castes like Brahmins, Kalita, Kaibarta, Ahom, Hira, Kumar, Muslims.

Assam has no sea coast and it is connected with the rest of India by a narrow corridor running between Bhutan and Bangladesh. This corridor is serving as a gate through which people enter North-East India. Cultural tradition of Assam, folklore, myth, legend and history, are very rich which carry traces of ancient civilization. *Bihu* dances are expressions of the joy of life which have got world-wide fame.

Geographically, Assam is a shadow of its earlier physique. Earlier the whole of North-East India was called Assam (except former princely states of Manipur and Tripura). Assam has been reduced to almost one-third of its original size. Till 1962, Nagaland, Meghalaya and Mizoram were districts of Assam. The Nagas declared themselves as independent on 14th August, 1947 (N.K. Das, 1982:45). But the first Prime Minister of India Pandit Nehru had a discussion with the leaders of the Naga people before deciding to create a separate State for them within India. Accordingly, the state Nagaland was born on 1st December, 1963. Thereafter, All Party Hill Leaders' Conference (APHLC) wanted their separate identity after Assam's Official Language Act, 1960, was introduced. Since 1965, Khasi, Jaintia and Garo Hills districts have been recognised as autonomous districts and on 21st January, 1972 Mizoram was separated from Assam to form a Union Territory and became a state on 20th February, 1987. Arunachal Pradesh, former NEFA, was constitutionally a part of Assam but not technically. For all practical purposes, it was regarded as a part of Assam and was specially administered by the Governor of Assam. In 1967, a traditional council was formed in NEFA with five ministers. On 21st January, 1972, it became a Union Territory and was renamed Arunachal Pradesh. It got its statehood as the 24th state on 20th February, 1987. Tripura and Manipur, former princely states, had entered, as a part of India on 15th October, 1949 and became Part-C States on 26th January, 1950. They were converted to Union Territories in 1956 and 1965, respectively and got their full-fledged status of States on 21st, January, 1972.

All these seven States, unitedly known as North-East India, came under a common forum, the North-East Council (NEC). The North-Eastern Areas Reorganisation Act No. 81 of 1971 was passed in the Parliament and was given the assent by the President of India on 30th December, 1971. As per this Act, NEC was formed and established at Shillong, Meghalaya, on 1st August, 1972 and was inaugurated by the then Prime Minister, Mrs. Indira Gandhi, on 7th November, 1972. NEC was constituted with the representatives of North-East States with a common Chairman. The NEC formulates regional plans to develop the North-East State Region as a whole.

Assam is the land of blue hills and dales covered with forest and luxurious vegetation, rich in minerals with the mighty Brahmaputra river flowing from east to west through the heart of the State. Perhaps, due to the beauty of North-East India, some old people of Assam say that those who comes to Assam from outside never go back, especially, without visiting goddess Kamakhya of Nilachal Hill, Guwahati. Otherwise, circumstances may compel them to come back again to Assam.

Among the States of North-East India, Assam is the land of Usha, who, as per *Mahabharata,* was enamoured of Anirudha, the prince of Dwaraka. Meghalaya, the abode of clouds, was the dreamland of Pramila. Arunachal Pradesh, where the sun rises above the snow-capped mountains was the homeland of Rukmini, daughter of Bhismaka, whose beauty enchanted Lord Krishna. Manipur, the dale of songs and dances, was the land of Chitrangada. In Nagaland, the eastern sentinel of our country, Arjuna's Ulupi was born. Tripura was the land of queen Tripura Sundari and Mizoram was the land of damsels of blue mountains and colourful river Dhaleswari (*Himalaya*, 1987:19).

1. Geography:—Assam is a frontier State of North-East India which lies on the north-eastern border of West Bengal. It lies approximately between 24°5'N-28°0'N latitudes and 89°42'E-96°0'E longitudes. It is the biggest State of North-East India with 78,438 sq. km area. (Census 1991). Assam is bounded on the north by Bhutan and Arunachal Pradesh, on the east by Arunachal Pradesh, Nagaland and Manipur, on the south by Mizoram and Tripura, Meghalaya is to its south and south-west and to the west are West Bengal and Bangladesh. Assam has an international border of 269 kms with Bangladesh. The shape of this State is more or less like a "standing bird" facing towards the north-west. The narrow corridor on its north-west in between Bhutan and Bangladesh is about 50 kms wide running through West Bengal (Jalpaiguri and Cooch-Behar districts) to connect Assam with other parts of India.

2. Name of the State:—Scholars are not agreed on the origin of the name Assam. The *Mahabharata, Vishnupurana, Kalika Purana* and *Yoginitantra* referred to the State of Assam as *Pragjyotisha* and in the medieval period it was called *Kamarupa.* The Allahabad pillar's inscription, during the reign of *Emperor* Samudra Gupta, referred to the State as *Kamarupa.* It is said that during the reign of Ahoms the name *Assam* was used to denote this region.

Actually, it seems that Assam is only the anglicised version of *Asom* which perhaps came from the word *Ahom* who ruled this region for almost six hundred years by conquering it in the 13th Century as *Shan* invaders. Some others say that the name Assam is derived from its unequal surface which is called *Asama* (*in Assamese*) as hills are interspersed with valleys in this region.

3. Physiography:—Assam is a land of criss-crossing mountains and valleys, hills and rivers. It has two physical divisions: the plains and the hills. It has three physiographic units: the Brahmaputra valley on the north, the Karbi Anglong and North Cachar Hills and plateaus in the middle, and the Barak valley on the south.

The Brahmaputra valley is 720 kms long and 80 to 100 kms wide in average ranging in height from 34 metres to 130 metres above sea level. It is made up of two parts—the Lower Assam Valley where the plains are broken by isolated groups of hills and the Upper Assam Valley with unbroken plains. Karbi Anglong and parts of North Cachar Hills form a part of Meghalaya (Shillong) plateau which is a range of mountains in the centre of Assam and divides the Brahmaputra valley from the Barak valley by the Barail range of Cachar. The plateau on the southern side faces the Barak valley and the northern edge slopes gently to the Brahmaputra valley. Karbi Anglong reaches an average elevation of about 450 metres above sea level. Higher average elevations of about 1,000 metres are to be found in the central portion of the hill district, east of the Kopili river. North Cachar Hills district is more hilly (about 90%) than Karbi Anglong district (about 70%). The main mountains of Karbi Anglong district are—Basundhari (774' 192 m), Raichang (737' 616 m), Mehekongthu (638'556 m), Kur (626' 364 m), Chengjehichan (1280' 16 m), Khunram (1310' 64 m). Karbi-Anglong's south-eastern part is known as Rengma hills. Mountains of North Cachar Hill district are straight and high. Barail hilly ranges pass through them. A few hills of Barail are higher than one and half kilometres. The Barak valley has mainly swampy flats broken by several low, isolated hills and ridges.

4. River:—Assam is dominated by the Brahmaputra river. It is one of the largest rivers in the world traversing a distance of about 2900 kms with a draining area of about 580,000 sq. kms (Madhab Sarma, 1977:43). It originates in Tibet and enters India from the north-east. This river's drainage is 640 kms from Kobo to Dhubri (K.G. Deb Krori, 1993:23). This river is known as Ya-lu-tsang-pu Chiang in Tibet and Brahmaputra, the son of Brahma (the creator), in Assam. After running 1609 kms through Tibet, the river turns south-east making a hairpin bend at a place, a few miles east of Namcha Burwa. Thereafter, it is joined by tributaries. At the town of Sadiya (Assam) the Brahmaputra enters Assam Valley of North-Eastern India as Dihang river. This river turns to the south-west and is joined by the two mountain streams of Luhit and Dibang. Below Dibrugarh, Brahmaputra river flows through the plain with a vast expande of water, broken by innumerable sandbanks or *chars.* This river is turbulent and mighty in Assam, even in the dry season. It receives several rapidly running Himalayan streams like Na-Dihing, Dibru, Buri-Dihing, Dichang,

Dikhong, Janji, Bhogdoi, Kapili, Digaru, Subansiri, Bharali, Dhansiri, Manas, Champamati, Saralbhanga, Sankosh, Kulsi, Shingra, Doodnoi, Krishnai, Jinjiram, etc. The main tributaries from the hills and the plateau to the south are the Jiadhal, Sowansiri, Ranganoi, Dikrong, Buroi, Bargang, Buri Dihing, Disang, Jiya Bhoroli, Jiya Dhansiri, Barnadi, Puthimari, Pagladiya, Mana, Champabati, Sonkosh, Dikhu and Kapili. Due to heavy monsoon rains, the narrowness of the valley and the heavy silting process, river Brahmaputra cannot maintain its normal channel and is prone to floods. This flood water has given rise to marshes like Dipar, Bildara, Roumari, Satdala, etc. The Bharali and Rupashi rivers are of much importance.

The main stream of the Brahmaputra also runs through Bangladesh to receive Surma river and is united with Meghna river. The upper part of Surma river is called Barak which runs through a narrow valley, shut in on either side by hills and forms the boundary between Nagaland and Manipur. At Tipaimukh, Barak turns to the north and divides Cachar from Manipur in a line almost parallel to that taken by the river in its downward sweep. The Barak river has over ten tributaries. Some of them are: Longlai, Shingra, Rakni, Sonai, etc.

The Barak valley is 200 km long and 96 km wide. The total catchment area of Brahmaputra (5.80 lakh sq. kms) is spread over Tibet (2.93 lakh sq. kms), India (2.95 lakh sq. kms), Bhutan (0.45 lakh sq. kms) and Bangladesh (0.47 lakh sq. kms) while the Barak basin extends over an area of 0.42 lakh sq. kms in Assam, Manipur, Mizoram, Meghalaya, Nagaland and Tripura and 751 sq. kms in Myanmar up to the Bangladesh border. Barak's main stream up to Lakhimpur has important tributaries such as Irrang (134 kms) or Tuilang and Tuival (139 kms) on the left bank and Makru (79 kms) on the right bank. Between Lakhimpur and Bhanga, Jiri, Chiri, Badri, Madura, Jatinga, Hareng, etc., join the right bank of the river Barak. The left bank of river Barak, is joined by Sonai, Ghagra, Sutarakhal, Katakhal, Pola, Hatia, Dhaleswari, Gomati (at Badarpur Ghat). The river Longai is known as Sonai at the town of Karimganj and joins Hakaluki Haor in Bangladesh and thereafter it joins Kushiyara. The river Longai is the main cause of sorrow of major parts of Karimganj district. It rises in the hills of Tripura and Mizoram and is threatening the NH-44, the only lifeline to Tripura, at a place called Lowairpoa which is very close to Tripura-Assam border. The river Surma, a branch of the Barak, passes along the Indo-Bangladesh border (K.G. Deb Krori, 1993:23-24).

5. Lake and Island:—Many swamps and lakes are found in both Brahmaputra and Barak. Truly speaking, there is no lake in Assam. Haflong lake, an artificial one, however, is situated in Haflong town. The Brahmaputra has an inhabited island named Majuli which is said to be the largest river island of the world (950 sq. km). It is to the north of Jorhat district formed by the diversion of the Kherkutia channel from the main stream of Brahmaputra. It is surrounded by the waters of Brahmaputra and Subansiri. There is another small river-island named Umananda near the city of Guwahati of the district Kamrup. This island has a rocky bed. There are several *chars* (sandbanks) in Assam.

6. Climate:—Assam escapes the normal Indian hot and dry season. The climate of Assam is moderately hot with humidity. It may be divided into four primary seasons, *viz.* (a) winter, (b) pre-monsoon, (c) monsoon, and (d) retreating monsoon. December to middle part of February is the winter season; the second part of December to January is the coldest month. The atmosphere is very humid and dense fogs are frequent in winter; especially fogs are very much common during mornings. The duration of foggy days varies from 60 to 100 days. The average minimum temperature was 8° C in 1995. The south bank of Brahmaputra and the Cachar plains have more foggy days than other parts of Assam. Cool gentle northern and north-eastern winds blow during the last week of January and first week of February. Rainfall is the lowest during this season and December is the driest month. Casual showers associated with western disturbances lowers the temperature and brings cold spells. March and April represent pre-monsoon season. Temperature gradually rises from the last week of February. This season is almost rainless but extremely windy. The winds very often become strong; sometimes duststorms occur. Duststorms occur especially in the western part of Assam valley. Casual thunderstorms are followed by rain. June to September is the monsoon season. Extremely high temperature is the main feature of the last part of July-August. Average maximum temperature is 36°C (1994). In July, 1994, Guwahati recorded its highest temperature for the month in the last 100 years. Maximum temperature of Guwahati on 18th April, 1996, was 39°C. But rising temperature is sometimes brought down considerably by rains which start in June. Mainly warm and humid weather is the feature of the monsoon season. Rain sometimes continues for three-four days together and sometimes accompanied by heavy storms. The last part of September to November is the retreating monsoon season, when monsoon gradually diminishes, rainfall is negligible and fair, sunny condition with very pleasant weather prevail and the hot temperature gradually decreases.

7. Flood and Drought:—Flood in Assam is common due to heavy monsoon rains. Floods comes in a series, time after time, from the early part of June till the middle of November. So far there is no arrangement to collect and store the surplus water for future use during drought. As such, crops are affected as much by drought as also by floods. This drought occurs as the rains cease suddenly.

The great earthquake of 1950, caused extensive landslides and silting up and changes in riverbeds in the plains. Thereafter, the rivers have regular floods, causing damage to crops, life and property.

8. Earthquake:—Geologists are of the opinion that Assam is within the belt of the eastern earthquake zone that spreads across and cross-connects the Pacific. Earthquakes are almost, common phenomenon in Assam. They may occur several times in a year. Ordinary earthquakes usually do not cause much damage. The earthquakes of 1869, 1897, 1930, 1950, had enormously affected the topography. The great earthquakes of 12th June, 1897 and 15th August, 1950, were the most devastating. The earthquake of 1897 had covered an area of about 200 miles in length and about 50 miles in width and Meghalaya

(Shillong) plateau was the epicentre. The earthquake of 1950 was worse which destructed about 15,000 sq. miles of Ch'a-yu (Rima) in Tibet and the Arunachal Pradesh border was the epicentre. It caused heavy landslides that blocked many hill streams and changed the riverbeds in the plains. It caused great loss of life and property. The history of earthquakes of Assam was started to be recorded since 1548.

9. Agriculture:—The soil of Brahmaputra and Surma (Barak) valleys is very fertile. It is composed of old and new alluvia forming a mechanical mixture of sand and clay. Red loamy soil is found in hilly tracts, and the yellow loamy soil of hill slopes is very much suitable for tea cultivation. Tea cultivation in Assam was started as early as 1835. The undivided districts of Sibsagar, Dibrugarh, Cachar and Darrang are important tea-growing areas. Tea is a major export commodity of India. Brahmaputra and Surma (Barak) valleys produce large quantity of raw jute. The hill districts practise *jhum* (shifting cultivation) and terrace cultivation. Tea of Assam was for the first time auctioned on 10 January, 1839 in the London market. Tea auction centres of India have opened branches in different places like Calcutta (1861), Cochin (1947) and Guwahati (1970).

Agriculture constitutes the major source of Assam's economy. Over 80 per cent of population depend on agriculture directly or inderectly. The total foodgrain production of Assam during 1990-91, was 3,442 thousand tonnes and in 1991-92, it was 3,380 thousand tonnes. Main cash crops are jute, tea, cotton, oilseeds, sugar-cane, fruit, and potatoes. Coffee cultivation has been started in North Cachar Hills and Karbi Anglong districts on a large scale.

The economy of Assam is predominantly agrarian. The crops of Assam may be grouped into—(1) wet or summer crops, (2) *rabi* or winter crops, and (3) the plantation crops. There are three important varieties of paddy—(1) *Sali* (Winter paddy), (2) *Ahu* (Summer paddy) and (3) *Bao* (Spring paddy). All these crops can be grown annually in the same field. Jute, sugar-cane, maize, gram, *tur*, etc., are cultivated in summer season. Pulses, oilseeds, cotton, tobacco, potato, sweet potato, chilli, etc., are winter crops. Jackfruit, mango, banana, orange, pineapple are the main fruits. Coconut and arecanut trees are very common in Assam.

10. Shifting (Jhum) Cultivation:—In Assam *jhum* cultivation is mainly practised in Karbi Anglong and North Cachar hills. The land at village level is distributed generally by the Village Council for shifting cultivation. In some cases, the Village Chief distributes the land among families. The jungles in the hills are cleared by them and burnt. This burnt ash serves as the only manure for shifting cultivation. The seeds are sown there by them. In this field they cultivate for a year or two and thereafter, they allow that field for about ten years to gather natural fertility of soil with a new growth of jungle on it. In dry region, it usually takes time to grow plants and trees. Shifting cultivation in the southern region of the two hill districts till the land for two to three years for cultivation and vacate it for about eight years for regeneration of forest. Paddy, is the main crop of shifting cultivation for them. Potato, cotton, ginger, chilli, etc. are also cultivated.

On gentle hill slopes at low altitudes they practise terrace cultivation of paddy by irrigating through artificially constructed channels. At the foot of the valley where there is plenty of water they practise wet paddy cultivation by dividing the land into small fields. The soil is churned into a thick paste by driving cattle on that field. Water is let in by artificial channels to wet the area of cultivation and to drain out the excess water which is not required. The individual ownership of land is mainly for permanent wet cultivation.

11. Irrigation:—Irrigation in Assam is troublesome both due to very little water and excessive water (drought and flood). The irrigation potential is created under State Government irrigation sector. At the end of 1991-92, there was 12,571 hectares under minor irrigation and 6,882 hectares under major irrigation.

12. Forest:—The forests of Assan. have enough raw materials. There are about 74 species of timber of which about 49 varieties are of commercially good quality. Fuelwood is found in abundance in Assam. The State has many plywood factories, sawmills and paper mills.

There were a total of 26 forest divisions in 1992. There are many groves of mangoes, jackfruits, etc. Bamboo trees are common in villages and semi-urban areas. Trees in the hill areas are gradually decreasing as people are using these for firewood, construction of houses and also for shifting (*jhum*) cultivation. In 1980-82, the forest area of this State was 19,796 sq.kms whereas it was 21,055 sq.kms in 1972-75. Thus, the forest area has gone down in Assam (Table I). However, it has at present improved again. In 1989-90, 1990-91 and 1991-92 the total forest area of Assam (excluding unclassified State forest) was 21,522.60; 21,412.24 and 21,684.52 sq.kms respectively.

Table I
Forest Areas

State	*Forest area in sq. km*		*Change of forest area in sq. km* (+) *Increased* (-) *Decreased*	
	1972-75	*1980-82*		
Assam	21,055	19,796	(-)	1,259
Manipur	15,090	13,572	(-)	1,518
Meghalaya	14,390	12,458	(-)	1,932
Nagaland	8,154	8,095	(-)	59
Tripura	6,330	5,138	(-)	1,192
Arunachal Pr.	51,438	58,104	(+)	666
Mizoram	13,860	11,971	(-)	1,889

Source: *Himalaya: Man & Nature,* VIII(XI), April, 1985.

The decrease in forest cover is mostly due to the exclusion of tea gardens from the forest category. In Assam there has been a decrease of 1,259 sq. kms of forest, out of which exclusion of tea gardens amounted to 1199 sq. kms

Assam lost about 81 sq. kms of dense forest to non-forest category due to severe degradation of the dense forest area in the Brahmaputra valley. Besides causing environmental imbalance, large-scale deforestation had resulted in problems like floods in the plains and soil erosion in the hills.

13. Flora:—The flora of Assam is common to that of the neighbouring states of North-East India and Bangladesh. Several varieties of flowering plants and trees are available in Assam. Some of the vegetation is similar to that of Bhutan and some plants are like those of Upper Myanmar. Many Ayurvedic medicinal plants are also available here. The hills of Assam are covered with dense evergreen forests of trees, plants, bushes, creepers and grasses. Evergreen forests are found in undivided Sibsagar, Lakhimpur and Dibrugarh districts. A total of 74 types of wood are available in Assam of which only 49 types are utilised for commercial purposes.

Rainfall and temperature of this State are suitable for the growth of vegetation like trees, plants, herbs, and creepers. Cotton, cane, *ikra,* bamboo, big grass, cactus, ferns, timber, mango, lichi, guava, sugar-cane, betel-nut, coconut, jackfruit, lemon, orange, banana, pineapple, tobacco, tea, coffee, etc. grow plentifully in Assam. There are varieties of flower plants such as rose, sunflower, lotus, water-lily, *bokful, karabi, kadam, sewali,* orchids, etc. Medicinal plants are *amlaku, thokra (O tenga), helencha, dumur, van-tulsi, basak, kalmegh, ghrita kumari, lajjabati, sarpa-gandha, thankuni, neem, kamranga,* etc. Rice, maize, wheat, millet, mustard, potato, *til,* betel-leaf, pulses, etc., are also grown here. Coconut, guava, betel-nut, betel leaf, banana are the most common garden crops of urban, semi-urban and rural areas.

14. Fauna:—The single-horned rhinoceros of Assam is famous in the world. The terrestrial fauna is richer than the aquatic fauna. These include varieties of insects, flies, mosquitoes, earthworms, leeches, crabs, snakes, toads, frogs, elephants, tigers, single-horned rhinoceros, leopards, deer, monkeys, cats, pigs, dogs, goats, buffaloes, jackals, butterflies, etc. Numerous varieties of fish include *Bhetki, Katla, Boal, Rohu, Koi, Goroi, Magur, Mrigal, Singi, Ghania, Puthi, Tengra, Soul, Chital,* etc. Water fauna like crab and tortoise are also found. Several types of birds are found especially *Salik, Charai, Bhatua, Tiya, Moina,* crow, cuckoo, etc. During October-November, birds of different species, including hooded or green-breasted pitta, three-toed forest king-fisher, Indian ruddy king-fisher, ashy-headed green pigeon, *koel,* spotted and emerald doves, migrate to Jatinga for breeding.

The wildlife of Assam has unfortunately fallen prey to the hunters. A portion of the reserved forest in Assam is devoted to wildlife sanctuaries. There are several such sanctuaries of which Kaziranga National Park is the main one which is famous for one-horned rhinoceros. But, every year a few of these rhinoceros are dying at the hands of rhino-horn smugglers' gang. There are wild buffalo, elephant, Indian swamp deer, sambar, hog deer, etc. Rajiv Gandhi Sanctuary (earlier name was Orang Sanctuary) is another, famous for one-horn rhinoceros. Manah Wild Life Sanctuary is known for the beauty of wildlife and also for fishing in the splendid river. Its main attraction is the wild buffalo, elephant, Indian bison, several species of deer, tiger and other carnivores. It is 95 kms west of Guwahati. Chakrasila is also a game sanctuary of Dhubri. There are also Soina-Rupai Sanctuary, Pabhoi Sanctuary besides several reserves such as Garampani, Laokhowa, Hahim, Kulsi, Chandubi, Rani, Dipar Beel, Ghaguwa, Chakarad Hill, Nambur, etc. which are the natural habitats of the wild animals and birds.

Here it may be mentioned that the famous site Jatinga is about 364 kms south of Guwahati. In Zemi Naga language, the word *Jatinga* means "pathway of rain and water". This area first came to be inhabited by the Nagas in 1890s. (*Shillong Times,* June 13, 1994:3). This site is famous for 'bird-mystery'. It is very near Haflong of North Cachar Hill district. Generally, the birds used to pass through Jatinga which is their migratory route. But it is strange as thousands of birds are believed to commit 'suicide' at Jatinga especially in September and November when a local festival is to start and people camp near the lake at the foothills of Jatinga. The light of camp-fire and other bright lights attracts the birds to flock there for their winter sojourn and perish in the fire and bright light. After they fall, they become motionless and lose all reflex action due to some unknown phenomenon. This type of 'suicide' is not reported elsewhere in India except for Longlu in Mizoram which reports a few such cases on certain occasions at regular intervals. The birds after their fatal fall lie in a listless condition and refuse to eat and die after a few days. The number of birds falling increases in dense fog and drizzle and also when the wind blows in a particular direction. It is stated that more birds fall around new moon days provided the weather condition remains the same. But common ***moina*** and ***bulbul*** also found in Jatinga, do not commit 'suicide' like other birds. The number of 'bird-fall' has been reduced especially after the devastating earthquake of 1950, in Jatinga though the reason is unknown. It seems that attracting force of light cause them to lose sense and fall down to earth to die.

Since human population is increasing day by day, the forest areas are decreasing accordingly as people construct houses by destroying the jungles. It results in lesser areas for the fauna. Here it may be mentioned that, on 5th March, 1995, (Sunday) a 6' 4" leopard was found in Ulubari near G.S. Road of Guwahati Municipal Corporation area. It came from nearby Narakasur hills at about noon and took shelter in an empty house. Instead of capturing it for Guwahati State Zoo, the City Police shot dead this helpless animal by firing 13 rounds from an AK-47 rifle through a window by bolting the door from outside. In this callous manner, the number of wild animals is gradually diminishing.

15. Minerals:—Assam has rich petroleum deposits. Oil was first discovered in Assam more than 100 years back in 1889, at Digboi. Thereafter, Digboi Oil Refinery was started in 1901, by Assam Oil Company. A second small scale petroleum refinery was established at Noonmati near Guwahati in 1962. Bangaigaon Oil Refinery and Petro Chemicals is the third one. Numaligarh, is another important one. Its foundation stone was laid on 3rd July, 1992.

After Digboi (1901), Naharkatia (1952), Moran (1956), many other oilfields have been found. In Lakoowa (1962), Rudrasagar (1962), Doom Dooma, Hoogriajan, Teok, Galeky, etc. oilfields have been found in Upper Assam. Layers of oil are also found in Jorhat-Golaghat area. In fact, more than 55 per cent of the area in Assam may be considered as oil-bearing. After the separation of Myanmar (Burma) in 1937, from India and the partition of India in 1947, Assam is now the main petroleum producing State of India.

Tengakhat (Dibrugarh District) Gas Crackar Project's, foundation stone was laid on 24th November, 1995. LPG bottling plant was under construction at Amingaon near Guwahati and commercial production was started in the early part of 1995. Titabar LPG bottling plant is in progress. ONGC discovered 1.05 lakhs cubic feet of gas at Adamtilla and Bashkandi in June 1994, in Barak valley. According to ONGC regional director, two gas turbine projects would be set up at these two places. Cachar project had also located three new oil and gas reserves at Bhubandhar, Patheria and Chatachura in Cachar, Karimganj and Hailakandi districts, respectively.

The total coal reserves estimated in Assam is 295.18 million tonnes (*Shillong Times,* May 26, 1994: p. 3). Coal is found in Makum, Dilly-Joypur, Jangi-Disai, Ledo, Margherita, Borgolai, Tipong, Namdang, Koilajan, Sheelveta, Khunbaman. Coal was first discovered in Dibrugarh in 1825, and commercially it has been used since 1882, for Assam Railways. Naharkatia and Moran oilfields have natural gas. Namrup fertilizer plant utilises a part of this gas. Assam has also gold as it appears in the sands of Sowansiri river (*Agradoot,* May 4, 1994: p. 1). Prior to 1960, not much information was available on mineral resources of Assam except crude petroleum, coal and limestone. Now a number of collieries are in existence.

Karbi Anglong and North Cachar Hills have limestone deposits. In 1981 and 1982, limestone produced was 269 and 232 thousand tons respectively. Bokajan Cement Factory of Assam produces annually more than 66 thousand tons. Production of coal was 982,000 m.t., crude-oil 4,838,000 m.t., natural gas 967 million cu.m., limestone 268,000 m.t. at Jiajuri, Lakhimpur and Sheelbheta; feldspar and quartz near Hahim; iron-ore at Chandardinga, Lengupara, Hahim and Kumari; fire-clay at Koilajan, Sheelveta, Ledo and Namdang indicates bright future for industry in Assam. Iron-ore deposits are found in Dhubri (GSI Report, August 10, 1994). Other discoveries include silver, gold-dust, white clay, lithomargic clay, glass-sand, etc.

Table II

Production of Mineral Oil and Natural Gas

	Mineral Oil (Lakh ton)		*Natural Gas (Cubic Metre)*	
Year	*Assam*	*India*	*Assam*	*India*
1974	39.4	74.91	539	1039
1975	41.9	82.83	621	1253
1976	42.9	84.50	848	1545
1977	44.7	86.96	824	1545

Year	*Assam*	*India*	*Assam*	*India*
1978	40.8	112.7	889	1731
1979	45.6	128.4	946	1929
1980	10.6	94.0	455	1462
1981	43.9 (Fixed)	149.0	869	1949
1982	51. 1 (Fixed)	—	875	—
1988	51.11	—	965	—
1989	54.09	—	1011	—
1990	49.27	—	987	—
1991	48.38	—	967	—

Source : *Asamiya Biswakosh, pt. I, 1987:277 and Statistical Handbook, 1992:182.*

16. Industry:—A number of industrial enterprises have been started in Assam. These include a fertilizer plant at Namrup, a jute mill at Silghat, a sugar mill at Dergaon, two paper mills at Jogigopa and Jagiroad, a spun-silk mill at Jagiroad, cement factory at Bokajan and Umrangsoo (N.C. Hills), match-factory at Dhubri, etc. There are several saw mills, and plywood factories also. The first plywood factory was set up at Sadiya by M/s Bird & Co. under the name, the Assam Saw Mill and Timber Co. in 1920. The Assam Match Co. was the first one to be set up at Dhubri under the name, WIMCO in 1926. A number of food-processing units for rice, oil and fruits were established in early 1970s.

Tea and oil industries are the main industries of Assam. In 1982, there was a total of 459 saw mills, 55 plywood factories, 4 match factories, 2 paper mills, and one hard board factories in Guwahati. The Sericultural Training Institute is situated at Titabar. Assam has a monopoly in the production of *Eri* silk (white colour), and *Muga*-silk (buff colour). They are unique in the world and are produced so far mostly in Assam. *'Pat'* i.e. mulberry-silk, *Tassar* (coarse silk, light buff colour) are also produced in Assam. Soalkuchi's *Muga* silk and *Pat* silk products are famous in India and abroad. Maulana Mohammed Tayebullah Government Textile Institute is situated at Guwahati for textile products. Assam is famous for its embroidered fabrics with figures of trees, leaves, flowers, animals and birds, triangular and linear geometric designs. *Bihuan, Manani Kapor, Khaniya Kapor, Bar-Kapor,* etc. and *foolam mekhela chaddar* are usually beautifully designed.

Brass-metal industry was famous in Assam. Titabar of Upper Assam was producing brass utensils but, now only Sarthebari and Hajo of Kamrup district produce these. Iron articles are made at Karanga in Sibsagar district. Gold ornaments of Assam look very beautiful and are made in most of the places of Assam.

There are bee-keeping, pottery, processing of cereals and pulses, oil, khadi, carpentry and blacksmithy, soap, leather, cane and bamboo industries, etc., in Assam.

Tea cultivation in Assam was begun as early as 1835, near the junction of the Brahmaputra and the Kundel rivers under the initiative of the British Government. In 1840, Assam Tea Company took charge of the Government tea plantations. Before the reorganisation of Assam in 1972, there were about 750 tea gardens, producing nearly 44,000 pounds of tea annually. In 1989, the total number of tea gardens in Assam was 848 with an area of 2,29,428 hectares and produced 1656 kg. per hectare (Census 1991, Assam-P). Tea Auction Centre for tea marketing was started at Guwahati in September, 1970. During 1980, Assam produced 305 million kg. of tea as against 575 million kg. for the country as a whole. Coffee cultivation in Assam is flourishing. In 1980, coffee was cultivated in a total area of 1148 hectares.

There are several varieties of wood in Assam and also varieties of bamboo trees. Minor forest products of Assam are—cane, thatch, grass, lac, rubber, honey, firewood, gum, orchids, and medicinal herbs, etc. There is a proposal to set up a paper-mill at Dhing (Nagaon district).

Sericulture, weaving and handicraft industries play an important role in Assam, particularly in the rural areas. Every Assamese household, in the rural areas of Assam, has handloom apparatus and women weave when they find time. Handicrafts made from bamboo, cane and palm leaves are beautiful. *Japi* (cultivator's hat), *mora,* chair, basket, toy, *sarai-bata,* etc. are their main products. Decorated *japi* beautifies the drawing-rooms of most of the people of Assam and also other regions. It indicates the aristocratic background of the family. Carpentry, wood-cut and wood-carving work testify to the glories of Assam. A modern planetarium in Guwahati has been set up on August 17, 1994.

17. Energy and Power:—Availability of electricity in Assam is inadequate. The total installed capacity of the generating plants is 5144 MW in 1991-92, of which thermal power is 512.4 and hydel power 2.0 respectively. The Assam State Electricity Board was constituted in 1958, under the Electricity Supply Act, 1941. It was bifurcated on 25th January, 1975, between Assam and Meghalaya as per provisions of the North Eastern Areas (Reorganisation) Act, 1971. As a result, two major hydel projects namely Umtru and Umium, due to their location in Meghalaya State, lowered the generation level of power for the reconstituted Assam.

During 1985, 53.6% villages of Assam were electrified. During 1991-92, 21,464 villages were electrified under the Rural Electrification Programme. The State has a target to electrify 95% villages by the end of the 8th Plan. Assam gas-based power project at Kathalguri would be started by April, 1995. Some gas based power projects of Assam are—Namrup, Chandrapur, Bongaigaon, Kapili, Lakwa. Amguri gas-based power project of 360 MW started on 13th June, 1993, and produced 280 MW. Assam will have plenty of power soon when proposed projects of lower Barapani, Kapili, etc., will start functioning properly. At present, the Assam State Electricity Board supplies power to a few neighbouring states also. Chandrapur TPS (Extension), Lakwa TPS

(Extension Phase-II), Karbi Longpi Hydro-electric Project, Dhansiri Hydro-electric Project and Dalaima Mini Hydel Projecte are located in Assam.

Bio-gas and solar-energy production is progressing in Assam. Assam Government has introduced in 1995 for about 2,150 families, a new power project *Kutir Jyoti* of solar energy. This was first introduced on 13th March, 1995 at Tetelia of Dimoriya, Assam. It is the cheapest power and energy project. It was extended to one lakh families in 1996. After the completion of the gas-based Adamtilla and Bashkandi projects of Barak valley 30 MW would be produced to meet the power requirement of the Barak valley in South Assam, Tripura and Mizoram.

18. Prehistoric Archaeology:—Almost every place of Assam has objects of historical and antiquarian interest. *Kamrup Annusandhan Samity* (Assam Research Society) was established at Guwahati in April, 1912 to carry out research on prehistoric archaeology of Assam and neighbouring states.

J. Coggin-Brown reported about grooved stone hammer from Assam in 1914. E.T. Dalton wrote in 1855 about the temple ruins of Assam. Hem Ch. Das Gupta reported in 1913 about two-shouldered stone implements from Assam. Frank Ede reported in 1902 about the sacred caves of Cachar district. C. Francis in 1902 wrote about the inscriptions on tombs in Assam. C. Von Furer-Haimendorf wrote about the megalithic culture of Assam in 1939. J.H. Hutton reported in 1925 about some carved stones in the Dayang valley of Sibsagar. A.H. Dani wrote in 1960 about the prehistoric tools of North-Eastern India. M.K. Dhavlikar reported in 1979 about boat burial.

Durga images were discovered at Surjya Pahar, an archaeological site in the district of Goalpara, besides the images of Siva. There was no scope for a systematic study of Archaeology uptil 1948, when the University of Gauhati was established. With the starting of Anthropology Department in Gauhati University in 1956, systematic investigation of Prehistoric Archaeology began in 1960-61 when T.C. Sharma with M.C. Goswami carried out explorations in the Langthing and Mahur river valleys of North Cachar Hills. These investigations discovered a stratified neolithic site at Daojali Hading. Prehistoric Archaeology section was started in Gauhati University's Anthropology department in 1966 along with the subject of Anthropology. Since then the department is regularly carrying out archaeological investigations. Anthropology department of Dibrugarh University is also taking interest in archaeological investigations soon after the creation of this department in 1969.

The North Cachar Hills and Kamrup zone have smooth stone tools made of sedimentary rock (shale). Generally, the tools are quadrangular axes and adzes and shoulder-celts. These neolithic site tools were found with cord-marked pottery. The richest archaeological site is Ambari (Guwahati) where excavation started in 1968-69. The antiquities of Ambari date from 7th to 17th century A.D. within which, two cultural periods are visible. Four old tanks and parts of four ramparts about 500 ft. in length, made of bricks, belonging to the 18th century were explored by State Archaeology Department at Dunaimukh (south-west of Golaghat town) in Upper Assam in January, 1993. The two tanks are historically important as they were dug out by Kachari king and Ahom king. These tanks are popularly known as *Juriat Pukhuri* (twin tanks).

A megalithic site at Makri, 15 kms far from Goalpara was reported in April, 1993. The sculptural art of Assam is found in stone door frame of the temple at Dah-Parvatia in Darrang district. At Kamakhya, a number of sculptures ranging from 7th to 17th century A.D. have been found. Numaligarh ruins in Sibsagar district of Upper Assam have a Siva temple of 10th and 11th century A.D. The remains and relics of the buildings, gateways, ramparts, pillars and numerous temples show the cultural development of the earlier period of Assam.

19. Currency of Assam:—In Assam, during the reign of different kings, they had their own small-sized currency of bell-metal. Different kings had different symbols on their coins. These coins indicate the artistic talents of that period. Ahom coins of Sudangpha alias Bamuni Konwar (1397-1407 A.D.) who struck coins in his own name while he ascended the throne were found. Ahom coins are generally octagonal in shape. The coins of Suklengmung alias Gorgoya Raja (1539-1552 A.D.) bear inscriptions in the Ahom language and Ahom script. Rudra Singha (1696-1714 A.D.) introduced Assamese script that continued till the end of the Ahom rule in 1824. The standard coin of the Ahom kings weigh a *tola* (two-fifths of an ounce) or 96 *ratis*. Gold currency was introduced only by Suklengmung, Udyaditya and Siba Singha of Ahom dynasty. A 9th century copper coin of Tyaga Simha of Mlechha dynasty was recently discovered in January, 1995. This coin bears the initial *Ta* in *Brahmi* script and the name of the king in full on the top of the coin. The seat of the dynasty was Hadapesvara, in modern Sonitpur district of Assam.

Koch coins are generally round in shape. The inscriptions are either in Sanskrit or Assamese script. Kachari coins are also round in shape. Govinda Chandra (1813-1832), the last Kachari King, issued modern type of coins. However, many more coins are yet to be discovered to write many more about the history of the earlier period.

A silver coin is obtained which bears a date equivalent to 1583 A.D. and was issued by Kachari King Jaso Narayan Deb (1580-1610 A.D.), and a worshipper of Hara-Gauri (Siva-Durga). *Ganapatrika* (Bengali daily from Guwahati) reported on 1st August, 1993 that some *Koch* coins have been found in Madgharia near Guwahati which had the engraved names of Naranarayan and Laksminarayan of Koch period. A few of these coins have the name of Emperor Jahangir. Along with these, two silver bangles have also been found which are 2.70 gm. and 5.35 gm. in weight. These were perhaps used as exchange in barter system in pre-Ahom period.

20. Historical Manuscript:—Old manuscripts are the main sources of history, literature and culture. Before the introduction of printing, writing was done on *Sanchi* bark which are available in the forests of Assam. The most illustrative manuscripts are—*Hasti Vidyarnava, Gita Govinda, Bhagavat* and *Lava Kushar Juddha.* To write these manuscripts, ink was made with *terminalia, citrina,* etc. The pen was a goose-quill or reed. Pictures are also available in all colours, especially yellow and green. *Sanchi* bark was used as early as seventh century. The earliest manuscripts are available in *Namghars* of Assam, written by Sri Sankardev and his disciple Madhabdev, which reflect the history and culture of fifteenth and sixteenth centuries.

21. Communications:—Assam serves as the eastern gateway for the commodities and communication of people. The transport system of Assam is now somewhat developed. There are four forms of transport rail, road, air and water. The isolated location of Assam—linked with the rest of India by only a narrow corridor between Bhutan on the one side and Bangladesh on the other—has prevented the quick development of efficient road and rail systems in the region. The growth of an inland water transport system has similarly been checked by the inclusion of the lower part of the Brahmaputra river in Bangladesh.

Assam is served mainly by a metre-gauge railway system. The history of the North-Eastern Railways in Assam is fairly old. By 1882, the only railway in the Brahmaputra valley was Dibru-Sadiya Railways (metre gauge) and 1883, Jorhat Provincial Railways (narrow gauge) was established. They were merged together in 1895, and was known as Assam-Bengal Railways and connected Assam with other parts of India. The work on Assam-Bengal Railways in Assam was first started in 1891-92. Gauhati-Jamunamukh section of the railways was started in 1897, for traffic. Chittagong (Bangladesh) was merged with Dibrugarh in 1904. But the railway links to outside were cut off after the partition of India and Independence in 1947. The railway link connecting Assam with the rest of the country was started in 1950, by North-East Frontier Railways. Now several trains are running to connect Guwahati directly with Delhi, Madras, Calcutta, etc. Some of the trains are—*Saraighat Express, Rajdhani Express, Cochin Express, Trivandrum Express, Bangalore Express, Dadar Express, Kanchanjunga Express, Avadh-Assam Express, North-East Express, Kamrup Express, Arunachal Express, Lohit Express, Brahmaputra Mail,* etc.

A broad gauge line has been constructed up to Jogigopa, which is being extended up to Guwahati on the bank of the Brahmaputra river. Within the State, all main towns and commercial centres are served by the railways. Some of the towns which have sprung up near railway junctions and other transportation centres are—Bongaigaon, Rangia, New Guwahati, Lumding, Mariani, Tinsukia, Badarpur, etc. The north-east region has a zonal Railway Headquarters at Maligaon near Guwahati since 1958. The present railway route length of North-East Frontier Railway is 3858.44 kms with 772.47 kms broad gauge, 2998.19 kms metre gauge and 87.48 kms narrow gauge (1991-92) track. The routes within Assam have 266.41 broad gauge and 2200.42 kms metre gauge (1991-92) track. A 350 kms long Rangapara-North Lakhimpur-Murkong

Selek railway line was constructed in the early and mid-sixties. The railways in Assam is the main communication and transport system for goods like coal, petroleum, petroleum products, tea, jute and also for passengers. The main railway line from Tinsukia to Guwahati and Westward handles a heavy traffic of more than 1000 metric ton miles per route mile per day each way. The State has been criss-crossed by the Brahmaputra and its tributaries. Brahmaputra bridge prevents a large number of ferries from plying to maintain the efficiency of railway and road systems. During the rainy season rail link of Assam is not satisfactory due to incidence of landslides in hilly areas and damages from floods. Kaliabhomora bridge was constructed across Brahmaputra river and was opened for public on 16th April, 1987. A-3 km long Naranarayan bridge is being constructed for crossing the Brahmaputra river at Jogigopa. It is said that it would be completed by March, 1997. When it is completed, a broad gauge railway line will be set up from Jogigopa to Guwahati. Construction work on a fourth railway bridge over Brahmaputra at Bogibill near Dibrugarh will be taken up by the end of 1997. Bogibill bridge will improve the road communication between north and south banks of Brahmaputra river.

There are three national highways. These are—NH 31, NH 37 and NH 36. The first two highways are the longest covering north and south banks of the river Brahmaputra from west to east. They cover Dhubri, Kokrajhar, Nalbari, Barpeta, Guwahati, Mangaldai, Tezpur, Nowgong, Lakhimpur, Dibrugarh, Tinsukia, Jorhat, Sibsagar, etc. NH 36 covers Diphu, Haflong, Silchar and southern part of Assam. But this is not fit for use by heavy vehicular traffic during the rainy season due to frequent damage by landslides, etc.

Total PWD road length in Assam is 30,086 kms of which 6,839 kms are surfaced and 23,247 kms are unsurfaced (1989-90). The total municipal road length in Assam is 1859 kms of which 497 kms are surfaced and 1362 kms are unsurfaced (1989-90). The condition of roads is not good during rainy season because of frequent damage by floods, existence of weak bridges, substandard surface, etc. State highways run from all the big towns of Assam. There are district roads, inter-village bridle paths, etc. Innumerable motor services have been commissioned on regular traffic roads for carrying passengers and goods.

Assam State Transport Corporation has operated maximum services on selected routes with its buses, cars and trucks. Since 1990, a great number of private transport buses and public carrier services ply regularly within the State and outside carrying passengers and goods. In 1991, the total number of motor vehicles on road in Assam were 2,49,323 of which there were 5,124 buses, 33,089 public carriers, 8,992 private carriers, 26,048 motor cars, 5,576 jeeps, 1,34,517 motor-cycles and scooters, 3,454 motor cabs, 7,455 tractors, 6,795 trailers, 336 omnibuses, 426 mini buses, 9291 government vehicles, 4,472 autorickshaws, and 3,748 other types. The development of road and bridge projects in Barak Valley in view of its topographical situation, a number of projects for construction of roads and bridges are being undertaken in the Barak Valley. Efforts are being made to develop inter-State communications between Assam and Mizoram by undertaking construction of roads like Kawnpui-Bhairabi-Gharmura, etc.

Assam's total navigable inland-waterways are approximately 4,065 kms, 2,193.6 kms throughout the year, the rest being navigable mainly during monsoons only and are served by two public sector organisations, namely—State Directorate of Inland Water Transport and Central Inland Water Transport Corporation (B.K. Sharma, 1993). The Brahmaputra is the main waterway of the State and its important tributaries, *viz.* Bharali, Manas, Buri-Dihing, Disang, etc. are also navigable for varying distances in their lower reaches. The earthquake of 1950 affected steamer navigation in the upper reaches of the Brahmaputra and the river port of Dibrugarh had stopped functioning till 1985. The Brahmaputra and its tributaries are mainly snow-fed while the rivers of the Cachar plain are rain-fed. So far country boats have been plying in the Barak river between Silchar and Karimganj on the border of Bangladesh.

The partition of India gave a blow to the steam navigation of the river Brahmaputra. Previously heavy export and import trades of Assam and Calcutta was carried on through this river. Light canoes were used. The Central Inland Water Transport Corporation is, however, now providing cargo services between Calcutta-Pandu and Calcutta-Karimganj. The State Inland Water Transport is moving goods since 1986 between Guwahati and Dibrugarh which has ferry services. Permanent water transport of goods between Guwahati and Dhubri has been started. At present waterways in Brahmaputra river from Dibrugarh to Calcutta function.

In 1848, the first steamboats were provided by the British East India Company which were plying between Calcutta and Guwahati. The India General Steam Navigation Company had started plying between Calcutta and Assam Valley ports in 1860. This steamer company was established in 1884 between Dibrugarh and Dhubri.

The direct air link between Guwahati and other parts of Assam with Calcutta is a post-Independence development. The first link between Guwahati and Calcutta was opened by air in 1947. Dakotas and Fokker Friendship planes were first introduced. At present, there are seven airports—Borjhar (Guwahati), Kumbhirgram (Silchar), Lilabari (Lakhimpur), Mohanbari (Dibrugarh), Saloni (Tezpur), Raraiya (Jorhat) and Dinjan (Chabua). There is Rupsi, a small airport at Gouripur. Indian Airlines serve regularly between Calcutta and Guwahati and vice versa. Since June, 1982 air services have improved and Airbus services have been intorduced to Borjhar. There are Indian Airlines flights from Guwahati to Delhi, Calcutta, Agartala, Silchar, Imphal, Dimapur, Dibrugarh, Tezpur, Jorhat, Lakhimpur, etc. Moreover, Vayudoot services are also available from

Guwahati to Rupsi, Barapani, Kailashahar, Kamalpur, etc. Helicopter services also connect Assam with the North-East States. There are at present a few private airlines flying passengers in east-west directions, like Sahara, East-West, Damania, Jet, and Modiluft.

In 1984-85, the total number of post offices was 3,312, and letter-boxes 12,524. The State had 159 telephone exchanges and an electronic exchange at Guwahati. There are now some private companies, other than Speed-Post and Posts and Telegraphs services, for quick communications system. There are at present five radio stations at Guwahati, Dibrugarh, Silchar, Jorhat and Haflong. Radio stations in Nagaon and Tezpur are likely to open by 1994-95 and a few more are to be started soon in Karimganj, Dhubri, and other places. Construction of Diphu Radio Station was started in 1988. Shillong-Guwahati Radio Station established in 1948 was the first one in north-east India. Independent T.V. centres are there in Guwahati (December 21, 1991), Dibrugarh and Silchar. A T.V. transmission centre was set up at Srikona near Silchar on October 11, 1991 and an independent T.V. Centre was opened in Silchar on April 30, 1993. A T.V. transmission centre was set up at Diphu.

Like Meghalaya, Tripura and Manipur, there is no Inner Line Restriction to visit Assam. For foreign tourists there was a Restricted Area Permit (RAP) system which has now been abolished since May 15, 1995 for Assam, Meghalaya and Tripura to improve the tourism industry as the Government of India is now trying to improve their Travel and Civil Aviation Department. Inner Line Permit was introduced in 1874 during the British days only for Arunachal Pradesh, Nagaland and Mizoram to prevent outsiders from exploiting the simple ethnic tribal groups of these regions. Tourist flow in Assam in 1988-89 up to December was 3,01,278 (domestic tourists) and 1,000 (foreign tourists) as surveyed by Indian Institute of Hill Economy (Basic Statistics of NEC, 1992:134).

22. Literacy and Education:—Literacy in Assam was not much satisfactory till 1961. There was only 27.39% literacy in 1961. This had increased very little in 1971 when it was 28.72% only. It however, increased rapidly till 1991and is now 43.20% (Census 1991).

Earlier, parents thought that girls did not need education. Girls' education was not only opposed by men but even by women. There was a general view that even the educated did not choose to marry an educated girl. Further, some others thought that it was sheer wastage of money to spend on a girl's education as she would go and work for her husband's family, after her marriage. The Christian Missionaries helped at the initial stage to improve women's education. Thereafter, the Government is continuously helping it to improve. Operation Blackboard Project was introduced to increase literacy among women.

The Government of Assam has declared education free in the State up to class Xth standard since April, 1978. Stress has been laid on the implementation of the National Adult Education Programme in the State. There are five Universities one each at Guwahati (1948), Dibrugarh (1965), Jorhat (1968), Silchar (Assam University, 1994), and Tezpur (1994). There are two Boards of Secondary Education, Art/Science/Commerce colleges 213, Law colleges 9, Engineering colleges 3, Medical colleges 3, Ayurvedic college 1, Agricultural colleges 2, Veterinary college 1, Teachers' Training colleges 9, Junior colleges (+2 stage) 11, Higher Secondary Schools (10+2 pattern) 367, High schools 3,065, Middle schools 5,703, Primary schools 28,876, Pre-Primary schools 482, Teachers' Training Schools 32, Polytechnics 7 and Technical and Industrial Schools 27 as on September, 1990. One Indian Institute of Technology (IIT) was opened at Guwahati during 1995-96.

Table III

Percentage of Literacy Rate Among Scheduled Castes and Tribes

	1961			*1971*		
	Total	*Male*	*Female*	*Total*	*Male*	*Female*
General Population	27.39	37.66	15.61	28.72	37.19	19.27
Scheduled Castes	24.42	31.77	16.10	25.79	35.00	15.74
Scheduled Tribes	24.35	33.76	14.31	26.03	34.62	17.16

Source : *Census of India, Assam 1971.*

Table IV

Percentage of Literacy Rate Among Rural and Urban Population

	Total			*Rural*			*Urban*		
Year	*Male*	*Female*	*Total*	*Male*	*Female*	*Total*	*Male*	*Female*	*Total*
1971	37.19	19.27	28.72	34.28	16.51	25.80	64.54	50.89	58.69
1991	50.62	35.18	43.20	47.53	31.88	39.96	74.17	63.26	69.19

Source : *Census of India 1971 and 1991 (Assam)*

Cotton College (Government), Guwahati was the first one to be established in Assam in 1901. It was named after Sir Henry Cotton, the then Chief Commissioner of Assam (1896-1902). B. Borooah College was next founded at Guwahati. It was a night college established in 1943. Thereafter, several colleges have been started at Guwahati. Some of these are—Handique Girls' College, Pragjyotispur College, Pandu College, Arya Vidyapeeth College, Commerce College, etc. Assam Medical College at Dibrugarh was established in November, 1947. Assam High Court (Guwahati) was established in 1948.

Mr Brown and O. Cutter came to India and brought with them a printing press. They established the first printing press in 1836, and Mr Brown was the first person to publish an Assamese newspaper *Arunoday* in 1844. The English Christian Missionaries Carey and Marshman with the help of Atmaram Sarma of Koliabor, Nagaon translated the Bible into Assamese and published it in 1873. In 1839, W. Robinson published a grammar book of Assamese language. In 1848, Brown published grammatical notes in Assamese and Mrs. O. Cutter wrote Assamese language vocabulary.

23. Language:—The Ahom dynasty was established in 1228 A.D., by Sukapha in Assam and ended with Purandar Singha in 1824 A.D. During this period, the Ahoms adopted Assamese language by rejecting their original *Tai* dialect. The hills and plains tribals have their own languages. It is said that the literature of Assam begins from the time of Sankardev (1449-1568 A.D.). Madhab Kandali and Mahendra Kandali appeared on the literary scene before Sankardev and translated Sanskrit Ramayana into Assamese. But, it seems that Sankardev brought about a revolution in Assamese literature by his voluminous writings. Madhabdev and Ram Saraswati enriched the Assamese literature by their writings. The British (India) Government introduced Bengali language in 1837 in schools and offices of Assam. But, in 1871, Assamese language was again imposed at the initiative of the American Baptist Missionaries in Assam and Anandaram Dhekial Phookan, Manik Chandra Barua, Gunaviram Barua, Hem Chandra Barua and others. The demand for Assamese as the official language of Assam is being made by Assam Sahitya Sabha since 1950. On March 3, 1960, the then Chief Minister Bimala Prasad Chaliha had appreciated the demand which was made by the Assam Sahitya Sabha and other institutions to declare Assamese as a State language (*AICEP March 3, 1960*: Speech of Bimala Prasad Chaliha: 49-50). On June 23, 1960, the Chief Minister announced that the Official Language Bill would be introduced as indicated by the APCC and the Assam Official Language Bill for Assamese was introduced on October 10, 1960, *(vide Act XXXIII of 1960).*

Most of the Assamese manuscripts of earlier days except the *Buranjis* (History) and the *Ankia Nats* (Dramas) were written in poetic form. It is said that Assamese prose literature developed in the sixteenth century while Bengali literature developed during the time of Iswar Chandra Vidyasagar and Bankim Chandra Chattopadhaya.

Assamese is a composite language. Assamese language has its roots in Magadhi Prakrit. Assamese language today has large elements of Sanskrit, Bodo, the Tai-Ahom and even Persian language (S. Gupta, 1984:93, 94). Indo-Aryan and Indo-Chinese words have entered into it. Pre-Aryan and non-Aryan influences are discernible not only in loan words but also in grammar, syntax and pronunciation.

The Kachari, Koch, Rabha, Hojai, Lalung (Tiwa), Moran, Chutiya, etc., belong to the Bodo family of languages. Most of them speak different dialects. But, the Assamese language is the *lingua franca* in Brahmaputra valley and Bengali language in Barak valley. The important languages are Assamese, Bengali, Bodo, and Hindi.

Table V

Bodo-speaking Tribes

Tribes	*Total*
Garo	307,000
Tripuri	300,000
Bodo	286,000
Bangdania	215,000

Tribes	*Total*
Mikir	154,000
Kachari	65,000
Riang	65,000
Jamatia	65,000
Rabha	44,000
Dimasa	32,000
Lalung	11,000
Others	10,000
Total	1,554,000

Source:—*Clarence Maloney (1974:422) and Census of India 1961.*

Table VI

Sino-Tibetan (or Tibeto-Chinese)-speaking family

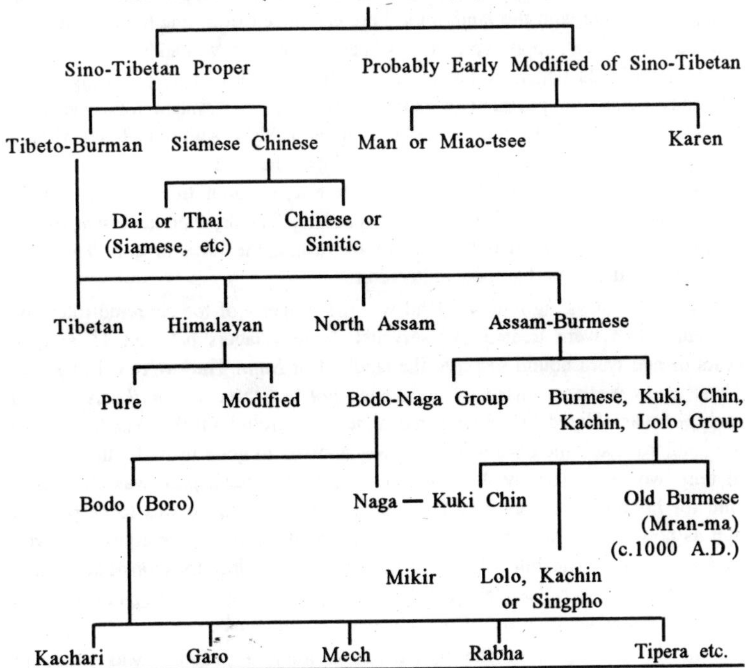

Source:—*Suniti Kumar Chatterjee (1951:14, 15)*

24. Land Reforms:—In Assam, the plain tribal land is not protected by the Sixth Schedule. It is supposed to be protected under the provisions of the Assam Land Revenue Manual of 1886, as amended in 1893. If the Land Revenue Manual of Assam government is properly followed, it will save the tribal economy. Assam Land Ceiling Act is perhaps a progressive law but it is said this was not of much help to the tribals of Assam.

There was no regular land revenue system in Assam till 1866. Acts and Rules were introduced in 1867, when land was divided into three classes—*Kheti* or *rupit* (wet low rice land), *bari* or *basti* (house land) and *pheringati* (dry high land, generally for bamboo). *Kheti* cultivation is divided into four categories—ownership, tenancy, landlord and tenant, and rice-supply type. *Kheti* rice land is either cultivated by the caste people themselves or cultivated on lease. The system of lease/tenant is called *adhi* (half). This *adhi* is of two types—*guchi adhi* (half the sheaves) and *guti adhi* (half the grain). The landlord provides only the land. The tenant is to bring bullocks, the cultivators and all other materials for cultivation. Under *guchi adhi* rice is to be divided equally after harvest between the landlord and the tenant and under *guti adhi* the tenant is to give a fixed amount of thrashed paddy to the landlord every year.

Under Assam *Adhiar* (*Bargadar* or share-cropper) Protection and Regulation Act, 1948, the tenant gets four-fifths of the crop if he supplies the plough and cattle, and the landlord's share is reduced from one-half to one fifth. According to rice-supply system a villager may borrow paddy from surplus paddy households which he has to repay either in paddy or by providing labour in paddy fields. No payment in money prevails in this system for co-villagers for *Sali* (including *Lahi*) and *Ahu* rice. Surplus paddy is sold outside the village. The *bari* or *basti* land is meant for house plots. The garden area or *bari* is used for the cultivation of vegetables. Areca-nut tree, coconut tree, banana, guava, mango, jackfruit, etc., are also found in house-land. The dry high land (*pharingati*) is used for dry crops such as mustard by raising the level of soil. This land is generally used for bamboo cultivation.

In earlier days, agricultural land was the property of the supreme ruler and the cultivators were treated like servants. Male villagers between 15 and 50 years of age were bound to serve the landlord or *Raja*. They were called *paiks*. These *paiks* were organised by *gots*. Each *got* had three/four *paiks*. A *paik* of each *got* was obliged to render personal service throughout the year to *Raja* or the landlord. Each member of the *got* was allowed to get a reward—that is, free of rent two *puras* (nearly three acres) of rice field. Each *paik* was also given land for his house and garden. For this, annually one rupee was to be paid by him as house tax. The land was chiefly cultivated by the village-cultivators who paid plough tax. The hill tribes paid hoe tax for growing dry crops like cotton. The other lands were 'estates' and they were generally granted to Brahmins and temples. These lands were also cultivated by the *paiks*.

In the later part of the nineteenth century, a proposal was made to introduce a type of 'feudal system' in Assam by the Board of Revenue. Colonel Hopkinson, the then Commissioner of Assam sought for Assam *raiyatwari* settlement and the Government decided in 1867, that the actual occupant of the soil can be protected, subject to payment of revenue to the Government at rates fixed for long periods and preserve the rights and obligations of proprietorship and the duties of fiscal and official administration (N.N. Bhattacharyya, 1991: p. 138). As per N.C. Dutta (1968), the British colonialists created different classes of landowners through the Assam Land and Revenue

Regulation Act, 1886. Two main types were—*Zamindari* and *Rayatwari.* Goalpara and Cachar districts of Brahma putra and Surma Valleys were under the *Zamindari* system.

At the time of Independence, the Government of Assam created thirty-seven tribal belts and blocks to protect the plains tribals and their land from intrusions by non-tribals. The whole area of each district was divided into blocks called *Mauzas.* The dues from the resident in a given *Mauza*, were collected by the Officer-in-Charge of it, who was called *Mauzadar/Chaudhuri/ Kagoti/Patgiri*. As per M. Hussain (1993: p. 267), a few Marwaris got appointments from the British rulers as *Mauzadars*—the land revenue collection agents for a cluster of villages known as *Mauza*, on a commission basis. The *Mauzadars* were normally appointed from the influential Assamese landed aristocracy. The appointment of the *Marwaris* as *Mauzadars* led to a conflicting situation in the mid-nineteenth century. Further, he wrote (1993: p. 39) that the colonial state introduced qualitatively different land revenue system as opposed to the pre-colonial *paik* system, known as *ryotwari* system in all districts of the Brahmaputra Valley with the exception of Goalpara which retained the *zamindari* system like Bengal. At present (1995) Assam has about 10 women *Mauzadars* out of more than 200 *Mauzadars.*

Assam *Adhiari* Protection and Regulation Act of 1948, was amended in 1952, 1955, 1957, 1960 and so on. The Assam State Acquisition of Zamindaries Act, 1951, was passed to abolish the Zamindari system in the permanent settled areas of Assam and brought the tenants directly under the Government. This was effected in June, 1954. The Assam Fixation of Ceiling on Landholding Act, 1956, came into force from February 15, 1958. This Act was amended in 1970 and 1975 and so on. There are other Acts such as Assam Non-Agricultural Urban Tenancy Act 1956; Assam State Acquisition of Lands belonging to Religious or Charitable Institutions of Public Nature Act 1959 Assam Consolidation of Holdings Act, 1960 Assam Gramdan Act, 1961 Assam Tenancy Act, 1971, etc.

Many Acts are amended from time to time in favour of the tenants. Temporary alienation of land from tribals to non-tribals, in the shape of *paiks, sukti, bandhak, khoi, mena,* etc. is increasing for want of money. Even Assam's temporary capital Dispur was built on a tribal village near Guwahati city. The increasing urbanisation in and around Guwahati has forced a good number of tribals, particularly the Karbis and the Bodos to sell their land. This has pushed them to the interior places. Land alienation has made a large number of tribals homeless in their own homeland (M. Hussain, 1992: p. 1049).

25. Population:—The Britishers started conducting population census from 1872. People of Assam can be divided into two categories— people living in the Brahmaputra and Barak valley and people living in the hilly areas of North Cachar and Karbi Anglong districts. The communities living in the valleys can be subdivided again into four groups—the Assamese and Bengali people of Brahmaputra and Barak Valleys respectively, the Bodo-speaking communities, the Mishings and the outsiders.

It is said that the Australoids came first to this region. After Australoids, Mongoloids came to Assam. According to the Mahabharata, the Mongolians were one of the earliest inhabitants of Assam. The geological history tells us that in the beginning of the late glacial period of Pleistocene era, about 25,000 years ago, the severity of climate forced the people of the South Central China to come closer to the warmer South. The entire South-East Asia was, thus, inhabited by these immigrants by the end of the first millennium. They, thereafter, proceeded to South-West and West and entered North-East India from Myanmar (Burma). It is said that some of the Caucasoid people entered Assam in pre-Vedic period and thereafter Indo-Aryans, before different Mongoloides such as Ahoms came to Assam.

Linguistically the Mongoloids belong to the Sino-Tibetan group of Tibeto-Burman. A group of them is Bodo people. This Bodo group comprises the Koch, Kachari, Lalung (Tiwa), Dimacha, Rabha, Mech, Chutia, Moran, apart from the Bodos themselves. Siamese-Chinese language speakers came to Assam at a later date. This Mongoloid people Tai or Shan migrated to Assam in the early part of the thirteenth century. They are known as Ahoms. The Ahoms, Khamyang, Phakiyals, Aitoniya, etc. speak Tai language which belongs to the Siamese-Chinese linguistic group. Tea-garden labourers have added another element. Large settlements of Hindu Nepali population are seen in the remote areas of the hills of Assam and also in the urban areas of the plains.

The total population of Assam is 222,94,562 (1991 Census-P) of which 115,79,693 are male and 107,14,869 are female. The growth rate is 52.44 % (1971-91). The urban population is 24,70,888 (11.08%) and rural population is 198,23,674 (88.92%); density of population per sq. km is 284 persons. In 1881, the area of Assam was 55,384 sq. miles and the population was 48,15,157 (*Encylopaedia Asiatica,* vol. I, reprinted in 1976: p. 189).

Table VII

Density of Population in 1991

States	*Area (Sq Km.)*	*Population (Persons)*	*Density (Per Sq. Km.)*
Arunachal Pradesh	83,743	8,58,392	10
Assam	78,438	222,94,562	284
Manipur	22,327	18,26,714	82
Meghalaya	22,429	17,60,626	78
Mizoram	21,081	6,86,217	33
Nagaland	16,579	12,15,573	73
Tripura	10,486	27,44,827	262
Total	2,55,083	313,86,911	123
All India	32,87,263	84,43,24,222	265

Source: *Geopolitics of NEI* by J. Hazarika (1996:38)

There are several tribal populations in Assam. These are the Aiton, Mech, Moran, Matak, Chutiya, Rabha, Hajong, Hojai, Rajbangsi, Koch, Turung, Man (Tai speaker), Mishing, Kachari, Deuri, Tiwa (Lalung), Karbi (Mikir), Tai-Pha-Ke, Bodo and Ahom. Besides them, Khasi, Garo, Mizo, Kuki, Naga, Manipuri, Tripuri, Arunachalese, Bhutiya, Lepcha, Oraon, Munda, Santhal, Bhil, Kaur, etc., are there. There are several caste population and they are the Assamese, Bengali, Bihari, Nepali, Marwari and Sikh communities etc.

Rise of population had taken place rapidly after the year 1941, due to the influx of the Bengalis from East Bengal (East Pakistan now Bangladesh) after a communal riot brokn out on the issue of religion, in the district of Dacca (East Bengal). After Independence and the creation of East Pakistan (East Bengal) in 1947, Hindu refugees came to Assam in large numbers from East Pakistan to settle. Since then, there has been a constant flow of refugees especially during Bangladesh War of 1971-72. A large number of Muslims and Hindu refugees came to Assam after the War and it seems they are not returning to their homeland. *Sentinel* reported in March 9, 1996 that Muslim population in India rose from 61.4 million in 1971 to 101.6 million in 1991. In Assam, the Muslim population rose from 3.6 million in 1971, to 6.4 million in 1991, registering an increase of 77.42 per cent. Muslims are in majority in four districts of Assam namely Dhubri (70.46 per cent), Goalpara (50.18 per cent), Barpeta (56.07 per cent) and Hailakandi (55.42 per cent). If the population of Muslims keeps on

Table VIII
Population of Assam

District	*Area in sq.km*	*Male*	*Female*	*Total*	*Density per sq.*	*Growth rate km 1971-91 (in per cent)*
Dhubri	2838	679,335	646,318	1,325,653	467	55.77
Kokrajhar		410,272	386,608	796,880	N.A.	75.94
Bongaigaon	7463	415,635	390,837	806,472	N.A.	64.43
Goalpara		338,323	323,478	661,801	N.A.	52.66
Barpeta	3245	712,861	669,854	1,382,715	426	42.71
Nalbari	2257	522,655	489,953	1,012,608	449	48.72
Kamrup	4345	1,056,525	931,137	1,987,662	457	64.69
Darrang	3481	663,596	623,037	1,286,633	370	54.17
Sonitpur	5324	742,455	676,029	1,418,484	266	56.49
Lakhimpur	2277	387,942	361,733	749,675	329	55.91
Dhemaji	3237	244,467	227,716	472,183	146	104.48
Morigaon	5535	329,977	310,399	640,376	N.A.	51.07
Nagaon		978,220	913,867	1,892,087	N.A.	51.17
Golaghat	3502	417,234	384,506	801,740	229	53.09
Jorhat	2851	453,001	415,444	868,445	305	32.68
Sibsagar	2668	467,610	427,502	895,112	335	36.80
Dibrugarh	3381	544,141	493,949	1,038,090	307	37.20

District	*Area in sq.km*	*Male*	*Female*	*Total*	*Density per sq.*	*Growth rate km 1971-91 (in per cent)*
Tinsukia	3790	508,703	454,473	963,176	254	47.16
Karbi Anglong	10434	343,649	311,766	655,415	63	72.79
North Cachar	4888	79,536	69,810	149,346	31	96.39
Karimganj	1809	424,118	401,433	825,551	456	41.82
Hailakandi	1327	232,236	216,270	448,506	338	45.76
Cachar	3786	627,202	588,750	1,215,952	321	47.65

Source: *Census of India 1991, Assam (P)*

increasing at the present rate, Marigaon, Nagaon and Karimganj will emerge as Muslim majority districts by 2001 A.D. This was reported to have been made by the former Director of Census Operations, Assam, in a seminar on the "Demographic Profile of Assam" on March 8, 1996. Further, the establishment of tea gardens during the second and third decades of this century led to the immigration of the Santal, Oraon and Munda tribes. Some Khasis had settled in Assam when the capital of Assam was shifted to Dispur (Guwahati) in 1972-73. It is observed that the population of Assam had abnormally increased in 1961-71, in comparison to other parts of India.

51.24 percentage (Census 1991-P), of the total population are cultivators. The rural population is now gradually decreasing and urban population is remarkably increasing.

Table IX
Population Growth

Year	*Population*	*Decadal variation in per cent*	
1901	3,290	16.99 %	
1911	3,849	20.48 %	
1921	4,637	19.91 %	
1931	5,560	20.40 %	
1941	6,695	19.93 %	
1951	8,029	34.98 %	
1961	10,837	34.95 %	
1971	14,625	36.05 %	52.44 %
1981	19,897*	12.05 %	
1991	22,295	—	

*Projected figure (as revised by R.G.I.)

Source: *Census of India 1991 (P)*

There are four main castes in Hindu society. These are—the Brahmin, Kshatriya, Vaisya and Sudra. The Sudras have suffered from various socio-economic and political disabilities in society. Some of them were called "untouchables" and referred to as "depressed" classes till 1935. Afterwards the term "Scheduled Caste" was applied to them in Government of India Act, 1935. Under Article 341 of the Constitution of Independent India, the President of India can specify the castes which are to be treated as Scheduled Castes.

Likewise, for tribal communities, the President of India can specify the tribes which are to be treated as Scheduled Tribes under Article 342 of the Constitution. Article 46 of the Constitution lays down that the State shall promote with special care the educational and economic interests of the weaker sections of the people, particularly, those of the Scheduled Castes and Scheduled Tribes and shall protect them from social injustice and exploitation. There are also special provisions in the Constitution for the benefit of these people. In Assam, the hill districts where Scheduled Tribes form the majority of the population, Autonomous District Councils have been formed with extensive powers of administration.

In the caste hierarchy the Brahmins occupy the highest position. Their traditional occupation is priesthood. Thereafter come the Kayasthas, who are traditionally writers or of derical cadre. In between Brahmin and Kayastha castes, there is the Kalita caste. Some are of the opinion that the Kalitas entered Assam from north-west India and they belong to the pre-Vedic Aryan group. However, Kalitas are divided into Bar-Kalita and Saru-Kalita. Bar-Kalitas think that they are superior to Saru-Kalitas. There are various Kalita castes, i.e, Kumar Kalita, Kahar Kalita, Sonari Kalita, Mali Kalita. There is another very important caste known as Keot caste. It is also divided into Halowa Keot and Jalowa Keot. Halowa Keots are higher in position than Jalowa Keots. Some think that, Kaivartas are a mixture of castes. They belong to Sudra group, lowest in the caste hierarchy. Traditionally they are the fishermen. There are Kumar and Hira castes. Kumars are in higher position than Hira. Kumars make pottery by wheel, whereas *Hiras* by hand. Tanti, Naoriya, Hari castes etc., are also there. There are Boishya caste doing different types of work. Some of them are known as Suri. In earlier days, the Suris used to make and sell wine. There are also Dhoba Boishya. They are divided into Rangoli Dhoba group who colour the cloth. There are Mukhi and Nath castes. Koch caste is also there. In earlier days, the Assamese were classified into two groups. Kalitas of Aryan people and Koch of Mongolian people.

Hindu caste system of Assam is different from other regions of India. These castes are not very strict in doing different types of work. It differs according to their original residential places in Assam. According to B.M. Das, the Koch is a caste (1987:284) and as per Sibendra Narayana Koch, it is a tribe in North-East India (198 :83). According to P.C. Saikia there are different types among Chutiyas, i.e. Hindu Chutiya, Deuri Chutiya, Ahom Chutiya, etc. (1984: p. 51).

In 1971, there were 16 Scheduled Castes in Assam. They were Bansphor, Bhuinmali or Mali, Britial-Bania or Bania, Dhupi or Dhobi, Dugla or Dholi, Hira, Jalkeot, Jhalo-Malo, Kaibarta or Jaliya, Lalbegi, Mahara, Mehtar or Bhanji, Muchi or Rishi, Namasudra, Patni, and Satradhar. Namasudra was numerically the strongest community; then came Kaibarta or Jaliya; thereafter, Patni and then Muchi or Rishi. The smallest community was Lalbegi. The proportion of Scheduled Castes was highest in Cachar district and then Nagaon district. The lowest proportion was in North Cachar Hill district.

The Scheduled Tribes are spread all over the districts. Karbi Anglong and North Cachar Hills, are inhabited by a large number of Scheduled Tribes. It is said that more than two thirds of the Scheduled Tribes are living in plains. Boro, Boro-Kacharis are numerically the strongest.

Table X

Distribution of Scheduled Caste Population

District	*Percentage of district population*	*Percentage of Scheduled Caste population*
Cachar	14.70	10.76
Karimganj	14.58	7.26
Marigaon	13.78	5.31
Hailakandi	12.05	3.26
Bongaigaon	10.74	5.23
Nagaon	10.00	11.43
Nalbari	8.78	5.38
Lakhimpur	8.01	3.63
Jorhat	7.61	4.00
Kamrup	7.54	9.10
Barpeta	6.54	5.47
Dhemaji	6.37	1.83
Somitpur	5.69	4.89
Golaghat	5.59	2.79
Goalpara	5.50	2.21
Darrang	4.95	3.88
Dhubri	4.82	3.87
Karbi Anglong	4.22	1.69
Dibrugarh	4.02	2.52
Kokrajhar	3.76	1.81
Sibsagar	3.56	1.94
Tinsukia	2.61	1.51
N.C. Hills	2.60	0.23

Source : *A.K. Neog (1995:2); 1991 Census*

Table XI

Percentage of Tribal Population

District	*Percentage of Tribal population*
Goalpara	13.85
Kamrup	10.44
Darrang	10.69
Nowgong	7.44
Sibsagar	6.82
Lakhimpur	40.23
Mikir Hills	55.37
North Cachar Hills	69.15
Cachar	0.89
Dibrugarh	5.77
Assam State = 22.07	

Source : *Joysankar Hazarika (1996:80) and 1971 Census*

The Muslims are grouped into the Syad, Garia (Sheikh) and Maria. They do not form a single homogeneous Muslim unit. According to M. Hussain (1993: p. 197), the Muslims of Assam are categorized into four groups—Assamiya Muslims, Na-Assamiya Muslims, Muslims of Barak Valley and North Indian Muslims.

As per B.M. Das (1987: p. 7), Muslims for the first time came to Assam in the early part of thirteenth century when Mohammed bin Bakhtiyar Khilji, a Muslim general of Kutubuddin led a Turkish army to this region. Following him, other Muslim invaders came to Assam. Every time they were defeated. A few Muslim soldiers preferred to live in Assam instead of going back with their defeated leaders. As per M. Hussain (1993:198-199), they may be regarded

Table XII

Main Tribes of Assam (1981)

District	*H.Qs.*	*Main Tribes*
Goalpara	Goalpara	Boro, Boro-Kachari, Rabha, Sonowal.
Kamrup	Guwahati	Boro, Boro-Kachari, Rabha, Sonowal.
Karbi Anglong	Diphu	Karbi, Dimasa-Kachari, Rengma Naga.
N.C.Hills	Haflong	Dimasa Kachari, Karbi, Zemi Naga, Kuki.
Nowgong	Nowgong	Lalung, Sonowal Kachari, Miri, Boro, Kachari.
Sibsagar	Sibsagar	Miri, Sonowal Kachari.
Cachar	Silchar	Barman Kachari.
Darrang	Tezpur	Sonowal Kachari, Boro Kachari, Miri, Rabha.
Lakhimpur	North Lakhimpur	Miri, Sonowal Kachari, Boro Kachari, Deuri.
Dibrugarh	Dibrugarh	Miri, Sonowal Kachari, Chutiya,Moran, Mishing, Phakial, Khamyang.

as the first batch of Muslim migrants to Assam. This had happened even before the arrival of the Ahoms who ruled Assam for 600 years. The Mughal emperors of India attacked Assam several times. But, the Ahom kings resisted the Mughal invasions. The Muslim prisoners of these wars were subsequently rehabilitated in different parts of the Brahmaputra Valley. According to E.A. Gait (1905:149), these Muslim prisoners did not obviously bring wives with them, and therefore, married local non-Muslim Assamiya women. M. Hussain (1993:199), reported that this had helped them to assimilate gradually into the medieval Assamese society. In course of time, they gave up their Hindustani language and became unilingual, that is, Assamiya-speaking people. Assam came into contact with the Muslims as early as 1203, but the systematic propagation of Islam in Assam started only in the early part of the 17th century. The second category of Muslims in Assam, as per M. Hussain (1993:200), are Na-Assamiya Muslims. They are also known as Pamua Musalman (the farming Muslims), Charua Musalman (the Muslims of river islands or banks seasonally submerged into river waters), Mian Musalman, Mymensinghia Musalman (Muslims from Mymensingh district of Bangladesh), "Immigrant

Muslims" and "Bengali Muslims". The third category of Muslims are the Barak Valley Muslims. As per M. Hussain (1993:198), linguistically they are Bengalis like their Hindu counterparts of Barak Valley. This community migrated from East Bengal (Bangladesh), particularly from Sylhet, during the pre-colonial and colonial period. The fourth and last category of Muslims are North Indian Muslims. As per M. Hussain (1993:197), they migrated to Assam during the later stage of colonialism and more so after Independence, mainly from Uttar Pradesh and Bihar in search of a livelihood. They are mainly washermen, butchers, barbers, *dhunias*, tailors, masons and carpenters and are also employed in retreading, vulcanizing and repairing of automotive tyres and tubes. This group in Assam has neither assimilated with the Assamiya Muslims nor with the Assamiya nationality.

26. Religion:—Assam was known as *Kamarupa* in seventeenth and eighteenth centuries. The *Vedic*, the *Pauranic,* and the *Tantric* have thrived here equally where primitive forms of worship, fetishism and animism also held their place. People of all races, Aryan, non-Aryan, Hindus, non-Hindus had equally contributed in building a prosperous Assam.

Vaishnavism, Saivism, Saktism, Buddhism along with Animism,and *Hinduism* were the earliest religions of Assam. The Chutiyas who lived in the Sadiya tract followed *Tantrism* (E.A.Gait, 1926:421). The Bhuyans, who inhabited both sides of the valley west of the Kachari kingdom followed *Tantrism* (B.K. Kakati, *Purani Kamrupar Dharmar Dhara,* 1955:90).The Hindus were either followers of *Vaishnavism* or *Saktism* (B.K. Kakati, *Mother Goddess Kamakhya,*1948:73—75, 82—87). *Vaishnavism* occupied an important place among the Hindus (G.C. Barua, *Ahom Buranji,* 1930:5-17). The Ahoms, a *Shan* tribe of northern Myanmar entered into Assam in the early part of thirteenth century (1228 A.D.) and formed a kingdom in Assam. They had their own religion, Taoism and worshipped various gods and goddesses. The *Phralong* sect of Ahom adopted Buddhism and followed Mahayana Buddhism. The Hindu influence was found among the Ahoms during the reign of Suhungmung alias Swarga Narain (1497-1539). During Pratap Singh's time (1603-1641) Hindu influence increased in Ahom kingdom and continued for a long time. The Ahoms had converted themselves to Hinduism by the seventeenth century before the arrival of the later immigrants and abandoned their language in favour of Assamese (Gait, 1963 edition). It is said that the first major stream of Muslims entered Assam in the thirteenth century (in 1203) when the first mosque came up (S. Gupta, 1984:92). Spread of Islam started systematically only in the early part of the seventeenth century. A Muslim saint Hazarat Shah Milan, Popularly known as Azan Faqeer, came to Assam in about 1630 A.D. He promoted Islam and helped it to take firm roots in Assam. He composed devotional songs, *zikir* and *Zaris* in Assamese language. This helped in popularising Islam in Assam. Azan Fakir was granted tax-free lands to set up his relgious institutions by the Ahom king. The kings did not interfere in Muslim *Madrasas* or mosques. Azan Fakir belongs to Syad group. All the Assamese Muslims belong to the *Sunni* sect of Islam. The highest proportion of Muslims are found in undivided Goalpara district and undivided Cachar and Nagaon districts. The Muslims of Assam have three broad 'caste-like' divisions. According to their social status, they are—the Syads (who claim to be the descendants of Prophet Mohammad), the Sheikhs and Garias (who form the major bulk of the population), and the Marias (the descendants of the captured Muslim soldiers). In Assamese community, at various socio-cultural gatherings the Assamese Hindus and Assamese Muslims mix with one another freely. There is less reservations among the Assamese Hindus about Muslims.

In the past, when the non-Hindu rulers embraced Hinduism, their subjects also followed them. After the Ahom kings became Hindus, the worship of goddess Durga, the celebration of Doljatra (Holi) and observance of Shiva Ratri were arranged at the capital town. Ahom king Suhungmung alias Swarga Narain witnessed the rise of neo-Vaishnavism under Srimanta Sankardeva who was born in a Bhuyan family (1487-1568). He started a new religion of Bhakti. He was a Kayastha by birth and a Sakta by family religion. He accepted socially depressed people of any caste, tribe and even Mohammedans in his religion. When initiated, these people were called Saranias. Sankardeva is worshipped by the people as an incarnation of God. The caste system in Assam is more flexible than in other parts of India. Tribe to caste mobility is a continous process. After the death of Sankardeva in Koch Behar (1569 A.D.) his followers split into Damodaradeva (1488-1598 A.D.) and Harideva (1493-1598 A.D.) sect of Bamun Gassains is held within the age of 12 to 17 years. Assamese Brahmins generally had converted the Brahmins to the new faith of Sankaradeva and named Damodariya group of Bhakti cult and Mahapurusiya group or the followers of Madhabdeva (1489-1596), a prime disciple of Sankaradeva, whose philosophy was Sankardeva's age-old tradition of social and ethical faith. However, Damodariya and Mahapurusiya groups joined together in all religious ceremonies of Vaishnavism concerned with Satras and Namghars. The Mahapurusiyas are against idol worship and worship of other gods while the Damodariyas perform the ceremonies. In social intercourse there is no difference between Damodariya and Mahapurusiya. The Satras and Namghars are two important religious institutions of Assam's Vaishnavism that control the morality and ethics of the Hinduised tribes and non-tribes (B.B. Goswami, 1972:277). The Satra (monastery, seat of a religious head, the Satradhikar) and Namghar (prayer halls) religious institutions of Assam were initiated by Sankaradeva at the end of fifteenth century.

K.N. Dutt (1958:21-22), reported that the word *Satra* derived from Sanskrit root *'troi'* (to protect) with prefix *'sat'* (meaning good) is a monastic centre where the *Guru* (preceptor) and his *Bhaktas* (devotees) reside devoting themselves to religious practices, studying and discussing the sacred literature and *Namkirtan* or congregational prayers. The campus of the *Satra* is sacrosanct and within it a *Namghar* or prayer-house with annexures, and residential cottages for the *Guru* (master) and the *Bhaktas* (disciples) are found. The *Satra* also ministers to the spiritual needs of masses or the laity surrounding it or paying homage to it. The *Namghar* or *Kirtan-ghar* is an essential feature of all *Satras*.

The Hindus are divided into Brahmin, Kayastha, Vaishya and Sudra. The Brahmins are considered as people of the highest status. Their traditional profession is the priesthood as stated earlier. Men wear sacred thread across their chest after their *Upanayana* ceremony which is held within the age of 12 to 17 years. Assamese Brahmins generally form only one endogamous group. Kayasthas of Upper Assam are not equal in status with those of Lower Assam. The Kalitas can marry the Kayasthas of Upper Assam; but, the Kayasthas of Lower Assam can marry only within their group. The Kalitas of Assam are below the Brahmins—long back, the Vaishyas used to prepare and sell wine. Vaishya washermen are also there. Among them those who colour the cloth are known as *Rangoli Dhoba*. There are those belonging to Hari caste who are considered as the lowest in caste hierarchy. Earlier, Assamese were divided only into Kalita and Koch, because, they wanted to divide people between Aryan (*Kalita*) and Mongoloid *(Koch)*. Among the Assamese caste system is not very rigid.

Non-Aryan tribes like the *Koch, Moran, Chutiya, Ahom, Kachari* were brought under *Vaishnavism*. *Satras* were established at different places in Assam. They had been looking after the religious and social well-being of the villagers as well as some urban dwellers for the last 400 years. In many places the community prayer halls (*Namghars*) of the Hindus are open to all.

Most of the hill tribes have been converted to Christianity by the Missionaries but, a majority of them still observe the customs and festivals of their traditional religion of *Animism* which has close affinity to the ancient form of Hindu worship. In 1971, 22 per cent of the population of North Cachar Hills and 8 per cent of Mikir Hills district followed Christianity. It is said that, some of the *Karbis* and *Kacharis* of Karbi Anglong and North Cachar Hills are Hindus.

As per the Census of India (1971), Hindus in Assam are 71 per cent of the total population of the State as against the all-India figure of 83 per cent, 24 per cent of the population are Muslims, a bigger number in the State compared with 11.20 per cent at the national level, 4.46 per cent of the population are Christians as against 2.60 per cent at the national level.

The Sikhs of Assam are divided into two categories. They are Punjabi Sikhs and Assamese Sikhs. The Punjabi Sikhs came to Assam a few years back in search of livelihood. The Assamese Sikhs are the descendants of Sikh soldiers, who came from Punjab to help one of the Ahom rulers to fight against the Burmese (Myanmar) invaders. Many soldiers settled in Assam after the war. They married Assamese girls. Most of the Assamese Sikhs reside in Borkhola of Nagaon district. Some of them live in Darrang, Kamrup and Dhubri districts.

Buddhism is adopted as the religion in some parts of North-East India specially Arunachal Pradesh, parts of Upper Assam, parts of Tripura and Mizoram. This religion has spread to Myanmar (Burma), Tibet, China, Japan and Sri Lanka (Ceylon). In some parts of Upper Assam, there are small populations of Buddhists, i.e. the Khamyang, Aiton, Tai Phake, Turung, Duania, the *Phralong* sect of Ahom, etc. According to their religion they are divided into four divisions. These are—(a) *Bhikku*, (b) *Rouli* (c) *Ojha* and (d) *Gankuli*. The *Bhikkus* are orthodox monks. The *Roulis* are the village priests who perform customary rites of the religion. The *Ojhas* (sorcerer) drive away the evil spirits by propitiating them. The *Gankulis* are the singers of narrative and sentimental songs who go round from village to village and give religious advice to the ordinary people. They have some customs which are similar to that of Animists. They have their own festivals which are held on the full-moon day of *Baisakh* (April-May) and *Kartik* (October-November) which are considered to be the anniversaries of Buddha's birth and attainment of *Nirvana* respectively. There are *Hinayana* Buddhists who eat fish and fowl if they are killed by others. The *Phralong* sect of Ahom are the offshoot of *Mahayana* Buddhist.

Jainism was first preached as a religion in Bihar and afterward it spread to other regions. The two principal sects of the *Jains* are the *Digambara* and the *Swetambara*, Digambara being the more numerous. Digambara means "Sky-clad" and Swetambara means "Clothed in white". The Jains are mostly Marwaris and Banias found all over Assam. Like the Brahmins, Jain boys are invested with the sacred thread which ceremony usually takes place at the boy's wedding or at the age of 22 years if he is unmarried. The thread is renewed annually at the time of the full moon of *Bhado* (August). Prior to that a fast for ten days is observed in honour of *Anant Nath*, the fourteenth *Tirthankar*. According to M. Hussain (1993:264), the Marwari traders arrived in Assam immediately after the colonization of Assam in 1826. He also reports (1993:271) about the famous Agarwala, the Marwari family of Tezpur and its contribution to the enrichment of modern Assamiya literature and culture. B.C. Allen reported that (1905), Marwari merchants used to trade in Gouripur (Dhubri district) since long back.

Table XIII

Population of Major Religions (1971)

Name of religion	*Proportion to total population per cent (Assam)*	*Proportion to total population per cent (India)*
Hinduism	82.72	71.04
Islam	11.20	24.03
Christianity	2.60	4.46
Sikhism	1.89	0.08
Buddhism	0.71	0.30
Jainism	0.47	0.09
Other religions and persuatsions	0.40	negligible
Religion not stated	0.01	—
	100.00	100.00

Source : *Census of India 1971.*

Table XIV

Three Major Religious Population Percentage of Three Decades (Assam)

Religion	1951	1961	1971
Hindu	60.31	69.75	71.04
Muslim	21.98	24.70	24.03
Christian	3.21	4.45	4.46*

Source : *Census of India 1971.*
*Including Mizoram (District of Assam, 1971)

Table XV

Major Religions in the District Headquarters of Assam (1971)

H.Qs.	*Population of the town*	*Percentage of Population to total Population*					
		Hindu	*Muslim*	*Christian*	*Buddhist*	*Jain*	*Sikh*
Dhubri	36,503	72.73	24.26	0.51	0.05	2.35	0.09
Gauhati	123,783	86.96	9.95	1.06	0.10	0.49	1.44
Tezpur	39,870	88.55	8.30	1.65	0.12	1.09	0.29
Nowgong	56,537	76.77	20.52	1.23	0.01	0.74	0.73
Jorhat	30,247	83.81	14.24	0.19	0.01	0.59	1.16
Dibrugarh	80,348	84.68	12.63	0.82	0.29	0.68	0.90
Diphu	10,200	88.37	4.88	5.41	0.20	0.07	1.07
Haflong	5,197	80.80	5.37	13.35	—	—	0.48
Silehar	52,596	88.62	9.77	1.07	0'02	0.48	0.04
Aijal*	31,740	6.34	1.22	92.36	0'07	—	0.01

Source : *Census of India 1971.*
*Mizoram District

Table XVI

Percentage of Population (1971, 1961)

State/Dist.	*Year*	*Hindu*	*Muslim*	*Christian*	*Buddhist*	*Jain*	*Sikh*
Assam	1971	71.04	24.03	4.46	0.30	0.09	0.08
	1961	69.75	24.70	4.45	0.32	0.08	0.08
Goalpara	1971	53.92	42.25	3.59	0.02	0.18	0.04
	1961	50.95	43.32	3.34	0.07	0.13	0.02
Kamrup	1971	69.96	28.93	0.88	0.04	0.10	0.09
	1961	69.19	29.30	0.89	0.02	0.11	0.05
Darrang	1971	78.45	16.19	5.06	0.17	0.07	0.06
	1961	75.72	19.35	4.64	0.12	0.09	0.07
Nowgong	1971	59.70	39.39	0.71	0.01	0.08	0.11
	1961	57.94	41.24	0.59	0.03	0.07	0.11
Sibsagar	1971	92.22	5.27	2.09	0.24	0.06	0.12
	1961	91.70	5.83	1.93	0.27	0.06	0.11
Lakhimpur	1971	91.45	4.59	3.21	0.54	0.07	0.14
	1961	89.97	5.64	3.47	0.53	0.10	0.17

State/Dist.	*Year*	*Hindu*	*Muslim*	*Christian*	*Buddhist*	*Jain*	*Sikh*
Mikir Hills	1971	90.27	1.30	7.99	0.35	0.01	0.08
	1961	81.64	1.34	7.54	0.39	0.01	0.10
North Cachar	1971	77.03	0.86	21.87	0.20	—	0.04
Hills	1961	79.49	0.87	19.44	0.03	—	0.01
Cachar	1971	58.71	39.89	1.32	0.02	0.05	0.01
	1961	59.60	39.14	1.10	0.02	0.03	N

Source : *Census of India 1971: Assam*

27. Superstitions, Magic and Belief:—Most of the people of Assam, both tribals and non-tribals, are superstitious. At one time, belief in the spirit-world was universal. The role of the exorciser—*bej* and *ojha*—are considered important among the common people. They believe in terrestrial, aerial, celestial and subterranean spirits. R.M. Nath (1948:59), reported that in 1337, the 1,00,000 strong cavalry of the valiant Mahammud Shah perished to a man in this land of witchcraft; and when a second army was raised, not a single soul would step beyond the border of Bengal into this dreaded land of *black art*... In 1530, Guru Nanak, the father of the valiant Sikh community, had the bitter experience of finding his brave Punjabi servant, Mordana, converted into a lamb in front of his eyes, by a woman of this country, who could reconvert the young man to his natural anatomical shape according to her personal and private needs. The faithful private secretary of the great religious preacher diligently recorded this sad incident in his memoirs, as a warning to the followers of his great master, against future entry of any of their progeny into this horrible country.

They worship *Sitala Ai* when they are seriously ill from pox. Pox is called *Ai-olowa* in Assamese (the visitation of mother Durga,who is also known as Sitala, Mahamaya, Bhagawati, Gouri, etc.). Further, they believe in *deo* (evil) spirit. *Deo* is a vulgar term for the goddess Kali. They also believe in the existence of *Bhoot* (ghost). According to them the victim suffers from an acute attack of fever due to *bhoot.* They have some faith in *baans* (Mantras). These are the Karsala Baan, Vishnu Baan, Sariah Baan, Kharika Baan, Chaka Baan, Nidra Baan, etc. The spirits, according to them are afraid of iron. So, they keep iron pieces when they want to drive away the spirits.

Superstition is unwritten social law. Some superstitions are based on medicinal properties of herbs and roots. Some think that if they light candles in dargahs of a Peer (mosque erected by or on the grave of a Mohammedan Saint), they may be cured of diseases. They believe in wearing amulets. Some of them promise an offering to a deity and fulfil their vow when they get positive results.

Superstition is inherent in the nature of man. Superstition shows the genius of the people. Most Hindus are superstitious about killing cows and cats. It was superstition which defeated Chila Rai, the general of the Koch king fighting against the Ahoms. It is said that the Ahoms won their famous battle against Chila Rai in 1562, because the Ahom general made all his men appear like Brahmins by making them wear the sacred thread, and Chila Rai was superstitious about killing Brahmins. It is said that the Ahoms were defeated by the Moamorias in 1769, because Radha-Rukmini, wife of the Moamoria general Raghaba, went with her husband to the field, and the Ahom soldiers were supersititious about the rumour that this lady possessed the supernatural power of arresting the entire hail of bullets by holding them in the folds of her costume (B. Rajkhowa, 1973:18).

Magic has great influence on the mind. In earlier days it was believed that the Assamese old women knew magic and mystical formulae. It was said that whoever entered Assam were overcome by the charms and never came out of the State. The outsiders used to call the inhabitants of Assam sorcerers and magicians. Assam was known as a land of magic and incantation. This is perhaps due to the *Tantrik* forms of Hinduism originating there. The Koch king Nara Narayan (1540-1587), conquered the Ahoms. He encouraged religion and rebuilt the temple of Kamakhya (1565 A.D.) which was demolished by Kalal Pahar, a general of Mohammedan army under Badshah of Gaur (Sulaiman Kararani, who ruled Bengal from 1563 to 1572 A.D.) during his invasion in 1553. E.A. Gait (1905:58), reported that when the new temple of Goddess Kamakhya was opened, the occasion was celebrated by the immolation of no less than 140 men, whose heads were offered to the Goddess on salvers made of no copper. Similar sacrifices were offered to various aboriginal deities. In earlier days, the magic of Assam induced fear psychosis among the ordinary people.

They believe in rebirth and the law of *Karma*, and dreams, specially early-morning dreams. Beggar, dead animal, fire, red-cloth, somebody laughing, gathering of men, etc., are considered bad symptoms in a dream. A dream about *puthi* fish means the dreamer is sure of getting wealth. Eating a particular type of fish during pregnancy indicates bad health for the child. It is further believed that eating a particular fish or animal when a woman is pregnant may affect her child's helth which is in her womb. It is, even believed that killing a fish, animal, bird, tree, etc. during pregnancy may badly affect the family. It is also believed that the women present nearby during childbirth should make the *uruli* sound (sound made by striking the tip of their tongue against the palate) for the happy announcement of the new-born baby.

28. Titles/Surnames:—The Brahmin titles are Barpujari, Sarma, Barthakur, Mahanta, Adhikari, Bhattacharjee, Chakravarty, etc. Goswami title is common among the Brahmins, but it is also used by the Kayastha "Gosains" of Damodariya sect of Sankaradeva's Vaishnavism. During the reign of Ahom rulers, some Brahmins were appointed as officers in the government and were given titles like Barua, Phukan, Barkataki, Kataki, Khound, etc. Their descendants still use these titles. The Bardoloi title is used by the *Surya Vipras, Ganaks* (M. Narimattam, 1988:41-42). The Ahom rulers distributed the top civic defence and administration posts among their men. There were "Gohains" next to the king who were Cabinet ministers and advised the king and in judicial, civil and military powers. They were the Bargohains, Bura Gohains and Barpatra Gohains. Bargohain was the king's stepbrother, the other two Gohains were top-ranked family members of the king. The word of local origin for the two ministers was Goswami or Gosain—the divine preceptor and they came to be known as Bura Gohain or Bargohain. The Gohains were given power over 10,000 *paiks* who were foot-soldiers and Rs. 90,000 as allowances. With the expansion of the Ahom kingdom, more Gohains were appointed in different regions like Sadiya-Khowa Gohains, Morongi-Khowa Gohains, etc. Their positions were normally hereditary. Next to Gohains, there were Bar-Barua and Bar-Phukan. Bar-Barua was in-charge of revenue and had judicial powers and Bar-Phukan acted as a viceroy. They were appointed from twelve classified families other than the families of Gohains. The Baruas with judicial powers were in-charge of treasury and known as *Bhandari* Barua; those in-charge of elephants and horses were Hati Barua and Ghora Barua respectively; physicians attached to the royal family were known as *Bej* Barua. Now, some of them omitted their prefix of titles *Bhandari, Hati, Ghora, Bej,* etc. Simply they are known as Barua.

After the Baruas, came the Rajkhowa title. Rajkhowas were governors of specified areas. There were twelve types of *Khounds.* They commanded small units of *paiks* (soldiers). The Hazarikas came next to Rajkhowas. They commanded 1,000 *paiks.* The Saikias were in-charge of 100 *paiks.* The *Boras* were the commanders of only 20 *paiks.* There were Katakis, Kakotis and Dolais. Katakis were emissaries of the king on foreign affairs and also dealt with hill-people of Assam. Kakotis were writers and record-keepers and Dolais were the astrologers. Barpujari, Bardoloi, Barbora, Barkataki, etc., have obvious meanings. The prefix *Bar* means "the great". There were several titles as per their work and function. *Khargarias* were guarding the armouries. *Khannikars* were the stone-sculptors. The Muslims were given many of these titles too. Even today, there are many Muslim Baruas, Saikias, Hazarikas, etc. The title *Rajbangshis* means men of the royal race of the Koch rulers.

Sometimes it is difficult to understand from the titles who are caste people and who are tribal, e.g., Choudhuri, Singha, Roy, etc. Again it is difficult to understand who are Brahmins and who are Kayasthas form the titles. So also, it is difficult to differentiate the Hindus from Muslims as some titles are common to both. There are Hazarika, Barua, Saikia, Sarkar, Mazumdar, Choudhury, etc., for both of them. There are titles like Dev Goswami, Mahanta, Kalita, Baishya, Keot, Kumar, Das, Hira, Tanti, Phukan, Talukdar, Senapati, Singha, Kakati, Nath, Katoki, Patgiri, Roy Choudhuri, Roy, Mehdi, Bezbarua, Saharia, Mukhi, Hari, Modoi, Bora, etc. There are tribal titles like Thaosen, Terang, Langthasa, Timung, Hagjer, Barman, Chootia, Kachari, Miri, Koch, Teron, Terang, Kemprai, Rangpi, Rajbansi, Boro, Sonowal, Basumatari, Doley, Doloi, Moormoo, etc., Islam, Haque, Ahmad, Ali, Hussain, etc., are Muslim titles.

As per E.A. Gait (1905:244), names of the Ahom kings usually started with *Su*, meaning "tiger" (*Singha*-lion) and ended with *pha*, meaning "heaven".

29. Festival:—Assam celebrates several festivals. *Janmashtami*, a religious festival is celebrated on the 8th Lunar day of the dark fortnight in the month of *Bhado* (August-September). Another festival *Ras-yatra* usually takes place on the full-moon day of the month of *Kati* (October-November). It is held in honour of Lord Krishna's amorous dalliance with the milkmaids in the autumn season. There are *Dol-yatra* (Holi), *Durga puja, Manasa puja, Kali puja* (Diwali), *Saraswati puja, Basanti puja, Sri Satya Narayan puja, Mangalchandi puja, Tusu Puja, Sani puja Tithi of Srimanta Sankardeva, Tithi of Sri Madhabdeva, Lakshmi puja, Amati,* etc.

The most important social and cultural celebrations are the three *Bihu* festivals. These are observed with great enthusiasm irrespective of caste, creed and religious affinity. All these are related to the starting of new harvesting season in their paddy fields. The *Bihus* were originally agricultural festivals. The *Bohag Bihu* is celebrated in mid-April with the commencement of the Assamese new year (first day of the *Bohag* month, which falls on the 14th of April) during the Spring. It is the main Bihu and also known as *Rangali Bihu* (*Ranga*-merry-making and fun). It is observed from 3 to 7 days with *Bihu-Husori* (a collective dance), song and music in open spaces. The ladies present hand-woven *fulam-gamocha* (towel) *Bihuan* to each and every male member of the family during this festival. In rural areas, cattle are taken to the river for bathing on the last day of *Chaita* (13th April) month and it is known as *Goru-Bihu* (*Goru*-cow). On the first day of *Bohag* (14th April) the people take bath and wear new clothes. Everybody generally pays respects to the elders who in turn bless the youngsters. Most of the Assamese Hindus offer their respect to God on this day. In *Namghar/Kirtanghar* offerings are made. This is followed by *Nam-Kirtan*. *Magh Bihu* is the second important *Bihu*. It is celebrated in mid-January. It is a harvest festival and performed with community feasts and bonfires. It is also called *Bhogali Bihu* (*Bhog* = feasting and enjoyment). January thirteenth night is *Uruka* night of *Agni* (fire). They arrange for a community feast at night with male friends and relatives where *boal, rou,* fish and vegetables are served with rice. They make *Meji* (conical- shaped temporary thatched constructions); one is a tall and big sized male *Meji* and another is a small and medium-sized female *Meji*. *Bhela-Ghars* are constructed with bamboo posts and walls made of dried banana leaves, hay, etc. The women are usually busy at home making *pitha* (cake) and sweets. At night, after the feast for *Uruka* is over, they burn down these *Mejis* and *Bhelaghars* early in the morning. They pay tribute to the fire by throwing betel-nut, betel-leaf, etc., on the burnt *Meji* and *Bhela-ghar. Agni* (fire) worshipping and eating *pithas* (cakes) is the main item in *Bhogali Bihu*. People take bath early in the morning of the first day of *Magh* (14th April) and pay their respects to the elders and make good use of the *pithas* prepared for this *Bihu* occasion. The third one is *Kati Bihu*. It is observed in mid-October. It is also known as the *Kongali Bihu* (*Kongali*-poor) which indicates that a common man is almost without foodgrains. It is observed before the *Tulsi* (basil) plant and in the paddy fields. The farmers run short of food during this *Bihu*. They believe that one gets a good yield (goddess *Lakshmi*) by performing *Tulsi puja* (worship). On the day of *Kati Bihu, Tulsi* plant is ceremonially planted. The act of planting and offering light at the feet of the plant constitutes the special function of the day. This *Bihu* is not widely observed by all the Assamese people. The urban youth has almost forgotten this *Bihu.* Dances of *Rangali Bihu* are not permitted in the *Satras* and *Bhogali Bihu* is observed in *Satras* with prayers and devotional songs only.

Death anniversaries (*Tithis*) of Sri Sankardeva and Madhadeva are observed in all *Satras* affiliated to *Purusa*, *Nika* and *Kala Samhatis*. In *Barpeta Satra*, Sankardeva *tithi* is celebrated for seven days and Madhabdeva's for ten days. *Satras* which are affiliated to the *Brahma Samhati* observe the *tithis* of Damodardeva, Harideva, Bhattadeva and other leaders of the sub-sect.

There are *Me-dum-me-phi* festival, *Chuka-Fa divas, Bir Chilarai divas, Lachit divas*, etc. Tea gardens' also have their own indigenous festivals. Every second Wednesday of February is observed the *Ali-Aye-Lingang* or Mishing festival. It starts at the premises of the *gum (gaon bura)* or *Murong Ghar. Liggad* is the main function of this. The Madhaba temple at Hajo in Kamrup district attracts not only the Hindus but also the Buddhist people of Bhutan who come every year to attend a month-long '*Daranga*' fair near Rangia, Assam. Hajo temple also enshrines the image of Lord Buddha. These types of fairs have developed into markets which attract visitors. The Bhutanese ignore the boundary lines of their country and pay visit to such markets situated in a foreign land. Hajo has a mosque on the Mukamara hill which is called as '*Poa-Mecca*' (i.e. one-fourth of the merit of Mecca). Near the mosque there is a tomb of Sultan Ghiyasuddin.

Good Friday, Easter, X-mas, etc., are the religious festivals of the Christians in Assam; Id-ul-Fitr, Id-uz-Zuha, Muharram, Fateha-Dohaz-Daham, etc. of the Muslims; Guru Nanak birthday, of the Sikhs Buddha Purnima of the Buddhists and Mahavir Jayanti of the Jains.

30. Dance:—*Bihu Hoosuri*, the *Bihu* dance is the main dance of Assam. People dance usually to the sound of their indigenous musical instruments like *Mohar singar pepa* (buffalo-horn flute), *dhol* (drum), and two horizontal cut pieces of bamboos (face to face striking of two cut pieces of bamboo lengthwise in the middle). In folk dances, imagination and instinct of the beautiful dancers are ensured as much by freshness and simplicity as by the music of the compositions.

'*Satriya*', is a form of dance of *Vaishnavite Satra*. It is said that this dance originated from seven/eight forms of Indian classical dances Kathak, Kathakali, Bharat Natyam, Odissi, Kuchipudi, Manipuri, Mohiniattam, etc. Vaishnava saint Sankaradeva and reformers introduced *Satriya* (*Chali*), dance to propagate the cult of Vaishnavism. There are twelve varieties of *Chali* dance which belong to the traditional Satriya dance, '*Ojapali*' dances are also there. It is a popular dance, illustrating scriptural stories.

Different tribes have their own folk-dances which we may classify into three parts—Ritual dance, Agricultural dance and Recreational dance. Among the Mishings '*Bhakat*' dance, '*Maiba*' (priest) dance-cum-prayer, dances in *Ali-aye-liagang* festival; Rabha dances, Karbi dances, Tiwa (Lalung) dances, etc., and in tea-gardens '*jhumur*' dances are performed. Naga dance, Mizo bamboo dance, etc., are also performed in North Cachar Hills and Karbi Anglong districts.

The Rabhas perform rituals when life comes to an end, *furkanti* dance with songs for eternal peace of a departed soul. *Bardaichikhla* is a folk-dance of the Bodos. They dance during *Bohag* month (April-May). In Bodo language *Bar* means wind or storm, *dai* means water and *chikhla* means a maiden or a deity. They believe that this Bardaichikla comes to save nature and gives life to her dry and dying plants and trees. *Deodhani* dance is a part of Maria-Puja. Generally unmarried girls dance in front of the deity Manasa. They dance to the drum-beat of *Joy dhol* (big-drum), *Bhortal* (big cymbal), etc. *Langkhon Fuja Mishawa* is a dance of the Tiwa related to their religious festival from November to January. *Jhummur* dance of tea garden labourers is associated with *Karam Puja* and other occasions.

31. Music:—The influence of Indian music on Assam was so great that not only did it influence Assamese songs in general but influenced its folk songs also. The use of musical instruments like '*Bansi*' (flute), *khol* (tom-tom), *mridanga* (cymbal), etc., influenced Assamese music and ultimately, folk-songs of Brahmaputra and Barak valleys.

The folk-songs and traditional devotional songs of Assam nurtured to many talents like Bishnu Rabha, Ambika Giri Roy Choudhuri, Joti Prasad Agarwala, Dr. Bhupen Hazarika and (Goalpariya folk-songs) Pratima Pandey (Barua) and so on. The influence of folk culture of Assam influenced the writings of modern poets and singers.

Assam started taking a new cultural turn in the fifteenth and sixteenth centuries. Srimant Sankardeva wrote a number of devotional songs. Every house of Assam today sings his songs from his *Kritans* and *Namghosas*. His songs were mostly written in *Brajabuli* language. Mir Sufi's *Sufism* (1614-1616 A.D.) of Assam created its own folk-songs, based on universal brotherhood and added glitter to Assam's culture. *Zikirs* of Ajan Fakir's philosophical secular choral songs of Assam are sweet to hear with typical rhythms. It echoes the spiritual ideals of Islam. Muslim saint Shah Milan, who migrated to Assam from Baghdad had composed the *Zikirs* to utter the name of God frequently by singing in a very simple manner. It is said that the tunes of these songs resemble the *Vaishnava* tunes as the saint Shah Milan (Azan Fakir) was influenced by the tunes of *Kirtan* and *Ghosa*.

Bargeet is a devotional song introduced by *Vaishnava* saints Sankardeva and Madhabdeva in the fifteenth century. *Bargeet* used to be sung to glorify the lord in various classical-*ragas* of Vaishnava traditional musical flavour. There are regional varieties of songs; *Kamrupia Lokageets* belong to Kamrup district. *Tokari geet* of Assam is popular. *Pal-Nam* of *Satras* are sweet to listen.

Bihu dances are performed with *Bihu* music and melodious *Bihu* folk-songs. Some songs are materialistic and some are deeply philosophic. Goalpara and Dhubri area of Assam have their own beautiful folk-songs for *Mahuts* (elephant tamers). All these songs have their own charm and sweetness.

Assamese are very fond of music. They have *Bihu-geet, Bargeet, Biya-Nam* (marriage songs), ritual songs, love songs, festival songs, *Nam-Kirtan*, etc. They usually sing to the accompaniment of their indigenous musical instruments and sometimes simply by clapping their palms. The *dhol* (drum) scooped out of a tree, specially from a jack fruit tree trunk is an important musical instrument in Assam, specially during *Bihu* festivals. They also use modern instruments. *Naoria geet* (boatman's song), *Nichukani geet* (cradle songs), *Bongeet* (wood man's ballade), etc., are quite popular.

32. Theatre:—*Bhawana, Mukha Deodha, Deodhani* are an integral part of the *Satra* activities. *Ankia-Nat* and *Satriya* dance drama are the theatres in Assam. All these are in true art form. They can be divided into two main types. One is the Vaishnava threatre called *Bhaona* and the other the modern stage-drama which started under the auspices of western education and British rule. *Bhaona* deals with on the life and deed of deities, gods-goddesses and Pauranic thems using. Brajabuli interspersed with Sanskrit words and *slokas* (recitation). The *Sutradhar* is an actor and stage-director of *Bhaona*. The *Oja* is the leader in the *Ojapali* dance of *Bhaona*. *Bhaonas* are popular in rural areas and, modern stage dramas are popular in urban areas. But it seems that T.V. serials, VCR/VCP, cable programmes, cinema, etc., are gradually edging them out.

33. Administration (Historical and Political):—The reconstruction of the ancient administration (historical) of Assam depends mainly on legends, myths, ancient dynastic chronicles and available relics of sculpture and architecture which have been discovered. In earlier days the territory and its surrounded areas were known as *Kamarupa*, a State that had its capital at *Pragjyotisapura* (modern Guwahati, on the southern bank of the Brahmaputra). Ancient *Kamarupa* included roughly the Brahmaputra valley, Bhutan, Rangpur district (now in Bangladesh), and Koch Behar of West Bengal (*N.E.B.* 1977, Vol. 2:207).

King Narakasura and his son Bhagadatta were the rulers of *Kamarupa* in *Mahabharata* period. The battle of Kurukshetra which was fought in 1449 BC, stands as a landmark in the history of India where all the kingdoms and the States, joined one or the other party. Bhagadatta was killed on the battlefield of Kurukshetra.

Huen Tsang, a Chinese traveller who visited the country during the time of the ruler Bhaskarvarman about 640 A.D., wrote about Assam and its people. After that, information about ancient Assam was insufficient for a few centuries. In the remote areas tribal chiefs were the rulers of their own territories. As they never maintained chronicles (except Ahom and Manipur kings) their past is somehow lost. But the discovery of copper plates, clay seals and stone inscriptions that date from 7th to mid-12th centuries, have thrown some light on the inhabitants of this region.

Kamarupa was ruled by various dynasties. These were the Naraka (c.2200-1389 BC), Varman (c.350-654 AD), Mlechh (c.655-985 AD), Pala (c.985-1130

AD), Deva (c. 1130-1500 AD), Sootia (c. 1194-1523), Kayastha (c.1340-1440), Khen (c.1400-1493), Eastern Kayastha (c. 1430-1512), Kalita (c. 1225-1430), Varahi (c. 1190-1390), Koch (1515-1772), Kachari (c. 1355-1832), Eastern Koch (1580-1640), Mohammdan rulers of *Kamrup* (1612-1658) and Tai *(Ahom)* (1228-1824 AD). There was no stable government until the Tai *(Ahom)* came to power in the early part of the thirteenth century.

The *Ahoms* crossed the *Patkoi* range from Burma (now Myanmar) and conquered the local Chieftains who ruled over the Upper Assam's plain area. Sukapha was the leader of the Shans (Tai Ahoms) who after defeating the Sootias (Chutiyas), etc., had laid the foundation of their kingdom (1228-1268 AD), in Upper Assam and continued to reign till 1824.

In the 15th century the Ahoms were the dominant power in Upper Assam. After two centuries of their rule in Upper Assam they extended their rule to lower Assam up to Goalpara by defeating the Koch, Kachari and other local leaders. But Goalpara was not a part of Ahom kingdom. The power and success of the Ahoms reached very high during the rule of the King Sukhrungpha or Rudra Singha (1696-1714). He maintained political relations with Bengal, Koch Behar, Tipperah, Manipur, Jaintia and Cachar. A cultural wave from the West swept over Assam and architects, painters, musicians, dancers and job-seekers from Bengal and other parts of India came to Ahom-capital Rangpur (Sibsagar). Rudra Singha shifted his capital from Garhgaon (near Nazira), to a place called Meteka, (near present Sibsagar town) and built a beautiful city called Rangpur or "city of palaces". This new city was decorated with tanks and temples. He died in 1714, leaving behind five sons and four queens. Rudra Singha had expressed his wish that all his sons should succeed the throne.

Rudra Singha's eldest son Sib Singha (1714-1744), was at Guwahati when Rudra Singha died. He ascended the throne in the capital Rangpur (Sibsagar) and assumed the Ahom-name Sutanpha. Pramata Singha, second son of Rudra Singha, ascended the throne (1744-1751), soon after the death of his elder brother. He assumed the Ahom name Sunenpha and was formally installed by the Deodhais (Ahom priests). Soon after that, a conspiracy was detected and the culprits were punished. He died in 1751. Rajesvar Singha (Surampha), the fourth son of Rudra Singha, became king and ruled from 1751 to1769. In July 1765, punitive action against the Mikirs was taken. In November 1768, a force was sent to Raha and the Kachari country. In 1769, the Jaintia Raja attacked the Ahom frontier with his troops. He could not succeed due to the strength of Ahom force and was compelled to withdraw his attack. Soon after this, Rajesvar Singha became ill and died. Lakshmi Singha (1769-1780), Namrup Raja, the youngest son of Rudra Singha became king and assumed the Ahom name Sunyeopha.

Disagreement in opinion and jealousy among the princes, senior officers, religious sects, gradually weakened the central administration of Ahom kingdom. The *Bargohain* (an officer with power next only to the king) and others denied Lakshmi Singha's legitimacy of kingship and supported the claim of Rajesvar

Singha's eldest son. As a result, King Lakshmi Singha before his death left the management of his kingdom in the hands of *Barbarua* (an administrator of eastern province from *Sadiya* to *Koliabar* and also commander of forces) and made his eldest son Jubaraj Gaurinath Singha (1780-1795) king, Lakshmi Singha died in December, 1780, at the age of 67 years. Gaurinath assumed the Ahom name Suhitpanghpa. Gaurinath was a bitter enemy of the Moamarias (a religious sect who played an important part in the downfall of Ahom rule). The Moamarias rose in revolt against him in April, 1782. In 1786, a more serious revolt was initiated by the Moamarias. As a result, the king fled first to Nagaon and then to Guwahati in panic. Before this, he sent urgent appeals for help to Barphukan (Viceroy) at Guwahati and also to Manipuri, Kachari and Jaintia kings.

In various parts of Assam the *Moamarias* set up, during their operations of 1786, numerous petty Rajas in Ahom-ruling areas. On the north bank of the Lohit, at Japaribhita the Moamarias set up their man as the Raja. Similarly, it happened in Majuli, east of Dihing at Bengmara, Sadiya, Rangpur, Darrang. They wanted to annex the northern part of Kamrup and even took possession of North Guwahati.

In 1786, Gaurinath sought the aid of the British from the neighbouring west. Captain T. Welsh was sent to Bengal by the British Governor-General of India who restored peace. Thereafter, Captain T. Welsh was called-back by the new Governor-General, Sir John Shore, as he had changed the policy of non-interference with the other territorial rulers since December, 1793. Gaurinath had requested the British Government several times so that Captain Welsh could stay at least for some more time. These appeals were seconded by Captain Welsh himself. But, Sir Shore ordered Captain Welsh to abstain from all further active operations and to return to British territory by July 1, 1784. Gaurinath's new capital was situated at Jorhat. He died on December 19, 1794, without any issue.

After the death of Gaurinath, Prime Minister Purnananda Buragohain appointed, without consulting anybody, the most powerful rival Kinaram, a descendant of Ahom king Gadadhar Singha's (1681-1696), line, as the next king (1795-1810). Kinaram took the Hindu name Kamaleswar and also the Ahom name Suklingpha. As soon as he became the king, a serious uprising was reported from Kamrup. In 1799, there was a revolt by the Moamarias. In 1798, the Singphos attacked the Ahom areas. The Khamtis tried to establish themselves at Sadiya and fought with the Ahoms in 1800.

The capital town at Jorhat was improved. The Bhogdoi channel was excavated. Kolia Bhomra Barphukan alias Protap Ballabh cleared Guwahati of all anarchist uprisings by murdering Kalita brothers, Haradatta and Viradatta who set up a revolutionary movement in North Guwahati. But, Sadiya area could not be recovered from the Khamtis and Dibrugarh area remained under the control of the Morans (R.M. Nath, 1948:154).

In 1810, King Kamaleswar died and Purnananda Buragohain nominated a young boy Chandrakanta, brother of late king Kamaleswar, as his successor (1810-1818), to the throne. He took Ahom name Sudinpha. Kolia Bhomra was succeeded by Badan Barphukan of *Dowerah* family as the Viceroy at Guwahati. Badan Barphukan was a power-greedy man.

In 1796, Bodaw Paya, the King of Burma planned to invade Assam to annex it with his territory. But he could not do so. King Chandrakanta was a mere puppet in the hands of his minister. He secretly encouraged Badan Barphukan (Viceroy/Governor) to get help from outside to oust the autocratic Prime Minister, Purnananda Buragohain. Bagyidaw, the grandson of Bodaw Paya was the King of Burma. He sent in 1816, a Burmese army of 8,000 men to help Badan Barphukan who advanced towards Jorhat and joined by his own recruits from Mukong, Hukong and Manipur on the way. Purnananda could not encounter this unexpected menace and died of heart failure in *Chaitra* (March/April), 1816 A.D. Purnananda's son Ruchinath Buragohain succeeded to his father's position but, he ran away with his family due to the fear of Burmese army to a safer zone at Guwahati. Shortly after that, Badan Barphukan was assassinated by the up-country Subedar Rupsingh. Ruchinath collected a force of his own and marched against the king Chandrakanta. He dethroned him and put Purandar Singha (1818-1819), as his new master on the throne at Jorhat in February, 1818.

Ala Mingi, the Burmese general attacked Assam in February, 1819, with his force and it compelled King Purandar Singha to run away to Guwahati and then to British territory. A new Burmese general Mingi Maha Bandula (Tilua) came to Assam. He installed Jogeswar Singha (1819-1824), as a puppet king and imposed (Burmese) rule on Assam. At that time, many Assamese people fled for safer zones in Rangpur, Koch Behar, Jaintia, Sylhet, Manipur, Cachar etc. Many Burmese soldiers got themselves local wives and created a new race themselves called the *Man* in Assam with Hinayan Buddhism as their religion and Assamese as their mother tongue. Britishers introduced their administration and rule in 1888 in Arunachal Pradesh and in 1838, in Assam along with Bengal.

The British had observed the developments in Burma. In March 1824, a formal war was declared against Burma by the British Government. The British force led by Col. Richards routed all Burmese centres in Assam. On 27th January, 1825, they were defeated at Sibsagar, a provisional treaty was concluded, through the intervention of the Buddhist priest Dharmadhar Brahmachari.

The British, however, had attacked the Burma's mainland. As the position was not secure the King of Ava Burma had to sign a treaty at Yandaboo on 24th February, 1826. He agreed, among other things, to abstain from all interference in the affairs of Assam. Thus, this treaty was concluded with Burma, and lower Assam comprising the districts of Kamrup, Darrang and Nagaon were annexed with the British India. These areas were placed in the hands of David Scott who, at that time, was in charge of the two Bengal districts of Goalpara and Garo Hills. These two districts of Bengal were tagged with Assam. The British Government gave kingship to Purandar Singha in 1833, to run the administration of Upper Assam except for Sadiya and Matak Rajya. Purandar Singha's administration proved a failure, both financially and generally, and in October, 1838, his territories were placed under the direct management of British officers, and Assam as a whole became a Non-Regulation Province of the Indian Empire (*A. Mackenzie*, 1989, *Reprinted*: 6). By 1839, Sibsagar and Lakhimpur districts were placed under the British administration. They extended their reign to South Cachar in 1832, Khasi Hills in 1833, Jayantia kingdom in 1835. By 1843, Khamti kingdom of Sadiya and Matak kingdom of Barsenapati were merged with the British dominion in 1854. In 1838, Assam was united with the British administered Province of Bengal and continued till 1874. By 1898, the whole hill and plain areas of Assam had come under British rule.

On February 6, 1874, a separate province of Assam was created to relieve the Lt. Governor of Bengal from his huge administrative responsibilities. The Province of Assam was placed under a Chief Commissioner with his capital at Shillong and the districts of Sylhet, Cachar, Goalpara and Garo Hills were merged with Assam. Prior to that, Assam had five districts ruled by the Ahoms. These were—Sibsagar, Lakhimpur, Darrang, Nagaon and Kamrup. Since 1874, the term "Assam" was applied to include not only these five districts but also the districts of Goalpara, Garo Hills, Cachar, Khasi Hills and Jaintia Hills, and Naga Hills. On September 12, 1874, Sylhet district was included in Assam.

In 1873, Assam was formed into a Chief Commissionership, with part of Koch-Behar added to it (*Encyclopedia Asiatica,* Vol.I, 1976, *reprinted*: 189). The following districts were under the Chief Commissioner of Assam (September, 1875). These were the Goalpara, Kamrup, Darrang, Lakhimpur, Sibsagar, Nagaon, Garo Hills, Khasi and Jaintia Hills, Nagar Hills, Sylhet and Cachar districts. In 1898, Lushai Hills district (Mizoram) was transferred to Assam. On October 16, 1905 after the partition of Bengal, Assam was combined with the eastern district of Bengal and constituted a new province under the name "Eastern-Bengal and Assam" as decreed by the British Viceroy, Lord Curzon. It was placed under a Lt. Governor. It had Rajshahi Division (Districts of Rajshahi, Dinajpur, Jalpaiguri, Malda, Rangpur, Bogura, Pabna); Dacca Division (Districts of Dacca, Mymensingh, Faridpur, Backergunge); Chittagong Division (Districts of Chittagong, Tippera, Noakhali, Chittagong Hill Tracts); Surma Valley and Hill Districts Division (Districts of Sylhet, Cachar, Lushai Hills, Naga Hills, Khasi and Jaintia Hills, Garo Hills) and Assam Valley Division (Districts of Goalpara, Kamrup, Darrang, Nagaon, Sibsagar, Lakhimpur). Two native independent States of Hill Tippera (Tripura) were in Eastern Bengal and Assam, and Manipur was lying to the east of the Province of Eastern Bengal and Assam. The capital was Dacca city, with Shillong as the Summer Sanitarium, and Chittagong as the seaport.

When the partition of Bengal was annulled in 1911, Assam was separated from Bengal but it retained Bengal's districts of Goalpara, Garo Hills, Sylhet and Cachar. It continued to have Khasi and Jaintia Hills. From 1912 to 1921,

Assam was again placed under a Chief Commissioner, Archdale Earle. In 1921, Assam became a Governor's Province with a Legislature and an Executive Council till the partition of India in 1947. Due to the partition of India in 1947, the Sylhet district (except Karimganj subdivision) was ceded to East Pakistan (now Bangladesh). An option was, however, given for the inclusion of Sylhet district of Assam. A poll was conducted on 6-7 July 1947. "The poll did not pass off peacefully. The police had to resort to firing on the Muslim mob who tried to capture the booth. In several places the Hindus were prevented from casting their votes. On 14th July, 1947, the result of the referendum was announced. The option for Pakistan entry was by a margin of 55,578 votes. The Muslim League celebrated the Pakistan entry of Sylhet district. The next step was the Boundary Commission's demarcation line of the Muslim and the non-Muslim majority areas in Assam. The Commission under the Chairmanship of Cyril Redcliffe, gave its award after three days of Independence. The award was, four thanas namely Patharkandi, Ratabari, Badarpur and half of Karimganj were to be retained in Assam, while the rest would pass on to Pakistan......" (Arun Bhattacharjee, 1993:99). On behalf of Cachar, the State Reorganisation Commission was (1954-56), urged to include Manipur and Tripura within Assam but, later on they decided otherwise, and the remained as Union Territories, later to become States (S. Bhat, 1975:104-105). Actually, in April/ May, 1954, the local people of Manipur and Tripura agitated against their annexation with Assam.

Sir Syad Sadulla formed the first Ministry in Assam in 1937. But after some time this Ministry was out of power and Congress leader Gopinath Bardoloi formed the ministry and stayed for 14 months till the resignation of his Ministry, at the instruction of the Congress Party of India. Again he formed his Ministry in 1946, and he was the Chief Minister till his death on August 5, 1950. Thereafter, Bishnuram Medhi was the Chief Minister of Assam. He resigned in 1957, and became Governor of Tamil Nadu. B.P. Chaliha succeeded as the Chief Minister of Assam in 1957. After that, in 1970, M.M. Choudhury became the Chief Minister and in 1972, Sarat Chandra Sinha was the Chief Minister till February 1978. In the beginning of 1978, Congress Party of India was split into Congress-I and Congress-B (Mrs. Indira Gandhi Congress-I; Brahmananda Reddy Congress-B; Devraj Urs Congress-U; Sarat Pawar Congress-S, etc.) Sarat Chandra Sinha was affiliated with Sarat Pawar Congress-S.

General Election was held in 1951, and Congress came to power with a big majority. Next election was held in 1957. Congress continued in power as it won, one after another, every election till February 1978. In March 1977, the Janata Dal came to power at the Centre, riding a popular wave against the excesses during the Emergency (June 26, 1975 to March 22, 1977). In General Elections of Assam in February 1978, for the first time in Assam Janata Dal (other than Congress) came to power. Sarat Chandra Sinha, Congress-S, Ministry, resigned soon after this election and, Golap Borbora Ministry assumed office on March 12, 1978. On June 8, 1979, All Assam Students' Union started its movement on "foreigner" issue, etc. Jogendra Nath Hazarika, who is famous for his declaration of "general amnesty" for ULFA militants on June 30, 1991, formed Assam Janata Dal Ministry on September 9, 1979. But it fell with the resignation of Hazarika on December 8, 1979. Thereafter, for the first time in Assam, President's Rule was imposed. Sayeda Anwara Taimur, Congress-I, became Chief Minister on December 7, 1980 but, she resigned on June 28, 1981. On June 30, 1981, for the second time in Assam, President's Rule was imposed till January 12, 1982. On January 13, 1982, K.C. Gogoi of Congress-I became the Chief Minister at 8.30 p.m. But, he continued only up to March 19, 1982, and President's Rule for the third time was imposed on March 19, 1982.

Congress-I came to power (101 seats secured out of 109) in February, 1983, election under the leadership of Hiteswar Saikia who defeated Congress-U. He was a member of Sinha Cabinet (1972-78), Taimur Cabinet (1980-81) and Gogoi Cabinet (1982). He belonged to the Ahom community.

Assam Accord was signed by Assam Movement leaders and the Government. A new political party Assam Gana Parishad (AGP) was formed on October 10, 1985. Election was held in December, 1985, and AGP came to power, Prafulla Kumar Mahanta, the most prominent student leader of the Assam Movement became the Chief Minister. He completed his five-year's term in office. President's Rule was imposed for the fourth time in Assam on November 27, 1990. Congress-I again came to power in June 1991, election, under the leadership of Hiteswar Saikia, ex-Governor of Mizoram. He continued till his death on April 22, 1996 and thereafter, caretaker Chief Minister Dr. Bhumidhar Barman (Congress-I) formed his ministry who submitted his resignation on May 10, 1996, as Congress-I could not win in the General Election of April 27, 1996, and he himself could not win from his own constitutency. AGP got the maximum number of seats and AGP-led coalition Government was sworn in on May 15, 1996, and Prafulla Kumar Mahanta became Chief Minister for the second time after his 1985 to 1990, rule in Assam.

In 1948, North East Frontier Agency (NEFA, now Arunachal Pradesh) was separated from Assam for security reason. The State Nagaland was carved out of Assam in 1963, Meghalaya was made an Autonomous Sub-State within Assam on 2nd April, 1970. Thereafter, it was converted to a State in 1972. Mizoram was separated from Assam to form a Union Territory on January 21st, 1972, and it became a full-fledged State on 20th February, 1987. Manipur and Tripura were formerly Princely States. These were first made Part-C States of India and Union Territories and finally States on 21st January, 1972, as stated at the beginning of this book. North East Frontier Agency (NEFA) was first made into a Union Territory and named Arunachal Pradesh on 21st January, 1972. Later on, it got its Statehood on 20th February, 1987.

34. Disturbances in Assam:—

(A) *Language Riot*:—Official Language of Assam Act, 1960, led to a riot in Assam. This Act was approved by the Governor on December 17, and was published in the Official Gazette on December 19, 1960. Language riot was experienced all over undivided Assam. It widened the rift among the people of Assam. However, language issue resulted in linguistic agitations in Cachar. As a result Bengali was made official language of Barak Valley and Assamese in Brahmaputra Valley. Language issue led to the exit of Chief Minister Bishnuram Medhi. He was succeeded by Bimala Prasad Chaliha (S. Bhat; 1975:99). Shekhar Gupta (1984:129), reported that P.N. Kar, an 85-years-old Congress leader from Cachar wrote in his publication entitled, "Invitation to the North-East Core". "Taking advantage of linguistic recognition of State and as there was no permanent language .....and the local languages, Bodo, Tai, Khasi, Jaintia, Mishing, Manipuri, Lalung, Garo, Karbi, Dimasa, etc., were without powerful political guard, the Kamrupias declared the local Kamrupia dialect as the Assamese language and as the only language of the entire region...."

Assamese, as the official language of Assam, caused a great rift as it was a sentimental issue and had greatly shaken the Hill People of Assam. The leaders of the various political organisations of the hill areas met in Shillong on July 6-7, 1960, and set up an organisation called "All Party Hill Leaders Conference (APHLC)". This party appointed a Council which submitted a memorandum to the President of India on 21st August, 1960, by opposing Assam's decision on official language; they put their demand for a separation of the Hill Districts from Assam as this was the only alternative left than to accept Assamese as the only language for official purposes. They repeatedly made their demand. Assam's Official Language Act 1960 was, therefore, further amended in 1964; English is permissible under Article 343 of the Constitution of India, section VIII.

(B) *Chinese Aggression*:—In 1962, Chinese armed forces crossed the McMahon Line, that demarcates the boundary between India and Tibet, occupied a part of Arunachal Pradesh (NEFA) and proceeded towards Tezpur in Assam. In December, 1962, however, they voluntarily withdrew from this area and went back to Tibet.

(C) *Anti-Marwari Riot*:—On 26th January, 1968, anti-Marwari riot took place in Guwahati. It is said that many Marwari trade and commerce establishments situated in Guwahati were destroyed.

(D) *Sipajhar Violence*:—This violence claimed about 20 lives but, actually it was more than that. S. Gupta (1984:18) mentions that "the rioteers forgot Assam's nearly 1000-year history of peaceful co-existence and, more recently, the 1980, linguistic clashes in Nalbari near Gauhati shows the intolerance of people towards other linguistic groups. While the agitation had remained peaceful in its basic approach there had been frequent incidents of violence. Even before the elections, there had been nearly 500 bomb blasts, including the one that killed 21 people in Guwahati's Fatasil market in mid-1982, and a year earlier that killed E.S. Parthasarathy, the former Commissioner of the Upper Assam

Division. Nearly 300 persons had died in the three-year agitation preceding the elections and it can be no one's alibi that one was taken by surprise..."

(E) *Doboka, Hojai and Jamunamukh Riots*:—Babri Masjid and Ayodhya issues created disturbances and about 60 people, mostly women and children were killed at Doboka, Hojai and Jamunamukh areas of Nagaon district during December 7-8, 1992.

(F) *Goreswar Massacre*:—In 1965, in Goreswar the government formally annunced a hundred people were massacred but it informally accepted a figure of around 600. Again on 21 February, 1983, about 33 people were massacred in Goreswar.

(G) *Gohpur Violence*:—On 14 February, 1983, at Gohpur, in Darang district, about 133 kms from Tezpur town, about a hundred people were killed. About 6000 became homeless in 17 villages. People died in attacks and counter-attacks.

(H) *Nellie Massacre*:—Government was determined to hold elections in Assam in February 1983 whereas Assam Movement leaders were determined to stop the election. On the morning of February 18, 1983, a mob surrounded Nellie, about 70 kms east of Guwahati in Nagaon district and massacred innocent people mercilessly. Nellie toll rose to 600, but people estimated it to be more than that.

(I) *Mangaldai Massacre*:—On 5 March, 1983, about 500 people died in Mangaldai massacre.

(J) *Chowlkhowa Massacre*:—After Nellie, in Chowlkowha Chapori in Darrang district about 500 people were massacred in February, 1983.

(K) *Silapathar Massacre*:—At Silapathar in Lakhimpur district iots of people were massacred.

(L) *Chamoria Riot*:—At Chamoria, west of Guwahati, several people died in a riot. It happened during and immediately after the February, 1983 election.

(M) *Khoirabari Massacre*:—In villages around the town of Khoirabari near Goreswar in Kamrup district south of Mangaldai, about 500 people were massacred.

(N) *Barpeta Violence and Bashbari Camp Massacre*:—On July 20th, 1994, violence started in Barpeta. Death toll rose to 21. People due to fear took shelter in different relief camps. On July 24th, 1994, more than a hundred people who took shelter in the relief camp at Bashbari near Manas Tiger Reserve were massacred. This is one of the biggest massacres after Nellie.

(O) *Kokrajhar and Bongaigaon districts riots*:—There was a big ethnic violence in Gossaigaon, Kachugaon, Sidli between Bodo and Adivasi (mainly Santhal) regions from 16/17 May, 1996 to 20/21 May, 1996. The toll in the ethnic violence in two districts rose to 136 as reported by AIR, New Delhi. It happened immediately after the installation of the new government in Assam.

There have been many more incidents of violence in Assam which were never reported.

There were several movements in Assam. A few of them are mentioned below—(a) Naga movement was started for their independence soon after 1947; (b) Mizo movement for their independence during mid-sixties; (c) movement for an oil refinery in Assam in late fifties; (d) movement demanding Assamese as official language of Assam in 1960; (e) movement for a tribal hill state for APHLC in 1962; (f) food movement of 1966; (g) movement for second oil refinery in Assam during 1969-70; (h) movement to make Assamese a medium of instruction up to the graduation level in Assam's two universities (Gauhati and Dibrugarh) in 1972; (i) All Assam students' union movement for economic development of Assam in 1974; (j) Bodo movement for Roman scripts; (k) Assam movement against the 'foreigners' issue during 1979-85; (l) Bodo movement for a separate Bodoland/Udayachal; (m) Karbi-Dimasa movement for an Autonomous State within Assam; (n) United Liberation Front of Assam (ULFA) movement to make Assam an independent State, etc. Thus, Assam is continuously involved in some movement or the other since Independence for political, ethnic, social, or economical reasons.

35. Local Self-government:—

(a) *Karbi Anglong Autonomous District Council*:—The district council is a corporate body. It consists of representatives elected by adult franchise to administer the functions and to exercise the power given to it. District Councils have elected and also a few nominated members.

As per the Census of India 1991, the area of Karbi Anglong is 10,434 sq. kms. This area is under Autonomous District Council, and Diphu is its headquarters. Until the Constitution of India came into force on January 26th, 1950, Karbi Anglong (Mikir Hills) was a part of the then districts of Nowgong and Sibsagar. Under the sponsorship of the Bardoloi Committee, the Central Government created the then United Mikir and North Cachar Hills district on June 23rd, 1951, and it was administered as a single unit. District Council general elections were held for Karbi Anglong in 1952, 1957 and 1962 for the first, second and third times respectively. There was no District Council general election for Karbi Anglong in 1967, but it was held in 1971. This district was called Mikir Hills District and renamed as Karbi Anglong in 1975.

The Mikir Hills district and the newly created North Cachar Hills district opted to remain with Assam instead of joining Meghalaya, an autonomous sub-State within Assam which was created on April 2, 1970, comprising only the United Khasi and Jaintia Hill districts and Garo Hills district.

Most of the developmental departments of Assam Government in the Mikir Hills district, have been functioning since June 1, 1970, under Mikir Hills District Council Administration. As per Assam Government Notification No. AAP 95/70/36, dated June 1, 1970, the following departments have been transferred under Mikir Hills Districts Council. They are—Agriculture, PWD (FC&I), PWD(R&B), TA & WBC Department (Soil Conservation), Animal Husbandry, Veterinary and Fisheries, Forests, Development of P. & CD, Industries (Cottage), Education (G.& PTM), Health & Family Planning (B), Health & Family Planning (A), Planning & Development (Social Welfare), etc,

This District Council comes within the purview of the Sixth Schedule of the Indian Constitution.

The Council is formed with three-fourths of the elected members, and the House is headed by a Chairman and a Deputy Chairman. The ruling body of the Council is the Executive Committee headed by a Chief Executive. The Executive Committee is constituted by the Executive members. In addition to this, chairmen of different departments have also been appointed for smooth running. The Secretariat Cell of the Karbi Anglong Autonomous District Council is headed by a Principal Secretary, who is an Indian Administrative Service personnel. Settlement fees on *Ghats, Hats, Bazars*, and licence fees are the major sources of revenue of the District Council.

The Karbi Accord was signed in September, 1994, and Karbi-Dimasa Accord was signed on April 1, 1995, to upgrade the two Autonomous District Councils.

(b) *North Cachar Hills District Council*:—North Cachar Hills, sub-division of the United Mikir and North Cachar Hills District was inaugurated on February 2nd, 1970, with Haflong as headquarters. As per the Census of India 1991, the area of North Cachar Hill is 4,888 sq. kms. This area is under Autonomous District Council. Until the Constitution came into force on January 26th, 1950, North Cachar Hills was a sub-division of the then Cachar district. Since September 16th, 1970, most of the developmental departments of Assam Government which were functioning in the newly formed North Cachar Hills District have been transferred to the administrative control of the North Cachar Hills District Council. As per Assam Government Notification No. AAP 95/70/100, dated September 10th, 1970, the following departments have been transferred under North Cachar Hills District Council. They are—Agriculture, PWD (Flood Control and Irrigation), PWD (Roads and Buildings), TA and WBC Department (Soil Conservation), Animal Husbandry, Veterinary and Fisheries, Forests, Development of Panchayat and Community Development, Industries (Cottage), Education (General and PTM), Health and Family Planning (B), Health and Family Planning (A), Planning and Development (Social Welfare).

North Cachar Hills was an excluded area under the Government of India Act 1935, during British period. The District Council general elections were held in North Cachar Hills in 1952, 1957, 1962 and 1968 for the first, second, third and fourth times.

The employees function primarily as the employees of the District Council and the District Council is associated with matters of recording of Annual Confidential Reports in accordance with the provisions prescribed by the Government of Assam. They are responsible to the State Government for implementing schemes which have not been transferred to the District Council, and are not entitled to any deputation allowances, etc. The Secretariat Cell of the Council is headed by a Principal Secretary belonging to the Indian Administrative Service (IAS).

Insurgents raised their demand for 'Dimaland' in North Cachar Hills (*Sentinel,* April 25th, 1995:1). Bombs were blasted near Diphu TV Station. No damage was caused to the TV tower (*Sentinel,* April 23rd, 1995:1).

(c) *Bodoland Autonomous Council:*—A new Autonomous Council for the Bodos was created by signing Bodo Accord on February 20th, 1993. The Council consists of forty members of which five members are nominated by the Assam Government. They took oath on May 20th, 1993. Law and order of this area is retained by the State Government. It was decided in June, 1994 that a total of 250 forest villages are to be included in Bodoland Autonomous Council. The Bodo area was not determined till July, 1994. The Bodos are demanding Dhubri (North Bank), Kokrajhar, Bongaigaon, Barpeta, Nalbari, Kamrup (North Bank), and Sonitpur districts. They are also demanding another ten in addition to five hundred fifteen villages to be included in Bodo Autonomous Council. The Assam Government is firmly committed to hold the first election in January, 1996 to the Bodo Autonomous Council for electing its thirty-five representatives. Bodo Autonomous Council is demanding inclusion in their area of about four hundred more villages along Assam-Bhutan border. Demand was also made for the inclusion of 10 km belt along the international border with Bhutan in Bodo Autonomous Council territory.

Executive, financial, administrative and legislative powers are with the Council. Bodo Regional Council and Gram Panchayats are also included in Bodoland Autonomous Council area.

(d) *Rava Hasong Autonomous Council:*—Assam Government decided to give autonomy to Rava communities (Rava, Mishing, Tiwa) as per Dr Bhupinder Singh Committee recommendation to set up Rava Hasong Village Council and Rava Hasong Autonomous Apex Council (*Purbanchal Prahari,* January 25th, 1995:1). Accordingly an "Accord" was signed on March 10th, 1995. It was decided to form a village council where more than 50 per cent population is Rava. The duration of this Autonomous Council will be for five years. A total of thirty-four departments have been transferred under Rava Hasong Autonomous Council and power of twenty-nine subject-matters have been transferred to Rava Hasong Village Council.

The State Assembly passed the Rava Hasong Council Act on 12th April, 1995, and an interim Rava Hasong Council was sworn in with fifteen members on 20the July, 1995, at Dudhnoi in Goalpara district. The Council is headed by Mr S. Rabha. Its headquarters is at Dudhnoi.

(e) *Karbi-Dimasa Autonomous District Council:*—Karbi-Dimasa accord was signed in New Delhi on April 1, 1995, to upgrade two earlier autonomous district councils by giving additional executive powers and legislative jurisdiction over a number of new subjects to Karbi Anglong and North Cachar Hill districts. The eight-year-old Karbi movement for autonomy came to an end with the signing of this agreement. The election to Autonomous District Council of Karbi Anglong was held in 1989. They secured 22 out of 26 seats to the District Council. Dr Jayanta Rongpi, Member of Parliament, however, ridiculed this accord and said the accord signed by the ASDC and the government was invalid and cannot be split into Karbi and Dimasa part (*Statesman*, May 23, 1995:8). The polling for Karbi Anglong and North Cachar Hill districts' Autonomous Councils were held on June 3, 1996, for twenty-six members in Karbi Anglong Autonomous District Council and twenty-two members in the North Cachar Hill Autonomous Council.

(f) *Lalung Autonomous Council*:—The Assam Government signed on April 13th, 1995, the Tiwa (Lalung) Accord with agitating Lalung leaders conceding the demands of the Lalung tribe, a Lalung Autonomous Council, with executive powers over thirtyfour subjects. It has also Lalung Village Council.

As per the accord, interim Lalung Autonomous Council include 144 villages in Kamrup and Marigaon district and all these villages will have village councils. An apex council will be formed with thirty members of which fifteen will be from Lalungs. A twenty-eight member interim Lalung Autonomous Council was sworn in at Nellie Pujathali on July 27, 1995. There will be no boundary to the council (Notification No. TAD/ST/276/94/55).

(g) *Mishing Autonomy*:—On May 2, 1995, Mishing Autonomous District Council sought an early accord and on June 14, 1995, the Mishing Autonomous Demand Committee signed an accord with the State Government granting autonomy to North Lakhimpur, Dhemaji, Jorhat and Golaghat districts. An interim Mishing Autonomous Council was sworn in North Lakhimpur on July 24, 1995. It headquarters is at Gusamukh in Dhemaji district. This autonomous district has no distinct geographical boundary.

36. Panchayats (Rural Local Government):—The Panchayat system means decentralisation of administration at the local government level. It lays special emphasis on land reforms. A major achievement of this is in agricultural production with the help of elected local bodies—the panchayat. Assam has adopted a three-tier panchayati-raj system under Assam Panchayat Raj Act, 1959. These are—*Gaon Panchayat* at village level, *Anchalik Panchayat* at Block level and *Mahakuma Parishad* at the subdivisional level. The Assam Panchayati Raj Act, 1959, was amended in 1968. Some changes have been made in Panchayati Raj Act, 1972. The acts are amended from time to time. Panchayati Raj is playing an important role in formulating plans for rural development. It is providing necessary policy guidelines to the State Government.

During Ahom rule, there were *Sarumel, Majumel, Dekamel, Gabharumel*, etc., organizations like Pachayat. The Bodo-Kachari had village committee which was similar to Panchayat. The *Satras* which were primarily formed for religious purposes had certain elements of panchayat administration. During British rule, the Patels and the Patwaris, the Mandals and the Gaonburas, the Mouzadars and theTahsildars were made official leaders in villages. As a result, *Sarumel* and *Dekamel* of the *Ahom* days lost their office. J.N. Das (1962:22) wrote in his *Democratic Decentralization in Theory and Practice* (Directorate of Panchayat and Community Development, Government of Assam, Shillong) that the *Satras* of Assam continue to dispense justice and resolve village disputes to this day.

In 1960, Assam Panchayati Raj had—rural population (in thousand) 8,629; total *Gaon Panchayats* (in plains only) 2,570; percentage of rural population covered 100; total villages covered 17,717; percentage of villages covered by panchayats 100; average population per panchayat 2,659; total number of *Anchalik Panchayats* 120 and total number of *Mahakuma Parishads* 16. Elections to the three-tier *Panchayati Raj* system of Assam were held in the early part of 1993, (Zilla Parishad, Panchayat Samiti, Gram Panchayat).

There are two types of paid employees in village council, viz. The *Deuri* caretaker of *Namghar* and the *Sara*, village messenger, to inform and invite the villagers to the public gatherings and to announce the decisions of the village council to the public. *Namghar* has a Secretary who consults its President. Some of the activities of the village council are: *Namghar*, village bank, weaving society, financial co-operative society, arts and craft centres, *Mahila Samity, Krishi Sahayak Samity, Krishi Samobay Samity* (co-operative agricultural society), *Pathar Parichalana Samity* (Field Management Society), granary, funds, *Jubak Sangha*, settlement of disputes, etc.

Table XVII

Subdivision-wise Panchayati Raj of Assam (1960)*

Name of Mahakuma Parishad	*Total No. of Anchalik panchayats*	*Total No. of Gaon panchayats*	*Total No. of villages covered*
Dhubri	7	162	1,349
Goalpara	6	115	1,463
Kokrajhar	7	76	1,666
Silchar	7	146	852
Karimganj	5	116	234
Hailakandi	3	71	1,681
Nowgong	18	213	1,046
Barpeta	8	174	1,902
Gauhati	17	387	836
Sibsagar	6	132	1,973
Dibrugarh	11	208	756
North Lakhimpur	6	123	1,190
Mangaldoi	6	159	1,025
Tezpur	7	135	536
Golaghat	5	118	745
Jorhat	6	127	848

**Excluded Nagaland, Meghalaya, Mizoram.*

Mahakuma Parishad is directly constituted with elected members from *Anchalik Panchayat*, deputy commissioner, subdivisional officer, members of Parliament and Legislative Assembly of the *Mahakuma Parishad* area, Municipal Chairman, Town Committee, and the Co-operative Central Bank of the area.

One representation from Scheduled Caste, Scheduled Tribe and two women members are included. The president and vice-president are elected from these members. The State Government deputes an officer to the *parishad* to act as its secretary.

Table XVIII

Mahakuma Parishad

Guwahati

Kamalpur —— *Anchalik Panchayats* —— *Dimaria*

Amingaon *Ghungsari* *Gaon Panchayat* *Barkhat* *Malyabari*

Source: *S.P. Jain (1976 : 20)*

Anchalik Panchayat has generally been established in the area covered by a community development block at block level. The *Gaon Sabha* is constituted in a specified area comprising of one or more villages having population of less than 5,000. An official is appointed by the State Government who functions as the secretary of *panchayat* and *gaon sabha.* He keeps records of properties, funds, sites of buildings, tanks, wells, schools, roads and other public property in possession of *gaon panchayat.* He also keeps records of all statistics relating to *gaon panchayat.* He prepares records about birth, death, marriage, tax and rates, etc.

Table XIX

Organisational Structure of Panchayat and Community Development (Assam Secretariat Level)

Agricultural Production Commissioner-cum-Secretary (P.&.CD.)

Director (P.&.CD.)

(State level)

Deputy Director Development (Grass-feeding) | **Deputy Director (Commissioner)** | **Deputy Director (Training)** | **Deputy Director (Panchayat)** | **Joint Director (Hills)** | **Special Officer (Composite)** | **Assistant (P. & CD)**

(Mahakuma Parishad level)

Secretary (Standing Committee) | **Secretary (M.P.)** | **M.P. Planning Officer**

(Block level)

E.O. (Veterinary) | **E.O. (Agri.)** | **Sub-Inspec. (Statistics)** | **E.O. (Co-op)** | **E.O. (Panchayat)** | **E.O (Overseers)** | **E.O. (Woman and Child).**

.....

Sr. Gram Sevak

Veterinary Field Asstt. | **Gram Sevak** | **Gram Sevika**

Source : *Director of Panchayat and Community Development, Assam and S.P. Jain (1976:16).*

As per Census of India 1991, (Series-I) Assam has 714 Gram Panchayats, 135 Development Blocks (1990-91), 21,995 inhabited villages (1971), and 93 towns (1991).

37. Municipality (Urban Local Government):—There is a statutory institution of urban local government, viz. the municipality in each town. It is said that, on November 1st, 1905, Gauhati Municipality had welcomed, Sir J.B. Fuller, the Chief Commissioner of Assam who assumed the charge of the new province "Eastern Bengal and Assam" as Lieutenant-Governor at Dacca.

The functions of the municipality involves water supply, sanitation, scavenging, drainage, roads, public health, etc. They get their income by imposing taxes on property, trade, business, water supply, house tax, fees from markets, revenues from vehicles, etc. At present (1992), there are in total twenty-four Municipal Boards in Assam and one Municipal Corporation in Guwahati. They are—Dhubri, Kokrajhar, Bongaigaon, Goalpara, Barpeta Road, Barpeta, Nalbari, Rangia, Palasbari, Mangaldoi, Tezpur, Dhekiajuli, North Lakhimpur, Nagaon, Hojai, Golaghat, Jorhat, Sibsagar, Sonari, Dibrugarh, Tinsukia, Karimganj, Hailakandi and Silchar. Each Municipal Board/Corporation has one elected Chairman/Mayor and one elected Vice-Chairman/Deputy Mayor.

The last election to Guwahati Municipal Corporation was held in 1979 immediately after the Janata Government came to power in Assam under the Chief Ministership of Golap Borbora. It was dissolved on October 12, 1982. After a gap of about 16 years again Guwahati Municipal Corporation's election was held on May 16th, 1995, for sixty constituencies where an Independent candidate won unopposed and joined Cong.-I. In this election, Cong.-I, AGP, BJP, CPI (M) and Independent candidates contested the poll but no one got majority. Cong.-I and AGP got equal number of seats—23 each, B.J.P.—9, Independent—4, and CPI(M)—1.

38. Chieftainship:—Some tribes have their own clan chiefs. These elderly leaders meet together to take decision and solve their minor disputes. They give suggestions regarding rules and regulations, as per social laws and customs, to their village people. They can punish guilty persons with a fine. They can outcast and expel the guilty from their society as a punishment. Villagers fear them for their unwritten powers. The head of each family participates in *Khel's* (chief) meetings and these meetings are generally held in *Namghars. Namghars* play religious as well as social roles to keep unity among the villagers. The amount of fine is credited partly to village fund and the other part is handed over to the victim of the case.

A *mel* in Assam was a time-honoured institution of Assamese social life. The *mel* or assembly of the people decided matters of common interest. Shrutidev Goswami (1989 in *Tenth Session*: 308), reported that "....in a statement recorded before *Mc. Cube,* Bijoy Chaudhari, a tenant of Pati Darrang *tehsil*, reported on 22 December, 1893, that one Monu *Gaon Bura* approached him with a message that he had been summoned by the *mel" (Raij nibo diche).* When he arrived at the place of the meeting he saw a few respectable persons of the area discussing something. On seeing him all of them began to reproach him for paying revenue against the direction of the *mel* and asked him to pay twenty-five rupees as fine... The poor villager had no power to defy the order of the *mel* and paid the fine (*Assam Secretariat Records, Home, A Proceedings,* September, 1894, No. 253, Memo. by Mc Cube, 11 January, 1894.)

39. Slavery:—V. Venkata Rao reported in his seminar paper on "*History and Culture of North East India*", 26-28 April, 1979, that there was no system of slavery or customs that had the slightest tinge of slavery, apart from the *boj* custom in Assam. But according to D.R. Banerji (1933, 2nd edition: 132-146) slavery in Assam started less than ten years after the Britishers began occupying the country. All the profits of a slave's work went to his master; the slave received nothing except food and clothing. Intermarriages between slaves were allowed. In the district of Darrang, the average cost of a good slave, belonging to the *Koletah, Kayot* and *Koch* castes, was twenty to twenty-eight rupees. Any slave or bondsman could emancipate himself, his wife and children at a sum fixed by a *Panchayat* appointed by the Magistrate.

Rules were proposed to be enacted in the Province of Assam for a gradual mitigation of slavery and bondage by F. Jenkins who submitted his letter of August 22nd, 1835, to R.D. Mangles, Secretary to the Government of Bengal in the Judicial Department Legislature Proceedings from 28 September to 28 December, 1835, (Imperial Record Department). M. Hussain (1993:39) reported that slavery was officially abolished in 1843.

40. Police:—During the British period, police force was needed to keep peace in the area. In 1853, the total force employed in Assam Valley was only 547 constables. In 1874, when Assam was separated from Bengal, the civil police force employed was 3,452 constables. Later on, the military police reduced this force.E.A. Gait reported (1905: 333-334) that in 1860, the general codes of Civil and Criminal Procedures were extended to the Brahmaputra Valley and in 1862 the Indian Penal Code came into force *proprio vigore.* In 1903, there were 384 officers and 2,289 men. One policeman was engaged to prevent and detect crime within 20 sq. miles and for 2,185 persons. The police force was under an Inspector General of Police, who was assisted by the Deputy Inspector General, District and Assistant Superintendent of Police, inspectors, sub-inspectors, head constables and constables. There was a large force of military police numbering 2,876 officers and constables in 1904, who were employed on quasi-military duties in Assam. Later on, Assam Government strengthened the police department by setting up police headquarters in towns with the Director General of Police as its head.

There were 221 police stations, 147 police outposts; 7 fire stations, 45 fire sub-stations, 13 railway police stations, 18 railway outposts; 4 river police stations and 6 river police outposts till 31 March 1992. Most of the police stations were set up after Independence. Silchar Police Station is the oldest one. Maximum cases were reported during 1992, at Kamrup district for offences—4675 cases—Nagaon district 2475, Sonitpur district 2154 for murder, kidnapping, dacoity, robbery, burglary, thefts, rapes, riots, cheating, etc. The village council exercises great influence on the social life of villagers in Assam. In the Guwahati High Court, till June 30, 1991, there were pending a total of 37090 civil cases and 208640 cases criminal and disposed of 12108 civil cases and 48234 criminal cases.

41. Games and Sports:—Assamese like all types of modern and indigenous games and sports. Young boys and girls are fond of modern sports. They also participate in all events of inter-State, national and also a few international games and sports. Some of them know judo, karate, wrestling, etc. They play carrom, table tennis, football, cricket, kabaddi, badminton, tennis, *kho-kho* etc. Women foot ball players participate in national competitions. In swimming and chess competitions they have brought international fame. They have succeeded in mountain trekking expeditions. They have their own mountain expedition teams. The Education Directorate is giving them physical education training. Rajiv Gandhi Sports Centre at Hengrabari (Guwahati) started on January 26 the, 1995, for youths of Assam to train them in sports, games and trekking expeditions.

The North-Eastern Council has taken up the scheme for development of sports and youth activities in the eighth Five Year Plan. It helps in organising adventure activities, youth exchange programmes, training, coaching camps, competitions/tournaments, etc., Boat races are also held. Horse-race, elephant race, tug-of-war, etc. are also some important sports. *Tel-Goch, Para-Bah,* etc., are indigenous sports of Boko area in *Suwari* festival. Bison fight is their popular game.

There are plenty of fishes in most of the rivers and *bills.* There are some good fish-catchers other than professional fishermen. They use fishing nets, fishing baskets, traps, spears, etc., to catch fish. In rural areas people in groups catch fish from ponds, etc. Sometimes some tribal women also catch fish in village areas. Fish are caught not only for sale but also for domestic consumption. In earlier days young boys used to go out with groups of friends, to forest to kill deer and other animals which they had to share with the participating members. Birds and animals are now gradually becoming scarce; jungles are becoming less dense and hunting is prohibited by the government. The villagers used to go out in groups for hunting animals and deer till 1945. A few of them are now illegally catching and killing birds also.

42. Weapons:—The main weapon is *dao* (dagger) which they use for all purposes. They use knife (*chakku/katari*), bow and arrow, etc. Some of them use guns and they are expert in using modern arms and ammunitions. The Ahoms, in earlier days, knew the use of gunpowder in firearms and, they were actually credited with using them first in India. Probably, they learnt this art from the Chinese. Iron had been used in ancient Assam. The Ahoms collected iron ore from Mikir Hills and made oval shaped-balls which were called *Messa.* Dhenkial near Golaghat was the centre for manufacturing firearms while Dadhara was the centre for manufacturing swords and sharp weapons (R.M. Nath, 1948:149). S.K. Chatterji (1951:57), wrote that Su-hung-mung introduced firearms in the Ahom army after the Mohammedan war. It is reported that some of them also now know how to make bombs. Some of them know guerrilla warfare. The latest insurgency has shown that the guerrillas are carrying foreign arms with country-made weapons.

43. Livestock and Poultry:—Agriculture is the main occupation in rural areas. Thus bull and buffalo find an important place in the agricultural life. Some of them keep cows for milk. Some have domesticated goats for milk and meat. A few lower-caste Hindus keep pigs. In rural areas some villagers keep duck for eggs and meat and pigeon for meat. In urban areas some keep fowls for eggs and meat including pigeons and ducks.

44. Health:—The climate of Assam is damp due to frequent rains and other natural causes. Pure drinking water is not available in all places. People of Assam suffer from goitre, malaria, asthma, pneumonia, tuberculosis, typhoid, diarrhoea, dysentery, cholera, skin diseases and other different types of diseases.

In Karbi areas a large number of people suffer from leprosy. In the past, the tribal superstitions stood in the way of doctors whenever they advised precaution against diseases. The Hindus dislike giving medicine to a person suffering from smallpox. They treat them with their indigenous medicine like *neem*-leaf, etc. They think it is a curse of *Ai* (*Devi*). In earlier days they used to allow the person who was suffering from smallpox, to eat fish, meat, egg and milk. There are people even today who prefer to die unattended than allow a doctor to touch them.

The condition of health services has progressed much. Hospitals, primary health centres, and dispensaries have been established throughout the State. There are also several private nursing homes. Less number of people now believe in magic and sacrifices as for curing diseases and have taken to indigenous medical care to cure diseases. It is reported that the rate of cancer in the North-East is higher due to tobacco-leaf chewing, bazar-made packet *'pan-masala'* having *zarda* (a kind of preparation of tobacco), and eating uncleaned vegetables. 10 AIDS cases have also been reported from Assam. A few of them have died. 16% HIV positive cases are found in North-East (*Sentinel,* January 24th, 1995 and February 8th, 1996).

B.C. Allen (1905), reported *Kala azar* to be most virulent in the countryside lying south of the Brahmaputra. *Kala azar* was high especially in 1892, 1896, and 1897, and there were outbreaks of cholera in 1834,1838-40, 1852-53 and 1861-62 (W.W. Hunter, 1879, Vol. I). Malarial fever is most prevalent in the month of May-June and again in October-November. Plague made its first appearance in the Brahmaputra valley in May, 1903. Dysentery and diarrhoea were common as also skin diseases and ring-worms. Smallpox, chicken-pox, measles were prevalent.

It seems that old diseases are reappearing. In 1994, plague spreadfrom Surat (Gujarat State) to the other parts of India. Malaria started in Assam in April-May, 1995 and the death toll rose to more than 200. In Sonitpur district it claimed 130 lives. Malignant malaria has again hit since May-June, 1996, in

Assam (Darrang, Sonitpur, Nalbari, North Guwahati, and Dhemaji). Forty-two people died till 11, June, 1996, and several persons suffer from malaria. Till May, 1995, five persons died due to AIDS in Assam. Nowadays, dysentery and diarrhoea are almost common diseases in Assam. Chicken-pox and measles are also common every year. Sometimes one or two eruptions of smallpox along with chicken-pox occur. Leprosy is another serious disease prevalent in Assam. It is caused due to the organism '*Mike Bacterium Lepa*'. At present, 32 lakh leprosy patients are there in India. In Assam their number is twelve thousand. Out of these, 1,359 are from Karbi Anglong. As per Dr Badan Chandra Krow, only 25 per cent of leprosy diseases are contagious (*Samai Prabaha,* February 8, 1995:3).

In 1990-91, there were in total 141 government hospitals, 482 primary health centres, 317 dispensaries with 12,303 beds, 143 rural family welfare planning centres and 5,111 sub-centres. In 1991-92, there were 4 tuberculosis hospitals, 3 leprosy hospitals, a cancer, a mental diseases, and an ayurvedic hospital each. *Sankar Nethralaya* (Eye) Hospital at Basistha Road, and another private eye hospital near Chowdhuri Cinema, A.T. Road, are in Guwahati. There are many Marwari private hospitals. The Missionaries of Charity of Mother Teresa laid the foundation stone for AIDS patient welfare home near Jalukbari, Guwahati on January 3, 1995. A Regional Medical Research Centre of North-East Region (ICMR) is situated in Dibrugarh. There are also Red Cross and Railway Hospitals. Neurological Private Hospital is also there. As per *Sentinel,* February 11, 1996, a Cancer Hospital will be started in Silchar.

In 1986, general fertility rate in urban area was 89.9, rural area 137.9 in comparison to India's urban 108.1, rural 145.6. Infant mortality rate per 1000 live-births was 78 in rural, 39 in urban, 76 combined, in comparison to India's 86 in rural, 50 in urban and 80 combined in 1990. Fertility of age group 15-19 was 45.7 in urban, 88.8 in rural; 20-24 was 145.9 in urban, 222.4 in rural; 25-29 was 161.9 in urban, 221.0 in rural; 30-34 was 104.9 in urban, 154.8 in rural; 35-39 was 39.5 in urban, 94.5 in rural; 40-44 was 10.2 in urban, 48.1 in rural; 45-49 was nil in urban, 2.4 in rural in 1986 in Assam.

45. Indigenous Medicine:—Some Assamese prefer indigenous medicine during the initial stage. If the disease is serious, then they go immediately to clinics and hospitals. Old people like indigenous medicines. A few of their medicines are as follows:—

1. *Mishmi Teeta*:—It is brought down from the hills for sale by the *Mishmis* (hill tribe of Arunachal Pradesh). This is a bitter aromatic tonic, valuable for treatment of fever, stomach pain, etc.

2. *Petroleum*:—It is used as a medicine for treatment of sores and wounds.

3. *Tulsi* (Ocimum sanctum, basil):—This is used to cure cough and cold, bronchitis, diarrhoea, malaria, several skin ailments, smallpox, measles, etc. Historical records say that Indian Ayurvedic physicians had prescribed this plant as a contraceptive since ages. It is perhaps true that it has anti-fertility property.

4. *Basak (Adhatoda vasica)*:—It is used to cure cough and cold.

5. *Dubba (Cynodon dactylon)*:—It is used to stop bleeding from outer parts of the body, and for several skin ailments.

6. *Neem (Melio axadirachta)*:—This is used to treat cure skin ailments, leprosy, stomach pains, etc.

7. *Sewali (Nyctanthes arbortristis)*:—This is used to treat bilious fever, faulty secretion of bile, stomach-pains, etc.

8. *Chirata* (Swerta chirata):—This is used to treat fever, intestinal worms, skin ailments, dyspepsia, stomach pain, etc.

9. *Amlaku (Phyllanthus emblica)*:—This is used to treat cough, resistance of urine, liver disorder, colic pain, eyesight, loss of hair, etc.

10. *Hartaki (Terminalia chebula)*:—This is used to treat constipation, pile, colic-pain, gallstone, vomiting, eyeailments, anemia, pox, skin diseases, swelling, etc.

11. *Bell (Aegle marmelos)*:—This is used to treat fever, pile, dysentery, dyspepsia, vomiting, swelling, etc.

12. *Karabi (Nerium indicum)*:—This is used to treat skin ailments, leprosy, fever, etc.

13. *Chandan (Santalum album)*:—This is used to treat severe fever, headache, skin diseases.

14. *Dhuna (Resin yellow)*:—This is used to treat dry pleurisy, hip rheumatism, wounds from fire, cracked skin of feet, mucus diarrhoea, etc.

15. *Pan (Piper betel)*:—This is used to treat constipation of child, headache, stomach ache, swollen gland, night-blindness, etc. Its root is used for sterilization, relief from cough and breathing trouble of children, cure from boils, etc.

16. *Thankuni (Hydrocotyle assiatica)*:—This is used to treat diarrhoea, leprosy, etc.

17. *Isabgul (Plantago ovata)*:—This is used to treat to relieve constipation.

18. *Tokma (Lallemantia royleana)*:—It is used to cure boils. It is also used to keep body cool.

19. *Amita (Carica-papaya)*:—It is used in cases of fever, jaundice, constipation, diarrhoea, etc.

20. *Narikal (Cocos nucifera)*:—This is used to treat stomach pain, dyspepsia, malaria, colic pain, gallstone, intestinal worms, ring-worms, hiccough, etc.

21. *Lasun* (*Garlic)*:—It helps to cure almost all types of curable diseases.

22. *Haldi (Curcuma longa)*:—It is used to cure diarrhoea, vomiting, pox, anemia, constipation, liver trouble, leprosy, all kinds of worm diseases including *Giardia lamblia*, allergy, jaundice, etc.

23. *Mati Mah (*Green Pulses, *Phaseolus rediatus)*:—Mixture of *mati mah*

and *muli* (*Rephanus sativus*) is said to cure kidney trouble. *Mati-mah* helps in discharging urine and stool, increases toleration. It helps in curing piles, rheumatism, colic pain, etc.

24. *Jackfruit*:—It is said that ripe jackfruit helps in curing AIDS.

25. *Thekra Tenga (Thouikal)*:—To stop stomach pain, indigestion, flatulence, dyspepsia, loss of appetite, diarrhoea, etc.

26. *Green Vegetables and Fruits*:—It is said that huge quantities of green vegetables like carrot *(gazor)* and tomato and plenty of fruit like orange helps to cure breast-cancer. A person suffering from cancer shall not drink coffee, wine nor use tobacco. Those who are suffering from blood pressure, need not eat bitter-tasting vegetables. They have to consume raw garlic one or two pieces daily. For anemia, lack of blood, etc., they have to eat stem of special type of pale-blue-stemmed *arum* as their food item.

46. Liquor, Drugs, etc.:—Many people are fond of foreign distilled liquor. In rural areas indigenous rice-beer is popular. This home-made liquor plays an important role in their life and culture. It is essential in some religious ceremonies, festivals and social functions. Some urban people are fond of indigenous rice-beer. A recent survey stated that rice-beer supplies all vitamins to keep the body healthy. *Ganja, Charas,* opium, narcotic drugs like heroin, nicotine, etc., are nowadays popular among the younger generation. Some of them have the habit of chewing dry tobacco-leaf. Most of them are addicted to betel-nut, lime and betel leaf. It is said that lime improves health. Some of them smoke bidi and cigarettes. It is stated that Assam has high esophagus-cancer that is caused by tobacco leaf chewing and smoking bidis, cigarettes. The Assamese middle class youth are fond of using *Sada (khoini)* which perhaps they have learnt from the Bihari/*Deshwali* people; the old generation never accepted it.

47. Food and Drink:—Rice is the staple food which is taken with cooked meat, fish, egg, vegetables and pulses along with spices. They prefer eating fresh fish to dry fish. Tribals like to eat dry fish. Plains' people of Assam take very small quantity of chillies. They like *salad* with their food. They specially like *mati-mah (Phaseolus rediatus)* pulse, *tit-kerela* (bitter-tasting vegetable), raw *amita (Carica papaya)*, gourd *(chalkumara)*, *Boal* and *Rohu* fish along with home-prepared *Khar*. *Khar* is not available in the market. They prepare it at home from dry banana leaves and coconut. *Khar* helps in making the food tasty. It is good for health if taken once in a month. They eat mutton, chicken, and meat of pigeon, duck, deer, etc. The Hindus and Brahmins do not eat beef and chicken. Muslims and higher class Hindus do not eat pork. Only the Christians and a few lower caste Hindus eat pork. It seems that the tribals eat a lot of meat. Assamese are fond of eating fruit. They like sour fruit and are also fond of coconut, mango, banana, papaya, pineapple, orange, guava, grapes, apple, jackfruit, lemon, etc. They prefer raw milk curd specially during *Bihu* festival. Tea is a popular drink with snacks. They drink tea quite often. After drinking tea, they generally chew *tamulpan* with lime. They are fond of milk and milk-made items. They prefer snacks made of flour and like papad. They often chew *tamul-pan* (unripe betel-nut and betel-leaf) with lime. They offer *tamul-pan* to every adult person.

48. Hospitality:—The tribals and non-tribals are frank and open-hearted with hospitality. No visitor can leave a village, specially a tribal one, without taking two meals. Now, due to lack of trust among people, they hesitate in showing hospitality. The urban people entertain visitors with tea and *tamul-pan.*

49. Physical Features:—The Assmese are a mixture of Mongolian-Tibetan, Aryan and Burmese ethnic origin (*AIAS, North Zone, Assam, Vol. I,* 1988:XVIII). The population of Assam entered the State at different times from different directions, in different successive waves. From the ethnic point of view, the Assamese population groups have been divided broadly into Caucasoids and Mongoloids. Mongoloids entered from north, east and south by different routes. They are scattered all over the hills of Assam and in pockets of plains. The Caucasoids are comprised of Hindus and Muslims. They have come mostly from western direction from the valleys of Ganges and Brahmaputra rivers.

The hill tribes of Assam show all the characteristics of Indo-Mongolian origin—a round face, more or less flat nose, prominent cheek bones, oblique set of eyes, sallow complexion, coarse hair. They are generally medium to above medium in stature, have mesocephalic to brachycephalic head, brownish yellow skin, well-developed limbs and are strong and sturdy. The women are medium to short statured. The Assamese of Upper Assam, especially the Ahoms, have typical Mongolian features. They have fair complexion, flat nose, straight hair (Leiotrichy), *epicanthic* fold (Mongolian-fold) of eyes, whereas of the Assamese of the lower Assam have dark to light brown complexion, *mesopic* (medium) prominent nose, coarse and straight hair, and prominent look without the Mongolian fold.

50. Dress and Ornaments:—Due to acculturation, modern educated young men have rejected wearing traditional dress. Traditionally men-folk of plains wear mill-made *dhuties* and small or big sized *sola/fatua* (shirt) and vest or *eri-chadar.* In villages, rich men use headgear. They use *japi* (hat) while working in paddy fields. The young boys nowadays use *dhuti, genji* only on some occasions but they prefer using Western dresses. They use *genji,* bush-shirt, T-shirt, *pajama*, trouser, coat, pant, knitted woollen jacket, leather jacket, fancy shirt, fancy pants with shoe, chappal, etc. Some of them use night-suit, jeans, etc. Earlier the Assamese used to walk barefoot at home but not so any more. Assamese ladies even enter the cooking room without chappals till today. The Assamese young boys use on occasions headgear with their *gamocha* (towel) which they tie to their hip, specially when they are dancing in *Bihu*, to cover the waist with the dhuti. Some young men use Punjabi-pajamas. Some use *khaddar* clothes.

The Assamese women use *riha-mekhela-Sador.* The long flowing skirt up to the ankles is known as *mekhela* and the upper garment is *riha.* The red coloured pattern at the end of the *riha* is graceful and symbolic. Designs are also found in the *pari* (border) of *mekhela* and *riha.* It is said that the dress of *mekhela* and *riha chadar* had been adopted from the Tibetan and Burmese women. Some are of the opinion that the long back *saree* was the dress of the Assamese ladies. The bride of lower Assam uses *saree* in the marriage ceremony. However, some Assamese ladies have started using *saree* at home and outside as it is cheaper than *mekhela-riha-Sador.* Ladies of Goalpara, Gouripur, Dhubri areas prefer *saree* for both outside and the home. The Bodo ladies of Kokrajhar, Darrang, Sonitpur, etc., use *dakhna* which is different from *Mekhela-riha-Sador.* Generally, *dakhna* has yellow colour body with some designs in brown colour, etc. Ladies do not use headgear. Married ladies cover their head with one end of the *riha-Sador* and it is called *orani* or *ghumta* (veil). The Hindu married ladies put vermilion on their forehead and on the parting of combed hair and wear bangles made of shell. Widows do not put vermilion or wear bangles of shell. Women wear *mekhela* covering waist to ankle. *Riha* covers the upper part. They wear *Sador* to cover the upper part and also use blouse and bodice. Assamese Muslims also use same dresses except vermilion. Modern ladies use all types of modern dresses like skirts, top, shirt, mini, midi, maxi, jeans, pant-shirt, ladies-suit, salwar-Punjabi, saree, *mekhela riha-chadar* with slippers, high heel shoes, etc. Some unmarried young girls are cutting their hair short but after marriage they grow the hair long. Women tie up their long hair into different types of beautiful *khopa* (hair-knot) on the back of their head. It seems that the ladies of Assam like to keep their own identity by using their traditional dresses. But men are much more influenced by Western dresses.

There are different types of dresses for the Brahmin priest, Mahanta, *Satradhikari, Kamla* (daily labourer), widow, unmarried/married ladies, girls, rich/poor, and different dresses for home/outdoor, puja offering, and different dresses for Bihu-dance, etc.

The Muslim women prefer silver ornaments and glass bangles. The Hindu women are fond of gold ornaments. But due to changes in economic conditions, influence of modernity, education, etc., they do not use these any more except on special occasions like marriages. Nowadays women use simple ornaments like earrings, chain, bangles, etc. Many of them use imitationes. Their traditional ornaments are—*thuria, kanphul, lokapar, keru, jangphai, gejera, dholbiri, bala, dugdugi, gamkharu, muthi kharu, anguthi* (ring), *zonbiri, sipatmani, birimani, magardana, galpata, kantha har, gereza, kareea, madali,* etc. Nowadays tribal women hardly wear ornaments. Some old ladies wear *gamkharu, thuria,* etc.

51. Weaving and Spinning:—Handloom weaving forms a cultural constituent of the women of Assam. In earlier days most of the cloth required for the family was produced at home. But now the scene has changed totally in urban areas. Mill products are gradually replacing the home-made products.

Home-made clothes are *mekhela* and *patani* (lower garment of women), *chadar* (upper garment of women), *gamocha* (towel), *dhuti*, bedsheet, *eri* (*endi*), etc. Some of them have fly-shuttle or throw shuttle and Assam-type loom. Throwshuttle loom antedates the fly-shuttle one. Spinning is generally not done by villagers. They get mill-product yarn from market. A few of them keep *eri* (*endi*) cocoons to produce *eri* (*endi*) cloth. The designs of the textiles are the tradition of the Assamese culture and they are initiated at the base level by the *Sipini* (weaver women) of Assam.

52. Sericulture of Assam:—Assam's handloom industry is basically silk-oriented. The salubrious climate of Assam is suitable for sericigenous flora and fauna. Four varieties of silkworms and their host-plants, mulberry (*Bomby mori*), Eri, Muga and Oak-Tasar are popular and important for economic and commercial purposes. Sericulture is an important cottage industry of Assam. Eri (*Philosamia ricine*) and muga (*Antherla assama*) have been producing silk traditionally since long back. Muga is the pride of the Assamese ladies. Oak-Tasar *(Antheria paphia* and *Antheria reyeli)* was introduced in Assam only in 1972. Nearly 90 per cent of the total silk production in the country is in the mulberry sector alone. As per B.K. Paul (*JNEC*, Vol. 13, No. 2, 1993:34) 16,000 families of Assam are engaged in raw silk production (in MTs), and, there are 7,020 sericulture villages producing seventeen mulberry raw silk (in MTs) whereas, Karnataka, the maximum producing State has only 14,742 sericulture villages with a production of 4,790 mulberry raw silk (in MTs). It is stated that about 50,000 persons are either directly or indirectly engaged in handloom industry in Sualkuchi village (*Sentinel*, May 7, 1995:1). As per A.N. Sarkar (*JNEC*, Vol. 13, No. 2, 1993:22), Assam is the largest producer of muga and eri silk in the country and sixth in ranking for production of mulberry silk. The production of eri and muga yarns are estimated at 200 tonnes and 75 tonnes respectively. Production of mulberry is around 30 tonnes per annum. Total production of silk fabrics in the State is estimated at 25 lakh metres annually.

53. Handicrafts:—Basketry among the Assamese is highly developed. They produce baskets of very fine designs for various purposes. The Assamese are experts in bamboo and cane work. But they have no professional basket-makers. In rural areas, men during leisure make baskets for domestic use. Among them, the bamboo and cane work have given way to the making of cane furniture. In urban areas few professional workers prepare a different kinds of armchairs, sofas, tables; variety of hats, etc. The State Government has established training centres for cane and bamboo work and toy-making for women trainees. A few of them are making pottery but gradually their number is decreasing due to the impact of modernisation. They are now interested in other professions. The blacksmiths have started manufacturing agricultural implements like *dao*, axe, hoe, sickle, etc. Some of them know wood carving. The carpenters are producing doors, windows, toys, bowls, cups, etc.

54. House and Compound:—In rural areas houses are made with wood, bamboo, mud and thatches. Walls are made of bamboo-splits, plastered with mud and inverted "V" shaped roof with thatches. Some houses in rural areas are now roofed with C.I. sheets, *ikra* wall, *pucca* floor of Assam type. Cemented buildings and Assam-type houses are seen in urban areas. Each household, in rural area, possesses a large compound, partially encircled by fencing. They have *chora ghar, bar-ghar, sarughar, maral-ghar, sowani-kotha, bulani chora ghar, pak-ghar* or *randhani ghar, dhekishal, tatsal, gohali-ghar, bharal ghar* and *Namghar* or *Kirtanghar,* etc.

Some households generally construct four houses on four sides of a big compound. Guests are entertained in the front house situated at the entrance from main road. It is call *choraghar*. This house may have one or more rooms. The second one is called *thoka-ghar* (living room). The head of the family, his wife and children live in this. It may have more than one compartment. The third one is called *thoka-ghar.* It has more than one compartment. One uses it for living purposes. The granary is constructed along with this and a separate shed, adjacent to this is constructed for kitchen. Sometimes the kitchen is constructed far from the living room. The fourth one is the cow-shed. The compound is swept everyday early in the morning. They use this cleaned compound for drying and thrashing paddy. The handloom is kept to one side of the living room. At the back of the house, they have water source and kitchen gardens. They plant flower trees in the vacant front-side of the compound to beautify their house. In the back, they plant coconut, betel-nut, banana, mango, jackfruit, bamboo, etc., trees. They have family *Namghar* which is a small sacred worshipping room for God. Every morning and evening they light a lamp (*banti*) in that room. Some of them have *Chang-ghar,* raised-floor house, and space underneath, for the pigs, poultry, etc.

Now due to acculturation, population growth and gradual progress and development of the State, lawn and open spaces are gradually decreasing and the houses in urban areas are constructed either with corrugated tin-roof of Assam-type or concrete. Multi-storeyed buildings are rapidly constructed in Assam discarding traditional Assam-type houses.

Ahom kings had constructed concrete houses in earlier days. It was customary not to allow the construction of the commoner's house to be like those of Ahom kings. Different tribes of Assam have constructed their houses in different ways. Some Karbis have built *chang-ghar* on wooden planks, etc.

55. Architecture, Sculpture and Folk Art:—In many ancient sites decorated temples, stone slabs of olden days with sculptures, terracotta plaques with designs are found.

Royal insignia and the seal of Ahom king reflect their artistic taste. Ahom royal palace (brick built) Gar-gaon, Kareng-ghar of Nazira, Sibsagar, reflect their skill in building palaces. Palace with underground cellars (*tola-toli ghar*), Rangpur, Sibsagar surprises the people of present day at the expertise of those workers.

Ancient sports pavilion (*Rang-ghar*), Rangpur, Sibsagar is an excellent example of this. Sibdole temple of Sibsagar town; Kamakhya temple of Guwahati; Mahabhairab temple of Tezpur; sculpture of Bamuni Hill of Tezpur; Da-Parbatia gate of Tezpur; wooden Singhasan pedestal of Vaishnava Satra of Barpeta; holy pedestal (wooden) Mahapurushia Satra of Barpeta; holy pedestal (silver) with stone image of Govinda of Auniati Satra; Devi temple's sculpture of Gaurisagar, Sibsagar; metal image of Mahishasuramardini Durga of Negheriting temple of Golaghat; Vasudeva stone image of Kuaritol, Silghat, Nagaon; Sibdole temple's sculptured panels in Negheriting of Golaghat are skilful efforts. There are a few painting manuscripts of Dakshinpat Satra, scenes of *Bhagavata Purana*, etc. Art in pleasure boat of Kamalabari Satra; timber roof-frame of *Kirtan Ghar* of Kamalabari Satra; Makara terracotta of Kamakhya temple, Guwahati; wooden painted sculpture on wall-panel of Barpeta *Namghar*; ivory image of Radha Krishna of Barpeta; wooden image of Vishnu on Garuda of Barpeta, etc. are great works of artistic skill.

Asans (low-seats) to sit before the idols of worship are beautiful. They are decreasing day by day. They are used for sitting on the floor while taking food. This is made of cane and sugar-cane and decorated with geometric designs. Articles of daily use like i.e., *chalani* (sieve), *pachi* (utensil), *duli* (utensil), *kula* (winnowing fan), *japi* (basket), *bichani* (hand-fan), *madur* (mat), *mora* (stool), *mukha* (mask), *phani* (comb), etc., are prepared from bamboo, cane, grass, etc. All these are still used by both urban and rural people. They look beautiful and are used for decoration. Decorated wooden *pira, barpira, chal or jal pira*, etc., are wooden low-seats with flowers, leaves, birds, and geometric designs. Low stools for bathing purposes have wood-cut designs.

The wooden, stone and mud-soiled images and figures are the result of beautiful workmanship. Wood-cut pictures on doors, village *Namghars* are also beautifully decorated. In earlier days people were using *dolas (Dooly*, cradle). They were different types with artistic works. Sargadeo, Satradhikar, officers were using *dolas* to go from one place to another, to attend marriages, etc. For ladies there were different *dolas* with beautiful designs. In earlier days, earthen dolls were made, especially in Kamrup district. They were given during marriage to idols in the month of *Bohag* (middle of April) with the hope of getting a son for a barren women. After this, the dolls of husband-wife were kept in a case of banana tree covers and a few eggs of a duck were kept and thereafter they were floated in a river. Earthen pitchers were painted with attractive designs. Present-day earthen censers are full of beautiful workmanship and skilful metal-work. *Kahi, Bann-kahi, maihang, bati, lota, chariya, sharai-bata*, etc., are decorative brass utensils which indicate the artistic mind of *Maria* people of Assam. Mainly they are made by the *Marias.* But all these are not much used by the urban people except *bata* to offer *tamul-pan* (betel-nut and leaves). All these brass utensils are used in rural areas along with aluminium and plastic utensils.

Artefacts of ivory were famous in Assam. It is said that Bhagadatta presented a sword made of ivory to Judhisthir. During the Ahom age, many artefacts of ivory like ring, comb, small artefacts, handle of sword, etc., were used. Village *Khanikars* are experts in fixing antlers of deer to wood heads of deer. Some of them keep the heads of deer, buffalo and their antlers in the drawingroom which indicate cultural richness of that person. They make combs and musical instruments *fani* and *paypa* from horns of buffaloes.

Pithas (cakes) are aslo examples of culinary art. These are not only sweet dishes but also indicate the artistic talent of the Assamese ladies.

56. Marriage:—Assamese are patrilineal, patrilocal and patriarchal. Each tribe of Assam has its own rule for selection of a mate. Marriage is generally of two types. These are through negotiation and sometimes through elopement. Elopement type of marriage exists only among the low-caste Hindus. Long back, marriage by exchange was prevalent in Assam. Marriage by capture is sometimes found among the tea-garden labourers in Assam. According to Mukunda Sarma (1973:31), the Rava people of Assam have *Nokdhangkai* (marriage by intrusion). The Karbis of Assam have cross-cousin marriage system (R.K. Mandal and M.N. Basu, 1936:110). This system is also popular among the Kukis of Assam. Among them the younger brother marries the widow of his elder brother but the elder brother cannot marry the widow of his younger brother. Love marriages and court marriages are also prevalent among the Assamese. Marriage is considered 'legal' soon after the formal marriage ceremony. In earlier days boys and girls could rarely mix but now, due to acculturation, they can interact with one another but still, there are some restrictions.

Marriage by service (*Chapania*) is said to be the best type of marriage among the Assamese people. In this, the would-be groom is required to stay and work in his would-be father-in-law's house for a certain period. This procedure applies also in the case of a negotiated marriage. As per B.M. Das (1987:285), there is another system of marriage called *dhemena*. In this, a man keeps a woman as his wife, who is either a widow or deserted.

The Assamese Hindus follow endogamy but they are exogamous in respect of clans. Marriage between members of the same clan is generally discouraged and they cannot marry a member within the last seven generations on the father's side and five generations on the mother's side. Morganatic marriage (a marriage in which the wife cannot enjoy the husband's rank) is rare. A higher-caste boy, however, can marry a lower-caste girl. It cannot be followed in reverse. Though it is seen sometimes in love-marriages. But, such cases are very rare.

The Kayasthas of upper Assam are not equal in status to the Kayasthas of lower Assam. The Kalitas and Kayasthas of upper Assam can inter marry. But the Kayasthas of lower Assam can marry only among them. (B.M. Das, 1987:284). In earlier days there was no dowry system. In some areas of Assam, Brahmin families used to receive bride-price from the groom's family. This depended on the age of the bride and her qualifications. In some castes, the bride's father gets a pair of cows from the groom's family. Nowadays, due to acculturation the grooms are demanding ornaments, household articles, luxury items, etc., from the bride's house. Traditionally no cash-dowry was received by them. But, at present, there is a change in their attitude and they accept cash amounts.

The Assamese are monogamous. Polygamy was prevalent in earlier days, among a few rich families. Child marriage was rare. In earlier days, an Assamese Brahmin girl used to marry a banana tree soon after her attainment of puberty. This was called *Tulani* or *Shanti Biya* (Puberty marriage). The age of marriage at present for girls is 20 to 28 years and boys 23 to 30 years.

In Assamese family, *sakha-sakhi's* (intimate friend's) place is very high, especially during the marriage ceremony. *Sakha-sakhi* wear the dresses exactly like the bride and the groom and sit near them. Most of the Assamese people fear the role of evil spirits in their marriage. These fake bride and groom, *sakha* and *sakhi*, actually help in performing the marriage ceremony smoothly by misleading the evil spirits and acting as the bride and groom. They have close relation with the bride and groom. Their children cannot marry the children of these friends and they observe the formalities for three nights when any of them dies (M. Sarma, 1973:83-84). Remarriage of widow and widower is allowed. But widows with children dislike to marry again. *Biya-Nam* sings in the bride's house for the ladies.

Marriage is generally celebrated for two days. On the morning of the first day, the groom's people go with marriage-clothes for bride, including ornaments, hair oil, comb, vermilion, pen, writing pad, scent, powder, *ulta, kumkum*, lipstick, betel-nut and betel leaves, big-sized *rohu* fish, varieties of sweets and curd, etc. These clothes and ornaments are worn by the bride during her marriage. These items are called *Zoran* or *Tekeli* from groom's house. In the groom's house, a *shradha* ceremony is performed on the morning of the marriage day, for the previous nine forefathers. The groom proceeds towards the bride's house in the evening with his relatives and friends. The bride and groom cannot eat on the day of their marriage till the marriage function is over. Women in the bride's-house keep "water in pitcher" from a river or pond for the bathing of groom before the initiation of marriage function. They collect and fetch this water early in the morning, on the day of the marriage. At night, when *lagna* (auspicious moment) comes the marriage is performed by Brahman Pandits. *Lagna* (auspicious moment) is selected from the almanac. Next day, after the marriage, the groom goes back to his house with his newly married wife. A *khoba-khubi* (feeding) function is observed in the groom's house on the (bride and groom) arrival day. Some of them perform a function at groom's house on the day of marriage before proceeding to the bride's house and they feed people.

The Muslims of Assam marry by *'nikah'* with the help of an Imam/ Maulavi. Some of the Muslims follow the marriage rites of the Hindus. But some are strict in following their own way.

Boro-Kachari are engaged in *Haba* (marriage) in which they follow the rule of clan exogamy. The Deoris are engaged in *Sajuba* (marriage). They have broadly four different forms of marriage. The Dimasa-Kacharis have *'Kalti'* (bride-price) depending on the means and the quality of the groom and the bride. But this system is disliked by the educated Dimasa people. Among the Mishings, two forms of marriages are performed. The Karbis are engaged in *Picho-Kapanori* (marriage). The Ahom marriage is called *Chaklang.*

57. Family Relations:—In the earlier days, people used to prefer living in joint families. Due to acculturation, education, limitation of economic conditions and lack of privacy, etc., nowadays people prefer staying in a nuclear family with wife and children after marriage. They do not want to take the responsibility of their old parents and avoid their duties towards parents, unmarried sisters, etc., and like to live separately. However, still a few joint-families, particularly in rural areas with old parents, uncles, aunts, cousins and many other relatives linked to each other through the male line live under the same roof. In a joint-family, generally the old father is the head of the family. After his death, the eldest son becomes the head. His instructions, suggestions, opinions are followed by other members of the joint family. He gets respect from other members of the family. The joint family protects and gives social security to its members; including the aged, invalid, sickpeople. It is the responsibility of the other members of the family to look after them.

When a close relative from the patrilineal side dies, all the close clan members observe common impurity for a certain number of days. But when somebody from the mother's side dies, this formality is not observed. If the father-in-law dies, the son-in-law need not observe it but, his wife has to maintain it generally for three days for her own father. For her father-in-law, she has to observe the same like her husband. During this period, there are some restrictions on food and drinks including the restriction to worship God, etc., and the entry into the sacred room.

In a Hindu family, a person can enter his relative's house, bedroom or kitchen, without permission. There is a joking relationship in between wife and brother-in-law; brother and grand-mother, grand-son, grand-daughter; sister's husband and wife's sister, younger brother of husband and the sister-in-law, husband and younger sister of wife, grand-father and grand-son and grand-daughter. Avoidance relationship is maintained between father-in-law and daughter-in-law, husband's elder brother and younger brother's sister-in-law. A brother's wife traditionally cannot come in front of her father-in-law or an aged person without covering her head with *oranee* (veil). She cannot call her husband and elder by name. In earlier days, a wife was prevented from speaking out the "name" of her husband. A husband was prevented from calling his wife by name. They were not expected to gossip in front of elder members.

Relatives, especially an elder one was called accordingly as per the relation and not by name. This relation was extended to their village people and their neighbours. Some of the kinship terms of the Assamese family are as follows :—

Kinship Terms	*Terms of address*	*Terms of Reference*
1. Father	Pita, Deuta	Pita, Deuta
2. Mother	Mai, Ai	Mai, Ai, Bou
3. Son	Bopa, by name	Lora
4. Daughter	Mai, by name	Ji, Jiori, Swoali
5. Elder brother	Kaka, Dada	Kaka, Dada
Kinship Terms	*Terms of address*	*Terms of Reference*
6. Younger brother	By name, Bhaiti	Bhai, Bhaiti
7. Elder sister	Bai, Baideo	Baideo, Danga Baini
8. Younger sister	By name, Bhanti	Saru Baini, Bhanti
9. Son's wife	Buari, Bou	Buari
10. Elder/Younger sister's husband	Bhindeo	Bhindeo
11. Father's elder brother	Dangar Pita, Khura	Dangar Pita, Khura
12. F.Y.brother	Saru Pita, Khura	Saru Pita, Khura
13. Father's mother	Aita	Aita
14. Father's father	Bar Pita	Bar Pita
15. Mother's elder sister	Jethei	Jethe
16. M.Y.sister	Mahi	Mahi
17. F.E.B.wife	Dangar mai, Khuri	Dangar Mai, Khuri
18. F.Y.B.wife	Saru mai, Khuri	Saru Mai, Khuri
19. F.E.sister	Jethi	Jethi
20. F.Y.sister	Pehi	Pehi
21. F.E.S.husband	Jesta	Jesta
22. F.Y.S.husband	Peha	Peha
23. Mother's brother	Moma, Momaideo	Moma, Momaideo
24. M.B.wife	Mami	Mami
25. Wife's younger brother	By name	Khursal
26. Wife's sister	By name	Khursali
27. Wife's elder brother	Bargiri	Bargiri
28. Wife's elder sister	Ai	Jesahu
29. Wife's s.husband	Salpati	Salpati
30. Husband's y. brother	By name	Deor
31. H.E.B. wife	Bai	Jayak
32. H.Y.B. wife name	Jayak	
33. H.Y.sister	By name	Nandiyak
34. Husband	Not addressed,	Giriak
35. Wife	Not addressed, sometimes Mayek	Ghainyak
36. Husband's father	Pita	Sahur
37. Wife's F.	Pita	Sahur
38. Husband's mother	Ai	Sahu
39. Wife's M.	Ai	Sahu
40. E.B.wife	Bou	Bou
41. Y.B.W.	Not addressed	Bhai Bou
42. M.E.S.husband	Jetha	Jetha

Kinship Terms	*Terms of address*	*Terms of Reference*
43. M.Y.S.H.	Moha	Moha
44. Son's W.F.	Bioi	Bioi
45. Daughter's H.F.	Bioi	Bioi
46. Son's W.M.	Biani	Biani
47. Brother's wife	Bhai Bowari	Nabou
48. Daughter's H.M.	Biani	Biani
49. One's intimate friend	Sakhi (for female), Sakha (for male), By name	Sakhi, Mita; Sakha
50. Father's male friend	Taoi	Taoi
51. F.friend's wife	Amoi	Amoi

**(F.=Father; M.=Mother; B.=Brother, S.=Sister, W.=Wife; H.=Husband; E.=Elder; Y.=Younger).*

58. Divorce:—Divorce is allowed by mutual consent. The bond of matrimony among the Assamese is very strong. Divorce is easy but very few cases of divorce have occurred because they do not want to break relations. Still a few of them desire divorce.

The tribals never go to court for divorce. They separate by mutual consent or the husband can send his wife back to her parents' house for good.

If a wife wants divorce she has to return her bride-price which she got from her husband. If it is sought by husband for reasons other than barrenness, adultery, sickness or incurable diseases, he has to pay some mutual fine to the village-elders and his wife. This fine is settled after mutual discussion by the parties concerned. A divorced wife is allowed to go only after leaving all children with her husband except for the suckling one and she is entitled to get some amount from her divorced husband to maintain the suckling infant.

59. Position of Women:—The position of tribal women, however, is higher. They enjoy a dominant status and in the market some of them are engaged in selling and buying. Both tribal and non-tribal women are happy; it is seen especially at the time of *Bihu* festival.

Domestic weaving and embroidery work seem to have become both a sacred duty and a compulsion for the Assamese ladies. Previously, no Assamese boy used to marry an Assamese girl who did not know loom-work. Even the Assamese society looked down on a girl who was ignorant of loom-work. In rural areas, most of the houses keep weaving apparatus to make cloth. But this custom is slowly disappearing due to acculturation. They now prefer to buy cloth from market including *Bihuan fulam gamocha* (towel with flower designs).

Earlier, the Assamese ladies used to respect their old folk, and used to cover their head with *orani* (veil). Even now, it a is practised in front of the elders. A young wife could not appear before the old and aged people, could not talk with them or menfolk or call them by name. Similarly, a mother-in-law could not come out and talk in front of her son-in-law.

A wife had her meal after her husband had taken. She could not eat along with her husband or before him. In olden days, women never participated in politics and administration as well as in community worship. With Britishers came with the Western culture and gradually women folk are getting emancipated. In the freedom struggle, Kanaklata, Mula Gavaru, etc., participated and before them, there was Sati Jaymati in 1679, during Lara Raja of Ahom kingdom. Now female politicians, administrators, engineers, physicians, industrialists, pleaders, teachers, scientists, sports-women, writers, artists, singers, dancers, police-women, etc., are emerging. Most of the urban women are now working both outside and inside the houses along with their menfolk.

In rural areas, young girls and women are allowed freely to dance *Bihu* with young boys. Even now, both in urban and rural areas remaining single is looked down upon.

They consider their kitchen as a holy place and do not allow women to enter with slipper/shoe or without bathing. During menstruation women are not allowed to enter or cook. There is no restriction on eating fish for the Assamese widows except among the Brahmins.

It seems that women got prestige, honour and respect from their menfolk in earlier days. Due to patriarchal form of society, everyone generally fears and obeys their menfolk and pay legitimate respects whether young or old, educated or uneducated, rich or poor, to the women. The women who are helpers of male partners in all spheres of life, are not allowed to participate in any religious function among *Satras.* Kanaklata, woman of Srimanta Sankar Deva's family, once became the head of a *Satra*; but, no one followed her example and even now, women are not allowed to enter any important *Satra* specially *Barpeta Satra.*

Tribal women of this region hold a high position. They have equal status with their men. Their men co-operate with them in household work and play an important role in agricultural activities. Bride-price is prevalent in a few tribal societies. In earlier days they gave *mithun* (wild bison) in exchange for brides. As *mithuns* are now becoming rare, marriages are settled on some price. A man returns bride-price if the woman leaves him or commits adultery. The *Karbi* woman have equal status with their men-folk. The bride, after her marriage, retains her surname. A Karbi woman works more than a man if one counts her devoted hours per day.

In every work of a tribal family—cleaning jungles for *jhum* (shifting) cultivation, collection of food material and fuelwood from the forests, washing clothe, cleaning utensils etc.—the women share work with the men. Above all, they cook food, attend to all domestic work, fetch water from nearby source, etc. They take care of the infants and children. They weave, knit, stitch clothes, etc. Brewing of rice-beer for the family is the responsibility of the women.

Tribal women are generally not allowed to attend a village court. In the community feast women are not allowed to take food along with men. They take food separately. In some tribal societies, women cannot attend the community worship for the well-being and prosperity of the village. The tribal married women have almost no right in the property of the father. All the movable and immovable property of her dead father is inherited by her brothers.

Parents in earlier days, were not in favour of education for their daughters. They believed that educated boys would not marry an educated girl and money spent on a girl's education was a waste as she worked for her husband's family after marriage. But this attitude is now changing in urban and semi-urban areas. A school-going girl generally helps her mother and takes care of younger brothers and sisters in a middle-class family.

60. Customary Law of Inheritance:—In an Assamese family father's property was inherited by the sons. But now, as per Government of India's law, daughters are also entitled equally to their father's property.

Among the *Deoris*, after the death of a man, his sons become the owners of his property which is equally divided among them. In case a man dies without having any son, his property goes to the nearest agnatic male relative. The wife and daughters are not eligible to share that property. Among the *Dimasa-Kachari*, cash, weapons, etc., are inherited by the sons. After the death of their mother, daughters get jewellery, mother's clothes, looms, etc. Cooking utensils, brass-metal dishes, bowls and other household articles are divided among sons and daughters equally at the death of their father. If there is no daughter, the maternal property is inherited by the nearest female relative who belongs to the same clan as the deceased woman. Among the *Tiwa (Lalung)*, after or before the death of a father, the land is divided equally among his sons. The father may keep one of share for his own use, which after his death, goes to that son who looks after him till his death. The daughters of Hill *Tiwa (Hill Lalung)* inherit the property of their mother. Among the *Mishings*, if a man has no son, his daughters may share his property on the condition that they bear the funeral expenses of their father. Among the *Bodos*, they prefer a male child to a female one, as sons are the sole inheritors of the parents, property.

61. Birth Rule:—In old days, they used to favour sons for better living. They welcome equally male and female child. Due to acculturation culture change now the Assamese are prefering male child.

A mother after the birth of a child cannot come out for 7 days and they consider the room as impure. This, however, varies among different castes and tribes. The tribals generally do not follow this. There are some ceremonies and sacrifices related with the birth of a child and it varies from clan to clan and tribe to tribe.

Some associate the birth of a child with the rebirth of a dead person in the family. Present-day women prefer to go to hospital for delivery than having it at home.

62. Name-giving ceremony:—The most important ceremony in connection with birth of a child is the name-giving ceremony which is performed two to nine days after the birth of a baby. It varies from people to people. Among some people a new-born baby is named immediately after the birth. The maternal uncle of a new-born child occupies an important place on rice cum name giving ceremony. This is performed either in the 3rd or 5th or 7th month and a feast is given by the parents.

Most of the tribals have no specific name-giving ceremony. Names are generally chosen later on. Children are given their pet names soon after birth. In the *Bodo* society they are not unduly concerned about formal names. Formal names are given without consulting others. Some tribals select the name of the child while baptising in a church.

63. Disposal of the Dead:—A dead body is cremated by the Hindus. The Muslims and the Christians bury their dead. They have common community cremation and burial ground. The dead body of a Hindu is burned near a river or stream with mango wood. Now, all types of woods are used. Even electric crematorium is used to burn the dead body at Guwahati. If a person dies an unnatural death, he is considered to be a sinner. The process of the disposal of the dead by tribals resembles that in the Hindu custom.

After the confirmation of death, the dead body is taken out and kept in the veranda or middle of the courtyard. Then it is bathed and new clothes are put on and a new white coloured cloth is wrapped around the body. Then it is placed on a bier which is made of raw bamboo. The projecting bamboo poles on four sides are put on the shoulders of four persons who carry the dead body. Generally, sons and relatives carry the dead body. Funeral procession with the dead body proceeds towards the cremation ground. The procession is led by a priest. Among the *Bodos* on the way from the house of the dead person to the cremation ground, the *deuri* or *oja* (priest) throws small pieces of yarn They believe the soul of the dead goes to the cremation ground from the house following the yarn. This custom is also seen among the *Deoris, Rabhas* and *Mishings*. Even a few Hindus also follow this but they use mustard-seed instead of yarn. In rural areas, one male member of each family is bound to go to the cremation ground with the dead body. Women and the children are not allowed to participate in the procession. If the dead one is an infant and below the age of five, the Hindus and some tribals bury them. Dead bodies of accident cases, pregnant women, drowned persons, epidemic cases, etc., are buried by tribals.

Before lighting the funeral pyre some traditional customs are followed. There is a system of placing five or seven stacks of woods, while the pyre is arranged. Thereafter the dead body is placed on the pyre. The eldest or the youngest son of the deceased lights the pyre. The relatives circumambute the funeral pyre; for a man, it is five times and for a woman, seven. After the cremation the funeral party takes bath in a river or a stream before returning to their respective houses. The funeral party has to purify themselves by sprinkling Ganga-water (pure water) or basil water on their bodies. This sacred water is kept ready for them to purify themselves before entering their houses. It is a custom among Hindus not to take food till the dead body is cremated. There is a custom among some tribals to serve drinks and food to everyone who comes to condole, as a mark of respect for the dead person.

The Bodo-Kacharis practise both cremation and burial. But cremation has come to be the normal practice. The Deoris, Dimasa-Kacharis, Karbis, Lalungs, Rabhas, Sonowals, etc., cremate the dead one. Burial is practised by the Mishings. They bury the dead bodies irrespective of age, sex and nature of death. Among the Bodos, after the cremation, all the members of the funeral party gather near the house of the dead one and are served with *Ju* or *Jumai* (rice-beer).

64. Shraddha Ceremony:—It is customary not to take fish, meat, egg, onion, garlic, *musur* pulse, etc., till the completion of death-rites (*shraddha*) among Hindus. This *shraddha* ceremony is performed generally on the eleventh day after the death of a person. Some of the non-Brahmins perform this ceremony on the thirtieth day after death. This eleven or thirteen or thirty-day period is called *Asuj* (impure) time for the family. In earlier days and even today the sons of the deceased person in a Hindu family tonsure their heads before the *shraddha* rituals. Some of the tribals perform a *shraddha* type ceremony, on the third or fourth or seventh day, after death. The Bodos observe this on the eleventh or thirteenth day of the death. As per *Encyclopedia of Religion and Ethics* (James Hastings, 1908, Vol. I:452), the *shraddha* is the custom of feeding the dead and is more highly developed from the primitive funeral feast.

Generally the eldest or the youngest son performs with the help of a priest, a *hom-yagga* (sacred-fire to sacrificial pit, as an offering to God) as a part of *shraddha* rituals without taking food. Some of them perform this *hom-yagga* of *shraddha* at Kamakhya temple with the help of *Panda thakur* (priest). He chants the *mantras* and the son of the deceased repeats it.

The Hindus serve vegetables with *luchi* (flour-made thin snacks fried in boiled *ghee*), sweets and curd at lunch on the day of the *shraddha* for friends, relatives and invitees. They cannot serve cooked rice, fish, meat or egg and *musur* pulse on the *shraddha* day. Next day, they observe *matsa-sparsha* (fish-touching and eating) day along with relatives during dinner. From that day, they eat all non-vegetarian items. If the family is not economically well off, the villagers contribute and arrange the *shraddha* ceremony.

The followers of the traditional Boro faith perform the *shraddha* ceremony with prayer before the altar of the *Bathou* and serve their relatives and villagers with *Ju* or *Jumai* (rice beer). Serving of meals are common in the *shraddha* ceremony. The responsibility of conducting the whole function rests on the eldest son. He has to perform these duties under the traditional customs. The followers of Brahma dharma perform *Ahuti* during the *shraddha* day. They serve vegetarian meals to all persons. Some of them serve rice-beer, at the end of the *shraddha* ceremony.

A day before at this ceremony a *preshraddha* or *daha* is observed by some Hindu families including the Bodos. Some are of the opinion that the word *daha* comes from Sanskrit word *dasaha* meaning ten. *Daha* is observed on the tenth day of the death. This is observed by offering some favourite dishes of the dead one, in open field or a quiet place. This ceremony is conducted by the priest who chants *mantras* (spell) facing south. The sons of the deceased chant the *mantras* along with the priest. The married daughters of the dead one in the Hindu family observe *shraddha* generally on the third day of the death. Sometimes, after one year of death, a family member can arrange an annual *shraddha*. They give *pindi,* globular lump of food offered as an oblation to a deceased relation in Puri (Orissa State) where the son offers one of his favourite fruit in the name of the dead one which he never eats in his life. But, nowadays, they do not observe all these customs rigidly.

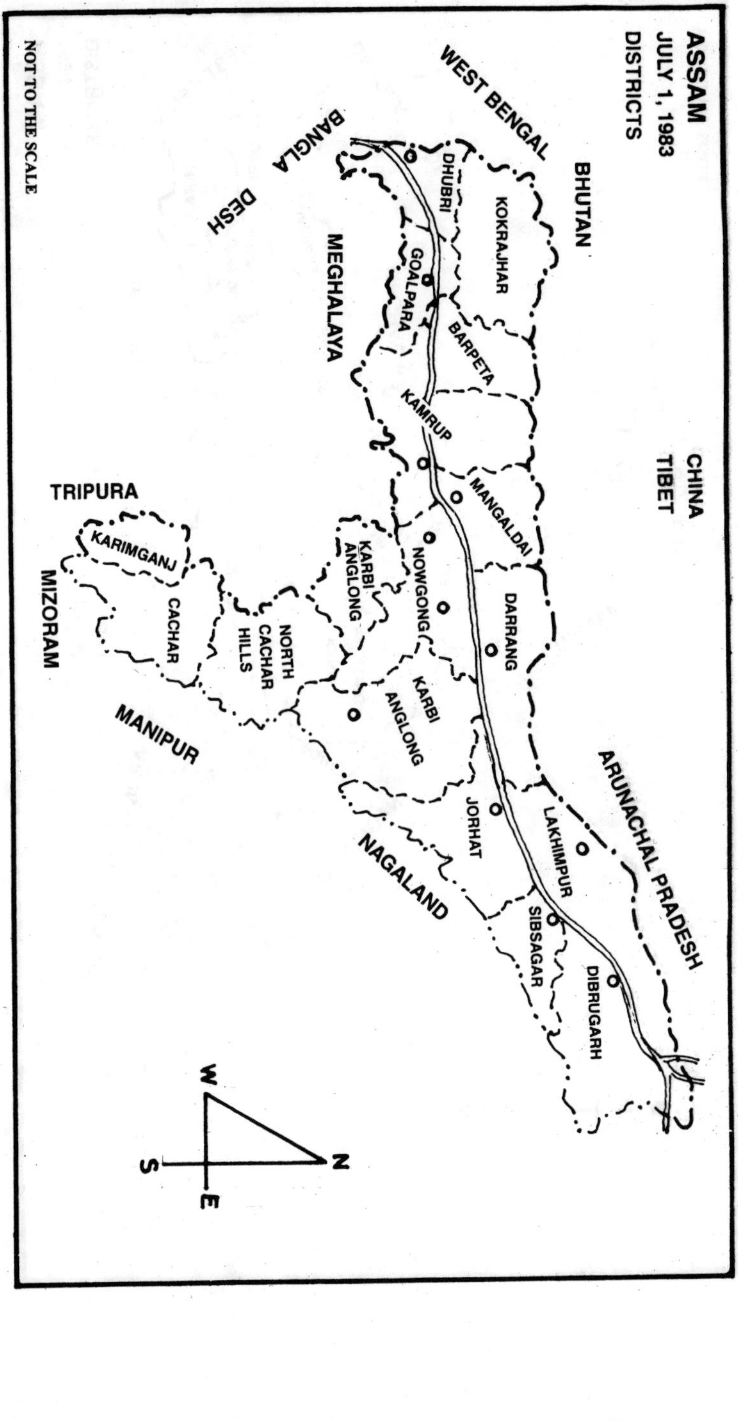
ASSAM
JULY 1, 1983
DISTRICTS
NOT TO THE SCALE
CHINA
TIBET
BHUTAN
WEST BENGAL
BANGLA DESH
MEGHALAYA
TRIPURA
MIZORAM
MANIPUR
NAGALAND
ARUNACHAL PRADESH
DHUBRI
KOKRAJHAR
GOALPARA
BARPETA
KAMRUP
MANGALDAI
NOWGONG
DARRANG
KARBI ANGLONG
KARIMGANJ
CACHAR
NORTH CACHAR HILLS
KARBI ANGLONG
JORHAT
LAKHIMPUR
SIBSAGAR
DIBRUGARH
W
N
S
E

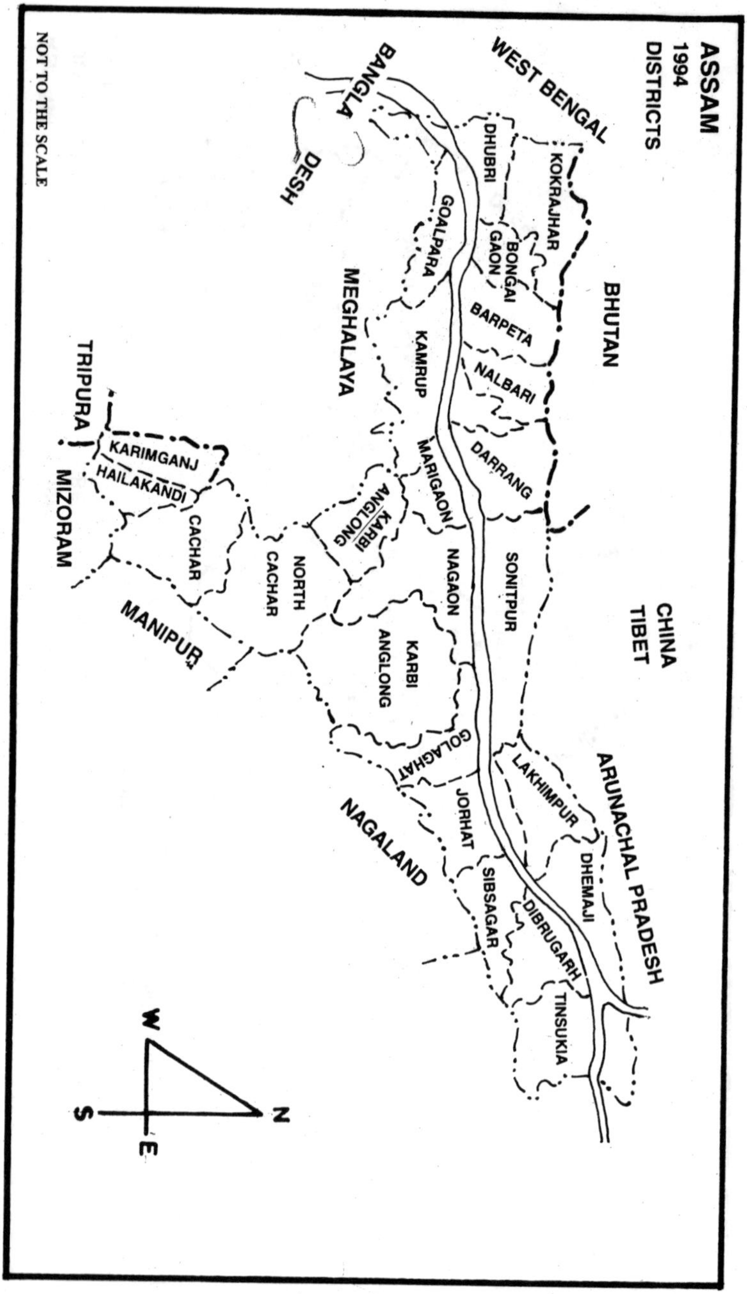
ASSAM
1994
DISTRICTS
WEST BENGAL
BANGLA
DESH
BHUTAN
CHINA
TIBET
ARUNACHAL PRADESH
MEGHALAYA
TRIPURA
MIZORAM
MANIPUR
NAGALAND
KOKRAJHAR
DHUBRI
GOALPARA
BONGAI
GAON
BARPETA
NALBARI
KAMRUP
DARRANG
MARIGAON
KARBI
ANGLONG
SONITPUR
NAGAON
KARBI
ANGLONG
NORTH
CACHAR
CACHAR
KARIMGANJ
HAILAKANDI
GOLAGHAT
JORHAT
LAKHIMPUR
DHEMAJI
SIBSAGAR
DIBRUGARH
TINSUKIA
W
N
S
E
NOT TO THE SCALE

2

Brief Description of the Districts

Assam was divided into twelve districts (Census of India 1951 and 1961). They were—Kamrup, Goalpara, Darrang, Nowgong, Cachar, Sibsagar, Lakhimpur, United Mikir and North Cachar Hills, Garo Hills, United Khasi and Jaintia Hills, Lushai Hills, and Naga Hills. The state Nagaland was born in 1963, from the Naga Hills districts, Meghalaya in 1972 from Garo, Khasi and Jaintia Hills districts, and Lushai Hills was separated from Assam and renamed Mizoram which became a Union Territory on 21 January, 1972 and a state on 20 February, 1987.

United Mikir and North Cachar Hills was bifurcated and constituted into two separate districts in 1970, i.e., Mikir Hills and North Cachar Hills (vide Notification No. AAP 134/68/22 dt. 1.2.1970 and AAP 134/68/10 dt. 30.1.1970 respectively). Later, Mikir Hills was renamed Karbi Anglong district.

All the districts have been grouped into "block" called *Mauza* and the residents pay revenue dues to *Mauzadar/Bishaya/Chaudhuri/Kagoti/Patgiri*. Present day *Mauzas* of Assam are different from the earlier territorial revenue units. For many reasons, the number of *Mauzadars* are gradually reducing. The areas assigned to them for each *Mauza* contains twenty to thirty, or even more villages (E.A.Gait, 1926 :294-295).

The land of Assam is upgraded by earlier subdivisions at district level. Now as per Census of India 1991 the total number of towns in Assam are 93, inhabited villages (Census 1971) 21,995, development blocks (1990-91) 135, Gram Panchayats (1991) 714. At present, Assam is divided into 23 districts. They are—Dhubri, Goalpara, Kokrajhar, Bangaigaon, Barpeta, Nalbari, Kamrup, Darrang, Sonitpur, Marigaon, Nagaon, Karbi Anglong, North Cachar, Cachar, Hailakandi, Karimganj, Golaghat, Jorhat, Sibsagar, Dibrugarh, Tinsukia, Dhemaji and Lakhimpur.

1. Dhubri District:—Dhubri district was a subdivision of earlier Goalpara district. Bangladesh is situated on its west and south-west, Garo Hills on its south-west, Goalpara on its east, Bangaigaon on the north-east and Kokrajhar on the north. River Brahmaputra passes through Dhubri, bifurcating the district and in the west the river turns south to enter the plains of Bangladesh. The town Dhubri is connected by rail with Calcutta, Guwahati and other cities. Steamers and steam-ferries ply on the Brahmaputra connecting Dhubri with

Dibrugarh by Inland Water Shipping Corporation. National Highway No. NH 31 passes through Dhubri. It is a well-connected place, but the development of this place suffers severely from the erosive action of the river Brahmaputra.

There are three subdivisions and eight revenue circles under Dhubri district. The subdivisions are—Bilasipara, Dhubri and North Salmara. The towns are—Sapatgram, Bilasipara, Gauripur, Mankachar, Golokganj, Chapar and Dhubri. The headquarters is Dhubri town. The area of this district is 2,746 sq. km. Total population is 13,25,653; male 6,79,335 and female 6,46,318. Rural population is 11,64,012 and urban 1,61,641. Educated persons are 29.44 per cent (1991). The main industries are match-sticks, aluminium workshops, etc. Rivers Gadadhar and Gangadhar are flowing on its north-west and join the river Brahmaputra.

Dhubri town:—It is the headquarters of this district. It is a class II town and a principal centre of trade. The town is well-lighted. It has a Municipal Board, College, High School, Library, Town Hall . In 1902, Dhubri was connected with Calcutta by rail. The total population of the town is 65,861; male 34,290 and female 31,571. It is a famous and popular place. The Municipality was constituted under Act V (B.C) of 1876, and subsequently Act III (B.C.) of 1884. Dhubri is 287 kms away from Guwahati.

Iron-ore deposits are found in Dhubri as reported by the Geological Survey of India (*Assam Tribune*, August 10, 1994:6).

Gauripur town:—It is a small town on the right bank of the Gadadhar river, about five miles away from the north of Dhubri. It has a College, School, Hospital, Post and Telegraph Office, etc. There are large and fine houses of Gauripur zamindars. Marwari merchants have been doing business in jute, mustard seed, etc., since long back. There are blacksmiths, wheelwrights, potters, goldsmiths, confectioners, shopkeepers etc. The total population of Gauripur is 19,945; male 10,374 and female 9,571.

Golakganj town:—It is an entrance station to Assam by railway. Total population is 6,220; male 3,246 and female 2,974.

2. Goalpara District :—This district was formed on 1 July, 1983. It is situated on the south bank of the Brahmaputra river. Garo Hills of Meghalaya are situated on its south, Dhubri district on its west and north-west, Bangaigaon on its north and Kamrup on its east and north-east. The undivided district of Goalpara had become a British possession in 1765, when the whole of the Mohammedan possessions in Bengal were ceded to the East India Company. At the time of these events, it formed a part of the district of Rangpur and was tagged with Assam in 1826.

There is one subdivision and five revenue circles. The subdivision is Goalpara and headquarters is Goalpara town. The area of this district is 1,911 sq. km. Total populations is 6,61,801; male 3,38,323 and female 3,23,478. There were no industries till 1994. Total educated population is 36.02 per cent.

Total rural population is 6,13,602 and urban 48,199 (1991). Dudhnoi, Krishnai, Jinari are the main rivers. All these are the tributaries of the river Brahmaputra. Goalpara and Lakhimpur are important towns. It has 3,136 hectares of land under tea cultivation with thirteen tea gardens (1989).

Goalpara town:—This is a class III urban area. The total population is 39,208; male 20,299 and female 18,909. Goalpara Sainik School (Military) is very famous. Goalpara Municipality was constituted under Act V (B.C.) of 1876 in 1878.

3. Kokrajhar District:—It was formed on 1 July 1983. It is surrounded by Bhutan on the north, Jalpaiguri and Koch Behar on the west, Barpeta on the east, Bangaigaon on the south-east and Dhubri on the north. There are two subdivisions and five revenue circles. Kokrajhar and Gosaigaon are the subdivisions. The headquarters is Kokrajhar. There were no forest and mineral wealth till 1994. 33.18 percent population are educated. The area of Kokrajhar district is 3, 498 sq. km. Total population is 7,96,880; male 4,10,272 and female 3,86,608. Buri Ai, Champamati, Saralbhanga, Sonkosh rivers flow through this district. Main towns are—Kokrajhar, Gosaigaon and Basugaon. Railways connect this district with West Bengal. Rural population is 7,46,198 and urban 50,682 (1991). Kachugaon Game Reserve is situated in this district.

Kokrajhar town:—It is a class III urban area. It is the headquarters of Kokrajhar district. Railway lines pass through this town and connect it with West Bengal. Total population of Kokrajhar is 28,240; male 14,937 and female 13,303. Kokrajhar is 276 km. away from Guwahati.

4. Bangaigaon District:—It was formed on 19 October, 1989. It is situated on the north bank of Brahmaputra river. Dhubri is situated on its south-west, Kokrajhar on its north and north-west, Barpeta on its east and Brahmaputra river and Goalpara on its south. There are three subdivisions and four revenue circles. Bangaigaon, Bijni and North Salmara are the subdivisions. There was no forest and mineral wealth till 1994. 40.24 per cent population are educated. The area of this district is 2,159 sq. km. Total population is 8,06,472; male 4,15,635 and female 3,90,837. There are paper factories and paper products, aluminium, rail-repairing industries. Manas river flows through this district. It is the boundary between Bangaigaon and Barpeta. It is perhaps the largest tributary in the western part of Assam that joins the Brahmaputra. Railway line goes through Bijni and Bangaigaon towns. Total population of rural area is 7,32,639 and urban 73,833 people. Bangaigaon, Bijni, Abhayapuri, Jogigopa are the main towns.

Bangaigaon town:—It is a class III urban area and headquarters' of Bangaigaon district. Railway line passes through this town and connects it with West Bengal and Assam. Total population of the town is 48,907; male 26,665 and female 22,242. It is 190 km. from Guwahati.

5. Barpeta District:—This district was formed on 1 July, 1983. It is situated on the north bank of Brahmaputra river. Bangaigaon is situated on its south-west and west, Kokrajhar on the north-west, Bhutan on the north,

Nalbari on the east, Brahmaputra river and Kamrup district are on the south. There are two subdivisions and eight revenue circles. Barpeta and Bajali are the subdivisions. The headquarters, is at Barpeta. Manas Game Sanctuary is situated here. There were no mineral products till 1994. 34.21 per cent are educated. The area is 3,307 sq. km. Total population is 13,82,715; male 7,12,861 and, female 6,69,854 (1991). Main industries are metal products and tusk-made handicrafts. Main towns are Barpeta Road, Barpeta, Howli, Sathebari, Bohari, Pathsala, Sarbhog. The main rivers are Chaulkhowa, Beki, Pomara, etc. They are the tributaries of Brahmaputra. Rural population is 12,85,455 and urban 97,260.

Barpeta town:—It is a class III urban area and headquarters of Barpeta district. Total population of Barpeta town is 25,345; male 12,949 and female 12,396. Barpeta is an important trading centre. Barpeta Municipality was formed under Act V (B.C.) of 1876 in 1886. Barpeta is famous for *Mahapurushia Satra* founded by the Vaishnavite reformer Srimanta Sankar Deva at the end of the fifteenth century. This *Satra* democratically elects its *Adhikari* or spiritual head. It is believed that the light that was first lighted in the *Manikut* of the Barpeta *Kirtan-ghar*, by Madhabdeva the founder of *this Satra*, has been kept burning ever since by an incessant supply of oil to the earthen vessel holding the light (K.N. Dutta, 1958:24-25).

Manas Game Sanctuary:—The sanctuary is about 105 sq miles, situated to the north at the foothills of the Himalayas and Bhutan. Railway station of Barpeta road is only 20 miles away. The road to the Sanctuary is motorable from October to May. It is 176 miles from Guwahati. It has tigers, pigmy hog, rhino, golden langur, elephant, wild buffalo, gaur (Indian bison), deer, hornbill, etc. as well as rare plants.

6. Nalbari District:—It is situated on the north bank of the river Brahmaputra. Barpeta district is in the west, Bhutan on the north, Kamrup district to the east, river Brahmaputra and a part of Kamrup district are on its south, Darrang district is partly on its north-east. This district has only one subdivision and nine revenue circles. 46.63 per cent are educated. Area of this district is 2,257 sq. km. Total population is 10,12,608; male 5,22,655 and female 4,89,953. Main towns are—Nalbari and Tihu. Main rivers are Pagladiya, Buradiya, etc. These are the tributaries of Brahmaputra. Rural population is 9,89,369 and urban 23,239 (1991).

Nalbari town:—It is a class IV urban area and headquarters' of Nalbari district. Total population of Nalbari town is 18,949; male 10,195 and female 8,754.

7. Kamrup District:—This district is surrounded by Meghalaya on its south, Marigaon on its south-east, Darrang on its north-east, part of Bhutan on its north, Nalbari on its north-west, Goalpara on its south-west. River Brahmaputra passes through this district bifurcating it. There are three subdivisions. They are Guwahati, Rangiya and Pragjyotishpur. Kamrup district has fourteen revenue circles. The area of this district is 4,345 sq. km.

Headquarters of this district is Guwahati town. Total population is 19,87,662; male 10,56,525 and female 9,31,137. Educated population is 54.60 per cent. Main industries areo, pipe, thread machine, cinema production, chemical industries, etc., Medical College, Ayurvedic College, Veterinary College, Guwahati University, Eye Institute, Engineering College, Engineering Institute, Deaf and dumb and Blind School, Physically Handicapped School are situated in this district. Main towns are Guwahati, Rangiya, Sualkuchi, Niz-Hajo, North Guwahati, Amingaon, Palashbari. Many ponds, *beels* are there. The *beels* are—Dipar beel, Chalchala beel, etc. Sualkuchi is 24 km. away from Guwahati. It is famous for Assam silk—*Muga, Pat* and other handloom fabrics. Till 1989, 3,550 hectares of land of Kamrup district were under tea cultivation with 15 tea gardens. Barnadi Game Reserve is situated in North Kamrup.

Guwahati town:—It is a class I urban area. Guwahati is the gateway to Assam and north-east region. It is a fast-growing metropolitan city. Kamakhya temple, Basistha Ashram, Nabagraha temple, Bhubaneswari temple, Ugratara temple, Umananda, Dolgobinda, Ashwaklanta, Pandunath Bisnu temple, etc., are situated here. Ahom ruler Gadapani who assumed the name of Gadadhar Singha (1681-1696) had erected the temple of Umananda in 1694, on the peacock island in the middle of the Brahmaputra river, near Guwahati and dedicated it to god Shiva. Ahom king Rajeswar Singha (1751-1769) had constructed Sukreswar temple in 1752.

Bharulu river passes through this town and joins Brahmaputra. The ancient name of Guwahati (Guwa=land covered with areca-nut trees) was Pragjyotishpura. It is situated on the bank of Brahmaputra (son of Lord Brahma) river. Narakasura had built this ancient city. National Highway No. NH 31 and 37 run through this town. Pragjyotishpura was the capital of king Bhagadatta of Mahabharata when Kamrup was conquered by the Ahoms. North Guwahati was said to have been built by the Koch king Parikshit, who flourished during the sixteenth century; and at the time of Mir Jumla's (1662 A.D.) invasion, Guwahati was described as lying north of the Brahmaputra (*JASB*, I, pt.I, 1872:69).

Guwahati Municipality was constituted under Act V (B.C.) of 1876 in 1878 and Act III (B.C.) of 1884 in 1887. North Eastern Railways headquarters' is situated at Pandu-Maligaon near Guwahati. Kamakhya temple, a place of pilgrimage, is situated 10 km. away from Guwahati on the top of the Nilachal Hills and is a vital centre of *tantric* form of Hinduism and Saktism. Kamakhya temple was damaged in sixteenth century by Muslim invaders. The present temple of goddess Kamakhya was built by king Naranarayan of Koch Bihar in 1665. In all the 51 *piths* or places it is believed that a portion of *Sati's* (goddess Durga) dismembered body fell. Bhubaneswari temple is also situated on the hilltop. The temple Ashwaklanta stands on the rocky promontory. It is said that Lord Krishna stayed here with Rukmini. Guwahati planetarium was opened for the public in 1994. Navagraha temple (nine planets) on Chitrachal hill depicts ancient astrology. It is situated in the eastern part of the town. Sukreswar is a notable place of Hindu pilgrimage. About nine miles south of Guwahati is the temple of Vasistha. This temple was built in 1751 A.D. in honour of Rishi Vasistha. There are two ashrams of Vasistha and Arundhati. Vasistha Temple Development Committee provides a *dharmasala* for visitors for accommodation. The temple and tank of Ugratara in Ujan Bazar (Guwahati) is also famous. Noonmati Refinery, Assam State Museum, Assam State Zoo, Chitraban Studio for cinema production, Gandhi Mandap of Sarania Hilltop, Regional Science Centre, etc., are situated in Guwahati. Chandubi lake is 64 km. away from Guwahati.

Hajo town:—It is a class I city under Sualkuchi and North Guwahati. Total population is 12,781; male 6,544 and female 6,237. There is a mosque on the Mukamara hill which is known as Poa Mecca, i.e. one-fourth of the merit of Mecca. The temple at Hajo is an object of veneration to Buddhists and Hindus. The image in the shrine is a representation of the man-lion (*Narasimha*) incarnation of Vishnu, but it is worshipped by the Bhutias under the erroneous impression that it is a statue of Buddha. The tomb of Sultan Ghiyasuddin is situated near the mosque. Hajo is 32 miles away from Guwahati.

Trans-frontier trade is carried on with Bhutan at Darranga (Bhutia fair). The Bhutias come down with lac, wax, wooden articles, blanket, ponies, donkeys and goats. They sell these and buy cotton thread, cloth, *eri* cloth, brass vessels, etc.

8. Darrang District:—Bhutan is situated on its north, Sonitpur in the east, Brahmaputra and Marigaon on its south, Kamrup is on the west. There are two subdivisions—Mangaldoi and Udalguri and nine revenue circles. The area of this district is 3,481 sq. km. Headquarters is Mangaldoi. Total population is 12,86,633; male 6,63,596 and female 6,23,030. Educated population is 34.58 per cent. It has four urban areas—Mangaldoi, Tangla, Kharupatia and Udalguri. Main rivers are—Baru, Noa, etc., and they are the tributaries of Brahmaputra. The area of tea cultivation was 39,670 hectares till 1989 with 93 tea gardens.

Mangaldoi town:—It is a class III urban area. Total population is 20,720; male 11,149 and female 9,571. National Highway No. NH 52 passes through this town. No railway line goes through this town. Mangaldoi is 70 km. away from Guwahati.

9. Sonitpur District:—Sonitpur, earlier Tezpur, was known as a city of blood (*Sonit* or *Tez*=blood, *pur*=city). As per legend, Sonitpur was the capital of the kingdom of Bana Raja, the mighty Asura king. His beautiful daughter Usha secretly married Aniruddha, grandson of Lord Krishna, the ruler of Dwarka, under Gandharva rites without her father's knowledge. After marriage they stayed in Agnigar on Bamuni hilltop which is 2 kms away from Tezpur. When Banasura learnt about this marriage he imprisoned Aniruddha. Lord

Krishna then came to Sonitpur to rescue his grandson where Banasura challenged Lord Krishna. A battle between *Hari* (Lord Krishna) and *Hara* (Lord Shiva in the form of Banasura) was fought and the whole city was flooded with blood, hence the name Sonitpur. Banasura was vanquished and Usha and Aniruddha were united forever.

Sonitpur district is situated on the north bank of Brahmaputra. This district was formed in July, 1983. It is surrounded by Arunachal Pradesh on the north, Lakhimpur in the east, Darrang in the west, Brahmaputra on the south. Nagaon and Golaghat are situated in the south. The area of Sonitpur is 5,324 sq.km. It has two subdivisions—Tezpur and Biswanath Chariali. It has seven revenue circles. Tezpur is its headquarters. Under this district: there are four urban areas—Tezpur, Rangapara, Dhekiajuli and Biswanath Chariali. Educated population is 39.84 per cent. Thread machine industry is situated here. A Central University in Tezpur (Tezpur University) was founded in 1994. Main rivers are Belsiri, Burigung, Bharali, Ghiladhari, etc. These are the tributaries of Brahmaputra. Total population is 14,18,484; male 7,42,455 and female 6,76,029. Rural population is 13,14,914 and urban 1,03,570 (Census 1991). Sonai Rupai wild life sanctuary is spread over 175 km. area in this district stretching along the Himalayan foothills. Elephant, Indian Bison, deer, various hill-birds are found in this sanctuary.

Tezpur town:—It is 181 km. away from Guwahati. This is a class II urban area. Total population is 54,999; male 30,055 and female 24,944 (Census 1991). It is said that Tezpur is the city of eternal romance. Kalia Bhomora bridge was constructed and opened for public on 3 April, 1987 over the river Brahmaputra. This bridge is 3.05 km. in length, named after the great Ahom general Kalia Bhomora Phukan. This bridge connects Tezpur with Nagaon district. The only national park of Assam, Kaziranga, is 82 kms away from Tezpur *via* Kalia Bhomora bridge. Various animals are found here. These are—one-horned rhinoceros, tiger, elephant, bison, water buffalo, leopard, jungle cat, hog-badger, cap langur, holluck, gibbon, swamp deer, sambar, hog deer, barking deer, sloth bears, geese, hornbill, ebiss, cormorants, egret, heron, eagle, pelican, etc. Orang wild life sanctuary was renamed as Rajiv Gandhi game sanctuary in 1994. It is known as a mini-Kaziranga. It is 65 km. away from Tezpur town. Various types of animals found are one-horned rhinoceros, buffalo, leopard, sambar, barking deer, tiger, different types of birds, green pigeon, florican, teal, geese and wild elephant.

Da-Parbatia gate is situated a few km. away from Tezpur. The carvings resemble early Gupta sculpture. Bhalukpung is 60 km. away from Tezpur a place of attraction for its hot-spring. The nearest river is Jia-Bharali. The large Hazara Pukhuri tauch preserves the name of Hazara Varman in Tezpur. It was excavated in the early part of the nineteenth century. This covers an area of seventy acres. A mental hospital is situated in Tezpur.

10. Marigaon District:—Marigaon was upgraded as a district from subdivision on October 1, 1989. It is situated on the south bank of Brahmaputra. Nagaon district is situated on its east, Darrang on the north, Kamrup on the west and south-west, Karbi Anglong on its south. Area of Marigaon district is 1,559 sq. km. It has one subdivision and five revenue circles. Headquarters is Marigaon. Educated population is 38.47 per cent. Total population is 6,40,376; male 3,29,977 and female 3,10,399 (Census 1991). Rural population is 6,05,758 and urban 34,618. It has three urban areas. These are Marigaon, Jagiroad and Jagiroad Paper Mill. Paper and fibre industries are the main industries of this district. Main tributary rivers are Kalong, Sonai, etc. Gauranga *Beel*, Mer *Beel*, are situated in this district.

Marigaon town:—Marigaon town is a class IV urban area. Its total population is 17,246; male 9,189 and female 8,057 (Census 1991).

11. Nagaon District:—Nagaon district is situated on the south bank of Brahmaputra, which Marigaon on its west, Sonitpur on its north, Karbi Anglong on south-west and south-east and North Cachar on its south. Total area of this district is 3,976 sq.km. Total population is 18,92,087; male 9,78,220 and female 9,13,867. Educated population is 44.24 per cent. This district has three subdivisions. These are—Kaliabor, Hojai and Nagaon. Headquarters is Nagaon. There are nine revenue circles. Total rural population is 16,86,493 and urban 2,05,594. There are six urban areas. These are—Nagaon, Lumding, Hojai, Lanka, Dhing, Raha. There are sugar and fibre industries. Dhing Paper Mill was set up during the eighth plan period. Fishery College is situated in this district. 7,767 hectares of land area were under tea cultivation till 1989 with 24 tea gardens. Laokhowa wildlife sanctuary is situated in Nagaon district spread over 60sq. kms area. It is only 15sq. km. away from Nagaon town. One-horn rhinoceros, wild buffaloes, swamp deer, ducks, etc., are found in this sanctuary. Pabitara Reserve Forest is situated in Nagaon district.

Nagaon town:—It is a class II urban area. The total population of Nagaon town is 93,324; male 50,013 and female 43,311.

12. Karbi Anglong District:—United Mikir and North Cachar Hills was bifurcated and constituted in 1970 into two separate districts, i.e. Mikir Hills and North Cachar Hills (Vide Notification No. AAP 134/68/22 dated 11.02.70 and AAP 134/68/10 dt. 30.01.70 respectively. According to these notifications they were named as North Cachar district and Karbi Anglong district. This finds mention in Article 6(2) of the 6th Schedule of the Assam Reorganisation Act, 1969.

The southern part of Nagaon district was bifurcated by the Karbi Anglong and formed into a broken "U" shaped valley. The western part of Karbi Anglong is surrounded by Nagaon district on north-east, North Cachar on the south-east, Meghalaya on the south and south-west, Marigaon on the north. Eastern part of Karbi Anglong is surrounded by Nagaon on its south-west and north-west, Golaghat on its east, north and north-east, Nagaland on south and south-east and North Cachar district on south and south-west. Total area of this district is 10,434 sq. km. Total population is 6,55,415; male 3,43 649 and female 3,11,766. Educated population is 37.48 per cent. It has three subdivisions. These are—Bokajan, Diphu and Hamren. Headquarters is Diphu. Limestone is the main mineral product. Plywood, cement, china-clay pottery industries, are there. Main tributary rivers are Kaliani, Dikharu, Nambar, Kalang, Barpani, etc. Karbi hill of this district is 4,456 ft. above the sea-level. There are several hills in this district. Some of them are—Neli Khala Hill, Lathuri, Bang Khang, etc. Rural population of this district is 5,85,129 and urban 70,286. It has six urban areas. These are—Diphu, Bokajan, Donkamokam, Dokmoka, Hamren, Howraghat.

Diphu town:—Diphu town is a class III urban area. Total population is 39,551; male 22,322 and female 17,229. It is 271 km. away from Guwahati by road. It is connected by railway and road with Guwahati. Dimapur (Nagaland) is its nearest airport.

13. North Cachar District:—This district is surrounded by Cachar district on the south, Meghalaya in the west, Karbi Anglong (western part) on the north-west, Nagaon and Karbi Anglong (Eastern part) on the north, Nagaland on the north-east, Manipur in the east. The area of this district is 4,888 sq. kms. There are two subdivisions. These are—Haflong and Maibong. Headquarters is Haflong. Educated population is 46.72 per cent. Total population is 1,49,346; male 79,536 and female 69,810. Rural population is 1,15,140 and urban 34,206 (Census 1991). It has three urban areas. These are Haflong, Maiong and Mahur. Main tributaries are—Diang, Kopili, Mahur, etc. Coal and lime stone are main mineral products. The biggest Hydel Plant NEEPCO (North East Electric Power Corporation) has come up in Kopili river. There is a hot-spring *Garampani* near Umransu. The water of this hot spring is believed to have medicinal value. Maibong is situated on the bank of Mahur river and 47 km. away from Haflong by road. Once it was the capital of Dimasa-Kachari kingdom and surrounded by stone-houses and temples of Kachari kings.

Haflong town:—It is the only hill station of Assam. Haflong is a class III urban area. Total population of this town is 26,191; male 14,634 and female 11,557. It is a hilly area about 3000 ft above the sea-level. It is covered with green trees, shrubs and herbs. Haflong is famous for sylvan beauty. Haflong lake is big, situated in Haflong town. Haflong is 345 kms from Guwahati by road. It is connected by railway and road with Guwahati.

Jatinga area:—It is famous as the birds' mysterious suicidal place. It is 9 kms. away from Haflong. Migratory birds come here from August to November. Birds, at night, attracted by street lights yield to their death-wish and their little plumage drops down near the light. It also happens during picnic parties at night. This may be compared with *Diwali* night, when large number of insects die at night when they come near the bright lamps of Diwali festival.

14. Cachar District:—It is surrounded on the north by North Cachar district, on the east by Manipur, on the south by Mizoram, Hailakandi and Karim-ganj on south-west, Bangladesh on the west and Meghalaya on the north-west. Cachar district has two subdivisions. These are Silchar and Lakhimpur. It has five revenue circles. Its area is 3,786 sq. km. Headquarters is situated in Silchar. Educated population is 48.65 per cent. Total population is 12,15,952; male 6,27,202 and female 5,88,750. B.T. College, Law College, Engineering College, Medical College, Assam University (Central University) at Silchar (1994), Polytechnic Institute, Industrial Training Institute, etc., are situated in this district. Rural population of Cachar district is 10,97,159 and urban 1,18,793 (1991). 18,706.66 hectares area was under tea cultivation till 1990 with 59 teagardens. Barak, Sonai, Rukni river tributaries flow in this district. It has two urban areas. They are—Silchar and Lakhimpur. Till 1992, there were 10 Community Development Blocks, 163 *Gaon Panchayats*, 8 Police Stations. Average maximum temperature of this district was 39.6 Celsius and minimum 6.8 Celsius in 1990. 632 villages were electrified till 1990-91. Five government hospitals and 68 Primary Health Centres were there in rural areas till 1990-91.

Silchar town:—Silchar is a class I urban area. Its total population is 1,15,045; male 59,941 and female 55,104. Silchar has road, rail and air communication. Kumbirgram airport is 24 km. away from Silchar town and Khaspur (Capital of Kachari kingdom) is 24 km. Bhubon (Shiv temple) is 40 km., Jarailtala (Borkhola) LPG bottling plant centre is 20 km., Engineering and Medical Colleges are 9 km. and 6 km. respectively, from Silchar. Dorgakona (Assam University) is 18 km. from Silchar town.

15. Hailakandi District:—This district was formed on 20 October, 1989. The south and south-east are surrounded by Mizoram. Cachar district is to its north and north-east, Karimganj on the west, Tripura is on south-west. It has one subdivision and four revenue circles. Headquarters' is Hailakandi. Educated population is 42.98 per cent. The area of this district is 1,327 sq. kms. Total population is 4,48,506; male 2,32,236 and female 2,16,270 (1991). Paper industry is situated here. Dhaleswari river passes through this district. Chatachura Hill is situated in the southern part of this district. Rural population in this district is 4,14,400, urban is 34,106. This district has two urban areas. They are—Hailakandi and Lala.

Hailakandi town:—This town is a class III urban area. Total population of this town is 25,475; male 13,135 and female 12,340 (1991). Hailakandi has road and rail communication.

16. Karimganj District:—This district was formed on 1 July, 1983. It is surrounded by Hailakandi district on the east, Cachar on north, Bangladesh on the north and west, Tripura on the south-west, Mizoram on the south. It has one subdivision and five revenue circles. Its area is 1,809 sq. km. Crude oil and natural gas are the main mineral products of this district. Educated population is 44.78 per cent. Headquarters is Karimganj. Total population is 8,25,551; male 4,24,118; female 4,01,433. Sugar industry is situated in this district. Rural population is 7,65,438 and urban 60,113. Langai river runs through this district. It has rail and road communications. This district has two urban areas Karimganj and Badarpur.

Karimganj town:—Karimganj town is a class III urban area. Total population is 43,623; male 22,679 and female 20,944.

17. Golaghat District :—This district was created on 23 October, 1987. It is situated slightly above Nagaland and on the south bank of Brahmaputra. The western part covers as a half moon the eastern part of Karbi Anglong district, Nagaland is situated on its south and south-east, Jorhat on its east, Nagaon on its north-west and Sonitpur on its north. It is spread over 3,502 sq. km. area. Total population is 8,01,740; male 4,17,234 and female 3,84,506 (1991). Educated population is 48.28 per cent. It has three subdivisions. These are—Golaghat, Dhanshiri, Bokakhat. It has five revenue circles. Headquarters is Golaghat. Crude oil is the main mineral product. Sugar industry and Police Training College are situated here. It has three urban areas. These are—Golaghat, Dergaon and Bokakhat. Rural population of this district is 7,53,821 and urban 47,919 people. Kakdonga, Dhansiri, Diyung, etc., are its tributaries.

Golaghat town:—It is a class III urban area. Total population of Golaghat town is 28,722; male 15,727 and female 12,995.

18. Jorhat District:—It is situated on the southern bank of Brahmaputra river. Sibsagar is on its east, Nagaland on the south, Golaghat on its west, Lakhimpur on the north. The area of this district is 2,851 sq.km. It has two subdivisions. These are—Jorhat and Majuli. It has five revenue circles. Headquarters is Jorhat. The main mineral wealth is crude oil and natural gas. Educated population is 55.16 per cent. Total population is 8,68,445; male 4,53,001 and female 4,15,444 (1991). Plywood factory and Agricultural University are situated here. An Engineering College is also established here. This district has two urban areas. These are—Jorhat and Mariani. This district has air, road and rail communications. Bhogdoi river passes through this district to Nagaland.

Jorhat town:—It is a class I urban area. Total population is 1,11,584; male 60,993 and female 50,591.

19. Sibsagar District:—This district was created on 1 July, 1983. It is situated on the south bank of the river Brahmaputra. Jorhat is on its west and north-west, Nagaland on the south and south-east and Arunachal Pradesh on north-east, Dibrugarh on the north. This district is spread over 2,668 sq. km. area. It has three subdivisions. These are—Sibsagar, Nazira and Charaideu. It has six revenue circles. Headquarters' is Sibsagar. Educated population is 54.23 per cent. Crude oil and natural gas are the main mineral wealth. Total population is 8,95,112; male 4,67,610 and female 4,27,502 (1991). This district has five urban areas. These are—Sibsagar, Sonari, Nazira, Moranhat and Amguri. Main tributaries are—Dikho, Namdang, Dichang, etc. Rural population of this district is 8,30,301; urban population is 64,811. 68,322 hectares of area was under tea cultivation till 1989 with 287 tea gardens. *Azan Pir's* Dargah at Dikhowmukh Saraguri Chapari is a famous one.

Sibsagar town:—It is a class III urban area. Total population of this town is 36,651; male 20,183 and female 16,468. It has rail and road communications.

20. Dibrugarh District:—It is situated in between Tinsukia and Sibsagar districts on the south bank of the river Brahmaputra. Dhemaji district is on its north, Tinsukia in the east, Sibsagar on the west and south-west, Arunachal Pradesh on the south. The area of this district is 3,381 sq. km. It has one subdivision and seven revenue circles. Headquarters is Dibrugarh. Educated population is 49.22 per cent. Total population is 10,38,090; male 5,44,141 and female 4,93,949. Coal was discovered in this district in 1825 and its commercial exploitation began in 1882 at the initiative of the Assam Railway and Trading Company. Natural gas is also available in this district. Main industries are plywood and repairing materials of rails. Medical college and university are situated here. This district is situated on the southern bank of Brahmaputra. Air, rail and road communications are there. 67,805 hectares area was under tea cultivation till 1989 with 280 tea gardens. This district has five urban areas. These are—Dibrugarh, Namrup, Duliajan Oil Town, Naharkatiya and Chabua. Railways were first introduced here in Assam in 1882 by the Assam Railways and Trading Company in the district. The length of that first railway route between Dibrugarh and Sadiya was 125 km.

Dibrugarh town:—It is a class I urban area. Total population is 123,885; male 67,540 and female 56,345.

21. Tinsukia District:—It was a subdivision constituted on January 26, 1973. It was upgraded as a district on 14 October, 1989. It has three subdivisions. These are—Tinsukia, Sadia and Margherita. It has four revenue circles. Area of this district is 3,790 sq. km. (1991). Crude oil, coal are the main mineral products. Headquarters is Tinsukia. Educated population is 41.19 per cent. Total population is 9,63,176; male 5,08,703 and female 4,54,473. Plywood industry is the main industry. It has Forest Training Centre. 8,04,772 population is rural and 1,58,404 urban. It has tea industry also.

It is situated in the extreme east of Assam on the south bank of Brahmaputra. Dhemaji district is on its north, Arunachal Pradesh is on its east and south, Dibrugarh district on its west. Digboi river, Doom Dooma river pass through this district. It has five urban areas. These are—Tinsukia, Digboi, Margherita, Doom Dooma and Makum.

Tinsukia district is encircled by hills and mountains and receives abundant rainfall. There are two rainy seasons, one from March to May is premonsoon and another from June to October is the monsoon one. The river becomes turbulent during monsoon and causes flood and erosion along its river banks.

Tinsukia town:—It is a class I urban area. Total population is 73,760; male 42,342 and female 31,418. Rail and road communications are there. It is an industrial and commercial area in Upper Assam. Sarbananda Singha Stadium is constructed in this town.

22. Dhemaji District:— It was upgraded to a district on 2 October, 1989. It has only one urban area and two subdivisions with four revenue circles. The area of this district is 3,237 sq. km. Headquarters' is Dhemaji. Educated population is 43.18 per cent. Total population is 4,72,183; male

2,44,467 and female 2,27,716. Dihang, Dibang rivers pass through this district and join Brahmaputra river. Several *beels,* i.e. Bangalmari *beel*, Kani *beel*, etc., are here. This district is situated on the north bank of the Brahmaputra river. Arunachal Pradesh is on its north and east, Tinsukia and Dibrugarh on its south, Lakhimpur on its west.

Dhemaji town:—Dhemaji town is a class V urban area. Total population is 8,826; male 5,139 and female 3,687.

23. Lakhimpur District:—It has two urban areas. These are—North Lakhimpur and Bihpuria. It is surrounded on the north by Arunachal Pradesh, Dhemaji is in the east, Majuli of Jorhat district is on the south, Sonitpur on its west. It has two subdivisions and six revenue circles. Its area is 2,277 sq.km. Headquarters of this district is North Lakhimpur. Educated population is 47.54 per cent. Total population is 7,49,675; male 3,87,942 and female 3,61,733 (1991). Rural population is 7,01,125 and urban 48,550. Main rivers are Soansiri, Ranga, Ziaghal, Kara, etc. The urban areas are North Lakhimpur and Bihpuria. It had 15 tea gardens in 4,152 hectares of area till 1989.

North Lakhimpur town:— It is a class III urban area. Total population is 40,044; male 22,590 and female 17,454. It has road communication.

Table XX

Districts, Subdivisions, Towns, Etc.

Districts and Headquarters	*Subdivisions*	*Towns and their Class*	*Revenue Circles*
1	*2*	*3*	*4*
1. DHUBRI H.Qs Dhubri town	1. Bilasipara 2. Dhubri 3. North Salmara	1. Sapatgram (IV) 2. Bilasipara (IV) 3. Gauripur (IV) 4. Mankachar (III) 5. Golokganj (V) 6. Chapar (IV) 7. Dhubri (II)	8
2. GOALPARA H.Qs Goalpara town	1. Goalpara	1. Goalpara (III) 2. Lakhimpur (V)	5
3. KOKRAJHAR H.Qs Kokrajhar town	1. Kokrajhar 2. Gosaigaon	1. Kokrajhar (III) 2. Gosaigaon (IV) 3. Basugaon (IV)	5
4. BANGAIGAON H.Qs Bangoigaon town	1. Bangaigaon 2. Bijni 3. North Salmara	1. Bangaigaon (III) 2. Bijni (IV) 3. Abhayapuri (IV) 4. Jogigopa (VI)	4
5. BARPETA H.Qs Barpeta town	1. Barpeta 2. Bajali	1. Barpeta Road (III) 2. Barpeta (III) 3. Howli (IV) 4. Sarthebari (V) 5. Bohari (V)	8

1	2	3	4
		6. Pathsala (V)	
		7. Sarbhog (V)	
6. NALBARI	1. Nalbari	1. Nalbari (IV)	9
H.Qs Nalbari town		2. Tihu (VI)	
7. KAMRUP	1. Guwahati	1. Guwahati (I)	14
H.Qs Guwahati town	2. Rangiya	2. Rangiya (III)	
	3. Pragjyotishpur	3. Sualkuchi (I)	
		4. Niz-Hajo	
		5. North Guwahati	
		6. Amingaon (V)	
		7. Palashbari (VI)	
8. DARRANG	1. Mangaldoi	1. Mangaldoi (III)	9
H.Qs Mangaldoi	2. Udalguri	2. Tangla (IV)	
town		3. Kharupatia (IV)	
		4. Udalguri (IV)	
9. SONITPUR	1.Tezpur	1. Tezpur (II)	7
H.Qs Tezpur town	2. Biswanath Chariali	2. Rangapara (IV)	
		3. Dhekiajuli (IV)	
		4. Biswanath Charia (IV)	
10. MARIGAON	1. Marigaon	1. Marigaon (IV)	5
H.Qs Marigaon		2. Jagiroad Paper Mill(IV)	
town		3. Jagiroad(VI)	
11. NAGAON	1. Kaliabor	1. Nagaon (II)	9
H.Qs Nagaon town	2. Hojai	2. Lumding (III)	
	3. Nagaon	3. Hojai (III)	
		4. Lanka (IV)	
		5. Dhing (IV)	
		6. Raha (VI)	
12. KARBI ANGLONG	1. Bokajan	1. Diphu (III)	
H.Qs Diphu town	2. Diphu	2. Bokajan (IV)	
	3. Hamren	3. Donkamokam (V)	
		4. Dokmoka (VI)	
		5. Hamren (VI)	
		6. Howraghat (VI)	
13. NORTH CACHAR	1. Haflong	1.Haflong (III)	
H.Qs Haflong town	2. Maibong	2. Maibong	
		3. Mahur (VI)	
14. CACHAR	1. Silchar	1. Silchar (I)	5
H.Qs Silchar town	2. Lakhimpur	2. Lakhimpur (VI)	
15. HAILAKANDI	1. Hailakandi	1. Hailakandi (III)	4
H.Qs Hailakandi town		2. Lala (V)	
16. KARIMGANJ	1. Karimganj	1. Karimganj (III)	5
H.Qs Karimganj town		2. Badarpur (IV)	

1	2	3	4
17. GOLAGHAT	1. Golaghat	1. Golaghat (III)	5
H.Qs Golaghat town	2. Dhanshiri	2. Dergaon (IV)	
	3. Bokakhat	3. Bokakhat (V)	
18. JORHAT	1. Jorhat	1. Jorhat (I)	5
H.Qs Jorhat town	2. Majuli	2. Mariani (III)	
19. SIBSAGAR	1. Sibsagar	1. Sibsagar (III)	6
H.Qs Sibsagar town	2. Nazira	2. Sonari (IV)	
	3. Charaideu	3. Nazira (V)	
		4. Moranhat (VI)	
		5. Amguri (VI)	
20. DIBRUGARH	1. Dibrugarh	1. Dibrugarh (I)	7
H.Qs Dibrugarh town		2. Namrup (IV)	
		3. Duliajan Oil Town (IV)	
		4. Naharkatiya (IV)	
		5. Chabua (V)	
21. TINSUKIA	1. Tinsukia	1. Tinsukia (II)	4
H.Qs Tinsukia town	2. Sadia	2. Digboi (III)	
	3. Margherita	3. Margherita (III)	
		4. Doom Dooma (IV)	
		5. Makum (IV)	
22. DHEMAJI	1. Dhemaji	1. Dhemaji (V)	4
H.Qs Dhemaji town	2. Jonai		
23. LAKHIMPUR	1. North Lakhimpur	1. North Lakhimpur (III)	6
H.Qs North Lakhimpur	2. Dhakuakhana	2. Bihpuria (V)	

3

Brief Description of Some Tribes and Castes

Assam is a melting pot of different races, languages and cultures. According to Kailash Sharma (Seminar NEICSSR, August, 1994). Assam is a museum of a large number of human species ever found on earth.

The people of Brahmaputra and Barak valleys are mainly of Indo-Iranian group, although many are of Mongoloid race, particularly in the Upper Assam region. By the time of their arrival in the Brahmaputra valley, the original Aryan people of Assam had become intermixed with other people. The tribes in the hills and the plains are of Mongoloid race *(Encyclopedia Britannica,* Vol. 2, 1977:208).

Suniti Kumar Chatterji (1951:55-56) states that when the Ahoms came to Assam, they met Hinduised Bodo States, the Chutiyas in the extreme east, the Dimasa or Kacharis in the Dhansiri valley. The exact situation in Western Kamarupa is not known. Probably the Lunar Dynasty of Vallabhadeva, an old Assamese-speaking dynasty of Bodo origin, was in power there. But in Kamarupa and the adjacent Kamata Bihar and Koch Bihar, the Western Bodos—the great Koch tribe—were going strong; and it was undoubtedly Koch and Mech resistance (probably under the leadership of the Lunar Dynasty) that brought disaster to the Turks. A branch of the Koches were in the royal house of Khens or Khyans, which was ruling Kamarupa till 1498 A.D., when Nilambar, the last king, was overthrown by Husain Shah of Bengal. After 1500 A.D., a great Koch chief and organiser, viz. Visva Simha rose to power and his son Nara Narayana and his house prevented the Ahoms from extending their power in Western Assam during the sixteenth century. Out of this struggle between the Tibeto-Burman Bodo and the Sino-Chinese or Thai Ahom, the Ahom emerged victorious. But by the time of this final triumph, the Ahom and the Bodo had both lost their independence and language and had merged into a single Aryan Assamese-speaking people. The Chutiyas had probably been receiving earlier Thai or Ahom immigrants from the East, and they had become considerably intermixed with them....They and the Bodo tribe of the Morans, living by the Dibru river, were conquered by the Ahoms; and the Chutiyas were absorbed by the Ahoms. The Ahoms were forced to take wives from among the Bados and utlimately integrated more and more with the original people....As per *Encyclopedia Asiatica* (Vol.I, 1976:190), Brahmins, Ganaks and Kayasths, are all of comparatively modern importation; Kalita are the only remnant of the early Aryan colonists; Keot are partly Hindu and partly proselytes raised to that position; The Dom are boatsmen and fishermen; the Hari, low caste immigrants; and converted Ahom, Chutiya, Lalung, Koch, Mech and Kachari. The Shan people were converted to Hinduism and adopted the language and customs of Hindus; their features mark them as of different origin. Indeed, it is stated that the Shans never brought women with them. The principal tribes on the frontier of Upper Assam are the Muttuk, the Khamti, and the Singpho. At the eastern end, near Saddiya, the tribes are mixed. As per B.M. Das (1987:5-6), certain populations have migrated to Assam mostly for economic reasons. This migration started mainly with the coming of the British, after the fall of the Ahom rule. Some of them have become Assamese and many of them have been Assamized.... In some of the districts of Upper Assam, there are small populations of Buddhists. They are the Khamyang, Aiton, Tai Phake, Turung, Duania, etc....... As per *Encyclopaedia Americana* (Vol.I, 1988:521) immigrants brought..... from the States of Bihar and Orissa to work in tea plantations have added another element to the population. As per Rabijit Choudhury (Feb.9, 1995), the stage is set for the inclusion of six backward communities in Assam in the list of Scheduled Tribes. These are Koch Rajbanshi, Ahom, Mottok, Moran, Chutiya and the "tea tribes". It is felt that change in the demographic picture of the State, with over one crore tribals, will have far-reaching consequences on the polity. He further stated that the list of Scheduled Tribes of Assam comprises fourteen communities in the Autonomous Hill Districts and nine communities in the plain districts. Under the 65th Amendment to the Constitution, 1990, it is mandatory for the Centre and the State Governments to consult the National Commission for Scheduled Castes and Scheduled Tribes on all major policy matters affecting them.

The main tribes of Assam are—Bodo, Boro-Kachari, Karbi, Rabha, Tiwa (Lalung), Hojai, Mishing (Miri), Deori, Dimasa, Mech, Hajong, Barman, Kachari, Sonowal Kachari, Phakial, etc. There are some other tribes who have mainly migrated from other States of North-East India to Assam. They are—Chakma, Garo, Khasi, Jaintia, Kuki, Mizo (Lushai), some Naga tribes, Lakher, Hmar, Pawi, etc. There are some tribes who have migrated to Assam for employment mainly in tea gardens from North Bengal, Bihar, Orissa, Sikkim, etc. They are Lepcha, Bhutia, Munda, Oraon, Santal, Bhil, etc. Many others of Mongoloid origin classified as "Other Backward Classes" live in Assam. They are—the Ahom, Chutiya, Moran, Tai Phake, Aiton, Turung, Duonia, Koch, Rajbanshi, Choudang, Moran, Matak, etc. There are also caste groups like Mahishya Das, Sudra Das or Dey, Gowala, Yogi (Nath), Suri, etc.

Some of the important Scheduled Castes of Assam are—Hira, Jalkeot, Kaibarta, Bania, Patni, Namasudra, Sutradhar, Dholi, Dhobi, Muchi, Bhangi, Bhuimali, Jhal/Malo, etc. There are Brahmin, Kayastha, Kalita caste groups of the Assamese Hindu along with some other races like Gurkha (Nepali), Bengali,

Bihari, Marwari, Sikh, Manipuri, Tripuri, South Indians, etc. A large number of Muslims are there in Assam.

According to Scheduled Castes and Scheduled Tribes List (Modified) of 1976, (No. 108 of 1976 dt. 18 Sept. 1976), there are a total of twenty-three Scheduled Tribes and sixteen Scheduled Castes in Assam.

1. Kachari:—L.A. Waddell (1901) states that the Kacharis are semi-Hinduised Mongoloid tribe. B.M. Das (1981) writes that the Kacharis are distributed throughout the Brahmaputra valley and also North Cachar Hill District of Assam etc. The tribe has several subdivisions like Thengal, Jharwa, Sonowal, Dimasa etc. The Kacharis of lower Assam districts are often referred to as the Boro Kachari. The Dimasa Kacharis are hill people and mostly live in North Cachar Hill District. B.N. Bordoloi (1988), mentions that the Dimasa Kacharis who live in the plains of the Barak Valley are known as the Barmans. According to U.C. Guha (1971, *reprinted* : 52,99) the Dimasas who consider themselves to be the descendants of Bhima, the second Pandava of the Mahabharata, and follow the Hindu religious principles and wear sacred threads like the Kshatriyas are called Barman. The Kacharis who consider themselves to be the descendants of Hidimba and follow traditional religion are known as Dimasa. J.B. Bhattacharjee (1977:219), says that in the plains the Dimasas were known as Barman who follow the system of wearing sacred thread like the Brahmins and the Kshatriyas. According to L.A. Waddell (1901), the Sonowal or Sadiola are mostly gold-washers in the Lakhimpur district of Upper Assam. G.C. Sarma Thakur (1988), writes that the Sonowal Kacharis belong to the Bodo group and nostalgically trace their close relationship with the Barmans of Cachar district, Boro Kacharis of lower Assam districts and Dimasas of North Cachar Hills district. In fact it is difficult to draw exclusive ethnic line between the Boro Kacharis and Sonowal Kacharis as both these sections originally came from the same stock. M.C. Saikia (1987), mentions that in Upper Assam they are identified as Sonowal and Thengal Kachari, while in the western Assam they are more popularly known as Boro or Boro-Kachari. As per E.T. Dalton (1872:81-82), the Kacharis are one of the most numerous and widely spread tribes on the Eastern Frontier. The majority call themselves "*Soronia*", i.e. purified Kacharis as they have adopted the customs of the Hindus. The *Soronias* keep fowls, but not pigs, and do not eat beef.

B.N. Bordoloi (1988) opines that the Kacharis had a long-standing enmity with the Ahoms. In 1536 A.D., the Ahoms occupied Dimapur, the capital of the Kacharis. Thereafter, the Kacharis established their capital in Maibang in North Cachar Hills. Again the Ahom armies crushed them as also the capital Maibang. Thus, the then Kachari king Tamradhaj fled for his life to Khaspur, in the plains of Cachar and formed the last new capital. Though the shifting of capital from Maibang to Khaspur was started during the reign of Tamradhaj, it was completed in 1750, during Kirti Chandra Narayan. In 1825, King Gobind Chandra abandoned Khaspur and established his capital at Haritika, about 6 kms west of Badarpur in Barak valley. Sonaram Thaosen (1962:47-48), states that King Indrapratap Narayan of Maibang (1637-1644), had renamed his capital Maibang as Kirtipur. The British annexed the Kachari kingdom and Cachar to its territory on August 14, 1932.

2. Barman Kachari:—The Dimasa Kacharis who live in the plains of the Barak valley are known as the Barman Kachari. They are peace-loving, patriarchal people. They have joint family system where the old father is the head of the family and married and the unmarried brothers, sons and daughters live in the same family. They have male and female clans known as *Semphong* and *Zulu*. When a boy is born he is included in *Semphong* and a girl in *Zulu*.

They are Hindus. All the gods and goddesses are worshipped by them. Their main occupation is agriculture. They generally practise cultivation of *sali* paddy. The other crops cultivated by them are cotton, mustard, sugar-cane, sweet potato, etc. Some of them are employed as teachers, doctors, engineers, etc. Weaving is a common cottage industry. Their women are expert weavers. Most of them have looms in their household. Some of them brew rice-beer for domestic consumption. They have *hedari* or *biba* system of mutual help. In this system, the village youths have to complete an assignment on a fixed date for a disabled family, i.e. childless couple, invalid villager, widow, sonless family, etc. In exchange, they get food and drinks.

Their language is Dimasa. which they speak among themselves. Almost all of them know Bengali language and prefer talking in Bengali with a Bengali. They know Assamese also. Nirupoma Hagjer (1974:68) states that the *Bihu* dances and *Bihu* festivals are not absent among the Barman Kacharis.

Traditionally they practise marriage by negotiation. Marriage by capture and elopement are dying out. The bride-price is called *Kalti*. Nowadays, parents of the girl do not take bride-price. Child marriage is not there. They follow monogamy. Divorce is very rare and for the widow remarriage is taboo. Sons inherit paternal property and daughters maternal property. Paternal properties are land, weapon, cash, cattle, clothes of the father etc. Maternal properties are jewellery, looms, clothes of the mother, utensils, etc. In a childless family, nearest male relatives and female members of female relatives inherit the property. This system is followed when the couple have no son or daughter. They do not allow inheritance of the father's property by daughters nor property of the mother by sons.

The houses are generally big-sized and spacious and built with timber posts, thatched roofs with mud-plastered walls. Many families have cemented buildings and Assam-type house with C.I. sheet roofed, *pucca* floor, *ikra* wall. They do not have bachelors' dormitory. In earlier days, they had *Kunang* (headman) and *Dilo* (assistant headman). Present-day, *Gaon Burahs* (village headmen) are appointed by the government. There are less number of disputes, elopements, thefts, etc. among them. They appeal to the courts for the settlement of a dispute only when the village councils fail to settle a dispute. They observe Rashleela, Holi, etc. Due to the impact of Manipuri culture, Kachari king, Krishna Chandra (1780-1813), married Manipuri princess, Induprava. Perhaps for this reason their traditional musical instruments like *khram* (drum), *muriwaitha* (flute), *suphin* (flute), etc., are gradually replaced by *khol* (Manipuri drum), cymbal, flute, etc.

Adult males use *dhuti*-type home-made *gamocha* (towel) at home. *Dhuti*, pant-shirt are used for outside. In earlier days, they used to wear eighteen-metre-long turban as their head-gear. Their ladies put *Rigu* (*Mekhela*) with *Rijamphai* (*Riha-Chadar*). They are fond of ornaments. Some of their ornaments are : *Poal* (necklace), *khamontai* (ear-ring), *chandrawal* (necklace), *rongborsa* (necklace), *khadu* (bracelet), and *eansidam* (nose ring). They use both gold and silver ornaments.

Rice is their main food. They eat both dry and fresh fish and vegetables. They eat less pulses. Mutton and meats of home-bred birds are taken less. They do not eat pork and beef. Tea is their favourite drink and they drink rice-beer occasionally.

The birth of a child is an occasion for joy. They happily welcome both male and female child and there is no discrimination. They give a feast on the purification day of the mother. They like being educated and thus their literacy rate is slightly high.

They have broad head, stumpy nose, languid eyes, prominent cheek-bone and are of medium stature, strong and muscular in appearance; the face is broad and round. Women are fairer than the men.

They cremate the dead and bury the infants. They believe in rebirth. In earlier days, they used to sing devotional songs when the dead body was taken to the cremation ground; paddy, cotton were dropped on the way. They purify themselves by performing post-funeral *Shraddha* (death rite) ceremony on the thirteenth day with the help of a Brahmin priest. They also perform annual *Shraddha*.

3. Boro, Boro Kachari:—The Boros belong to Indo-Mongoloid ethnic group of Tibeto-Burman language family. As per R.M. Nath (1948:15-16) this country was known as the *Bod* (homeland). Earlier the inhabitants of the *Bod* country were known as *Boddo-Ficha* or *Boddo-cha* (*Ficha*—*cha*—children) and later simply as the Boddo or the Bodo. As per Bijoy Daimary (*PNEIHA* 1987:531), the term "Bodo" adopted by Brian Hodgson is an English transliteration of the word Boro. G.A. Grierson (1903, *LSI*, Vol.I, pt.I:63) stated that Bodo is only a mispronunciation of the word Boro.

The Bodos live in North East India. A few Bodos are found in Burma, Nepal, Bangladesh, Sikkim and Bhutan. K.L. Barua (1966:14) mentions in his *Early History of Kamrupa* that during the time of the Mahabharata or even earlier, the Bodo tribes constituted the bulk of the population of Assam, northern and eastern Bengal and the surrounding and intervening hills. They are now largely concentrated in Kokrajhar district, northern belt of undivided

Kamrup and Darrang districts and so on. As per T.C. Sharma (1983:57) they introduced the technique of food production by plant cultivation and domestication of animals. They also introduced the art of rearing silkworm, and spinning and weaving silk clothes.

The clan is divided according to traditional work. Nowadays such traditional work is not recognised. A clan name ends with the word *'ari'*. There are about twentythree *aris.* They are—Basumatari, Masari, Doimari, Narzari, Ramsari, Borogaori, Swargiari, Khangkhlari, Gayari, Mahilari, Ouari, Joyoari, Ishari, Kahari, Sibiugari, Sibiziari, Babaiari, Biugbiugari, Ganjlerari, Fadangari, Samphrangari/Mao-Marari, Kherkatari and Thaletari. In earlier days Basumataris were landowners, Gayaris were in-charge of betel-nut cultivation, etc. Now since there is no stratification the clan plays no role in regulating the marriages. The clan names are now used as surnames by the Bodos. The followers of *Brahma* cult use *Brahma* surname.

They are patriarchal and prefer living in a joint family. Father is the head of the family. All the members enjoy equal status within the family. A son can leave the joint family during the lifetime of his father to live separately. Unmarried sons living in the family get double share in the family-property compared to the married sons who stay separately. The eldest son assumes the charge of the house after the death of his father and he fulfils his duties after consulting his mother. The eldest son gets a big share of property in view of his family responsibilities.

They have two important institutions—*Hadengoura* and *Hachung-goura.* The common institution in Boro villages is the village council. The *Gaonbura* (village headman) and his assistant *Halmazi* perform the social duties of the village.

Marriage within the same clan is said to be prohibited but it is not so in actual practice. They dislike marrying people other than Boro-Kachari. In earlier days, there was cross-cousin marriage (MBD/FSD), but now it is completely abolished. Widow marriage is recognised and after remarriage she loses the right to property of her deceased husband. She can take a child below one year to her new husband. A widower can remarry his deceased wife's younger sister but not the elder. Similarly, a widow can marry her deceased husband's younger brother, but not the elder.

They have six types of marriages but marriage through negotiation has become the normal social custom. The different types of marriages are—1) *Sangnanoi lainai haba* (negotiated marriage), 2) *Gorjia lakhinai haba* (Marriage by service), 3) *Kharsonnai haba* (bride enters groom's house before the settlement of marriage), 4) *Bonanoi lainai haba* (bride is forcefully taken), 5) *Donkhar langnai haba* (elopement marriage), 6) *Dongkha habnai haba* (widow marriage). The Bodos who follow *Brahma dharma* perform the wedding ceremony in a reformed manner which is a little different from other systems of marriages. They had *Phon* or *Phon thaka* (bride-price), but it is gradually being abolished. Divorce is rare among them. If a couple wants to divorce, the case is placed before a big gathering (*Samaj*) for solution. It may take place by mutual consent of husband and wife. This is performed by tearing a betel-leaf which is called *Pathoi-lai bisinai* in Bodo. If the husband divorces his wife for inadequate reason, he has to bear the responsibility of her livelihood for a certain period. A divorced wife cannot take any children with her, except a child below one year.

The Boros are agriculturists. They cultivate both *Ahu* and *Sali* paddy. The Bodos rear the *eri* silk cocoons. The Bodos of Kokrajhar area rear a special type of *eri* cocoon which is red in colour. The Bodos of Upper Assam rear *muga* and mulberry silk cocoons. Menfolk are experts in making cane and bamboo products. *Pachi, dala, chalani, chepa, palo, jakoi, khaloi*, etc., are the result of their skilled work.

Boro language has no script of its own. Devnagari script is used for Boro language from April 1975. The Boro language has been declared as an associate official language by an Ordinance issued on December 28, 1984. They talk in Assamese. The Boro literature came into prominence during the Brahma movement led by Guru Kalicharan Brahma and has been developed by Sahitya Sabha since 1952. The influence of Assamese language is noticed in most of their songs.

In old days, they were animists. Later Guru Kalicharan Brahma introduced the faith of Srimat Paramhansa Sibnarayan Swami of Calcutta among Bodos. This ushered in a social change among them and they accepted Vedic Sanatana Dharma's Brahma cult. Some of them accepted Hindu religion and converted to *Sarania*, whereas Barman and Brahma became the followers of Christianity. A large number of them are followers of *Bathou* or *Siva*. The *Sizu* plant (*Euphorbia splendens*) is the symbol of the *Bathou* which is planted with a sapling of *jatrasi* and *tulsi* in the north-eastern part of the courtyard. *Sizu* plant and *chaki-banti* (light) are offered every evening. They have goddesses, i.e., *Mainao* (Lakshmi), *Bathou Buri* (Gouri) and god *Bathou Bura* (Hara), *Bathou Bura* and *Bathou Buri* are the protectors of this world. *Bathou* represents the earth, air, water, ether and fire. Another religious institution is known as *Kherai*, which is a symbol of hope and desire. This puja is performed either individually for the welfare of a family or collectively for the welfare of the villagers. Generally, they perform *Kherai Puja* before and after cultivation for good harvest. This is of four types namely, *Darshan, Umrao, Phalo* and *Noani*.

The Boro-Kachari celebrate *Bihu* festivals. Baisagu (mid-April) Bihu, Bohag Bihu/Rangali Bihu, Domashi (mid-January) Bishu, Bhogali Bihu/Magh Bihu, and Katrigacha (mid-October) Bihu, Kangali Bihu/Kati Bihu, are some of the main Bihus. Katrigacha is not important and no merriment is observed. Their traditional musical instruments are—*Kham* (madal), *jotha* (manjari), *khawbang* (tal), *gagana, siphuri* (flute), *thorkha* (drum), etc.

It is said that the converted Boro Kacharis of *Brahma dharma* are educationally and culturally more advanced. The Boro Kachari women wear *Dakhna*, a single piece of garment covering from breast to ankles. They use blouse to cover the upper part of the body. During dance rituals they wear special dresses. The art of dyeing yarn and clothes were community secret. They prefer yellow and orange clothes. Men wear *dhuti*, shirt, trouser, etc., like the Assamese. They wear a scarf called *patani* which has geometrical designs on the borders. *Patani* is actually a symbol of the Boro Kachari tribe.

Rice is their staple food. They prepare home-made rice-beer called *jumai*. The Brahma group of Boro Kacharis generally do not drink this *jumai*. They eat both fresh and dry fish (*nakam*). The *Saranias* keep fowl, but not pigs and never eat beef.

The Boro girls are fond of ornaments. *Enti* is made of brass or gold. Some of them do not like wearing ornaments. As per Haddon, they have dolichocephalic platyrrhine (pre-Dravidian) racial elements in the tribe. In physique, men and women are medium-statured and well-built, strong and healthy.

They do not celebrate the birth of a child. However, a woman is considered unclean for about a month after giving birth. After the birth of a child, they offer a fowl to the household deity.

They follow both burial and cremation for the disposal of the dead body. Now, they prefer cremation only. On the tenth day (from the day of death) *Daha* (a funeral ceremony) is performed; but, *shraddha* ceremony is performed on the eleventh or thirteenth day by *Douri* (*Deuri*), or *Oja* (medicine man), who chants the *mantras*.

4. Dimasa Kachari:—They inhabit mainly the North Cachar Hill district. They are also found in Karbi Anglong and Cachar districts—Meghalaya and all over Assam. In Cachar, they are known as the *Barman Kachari*. Economically and educationally they are backward.

Linguistically the Dimasas belong to Tibeto-Burman and Indo-Mongoloid ethnic group. As per P. Gupta and P.C. Dutta (1966), the Dimasa Kacharis are short to medium-statured people. The mean stature is 163.9 cms. and mean value among the Kacharis are 1630.5=5.9 cms. As per S.T. Das (1987), most of them have medium brown colour with low waves of hair. They have shallow to medium-nasal-root. Epicanthic folds and eyeslits are considered non-Mongoloid. They have round and broad face with prominent chins.

The term *Dimasa* literally means the son of a big river (Di=water, ma=big, sa=son). As per B.N. Bordoloi (1987), Dimasas consider themselves to be the descendants of the Brahmaputra river in Assam. They might have lived once on the banks of this river, prior to the establishment of the capital at Dimapur (now in Nagaland).

They speak Dimasa Kachari language. G.A. Grierson (*LSI*, Vol. III, pt. II, 1903), classified the Kachari language as Naga-Bodo group. Dimasa language uses Bengali script. They do not have written history but the legends are rich. It is said that, the term *Dimasa* is derived from Hidimba, wife of Bhima, the second Pandava, of the *Mahabharata* who married her while in exile. Their son Ghatotkacha showed heroism during the battle of Kurukshetra. They think they are the descendants of them. Some scholars are of the opinion that the *Bodasa* or *Bodos* came to be known as *Dimasa* soon after the establishment of their capital at Dimapur on the bank of the river Dhansiri which is known as river Dima in their language.

They are patriarchal, patrilineal, patrilocal people. They do not give equal status to their women. That is why they do not give importance to female education. They are peace-loving people. They have been influenced by the Assamese and the Bengalese. They are not influenced by Christianity. The family consists of husband, wife, unmarried children and unmarried brothers and sisters. As soon as the unmarried son or brother marries, they start living separately. This happens in the case of sisters and daughters.

They have forty ***Sengphong*** male clans and forty-two ***Zuluk*** female clans. The sons belong to the father's clan and daughters to the mother's clan. As they follow the patriarchal system of family, the female clan does not occupy a significant position. The clan is exogamous and no marriage is possible between the bride and groom of the same clan and none can marry within his or her father's and mother's clans. In earlier days actually, they had no clan system.

They practise monogamy and marriage by negotiation is the normal practice. Marriage by capture is rare. They have bride-price called *Kalti.* But now they do not follow this custom. They have no child-marriage system. Marriage outside their community is looked down on and parents drive them away from their home. A younger brother can marry his elder brother's widow but an elder brother can't marry the widow of his younger brother. If the wife dies, her husband can marry the wife's younger sister but not the elder. They prefer cross-cousin marriage (MBD or MBS with SSS or FSD). The clan names are often used as surnames. A *Thaosen* clan boy cannot marry a *Thaosen* clan girl. Similarly, a ***Diunma*** girl cannot marry a ***Diunma*** boy and so on. For marriage ceremony they do not require a priest. Divorce is rare. A man can divorce his wife on reasonable grounds and vice versa. If the divorce proposal comes from the husband then he won't get back his *Kalti* (bride price), if it comes from the wife's side then she should return *Kalti* to her divorced husband.

Most of the Dimasa villages are on hill slopes with a river or a stream running by. The houses of the Dimasas are made of timber, mud-plastered bamboo walls, and thatched roof. The houses are built on ground. They have bachelors' dormitories for unmarried young boys called *Nodrang.* For girls there is no provision of a *Nodrang.* At present, no one stays at night in a bachelor's dormitory. Now, the empty *Nodrangs* reminds of the Dimasa's glorious past.

They have their traditional village headman called *Kunang* who discharges his duties with the help of his assistant *Dilo.* They, along with some village elders, settle disputes and minor cases like theft, elopement, etc. When women are involved, the elderly women of the village are invited for the trial, otherwise ladies are not invited. Without the permission of the *Kunang* (*Gaonbura*, headman) no community function in the village is performed. Village headman is selected by the village elders in a formal meeting.

Agriculture is the principal occupation. They practise wet paddy cultivation in low plain areas and *jhum* (shifting) cultivation in hilly areas. The crops are paddy, maize, sesame, cotton, chillie, pumpkin, gourd, ginger, brinjal, mustard, pineapple, orange, etc.

They rear buffalo, goat, fowl and duck. As they dislike drinking milk, they do not rear cows. They do not drink she buffaloes milk. Now, they have started drinking and eating milk-made items. The Dimasa girl who does not know weaving finds it hard to get married. Perhaps because this, every Dimasa woman is an expert weaver.

The male dress consists of a *Risa* which is generally a deep green-coloured one-metre-long cloth, a shirt and an artistically designed scarf called *Rinsao.* Sometimes they use cotton or *endi* silk turban of nineteen metres length. They also use dhoti, trouser, shirt, etc. Women wear a *mekhela*-type cloth called *Rigu,* made of cotton or *endi*-silk. An artistically designed scarf called *Rijamphai* is used to cover the upper part of the body. For dancing, the young girls use a designed scarf called *Rikhaosa.* Women keep long hair and tie it in a bun. Ladies are fond of ornaments. Some of the ornaments are *Poal* (necklace), *Khamontai* (ear-ring), *Chandrawal* (necklace), *Rongborsa* (necklace), *Khadu* (bracelet), *Eansidam* (nose ring), etc. They use ornaments made of silver, gold, beads, sea-shells, etc.

Rice is their staple food which they eat with chillies, vegetable curry and sometimes with fish and meat. Deer's meat and dried fish are favourite food items. They do not eat beef. They prefer milkless tea. *Zou* (rice-beer) is their favourite beverage which they prepare at home. They consume betel nut with betel leaves. Men smoke a lot.

They are always cheerful as they are satisfied with what they have. They fight only when they are provoked. They have *Pathri* or doctor who predicts the future and cures diseases by his magical power. The *Pathris* also perform ritual dances with *Khram* (dram) and *Muri* (flute). They have several types of dances and music. They do not sing while dancing. They have rich folk stories.

In rural areas, the Dimasa men make bamboo and cane goods in their leisure time. They are animists. They also follow Hinduism in crude form. They have six *Madais* (god) namely, *Sibrai, Doo Raja, Naikhu Raja, Waa Raja, Ganyung Braiyung* and *Hamiadao*. They respect Sibrai (Hindu god Siva) very much and mention Sibrai in all types of worship of god. They sacrifice pigs, fowls, etc., while worshipping gods. Earlier they used to sacrifice human beings once in a year. Christian Missionaries tried to convert them into Christianity, but were unsuccessful.

Before they start cultivation, *Rajini Gabra* and *Harni Gabra* festivals are observed once in a year. *Busu*, the harvesting festival, is an important one. The paternal property is inherited only by the sons. The eldest son gets the largest share. The maternal property is inherited by daughters. If a man does not have a son, at his death the paternal property is inherited by his nearest male relative, but not by his daughters. Similarly, if a woman does not have a daughter, at her death, the maternal property is inherited by her nearest female relative but, not by her sons. Paternal properties include land, cash, cattle, weapon, etc., and maternal are jewellery, looms, mother's clothes, etc.

They believe that the birth of a child is in the hands of god. In rural areas, they take the help of two elderly women for the delivery of a child but in urban areas they prefer going to hospital. The dead bodies are cremated. A man is allowed to die inside his room. At the death of a husband, wife unties her hair till the cremation is over. They bury an infant, if it is below two months of age.

5. Sonowal Kachari:—They inhabit Lakhimpur, Dibrugarh, Dhemaji, Sibsagar and Jorhat districts. They belong to the Bodo group and have close relationship with the Barmans of Cachar district, Boro Kachari of lower Assam districts and Dimasas of North Cachar Hills district.

Sonowal Kacharis are short to medium-statured; they have flat nose. almond shaped eyes and light olive complexion. It is said that they used to make gold (*son*) ornaments, etc., during the reign of the Ahom kings and were known as *Sonowal.* They are also known as *Soronia,* 'purified Kacharis'. They have accepted the customs of Hindus and abstain from taking forbidden food (E.T. Dalton, 1872:81-82). G.C. Sharma Thakur (1972:20), stated *Sonowals* now profess Hinduism and, the traditional tribal beliefs and practices are disappearing. According to him (1988:89) the *Saranias* referred to by S. Endle (1910), are the *Sonowals.*

There is a headman (*Gaon Bura*) who looks after village administration. They have *Barik* (in-charge of Namghar), *Pathek* (reader of religious scripts in public), *Asirbadia Bura* (blessing offerer), *Gitghai* (expert in songs specially Husori), *Medhi* (chief in all religious functions), *Tamuli* (supplier of betel-nut to the audience), *Randhani* (cook), *Bilonia* (distributor of feast), *Gayan Bayan* (religious dancer). *Namghar* is also used for solving village disputes placed before the village elders.

They cultivate *Sali* and *Ahu* paddy. Men and women both work in the paddy field. They also grow mustard, potato, sweet potato, *mati mah* (Pulses), etc. Rice is the main food which they eat with pulses and vegetable curry. Fish, mutton and chicken are delicacies. They do not rear pig and do not eat pork and beef. Earlier they used to consume home-made rice beer but now they prefer tea. They eat betel leaves and nuts.

Their dresses resemble those of the Assamese. Every house has a loom. They are simple in their dress. Women are not fond of ornaments. Hindu *Sonowals* use non-tribal titles like Hazarika, Saikia, Bora, etc. Now they prefer to use only the *Sonowal* title.

They follow monogamy. They have four types of marriages namely, 1) *Nowa Dhowa* (Bor Biya), 2) *Hom Diya* (traditional Hindu marriage by employing Brahmin priest), 3) *Gandharba* (love marriage, when couples take the initiative without parent's consent and after three days, information is sent to the parents of the girl) and 4) *Churchuria or Rabha Sarakai diya* (marriage by running away; an unceremonious feast is given to some elders for legalisation of the marriage). There is no fixed bride-price. It varies according to the status of the groom. Now only for Gandharba marriage bride-price is charged. Marriage within the same clan is prohibited.

Both nuclear (husband, wife, unmarried children) and joint family (father, mother, unmarried brothers, sisters, children, etc.), systems are found among them. The eldest male member of a family runs the house. After the death of the father the land is divided equally among the sons and the house of the father goes to the eldest son.

They are divided into seven exogamous *bangshas* (clan) namely, Bali Khitiari, Chiri Puriya, Amarabamiya, Dhulial, Ujani Kuchiya, Namani Kuchiya and Tipamiya. These clans are subdivided into fourteen subclans (khols), namely, Hagral, Muktal, Madan, Manikiyal, Ahmal, Formal, Bor Hajoal, Saru Hajowal, Kumral, Dhekial, Dingial, Lothial, Dangral and Chetial. Again there are subdivisions of these subclans namely, Makrari, Daphlari, Nezkatari, Daimari, Khakhlari, etc. There is no higher or lower rank of a clan. The origin of the clan is traced from the characteristics of their ancestors.

The *Sonowals* are fond of cleanliness. Most of them are the followers of Mahapurushia Vaishnav Dharma and disciples of *Auniatic Satra* and *Checha Satra.* Sonowals are divided into *Sarania* and *Bhajania.* Sonowals above the age of sixteen are regarded as *Sarania* and those above fifty are known as *Bhakats* and divided into various grades and the seniormost may be a *Medhi* (G.C.Sharma Thakur, 1988:88). Like other Kacharis, they worship Siva, Bathou, Bura Poha, Saragdeo, Pir Diya, Morak Diya, Laksmi Diya, etc. They observe Janmashtami, *tithis* of Sankardeva and Madhabdeva, etc.

Rangali Bihu is the traditional community festival. They observe also *Bhogali* and Kati *Bihus.* Their culture resembles that of the Assamese. They speak Assamese. The birth of a child is an occasion of joy for the family.

They cremate the dead bodies. Before 1921, some of them used to practise the burial system. Now only children below five years are buried. Dying inside the room is not considered a good men. The *Medhi* (priest) presides over all the functions of death rites. They observe *tilani* (third day), *dahdinia daha* (tenth day) and *Kuridinia kaj* (twentieth day). They arrange *Namkirtan* and a common feast on *Kuridinia kaj.*

6. Mech Kachari:—According to B.K. Roy Burman (1970:48), Mech are the same as Kachari who are seen in some parts of Assam and West Bengal. L.A.Waddell (1901:57), stated that this tribe of lower Assam appears to be a branch of the Kachari family. They inhabit the Mechpara area, Salmara subdivision of the Goalpara district. They are found in Khowang area of

Dibrugarh district and in Parakhowa area of the Karbi Anglong district. On the border of Nagaon district. Some of them are found in Sonitpur district, and in North Bengal.

They belong to Tibeto-Burman family of Bodo group. As per N. Vasu (1922:98) in ancient times the Kiratas in Kamrupa (ancient Assam) were called 'Mlecchas' and the term 'Mech' is a corruption of the term 'Mleccha'. G.A. Grierson (*LSI*, 1903, Vol. III/II/:1) also opined that Mech is a corruption of Mleccha. B.N. Bordoloi (1991:83) argues that the scholars have failed to prove why only a section of a specific ethnic group was called Mech. Hence Mech is not a corrupt term of *Mleccha*.

Mech culture is rapidly changing and they do not like introducing themselves as Mech. They prefer identifying themselves as Kachari. The percentage of literacy is high among them. The clan is called *Ari*. It is divided into five main clans namely, Sampramari or Campramari, Narzinari or Narzenari, Basumatari, Mochari or Mashari and Hajoari. Sampramari are highest in rank and they are the priests. They have four more clans which are based on occupation. They are—Borgaoari, Doimaari, Goyaari and Khatlouari. The first three occupational clans are also found among the Bodo Kacharis. The clan names are used as surnames.

Their clan is exogamous and marriage is not possible within the same clan. They marry within their own tribe. Inter-tribal marriages with the Bodo-Kachari and other backward classes are seen. E.A. Gait says that inter-tribal marriages between the Meches and the Koches were held freely. They have bride-price called *jan*. This is paid in cash and varies according to the beauty of the bride. The bride-price is now abolished. Marriage by negotiation is the traditional system of marriage. Divorce is rare. Child-marriage is not in practice.

Rice is their staple food which they take with chillie, burnt-fish, vegetable curry, etc. Occasionally they consume pork, pigeon, fowl, duck, etc. Earlier they used to eat buffalo meat. They prefer tea without milk. *Jou* (rice beer) is their favourite drink. They smoke tobacco and chew betel-nut with betel-leaves and lime.

In earlier days, they were animists. They used to worship the traditional gods and goddesses even after accepting Hinduism. *Bathou, Ailung, Agrang, Khaila, Khungri, Kazi, Brali, Laithu, Jamuna, Shali Jamanai, Maenow*, etc., deities are worshipped by them. Some of these are treated as Siva, Parvati, Lakshmi, Saraswati, Kartik, Ganga, etc. They observe all the three *Bihu* festivals. Some of them are followers of Vaishnavism.

They dress in a simple manner. Men used to wear *dhuti* called *gamocha*, turban, and *endi* shawl or *chaddar*. But now they wear modern European dresses like trousers, shirt, etc. Women wear *mekhela,* which is tied around the chest just below the armpit that hangs up to the knees. It is called *Dokhna Thinthai* and *Dokhna Ashar*. They wear blouse. Simple ornaments are used by them.

Like the Boro Kachari, the Meches also follow the patrilineal system. Sons inherit the property of the father. If there is no son, the nearest male kin of the deceased gets the property. Daughters can't inherit the father's property.

The Mech families which have not converted to Christianity, or Hindu faith of Brahma cult, or Vaishnava cult keep a *Siju* tree in the north-eastern corner of their courtyard which is considered as *Bathou* (Siva). They do not celebrate the birth of a child and it is only an occasion of joy. They do not practise *jhum* cultivation. They cultivate paddy, pulses and vegetables. They are experts in rearing silkworm particularly *eri*. *Kanti* (bamboo-made loom) are used by most of them. They are fond of songs and music. They have several musical instruments namely, *kham*, *chifang* or *siphang*, *thorkha*, etc., Some of them are experts in fishing.

They believe in evil spirits. The doctor is called *Ojha* or *Dousi*. In earlier days, they used to take herbal medicines, etc. from the *Ojha*. Now they prefer modern medicines.

They cremate as well as bury when unnatural death occurs. Death rite (*Shraddha*) is performed on the eighth or twelveth day as fixed by the village headman after consulting village elders. On the day of the *shraddha* the village people and the relatives are invited to a feast. Help and co-operation are extended by every family with manual labour and food and drink.

7. Hojai Kachari:—They reside in Nagaon district and belong to Bodo linguistic group and speak the Tibeto-Burman language. Both Assamese and Roman scripts are used by them. L.A.Waddell (1901:44), reported that the purest tribe is the *Hojai* or *Hajong* who live in the hills. The word *Hajo* means *'a hill'* in both the *Kosari* (*Kachari*) and the *Kos* (*Koch*) dialects.

They are divided into two groups, namely, *Sangskari* (Hinduised people) and *asangskari* (*Adi*, traditional people). All these groups, have forty patrilineal clans (*Sengphong*) and forty-two matrilineal clans. They use clan names and Barman as surname. They are endogamous. Marriage is not possible within the same clan. Mainly marriage by negotiation and marriage by elopment are seen among them. Bride-price (*Kalti*) is given. *Sangskari* women use vermilion as a symbol of marriage. Divorce is rare. Monogamy is the prevailing practice.

Agriculture is their main occupation. They select the headman (*Gaonbura*) at a meeting of elders. They believe in spirits. They are closely related to the Dimasa, Barman Kachari and Boro Kachari people. Their customs are some what similar. Hinduised Hojai cremate the dead body. They perform the death rites (*Shraddha*) on the thirteenth day.

8. Hajong:—They inhabit Lakhimpur area of Goalpara and South Salmara of Dhubri districts. But most of them live in Garo Hills of Meghalaya. A small number of Hajongs are at present to be found in Miao subdivision of Tirap district of Arunachal Pradesh. A few scholars are of the opinion that the word

Hajong is derived from the Kachari word *Haju* which literally means the people who live in high hills. Some other scholars are of the opinion that the word *Hajong* originats from Garo word *Ha-Jong* (*Ha*=land, *Jong*=ant/worm). As the Hajongs, main occupation is agriculture, so this word is used for them.

As per E.T. Dalton (1872:86-87), the Rabhas and the Hajongs of Goalpara district are branches of the Kachari race and connected with the Garos. Further, he states that the Hajongs appear to be identical with the *Hazai* (*Hojai ?*), Kacharis of North Cachar. According to L.A.Waddell (1901:43), Hajong is the primitive *Kachari* of the hilly tracts. R.K. Rai Hajong (1982:17) reports that the Hajongs like to introduce themselves as *Kshatriyas*. But, Garo and the Kachari do not consider themselves so. E.A. Pakyntein (1965:63), cited from *Report of the Census of Assam 1891* that the Hajongs, like the Rabhas, are closely associated with the Garos and Kacharis, but want to have a separate identity. Further, the Hajongs are divided into two sections—the Byabahari or ordinary Hajong and the Paramarthi or seeker of God. The latter are more Hinduised and belong to the Vaishnava sect while the others are Sakta. The Vaishnava sect does not believe in spirits and abstains from eating flesh. They are beginning to describe themselves as *Rajbansis*. K.R. Hajong (*Assam Tribune*, March 13, 1994:I), reported that according to P. Bhattacharya, the Hajongs physically having dark complexion belong to the Mongoloid tribe and are related to the Garos and the Boro-Kacharis. R.M. Nath (1948), opined that the Kachari, Koch, Hajong, Rabha, Tipra of our country are, *Kirata* race. However, it seems that the *Hojais* and the *Hajongs* are the same people.

As per G.K. Ghosh (1992:37), the original home of the Hajong was Mymensing district of East Pakistan (now Bangladesh). The Hajong belong to Tibeto-Burman, Mongoloid-featured Bodo group. They have their own language that is a mixture of Assamese and Bengali. According to D.N. Majumdar (1984:151), this language is known as *Jharua* dialect of Assamese. As per M. Barman (1987:40), the language spoken by the Hajongs at present, is a branch of *Kamrupi* language. According to R.K. Rai Hajong (1982:17), the Hajongs had their own language in the distant past, when and how that disappeared, nobody knows. But a few original Hajong words are used by them.

Men wear *dhuti* called *Ningti*. It is a home-woven cloth bigger than *Gamocha*. During winter, they use *chaddar* to cover their bodies. They use a scarf known as *kampesh*. Women wear *mekhela* called *Patin* and it covers their bodies from the waist to the ankle. It has mainly blue colour designs of flowers. At home, they do not use blouse. They cover the upper part of the body with cotton *chaddar* called *Pachhra* or *Agrun* with designs. During festivals they use another cloth called *Kamarbandha* around their waists. Hajong ladies are fond of traditional ornaments. Some of their ornaments are—*kata baju* (armlet), *baghh* (anklet), *harsara* (necklace), *gunjar* (anklet), *kairu* (ear-ring), *nala* (nose ring), *kanful* (ear-ring), etc.

Their traditional loom is called *Bana*. Most of their clothes are woven at home by women. They use several musical instruments, namely, *dhuluk* (drum), *khul* (cylindrical drum), *rasamandali* (string instrument), *dotara* (string instrument), *bansi* (flute), *gubua'* (gagana), etc. The Hajongs are rich in folk music. They sing during dance, *puja*, etc.

The Hajongs are cultivators. They produce paddy along with jute, mustard and other agricultural items. Both men and women work in the field. Women, however, do not plough land and it is the duty of men. They rear cattle, goat, duck, pigeon, etc. They do not rear pig and fowl.

The Hajong men are darker in complexion than their women. Average height is below medium to short (1.60m. male and 1.40m. female). Their eyes are not small. They are strong and stout. They have patrilineal exogamous *Nikni* (clan). Some of the clan names are—Chondi, Kendagaiya, Baliati, Dinjar, Koitar, Sonamukhi, etc. As per D.N. Majumdar (1984:159), the matrilineal clan organisation of the Hajong was lost long back. However, the father is the head of the family. After the death of the father, his sons inherit his property. If there is no son, the nearest male relative gets the property, but not his daughters. This customary law is, however, relaxed in educated families; because the sonless father's property is nowadays inherited by the daughters. Their *nikni* (clan) is exogamous. Marriage by negotiation is practised. In earlier days they had dowry and bride-price system, which is now abolished. Divorce is allowed but it is rare. A widow and a divorcee can remarry with the consent of the village elders. Child marriage is absent. They observe *sua* (pollution) after birth and death. Between seventh to tenth day of the birth, they tonsure the head of the new-born baby to end the pollution period.

They were animists. Most of them are now Sakta, and worship Durga, Kali, Lakshmi, etc. Some of them are Vaishnava, the devotees of Vishnu. They worship gods and goddesses of the Hindu faith along with some traditional deities. Some of their deities are—*Bash* (bamboo), *Padma* (*manasa,* snake), *Kartik*, etc. They believe in *Jarang Deo, Maila, Bhut*, etc., spirits. During religious festivals they sing devotional songs (*sankirtan*).

They cremate the dead. They observe *Shraddha* (death rite) on the eleventh or the thirteenth day after death.

9. Tiwa (Lalung):—Tiwa are mostly plain tribes of Assam and are settled in Nagaon district. Some are found in Amri area of Karbi Anglong district, south-east part of Kamrup, and eastern part of North Lakhimpur. There are also Hill Tiwas (Hill Lalungs).

They belong to Mongoloid-featured Tibeto-Burman speaking Bodo subgroup. Some rural Lalung octogenarians believe that their forefathers were the *Jaintias* (G.C. Das, 1962:173). There is a mythological story that once Lord Mahadev was heavily intoxicated with rice-beer and was lying unconscious on a road with saliva (*lal*) coming out of his mouth. From this saliva, he created one male and one female human beings. They were created from saliva (*lal*), so they were known as *Lalung*. In Lalung (Tiwa) language *Tiwa* means superisor or elevated. As they came to Assam following the river Brahmaputra, they might have introduced themselves as Tiwa. As per G.C. Sharma Thakur (1972:90), they entered Assam through the north-eastern hilly tract from their original habitat, the Tibetan Plateau. According to him, they are perhaps the last Bodo group entering Assam through this tract.

According to the Tiwas, there were two races *Dev* and *Daitya* and they are descended from the *Daitya* race. They call non-Tiwas as *Midu*. They are divided into twelve exogamous clans (*Kul*). These have been subdivided into a number of sub-clans (*Dhan-Bangah*). As per G.K. Ghosh (1992:50-51), the Tiwas of each clan can be identified by certain common surnames. He mentions their clans, sub-clans and surnames as follows :—

Clan	*Sub-clan*	*Surname*
Macharang	Machereng, Magor	Deoraja
Madur	Ladur, Puru, Sagara	Dekaidoloi, Gaonkhza
Maloi	Fangsong, Pumbe (une)	Bordoloi, Konwar
Dafor	Mithi, Lonfoi	
Sukai	Kharai	Senapati, Das, Deori
Amfli	Aagara, Chanchara	
Lasa	Mithi	
Chalang	Muni, Metang	Deori, Konwar
Amchong	Amchi	Amsi, Pator
Kakhor	Aagari	
Darnong	Damlong, Kholre	Lora
Lorom		Bordoloi
Common Surnames		Kakati, Manta, Doloi, Bharali, etc.

Later these clans broke up and formed into new clans and sub-clans. The status of Macharang and Machereng clans seems to be superior. There is reason to believe that the Tiwas were once a matriarchal tribe and the wife and not the husband was the head of the family. The line of descent was traced through the female members only. The Tiwa festivals are mostly related to religion. Their important festivals are—*Mal puja, Bison Kunwari puja, Thal puja, Sani puja, Dewali puja, Jankang puja*, etc. All these are performed in forests. There are other *pujas*—*Garakhia puja, Nam Bhatima puja, Kalika puja*, etc. These are held in *Thanghar* (sacred place of worship). Every January to April, they observe the following festivals at home—*Mahadev puja, Lakshmi puja, Sukil Bhakat Sewa, Madahi Bhakat Sewa, Najaniya Bhakat Sewa.* They have also *Gobha Raja's Mela, Magh Bihu, Bohag Bihu*, etc. Their gods are—*Mahadev, Ganesh, Parameswar, Badarmaji, Baolakong* and their goddesses are—*Ai Gosani or Devi, Lakshmi, Padumi, Kalika, Kamakhya, Saru Ai, Bor Ai*, etc. Lord *Mahadev* is their benevolent god. They consider "Wednesday" as auspicious to perform marriages and for festivals.

They follow Hinduism. Among them a few Christians are also there. The room where they worship the household deities is called *Barghar*. There is no idol of god or goddess in this room. The Tiwa have their own dialect. Their clans are exogamous. No marriage can take place between members of the same clan. Monogamy is practised. A younger brother can marry the widow of his elder brother, but not vice-versa. Cross-cousin marriage is preferred. Marriage between the Tiwa and the Karbis is allowed. Some of the manners, customs and traditions of the Tiwas resemble those of the Karbis. Their marriage system also resembles those of Hindus. But they do not observe *'hom'* (sacred fire as an offering to god) at the time of presenting the bride at marriage.

All the complicated disputes are settled by the Village Council which is formed with the elder persons of the village and presided by the *Gaonbura* (village headman). Ordinary disputes are settled by the *Gaonbura*. In earlier days they had a king. He resided in a village called Na-Khola near Jagiroad. Only on *Darbar* (meeting) day he used to wear his royal dress for the proceedings.

The Tiwas linguistically and socially belong to the Bodo group. They are yellow-skinned Mongoloid Asiatics. The face is almost broad, with a mesocephalic head. They are medium-statured with prominent eyes and mesorrhine nose. They are strong and healthy. Plain Tiwa men wear *dhuti, genji* and sometimes *Nimai sola* and shirt. The Hill Tiwa men use a narrow strip of cloth called *lengti*. It is also called *Tangali* and has embroidered designs. According to their status, they lengthen the ends of the *Tangali*. The elderly men use *lagri* (turban). The Hill Tiwa women use *Mekhela* extending up to the knees and a *chaddar* covering the upper part. The winter clothes are *Khania Kapor* and *Bor Kapor*. The plain Tiwa women use dresses like the Assamese women. Their traditional dresses are *Mekhela, chaddar* and *riha*. They wear special dresses for various festivals. These dresses are—*Singkhap Mekhela, Riha, Sondia Kapor, Thenus (chaddar), Seleng, Sakathia, Farke* (blouse), *Mankapor* and *Borkapor*. Thongali is a waist band which they wear while working at home. They use traditional ornaments. The women weave clothes on their looms. They have their own dance, music and musical instruments. In the earlier days they used to have *deka-chang*, youth dormitory, for young boys. Men in leisure time prepare cane products. Plain Tiwas practise wet land cultivation and the Hill Tiwas *jhuming*. In *jhum* they cultivate mixed crops.

After the birth of a child, the mother observes her impure period till the umbilical cord of the new-born drops off. Soon after this, the purification ceremony is observed. They cremate the dead. The Christian Tiwas bury the dead. They do not have any fixed day for *shraddha* (death-rite) or purification.

10. Rabha:—The Rabhas are scattered in the undivided districts of Goalpara, Kamrup and Darrang. They inhabit Meghalaya, Bangladesh, West Bengal, etc. The Rabhas have some cultural similarities with the Bodo linguistic groups like Garo, Kachari, Mech, Hajong, Koch, etc. As per L.A. Waddell (1901:65), the Rabhas are the offshoot of the *Kachari* tribe. According to B.M. Das (1960:117), the Rabhas are closely associated with the Garos.

As per L.A. Waddell, the Rabhas are divided into Pati (whose status is highest), and who live mostly in Kamrup and Darrang, Rangdani and Totala (the lowest in status) who live in undivided Goalpara district. As per B.M. Das (1981:34), the Rabha tribe is divided into several groups, namely Pati, Maitori, Rangdani, Totla, Bitlia, Dahuri, Shonga, etc., of which the first three constitute the major bulk of the Rabha population. Each group consists of several exogamous clans, termed as *Bar* or *Barai*. Two or more *bars* are united to form a lineage called *Hur* or *Huri*. *Hur* is exogamous. The *Bar* is matrilineal. But the Rabha residence is patrilocal. The father is the head. It appears that the Rabhas are in transition from matriarchy to patriarchy.

The Rabhas show all the Mongolian physical characteristics. They have round face, flat nose, prominent cheek bones, oblique eyes, scanty beard and good health. As per B.M. Das (1981:40), one section of the Rabhas have abandoned their own dialect in favour of Assamese. The Rabhas were animist, but now have adopted Hinduism. Hinduism has brought about changes in their habits, manners and customs. They do not touch beef but are fond of pork. Goats and fowl are reared in rural areas. They observe Durga Puja, Kali Puja, Ganesh Puja, Lakshmi Puja, Siva Puja, etc. In Nagaon, they are devoted to *Biswahari,* the goddess of snakes. Pati Rabhas are the followers of both Saktism and Saivism along with their traditional faith in animism. Some of them are Vaishnavites of Mahapurusia sect and have faith in *Ek-saran Nam Dharma*. Some of the Rabhas have adopted Christianity. They are mostly from Loharghat and Rani areas of Kamrup district and Dudhnoi of Goalpara district.

The Pati Rabhas speak the Kamrupi dialect of the Assamese. The Rangdani speak a language known as Rangdani Rabha. It belongs to the Bodo group of languages and resembles the Atong dialect of the Garo language. They celebrate Rongali Bihu, Bhogali Bihu and Baikho or Khosi festival. The Rabhas consider themselves superior to the Kacharis and, the Garos. No intermarriage between the Rabhas and the Garos is possible. They can marry a Kachari girl on payment of bride-price but a Kachari boy cannot marry a Rabha girl until he goes through a ceremony of purification. Cross-cousin marriage is allowed among the Rabhas. They have traditionally only one type of marriage i.e. marriage by negotiation. No marriage can take place between the same *Barai* (equivalent to *Gotra*) including a *Hur* (*mitr Gotra*). A younger brother can marry the widow of his elder brother but the reverse is not possible. Similarly, one can marry the younger sister of one's wife but not the elder sister. They do not have child-marriage system. Divorce and remarriage of divorcees, widows and widowers are allowed. Both extended and nuclear families are found among them. All sons get equal share of the father's property. A daughter is not entitled to inherit property, unless the father will it for her before his death. A widow is not entitled to inherit the property of her husband.

Agriculture is the main economy. They practise both wet and dry cultivation with plough and paddy, jute, tobacco, mustard, pulses, sugar-cane, etc. The Rabha women are expert weavers.

Rice is their main food which they eat with vegetable curry, pulses, etc. Dried fish is a delicacy. Beef is prohibited. Rice-beer is their favourite drink. In earlier days, they never used to drink cow's milk as it was considered an excrement. Fishing and hunting were important games for every family. When a woman found herself pregnant, sacrifice was offered to *Bai, Ma-bai,* for safe delivery of the child. It was a popular belief among them that if the embryo moved to the right side, the child would be a boy and if to the left, a girl. They welcome both boy and girl happily and hold no discrimination. A fortnight or a month after the birth of a child, a feast is given. The mother of the child selects the name for her child.

They cremate the dead bodies. In case of death by epidemic disease, violent death, or if an infant died, they were buried and not cremated. They observe death pollution for fifteen days and during this period they eat only vegetarian food.

11. Karbi:—In earlier days, the Karbis were known as the *Mikirs.* The term *Mikir* was given by the Assamese. But they call themselves *Arleng* (i.e. the Man) in their own dialect. They belong to the Mongoloid group and linguistically to the Tibeto-Burman group. The Karbis entered Assam from Central Asia, in one of the waves of migration.

As per G.C. Medhi (1974:17), earlier they inhabited the hilly region, between Nagaon and Sibsagar (present Jorhat) districts in and around Kaziranga forest. N.N. Barua (1976), opined that the area between Dimapur and the Kopili river was inhabited by the Karbis, in their earliest migration. They inhabit the adjoining Nagaland, North Cachar Hills, Nagaon and south of Jorhat and Sibsagar and Karbi Anglong districts. Racially the Karbis belong to the Mongoloid and linguistically to Tibeto-Burman group.

Men are 5 ½' to 6' and women 5' to 5'2" in height; complexion is yellowish *(xanthoderms)*. Dark complexioned Karbis are rare. They possess flat nose, small eyes and resemble the Lepcha, Mizo, Kuki, etc., in appearance.

According to their regional habitation, they are divided into Chinthong, Ronghang and Amri. Those who live in plain districts are called Dumrali. They have five ***kurs*** (clans). These are Terang, Teron, Lekthe, Ingti and Timung. Each of these, has sub-***kurs*** (sub-clans). The clan are exogamous. *Ingti* is a priestly clan and in earlier days it had a higher status. They have marriage by service and cross-cousin marriage. They have no bride-price system. The bridegroom (would-be) lives with his would be father-in-law for two years and works for him to get his daughter as wife. After marriage the wife uses the surname of her father. But the children assume the title of her husband. Marriage is generally arranged with the consent of the parents. Divorce is rare. Child marriage is not practised although widow re-marriage is allowed. They give equal status to their women. They help each other in cleaning the jungles, collecting firewood, cultivating the field, and to fire the jungles on hilltops for *jhum* cultivation, etc. Before marriage young boys and girls are allowed to know each other and dance together. They are frank and open-hearted with each other. Now, due to lack of trust, they are hesitant in showing their hospitality.

They follow patriarchal system where father is the head of the family. The line of descent is traced through the male member. In a family they have father, mother, children, unmarried brothers and sisters; after marriage, brother/sister live separately. At the death of father, his sons inherit his property; daughter cannot get father's property. In the absence of a son, the nearest male relative gets the property.

They have Village Council called *Me*. Each revenue village has a village-headman *(Gaonbura)* appointed by the District Council Authority. They generally live in a house on hills. They practise permanent cultivation in the plains area and *jhum* cultivation in the hilly areas. And sometimes the whole village is shifted to the newly selected site of their *jhum*. In order to stop this habit and also to avoid *jhum* (shifting) cultivation, the Karbi Anglong District Council, in 1963, established some model villages on hill slopes where each family was provided with a house, land for permanent cultivation, etc. Karbi houses in hilly areas are built on a bamboo platform with timber posts. But in plain areas, the houses are constructed on ground.

Their traditional religion is a crude form of Hinduism. Hindu Karbis call themselves *Hanghari* (family men). They believe in one supreme being, *Arnam Sansar Recho* (creator of universe). They have some benevolent and malevolent deities. They sacrifice pigs and fowl in rituals. They believe in witchcraft and black magic. A few Karbis are followers of Christianity.

Karbi women are expert weavers and produce most of the clothes needed for their family. Many families rear *Endi*. Cane and bamboo articles are made by the men at their leisure time.

The ordinary dress of the Karbi man is a strip of cloth about six inches wide and six feet long covering the loins and thighs. They also use a sack-like armless shirt of coarse blue or white colour. It is slightly embroidered in various colours. Sometimes they use a turban. The women wear *pini,* a long sheet covering the upper part of the body and descending to the knees. It is tied at the waist by an embroidered tape like a lamp-wick, the long ends hanging low down. It is called *khichu*. They also use the Assamese dress. The educated men and women have almost given up their traditional dress and ornaments.

In earlier days they had bachelors' dormitory, *Farla (Jirkedam)*. It is gradually vanishing due to acculturation. They have many festivals, namely *Rangker, Hacha, Rongker*, etc. Dance and music play an important role in their life. They do not generally observe *Bihu* festivals.

It is observed that the women work more than their menfolk if the devoted hours of her work per day are calculated. Women are not allowed to attend the village court for trial; they are not allowed in the community feast along with men. Women are taboo in *Rangker* festival. The Karbi women are gradually improving their status by accepting the challenge of transition.

They welcome the birth of both boy and girl child. The name of a child is given by the oldest woman of the village. They cremate the dead.

12. Mishing (Miri):—They call themselves *Mishing*, but are known to the Assamese as *Miri*. In their language *Mi* is man, *shing* is white/good. Thus, it stands for *good man*. They are divided into Hill *Miri* and Plain *Miri*. Those who live in hilly areas are Hill *Miri* and the *Mishing* or Plain *Miris* are those who live in plain area. People believe that in earlier days, they inhabited Arunachal Pradesh and had blood relations with the *Padam-Minyong*. Later on, a section of them came down to the plains of Assam and inhabited the riverine areas of Lakhimpur, Dibrugarh, Sibsagar, Jorhat and Sonitpur districts. They also inhabit Siang and Lohit districts of Arunachal Pradesh. They have many similarities in appearance with the *Nishis (Dafla), Padam-Minyong,* etc. The *Adis (Abors)* call the plain *Mishing* as *Aying Birrang* (plain brother), and the plain *Mishing* call the *Adis (Abors), Adi Birrang* (Hill Brothers).

They belong to the Tibeto-Burman family of Indo-Chinese group. This Mongoloid group has fair complexion. They are physically sturdy and well developed and are medium-statured with Mongoloid features. They possess wide chest and broad shoulder. The lips are thick and the nose is flat. They do not have their own script and most of them do not know their own language. Some speak Assamese very well.

As per their habitat, they are broadly divided into two sections—*Barogam* and *Dahgam*. Among *Barogam* there are several clans namely, Doley, Kutum, Kuli (Kouli), Pait, Patir, Basar, Pasar, Kardong, Misong, Pegu, Kumbang, etc. and among Dahgam—Moying, Chayang, Taye, Pamegam, Murung, Bori, Pangging, Yein, Panchang, Noroh, Koman, Pogag, Paow, Bosing, Ayan, Padun, Saro, Nagate, Regon, Darik, etc. Generally they use these clan names as surnames.

The clans are exogamous and patrilineal. They have two types of *midang* (marriage)—formal marriage and informal marriage. The marriage ceremony continues for two days. In a formal marriage, the boy's party always takes the initiative. It is an expensive one. They have informal marriage by elopement. They have bride-price called *Alig* and marriage by service which is called *Magab Dugnam*. They prefer cross-cousin marriage.

They establish their village on the bank of a river. Thus their villages are not far away from rivers. Every village has a *Kebang*, which is supreme in all matters within a village. The head of each *Kebang*, is called a *Gam*. His post is not hereditary. He conducts the proceedings of the *Kebang*. Of late *Kebang's* position has been considerably eroded by *Gaon Panchayat*. The role of *Gaonbura* (Panchayat President) is more important than *Gam*. But still they obey the decision of *Kebang*. Outsiders are entertained with hospitality. They are simple people.

They have an institution called *Yame Mimbir*. All young boys and girls are members of this institution. *Deka Bora* and *Tiri Bora* are two officials who organise this in a village and it is still there in most of the villages.

They follow Hinduism, animism, and the *Bhakatia* cult. They worship Hindu deities and spirits, i.e., thunder and lightening, storm, drought, etc., with occasional offerings of fowl, pigs and *apong* (rice-beer). The Mishing religious rites are performed by the priest called *Mibu.* They profess the cult of *Mirui,* worship Donyi-Polo (sun and moon) and the principal deities like the *Adis* (*Abor* of Arunachal Pradesh and call themselves *Ami* or *Tani* (man).

They live in huts raised on piles. They keep pigs under the plank *(chang)*, and the cattle in a separate shed adjacent to their houses. They are gradually adopting Hindu habits and have started living in mud huts built on the ground. The *Mishing Morung* (bachelors' dormitory) celebrates annual *Porag,* and other festivals. In earlier days, the women used to tatoo their faces. The men wear mill-made dresses. *Kaping,* a traditional long narrow piece of cloth is wrapped round their waists. The women wear a *Sumpa* around their waists extending down to the knee. They cover the upper part of their bodies with *Galuk* a narrow strip of cloth around their breasts. Sometimes they use *Hura,* a small piece of cloth for head. The married use a small piece of cloth around their hips. On special occasions both men and women use various colourful dresses. Women also use *mekhela* which they call *Ege*. The women are good weavers.

In their society no one is treated as big or small, rich or poor in status. According to them, all are equal and they eat food with all. They are straightforward and firm but superstitious. The folk-songs and tales are rich. Some of their musical instruments are—*Doom Doom* (drum), *Taktak (Taka), Pempa (Pepa), Ke-kung (Beena), Dotara, Gagana,* etc.

They bury the dead irrespective of age, sex and nature of death. Every village has a common burial ground. They observe purification, *'Tilani'* on the third day after the death, without having feast and fun; *Mahekia* is an important purification ceremony, when a feast is arranged. Then they observe *Daha* which is held after one year or so after death.

Father's property is inherited equally by all sons. Daughters are not entitled to get the property of the father. If there is no son, then daughters get the property if they bear the funeral expenses of their father. *Apong* (rice-beer) is their favourite drink.

13. Deori:—They are one of the four divisions of the *Chutiyas* namely *Hindu Chutiya, Ahom Chutiya, Borahi* and *Deori*. The *Deoris* have been successful in keeping their traditions, religious belief and practices intact. As per L.A. Waddell (1901:42), the *Chutiyas* are divided into three sub-tribes—the *Deori,* the most primitive; the *Borahi,* semi-Hinduised, and the more Hinduised, the *Ahom Chutiyas.* According to him, the Chutiyas of Shan origin, though E.T. Dalton believed them, from their language, to be closely related to the Kacharis.

U.C. Goswami (1962:87), stated as per *Imperial Gazette* of 1909, that Pal dynasty's Hindu kings were the first administrators of Lakhimpur. Their capital was near Sadiya. The *Chutiyas* had dethroned them in approximately eleventh century. They entered Assam through the north-eastern passes and established their kingdom in the upper regions of the Brahmaputra. When the Ahoms entered Assam in 1224 A.D., the *Chutiyas* were settled at Sadiya and were masters of the western part as far as the Desang river. Hostility broke out between the *Chutiyas* and the *Ahoms* in the middle of the fourteenth century and in 1523; the *Ahoms* finally defeated the *Chutiyas.*

The original abode of the Deoris was on the banks of Subansiri river of Arunachal Pradesh. Their present habitations are in the riverine areas of Lakhimpur, Dibrugarh, Sibsagar, Jorhat and Sonitpur districts of Assam. The Mongolian characteristics are seen among the Deoris. They are strong and possess charming features. They maintain cordial relations with the non-tribals and people are charmed by their simplicity and hospitality. They have three divisions—Dibangia, Borgonya and Tengapani. Only the Dibangias know Deori language, whereas the other two divisions have almost forgotten their traditional language, Deori and instead speak Assamese language fluently.

The Deori's Dibangia group has 14 *Jakus* (clan), Borgonya has 6. They prefer joint family. After the death of the father, his property is inherited equally by all his sons. In case a man dies without any survivor, his property is inherited by his nearest male relative. The wife and daughter cannot share the property.

Their staple food is rice which they eat with boiled green vegetables, chillies and salt. They eat fowl, pig, duck, goat and also fish. Rice-beer *(Suze)* is prepared in most of the Deori houses. Generally, they are pile dwellers. Clan exogamy is strictly followed in case of marriage. Deori marriage *(Sajuba)* is of four types—*Barbiya, Sarubiya, Dharam Biya* and *Tamolkata Biya*. Child marriage is not prevalent but widow remarriage is accepted. *Barbiya* is arranged by the parent and it continues for three days. *Majubiya,* another kind of marriage, is arranged by the parents. Expenses are slightly less than *Barbiya.* Duration of this marriage is two days. For these two types of marriages, the groom gets dowry. *Dharam biya* is completed in one day and expenditure is low. They have *Tamolkata biya* which is solemnised before a girl attains puberty. The widely popular marriage among them is marriage by elopement *(Gandharba).*

The Deories are still maintaining their traditional beliefs and practices. The influence of Vaishnava Gosains is found in Deori villages. They worship Siva-Parvati *(Kundi Mama)* and the common place of worship is known as *Than.* They have many household deities. They observe *Bihu* and Wednesday, according to their belief, is the most favourable day of the week. They are very superstitious.

Among the Deori cremation is the rule. Infants, pregnant women and epidemic cases are buried.

14. Phakial:—As per Sarbananda Rajkumar (1962:112), there is no separate tribe or caste named *Phakial. Tai* people are divided into Tai Khamti, Tai Turung, Tai Khamiyang, Tai Aiton, Tai, Phake, etc. Like Ahom, Khamti, Turung, Khamiyang, Aiton, etc., the Phakial is the biggest section of Tai population. Their actual name is Tai Phake. As per G.K. Ghosh (1992:67), *Pha* means king and *ke* means a great man or high official. G.C. Sharma Thakur (1972:37), states that the Assamese people who live near the Phakial village in Naharkatia, Joypur and Margherita, define the word Phakial in their own way. According to them, Phakials were originally Burmese who managed to stay in Assam by telling a lie *(phaki)*. They gave their identity as Phake. The word "Phake" was later recognised as Phaki and the people were known as Phakials. They came through Patkai range and resided in Mogoung till 1700 A.D. They are the main people of the present Tai race. Further, he reports (1972:41), that in October, 1952, a representation signed by Sri S. Gohain, Sri A.M.K. Gohain and Sri C. Gohain was sent to the Government of Assam in which they had demanded the inclusion of the Phakials in the list of Scheduled Tribes. As per G.L. Borooah (1985:52), they are said to have immigrated to Assam in about 1760 A.D.

According to L.A. Waddell (1901:67), the *Tai* are the *Shan* people. The Northern Shans (1901:65), in Assam, call themselves *Tai Shyams*, and are commonly known as Shans. They may be grouped as—*Ahom* or *Tai Mau; Khamti* and *Khamjang* (who resided in a small colony at Jorhat and Titabar), *Fakial* (residents in a colony of Hukong Shans at Dihing near Makum), *Aiton* (who resided in a colony of Sibsagar district), *Nora*, mixed with Assamese. They resemble *Khamptis*, in culture and religion.

Phakials are of four types—Nam Fakials (they are mainly residents in Naharkatia); Tipam Fakial, Bar Fakial (reside in Margherita area) and Manmou (reside in Lidu area). They have some divisions like Thamung, Man Hai, Tumten, etc. They are pile dwellers.

They are Buddhists. They have Buddha Vihar (monastery) in their villages. An image of Lord Buddha and a few monks *(Bapu)* reside in each monastery. These monks *(Bapu)* follow the almanac of Myanmar (Burma). In a Phakial village, socio-cultural activities are performed in Buddha Vihar. In earlier days Pali language was taught to the students which helped in studying the religious scriptures. They follow the spiritual advice laid down by *Pancha Sheela* and *Ashta Sheela*. *Ashta Sheela* disciples never kill aninmals.

Their complexion is light with Mongolian features. The village houses are traditionally constructed on high wooden platforms raised about 5' above the ground. These houses are mainly strengthened with wood and bamboo. Palm leaves are used for roof and canes for walls. Every house has a ladder to enter the house. Assamese folk-songs are sung by them. They burn *Meji* (like the Assamese *Uruka* in January) and eat rice on the full-moon day in the month of February. They collect feast materials by singing *Huchori* from each house. During *Bohag Bihu* they bathe the image of Lord Buddha and the disciples of Ashta Sheela to receive their blessings. Thereafter, they celebrate *Pani-Bihu* which is the Holi festival. According to custom, they observe Bihu for seven days.

Males wear a *lungi (fatong)* round their waists which is extended up to the ankle. They use shirt and pull over. White turban *(fahoho)* is the headgear of both men and women. Aged men use white shirt with long and loose sleeves, and a white *chaddar* (*fafekmai*), while going to temple or a distant village. The *chaddar* has plain border. It is two and a half yards long and one yard wide. The women wear *mekhela* (*Chin*) and *fanangwat* to cover the upper part and a cloth-belt (*chairchain*) round the waist. Girls wear frocks, *fafek*, *chaddar*, etc. Boys wear *lungi*, pant, shirt, etc.

They have *Gaonbura* (headman), *Pathek* (expert in religious matter), *Vikshoos* (monks), *Sramans*, etc. Minor cases are judged by the *Gaonbura* with the help of elders. The women keep themselves busy with looms. They produce *Sali* paddy. Rice is the main food which they take with vegetables, fish and meat. They eat dry fish and dry meat. They do not kill animals for consumption but they eat meat whenever it is killed by others.

They have several clans. A few of these are—Thumung, Wingken, Manhai, Chowhailung, Kangmung, Chekhen, Mungnoi, Mahao, Homa, Homen, Chekhap, Choton, Tumten, Lokho, Misa, Tonkha, Pomung, Kolo, etc.

Father is the head of the nuclear family. After his death, the land and property is divided equally among the sons. The house is given to the youngest son, as he is the last one to remain with his father. The daughters and widow cannot inherit this property.

They are monogamous. Clan exogamy is the rule. Cross-cousin and parallel-cousin marriages are prevalent. Child marriage is absent. When a man dies without a son, his widow can marry the younger brother of the deceased. Divorce is rare. Among them, bride-price (in cash) is prevalent. There is marriage among the Phakials with the Khamtis, Turungs, Aitonia and the Khamjang who have similarities in their religion, custom, etc.

They cremate the dead body except for children below ten years of age, accidental cases, victims of diseases like typhoid, cholera, smallpox, etc. These are buried. The purification ceremony is observed on the sixth day of the death.

15. Aitonia:—They are a small section of the Tai people. L.A.Waddel (1901:19), says that they are a small branch of a *Shan* tribe settled in Sibsagar district. Aitonia are also known as *Shyam* people. They have settled in the plains of Barpathar and Balipathar of Karbi Anglong district. The Aitonia or Shyams are not declared as a Scheduled Tribe under the Sixth Schedule of the Constitution of India.

The Shyams or Aitonia originally belong to Siam or Thailand. It is believed that they migrated to Assam in the thirteenth century along with the Ahoms. They make their houses on raised platforms 4' to 5' above the ground. They have few rooms in their houses. The space between the platform and the ground is used by their women for weaving looms. Buddha Vihar (temple) is constructed in a central place of the village with superior materials of construction.

Some excellent social customs are found among them. These are the principles of self-help and co-operation of Aitonia with others. This type of attitude is found among the Mizos. Mutual co-operation among Aitonia is evident in house-building, solemnising a marriage ceremony, observing the death rites, fishing and cultivating paddies, etc.

Generally they cultivate *Sali* paddy. Now they are also growing *Ahu* paddy. They do not practice *jhum* cultivation. Potatoes, brinjals, arums, betel-nuts are produced. They do not kill animals to eat. They rear cows and buffaloes for milk. Rice is their main food which they take with boiled vegetables, *dal*, fish, etc. Aitonia women are expert weavers. They weave cloth with the help of either traditional *kanti* loom or shuttle loom. It is believed that weaving was not their original vocation, but they learnt it from their neighbours.

There is a *Gaonbura* (*Hoban*) in Aitonia village who presides over the assembly of the elders. His post is honorary. Aitonia have *Pathek* (*Trayo*) who guides the religious activities and *Barik* (*Chacho*) who informs the villagers about village-council's socio-religious plans and programmes.

The tribe is divided into a number of clans. Only in marriage, reference to clan name is made. Marriage within the same clan is prohibited. They are patrilocal and patrilineal people. Both primary and extended families are found among them. Property is divided equally among the sons. Daughters and widows cannot inherit property. If a man dies without having a son, his property is inherited by a close male relative on the father's side.

Child marriage is absent. Divorce is rare. Cross-cousin marriages (MBD type) are preferred. Cross-cousin marriage with paternal aunt's daughter is prohibited. Widow remarriage and both formal and informal types of marriages are prevalent. *Pasag* (mediator) plays an important part in marriage negotiation talks between the bride and groom parties. Bride-price *(Tanka Tangho)* is given. They practise monogamy.

They follow Buddhism. They have Pagoda like monasteries where all religious festivals are held. *Chamun* is their head priest who reads out the Buddhist scriptures *Pancha Sheela, Ashta sheela* and *Dasha sheela* almost every evening and on special occasions. They observe three *Bihus* and *pujas* of Hindu Gods and Goddesses. They do not celebrate childbirth, but perform the name-giving ceremony of a new-born baby.

The dead body of an aged person is cremated but children, suicide cases, victims of diseases like cholera, small pox, etc., are buried. The purification ceremony is observed on the sixth day after death and a feast is offered to the villagers. A less important ceremony is observed on the seventh day after death. Monks perform the *Mangal Sutra* in the house of the deceased on both the sixth and seventh days of purification. On these two days gifts are given to monks of the temple.

16. Duonia:—As per Sarbananda Rajkumar (1962:108), there is no tribe called Duonia. However, they are the Assamese community of plain tribes of Margherita and Ledo areas of Dibrugarh. They have ten villages namely Duarmara, Enthem, Mungyong, Muk, Ulup, Bahbari, Ketetong, Enthong, Dibang and Khujan. As per H.K. Borpujari (1882:42), the admixture of the Singphos and the Assamese are known as the Duonia. They were brought under the control of the Singphos in 1791. Living with the Singphos for a long time, they forgot their own dialect. They speak Singpho dialect (*Duon*) and are hence known as Duonia (one who knows *Duon*). According to Singpho dialect, *Duonia* means people under a king or chief. As per E.T. Dalton (1872:14), from the intercourse between the Singphos and Assamese female slaves, a mongrel race has sprung up, well-known in Upper Assam under the denomination Duanias. They have been found to be very useful auxiliaries in frontier wars because of the Singpho language and tactics.

Their houses are built on bamboo platforms raised about 5' above the ground. A ladder is used to enter their houses. The women besides helping their men folk in agriculture, weave clothes and help in house-hold matters. Their food items resemble those of Assamese people. According to their religion, rice-beer or any alcoholic product is prohibited.

Originally the Duonias were known as the Moran, Matak, Miri, Kachari and Ahom people but they lost their identity as they spent many years under the Singphos as serfs. Now the Singphos marry them.

The Duonias are divided according to the name of the Singpho leader who had captured them in old days *viz.* Umban, Mache, Nungree, Ginsang, Gumju, Ulup, Ningda, Lajum, Lachai, Gazu, etc. They have *Gaonbura* (headman) who is the head of socio-cultural activities. His power of administration is now wielded by village panchayats.

They have two types of marriages *viz.* formal and informal. Formal marriages are expensive. Marriages are arranged by parents. They have bride-price system. In the informal marriage, no formalities are maintained and the girl is taken away secretly, though later on the boy must establish good relationship with the girl's parents by paying the bride-price.

Long back, they were animists; now they are Buddhists and are divided into two groups. A group follows *Panch Sheela* and another *Ashta Sheela.* They worship Buddha on every full-moon and new-moon day. Their main festival is *Pani Bihu* which they observe during *Rangali Bihu* of the Assamese. It continues for three days. Young boys and girls sprinkle water among themselves during Pani Bihu. At that time all the villagers bathe the image of Buddha.

They practise both cremation and burial of the dead body. Dead bodies above 20 years of age are cremated and below that age are buried. The purification ceremony is observed on the sixth day after death. A less important function is held on the seventh day.

17. Turung:—There are several people of the *Tai* origin like the Ahom, Khamyang, Aitonia, Khampti, Singpho, etc. The Turung is another tribe of *Tai* origin settled in Assam which is numerically a small community. They are Mongoloid people of Tibeto-Burman origin, who migrated to India from Myanmar (Burma), following almost the same route as other Tai people. They migrated to Assam perhaps in the middle part of the eighteenth century. As per E.A. Gait (1926:78), the Turungs in fact did not reach the plains of Assam until the beginning of the nineteenth century. According to administrative report of Assam of 1892-93 and 1901-02, they were remanded slaves for five years to the Singphos and were released by the British army. The Turungs, however, deny this report although they admit their relationship with the Singphos (G.K. Ghosh, 1992:69).

They are now settled in the south-western villages of Titabar and Sarupathar of Assam. Their main residential areas are—Tipomia, Pathargaon, Pohukatia, Kohukhat and Rajapukhuri. They speak a dialect which is a mixture of Singpho and Tai languages. Till now, there is little change among them. In spite of urbanisation, modern education and developmental activities they retain their cultural and ethnic identity intact.

They construct their houses generally in traditional pattern on raised platform with bamboo wall, *machan* and thatched roof. Most of the houses possess cowshed-cum-granaries. The space between the raised platform and the ground is used for weaving by their women.

The Turungs are Buddhists. They observe Buddhist rituals and festivals. Buddhist scriptures of *Panch Sheela, Ashta Sheela* and *Dasha Sheela* are recited in their monasteries (Buddha Vihar) in Pali language by *Tripitaka.* They observe religious and cultural festivals like *Buddha Purnima*, Bihu, etc.; and are similar to the Aitonia.

In social activities, the Turungs are very co-operative with villagers. They grow *Sali* paddy. Potato, brinjal, arum, betel-nut, etc., are also produced. Rice is their main staple food. They do not kill any animal but eat fish and meat. They eat pork but beef is strictly prohibited.

They have *Gaonbura* (*merengdingla*, headman). Who occupies an honorary position. They have *Pathek* (*Zare*) who guides the religious functions. There is *Barik* who informs the villagers about the socio-religious activities of the village council. It is said that the Turungs were divided into Tailung or Taioi and Durung or Drarai. Now these divisions are hardly found. They have several clans *viz.* Lungking, Namchom, Chaopu, etc. They have primary and extended families. Sons get equal share of their father's property. The widow and daughters are not eligible to the property. If a man dies without having a son, his nearest male relative gets his property.

Child marriage is not prevalent. Marriage within the same clan is prohibited. Divorce is rare. Both formal *(Nom Chaw)* and informal *(Frongwa)* marriages are accepted. They have bride-price *(Pho)* system which they pay in cash.

They cremate the dead. A child below ten years of age, suicide cases, pregnant women, victims of diseases like cholera, smallpox, etc., are buried. A purification ceremony is observed on the sixth day after the death.

18. Khamyang:—These are the *Tai* people and are also known as the *Noras*. As per E.A. Gait (1926:80-81), there was a war between the Noras or *Shans* of Mungkong... the Noras are regarded by the Ahoms as close kinsmen. They are Buddhists and are generally employed as astronomers and writers. Their religious activities are similar to the *Phakials.*

It is not known when the Khamyangs came to Assam. Now they reside in Desangpani and Cholapather villages of Sibsagar and Titabar in Jorhat districts. They are also settled in Arunachal Pradesh. They construct their houses traditionally on raised platform of 4' to 5' high from the ground. Some of them are also constructing their houses on the ground. They cultivate *Sali* paddy. Vegetables are also produced by them. They rear cow and buffalo for milk. They like fish very much and also eat pork.

They have *Gaon bura* (head man) who presides over the meetings of the village elders. They have *Barik* (informer) and *Pathek* (religious guide). All these three posts are honorary. They have nine clans *viz.* Thumung, Bailong, Pangyoik, Chowlu, Chowlek, Chowlik, Tungkhang, Chowhar and Chowchong. They have both primary and extended families. The property of the father is inherited equally by the sons. The widow and daughters are not entitled to get property. If no son is there, property is inherited by the nearest male relative on the father's side.

Child marriage is not prevalent and marriage within the same clan is prohibited. Formal and informal types of marriages are in practice. In earlier days, they had bride-price system which is now gradually disappearing.

They cremate the dead bodies. Dead bodies of children, suicide cases, pregnant women, victims of diseases like cholera, typhoid, smallpox, etc., are buried. Purification ceremony is observed on the sixth day of death. Monks perform the purification and a feast is offered to the villagers.

19. Khampti:—They are mostly found in Arunachal Pradesh. But some of them are settled in Bihpuria and Narayanpur areas of North Lakhimpur and Sadiya. They are a section of *Tai* people who are regarded as *Shanghai*, i.e. the greatest of the *Shans.* Originally they came from Mung Khamti Long or Bor Khampti or Manshi in Upper Myanmar (Burma) from the source of Irawady river. As per E.T. Dalton (1872:10), their first settlements in the valley were on the river called Tengapani; but during King Gaurinath Singha's time (A.D. 1780-1790), because of civil wars they pushed on to Sadiya. It is said that after settling in Assam, the Khampti chiefs frequently took Assamese wives, and in some families the effect of this is marked in softening and improving the features of the later generations (G.C. Sharma, Thakur, 1972: 54-55).

They construct the houses on raised platform like the Duonia, Khamyang, Singpho, etc. They have several clans. Marriage is not possible within the same clan. Child marriage is not in vogue. Divorce is rare. Formal and informal marriages are accepted. There is bride-price system but it is gradually disappearing. They are Hinayan Buddhists.

They cremate the dead bodies. But children below 10 years of age, suicide cases, victims of diseases like cholera, smallpox, etc., are buried. Purification ceremony is observed on the sixth day after death.

20. Singpho:—As per E.T. Dalton (1872:14), the Singphos are called by the Myanmarese (Burmese) as *Ka Khyen* or *Kaku* whose original settlements were on the eastern banks of the Irawady river. It was only after entering the valley of Assam that they assumed the name of Singphos, which in their own language means *man*. It is said that the Singphos were the original inhabitants of Shan States in Upper Myanmar and they came to Assam in 1793. At first they settled in Tengapani and Namrup areas, thereafter during the Myanmarese invasion, they went towards Sadiya with a number of Assamese captives who were later on released by Captain Neufville in 1826. They are now settled in Margherita and Ledo area's Bisagaon, Kathagaon, Kumsai, Pangsum, Hasak, Ninggam, Langgam, Ulup, Dibang, Uban and Manggong. They are an important tribe of Arunachal Pradesh.

They have Mongolian features with medium stature, oblique eyes, high cheekbone, and the complexion varies from dark brown to yellow. They make houses on raised platform similar to those of Duonia, Khamiang, Khampti, etc. They produce *Sali* paddy. *Jhum* cultivation has almost disappeared. Rice is the main food. They like pork and chicken. Earlier they were addicted to opium. They have several clans and are exogamous. Formal and informal types of marriages are prevalent. They have bride-price system. It varies according to the status of the groom. They are Buddhists. They believe in spirits.

They have *Gaonbura* (head man). Both nuclear and joint families exist. The eldest son gets landed property, the youngest son gets movable property. Wife, other sons and daughters do not get property.

They cremate the dead bodies. Poor people bury the dead body. Purification ceremony is observed on the sixteenth day of the death.

21. Ahom:—As per L.A.Waddell (1901:17), they are a tribe of *Shan* family. It is said that they are descended from a batch of the *Mau (Man)* tribe of Shans who are known as Myanmaries (Burmese) in the Mogoung district of the Upper Irawady, who crossed over the *Patkoi range* about 1228 A.D., into the Brahmaputra valley, near Dibrugarh under the leadership of Chukapha (ACR, 1881:82). They gradually extended their territory down the river banks about 1500 A.D., the Chutiya tribe who inhabited the rich plains along the river, about 1615 A.D., and extended the rule over the Hinduised *Kacharis* along the great river as far as Guwahati in lower Assam. And the conflict with the Mohammedans and Myanmarese lead the British to annex Assam by the treaty of Yandaboo on February 24, 1826. In 1662 A.D., Mirjumla, the Mohammedan general of Dacca, came to Assam with a strong force. He advanced up to Ahom capital at *Gargaon* and captured it on March 17. He signed a treaty with the Ahom king Jayadhwaj Sinha. Mirjumla died on his way to Dacca.

The Ahoms entered through Patkoi range from the south-east district of Dibrugarh and conquered the Borahis, the Moran tribe. During the reign of Suhung *alias* Swarga Narain (1497-1539), the Chutiya territory centring round its capital, Sadiya, was annexed in 1523. They defeated the Kacharis and extended the western region of Sibsagar District in 1536. They signed peace treaties with the Nagas (1655), Deuri-Chutiyas (1673), Mishmis (1675), Singphos (1798), Khamptis (1800) and others who lived around the kingdom.

They identify themselves with the Assamese Hindu. They are mainly found in the districts of Dibrugarh, Lakhimpur, Sibsagar and Jorhat districts of Upper Assam. They had their own language of Tibeto-Burman origin but they gave up that and accepted Assamese as their own language. But a few *Tai* words have entered into Assamese language.

Their main occupation is agriculture. They construct their houses with bamboo although designs of the houses are now changed due to the influence of the Assamese culture. Betel-nut and coconut trees are grown within the compound.

The Ahom king Sib Singha was an orthodox Hindu ruler who ruled in 1714 A.D. The common people have converted to Hinduism long back. Earlier they were animists and were not Buddhists. They have *Chaklong*-type of marriage ceremony. This marriage has three essential items, *viz*., the exchange of lime box and betel-knife and the smell of turmeric and the tying of the nuptial knot. It is performed by an Ahom priest (*Mohan or Deodhai*) in Tai language. They have ordinary type of simple marriage called *Gur-Pithaguri* (molasses-pounded rice). A man cannot marry a girl of his own sect., i.e., a Buragohain boy can't marry a Buragohain girl. Divorce is rare. Widow remarriage is allowed.

L.A.Waddell (1901:18-19), mentioned the following subdivisions of the Ahoms :—

Sub-tribes (endogamous)	*Sects (exogamous)*
Chamua (the descendants of the chiefs and nobles)	Kunwar (Ruler)
	Bor Gohain (Ministers)
	Bura Gohain (Ministers)
	Duara
	Lohon
	Sandikai or Handikoi
	Dangoriya
Kelua (the bulk of people)	Cheliya or vetiya
	Pator
	Dihingia
	Hatimuriya
	Deodhai
	Mohan (Priests)
	Bailung (Astrologers)
Melua (menials and slaves)	Chaddang (executioners and others)

They are medium to tall in stature with regular features of a Mongoloid race. Face-hair of man is scanty. The dress pattern of both men and women resemble that of Chutiya and other Assamese. *Umpha puja* is one of the important ceremonies and was considered as a State-ceremony during the Ahom rule. It was performed once in 10/12 years, and pigs, cows, dogs, etc., were sacrificed (G.K. Ghosh, 1992:65). They have Rik-Khwan ceremony. They celebrate it with the help of their priest *Deodhais* by offering chicken, egg, banana, betel-nut its leaves and boiled rice. Hinduised Ahoms used to celebrate Hindu ceremonies and Vaishnava sects used to follow Vaishnava religious ceremonies. Some of them are strict vegetarians but it is said that the Deodhais and Mohans were the last to be converted to Hinduism who eat fowl and pork.

They do not have much interest in music and dance. Some traces of Ahom tradition in their ceremonies are observed. The Ahoms practise cremation, but a few lower classes bury their dead. The priest performs the Hindu funeral ceremony. It was only in 1769, that the dead body of king Rajeswar Singha was cremated according to his will and since then regular Hindu funeral ceremonies are performed (G.K. Ghosh, 1992:64). Long back, before accepting Hinduism, the Ahoms used to bury their dead bodies in boxes along with a water-pot, cup, *dao, japi* and a *pira* (dwarf wooden stool) and a huge earth-mound of pyramid type *(Maidam)* was raised over their graves.

22. Chutiya:—They are called both Sootia and Chutiya. They are included in 'Other Backward Classes'. They are a branch of the Bodo group of Tibeto-Burman linguistic sub-family. They inhabit Dibrugarh district. The Chutiyas had been already settled before 1228 A.D., at Sadiya and were masters of that region up to the river Burhi Dihing. The Chutiyas established their power in 1189 A.D., and their leader was Birabar or Bir Pal (*c.* 1194-1224), who became the king of present Sadiya region. During the reign of king Nitya Pal in 1523, the Chutiyas were defeated by the Ahoms. The Chutiya kingdom was annexed with Ahom area and an officer known as the Sadiya Khowa Gohain was appointed to look after the administration of this area.

As per R.M. Nath (1948:68), they lived originally near Swat lake, to the north of the Himalayas and to the east of the great Manas lake, then migrated to the south along the Subansiri river that joins the Lohit river in the north-east of North Lakhimpur in the middle of the seventh century A.D. during the reign of Varman dynasty of Kamrupa. They were termed Swatias by the people of Kamrupa and presently the term Sootia or Chutiya has come into use.

As per L.A.Waddell (1901:42), they are divided into three sub-tribes:—

Sub-Tribes (Endogamous)	*Sects (Exogamous)*	
Deori	Dibongia	
	Zonga-pani	(? Territorial)
Borahi (Semi-Hinduised)	Pator-hat	(? Territorial)
Ahom-Chutiya caste (Hinduised)		

In olden days they practised human sacrifice before the deity until the British occupation. The Deori have never employed the services of Brahmins. They build houses on bamboo platforms raised about 5' from the ground. They are medium to tall in stature like the Kacharis. They eat meat except for beef. Child marriage is not in vogue but both formal and informal marriages are prevalent. They have bride-price system and burn the dead bodies.

23. Matak:—As per S. Dutta (1985:1), the Mataks formed a community and have certain cultural traits and patterns of social behaviour under Vaishnava sect. Prior to 1251 A.D., the region between the Brahmaputra and the Burhi Dihing in Dibrugarh district, was called Matak country and was ruled by Bor Senapati. The Singphos began to raid Assam. They found that in Sadiya area, the Bor Senapatis were better able to defend themselves than those residing under the crumbling power of the Ahoms and, therefore, they called them *Matak* meaning "strong". The Mataks are mainly known for popular rebellion against the Ahom kingdom (1769). In 1786, in alliance with the hill-tribes they occupied the Ahom capital at Rangpur and compelled the king Gaurinath Singha (1780-1795), to take shelter in Guwahati. After occupying Assam, the British recognised the autonomy of the Matak kingdom which was annexed to the British kingdom in 1839.

There is confusion between the terms Matak, Moran and Moamaria. S. Dutta (1985:20), opines that Moran is a tribe, Moamaria or Mayamaria is a sect whose followers are called Moamarias or Mayamarias and Matak is a community which includes all the disciples of the Mayamara *Satra* belonging to different castes, tribes and professional groups.

The Moran is a branch of Bodo group of Tibeto-Burman linguistic sub-family. Moran, Borahis, Kacharis and Chutiyas were the main tribes of the Matak community. As all of them were Bodos in origin, they had a common pattern of living too. They lived in joint families (S. Dutta, 1985: 45). They have a *Gaonbura* (head man). He is elected by the elders of the village, taking into consideration his moral integrity, intellect, etc. Their *Raij mel* (meeting) is called to take a common decision where *Gaonbura* presides. It settles the minor disputes of the village people.

Child marriage is absent. They have no dowry system. The groom has to pay a bride-price called *Ga-dhan.* They have two types of marriages : negotiation (settled) marriage and love marriage. The family is monogamous. Girls are free to choose their partners and widow remarriage is prevalent. The women have equal status with their menfolk. Perhaps due to this equal status women like Radha and Rukmini along with other women participants took the leading part in the rebellion against the Ahom reign.

After the birth of a child, they offer fowl to the deities. The menfolk wear a *churia* and tie *gamocha*, a piece of black cloth on their head. The Matak women use *thia-mekhela*, tied from breast to ankles and wrap black-coloured *gamocha* on their heads. They use blouse, *parkani* (upper garment) to cover their body. Their garments are made of coarse cotton and *Endi.* While offering *puja* (prayers) to the God, the women cover their head with a veil.

They are mainly agriculturists. Most of their social functions are related to agriculture or hunting. Before and after harvesting the villagers make merry when they sing, dance and arrange feasts among themselves. They observe *Bihu* type festival in connection with the worship of their goddess *Primal,* though they do not observe *Bihu.*

Before their conversion to Vaishnavism they were animists. They now worship *Primal* male deity and *Primal* female deity. They also worship some other deities. Weaving and sericulture are the most important cottage industry. They have their professional spinners of *Pat* silk called *Yogi* and *Katani* and professional weavers are called *Tatis.* They have the Assamese caste groups of Hinduism from Brahman Mataks to Sudra Mataks. With the introduction of neo-Vaishnavism, they consider it unclean to keep pigs and fowl and they do not eat meat. *Lao-pani* (rice-beer) is also considered as unclean.

They burn the dead bodies. "The bereaved family performs the death rites jointly along with some other bereaved parties, and for this, a bereaved party sometimes had to wait for a year or so" (S. Dutta, 1985:46).

24. Borahi:—The tribe *Borahi* is akin to the Chutiya. Like the Chutiya, they also represent a group of the Bodo tribe. They inhabit Borahipathar in Dibrugarh district and they have a small population. They speak Bodo language. Perhaps they are a section of the Chutiya tribe. A few scholars opine that their name *Borahi* is derived from *Varabha* which they originally used to worship (an incarnation of God Vishnu). R.M. Nath (1948:60), is of the opinion that during the reign of the kings of the Varaha Pala dynasty many princes had an admixture of blood with the Bodos, and thus a race of children, of Varaha Pala fathers and Bodo mothers grew up, and was known as the "Vrahis".

The Borahis were defeated by the Ahoms in 1228 A.D. The Ahoms married them. Later on, many *Borahis* married the Ahoms. The first ruler of the *Borahi* accepted the initiation from the *Mayamara Mahanta*. The *Borahis* dynasty was Babhru-vahana (c. 1190-1220), and Pokharna (1385-1390), was the last ruler. Babhru-vahana established his kingdom with headquarters at Ghughuragarh, north-west of Dibrugarh. Afterwards, the kingdom was extended towards the south and founded in *Majuli* area the southern capital or *Dakshin pat.* Later on, the main capital was shifted to Simulguri and the kingdom was surrounded by Sibsagar district and Majuli. R.M. Nath (1948:61), states that the king was selected from the Varahi race, but the ministership was given to a man of the pure Bodo race. The king Thakumutha (1260-1270), fled with his followers to escape from the Ahom intruders and settled in the eastern part of the Darrang district and established a capital called Brahmapur, on the bank of Brahmajan river. This capital was shifted to north-east and named Viswa-Karmapur (now it is called Bihpur or Bihpuria). Finally, their capital was shifted to Brahma-Tezpur.

The *Borahis* are fond of songs and music. They play on drums, flutes and cymbals. They worship *Siju* (Cactus) trees. They are the followers of the Bodo culture.

25. Koch/Rajbansi:—As per J.H. Hutton (1946:251, 257), the *Koch* is a tribe of Assam and northern Bengal; in the latter area it is generally Hinduised as the caste of Rajbansi, but in Assam *Koch* is used for several tribes when Hinduised, particularly for Kacharis, Lalungs and Mikirs. Rajbansi is a caste formed from the Koch tribe, in northern Bengal and Assam. L.A. Waddell (1901:48), mentions that this semi-Hinduised people occupied the plains of the Brahmaputra between lower Assam and north-eastern Bengal. Census Report of 1881, stated that the Koch invasion of Assam occurred in the middle of the sixteenth century. The term *Koch,* according to Waddel, has become more of a caste title, than a tribal appellation. Any tribe of the Kachari, Garo, Rabha, Lalung and allied tribes can become a *Koch* by establishing a Brahman priest and giving up eating beef and pork. There was a resident king at Koch Bihar, Darrang, Bijni, Mechpara, Sidli, Beltola, Jalpaiguri and Lakhi. A large number of Koch people call themselves *Rajbanshi* or clanmen of the Bijni king and claim their alliance with the royal race of Koch Behar. According to Census Report (1891), Assam *Rajbanshis* are mainly Koch and Mech tribes who have assumed this name on conversion to Hinduism. The Koch *Rajbanshis* are recognised by the Government as Other Backward Classes. The Centre has included on 28 January, 1996, the Koch *Rajbanshis* in the list of Scheduled Tribes of Assam, excluding those in the autonomus districts. Actually they were agitating since 1967, to get the status of Scheduled Tribes.

The name Koch is said to be the *Prakrit* form of *Kavach,* a word used in the *Yogini Tantra* to designate the non-Aryan tribes of northern Bengal. Perhaps *Kavach* is the *Sanskritized* form of *Koch.* It is further said that the Koch is a branch of the Bodo who were Hinduised at an early stage. As per B.M. Das (1987:284), long back, people of Assam were divided into two groups viz. *Kalita* and *Koch.* Kalita are the Aryans and Koch are of Mongoloid origin. People have several opinions about the origin of Koch. However, there is now an Assamese race called Koch. Their surnames are—Ray, Sarkar, Singha, Varma, etc. Sudeshna Sarkar has stated (*Statesman,* Feb. 20, 1996:6), that Koch Rajbanshi claim they form 33 per cent of the total population of Assam. The clan is said to be the descendants of king Bhishmadeb Singha, ruler of Koch kingdom that was extended from eastern Bihar to Manipur.

They claim themselves to be the Kshatriya in the *Varna* system. The married women put vermilion and wear shell-bangles as marriage symbols. Rajbanshis have *gotras,* i.e., Kashyap, Batsya, Alambyan, Parashar Matgaulya and Sandilya. They speak Bodo language which resembles the Assamese and Bengali languages and use Assamese script. They are generally agriculturists.

The Koch are divided into several endogamous divisions. Each of these divisions has a set of exogamous clans (nikini). According to Risley (1891), Rajbansi (Surbansi) is their sub-caste. They follow monogamy. Marriage by negotiation with mutual consent is prevalent. Bride-price (*bou-pan*) and dowry (*jamai-pan*) are not customary. Widow remarriage is allowed but not favoured by the society. Both nuclear and extended families exitst. They observe seven days of pollution after the birth of a child.

They are animists and follow Hindu religion. They worship Kamakhya, Shiva, Kali, etc. *Astha Prahar, Holi*, etc., are their festivals. They cremate the dead. A period of mourning is observed for thirteen days.

26. Choudang:—They are a part of the Ahoms. Most of them had settled in Sibsagar district as early as 1872. In earlier days, they were the guards or executioners of the Ahom kings and they lived within the boundary of the Ahom court. They drink liquor, eat pork and fowl. They bury their dead.

There are some ethnic caste groups who inhabit Assam. They are the Brahmins, Kayastha, Kalita, Kaibarta, Namasudra, Bhuyan, Kewot, Hira, Jalkeot, Bania, Patni, Sutradhar, Dholi, Dhobi, Muchi, Bhongi, Bhuimali, Jhalo/Malo, Mahishya Das, Sudra Das or Dey, Gowala, Yogi (Nath), Suri, Harijans, Tea Garden Labourers, etc. There are communities like the Assamese, Bengali, Bihari, Marwari, Nepali, Sikh, Manipuri, Tripuri, South Indians, etc. There are different religious groups like Hindus, Muslims, Christians, Buddhists, etc.

27. Brahmins:—They are among the oldest of the Hindu settlers in the Brahmaputra valley. The king of Kamatapur, whose dominion extended up to Kamrup, imported a number of Brahmins from Mithila or Bihar in the thirteenth or fourteenth century. Some of them settled permanently in Assam. In the sixteenth century Koch ruler Viswa Singh (1515-1540), brought Brahmins from Oudh and Sylhet, whose descendants were known as Kamrupi Brahmins. The Ahom kings drove back the first attack on Viswa Singh's successor by an army of Sudras disguised as Brahmins, wearing the thread. About 1640 A.D., the Ahom king rejected the sacred threads of pseudo-Brahmins and restricted their movements in different parts of Upper Assam. They turned to Vaishnavism.

The worship of god Vasudeva during *Kalita* dynasty was popular and a Brahmin of *Kasyap gotra*, Narayan, got from king Satya Narain (1390-1400), a grant of eight hundred acres of land on the bank of the Dholi river in North Lakhimpur in 1390 A.D. In 1401 A.D., another Brahmin Rabi-Deva of *Sandilya gotra* received from Lakhmi Narain (1400-1430), a grant of about 260 acres of land on the bank of the Subansiri river. The Brahmins evolved a simple way to worship *Narayan* or *Vasudeva* by reciting stories of god. This is called *Satya Narayan Vrata*.

An Ahom king in 1399 adopted as one of his gods the *Saligram* of a Brahmin living on the *Dihing* who had sheltered him and his mother during the days of exile. Suklengmung *alias* Gorgoya *Raja* (1539-1552), had built two temples of *Song Deo* and *Laksmi Narayan* and the deity honoured by the Ahom kings during their initiation into Hinduism under the guidance of Brahmins in the seventeenth century was described as Govind Thakur.

The majority Brahmins of Upper Assam claim a more recent origin than the earlier settlers and are doubtful about their connection with *Kanaaj.* The *Tantrik Brahmins* traced their origin from the village of *Simla* in the *Santipur* Pargana (subdivision), of Nadiya district around seventeenth century. Ahom king Rudra Singha (1696-1713), selected one of them as *Rajguru* (court confessor), while others had temples and lands assigned to them in Kamrup. There are also *Ganak Brahmins (Bailung)* in Assam who enjoy more status here than in Bengal and the Brahmin Goshain of the great *Satras* of Upper Assam have lately established their claim as brothers of the Brahmins. Their profession is astrology. They reside in Darrang district.

The Brahmins of Assam are said to be of either *Baidik* or *Saptasati* sub-caste. Sharma, Sarma, Deb Sarma, Goswami, Chakraborty, etc., are common titles of Brahmins. The title *Bhat* is of Brahmin genealogy. Most of the Brahmins are from Bengal and elsewhere. The Brahmins of Brahmaputra valley are ignorant of their status which the Brahmins are conscious of in Barak valley of Assam, Bengal and other parts of India. They don't have *Kulin* or *Ghataks* (except in Barak valley). Subsequent immigration of Brahmins have taken place from Bengal and other parts of India to Assam.

The traditional occupation of the Brahmins is priesthood.The Brahmin priests are called *Barna* Brahmin (*Deodha* or priestly class). The Brahmins retain their tradition of old faith and hierarchy in all aspects. They learn the *Gayatri mantra,* undergo the ten purifying ceremonies and wear the sacred thread. They do not take cooked food and drinking water from lower-caste people.

28. Kayastha:—They are the writer caste, found mainly in Barak valley and Kamrup. The Kayasthas of Kamrup district claim that they are the descendants of the seven houses of Kayastha. The Kayasthas had settled in Assam before the period of Durlabha Narayan (1345-1380), who ruled under the title of *Baro Bhuiya.* The Vaishnava reformer, saint Sankar Dev was the grandson of Chandibar Kayastha. His descendants live in Nagaon district, where they are known as *Mahajan* or *Thakuria.*

Pratap Dhwaja (c. 1340-1345 A.D.), a Kayastha, took over the reigns of the Kamota kingdom and divided it into two administrative portions—the headquarters of the western portion, Kamota or Gaud was in Rangpur at Kamotapur and the eastern portion of Kamapur was at North Gauhati. The Kayasthas had been politicians, diplomats, court-officials, etc., in most of the kingdoms in the east from the sixth century A.D. It is stated by R.M. Nath (1948:51), that Dharmapala from 1345, to 1370, brought seven families of Kayasthas from Kamota and settled them in various areas with extensive land grants, investing them with a kind of feudatory power over their areas....

Dharmapala wanted to possess supernatural powers like Kendu-Kolai—the chief *tantric* priest of Kamakhya. This is said to have brought about his ruin. He had to leave the country leaving it in the hands of the feudatory immigrant chiefs from Kamota—who were known as *Bhuyans*. The Kayasthas used to follow the traditional cultural norms in all aspects of life.

29. Kalita:—After the Brahmins, the caste Kalita occupies the highest grade. They are supposed to have migrated to Assam long before the Aryan invasion of India and resided in Brahmaputra valley. There are other Kalitas, who live in Sambalpur (Orissa), and Chota Nagpur (Bihar). Their history, however, is not known. There is a mythological story that they are the descendants of the Kshatriyas who fled from the wrath of Parasurama and threw away their sacred threads *(uttari)* to conceal their caste. That is why they were called *Kul-lupta* (vanished clan) or *Kalita*. According to another story, they are Kayasthas who have been degraded for taking to cultivation.

They are expert artisans in masonry, carpentry, metal work and are hard-working, and expert agriculturists. They are scattered in undivided Kamrup, Darrang, Nowgong, Sibsagar, Goalpara and Lakhimpur districts of Assam. There was all-round development in social, religious, political and industrial fields of their occupied area. They are divided into Bar Kalita, Saru Kalita, Kumar Kalita, Mali Kalita, Kahar, Kalita, Sonari Kalita, Nat Kalita, Bez Kalita, etc., as distinguished from dancers and potters. Bar Kalita are proud of their high status and declare themselves as the actual Kalitas. "The Kumars or Sonari are different from Kumar Kalita, Sonari Kalita" (B.M. Das, 1987:284).

30. Bhuiyans:—The *Bhuiyan* name occurs in the south of Gaya district, in Champaran, Santhal hills, Chota Nagpur where it seems to be used in the sense of *Children of the Soil*. In Assam, the word *Bhuiya* means land-owner. The Census of Assam 1881, mentioned that the *Bhuiyans* of the Brahmaputra valley are similar to the *Bhuinhar* or land-owning Brahmans or Rajputs who form a large community in Bihar and the eastern districts of the North-Western Provinces.

R.M. Nath (1948:51), reports that the Bhuiyans became masters of their limited areas though the various successors to Dharmapala's throne retained nominal supremacy over them. There were constant quarrels amongst them especially at the time of each succession; and at last one of them shifted his capital, to the east of modern Tezpur and established a new capital, Protapgarh, being named after the ruler, in about 1385. This kingdom continued till 1498 A.D. It is said that the Bhuiyans were the head of twelve families *(Barah Bhuiya)*. Six of the families were Brahmans and six were Kayastha. As per the Census of Assam 1881, the Bhuiyans of the present day are all Kalitas, but they claim their superiority over the ordinary Kalita. They seem to have been in Sibsagar, Lakhimpur in 1872, and in Kamrup, Darrang and Nowgong in 1881. They settled both in plain and hilly areas.

They follow both Hinduism and animism. They eat meat, fish, egg, etc., and drink rice-beer. They practise endogamy at the sub-group level and exogamy at the village level. Child marriage is absent. Their traditional marriage is performed by negotiation with mutual consent. Marriage by elopement is also common. They are monogamous. Bride-price is paid in cash and kind. Dowry system is introduced recently. Divorce is rare. If the village council allows then only divorce can be sought. For this, parents of the bride have to repay the bride-price. The children in divorce cases stay with their father. Widow remarriage is allowed. Their family is generally of nuclear type. Sons get father's property. The eldest son succeeds to his father's authority of responsibility to run the family. The family is patrilocal and patriarchal.

Generally dead bodies are cremated. The pollution period is observed for ten days after death. E.T. Dalton and others had concluded that the Bar Bhuiyans of Assam are allied to the aboriginal Bhuiya caste of Bengal. Assamese Bhuiyans are known as Kayastha. Dr. Wise shows that at least one of these Bhuiyans or Chiefs is Muslim. The term is freely used as the equivalent of zamindar and applied to persons of any caste without implying any connection with the aboriginal tribe of that name.

31. Kaibarta and Kewot:—The Kaibartas are scattered all over the plain districts of Assam. They are divided into two subdivisions—*Halwa* (cultivators) and *Jaliya* (fishermen). Halwa Das of Barak valley or Halwa Kaibarta of Brahmaputra valley seems to get higher status and better privileges than the Jaliya Kaibarta. The Jaliya Kaibarta has one *gotra* i.e., *Kasyap*. Their titles are Das, Hazarika, Saikia, Baishya, etc. They are settled mainly near rivers, ponds, etc.

The Kewots are Kaibartas. They are mainly a fishing community and sell fish. In Assam their rank is superior to the Sudra caste. They are scattered in Brahmaputra valley. Like the Kalitas, they are also divided into a number of functional sub-castes. The main division is in between the *Halwa* (cultivator) and the *Jaliya* (fishermen) Kewots. The Halwa Kewots are considered superior to the Jaliya Kewot. They want to upgrade their position in the social hierarchy of Hindu society. The Jaliya Kewots are found mostly in the plains of Assam. There are Mali Kewot, Kumar Kewot, Saru Kewot, etc. Halwa Das and Kaibarta are mentioned by Manu as alternative designations of the same people. Dr. Bhupen Hazarika, the famous singer, belongs to the Kaibarta community of Assam.

32. Namasudra:—As per Manu, the term *Namasudra* indicates a fourth group of caste. The term seems to have no meaning. Namasudra is the title under which the Chandals try to hide their true caste. A large number of Namasudras migrated to Assam and settled in Goalpara, Dhubri, Cachar districts. Many Namasudras came to Assam as refugees from East Bengal (now Bangladesh) and permanently settled here. As per Bhakta Das (1986:31), the Namasudras are the aborigines of Uttar Pradesh. On different occasions they migrated to different places of India. A branch of this community came to Assam and some of them were converted to Christianity. Namasudra has links with Mahisya Das, a fishing community.

They are scattered in Assam and settled mostly in Nagaon, Barpeta, Nalbari, Goalpara, Dhubri, Karimganj districts. They are found in Rangia,

Nagrijuli, Chaygaon, Panikheti, Chamaria Boko, Palashbari, Guwahati, Kalaigaon, Dhekiajuli, Tezpur, North Lakhimpur, Sapatgram, Bijni, Abhayapuri, Mankachar, and other places. Their surnames are Das, Bhowmik, Sarkar, etc.

Their occupations are boating and cultivation. Their priest is not a Brahmin. They have separate priests of their caste.

The *Tokar* caste of Kamrup and Mangaldai occupied the position of *Hira* and *Hari* and is inferior to *Katani* sub-caste of *Jogis.*

33. Bania:—This word is used for those who are tradesmen and jewellers. They make gold ornaments. Now some of them have adopted agriculture as their occupation. They are settled mainly in Darrang, Sonitpur, Nagaon, Abhayapuri.

34. Hira:—The Hiras make earthen pots. They differ from other potters in that, their women are engaged in pottery work and they shape pots by hand instead of wheel. They prepare four layers of clay, each of which is partially dried before the next layer. When this process is completed they pile the pots in a heap, with straw between each pot and set fire to bake the clay. This clay is known as *Hiramati* after the name Hira Devi. There is a story that a pilgrim from Orissa named Mohendra Mahapatra came with his family to Kamakhya temple about 500 to 600 years back. He died there and his wife Hira Devi with her two minor sons could not go back to Orissa. When she went out to the bank of Brahmaputra in search of livelihood she found shining flexible clay with which she made various forms of earthen pots. That is why it is called *Hiramati* clay. The utensils made of this clay do not crack while cooking.

Though they were Brahmins of Orissa, the Brahmins of Assam did not allow her two minor sons to put on sacred thread *Lagun* as they took to *Kamar* profession. They resided in Pandu near Guwahati and afterwards migrated to village Bahati (Goalpara) in search of livelihood. Their descendants are known as the *Hiras* and they are spread throughout Assam.

35. Patnis:—They claim to be the offsprings of Madhab Patni who ferried Rama Chandra of *Ramayana* across the Ganga. The Patnis and Kaibarta originally belonged to the same stock. In the Census of 1901, the Patnis were recorded as *Nadiyal* with a view to maintain their identity from *Dom.* They succeeded in establishing their identify on the eve of the Census of 1921, from the *Dihing Satradhikar* of Nagora Satra (Golaghat) to be designated as Kaibarta and the Government of Assam identified the Nadiyals as Kaibarta. They now reside in Karimganj and Silchar areas of Barak valley. In 1921, Census, *Patnis* of Barak valley were shown as *Mahishya.* Again in 1931, Census, it was described that, "The Patnis in Cachar have assumed the nomenclature of 'Mahishya Das". Das, Bhowmik, Sarkar, etc., are surnames of Mahishya Das.

36. Sutradhar:—They are carpenters by profession. They reside mainly in Barak valley, Goalpara and Dhubri districts. There is a story that they failed to supply fuel to the Brahmins during *puja.* Thereafter, they were degraded and given a low position in the society. Generally, the *Ganaks* are their priest.

37. Jalo/Malo:—As per H.H. Risley, they are Dravidian boating and fishing castes and as per W.H. Wiser (1958), they are the Kaibarta people. They inhabited the Barak valley. Some of them reside in Goalpara and Dhubri districts.

38. Dhobi/Dhoba:—They are not indigenous people of Assam. They came from Bengal, Bihar and Orissa. Dhobi and Dhoba are termed according to their original residential areas. *Dhoba* are the washermen from Bengal and Orissa and, the *Dhobi* from Bihar. In Assam, Muslim washermen are called *Dhobi* and the term *Dhoba* is applied to the Hindu washermen.

39. Mahara:—Their traditional occupation was bearing *Palki*. They prepare *Hookah* (smoking apparatus) for their *Zamindars* (landlord) to smoke. The *Zamindars* employ them also as peons, Mandals, etc. They were degraded in caste hierarchy and placed in *Sudra* category. Most of them reside now in Barak valley. They are originally from Bengal.

40. Dholi:—They are drummers. They immigrated from Bengal and settled mostly in Barak valley. Some of them are cultivators and some rear cows. They were degraded in caste hierarchy. They have no Brahmin priest. The priests are chosen from their own caste, *Sudra*.

41. Muchi:—They are cobblers and do leather work, particularly sewing. They are mainly found in Barak valley. They are scattered all over the districts of Assam. They are mainly migrants from Bihar, Gujrat and U.P. They belong to *Chamar* caste. Ivory bangles are the symbol of marriage for women.

42. Bansphor/Bhangi/Mehtar/Lalbegi:—They are scavengers and sweepers. They migrated to Assam from Punjab, Bihar, etc. They follow the customs of Hindus, Muslims and Sikhs. Most of their men-folk are skilled in basket work. The Lalbegi follows half Hindu and half Muslim customs and beliefs.

43. Bhuimali:—Their traditional occupation is gardening, and they sell flowers in the temple for *puja* purposes. Now most of them are living in Hajo and Palasbari area. Some of them live in Barak valley. Some of them are taking to agriculture as their occupation.

44. Jugi (Nath):—1881, Census says that it is doubtful as to how far Jugi (Nath) may be classed among Hindus. The genuine Jugi eats all types of meat, lives without a Goshain, and buries the dead body. The name *Nath* suggests some link to the gypsy caste of India. The great majority have enrolled themselves among Hindus by the name of *Katani*, which means spinners or reelers of thread. Katani caste is distinguished from Jugi in Brahmaputra valley.

45. Dom:—Doms of Brahmaputra valley are mainly Vaishnavas and a large number of them are disciples of the Moamoris Gosain. The Assamese Dom is a fisherman. The Dom name is euphemised into *Nadiyal*. They are akin to the Keots. They have *Halwa Dom*, who have taken agriculture as their occupation, and *Jalwa Dom* (Nadiyal Patni) who still follow the trade of fishing. *Halwa Dom* is considered more honourable than *Jalwa Dom*. It is said that the *Panis* and *Haris* are the Dom caste. Those who remove dead bodies and rear and sell pigs are called *Suariya Dom*. Halwa and Jalwa Doms deny all knowledge of their relationship with Suariya Dom.

46. Napit:—Traditionally they are barbers. They reside in Barak valley and Goalpara, Kamrup and a few other districts of Assam. They use Sil, Seel etc., as their titles. It is said that the central and eastern districts of Brahmaputra valley are claimed by Kalitas. In Darrang, they are known as Barber Kalita (Census 1891). Some other communities of this profession reside in Assam. They have migrated from Bihar and Orissa and are known as Muslim *Hajam* and *Bhandari*, respectively. Some of the *Napit* community have abandoned their hereditary profession and taken to other professions.

47. Madak:—They belong to the *Nava-Sakha* group. They are mainly migrants from Bengal. They are also called *Mayara*. They are confectioners. Some of them are settled in Barak valley and Goalpara district.

The tea-garden labourers of Assam comprise diverse ethnic groups. They were recruited from undivided Bengal, Bihar, Orissa and Madhya Pradesh in the nineteenth century. Recruitment of labourers from outside Assam started around 1890, and continued till 1960. In 1837, the first Tea Community was formed and the first tea-garden was started in 1837. Those tea-garden labourers who settled outside the tea-plantations were known as the ex-tea garden labourers. They were dislodged from the tea-gardens and started residing in rural parts of Assam. There are about 68 communities of tea-garden labourers. Among them the Munda, Santhal and Savaras are the major ethnic groups.

48. Munda:—The Mundas are almost similar to the Hos, Santhal and Kharias. The Mundas represent the main body, the other three being the offshoots. They are mainly found in Bihar and Orissa. Some of them migrated to Assam either as tea-garden coolies or ex-tea garden labourers, now they are settled permanently in Assam.

The Mundas are found in pure form but their brethren have been partially Hinduised and are known as *Bhumij*. The *Bhumij* have retained the Munda burial custom but have forgotten the Munda speech. They migrated to Assam from Baghmundi of Manbhum district as tea-garden labourers. The *Kols*, who were originally Mundas had also come as tea-garden labourers from Purulia of Manbhum district. The *Lohar* or blacksmiths also migrated to tea-gardens as workers. These Bhumijs, Kols and Lohars are the Munda group of people.

The Munda language is known as Kolarian. In Mundari there are no parts of speech. The language has a number of words which they use as nouns, verbs, etc., according to their position in a sentence. They speak in Assamese which is a mixture of Hindi, Assamese and their own dialect. The Mundas call themselves *Horoko* (*Horo*=man; *ku*=is a plural sign). The Mundas are divided into exogamous sects *(killi)*; each sect worships a distinct totem. The Mundas are agriculturists. Their festivals are—*Magh Parab, Phagua, Ba-Parab, Hon-*

Ba Parab, Batauli, Sohrae, etc. Some of them have been converted to Christianity. They marry within their own group of people. The bride adopts the totem of her husband along with her own totem. Bride-price is prevalent. Widow remarriage is permitted which is called *sagai* or *Sangha*. Divorce is easy which usually entails in a repayment of bride-price. Rice-beer is commonly used. After the birth of a child, the mother observes purification till the sixth day (*chathi*). The bodies of the deceased are generally cremated and selected bones are buried under the stone of the ancestor. The Christian Mundas bury their dead.

49. Santal:—Santal is widely distributed of the Munda group which is found in Santal Parganas, Hazaribagh, Manbhum, Singhbhum, Bakura, Midnapur, Sambalpur, Birbhum, Bhagalpur, etc. Their legendary origin is similar to that of the Munda and Ho. The Santali language is allied to the Mundari. They call themselves *Horko* (Mundari *Horoko*). Their vocabulary is very rich. They speak a mixture of Hindi, Assamese and their own dialect. The Santals are divided into totemistic *septs* (*killis*) like the Mundas and the *septs* are mainly exogamous. Marriage within the same *killi* is not allowed. Marriage by service is not uncommon. Marriage by capture is common. Widow remarriage is possible. Divorce is allowed. *Sohrai* is the main festival. They celebrate *Sakrat, Baha, Brck-Sim, Hanai-Sim, Nagh-Sim,* etc., festivals. Their religion is animism and they believe in witch craft and think their sickness is due to a *Bonga*. Some of them have been converted to Christianity. After the birth of a child, they observe impure period. Their occupation is agriculture. Their customs are similar to Hinduism. A large number of Santals are settled in Dhubri (Assam) and lost their of customs burial. Santals, except the Christians cremate their dead.

50. Savara:—The Savara or Saora are Dravidians and inhabitant from Orissa, West Bengal, Madras, etc. Linguistically they belong to Kolarian group. Their women wear few clothes and are always happy and cheerful. They like dancing and sports. They are extremely superstitious. The arrow has some religious significance for them. Majority of them are bilingual and speak in Assamese which is a mixture of Hindi and Assamese. They build houses on a *machan* (platform), two/three feet above the ground. They have also *Katcha* ground houses with bamboo and thatch. Most of them follow Hinduism. Some of them have been converted to Christianity. They marry by negotiation. Divorce is permitted. Widow remarriage is found among some of them. Except the Christians, others consume liquor they cremate their dead.

51. Muslim Community:—They are mainly found in Barpeta, Nagaon, Cachar, Karimganj, Hailakandi, Goalpara, Mangaldai, Kamrup districts of Assam. The Muslims immigrated to Assam during the early part of the thirteenth century. They adopted the Assamese language and followed the Assamese way of life. The Muslims of Assam are mostly the *Syad*, the *Garia* (Sheikh) and the *Maria* groups. The *Fakirs*, of course, are all Muslims. The *Garia* probably introduced the faith by Gaur of Bengal. The *Marias* are traditionally brass workers. Like Doms and Hiras, the *Marias* lived in Assam even before the arrival of the Ahoms. They gave up eating pork and liquor.

The kingdom of Kuch Behar, including Goalpara, Kamrup and the western border of Darrang were overrun by Muslims in 1603, and after sixty years they advanced as far as Garhgaon, the capital of the Ahom kings, and imposed a tribute upon its ruler. In 1669, a second invading force was defeated, and the Muslims were driven back behind the Manas. But, they regained Guwahati after ten years and were finally expelled in 1688 (Census of Assam, 1888). Muslim invaders came to Assam on different occasions. A few Muslim soldiers preferred to live in Assam instead of going back with their defeated leaders. Later on, they adopted the Assamese language and followed the Assamese culture through marriage to local girls.

A Muslim saint Azan Fakir (Hazarat Shah Milan) came to Assam in the middle of seventeenth century. He was a *Syed* and married a local Ahom girl. He promoted Muslim religion in Assam. It is said that the Ahom kings encouraged some Muslim artisans to migrate to Assam to promote art and culture. Most of the Assamese Muslims belong to the *Sunni* sect of Islam. The Assamese Hindus and the Muslims interact freely. The Syeds claim to be the descendants of Prophet Mohammed and occupy the topmost position in social hierarchy. The Garia (Sheikh) and the Maria who are the descendants of the captured Muslim soldiers during the Ahom age in Assam occupy the second position. The Garia and Maria are different from the Bihari Muslims who have not yet been Assamised. As per J.H. Hutton (1946:28), the bulk of the Muslim population are no doubt more or less of aboriginal extraction converted to Islam. The Muslims bury the dead in their own community burial ground; recitation of holy *Koran* for seven to eleven days continues, in some houses of the deceased.

52. Harijans:—They belong to the Arya-Dravidian group and are all Scheduled Castes. They came to Assam from U.P., Haryana, Delhi, Bihar, etc., and engaged themselves in various menial works. They occupy the lowest position in caste hierarchy. As per Bhakta Das (1986:12-13), a few restrictions in rural areas imposed on them were as follows—They were required to tie a black thread around their neck as a mark of identification; required to walk barefoot as wearing shoes would insult others; prohibited from sitting on elevated portion of land, not to talk of using cot, chair, etc. Many other restrictions were imposed on them. They cremate their dead.

53. Assamese Community:—The Assamese are scattered all over Assam and other neighbouring States. They are, however, less in numbers in Barak valley districts including North Cachar and Karbi Anglong districts. They speak Assamese which is an Indo-Aryan group of languages and has its roots in Sanskrit. It is said that some of them have been Assamised. "The population of Assam has increased from 3.3 million in 1901, to nearly 15 million in 1971,.....the Assamese find themselves in the position of becoming a minority, although the largest minority in their own State". (Andrey Cantlie, 1984:XI).

The high-caste Assamese are by and large mesocephalic showing a tendency towards mesorrhine nose (B.M. Das, 1987:56). Many researchers opine that the caste Kalita have more Dravidian blood than Aryan. According to R.M. Nath, the *Kalitas (Kal-tons)* originally migrated from Southern India. They are said to have originated from a priestly class because in ancient times Kalitas acted as priests in converting people to Hinduism (M. Narimattam, 1988:30-31). The Kalitas are in large numbers all over Assam. The Assamese have a number of *gotras* namely—Bharadwaja, Gautama, Kaushika, Sandillya, Kashyap, Modgulla or Madhukalya, Batsya, Parasar, Alambyan, etc. The Assamese handloom products are famous in the world. Loin loom and handloom are among the artistic traditional crafts. Most of the village women know how to weave. Bamboo and cane products demonstrate their artistic skills. *Bihu* is their main festival. They celebrate other festivals also. They observe Sankaradeva, Madhabdeva *tithis*, etc. They perform *Durga Puja* and other *pujas*. The females wear *eri, muga* and *pat Mekhela-chaddar* with blouse. The lower part of the body from waist to ankle is covered with a *mekhela* and a *chaddar* covers the upper part along with a blouse. The young girls wear frock, midi, maxi, salwar, pants shirt, etc. Men wear pants, shirt, *pyjama*, genji, lungi, *fatua, dhoti*, etc. Women like ornaments. They generally follow endogamy. They have several types of marriages. These are—arranged marriage by negotiation (*bar-biya*, fire sacrifice in *hom*), elopement (*poluai ni biya*), *joran-biya* (marriage by exchange of gifts), love-marriage (civil marriage in a court), intercaste marriage, etc. Some non-Brahmins observe *Tolani biya* and Brahmins *Shanti biya*. Both these marriages are observed on the seventh day of a girl's first menstruation with a banana tree as husband. This is a "fake" marriage; when she grows up she marries a man as usual.

In some castes, father offers honey to the newborn child soon after the birth. It is said that purification ceremony is performed by the Brahmins on the eleventh day after the birth of a child. The non-Brahmins perform it on the thirteenth day or so. The mother is considered impure up to this period. The family priest gives two names of the child on the day of purification. A special *puja* is offered to God on this occasion. During the age of 8 to 16 years a Brahmin boy observes *Upanayana* and puts holy thread (*lagun*) and is initiated into *gayatri mantra* (secret spiritual advice). Brahmin titles are—Sarma, Borpujari, Borthakur, Bhattacharjee, Chakravarty, etc. Goswami title is used by the Brahmins as well as Kayastha Gosains. It is said that the Kayasthas were born from Kshatriya father and Sudra mother. The Kayasthas and Kalita have little difference between them and they come next to the Brahmins in the social hierarchy. The Assamese Hindus do not eat pork, beef and chicken. A few lower-caste Assamese eat pork. They do not like dry fish. Some of them like rice-beer, wine, etc. They prefer ***khar*** made cooked foods. They eat papaya, gourd, cucumber, *mati-ma (maskalai dal)*, gram, *Boal* fish, unboiled milk curds, etc. They drink unboiled milk. They do not consume much chillies. They prefer ***papad***, snacks made of ***atta*** or ***maida*** to milk-made sweets. Most of the time they chew raw areca-nuts and betel leaves with lime. They like tea very much. Bathing is compulsory for a lady before entering the kitchen to cook. During menstruation a wife is not allowed to cook. She is prohibited from touching water or cooked food and is treated as untouchable. But this custom is slowly disappearing among modern, educated, urban women. Early in the morning they sweep their courtyard. *Bargeet, Kirtan Ghosa, Oja-puli, nam-ghosa,* etc., are their music in *Satras*.

They cremate the dead bodies.The Brahmins purify themselves by performing post-funeral *shraddha* (death rite) on the eleventh day of the death. All of them observe yearly death rite, *shraddha* (*basarekia/batsariki*) at the end of every year.

54. Bengali Community:—The Bengalis are scattered all over Assam, West Bengal, Tripura, Meghalaya and Bangladesh. In Assam they are mainly found in Barak valley districts, Dhubri, Goalpara, Sonitpur, Dibrugarh and Tinsukia districts. They speak the Bengali language.

All the four groups of castes are found among them. These are—*Brahmin* (priest), *Kshatriya* (warrior), *Vaishya* (merchant, cultivator), and *Sudra* (menial and labourer) and it is said that they are born respectively from the mouth, arms, thighs and feet of Brahma. They have a number of *gotras* namely—Bharadwaja, Gautama, Kaushika, Kashyapa, Modgulla or Modhukulya, Parasar, Dhanvantari, Shakti, etc. *Durga Puja* is their main festival. They celebrate other festivals also. The women wear *saree* with blouse. The young girls wear frock, midi, maxi, salwar, etc. Men wear pants, shirt, *pyjama, genji, lungi, fatua (nima), dhoti*, etc. Women like ornaments. They generally follow endogamy. Marriages are mainly arranged by negotiation (fire sacrifice in ***hom***), love marriage (civil marriage in a court), intercaste marriage, son-in-law-of-the-house (*ghar jamai*), etc.

In some castes an elderly lady puts a drop of honey in the mouth of a new-born baby soon after the birth in the belief that the baby will grow up as sweet as honey. Birth purification is observed on the seventh and eleventh days after the birth of a child. The mother is considered impure up to this period. The family gives names to a child on *Annaprasan* (rice-giving ceremony) day which is performed during third to ninth month. *Upanayana* is performed for a Brahmin boy to put the holy thread (*logun*) and to teach the *gayatri mantra*.Brahmin titles are—Banerjee (Bandopadhya), Chatterji (Chattopadhaya), Bhattacharjee, Chakraborty, Goswami, etc. The *Baidya* (or physician) caste is said to be lower in position in Sylhet (Bangladesh) who generally do not intermarry with the Kayastha caste like the Sylheti *Baidyas*. The Baidyas claim to be the descendants of Aswini Kumar, the physician of heaven, and a Brahmin female. In social rank, they appear to be slightly superior to the Kayasthas. H.H. Risley treats the *Halwa Das* of Bengal as a sub-caste of Kaibarta. Their position is much higher than that of the ordinary Kaibarta. They claim to be the Sudras or Kayasthas. Das and Kaibarta are mentioned in *Manusanghita* as alternative designations of the same people. The occupation of fishing is assigned to the ordinary Kaibartas, by *Manu.*

The Hindu Bengalis do not eat pork, beef and chicken. Barak valley Bengalis favour dried fish. Most of them do not like to drink rice-beer, wine, etc. They like milk-made sweets very much. Some of them chew dry *supari* (areca nuts) and betel leaves with lime, etc. They like drinking tea. Bathing is compulsory for all before entering the *puja-ghar* to worship. Every morning their ladies have to sweep all the rooms. *Bhajans, Rabindra Sangeet, Nazrulgeet, adhunik* songs are sung by them.

They cremate their dead. Eleven days or thirty days *asuj* (impure) is observed by the Brahmins and Kayasthas respectively. After one year, they observe annual death-rite (*batsariki*) either in *Kamakhya* temple or in their houses.They give *pindi* in Puri (Orissa).

55. Bihari Community:—They are the largest group among the Hindi-speaking population in Assam. They are mainly labourers, rickshaw—pullers, *thelawala*, porter, brick-maker, earth-filler, mason, electric mistry, etc. Some of them run small hotels, grocery, and *pan*-shops, vegetable and fruit shops. A few of them are working as sweepers, etc. Some of them are professionals, teachers, etc., in Assam. They are scattered all over Assam. They migrated mainly from Bihar (Hazaribagh, Muzaffarpur, Boishali, Deoghar, Chhapra, Samastipur, Darbhanga, Katihar, Purnia, etc.).

Some of the Bihari Brahmins do not eat non-vegetarian items. They prefer *chapati* to rice. Low-caste Biharis eat fish, meat, egg, etc., and prefer pork meat. But, they do not eat beef except for the Bihari Muslims, who do not eat pork. The Bihari titles are—Singh, Sharma, Jadav, Rai, Chowdhury, Das, Prasad, Tewari, Jha, Kumar, etc. They worship Durga, Lakshmi, etc., and observe specially *Chat Mai Puja.*

They have exogamous clans. Two types of marriages are in vogue *viz.* marriage by negotiation and love marriage. They are monogamous and prefer joint family. In earlier days the low-caste people used to get their daughters married before the attainment of puberty. It was also observed in case of sons. Again it is observed in a few cases, that the bride is elder than the groom. In earlier days, the low-caste Bihari people had to kill pork to eat by driving out the pig from sty then hunt it with stick and spear.

They cremate their dead except the Muslim Biharis who bury their dead. A few low-caste Hindus in earlier days used to bring "criers" for mourning people of the within seven to eleven days after the death. Most of the people of the same clan of the area shave their heads as a symbol of mourning.

56. Marwari Community:—The Marwari traders migrated long back from North Bengal into Assam. They emerged very strong in trade and commerce in Assam. From the westernmost Goalpara district to the easternmost small town of Sadiya, the Marwaris established their supremacy in trade and business (M. Hussain, 1993:265). They are now scattered all over Assam, specially in Dibrugarh, Tinsukia, Dhubri, Goalpara, Kamrup districts. They migrated to Assam from Rajasthan, Haryana, Punjab, U.P., Delhi, etc. The *Agarwalla* family of Tezpur has uplifted modern Assamese literature and culture. Haribilas Agarwalla (1842-1916), and his son Chandra Kumar Agarwalla helped in making Assam a culturally rich State in late nineteenth century and early twentieth century respectively. Jyoti Prasad Agarwalla (1903-51), of the same family is one of the famous Assamese poet, music composer, freedom fighter, etc. The Marwari titles are—Agarwalla, Bajaj, Birla, Gupta, Jain, Dalmia, Goenka, Jalan, Kanoi, Tata, Bajratia, etc.

They do not eat fish, meat, egg, etc. They are followers of *Jain* religion. The *Jains* are of two sects—*Digambara* and *Swetambara.* The former means "sky-clad" and Swetambara means 'clothed in white'. Yellow garments are now adopted by the Digambara. They have *Yati* who reads and explains the sacred books to the crowd of *Sravakas* or Jain laymen in the mornings and evenings, such functions being known as *Sandhya.* There is very little to distinguish them from ordinary Hindus. Diwali marks the commencement of new year and Lakshmi, the goddess of fortune is worshipped. The wedding ceremonies are generally simple. Their boys use the sacred thread. This thread is renewed annually at the time of the full moon of *Bhado* (August). Before this, a fast is observed for *Anant Nath*, the fourteenth *Tirthankara.*

The Assamese Marwaris ran shops on tea plantations and financed the tea planters by means of the *hundis* used for remittances to and from Calcutta (Thomas A.Timberg, 1978:199). "Almost the entire internal trade, the procurement of such export goods as rubber, cotton, long pepper, silk, etc., and the distribution of various manufactured goods were in the hands of the Marwari community right from the beginning of British rule". (Amalendu Guha, 1969: 572).

They cremate their dead. They do not observe the *shraddha* ceremony like the Hindus.

57. Nepali Community:—The Brahmin, Chhetri, and Gurung population of Nepal have been in larger numbers than any other community in Assam. Magar and Newar are comparatively lesser in numbers. Some prefer to call them *Gurkha* rather than Nepali. They have several castes *viz.* Thakuri, Chhetri, Rana, Damai, Sarki, Kami, Sunar, Sanyashi, Gharti, etc. They have several *gotras.* They came to Assam mostly with the Gorkha Regiment. Now, they are scattered all over Assam and the neighbouring States.

The status of the Nepalis in India has been diminishing both legally and sociologically. There is a distinction between (1) the Nepalis of Nepal; and (2) the Indian Nepalis, that is, the people of Nepali origin living in India for a reasonably long period of time and participating in the socio-economic and political processes in India. The second group of Nepalis has been experiencing the process of assimilation, of course, in uneven degrees, depending on the demography, place and areas of their residence in India. Though technically Nepal is a foreign country, the Nepalis were never treated as foreign nationals in India. So was the status of the Indians in Nepal. The ongoing trends found manifestation formally in the Indo-Nepal Friendship Treaty of 1950, the Tripartite Delhi Agreement of 1951, and the revised Indo-Nepal Agreement of 1956. Therefore, a Nepali can come to India without a passport and visa, and an Indian can similarly go to Nepal without a passport and visa. (M.Hussain, 1993:254).

The Nepali titles are—Sharma, Nepali, Thakuri, Gurung, Thapa, Chettri, Rana, Sunar, etc. Brahmins are the highest in the caste hierarchy along with Chhetris. Nepali, an Indo-Aryan language, is their mother tongue. The progeny of a Brahmin and a *Khasi* hill woman was referred to as *Khatri*. The term Khatri is a corrupt word of the Sanskrit form Kshatriya-Kshatri. Their occupation is farming, selling cow-milk, civil and military services, porter, etc. Some Brahmins act as family priests of the Nepalese. Marriage among the Brahmims and the Chhetris is, as a rule, monogamous; yet a few cases of polygamy are found. Many Brahmin girls marry at an early age while the Chhetri girls marry only when they reach a mature age. A relative acts as a middleman *(lami)* in marriage negotiations. They worship gods and goddesses. Dashain or Durga uja is the most important festival. *Tihar* is another festival which is celebrated with merriment. They cremate their dead on the bank of river. Mourning is observed for thirteen days by all members of the family and relatives.

58. Sikh Community:—"There were small groups following Sikhism and Buddhism in Assam. Though they were not a very large group, they added to the variety in demographic composition and richness of culture". (M.Hussain, 1993:30). They are scattered all over Assam specially in Nagaon district. Some of them have married Assamese girls and speak Assamese. They follow the Assamese culture and have been staying in Assam for the last three to four generations. The term *"Sikh"* means "disciple". They depend upon their spiritual teachers or "gurus" in religious matters. Sikhism was founded by Khatri saint Guru Nanak in fifteenth century. But Nanak was a religious reformer like Kabir, Ramananda and others. He preached the unity of God, the abolition of idols and disregard for caste distinctions. Guru Govind Singh (1675-1708) preached the *Khalsa* (the pure). He propounded the equality of all men who joined him and named it *pahul* (gate) and *prasad* (communion) was taken by four castes from one dish. The higher castes deserted him. He advised his followers to have unshare hair, blue dress, title of Singh with two-edged dagger. A true Sikh has five *Kakkas* or K's, i.e., the *kes* or uncut hair and unshaven beard, the *kachha* or short drawers ending above the knees, the *kada* or iron bangle, the *kripan/khanda* or steel knife and the *kanga* or comb. They follow all rules of conduct laid down by Guru Govind Singh, i.e., dress in blue clothes and caps of all sorts, to observe personal cleanliness, especially of hair use ablutions, to eat meat when killed by *jatka* (decapitation), to abstain from using tobaco, never to blow out a flame nor extinguish it with drinking water, to take food by covering the head, pray and recite passages of the *Granth* in every morning and evening before having meals, reverence to cow, not to worship saints and idols and to avoid mosque and temple and worship to only one God, neglecting Brahmins and Mullas, and their scriptures, teachings, rites and religious symbols. Their titles are—Singh, Jaswal, Bhalla, Gill, etc.

They are mainly truck drivers and three-wheeler drivers in Assam. Some of them are businessmen, employed in government serivce, etc. They cremate their dead.

59. South Indian Community:—Before the Kiratas, the Dravidians and the Austrics were the only people living in North-East India. Dravidian features of dolicocephalic are also found among some people of this area. Dravidians lived here around tenth to second century B.C. Some south Indian communities are now scattered in Assam. They are mainly in government service, teachers of Convent Schools, businessmen, etc. They speak a language with distinct Dravidian affinity. *Dravidian* is the name assigned to the group of languages which include Tamil, Telegu, Khond and Oraon. The Dravidians have prominent cheekbones, long head; more hair with black colour and thick lips.

Most of them follow Hindu religion. A few of them are Christians and Muslims. The Brahmins do not eat non-vegetarian items except Christians and the Muslims. Most of them like vegetables specially sour tasting items like lemons, tomatoes, milk-curd, etc. They prefer to eat *sambar, dhosa, idli.* The men wear *lungi,* a type of plain cloth at home and pants, shirt etc., while going out. Their women wear saree. Their titles are Rao, Aiyappan, Subramanium, Padmanabha, Srinivas, Rajan, Pillai, Annapurna, Mariamma, Chittaranjan, etc.

They cremate their dead except the Christians and the Muslims who bury the dead bodies.

SHARAI

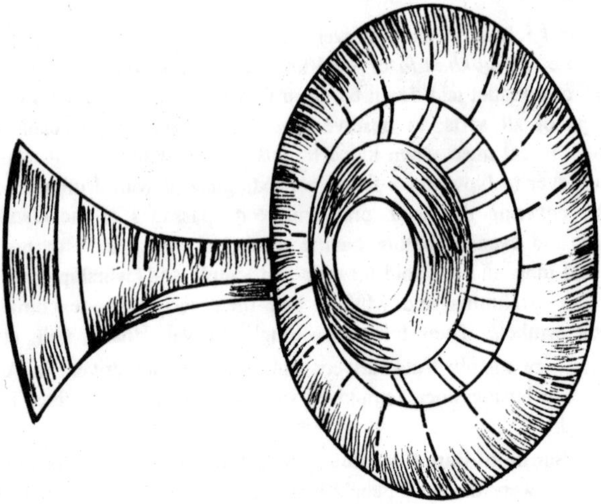

SHARAI

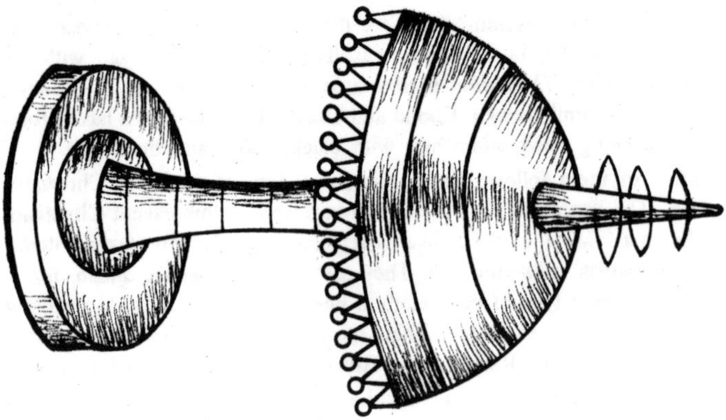

BATA

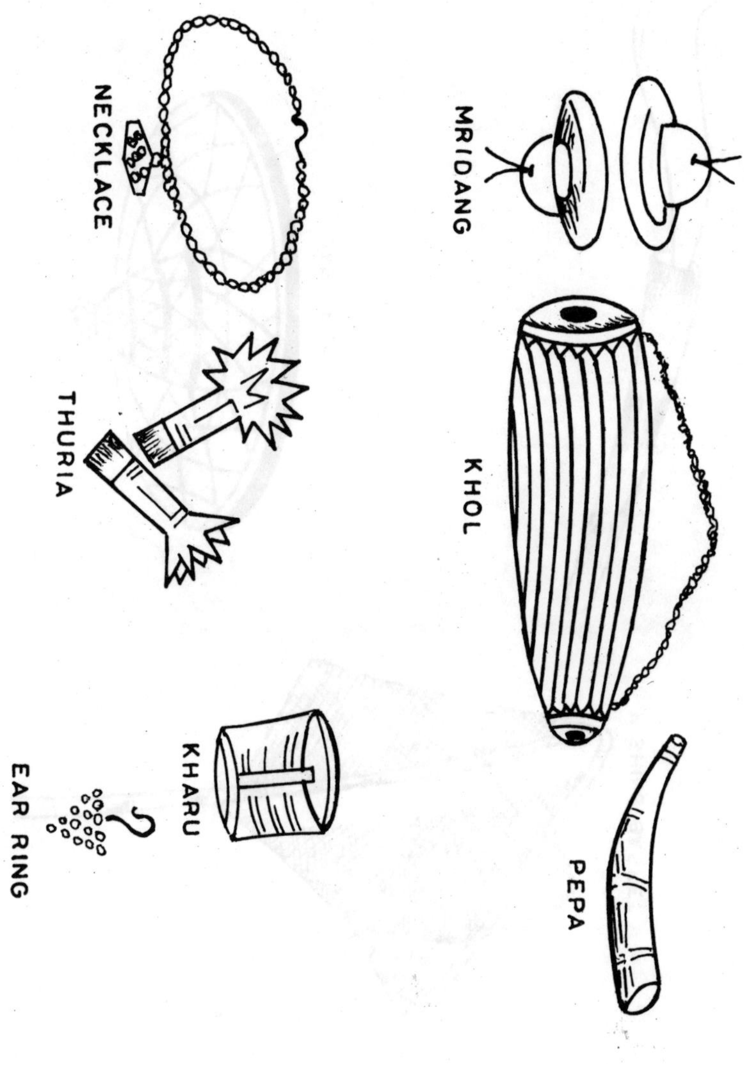
NECKLACE
MRIDANG
THURIA
KHOL
KHARU
EAR RING
PEPA

DAO

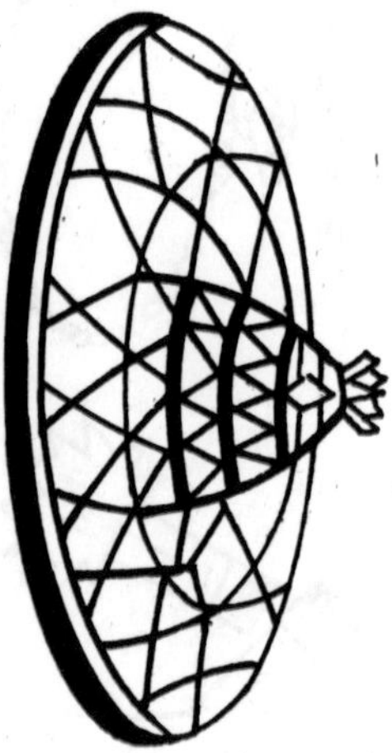

JAPI (HAT)

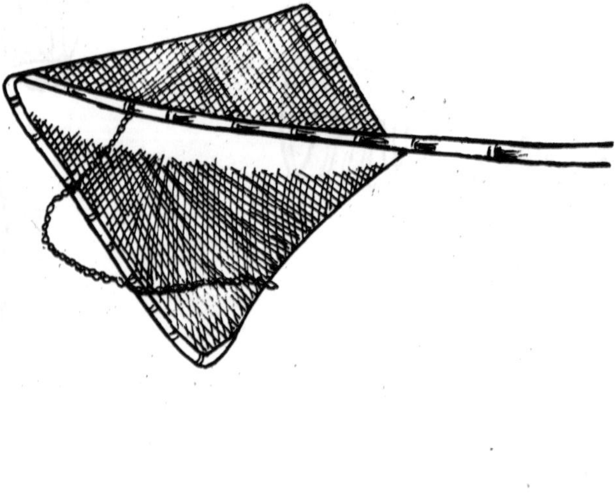

FISHING BASKET

PART-II (A)

FULL BIBLIOGRAPHY OF CULTURAL, SOCIAL ANTHROPOLOGY AND SOCIOLOGY

1. **Aberystwyth Wales** : 1913 : *Slavery on British Territory:Assam and Burma.* Wales, National Library of Wales of Calvinistic Methodist Archives.

2. **ABIL** : n.d. : *Boro chuti galpa.* Guwahati, Anundoram Borooah Institute of Language, Art & Culture, Assam (*in Assamese*). (18 stories).

3. **Acharya, S.K.** : 1986 : Ethnic aspects of the National Processes in India: Castes, tribes and ethnolinguistic entities. (Contributed to the *Social Scientist. Seminar on the Indian National Movement: Its Political, Social and Ideological Dimensions,* New Delhi).

4. ———— : 1988 : Ethnic Processes in North-Eastern India. *Economic and Political Weekly,* XXIII(21), May 21: 1068-77.

5. **Agnihotri, Malti**: 1972 : The story of Chawngchilhi. *Folklore,* XIII (4), April: 152-55.

6. **Agnihotri, S.K.** : 1974 : The Phakials of Assam. *North-Eastern Research Bulletin, V,* Summer: 36-44.

7. ———— : 1980 : The changing village scene in Assam. *(In) Family, Marriage and Social Change. (Eds.)* S.M. Dubey, P.K. Bordoloi and B.N. Borthakur. New Delhi, Cosmo Pubs.: 139-46.

8. ———— : 1996 : *Phakials and other minor Thai communities of Assam.* Lucknow, S.Kumar & Association.

9. ———— : A note on folklore of the Phakials. *Seminar paper on Traditional Culture and Folklore in North-East India,* 18-19 Nov., Shillong, NEICSSR.

10. **Agnihotri, S.K.** *and* **S.A. Khan** : 1985 : The status of children in Assam. *Social Welfare,* 31(10), Jan. 17-20.

11. **Agrawal, Binod C.** : 1977 : Interaction between tribes and non-tribes. *(In) Tribal Heritage of India, Vol. I: Ethnicity, Identity and Interaction. (Ed.)* by S.C. Dube. New Delhi, Vikas Publishing House: 123-28.

12. **Ahmad, Ramesh** : 1990 : Asomia jatiya utsav Bihu ek krishi utsav hain. (Translated into Hindi by Arvind Kr. Sharma). *Pur. Pra. (Lohit Bharati).* April 14: 3(1-6).

13. **AIRTSC** : 1994: *The Socio-Economic conditions of the Kaibartas of Assam:* (A case study). Guwahati, Assam Inst. Res. for Tribes and Scheduled Castes.

14. **Alam, Ajhar** : 1995 : Ambubachi Mela ka pouranik mahatta *(in H.). Pur. Pra.,* June 21: 5(1-6).

15. **Ali, A.N.M. Irshad** : 1973 : Adoption among the Boro-Kachari. *Social Welfare,* 20(8), Nov.: 17-28.

16 **Ali, A.N.M. Irshad** : 1974 : Occupational change through generations among the Assamese Muslims. *(In) Contemporary Anthropological Research in North-East India. (Ed.)* B.M. Das. Dibrugarh, Dibrugarh University: 93-100 (This is also *Bulletin of Anthropological Deptt.*, Dibrugarh University, Vol. III, 1974).

17. ———————— : *Social relations among the Assamese Muslims in rural and urban situation.* Unpublished Ph.D. Thesis, Deptt. of Anthropological, Gauhati University.

18. ———— : 1975 : Hindu-Muslim relations in an urban setting of Assam. *The North Eastern Research Bulletin*, VI, Summer: 16-29.

19. ———— : 1976 : Kinship and marriage among the Assamese Muslims. *(In) Family, Kinship and Marriage among Muslims in India. (Ed.)* by Imtiaz Ahmad. New Delhi, Manohar Book Service: 1-23.

20. ———————— : Social Change among the Assamese Muslims. *Proceedings of a Seminar on Social Change in North-East India,* organised by the Deptt. of Anthropology, Dibrugarh University, March 26-27.

21. ———— : 1977 : Asamiya Musalmanar Sanskriti. *Asam Sahitya Sabha Patrika*, 34(4): 67 (*in Assamese*).

22. ———————— : Marriage among the Assamese Muslims. *(In) North-East India: A Sociological Study. (Ed.)* by S.M. Dubey. New Delhi, Concept Publishing Company: 111-24.

23. ———— : 1978 : Marriage among the Assamese Muslims. *(In) North-East India: A Sociological Study. (Ed.)* by S.M. Dubey. Delhi, Concept Publishing Company: 111-24.

24. ———————— : Immigration and assimilation: The case of the immigrant Muslims in Assam. *(In) Cultural and Biological Adaptability of Man with special reference to North-East India. (Eds.)* A.C. Bhagabati and R.K. Kar. Dibrugarh, Dibrugarh University: 65-72 (This is also *Bulletin of Deptt. of Anthropology,* Vol. 6, 1977).

25. ———— : 1979 : Social groups among the Assamese Muslims. *Proceedings Section of Anthropology, and Archaeology, Annual Session, Indian Science Congress, 66th Session*, Hyderabad.

26. ———————— : Hindu Muslim relations in Assam. *Man in India* 59(4), Oct.-Dec.: 361-82.

27. **Ali, A.N.M. Irshad** : 1981 : Family and kinship in an urban Assamese Muslim community. *Bulletin Deptt. of Anthropology,* Dibrugarh, Dibrugarh University, Vols. 7-8 (1978-79): 151-61.

28. **Ali, A.N.M. Irshad** : 1982 : Some aspects of social relations in a semi urban Assamese Muslim community. *Bull. Deptt. of Anthropology,* Dibrugarh, Dibrugarh University, 9 (1980): 1-13.

29. ———— : 1985 : Influence of indigenous folk traditions on the Assamese Muslims. *Assam Academy Review.*

30. ———— : Variation in the culture of the Assamese Muslims. *(In) Anthropological Perspectives on North-East India.* Dibrugarh, Dibrugarh University: 1-8 (This is also *Bulletin Deptt. of Anthropology, Dibrugarh University,* Vol. X, 1981).

31. ———— : 1986 : Asamat Islam Dharmar Bistar: Asamiya Musalman Janasankhyar Gathan Aru Sanskritar Sangmishran. *(In) Asamar Manuh. (Ed.)* by B.M. Das. Jorhat, Asam Sahitya Sabha: 91-106 (in Assamese).

32. ———— : 1992 : Islam in tribal societies of North-East India: Some aspects of the process of cultural contact. *Bulletin Deptt. of Anthropology,* Gauhati University, Vol. VI, March: 46-52.

33. ———— : 1994 : Social groups among the Assamese Muslims. *Bulletin Anthropology Deptt.,* Gauhati University, VIII: 6-13.

34. **Ali, A.N.M. Irshad** *and* **A.C. Bhagabati** : 1971 : Kinship and marriage in a rural Assamese Muslim community. *Jour. Assam Science Society,* XIV (1): 27-32.

35. ———— : 1972 : Hindu Muslim relations in an Assamese village. *Bulletin Deptt. of Anthropology,* Guwahati, Gauhati University, I, Dec.: 69-80.

36. **Ali, A.N.M. Irshad** *and* **Birinchi K. Medhi** : 1993 : Sikhism in an Assamese village. *Bull. Deptt. of Anthropology,* Gauhati Univ., VIII: 1-11.

37. ———— : 1993 : The Assamese Sikhs: An ethnographic profile. *Bulletin Deptt. of Anthropology,* Dibrugarh University, 20-21 (1911-92): 1-11.

38. ———— : The Assamese Sikhs: Profile of a minuscale community. *(In) Profile of India. (Ed.)* by S.B. Roy and A.K. Ghosh. New Delhi, Inter India Pub.: 277-57.

39. **Ali, A.S.M. Idrish** : 1985 : Tiwa and Lalung: Two names of a tribe and the folklore connected with them. *(In) Folklore, in North-East India. (Ed.)* by Soumen Sen. Delhi, Omsons Publishing: pp. 113-20.

40. **Ali, Meer Hasan** : 1832 : *Observations on the Musalmans of India: Description of their manners, customs, habits and religious*

opinions made during twelve years residence in their immediate society. London, Parbury, Allen and Co. (*2 vols*).

41. **Ali, M. Ibrahim** : 1975 : Asamiya Musalmanar Samaj Sanskritiloi Abadan. *Souvenir (Ed.)* by Habibul Haque (*in Assamese*).

42. **Ali, Rahmat** : 1932 : Contribution a l' etude du Probleme Hindou Musulman. *Revue des Etudes Islamiques,* Vol. 6: 269-414.

43. **Ali, Syed Mohammed Ameer** : 1892 : *The Moslem festivities.* Calcutta. Printed and Published for the Author and Proprietor by Messrs H.C. Gangooly and Co., 76p.

44. **Ali, Tafazzul** : 1979 : The enchanted drums. *Folklore,* 20(11), Nov.: 264-69.

45. **All Assam Koch Association** : 1989 : *Koch aru Rajbonshi ekey jati nohai* (*in Assamese*). Gopalpur (Dhubri), All Assam Koch Association.

46. **All Assam Tiwa Yuva-Chatra Sanmilan (Ed.)** : 1975 : Tiwa sampradayar parichaya. Jorhat, *Asam Sahitya Sabha,* 115p (*in Assamese*).

47. **All India Handicrafts Board** : 1958 : *Handicrafts of Assam.* New Delhi, All India Handicrafts Board, 8 p.

48. **Amarnath** : 1990 : Boro sanskriti par sankat *(in Hindi). Pur. Pra. (Lohit Bharati),* July 9: I(1-8).

49. **Amrita Bazar Patrika** : 1985 : Tai Ahoms show signs of socio-cultural revivalism. *Amrita Bazar Patrika,* Feb. 12 : 12 (Annual Ritual: Mey-Dam-Mey-Fi-Ahom).

50. ——————— : Bonded labour still remains in N-E region. Nov. 13: 9.

51. ———— : 1986 : Plight of Reang tribals in Assam. April 24: 7(1-4).

52. ——————— : Bihu: A unifying force. April 26: 7(1-4).

53. ———— : 1987 : Wild wealth of North Cachar Hills remains untapped. Aug. 9: 7(2-4) (About Dimasa, Karbis, Khelmas).

54. ———— : 1988 : Recognition of 'Chutiyas' as scheduled tribes. Nov. 13: 7(3).

55. ———— : 1989 : Life of Lalung tribe in Assam. March 21: 7 (1-4).

56. ——————— : Karbis: A tribe of N.E. Assam. April 1: 7(2-5).

57. **Anam, Nazmeen** : 1895 : A Collection of Kachari Folk Tales and Rhymes. *(In) Kachari Grammar* by S. Endle. Shillong, Assam Secretariat Printing Office (Supplement), 61p.

58. ——————— : A Collection of Kachari Folk Tales and Rhymes, Shillong, Assam Secretarial Record Room, No. Home B, 1097/ 1116-1895.

59. ————— : 1896 : Kachari Folk Tales. *Jour. of the Buddhist Text Society*, 4, Pt. I, Appendix-III: 17-36.

60. ————— : 1910 : Bodos. *(In) Encyclopaedia of Religion and Ethics, Vol. 2. (Ed.)* by James Hastings. Edinburg, T & T Clark (Reprinted in 1921 from London again in 1973 from New York): 753-55.

61. ————— : 1994 : The Karbi Ramayana. *Assam Tribune (Sunday Reading)*, Nov. 13: IV (4-8).

62. ————— : 1995 : The dying art of Dhubri. *Sentinel*, June 4: 4(3-8) (Sola art, masks of goddess, pith craft).

63. ——————— : The Rengmas of Karbi Anglong. *Sentinel*, Oct. 15: I (1-8); Oct. 22: 4 (1-8).

64. **Anand, Manoj** : 1994 : Satras face extinction due to Assam govt's lackadaisical attitude. *Shillong Times*, Jan. 19: 1(2-8).

65. **Anand, Mulk Raj** : 1960 : Dances of Assam. *March of India*, 12(5), May: 23.

66. **Anderson, J.D.** : 1911 : *The Kacharis*. London, Macmillan & Co.

67. **Anonymous** : 1827 : Notice Dur Divers Peuples de l'Assam et des Contrees Voisines. *Nouvelles Annales des Voyages*, 33: 228-38.

68. ————— : 1847 : *A Sketch of Assam: With some account of the Hill Tribes*. London, Smith Elder and Co., 220p.

69. ————— : 1854 : Assamese matters, past and present. *Calcutta Review*. 23: 38-65 (Regarding Social Organisation and Religion).

70. ————— : 1872 : Kaibarta. *(In) Census of India 1871. Report, Vol. V: Dacca Division*, 55p.

71. ————— : 1881 : Rabhas, Hajongs, Mech. *(In) Census of India 1881, Report, Assam*, 73p.

72. ——————— : Kachari. *(In) Census of India 1881 Report, Assam*: 67-71.

73. ————— : 1891 : Poliyas, Koch. *(In) Census of India 1891, Bhagalpur Division, Purnia District*. Patna, Govt. Press: 57.

74. **Anonymous** : 1891 : Koch. *(In) Census of India 1891, Presidency Division, Murshidabad District,* 53p.

75. ——————— : Koch. *(In) District Census Reports, 1891, Rajshahi Division, Patna District,* 49p.

76. ——————— : *Koches. (In) District Census Report, 1891, Rajshahi Division, Rangpur District,* 10p.

77. ——————— : Kewat. *(In) District Census Report, 1891, Orissa Division, Cuttack District,* 13p.

78. ——————— : Kewats. *(In) District Census Report, 1891, Patna Division, Darbhanga District,* 154p.

79. ——————— : Kaibarta. *(In) District Census Report, 1891, Rajshahi Division. Patna District,* 146p.

80. ——————— : Kaibartas. *(In) District Census Report, 1891, Rajshahi Division, Rangpur District,* 111p.

81. ———— : 1897 : Ciamowie-Wymierajacy Lud W Assamie. *Missye Katolickie* (Kracau), Vol. 16: 119-26, 160-65, 182-87, 210-17.

82. ———— : 1924 : ***Handbook of Castes and Tribes Employed in tea estates in North-East India.*** Calcutta, Tea Districts Labour Association, 360p.

83. ———— : 1925 : L'Assam. *Nouv. Ann.Voyages,* Vol. 26: 309-16.

84. ———— : 1956 : ***Brochure of Cultural Research Institute, West Bengal.*** Calcutta, Cultural Research Institute (Mech. etc.).

85. ———— : 1957 : Traditional arts and crafts: Tripura, Manipur and Assam. ***Bulletin of the Institute of Traditional Cultures*** (Madras): 200-05.

86. ———— : 1958 : The Hill Tribes of Assam. *Modern Review,* Vol. 103(3), March: 245.

87. ———— : 1961 : Aided institutions work for tribal welfare in Assam. *Social Welfare,* 8(9), Dec.: 27.

88. ———— : 1965 : Two marriage songs from an Assamese, *Folklore,* 6: 27.

89. **Anthropological Society** : 1988 : Symposium on Anthropological perspectives on the tribes of Assam Hills, *23rd Annual Session. Anthropological Society of North-East India, Feb. 26-28,* Hamren (Karbi Anglong District), organised by Gau. Univ. Anthropology Deptt.

90. **Aonok, S.W.** : 1956 : Morung organisation among the Mikir Nagas. *Vanyajati*, 4(2).

91. **Archer, Mildred** : 1948 : Book Review: Dalton's Descriptive Ethnology of Bengal. *Man in India*, 28: 170-71.

92. **Arkell, A.J.** : 1935 : Some Tuareg Ornaments and their connection with India. *Jour. Royal Anthropology Inst.*, 65: 297-306.

93. **Arunodoi** : 1857 : Islam Dharma. *Arunodoi*, Vol. 12 (2), Feb. (*in Assamese*).

94. **Asam Sahitya Sabha** : n.d. : *Asamar Ojapali* (*in Assamese*). Jorhat.

95. ——————— : *Rava Sadhu* (*in Assamese*). Jorhat, A.S.S.

96. ——————— : *Boro Sadhu; Deuri Sadhu; Sonowal Sadhu* (*in Assamese*). Jorhat, A.S.S.

97. ——————— : *A few aspects of Assamese literature and culture*. Jorhat, 76p.

98. ——————— : *Tradition and style*. Jorhat, 28p.

99. ——————— : *Madhav Kandali Ramayanar Bhasha* (*in Assamese*). Jorhat, 23p.

100. ——————— : *Mayong anchalar lok-sanskriti* (*in Assamese*). Jorhat, 35p.

101. ——————— : *Asamar tatshal* (*in Assamese*). Jorhat, 25p. (Weaving).

102. ——————— : *Asamar badya jantra* (*in Assamese*). Jorhat, 28p. (Musical instruments).

103. **Ashiana, Abhay** : 1996 : Surya ka Makar men jana Makar Sankranti hai. *Purbanchal Prahari*, Jan. 14: 5 (1-6) (*in Hindi*).

104. **Assam, Economic** *and* **Statistics** : 1962 : *Deptt., Report on the socio-economic survey of the Chaudang community in the Jorhat sub-division*. Shillong, Assam Economics and Statistics, Dec., 43p.

105. **Assam Information** : 1990 : Songs and dances of Assam. *Assam Information* XXXXI, Feb.: 30-1.

106. **Assam Quarterly** : 1961 : The Bohag Bihu. 1(2), April: 1-5.

107. ——————— : Tribal Wisdom: Kachari Folk Tales. 1(2), April: 70-2.

108. ——————— : 1962 : Asam Sahitya Sabha; Cultural notes on literature. II(4), Oct.: 57-59.

109. **Assam Research Society** : 1984 : Readings in the history and culture of Assam (A collection of articles on indological topics from *Jour. Assam Research Society* since 1933), Guwahati.

110. **Assam Sahitya Sabha** : 1980 : *Assam and Assamese mind: A Collection of Essays.* Gauhati, Assam Sahitya Sabha.

111. **Assam Tribune** : 1982 : Karbi role in Assamese culture stressed. April 25: 1 and 3.

112. ———— : 1985 : Different ethnic groups of Assam. March 29: 4(2).

113. ———— : Symposium on Kamrupi folk literature, held on May 17. May 26: 5(4).

114. ———— : Editorial: Bihu Musings. April 14: 4(1-2).

115. ———— : First Karbi Geeta released. Nov. 22: 3(3).

116. ———— : 1987 : Me-Dam-Me-Fi at Talatalghar. Feb. 14: 5(2) (Tai Ahom).

117. ———— : Doul Yatra at Barpeta. March 22: 7(5) (Four days festival at Barpeta).

118. ———— : Bihu troupe for USSR. *Assam Tribune*, June 10: 1(3), 8(6).

119. ———— : Review of "Bhaona": Ritual play of Assam by Maheswar *Neog.* June 19: 4 (7-8).

120. ———— : Govt. urged to declare Assam as "Tribal Land", June 25: 5(3-4).

121. ———— : Significance of Krishna's Ras Lila. Nov. 12: 5(3).

122. ———— : 1988 : Editorial: Magh Bihu. Jan. 14: 4(1-2).

123. ———— : Ali-Aye-Ligang: A festival of Mishings. Feb. 15: 4(7-8).

124. ———— : Report on Backlog of posts for the ST and SCs in Assam. March 27.

125. ———— : Editorial: Thoughts on Bohag Bihu. April 13: 4(1-2).

126. ———— : Untouchability unknown to Assamese Society. Aug. 7: 2(7-8).

127. ———— : 1989 : Plea for solidarity of plain tribals. Jan. 19: 1(7-8) 6(6) (Lalung).

128. ———— : Demand to include Muslim fishermen in SC list rejected. May 7: 3(3) (Cachar, Karimganj OBC).

129. **Assam Tribune** : 1989 : Tiwas inclusion in 6th schedule demanded. Sept. 8: 6(7-8).

130. ———————— : Ras festival at Palasbari. Nov. 16: 3(5).

131. ———————— : Ras festival at Tihu. Nov. 17: 3(2).

132. ———————— : 1990 : Me-Dam-Me-Fee celebrated. Feb. 8: 5(4).

133. ———————— : Hojai Round Up: Holy bath by Dimasa people. March 2: 6(3-4).

134. ———————— : Land allotted to Mishing Kebang. March 9: 6(5) (Mishing Murong-Ghar).

135. ———————— : Dol Jatra celebrated at Barpeta. March 17: 7(1-3).

136. ———————— : Manasa puja at Ranakuchi from March 28. March 22: 5(6) (Tihu, Assam).

137. ———————— : Inclusion of Kock Rajbonshis in ST list urged. April 10: 5(1-2).

138. ———————— : Sati Sadhani utsav observed. May 1: 2(7-8) (Chutiya Rani).

139. ———————— : First tribal community centre opened. May 24: 3(4-5) (Guwahati).

140. ———————— : Tiwas want ST status. June 28: 6(4) (Lalung).

141. ———————— : Manasa Puja on July 12. July 7: 5(4) (Ugratara temple at Uzan Bazar Jorpukhuri, Guwahati).

142. ———————— : Inclusion of Koch-Rajbonshis in SC and ST list demanded. July 7: 5(5-8).

143. ———————— : Cultural awakening in North Cachar Hills. Aug. 18: 5(3-5). (Dimasa, Karbi, etc.).

144. ———————— : Plea to include Chutiyas in Plains ST list. Sept. 12 : 3(4-5).

145. ———————— : End of traditional boat-race at Barpeta. Sept. 24: 3(4-5) (Cultural tradition).

146. ———————— : Sankar Janmotsav at Barpeta. Oct. 3: 5(3-4) (542nd Birth Anniversary).

147. ———————— : Asom Satra Sangha meet opens. Nov. 10: 1(7) 2(8).

148. ———————— : Diamond Jubilee of Kamrupiya Sanatan Dharma Mondolee. Nov. 12: 3(4) (Tezpur).

149. **Assam Tribune** : 1989 : Seminar on Devadasi Culture. Nov. 14: 5(4-6) (Hajo).

150. ———————— : Kuki chavang-kut festival celebrated. Nov. 15: 5(5-7) (Hoflong, Assam).

151. ———— : 1991 : Bhogali Bihu gaiety missing. Jan. 13: 1(5-7) 8(5-6).

152. ———————— : Editorial: Magh Bihu. Jan. 13: 4(1-2).

153. ———————— : 50 Years Ago: Tribals and ex-labourers, protested against exclusion from Hindu fold. (*Assam Tribune*, Oct. 10, 1941). March 24: 4(1-2) (Kachari and ex-tea garden labourer of Tezpur).

154: ———————— : Manasa image installed. April 2: 5(4-5) (Palasbari).

155. ———————— : A cultural extravaganza. Sept. 22: 4(3-6).

156. ———————— : Plea to include in ST list. Nov. 7: 3(3) (Koch Rajbonshi of Assam).

157. ———————— : In quest of a new Assamese society. Nov. 9: 4(3-8) (Barak Valley, Bodo).

158. ———— : 1992 : Manikut utsav at Hajo. Jan. 17: 8(6).

159. ———————— : Sati Sadhani utsav celebrated. May 7: 5(5-6). (Sibsagar Dist. Chutia Jati Sanmelan).

160. ———————— : Preservation of Hajong culture demanded. May 23: 5(1-2).

161. ———————— : Inclusion of Bodos, Tiwas in Hills list urged. Aug. 4: 3(3).

162. ———— : 1993 : Editorial: Salani Bihu. Jan. 13: 4(1-2) (Bhogali Bihu).

163. ———————— : Mishing festival celebrated. Feb. 18: 1(5) 2(6).

164. ———————— : Doul festival celebrated at Barpeta Satra. March 14: 3(1-4).

165. ———————— : Inclusion of Matak-Moran in 6th Schedule demanded. May 8: 5(6-8).

166. ———————— : A sad profile of Mayong. May 22: 5(4) (Mayong, an ancient place of Assam, popular for its spiritual and mystical power which is now about to die).

167. ———— : 1994 : Editorial: Bohag Bihu. April 14: 4(1-2).

168. **Assam Tribune** : 1994 : Call to preserve Chutiya Culture. May 11: 3(5-8). (Marigaon).

169. ————————— : Mishings, Ravas, Tiwas to get autonomy soon. July 2: 1(7-8).

170. ————————— : Ras festival at Palasbari. Nov. 17: 5(1).

171. ——————— : 1995 : Heralding Spring. *(Sunday Reading),* April 9: 1(1-8) (Rongali Bihu).

172. ——————— : 1996 : Magh Bihu musings. *(Sunday Reading),* Jan. 14: III (5-6).

173. ————————— : Bohag Bihu festival. April 14.

174. **Aswini** : 1996 : Assam: A changing culture scape. *Sentinel (Sat. day Fare),* Feb. 3: I (1-8) (Assamese dress, dhuti, mekhela-sadar of pat, muga; food habit, etc.).

175. **Athparia, R.P.** : 1972 : *Marriage system of the Mikir.* Unpublished M.Sc. Dissertation, Anthropology Deptt., Dibrugarh University.

176. ——————— : 1978 : *Customary Laws of the Karbi.* Shillong, Anthropology Surv. India (*Mimeo*).

177. ——————— : 1984 : Karbi. *(In) Tribal Education in India. (Eds.)* by Biman K. Das Gupta and Ajit K. Danda. Calcutta, Anthropology Surv. India: 17-9.

178. ————————— : The Chomangkan: Death ceremony of the Karbis. *Human Science*, 33(3), Sept.: 257-62.

179. ——————— : 1992 : *A study of two interacting political systems among the Karbi in the district of Karbi Anglong and Assam.* Unpub. Ph.D. Thesis, Anthropology Deptt., Dibrugarh Univ.

180. ——————— : 1993 : Reorganisation of the Hill areas of Assam: A study of Karbi Anglong District. *Proceedings of a Seminar on Reorganisation of NEI since 1947*, held on 22-23 Feb., organised by NEICSSR, Shillong (*Mimeo*).

181. ————————— : Amity and development: Some observations among the Karbis. *Procg. of a Seminar on Social Health, Amity and Development*, held on 24-25 March, organised by NEICSSR and Voluntary Health Association, Shillong (*Mimeo*).

182. ——————— : 1996 : Traditional political system: A case study of the Karbis of Assam. *(In) Peoples of North-East India: Anthropological Perspectives. (Ed.)* by Sarthak Sengupta. New Delhi, Gyan Publishing House: 199-220.

183. **Athparia, R.P.** : 1996 : Traditional Institution of the Alongri and Ethnic solidarity among the Karbis, Assam. Paper of *Golden*

Jubilee of Anth. Survey of India, Shillong, 13-14 Sept. '96 *(Ethnic Situation in North East India, Fields & Frontiers).*

184. **Athparia, R.P.** : 1996 : Book Review: Kinship and Family in the North-East. *Jr. NEICSSR,* 20(2), Oct.: 68-70.

185. **Athparia, R.P.** *and* **G.C. Ojah** : 1995 : The problems of economic development among the Hiras of Assam. *(In) Core Problems of the Scheduled Castes of Assam. (Ed.)* by Bimal Kr. Hazarika. Guwahati, AIRTSC: 70-7.

186. **Athparia, R.P.** *and* **M. Buzarbarua** : 1991 : Social and Cultural life of the Mishing of Assam. *Social Research,* 10(2-3): 6-11.

187. **Athparia, R.P.** *and* **N.K. Das** : 1979 : The Karbi and Angami Naga political system: A preliminary compositive analysis. *Procg. of Bio-Cultural Profile of North-East India,* April 26, Anthropology Surv. India, Shillong (*Mimeo*).

188. ———— : 1994 : The Karbi and the Angami Naga Political Systems: A comparative analysis. *(In) Tribal Situation in North-East India. (Ed.)* by Sarthak Sengupta. New Delhi, Inter-India Pub.: 215-21.

189. **Athparia, R.P.** *and* **S. Sengupta** : 1990 : The Hmars of Assam: A Preliminary appraisal on identity orientation. *(In) Nationality, Ethnicity and Cultural Identity in North-East India. (Ed.)* by B. Pakem. New Delhi, Omsons: 187-90.

190. **Bagchi, Tilak** : 1991 : Book Review: Stratification, hierarchy and ethnicity in North-East India. (*Eds.*) by R.K. Bhadra and S.R. Mandal. Delhi, Daya Publishing House, *Man and Life,* 17(3-4), July-Dec.: 183-85.

191. ———— : 1992 : Book Review: Transfer and alienation of tribal land in Assam with special reference to the Karbis of Karbi Anglong District, by B.N. Bordoloi, Western Book Depot, Guwahati, *Man and Life,* 18(1-2), Jan.-June: 101-03.

192. ———— : 1995 : Book Review: Kinship affinity and domestic group: A study among the Mishing of the Brahmaputra valley, by J.S. Bhandari, Gyan Publishing House, New Delhi ix+280pp., 1992. *Man and Life,* 21 (3-4), July-Dec.: 175-76.

193. **Bahadur, K.P.** : 1977 : *Caste, Tribes and Culture of India: Assam.* Delhi, Ess Ess Publishers: 16-8, 27-8, 32, 39, 43, 66.

194. **Baines, Athelstane** : 1976 : *Ethnography (Caste and Tribes).* Delhi, Concept Publishing Comy. (*Reprinted,* 1st Published in India in 1912): 126, 130-32.

195. **Baishya, Alakesh** : 1992 : Bihu: Assam's cultural highpoint.

North Eastern Times, April 14 (*Rongali Bihu Supplement*): IV (1-8) (*Tr.)* into English by Haribhau Joshi.

196. **Baishya, Alakesh** : 1994 : Bihu in a changing scenario. *Assam Tribune*, April 15: 4(3-6) 8(3-4).

197. ―――――― : 1995 : The essence of Assamese culture: Bihu. *Sentinel*, April 8: I(1-8).

198. ―――――――― : Bihu jatiya ekata ka vahak *(Tr.)* by Labanya Goswami. *Pur. Pra.*, April 14: 5(1-6) *(in Hindi)*.

199. ―――――― : 1996 : Folk culture of Assam: Problems and prospects in present day context. *North-East Times (Highpoint, Sunday)*, March 24: (2-8).

200. ―――――――― : Traditional rituals and age old beliefs. *Sentinel, Saturday Fare,* April 13: 1 (1-8) (Bihu).

201. **Baishya, Dinesh** : 1992 : Environment management in folk literature. *Assam Tribune* (*Sunday Reading*), April 26: I(1-8) (Ahom).

202. **Baishya, Hiren** : 1990 : Bihu giton men upama (*in Hindi*). *Pur.Pra.*, April 14: 5(6-8).

203. **Baishya, Paresh** : n.d : *Folk culture of the districts of Kamrup, Nalbari and Barpeta*. Guwahati(?).

204. ―――――― : 1992 : *Asomat Nao-Khelar Parampara (in Assamese)*. Dadara, Manikoot Prakashan.

205. **Baker, E.C.S.** : 1892 : Mikir in North Cachar. *(In) Census Report of Assam*, 1891. Shillong: 254.

206. **Bakht, Humayan** : 1989 : *A Sociological Study of Bodo Movement*, Unpub. M.Phil. Thesis, New Delhi, JNU, School of Social Sciences.

207. **Baldev** : 1986 : Asom me jadu abh vi hai (*in Hindi*). *Vanyajati*. 34(1), Jan.: 11-2.

208. **Balfour, H.** : 1897 : The life history of an Aghori Fakir. *Journal of the Anthropological Institute,* 26: 340-56.

209. ―――――― : 1923 : Welfare of primitive peoples. *Folklore,* March.

210. ―――――― : 1929 : Concerning thunderbolts. *Folklore,* 40: 37-49, 168-72.

211. **Bandopadhyay, Biswanath** : 1961 : Hira potters of Assam. *Man in India*, 41(1), Jan.-March: 25-44.

212. **Bandopadhyay, P.K.** : 1983 : Book Review: The Tai Phakes of Assam, by G.C. Sharma Thakur. B.R. Publishing Corporation, Delhi, 1982, *Jr. NEICSSR*. 7(1), April: 46-7.

213. **Banerjee, A.C.** : 1971 : Sadiya, the headquarter of the Khamtis. *(In) The Tai Khamtis, (Comp.)* by Lila Gogoi. Chowkham(NEFA), Chowkhamoon Gohain (Namsoon): 123.

214. **Banerjee, Biswanath** : 1968 : Relation between environment and culture among some Indian Primitive communities living in the Hills. *Bull. Cul. Res. Inst.* (Calcutta), VII (1-2): 55-7 (Koch etc.).

215. **Banerjee, Sudhansu Mohan**: 1960: A few anecdotes about Kamrupa-Kamakhya. *Modern Review* (Calcutta), 107: 233-36.

216. **Banerji, D.R.** : 1933 : Slavery in Assam. *(In) Slavery in British India,* by D.R. Banerji. Bombay, D.B. Taraporevala: 77, 132, 134, 136, 137-40, 146, 198, 284, 310-13.

217. **Bantha, J.N.** : 1984 : The Koch-Rabha. *Assam Tribune*, Nov. 24.

218. **Bantho, J.** : 1974 : Rabha jatir itibritta (*in Assamese*). *Naguapara, Garo Hills* (*2nd ed.*).

219. **Bara, Birinchi Kumar** : 1952 : Notes on sorcery and its practices in Assam. *Jr. Univ. of Gau.*, I: 41-51.

220. **Barah, Durgeswar** : 1988 : *A study of socio-economic conditions of Dimasas with reference to their agricultural practices.* Unpub. Ph.D. Thesis, Jorhat, Assam Agricultural Univ.

221. **Barbarua, S.S. (Ed.)** : 1970 : *Chaklong Bedi*. Jorhat.

222. **Bardoloi, Buddhiman** : 1975 : Datipariya Tiwa Kristi. (*In*) *Tiwa Sampradayar Parichaya. (Eds.)* by All Assam Tiwa Yuba Chatra Sanmilan. Jorhat, Asam Sahitya Sabha: 92-115. (*in Assamese*)

223. **Bardoloi, Dharmaram** : 1975 : Tiwa Sampradaya. (*In*) *Tiwa Sampradayar Parichaya. (Eds.)* by All Assam Tiwa Yuba Chatra Sanmilan. Jorhat, Asam Sahitya Sabha: 1-13 (*in Assamese*).

224. **Bardoloi, G.C.** : 1923 : Notes on certain frontier tribes. (*In*) *Census of India 1921, Vol. III, Assam*. Shillong, Govt. Press (Part-I, Report, Appendix-B: XV; XVI).

225. **Bardoloi, N.** : 1983 : *Asamar Loka Sanskriti* (*in Assamese*). Guwahati, Bina Library.

226. **Bardoloi, Nirmal Prabha** : 1996 : Devi worship among the Bodos. *Sentinel, Saturday Fare*, October 19: 1(1-8).

227. **Barkataki, Annada Devi** : 1948 : *Biyanam* (Collection of

marriage songs of the Jorhat sub-division of the Sibsagar district; *(in Assamese)*.

228. **Barkataki, Kakoli** : 1983 : A spurt of revival than obscurity: Assam's Vaishnavite Illustrated Manuscripts. *Indian Magazine*, 3 (9), Aug.: 220-33.

229. **Barkataki, Padma** : 1958 : *Hidden facts from the magic land of Assam*. Calcutta, ABC Pubn., 90p.

230. **Barkataki, S. (Comp.)** : 1969 : Festivals and Folk Dances. *(In) Assam* New Delhi, NBT (India): 96-106.

231. —————— : Assam through the ages. *(In) The Land and People: Assam. (Comp)* New Delhi, NBT (India): 6-7.

232. —————— : Some aspects of tribal life. *(In) The Land and People: Assam (Comp)* New Delhi, NBT (India): 127-37.

233. —————— : The Cachar District, *(In) The Land and People: Assam, (Comp)* New Delhi, NBT (India): 138-40.

234. —————— : Fairs and sacred shrines. *(In) The Land and People: Assam. (Comp)* New Delhi, NBT (India): 107-11.

235. —————— : Art and Craft. *(In) The Land and People: Assam. (Comp)* New Delhi, NBT (India): 74-80.

236. —————— **(Ed.)** : *Tribes of Assam*. New Delhi, NBT (India): 50-62 (Mikir) 63-80 (Tribes of N. Cachar), 63-71 (Dimasa Kachari), 122-28 (Mikir), 128-35 (Dimasa).

237. ———— : 1970 : *Tribal Folk Tales of Assam (Hills)*. Gauhati Pubn. Board Assam, 244p (Mikir, Dimasa-Kachari etc.).

238. **Barman, Bhanu Bhusan** : 1983 : Letters to the Editor: Koch Rajbanshi Sanmilani. *Assam Tribune,* July 15: 4.

239. **Barman, Matilal** : 1987 : Hajong samaj aru sanskriti (*in Assamese*). *(In) Golden Jubilee Souvenir of Uttar-Pub. Bharat Hajong Unnayan Samiti, Lakhimpur*: 38-40.

240. **Barman, Sibnath** : 1982 : *Loka Kristir Utsa*. Gauhati, Pub. by the author (*in Assamese*).

241. **Barmudoi, Ananda** : 1995 : Bozbaroa, Bihu and the Middle Class. *Assam Tribune*, April 15: 4(3-6).

242. **Barooah, J.** : 1955 : *Folk tales of Assam* (2nd ed). Guwahati, Lawyers' Book Stall, 121p.

243. **Barooah, Jeuti** : 1993 : *Single Women in Assamese Hindu Society*. New Delhi, Gyan Publishing House, 231p.

244. ———— : 1996 : Divorce and its consequences in

Contemporary Assamese Society. *(In) Communities of North-East India: An Anthropological Perspective. (Eds.)* by Farida Ahmed Das and Indira Barua, Delhi, Mittal Pubn.: 154-60.

245. **Barooah, Nirode K.** : 1969 : David Scott and the question of slavery in Assam: A case study in British Paternalism. *I.E.S.H.R.*, 6: 179-96.

246. **Barpujari, H.K.** : 1964 : Early judicial panchayats in Assam. *Jour. Indian History,* 42, August: 343-49.

247. ————— : 1979 : *Slavery in Assam: Problem of its emancipation*. Gauhati, Deptt. of Historical and Antiquarian Studies, Assam (*Golden Jubilee Volume*).

248. ————— : 1985 : Vaishnav Niryaton Aru Moamoria Bidroh (*in Assamese*). *Prakash,* Feb.-April (Guwahati, Pubn. Board, Assam).

249. **Barpujari, Utpal** : 1989 : Hajo: A Fusion of Faiths. *Assam Tribune* (*Sunday Reading*), Dec. 17: 1(1-8).

250. **Barthakur, B.N.** : 1993 : *Community and village development.* Calcutta, Institute of Social Research & Applied Anthropology, 227p.

251. **Barthakur, S.K.** : 1980 : Certain plants in the *Folklore,* and folk life of the Karbis (Mikirs) of Assam. *(In) Glimpses of Indian Ethnobotany. (Ed.)* by S.K. Jain. New Delhi, Deep Publications.

252. **Barthakur, Sarat** : 1989 : Textile art of Assam. *Assam Information,* XXXX, April-May: 27-8.

253. **Barua, A.** : 1989 : Religious outlook of the Ahoms. *North-East India History Association. (Ed.)* by J.B. Bhattacharjee. Shillong, NEHU Hist. Deptt., Vol. 10: 143-46.

254. **Barua, Abhay** : 1990 : Krishi sanskriti ki shuruat aur Bihu ki utpatti (*Tr.*) into Hindi by Vimal Agarwal. *Pur. Pra.*, April 14: 5(1-3).

255. **Barua, Anil** : 1988 : The Kamakhya Temple. *A.B.P.* (Call for Travel Supplement), Oct. : 6(5-8) (No date was printed in *A.B.P.*).

256. **Barua, Archana** : 1991 : *The religious form of life in Assam with special reference to Vaishnavism of Sankardeva.* Ph.D. Thesis, N.E.H.U., Shillong.

257. ————— : 1993 : Shankardeva: The Vaishnavaite saint of Assam. *Shillong Times,* Aug. 25: 4(3-6).

258. **Barua, Arun** : 1976 : The Ahom rulers and the neighbouring tribes. *The North Eastern Spectrum,* 1(3-4), Sept.-Oct.: 16-8.

259. **Barua, Atul Chandra** : 1963 : *Sandhiyar Sadhu*. Shillong.

260. ―――――― : 1966 : Mangaldair Dhuliya aru Kaliya (*in Assamese*), *Asom Bani*, April 10.

261. ―――――― : 1974 : *Manasa Kavya aru Ojapali* (*in Assamese*). Mangaldai, Pub. by author (on *Folklore,*).

262. ―――――― : 1985 : *Asamiya Loka Sahitya* (*in Assamese*). Guwahati, Pub. by author.

263. **Barua, B.K.** : 1941 : *Assamese Literature*. Bombay, International Book House, 102p.

264. **Barua, B.M.** : n.d. : Common Ancestry of the Pre-Ahom Rulers. *Indian History Quarterly*, XXIII: 200.

265. **Barua, Bhaben** *(Ed.)* : 1971 : A linguistic study of Assam. *Assam Academy Review* (Calcutta), 1 (A), Navanna Printing Press.

266. **Barua, Birinchi Kumar** : 1942 : Bihu and its probable relation with Fire Festivals. *Jr. Assam Research Society*, 9: 73-7.

267. ―――――― : 1943 : Bihu songs. *Triveni Quarterly*, 15: 161-63.

268. ―――――― : 1951 : *A Cultural History of Assam* (Early Period), Vol. I. Nowgong, K.K. Barua, 223 p.

269. ―――――― : 1952 : Notices of sorcery and its practices in Assam. *Jr. Univ. of Gauhati*, 1: 41-51.

270. ―――――― : 1956 : *Assamese literature (Modern Period). March of India*, 8(6), April: 39-42.

271. ―――――― : 1957 : *Modern Assamese literature*. Gauhati, Lawyers Book Stall.

272. ―――――― : 1959 : Assamese language and early Assamese Literature. *(In) Souvenir on aspects of the heritage of Assam (Ed.)* by K.N. Dutt. Gauhati, 22nd Session of Indian History Congress, December.

273. ―――――― : 1960 : *Sankaradeva Vaisnava saint of Assam*. Gauhati, Assam Academy for Cultural Relations.

274. ―――――― : 1961 : *Asamar Loka-Sanskriti*. Gauhati, Lawyers Book Stall.

275. ―――――― : 1962 : Sankaradeva, the Vaisnava Saint of Assam. Gauhati Lawyers Book Stall.

276. ―――――――― : Weaving in Assam. *The Assam Quarterly*, 11(2), April: 45-9.

277. ―――――――― : Rabindranath and Modern Assamese Poetry. *The Assam Quarterly*, II(I), January: 64-9.

278. **Barua, Birinchi Kumar** : 1963 : Change in meaning of some O.I.A. words in Assamese. *Jr. Univ. of Gauhati* (Arts), 14(1): 171-76.

279. ———————— : *Asamia Bhasa Aur Sanskriti.* (*in Assamese*) Gauhati, Lawyers Book Stall, 187p.

280. ————— : 1964 : *History of Assamese Literature.* Delhi, Sahitya Academy. (Bodo, Chutiya, Kachari, Koch, Lalung, Dimasha, Rabha, Moran, etc.).

281. ————— : 1969 : *A Cultural History of Assam* (Early Period), Vol. I. Gauhati, Lawyers Book Stall, 144p.

282. ————— : 1989 : *Asamar Loka Sanskriti.* Guwahati, Bina Library, 242+108p (in A, 3rd ed., reprinted).

283. —— **(Ed.)** : 1954 : *Ankyya Nat.* Gauhati.

284. **Barua, Birinchi Kumar** *and* **H.V.S. Murthy** : 1965 : *Temples and Legends of Assam.* Bombay. Bharatiya Vidya Bhawan.

285. **Barua, Birinchi Kumar** *and* **Satyendra Nath Sharma (Eds.)** : 1964 : *Manasa Kabya* (*in Assamese*). Gauhati, Dutta Baruah and Co.

286. **Barua, Chandra Kr.** : 1968 : *Kayastha ganar parichay.* Gauhati, Lalit Press (*in Assamese*).

287. **Barua, D.K.** : 1976 : Aspects of change in a Vaishnavite Satra: Barpeta. *Proceedings of a Seminar on Social Change in North-East India,* organised by the Deptt. of Anthropology, Dibrugarh Univ., March 26-27.

288. ————— : 1994 : Barpeta Satra: An insight into its relations with the local community. *Bull. Deptt., Anthropology G.U.,* VIII: 20-3.

289. **Barua, D.K.** *and* **Indira Barua** : 1995 : A glimpse into the communal life of the Tai Turungs. *Bull. Deptt., Anthropology D.U.,* 23: 118-31.

290. ————— : 1996 : Deori. *(In) Encyclopaedic Profile of Indian Tribes. (Eds.)* by Sachidananda and R.R.Prasad. New Delhi, Discovery Publishing House: 206-08.

291. ———————— : *Socio-Cultural and Demographic study of the Tai Turungs of Assam.* Calcutta, K.K. Pubn.

292. **Barua, Deepali** : 1992 : Social status of working women in Assamese Society. *(In) Status of Women in Assam. (Ed.)* by S.L. Baruah. New Delhi, Omsons: 16-21.

293. **Barua, Gautom Prasad** : 1992 : Forces of Assamese literature. *Assam Tribune,* Feb. 19: 4(3-6) 7(3-4).

294. **Barua, Gautom Prasad** : 1992 : 'Bangladeshisation' of Assamese culture. *Assam Tribune*, May 18: 4(3-6) 7(1).

295. **Barua, Girish** : 1993 : *Asamar Jati Samashya Aru Joti Bisnur Chinta (in Assamese)*. Guwahati, Naya Sahitya Parishad.

296. **Barua, Gitanjali** : 1985 : Maamura Matak Community of Assam. *Proceedings of People of India, Pre-Test Seminar of Anthropological, Surv. of India, Shillong* on Dec. 5.

297. ——————— : Social change among the Deori: The attitudinal angle. *Proceedings of a Seminar on Sequences in Development in North-East India (A Study of tradition, continuity and change)* organised by NEICSSR, Shillong on 9-10 December (*Mimeo*).

298. ——————— : 1989 : Asamar chaha banuar Loka sanskritir eti Chamu avas (*in Assamese*). *Social Sciences: An Interdisciplinary Journal* (Silchar), 2(2). Dec.

299. ——————— : Social change among the Deori: The attitudinal angle. *(In) Sequences of development in North-East India (Ed.)* by J.B. Bhattacharjee. New Delhi, Omsons Pubn: 125-30.

300. ——————— : 1990 : On Khamyang ethnography: Some observations. *Jr. NEICSSR*, 14(1), April: 47-53.

301. ——————— : The scenario of social change: Special reference to religious place (A case study among some tea garden communities of Brahmaputra valley). *Proceedings of a Seminar on Status of Religion in tribal areas in North-East India* sponsored by NEICSSR, Shillong on 15-16 Feb (*Mimeo*).

302. ——————— : 1993 : The scenario of social change with special references to religious place: A case study among tea garden communities of Brahmaputra Valley. *(In) Religion in North-East India. (Ed.)* by Soumen Sen. New Delhi, Uppal Publishing. House: 166-73.

303. **Barua, Hem** : 1960 : Tribes and Races: North-East Frontier. *United Asia* (Bombay), 12: 323-27.

304. ——————— : 1962 : *The Red River and the Blue Hill*. Gauhati, Lawyers Book Stall (3rd revised edition, 1st pubd. in 1954), 205 p.

305. ——————— : Rangali Bihu. *Illustrated Weekly of India*, 83(30), July 29: 69.

306. ——————— : 1963 : Rural Themes in Indian Literature: *Assamese. Ill. Weekly of India*, Aug. 8.

307. **Barua, Hem** : 1967 : Aspects of Assamese Literature. *Ill. Weekly of India*, 88(17), May 28: 55-6.

308. ———— : 1971 : *Assamese literature* (2nd ed.) New Delhi, NBT (India), 271 p.

309. **Barua, H.C.** : 1908 : *Marriage systems of the Assamese people*. Gauhati, Pub. by the author.

310. **Barua, Hem Chandra** : 1908 : *Notes on the marriage systems of the people of Assam*. Sibsagar, Ananda Ram Barua, 60 p. (2nd ed., 1st ed. 1892).

311. **Barua, Hem** *and* **J.D. Baveja** : 1956 : *The Fairs and Festivals of Assam*. Gauhati, Lawyers Book Stall, 62 p.

312. **Barua, Indira** : 1972 : Notes on family structure of an Ahom village. *Bull. Deptt. of Anthropology, Dibrugarh Univ.*, 1: 28-32.

313. ———— : 1973 : Mortuary rites among the Mohans and Deodhais. *Bull. Deptt. of Anthropology, Dib. Univ.*, II: 22-6 (Ahom).

314. ———— : 1974 : The Ahoms of Moranjan village. *(In) Contemporary Anthropological Research in North-East India. (Ed.)* by B.M. Das (*Bull. Anthropology Deptt.*, Dib. Univ., III). Dib. Univ., Anthropology Deptt.: 105-12.

315. ———— : 1975 : *Moranjan : Social Relations in an Ahom Community of Assam*. Ph.D. Thesis, Anthropology Dib. Univ. Deptt.

316. ———— : 1976 : A study on some aspects of social change in an Ahom village. *Proceedings of a Seminar on Social Change in North-East India,* organised by the Deptt. of Anthropology., Dib. Univ., March 26-27.

317. ———————— : Opinion leaders in a village community. *Bull. Deptt. of Anthropology, Dib. Univ.*, 4 (1975): 7-10.

318. ———————— : Religion in an Ahom community. *Proceedings of a Seminar on Social Change in North-East India*, organised by the Deptt. of Anthropology, Dib. Univ., March 26-27.

319. ———— : 1977 : Family: A comparative study of a rural and an urban village. *Bull. Deptt. of Anthropology, Dib. Univ.*, 5(1976): 34-9.

320. ———— : 1978 : The Ahom: An appraisal of a reviving and revitalizing trend. *(In)* Cultural and Biological Adaptability of Man with special reference to North-East India. *(Eds.)* by A.C. Bhagabati *and* R.K. Kar (*Bull. Deptt. of Anthropology*, 6, 1977, Dib. Univ.): 59-64.

321. **Barua, Indira** : 1978 : *Social Relations in an Ahom Village.* New Delhi, Sterling Pubs.

322. ———— : 1979 : Changing occupational structure in two villages in Assam. *Man in India,* 59(2), April-June: 106-19.

323. ———— : Some aspects of kinship relationship in an Ahom village. *Eastern Anthropology,* 32(1), Jan.-March: 1-9.

324. ———— : 1981 : Marriage among the Ahoms: A study in two Ahom villages. *Jr. Ind. Anthropology Soc.,* 16(1), March: 35-43.

325. ———— : 1982 : Tai elements in Assam. *Jr. Social Research,* XXV(II), Sept.

326. ———— : Kinship system of the Tai Turungs of Assam. *East. Anthropology,* 35(1).

327. ———— : Salient features of kinship system of the Tai Turungs of Assam. *East. Anthropology,* 35(3): 201-12.

328. ———— : 1992 : The Tai Turungs of Assam: A Study of Socio-demographic Profile. *Man in India,* 72(3), Sept.: 317-29.

329. ———— : 1994 : Family and socialisation processes: A study among the Tai Buddhist Communities of Assam. *Jour. Indian Anth. Society,* 29(1-2), March-July: 151-61.

330. **Barua, Indira** *and* **Minati Chutia** : 1991 : The Chaudang of Assam: Ethnicity and Social Change. *East. Anthropology,* 44(3), July-Sept.: 225-40.

331. **Barua, Indira** *and* **Runumai Phukan** : 1994 : Socio-cultural roles of Deori women. *Bull. Deptt. of Anthropology,* D.U., 22: 54-66.

332. **Barua, Induprava** : 1975 : Asamat mahila jagaran aru mahila samitir bhumika. *(In)* Smaranika. *(Ed.)* by Indira Miri (*in Assamese*). Gauhati, *Souvenir of International Women's Year:* 22-31.

333. **Barua, Jagaram** : 1875 : *Sree Sree Gopal Deber Bargit.* Tezpur, Bharati Press.

334. **Barua, Jamini Kumar** : 1951 : Rabhas. *(In) Tribes of India.* Delhi, Bharatiya Adimjati Sevak Sangh, 2: 35-8.

335. **Barua, K.L.** : 1936-37 : Alpines in Eastern India. *Indian Culture,* 3: 161-71.

336. **Barua, K.L.** : 1938 : Human sacrifice in Assam. *Jr. Assam Research Society,* 6: 4-11.

337. **Barua, Kalyan** : 1994 : Beyond the horizon of Vaishnavism: The Sonowal Kachari Case. *Bull. Deptt., Anthropology G.U.*, VIII: 24-33.

338. —————— : The Sonowal Kachari: Some aspects of their social life. *(In) Tribes of North-East India. (Ed.)* by Sarthak Sengupta. New Delhi, Gyan Pubg. House: 120-26.

339. ———— : 1996 : Problem of ethnicity among the Patri-Matri Rabhas: A search at the Twilight zone. *(In) Communities of North-East India: An Anthropological Perspective. (Eds.)* by Farida Ahmed Das and Indira Barua. Delhi, Mittal Pubn.: 41-8.

340. **Barua, Khanin Ch.** : 1960 *: Assam: Her people and her language.* Gauhati, Lawyers Book Stall (2nd ed), 22 p.

341. **Barua, M.** : 1977 *: Matak Jati aru Matak Sanmillan.* Chabua, Sadau Asam Matak Sanmillan aru Sadau Asam Matak Chatrar Sanmillan (*in Assamese*).

342. **Barua, Mary** : 1995 : Bihu festivities in Vaisnavite centres. *Assam Tribune*, April 14: (3-8).

343. **Barua, Nabakanta** : 1962 : Humour in contemporary Assamese literature. *The Assam Quarterly*, II (3), July: 31-5.

344. ———— : 1990 : Jati, Bhasha va Dharma ke visheile kanton se paramparagat marg ko koi band na kare (*in Hindi*). *Pur. Pra. (Lehit Bharati)*, Feb. 25: I(1-8).

345. **Barua, Nagendra Nath** : 1973 *: Dimasa deshar sadhu* (*in Assamese*). Karimganj (about *Folklore,*).

346. ———— : 1976 : *Kabi* sanskrit dhara. *Saptahik Janambhumi* (Jorhat), June 30.

347. ———— : 1980 *: The Dimasa Society and their folk songs.* Gauhati, Pub. by the author.

348. ———— : n.d. *: Dimacha sakalor git-mat* (*in Assamese*). Guwahati, Asam Prakashan Parishad.

349. ———— : 1992 *: Dimasa bhashar bharal* (*in Assamese*). Guwahati, Asam Prakashan Parishad.

350. **Barua, Nakul** : n.d. : *Memi-mang-phura.* (*in Tai-Ahom language*). Jajalihab (Sibsagar, Assam). Unpub. Tai-Ahom Language MSS.

351. **Barua, Nihar** : 1967 : Songs that grew out of a legend : Mahut songs from Goalpara. *(In) Folk music and folklore Anthropology. (Ed.)* by Hemanga Biswas. Calcutta, *Folklore,* Research Institute, I: 93-105.

352. **Barua, P.K.** : 1945 *: Kamarupiya Biyar Git* (*in Assamese*). Gauhati, Pub. by the author.

353. **Barua, Prafulla** : 1965 : *Fundamentals of Assamese Culture.* Gauhati, P.C. Barua, Rehabari.

354. **Barua, R.** : 1963 : *Seuji Pator Kahini (in Assamese).* Shillong, Chapala Sahitya Sadan (about tea leaf).

355. **Barua, S.** : 1994 : Marwari Muslim; Nepali; Marwari. *(In) People of India: Meghalaya. (Ed.)* by K.S. Singh. Calcutta, Seagull Books: 187-88; 189-96; 197-202.

356. **Barua, Suparna** : 1996 : A Woman in Dimasa Society: A Note. *(In) Communities of North-East India: An Anthropological Perspective. (Eds.)* by Farida Ahmed Das and Indira Barua. Delhi, Mittal Pubn.: 144-53.

357. **Barua, T.C.** : 1975 : Cultural Heritage. *Link,* 17(21), Jan. 5: 27-30.

358. **Baruah, A.K.** : 1990 : *The Karbis of the Hills.* Guwahati, Abhiyatri Mudran aru Prakashan.

359. ———— : 1994 : Aspects of Jyoti Prasad's views on Assamese Culture. *NEIHA, 15th Session,* Shillong, Hist. Deptt., NEHU.

360. **Baruah, Bhuban** : 1990 : Marwaris: A sage of enterprise. *Assam Tribune,* (Sunday Reading), Feb. 18: 1 (1-8).

361. **Baruah, Bijoya** : 1989 : Castes and Professions in the Fourteenth Century Assamese Society as reflected in Madhava Kandali's Ramayana. *NEIHA (Ed.)* by J.B. Bhattacharjee. Shillong, NEHU Hist. Deptt., Vol. 10: 68-73.

362. ———— : 1990 : Costume, Coiffure and Ornament in the Medieval Assamese Society. *NEIHA (Ed.)* by J.B. Bhattacharjee. Shillong, NEHU Hist. Deptt., Vol. 11.

363. **Baruah, Binita** : 1981 : *A study on professional pattern in an Assamese Muslim village of Natun gaon Bairagimoth in the dist. of Dibrugarh.* Unpub. M.Sc. Dissertation, Anthropology Deptt., Dibrugarh Univ.

364. **Baruah, Chitralekha** : 1996 : A peep into the Nepali society in Assam: Brothers and Sisters. *Sentinel* (Sunday), April 28: I (1-5) (Relationship, parasama, bratabanda, bhratridwitiya, Ganeshchouthi, teej, etc.).

365. **Baruah, Dipendra Kr.** : 1974 : A note on the Socio-Religious aspects of Barpeta: A Satra based township in Assam. *(In) Contemporary Anthropological Research in North-East India. (Ed.)* by B.M. Das (It is also *Bull. Anthropology Deptt.,* Dibrugarh University, Vol. III), Dib. Univ., Anthropology Deptt.,: 113-21.

366. **Baruah, Geetanjali** : 1980 : Family structure among some tea garden labourers of Assam. *Bull. Cal. Res. Inst.*, XIV (1-2): 73-9.

367. **Baruah, Jeuti** : 1991 : *Single women in contemporary Assamese Hindu Society: An Anthropological study of their problems and status.* Ph.D. Thesis, Anthropology Deptt., Gau. Univ.

368. ————: 1992 : Emergence of single women in modern Assamese Hindu society. *Bull. Deptt. of Anthropology,* (Gau. Univ.), VI, March: 28-32.

369. **Baruah, Kalyan** : 1980 : *Some aspects of family life of the Sonowal Kacharis* (based on field study of Dainijan village, Dibrugarh). Unpub. M.Sc. Dissertation, Anthropology Deptt., Dib. Univ.

370. ———— : 1991 : Problems of a village economy in Assam: A case-study of Sonowal Kachari. *Social Sciences*, 4(1-2), June-Dec.: 231-36.

371. ———— : 1992 : Cultural Adaptability of the Achik Mande: A comparative study in Assam and Meghalaya. *Bull. Deptt. of Anthropology,* (Gau.Uni), VI, March: 33-9.

372. ———— : 1993 : Family structure among the Sonowal Kacharis: Continuity and change. *Bull. Anthropology Deptt., Gau. Univ.*, VII: 30-8.

373. **Baruah, Kalyan** *and* **Geetanjali Baruah** : 1986 : The problem of ethnic identity: A caste-study among the Moran. *Proceedings of a Seminar on the question of Nationality, Ethnicity and Cultural Identity in the context of North-East India*, 5-6 Dec., organised by NEICSSR, Shillong (about Matak, Moran, Moamaria).

374. ———— : 1990 : The Problem of Ethnic Identity: A case-study among the Moran. *(In) Nationality, Ethnicity and Cultural Identity in North-East India. (Ed.)* by B. Pakem. New Delhi, Omsons: 181-86.

375. **Baruah, Kanaki** : 1980 : *The Sonowal Kachari of Lepetkata village Dibrugarh Dist. with special reference to fishing, birth and pregnancy and religious organization.* Unpub. M.Sc. Disser., Anthropology Deptt., Dib. Univ.

376. **Baruah, M.K.** : 1983 : North Guwahati: The place and the people. *(In) Souvenir: Anthropological Society of North-East India. (Eds.)* by H.C. Sharma *and* B. Choudhury. Gau. Uni., Anth. Deptt.: 51-8.

377. **Baruah, Prasanta J.** : 1990 : NEZCC: Researching through culture. *Assam Tribune*, (*Sunday Reading*), Feb. 11: I(1-8).

378. **Baruah, R.M.** : 1980 : *A study on some aspects of Sonowal Kachari of Lepetkata village, Dibrugarh.* M.Sc. Dissertation, Anthropology Deptt., Dib. Univ. (In A.).

379. **Baruah, Rita** : 1982 : The spatial distribution of Mongoloid population in North-East India. *North Eastern Geographer* (Gau. Univ.), XIV(1-2): 52-6.

380. **Baruah, S.L. (Ed.)** : 1992 : *Status of women in Assam (with special reference to non-tribal societies).* New Delhi, Omsons Pub.

381. ———— : 1994 : *Last days of Ahom Monarchy.* Guwahati, Distributed by United Pubs.

382. **Baruah, Sanjib** : 1995 : Western Cultural boundary of Assam. *E.P.W.*, XXX(44), Nov. 4: 2783-2784.

383. **Baruah, Unnat Kr.** : 1981 : *Urban impact and socio-economic change in a pre-urban fishermen community.* M.Sc. Disser., Anthropology Deptt., Dib. Univ. (Unpub.).

384. **Basanti** : n.d : Tea pluckers in Assam. *Manushi*, IV(4), May-June: 8.

385. **Bastian, A.** : 1881 : Huge estamme Assam. *Zeitschrift fur Ethnology*, 13: 149-60.

386. **Basu, K.** : 1888 : Customs and practices among the Koch. *Jr. Anthropology Society of Bombay*, 3(2): 103.

387. **Basu, Kedar Nath** : 1888 : Some curious customs among Kochs. *Jr. Asiatic Society of Bengal*, 3(2): 102-03.

388. **Basu, P.C.** : 1929 : Head dress of the hill tribes of Assam. *Jr. Asiatic Society of Bengal*, 25: 103-14.

389. **Basu, Pravash Ch.** : 1931 : The social and religious ceremonies of the Chakmas. *Jr. and Proceedings of Asiatic Society of Bengal (N.S.)*, 27 (2); 213-23.

390. **Basumatari, D.R.** : 1986 : *Boro Kachari Bathau Dharma Aru Samaj Sanskriti.* Nalbari, Pub. by author.

391. **Basumatàri, Gahin** : 1963 : Boro lipi (*in Assamese*). *Asom Bani*, Nov. 22.

392. **Basumatari, Joy Narayan** : n.d. : *Bathou Ashram.* Aflagaon (Kokrajhar, Assam), Pub. by the author.

393. **Basumatary, A.** : 1946 : Koch Kacharir parichaya. *Khada.*

394. **Basumatary, Ani Ram** : 1957 : *Kristi.* Gauhati, pub. by the author.

395. **Basumatary, Dhuparam** : 1955 : *Bore Kachari Sanskritir Kinchit Abhas* (*in Assamese*). Nalbari, Pub. by the author.

396. **Basumatary, Jaynarayan** : 1985 (B) : *Boroni Bathou Dharam Bijab* (in Bodo). Kokrajhar, Pub. by author, 56p.

397. **Basumatary, Ramdeu** : 1978 : Some idea on "Bathou". *(In) The Bodosu (Ed.)* by Ram Mochari Mani. Gauhati.

398. **Basumatary, Ram Das** : 1993 : Bathou Dharam Aru Santhou (*in Assamese*). *Laithun*, VIII: 3.

399. **Basumatary, Rupnath** : 1986 : Bag Duarni Birgashri Sikhla (*in Bodo*). *Nisima, A Souvenir of 12th Annual Conference, Kokrajhar District, Bodo Sahitya Sabha*; 24-5.

400. **Basumatary, Sukumar** : 1996 : Bodo Ridelle. *Seminar paper on Traditional culture and folklore in North-East India*, 18-19 Nov., Shillong, NEICSSR.

401. **Baveja, J.D.** : 1956 : *Fairs and Festivals of Assam*. Guwahati, Lawyers Book Stall.

402. ———— : 1960 : *Across the golden heights of Assam and NEFA*. Guwahati, Modern Book Depot. 144.

403. ———— : 1982 : *New Horizons of North-East*. Gauhati, Western Book Depot, 152 p. (Ahom, Dimasa, Kachari, etc.).

404. **Baviskar, B.S.** : 1975 : Tribes and nation building in the North-East. *Vanyajati*, XIII(2-3), April-July: 16-7.

405. **Baxla, Zepherinus** : 1993 : The Adivasis in Assam. *(In) The Catholic Church in North-East India, 1890-1990 (A Multidimensional Study). (Ed.)* by Sebastian Karotemprel. Shillong, Vendrame Institute (Calcutta, Firma KLM Pvt. Ltd.): 452-459.

406. **Bayan, Jogen** : 1992 : Sankardeva and dawn of Assamese drama. *Assam Tribune*, Aug. 29: 4(3-6).

407. **Beck, Brenda E.F.; Peter, J. Claus; Praphulladatta Goswami** *and* **Jawaharlal Handoo (Eds.)** : 1987 : *Folk Tales of India*. London, The Univ. of Chicago Press: 35-7, 99-102, 139, 153-54, 202, 204-06, 209-11, 240-41, 289 (Assam).

408. **Becker, C.** : 1980 : *History of the Catholic Missions in North-East India (1890-1915)*. Translated by G. Stadler and S. Karotemprel. Calcutta, Firma KLM: 28-91 (Brahmaputra valley): 92-138 (Surma valley).

409. **Begum, Anarkali** : 1980 : *Economic and society in an urbanised Assamese Muslim village*. M.Sc. Disser., Anthropology Deptt, Dib. Univ. (Unpub.).

410. **Begum, Eliga** : 1983 : *Anthropological field report on the people of Kolowlowa Deuri gaon, with special reference to family, clan, housetype, marriage, village organisation*. M.Sc. Disser., Anthropology Deptt., Dib. Univ., (Unpub.).

411. **Begum, Farida** : 1995 : Ullasita man ki madakata ka pratik Bihu parv. (*in Hindi*) *Pur. Pra.* April 14; 5(7-8).

412. **Behal, Monisha Agarwala** : •1987 : *The Vaishnava Monasteries 'Assam in relation to Folk Religion'*. Ph.D. Thesis. Unpub. Gau. Univ.

413. **Behera, D.K.** *and* **N. Nanda** : 1990 : Status of women among the plain-Bhuiyans. *East. Anthropology,* 42(2).

414. **Bejbarua, L.** : 1963 : *Mahapurush Sri Sankardev aru Madhab Dev.* (*in Assamese*) Gauhati Sahitya Prakash, 329 p.

415. **Beverley, H.** : 1872 : Koch, Kaibarta, Rajbansi and Kachari. (*In*) *Report on the Census of Bengal 1871*. Calcutta: 182-84, 186, 201-03.

416. **Bey, Warten** : n.d : *Thai Avo Mongvo* (*in Karbi*). (A collection of songs).

417. **Bezbarua, L.** : 1911 : *Burhi Air Sadhu.* (*in Assamese*) Gauhati, Sahitya Prakash, B.N. Bordoloi.

418. ———— : 1950 : *Burhi Air Sadhu,* (*in Assamese*). Gauhati (3rd ed. about *Folklore*).

419. ———— : 1951 : *Kakadeuta aru Natilora* (*in Assamese*) Gauhati (3rd ed. about *Folklore*).

420. **Bezbarua, Lakshminath** : 1911 : Collection of tales, ballads, etc. (Eng. Tr., 1915).

421. **Bezbaruah, Bandana** : 1992 : Family structure of the Mataks: A case study. *Bull. Deptt. Anthropology, Dib. Univ.*, 18-19(1989-90): 98-106.

422. ———— : 1993 : Kinship system among the Mataks: Some aspects. *Bull. Deptt. of Anthropology, Dib. Univ.*, 20-21 (1991-92): 74-83.

423. ———— : 1996 : The Matak as an ethno-religious sect. *(In) Communities of North-East India: An Anthropological Perspective. (Eds.)* by Farida Ahmed Das and Indira Barua. Delhi, Mittal Pubn.: 204-11.

424. **Bezbaruah, Rama** : 1975 : Dance of Assam. *Link*, 17(21), Jan. 5: 31-2.

425. **Bezbaruah, Ramananda** : 1992 : Assamese society and culture. *(In) Glimpses of the Indian Tribal Life. (Ed.)* by D.P.S. Khanna. Delhi, Sarita Book House: 51-3.

426. **Bezbaruah, Sadanand** : 1993 : Joginitantra Shakti Rupini Mahakali (*in Assamese*). *Ajir Asom*, Oct. 17: 6(1-6) (Kamakhya).

427. **Bhadra, Ranajit** : 1979 : Rural class structure in post-independence Assam. *Eco. and Pol. Weekly*, XIV(4), Jan. 27: 165-67.

428. **Bhadra, R.K.** : 1974 : Indian tribes and their modernization. *Vanyajati*, XXII(2), April: 40-9 (Assam etc.).

429. **Bhadra, Ranjit K.** : 1979 : Rural class structure in post-Independence Assam. *Eco. and Pol. Weekly*, 14(4), Jan. 27: 165-67.

430. ——————— : Emerging patterns of agrarian class in rural Assam. *Eastern Anth.*, 32(4), Oct.-Dec.: 272-85.

431. **Bhadra, Ranjit K.** : 1991 : *Caste and Class: Social Stratification in Assam*, Delhi, Hindustan Pubg. Corp.

432. **Bhadra, Ranjit K.** *and* **S.R. Mandal (Eds.)** : 1991 : *Stratification Hierarchy and Ethnicity in North-East India*. Delhi, Daya Publishing House, 310 p.

433. **Bhagabati, Anandamohan** : 1981 : Dances of Assam. *Assam Information*, 32, Jan.-March: 39-46.

434. **Bhagabati, A.C.** : 1962 : The Khamyangs of Upper Assam. *The Assam Quarterly*, II (I), Jan.: 70-1.

435. ————— : 1968 : An Assamese fisherman's community in Pre-Urban setting. *Report of the Commissioner for S.C. and S.T.*, No. 18.

436. ——————— : *Anthropology and the Assam Region: A plea for field research in the plains.* Simla, IIAS (*Mimeo*).

437. ——————— : The Tribes of North-Eastern India. *(In) Assam: An outline. (Ed.)* by M. Borthakur. Gau. Univ., Geog. Deptt.,: 40-4.

438. ——————— : Village Padumbari, *(In) Sixteenth Report of the Commissioner for Scheduled Castes and Scheduled Tribes*, Vols. I-II. Delhi, Manager of Pubn.

439. **Bhagabati, A.C.** : 1969 : Anthropological Research in the Assam Region: Some proposals. *(In) Urgent Research in Social Anthropology. (Eds.)* by B.L. Abbi *and* S. Saberwal Simla, Indian Inst. of Adv. Study: 54-60.

440. ————— : 1970 : *Social Change in Rural Assam:* (A Project Report). Gau. Univ., Anthropology Deptt.

441. ————— : 1974 : Research in Social Anthropology in North-East India: Problems and prospects. *(In) Contemporary*

Anthropological Research in North-East India. (Ed.) by B.M. Das (*Bull. Anthropology Deptt.,* Dib. Univ., III): 158-65.

442. **Bhagabati, A.C.** : 1975 : Social Change in the Hill areas of North-East India. *Bull. Deptt. of Anthropology, Gau. Univ.,* IV.

443. ———— : 1981 : Some aspects of emerging tribal identity in North-East India. *Bull. Deptt. of Anthropology, Dib. Univ.,* 7-8(1978-79): 78-95.

444. ———— : 1982 : Emerging tribal identity in North-East India. *(In). Tribal Development in India: Problems and Prospects. (Ed.)* by B. Chaudhury. New Delhi, Inter-India.

445. ———— : 1983 : Ethnic cultural identity: An anthropological assessment. *Assam Tribune,* May 1: 3.

446. ———— : 1988 : Tribal transformation in Assam and North-East India: An appraisal of emerging ideological dimension. *75th Indian Sc. Congress and The Anthropology Sec.* (Platinum Jubilee), Pune: 1-26.

447. ———— : 1990 : Anthropological perspectives on tribal development in the Assam Hills: A preliminary statement. *(In) Constraints of Tribal Development in North-East India. (Ed.)* by B.N. Bordoloi. Guwahati, Tribal Research Inst.: 6-16.

448. ———— : 1992 : *Proceedings of a Seminar at Guwahati on Growth and Justice on tribal studies* organised by the Inst. of Social Change and Development, Guwahati, sponsored by NERC of ICSSR, Shillong on Nov. 23.

449. ———— : Perspectives on ethno-cultural identity movements in North-Eastern India. *(In) Ethnicity, Caste and People: India and the Soviet Union. (Ed.)* by K.S. Singh. New Delhi, Manohar Pub. for Anthropology Surv. of India: 139-66.

450. ———— : Social formations in North-East India. *Bull. Deptt. of Anthropology, Gau. Univ.,* VI, March: 9-27.

451. ———— : 1993 : Tribal Transformation in Assam and North-East India: An Appraisal of emerging ideological dimension. *(In) Tribal transformation in India,* Vol. III, Pt. VI. *(Ed.)* by Buddhadev Chaudhuri. New Delhi, Inter India.

452. **Bhagabati, A.C.** *and* **Bibhash Dhar** : 1977 : Tribesmen as townsmen: A case study in Assam. *Bull. Deptt. of Anthropology, Dib. Univ.,* 5(1976): 62-70.

453. **Bhagawati, Simanta** : 1996 : A time to celebrate. *A.T., (Sunday Reading),* Jan. 14: I (1-8) (Magh Bihu/Bhogali Bihu).

454. **Bhakat, Dwijendra Nath** : 1992 : *The Assamese Vaisanavite Satra of North Bengal and Goalpara.* Ph.D. Thesis. Unpub. Assamese Deptt., Gau. Univ.

455. **Bhandari, J.M.S.** : 1962 : Family organization of the Mishing(Miri) of Assam. *Bull. Deptt. of Tribal Culture and Folklore, Research*, Gau. Univ.: 46-56.

456. **Bhandari, J.S.** : 1961 : Miri dances. *Assam Quarterly*, I(4), Oct.: 38-40.

457. ———— : 1968 : Land and social structure: An economic study of a Mishing village. *East. Anthropology*, XXI(1), Jan.-April: 21-36.

458. ———— : 1973 : Changing emphasis on the religious beliefs: Study in ideological conflict among the Mishing. *(In) Studies in Social Change. (Ed.)* K.S. Mathur. Lucknow, Ethnographic and Folk Culture Society.

459. ———— : 1974 : Land and social structure: An economic study of a Mishing village. *(In) Tribes, Caste and Peasantry. (eds.)* by K.S. Mathur *and* B.C. Agarwal. Lucknow, Ethnographic and Folk Cultural Society: 8-20.

460. ———— : 1984 : Ethno-history, ethnic identity and contemporary Mishing society. *Indian Anthropologist*, 14(2), Dec.: 79-104.

461. ———— : 1992 : *Kinship affinity and domestic group: A Study among the Mishings of the Brahmaputra Valley.* New Delhi, Gyan Pubg. H., 280 p.

462. ———— : 1996 : *Kinship and family in North-East India.* New Delhi, Cosmo Publication, 325p. (Compilation of papers on kinship and family).

463. ———— : The principle of descent and structure of descent groups among the Pagro-Mishing of Brahmaputra valley. *(In) Kinship and Family in North-East India. (Ed.)* by J.S. Bhandari. New Delhi, Cosmo Publications: 285-328.

464. **Bhandary, B.K.** : 1950 : *Tribes of India.* New Delhi, Bharatiya Adimjati Sevak Sangh: 11-5 (Kachari, Mikir etc. *Ed.* by V. Raghaviah).

465. ———— : 1995 : Letters to the Editor: Rallying behind Rickshaw-pullers. *Sentinel*, Oct. 5: 4 (7-8).

466. **Bharali, Arunima** : 1988 : Some aspects of *Medieval Assamese culture as reflected in Medieval Assamese Literature.* Unpub. Ph.D. Thesis, Gau. Univ.

467. **Bharali, P.N.** : 1985 : Economic Transition of Tribal Society: Case studies of two Deuri village. *Bull. TRI* (Guwahati), I(III).

468. **Bharali, P.N.** *and* **A.K. Borah** : 1990 : Status of traditional religion in the midst of the Deori tribe: A case study of three villages in Assam. *Proceedings of a Seminar on Status of Religion in tribal areas in NEI*, sponsored by NEICSSR, Shillong on 15-16 Feb. (*Mimeo*).

469. ———— : 1993 : Religion of the Deori tribe: A case study of three villages in Assam, *(In) Religion in North-East India. (Ed.)* by Soumen Sen. New Delhi, Uppal Publishing House: 148-59.

470. **Bharali, S.** : 1987 : Assamese literature in the doldrums. *Assam Tribune*, Feb. 15: 4(3-6).

471. **Bharali, Sailen** : 1984 : *Asamiya Loka-Natya Parampara* (*in Assamese*). Pathsala Bani Prakash.

472. ———— : 1991 : Madhavdeva the dramatist. *Assam Tribune (Sunday Reading)*, July 14: I(1-5).

473. **Bharati, Madan** : 1996 : Makar Sankranti ka pouranik mahatta. *Pur. Pra.*, Jan. 14: 5(1-3) (in H).

474. **Bharati, Tarak Deb** : 1973 : Eastern Indian handicrafts: A preliminary survey. *Folklore*, XIV(9), Sept.: 354-59.

475. **Bharatiya Adimjati** : n.d. : *Souvenir All India Tribal Conference in Assam*. New Delhi, Bharatiya Adimjati Sevak Sangh.

476. **Bhatra, Roshan** : 1995 : *Socio-Economic Profile* of the Rickshaw-puller (Survey Report for Ph.D. on-going project)

477. **Bhattacharjee, Amalendu** : 1985 : Marriage songs of the Bengalee Hindus of Cachar District of Assam. *(In) Folklore, in North-East India. (Ed.)* by Soumen Sen. Delhi, Omsons Pubs.: 146-55.

478. ———— : 1988 : First World War as reflected in Bengali folk songs of Barak Valley. *NEIHA*, 9: 109-17.

479. **Bhattacharjee, Amalendu** : 1992 : Marriage songs of the Bengalee-Hindus of Cachar District of Assam. *(In) India through ages, Vol. V: Folklore of India. (Eds.)* by T.R. Sareen *and* S.R. Bakshi. New Delhi, Anmol Pubs.: 261-78.

480. **Bhattacharjee, Anjali** : 1977 : *Cachar under British Rule in North-East India.* New Delhi, Radiant Pubs., 353p.

481. ———— : 1990 : Animals in Assamese folktales: A comparative study of the characteristics of animals. *Folklore*, 31(2), Feb.: 37-43.

482. **Bhattacharjee, Anjali (Ed.)** : 1980 : *Proceedings of North-East India History Association,* Vols. I-13, 1980-1991, 1993. Shillong, NEHU, History Deptt.

483. ———— : 1981 : Dimasa State formation in Cachar. *Proceedings of a workshop Seminar on Tribal Politics and State System in Eastern and North-Eastern India*, July 24-27, 1981 by Centre for Studies in Social Sciences, Calcutta (Reported by S.C. Sinha in *Jr. Ind. Anth. Society,* 16(1), March: 93-4. Also *(In) Tribal Politics and State Systems in Pre-Colonial Eastern and North-Eastern India. (Ed.)* by Surajit Sinha. Calcutta, K.P. Bagchi, 366p.

484. **Bhattacharjee, J.B.** : 1985 : History and *Folklore,* in the Context of Cachar valley. *(In) Folklore, in North-East India. (Ed.)* by Soumen Sen. Delhi, Omsons Pubs.: 156-58.

485. ———— : 1987 : Dimasa State formation in Cachar. *(In) Tribal Politics and State Systems in Pre-Colonial Eastern and North-Eastern India. (Ed.)* by S.C. Sinha. Calcutta, K.P. Bagchi.

486. **Bhattacharjee, Kishore** : 1980 : *Economic life of Karbi people of Rongkargthir.* Unpub. B.A. (Honours) Dissertation, Gau. Univ.

487. ———— : 1996 : Psychological Interpretation of two Assamese tales. *Seminar paper on Traditional Culture and Folklore in North-East India,* 18-19 Nov., Shillong, NEICSSR.

488. **Bhattacharjee, Kishore** *and* **Annada C. Bhagabati** : 1996 : Kinship of the Assamese: Symbols and structures. *(In) Kinship and Family in North-East India. (Ed.)* by J.S. Bhandari. New Delhi, Cosmo Pubns.: 373-92.

489. **Bhattacharjee, M.** : 1996 : Bihu Asam ki Lok Sanskriti ka Pratik. (*in Hindi*). *Pur. Pra.* Jan. 14: 5(1-6).

490. **Bhattacharjee, Monorama** : 1987 : Asomar astitya raksha andolonat nari bhumika. (*in Assamese*) *Satsari,* 1(1), Feb.: 23-9, Guwahati.

491. **Bhattacharjee, Padma Nath** : 1930 : Folk custom and folklore of the Sylhet district of Assam. *Man in India,* 10(2-3), April-Sept.: 116-49.

492. **Bhattacharjee, T.** : 1986 : *Sociology of the Karbis.* Delhi, B.R. Pub., 198 p.

493. **Bhattacharjee, Tanmay** : 1996 : Barman *(In) Encyclopaedic profile of Indian Tribes. (Eds.)* by Sachchidananda and R.R. Prasad. New Delhi, Discovery Pubg.: 72-5.

494. **Bhattacharya, A.** : 1991 : The tribal problem in North-East India. *Marxist,* 9(2), April-June: 26-41.

495. **Bhattacharya, B.K.** : 1973 : Bihu-names: A unique feature of Assamese oral poetry. *Assam Tribune*, April 13: 4(3-5) 7(5).

496. ———— : 1978 : Tribal societies in flux. *(In) Souvenir All India Tribal Conference and National Seminar on Tribal Welfare.* Guwahati: 1-2.

497. **Bhattacharya, Basanta Kr.** : 1996 : Aspects of Assamese culture. *Seminar paper on Traditional Culture and Folklore in North-East India*, 18-19 Nov., Shillong, NEICSSR.

498. **Bhattacharya, Birendra Kr.** : 1968 : The Assamese Bihu Festival. United Asia, 12(2), March-April: 115-17.

499. ———— : 1978 : *Dersa Basarar Asamiya Sanskritit E bhumuki.* Gauhati. (*in Assamese*)

500. **Bhattacharya, Jogendra Nath** : 1896 : Kaibartas. *(In) Hindu Castes and Sects.* Calcutta : 279-81.

501. **Bhattacharya, Manoranjan** : 1991 : Asamiya sanskriti ka ek mahattapurna ang: Magh Bihu ya Bhogali Bihu (*in Hindi*). *Pur. Pra (Lohit Bharati)*, Jan. 13: I(1-8).

502. ———— : 1993 : Bihu ke rang antarik hain aur bahya vi. (*in Hindi*) *Pur. Pra (Lohit Bharati)*, April 13: 1(4-8).

503. ———— : 1995 : Bihu ka rang antarik hi nahi vahaya vi hai. (*in Hindi*) *Pur. Pra.*, April 14: 5 (1-6).

504. **Bhattacharya, N.** : 1964 : Life at standstill in Gauhati. *New Age*, 12(40). Oct. 4: 2.

505. **Bhattacharya, Pramod Chandra** : 1955-56 : Glimpses from Boro folksongs. *Indian Linguistics*,. Vol. 17 (Taraporewala Memorial volume): 240-44.

506. ———— : 1957 : *Boro folksongs and tales.* Guwahati.

507. ———— : Boro folksongs on love. *Indian Folk Lore*, 2(1), April-June: 41-5.

508. **Bhattacharya, Pramod Chandra** : 1962 : A sheaf of Boro folksongs. *Assam Quarterly*, II(I), Jan.: 57-9.

509. ———— : Nara-Turung-Aitoniya. *(In) Asamar Janajati (Ed.)* by Pramod Ch. Bhattacharya. Jorhat, Asam Sahitya Sabha: 233-35 (*in Assamese*).

510. ———— : Pahar Bhoiamar annanya janajati. *(In) Asamar Janajati. (Ed.)* by Pramod Ch. Bhattacharya. Jorhat, Asam Sahitya Sabha: 322-34 (*in A., Hajong etc.*).

511. ———— **(Ed.)** : *Asamar Janajati.* Jorhat, Assam Sahitya Sabha (*in Assamese*).

512. **Bhattacharya, Pramod Chandra** : 1969 : *Asamar Loka Utsav*. Gauhati (*in Assamese*).

513. ———— : 1973 : Asamar thaluwa sanskritir samannay: Garo-Rabha Bodo sakalar loka nritya : Hanaghora. *Jhankar* (Guwahati) (*in Assamese*).

514. **Bhattacharya, Sarmistha** : 1994 : Koch. *(In) People of India: Meghalaya. (Gen. Ed.)* by K.S. Singh. Calcutta, Seagull Books: 140-47.

515. **Bhattacharya, Suryyatara Pramodehandra** : 1969 : *Asamar Lok Utsav*. Guwahati, Pub. by the author, 108p.

516. **Bhattacharyya, Harichandra** : 1964 : *Origin and development of the Assamese drama and the stage from the earliest times up to 1940*. Guwahati, Barua Agency, 251p.

517. **Bhattacharyya, Kishore** : 1991 : *Structure and individual in Assamese society: A study of family, kinship, caste and religion*. Unpub. Ph.D. Thesis, Anthropology Deptt., Gau. Univ.

518. ———— : 1992 : Cultural construction of persons in Assamese society. *Bull. Deptt. of Anthropology, Dib. Univ.* 18-19(1989-90): 10-20.

519. **Bhattacharyya, Mini Thakur** : 1991 : Planned development, change and nature of ethnic identity: A study on the Dibongiya Deoris. *Bull. Deptt. of Anthropology, Dib. Univ.*, 16-17 (1987-88): 89-93.

520. **Bhattacharyya, Nandalal** : 1992 : *Asamer Lokakatha*. Calcutta, Best Books, Publication Division.

521. **Bhattacharyya, P.C.** : 1975 : Asomiya Sanskriti Jana Jatir Barangini. *Asomiya Sanskriti*, Asom Sahitya Sabha, Jorhat. *(Ed.)* by H.P. Neog and Lila Gogoi.

522. ———— : 1976 : Elements of Indo Mongolis Boro culture. *(In) The Common Quest. (ed.)* by D.N. Chakravarty. Guwahati, Directorate of Infor. and Pub. Relation, Govt. of Assam.

523. ———— : 1978 : Religious beliefs among the tribes of Assam. *Bodosa, 19th Conference of the Bodo Sahitya Sabha*.

524. ———— : Some socio-religious aspects of the tribes of North-East India. *All India Tribal Conference*.

525. ———— : 1983 : Boro and Dimasa: A comparative study. *Bull. of the Tribal Research Inst.* (Guwahati), II.

526. ———— : 1985 : An introduction to Boro-Kachari society and culture. *(In) Boro-Kachari Samaj aru Sanskriti* by Bhabendra Narzi. Guwahati, Bina Library: XI-XVIII (*in Assamese*).

527. **Bhattacharyya, Padmanath** *(Ed.)* : 1929 : *Heramba Rajyer Dandavidi* (in B.). Guwahati, Samatater Prube: *Sahitya Parishad Patrika*, XVI, 1326 B.S., N.1.

528. **Bhattacharyya, Parag Kumar** : 1987 : *Treatment of love in Assamese short story: A study of its origin and development.* Unpub. Ph.D. Thesis, Gau. Univ.

529. ————— : 1987 : Oral Human of Mother Goddess. *Assam Tribune*, Oct. 1: 4(3-6) (About Kamakha).

530. **Bhattacharyya, Pramod Ch.** *(Ed.)* : 1995 : Rabha jati, atit aru bartaman. *History Conference on 27th Feb. 1995 at Kairabari, Darrang Dist., Xth Rabha Sahitya Sabha Session (Mimeo).*

531. **Bhattacharyya, S.C.** : 1994 : *Arunodaya yugar sahityat Asamiya samaj aru sanskriti: Eti adhayana.* Unpub. Ph.D. Thesis, Assamese Deptt., Gau. Univ. *(in Assamese)*

532. **Bhattacharyya, T.K.** : 1983 : *Sociology of the Karbis.* Ph.D. Thesis Gau. Uni.

533. **Bhorali, D.** : 1982 : Occupational division : Case study of Mriya community of Guwahati. *(In) Guwahati: Its past, present and future.* Guwahati, Handique College, Traders Unit: 21-4 (*Mimeo*).

534. **Bhowmick, Atul Ch.** : 1996 : Mech. *(In) Encyclopaedic Profile of Indian Tribes. (Eds.)* by Sachchidananda and R.R. Prasad. New Delhi, Discovery Pubg. House : 669-71.

535. **Bhowmick, P.K** : 1989 : Book Review: Matriliny to Patriliny: A study of the Rabha society by Manis Kumar Raha, New Delhi, Gian Pubg. House, 375pp, *Man and Life*, 15(3-4), July-Dec.: 197-200.

536. ————— : 1990 : *Applied Action-Development Anthropology.* Calcutta, Institute of Social Research & Applied Anth.: 182-94 (It has also on *Tribal development in North-East India).*

537. **Bhowmik, D.C.; Sipra Sen** *and* **S.K. Mukherjee (Comp)** : 1979: *Silver Jubilee Celebration, North-East India, Shillong, 1953-1978: Anthropological Literature of North-East India(Researches conducted by Anthropology S.I.).* Shillong, Anthropology S.I. (*Mimeo*).

538. **Bhowmik, P.K** : 1994 : *Primitive tribal groups in Eastern India.* Calcutta, 260 p.

539. **Bhowmik, Sharit Kumar** : 1988 : Development perspectives for tribals. *EPW*, XXIII (20), May 14: 1005-07(Assam and NEI).

540. **Bhuiyan, N.C.** : 1960 : *Cha bagichar banua* (In A.). Jorhat, Asom Sahitya Sabha.

541. **Bhuyan, B.C.** : 1995 : *The Tribal Women*. New Delhi, Omsons Pubn., 102p.

542. **Bhuyan, Banti** : 1980 : *A study on fishing, death and disposal, religious beliefs and practices of the Sonowal Kacharis of Lepetkata*. M.Sc. Disser. Unpub. Anthropology Deptt., Dib. Univ.

543. **Bhuyan, Girin** : 1980 : *The Sonowal Kachari of Lepetkata: An investigation into house type, death and disposal and village organization*. M.Sc. Disser. Unpub. Dib. Univ.

544. **Bhuyan, Hiranya Kr.** : 1996 : The scintillating folk dances of the Bodos of Assam: (Culture). *Eastern Panorama*, April: 26-7 (Bodo).

545. **Bhuyan, Jadav** : 1979 : Handicrafts of Assam. *Times of India*, Dec. 7: 8 (1-3).

546. **Bhuyan, S.K.** : 1918 : *Ahomar Din, or, an account of the social and political condition of Assam during Ahom regime (in Assamese)*. Guwahati, DHAS, Assam.

547. ———— : 1959 : The administrative system of the Ahoms. *(In) A Souvenir: Aspects of the heritage of Assam. (Ed.)* by K.N. Dutt. Guwahati, Indian History Congress, 22nd Session: 89-95.

548. **Bhuyan, Sattyakee (D'Com)** : 1996 : Karbi youth festival. *Sentinel*, Feb. 24: 4 (2-5).

549. **Bista, Dor Bahadur** : 1967 : *People of Nepal*. Kathmandu, Ratna Pustak Bhandar (Reprinted, 2nd edition in 1972): 37(Koch), 134-37(Rajbanshi): 142-45 (Bodo).

550. **Biswas, C.K.** : 1990 : The Hindu identity of the Barmans of Cachar. *Proceedings of a seminar on Status of religion in tribal areas in NEI* organised by NEICSSR, Shillong on 15-16 Feb. (*Mimeo*).

551. **Biswas, Hemanga** : 1385BS : *Lok sangeet samiskhya* : Bangla O Assam. Calcutta, A. Mukherjee (*in Bengali*).

552. **Bloch, T.** : 1898 : On an Assamese drum or "Doba" (foreward by J.F. Needham). *Proceedings of the Asiatic Soc. of Bengal*, 186p.

553. **Boissya, C.L.** *and* **R. Majumder** : 1980 : Some folklore claims from the Brahmaputra valley (Assam). Ethnomed (W.Germany), VI(1-4): 139-45.

554. **Bonin, C.E.** : 1911 : Les Tribes de Frontiere et la Penetration Anglaise du Haut-Assam. *Asie Francaise*: 284-93.

555. **Bonnerjea, B.** : 1932 : An inquiry into the position of women in Hindu Society. *Indian Antiquary*, 61: 145.

556. **Bora, A.K.** : 1985 : Review of legal provisions relating to the employment of children in tea plantations and its enforcement. *Unpublished paper presented in a Seminar on Child Labour in tea plantation of Assam* (Guwahati), Feb. 12-14 (*Mimeo.*).

557. **Bora, Astam** : 1995 : Dimasa Janajati. *Pur. Pra.*, Jan. 10: 5(1-2) *(in H.)*

558. **Bora, Bibha** : 1994 : *Society in Medieval Assam with special reference to women*. Unpub. Ph.D. Thesis, History Deptt., NEHU, Shillong.

559. **Bora, Dipalima** : 1987 : Assam and Tribal Problems-I. *Shillong Times,* Oct. 14: 2(3-6).

560. ———— : 1987 : Assam and Tribal Problems-II. *Shillong Times,* Oct. 15: 2(3-6).

561. **Bora, Dipanjali** : 1996 : Harsa aur ullas ka Vaishakhi parva (in H). *Pur. Pra.,* April 14: 5 (1-6).

562. **Bora, K.P. et al** : 1962 : A sociological study of postgraduate students of Guwahati University. *Jr. Univ. Gau.* (Arts), 13(1): 109-44.

563. **Bora, Mrinal Kr.** : 1996 : Traditional folk costume of the Pati Rabhas of Assam. *Seminar paper on Traditional Culture and Folklore in North-East India*, 18-19 Nov. Shillong, NEICSSR.

564. **Bora, N.N.** : 1981 : *Dyarchy in Assam*. Ph.D. Thesis, G.U.

565. **Bora, P.P.** : 1990 : Letters to the editor: Committee on Art and Culture. *Assam Tribune*, March 13: 4(3-4).

566. **Bora, Shiela** : 1994 : The Nowgong Orphan Institute: A reflection on miles Bronsons work for women (1843-1854). *Seminar on Social Movements in North-East India with special reference to women, youth and religion,* organised by NEICSSR, Shillong on 26-27 August, 1994 (*Mimeo*).

567. **Borah, D.** : 1975 : Religious practices in a Chaudang village. *The North Eastern Research Bulletin*, VI, Summer: 69-76.

568. ———— : 1977 : Social organisation among the Dimasa Kacharis with special reference to family and marriage. *Seminar and 3rd Conference of North-East India Sociological Association*, Deptt. of Sociology, Dib. Univ. February.

569. ———— : Occupational differentiation and political Organisation in a Village in Upper Assam. *(In) North-East India. (Ed.)* by S.M. Dubey. New Delhi, Concept Publishing House.

570. ———— : Village leadership in a Dimasa Kachari

village. *Seminar on Social and Political Institutions of the Hill People of NEI,* organised jointly by Anthropology Surv. of India and NEICSSR, Shillong, July 1977.

571. **Borah, D.** : 1978 : Occupational, Differentiation and Political Organization in a village in Upper Assam *(In) North-East India: A Sociological Study. (Ed.)* by S.M. Dubey. Delhi, Concept Publishing House: 135-48.

572. ———— : 1985 : *Khejurbond : Socio-Economic Resurvey of a Tribal Village in North Cachar Hills District of Assam*. Jorhat, Agro Eco. Research Centre (NEI), 120 p. (*Mimeo*).

573. ————: 1986 : *A study of the Socio-Economic conditions of the Dimasas with reference to their agricultural practice.* Unpub. Ph.D. Thesis, Assam Agricultural Univ., Jorhat.

574. ———— : 1990 : Village leadership in a Dimasa Kachari village. *(In) Social and Political Institutions of the Hill People of North-East India. (Eds.)* by Jayanta Sarkar and B. Datta Ray. Calcutta, Anthropology Survey of India: 29-35.

575. **Borah, D.** *and* **S.N. Buragohain** : 1979 : *Khejurbor: A Socio-Economic Survey of Dimasa Village.* Jorhat, Agro Eco. Res. Centre (*Mimeo*).

576. **Borah, D.K.** : 1983 : Itafort and the Chutias. *Arunachal News,* 12(5), Aug.-Sept.: 26-8.

577. **Borah, J.N.** : 1989 : Letters to the Editor: Madhupur Satra. *Assam Tribune,* Sept. 4: 4(3-4) (Near Kokrajhar).

578. **Borah, Meena** : 1988 : Neo-Vaisnavism of Sankaradeva. *Assam Tribune,* Sept. 21: 4(7-8).

579. ———— : 1989 : *Later history of Vaishnava faith and movement in Assam.* Unpub. Ph.D. Thesis, Gau. Univ.

580. ———— : 1992 : Image worship in Neo-Vaisnavism. *Assam Tribune,* Aug. 29: 4(3-6).

581. **Borah, Sadhana** : 1967 : Bihu, festival of seasons. *Illus. Weekly of India,* 88(17), May 28: 61.

582. **Borah, Sonmoni** : 1993 : *Influences of the West on Assamese culture.* Rongpur (Sibsagar). Asam Sahitya Sabha.

583. **Bordoloi, B.N.** : 1983 : An ethnographic note on the Hmars of North Cachar Hill district of Assam. *Bull. Tribal Research Institute, Assam,* 1(1).

584. ———— : 1984 : Strategies from tribal development in N.E. India with special reference to Assam. *Proceedings of a Seminar*

on Anthropology and Development with Spl. Reference to N.E. India, Dib. Univ.

585. **Bordoloi, B.N.** : 1984 : Some aspects of etymology of the term "Dimasa Kachari". *(In) The Tribes of North-East India. (Ed.)* by S. Karotemprel. Calcutta, Firma KLM: 245-51.

586. —————— : *The Dimasa Kacharis of Assam.* Guwahati, T.R.I. (2nd edition), 103p.

587. —————— : 1985 : Assam's special component plan for Scheduled Castes: Retrospective and Perspective. *(In) Planning in North-East India. (Ed.)* by K. Alam. New Delhi, Omsons Pub.: 63-78.

588. —————— : Masira Kohir: The Holiest verse of the Karbis and its significance. *(In) Folklore in North-East India. (ed.)* by Soumen Sen. Delhi. Omsons Pub.: 93-6.

589. —————— : The Karbis: Their origin and migration. *Bull. of TRI* (Guwahati).

590. —————— : Strategies for tribal development in North-East India with special reference to Assam. *Bull. of TRI,* I(III).

591. —————— *et al* : Traditional Tribal Institutions. *Bull. TRI,* Assam, Guwahati, Vol. I(3).

592. —————— : 1987 : The Dimasa Kachari; the Karbis. *(In) Tribes of Assam,* I, by B.N. Bordoloi, G.C. Sharma Thakur and M.C.Saikia. Guwahati, TRI(Assam): 36-51; 52-73.

593. —————— : 1988 : The Barmans of Cachar: The Zemi Nagas of N.C. Hills. *(In) Tribes of Assam,* II, by B.N. Bordoloi and G.C.Sharma Thakur. Guwahati, TRI (Assam): 1-19: 94-110.

594. —————— : Women's education in the tribal areas of Assam: A few basic issues. *(In) Tribal Women and Development. (Eds.)* by J.P. Singh, N.N. Vyas and R.S. Mann. Udaipur (Rajasthan) MLV Tribal Research and Training Institute: 209-20.

595. —————— : 1989 : Tribal Development Plans and Programmes in the Sixth Schedule Areas of Assam with special reference to Management of land: A Critical Appraisal. *Paper presented in the National Seminar on Nehru and Evolution of Tribal Policy in India.* New Delhi, Sept. 1989.

596. —————— : 1990 : Constraints of tribal development in North-East India: A few basic issues from Assam experiences. *(In) Constraints of Tribal Development in North-East India. (Ed.)* by B.N. Bordoloi. Guwahati, TRI : 51-67.

597. —————— : Constraints of tribal development in North-East India. Guwahati, TRI, 222p.

598. **Bordoloi, B.N.** : 1991 : Hajongs. *(In) Tribes of Assam,* III, Guwahati, Assam Inst. of Research for Tribals & Scheduled Castes: 18-42.

599. —————— : The Meches. *(In) Tribes of Assam,* Pt. I, *(Ed.)* by B.N. Bordoloi. Guwahati, Assam Institute of Research for Tribes and Scheduled Castes: 79-97.

600. ————— : 1992 : *Proceedings of a Seminar on Tribal Women and Development*, organised by Assam Institute of Research for Tribals and Scheduled Castes, Guwahati on 4-6 April, 1992 (*Mimeo.*).

601. —————— : Tribal development in Assam : Some visible and invisible constraints. *(In) Constraints of Economic Development in North-East India. (Eds.)* by P.D. Saikia and D. Borah. New Delhi, Omsons Pub.: 25-36.

602. ————— : 1993 : On the composite Assamese culture with special reference to tribal elements. *Proceedings of a Seminar-cum-Workshop on the Cultural Heritage of the North-East India*, held at Gouri Sadan, Guwahati on 25 Sept. 1993 by Vivekananda Kendra Institute of Culture (*Mimeo*).

603. ————— : 1996 : Hajong. *(In) Encyclopaedic Profile of Indian Tribes. (Eds.)* by Sachchidananda and R.R. Prasad. New Delhi, Discovery Publishing House: 314-16.

604. —————— : Rabha. *(In) ibid*: 860-62.

605. **Bordoloi, B.N. (Ed.)** : 1986 : *Alienation of Tribal Land and Indebtedness*. Guwahati, AIRTSC.

606. ——— **(Ed.)** : 1988 : *Proceedings of a Seminar on Constraints of Tribal Development in North-East India*, organised by TRI, Guwahati on May 16-18.

607. —————— **(Ed.)** : *Application of Science and Technology for Tribal Development.* Guwahati, TRI, 203p.

608. ——— **(Ed.)** : 1991 : *Tribes of Assam,* III. Guwahati, Assam Inst. of Research for Tribals & Sch. Castes, 99p.

609. **Bordoloi, B.N.** *and* **G.C. Sharma Thakur** : 1986 : *Alienation of Tribal Land and Indebtedness.* Guwahati, Assam Inst. of Res. for Tribals & Sch. Castes.

610. ————— : 1988 : *Tribes of Assam,* Part II. Guwahati. TRI, Assam, 111p. (Barman of Cachar, Sonowal Kachari, etc.).

611. **Bordoloi, B.N., G.C. Sharma Thakur** *and* **M.C. Saiki** : 1987: *Tribes of Assam. Part I.* Guwahati, TRI, 142p (Boro-Kachari, Deori, Dimasa Kachari, Karbi, Lalung, Miri, Rabha, etc.).

612. **Bordoloi, Buddhiman** : 1896 : Shaka: Mor jatir samparke asar serek. *Ringchang* (Jorhat), I(II), Bhadra 1. (*in Assamese*).

613. ———— : 1973 : Tiwa sakalar Krishti, Ringsang. *A Jr. of the All Assam Tiwa Yuba Chatra Sanmilan*, 1(1).

614. **Bordoloi, Budhindra Nath** : 1966 : A night among the Dimasa Kacharis with special reference to the dance performed by them to welcome outside guests (*Assamese*). *Janasikhya*, 27(1).

615. ———— : Bachelors' dormitory: Mikirs. *Janasikhya*, 26(6).

616. ———— : 1967 : The case study of a rice brewing Mikir family. *Assam Tribune*, (*Sunday Magazine*), June.

617. ———— : 1974 : *A case study of a rice brewing Karbi (Mikir) family*. Diphu, Diphu Govt. College, Pub. in the Historical Survey of Diphu.

618. ———— : 1976 : *(The) Dimasa Kacharis of the North Cachar Hills District of Assam*. Gauhati, Dir. Inf. and Pub. Rel., Govt. of Assam, 99p.

619. ————: 1982 : *Chomangkan : The death ceremony performed by the Karbis*. Gauhati, Tribal Research Institute, Assam, 54p.

620. ———— : 1983 : The Veipheis of North Cachar Hills District of Assam: A brief ethnographic note. *(In) Souvenir: Anthropological Society of North-East India. (Eds.)* by H.C. Sharma and B. Choudhury. Gau. Univ., Anthropology Deptt.: 37-40 (Any Kuki tribe).

621. **Bordoloi, Dharmaram** : 1965 : Lalung jatir parichay. *Tiwa Sampradayer Parichay*, Jorhat: 6-7 (*in Assamese*).

622. ———— : 1973 : Tiwa jatir parichay. *Ringsang*, I(I) (*in Assamese*)

623. **Bordoloi, M.N.** *and* **B.M. Das** : n.d. : *Assamiya Sanskriti* (*in Assamese*).

624. **Bordoloi, N.** : 1975 : Costumes and Ornaments of Assam. *Link*, 17 (21), Jan. 5: 32-4.

625. **Bordoloi, Nirmal Prabha** : 1972 : *Asamar Loka Sanskriti*. Guwahati.

626. **Bordoloi, Nirmal Prova** : 1982 : *Karbi samaj aru sanskritir e cherenga*. Jorhat, Asam Sahitya Sabha, 68p (*in Assamese*).

627. ———— : 1986 : *Tantra and tantrism of ancient Assam*. Guwahati, Sahitya Prakash, 522p.

628. **Bordoloi, P.K.** : 1970 : *Research Project on Urbanisation in Tribal Areas (Namrup and Dimapur)*. Sociology Deptt., Dib. Univ.

629. ——————— : A village in Upper Assam. *North Eastern Research Bulletin* (Dib. Univ.), 1 (Summer): 72-80 (Brahmin; Koch, Chutia; Muslim-Sayed, Sheik; Kalitas-Kahar (Brass), Kumar (Potter), Sonar (Goldsmith).

630. **Bordoloi, Prasanta Kr.** : 1977 : Study of organization and social relationship in a factory in Upper Assam. *(In) North-East India: A Sociological Study. (Ed.)* by S.M. Dubey. New Delhi, Concept: 89-98.

631. **Borgohain, Hiren** : 1980 : The Turungs and their social and cultural life: A Mongoloid population of Assam. *Jr. NEICSSR*, IV(II), Oct.: 16-8.

632. **Borgohain, Rooplekha** : 1994 : *Politics of land reforms in Assam.* New Delhi, Reliance Publishing House.

633. **Borkakati, Sanjib Kr.** : 1994 : Caste definition and caste conflict. *Assam Tribune*, July 1.

634. **Borkataky, Anju** : 1992 : Women and violence in non-tribal societies of Assam. *(In) Status of Women; Assam. (Ed.)* by S.L. Baruah. New Delhi, Omsons Pubs.: 127-32.

635. **Borkataky, Biren** : 1992 : Folk culture : Its nature and future. *Assam Tribune*, April 13: 4(3-8) (Ahom).

636. ————— : 1994 : Place of assimilation in Assamese culture. *Assam Tribune*, April 14: 4(3-8).

637. **Borman, B.M.** : 1968 : *Early Political Institutions of the Tai: Synthesis and Symbiosis.* Unpub. M.A. Thesis, University of Washington.

638. **Boro, Anil** : 1996 : The traditional religion of the Boros: A fusion of Indian and ethnic specific tradition. *Seminar paper on Traditional Culture and Folklore in North-East India*, 18-19 Nov. Shillong, NEICSSR.

639. **Borooah, Anundoram** : 1994 : *Boro Chuti Galpa (in Assamese).* Guwahati, Inst. of Language, 35p.

640. **Borooah, Jnandabhiram** : 1963 : *Folk Tales of Assam.* Gauhati, Lawyer's Book Stall, 136p(3rd *Reprinted*; 1st edition Pub. by Timber and Stores Agency, Howrah, 160p in 1915 and 2nd edition by L.B.S., Guwahati in 1955, 121p.

641. **Borthakur, Nandita** : 1995 : Utility of Bamboo in Households of Assam. *Jr. NEICSSR*, 19 (1), April: 43-7.

642. **Borthakur, S.K.** : 1976 : Traditional weaving implements among the Mikirs (The Karbis) of Assam. *Indian Museum Bulletin*, XI (2), July: 46-50.

643. **Borthakur, Sarat** : 1988 : Textile Art of Assam. *Assam Tribune (Sunday Reading)*, Sept. 11: I(1-8).

644. **Borua, Prafulla Kumar** : 1990 : Human sacrifice in Kamakhya. *Assam Tribune (Sunday Reading)*, Oct. 7: 2 (1-8).

645. **Boruah, Aswini** : 1994 : Epitome of composite culture. *Assam Tribune (Sunday Reading)*, Jan. 16: I (1-8) (Religion of Assam: Hajo).

646. **Boruah, B.K.** : 1960 : *Sankardeva : Vaisnava saint of Assam*. Gauhati, Assam Academy for Cultural Relations.

647. **Boruah, Hemanta Kr.** : 1991 : *Asamor Bihu utsav eyar Sanskritik disar vislesanatmak adhyayan (An analytical study of the cultural aspects of the Bihu festival of Assam)*. Unpub. Ph.D. Thesis, Dib. Univ.

648. **Boruah, Prafulla** : 1965 : *Fundamentals of Assamese culture*. Gauhati, P.C. Barua, 36p.

649. **Boruwa, Pallav** : 1995 : Principal Satras in Assam. *Assam Information*, XXXXVI, Jan.-March: 39-40 (Brahma Samhati, Kala Samhati, Purusa Samhati, Nika Samhati or Sampradai).

650. **Bose, J.K.** : 1934 : Dual organisation in Assam. *Jr. Deptt. of Letters*, Cal. Univ., Vol. 25: 1-29.

651. ———— : 1936 : Origin of levirate in Assam. *Nature*, June 6.

652. ———— : 1942 : Anthropological notes and news: Levirate in Assam. *Man in India*, XXII(1), Jan.-March: 71.

653. ———— : 1980 : *Glimpses of Tribal Life in North-East India*. Cal., Inst. of Soc. Res. and App. Anthropology (Mikir: 25, 63; Mantak : 75; Kachari: 86; Miri: 25; Ahom: 25; Rabha: 65, 87).

654. **Bose, N.K.** : 1959 : *Slave Trade in Assam*. Calcutta, Modern Bengal: 67-8.

655. ———— : 1960 : *50 years of Anthropology*.

656. ———— : 1971 : *Tribal Life in India*. New Delhi, NBT India (*Assam etc.*).

657. ———— : 1972 : *India—The Land and People: Some Indian Tribes*. New Delhi, NBT India: 1, 3, 6, 9, 11, 14, 39, 55, 70, 72, 75, 84, 108, 135.

658. **Bose, N.K.** : 1972 : *Anthropology and some Indian problems.* Calcutta, Inst. of Soc. Res. and App. Anthropology

659. **Bose, Nirmal Kr.** : 1967 : National Seminar on Hill People. *Man in India,* 47(1), Jan.-March: 1-7.

660. **Bower, Ursula Graham (Betts, Ursula)** : 1940 : The founding of Chingjaroi. *Folklore,* 51: 211-13.

661. **Bowmik, K.L.** : 1971 : *Tribal India: A profile in Indian Ethnology.* Calcutta, The World Press.

662. **Brahma, C.M.** : 1993 : Literature and social reality in the tribal societies of North-East India (1968-1993)—So far as it relates to the Bodo society. *Proceedings of a Seminar on Literature and Social Reality in Tribal Societies of North-East India* (1968-93) held on 24-25 Nov. 93 in NEHU, organised by Centre for Literary and Cultural Studies, NEHU; NERC; ICSSR (Shillong).

663. **Brahma, Dhananjay** : 1984 : A significance of the *Siphung* (flute) in the Bodo Kachari society. *Souvenir, 25th Annual Conference,* Bodo Sahitya Sabha, Gossaigaon Session.

664. ————— : 1985 : A significant place of Sijau in the Bodo Kachari Society. *Souvenir of the 26th Conference of the Bodo Sahitya Sabha,* Boko, Kamrup, Assam.

665. **Brahma, K.** : 1983 : Gods and Goddesses of the Bodos: How they are worshipped. *Jr. NEICSSR,* 7 (2), Oct. : 35-9.

666. **Brahma, Kameswar** : 1985 : "Hathasuni", a primitive system of marriage of the Bodos: Special reference to the Bodos of Kokrajhar and Goalpara districts. *Jr. NEICSSR,* 9(1), April: 44-7.

667. ————— : 1988 : Bathou: Its impact on Bodos. *Laithun,* III: 86.

668. ————— : 1989 : Status of Bodo women in the Society. *Seminar on Status of women in the plain tribal societies of Assam: Tradition and change,* organised by Folklore Res. Deptt., G.U.

669. **Brahma, Kameswar** : 1989 : *Aspects of social customs of the Bodos.* Gossaigaon (Kokrajhar, Assam), Chiranjib Brahma, 81p.

670. ————— : 1992 : *A study of socio-religious beliefs, practices and ceremonies of the Bodos : With special reference to the Bodos of Kokrajhar District.* Delhi, Mittal Pub., 310p.

671. **Brahma, M.M.** : 1979 : *Boro Kacharir Samajar Khel, iyear utpatti aru bibheg.* Jorhat, *Asam Sahitya Sabha* (*in Assamese*).

672. **Brahma, Mohini Mohan (Ed.)** : 1960 : *Folk songs of the Bodos.*

Gau. Univ., Pub. Deptt., Deptt. of Tribal Culture and Folklore, Research.

673. ———— : 1976 : *Kherai : The main festivals of the Bodos.*

674. ———— : 1983 : A brief introduction of the Bodo-Kacharis of Assam. *Bull. TRI* (Gau.), I(I).

675. **Brahma, Mohini Mohan** *and* **Praphulladatta Goswami** : 1972: *Bodo Kachari Sola.* Gau. Univ., Folklore, Research Deptt., 261p. (*in Assamese*).

676. **Brahma, R.C.** *and* **B.B. Gayary (Eds.)** : 1976 : *The Khamrub Bisombi (Kamrup Smriti)* : Souvenir, the 17th Conference of All Bodo Sahitya Sabha, Barama, Kamrup, 83p.

677. **Brahma, R.N.** : n.d. : *Boro Jatir Sangkhipta Parichay.* 16p.

678. **Brahma, Rupnath** : n.d. : Boro-Kacharir Sanskriti (*in Assamese*). *Asom Sahittya Sabha Patrika* (Jorhat), 13 (3).

679. **Briffault, Robert** : 1927 : *The Mother: A study of the origins of sentiments and institutions, vol. III.* London, George Allen & Unwin Ltd.

680. **Brigumuni** : 1970 : *Mising Sanskritir alekhyo* (*in Assamese*). Guwahati, Brigumuni Kaguyung.

681. **Brownlow, C.** : 1874 : Description of a Bachelor's Hall among the Mikir tribes, Assam, with certain symbols connected therewith. *Jr. and Proceedings of the Asiatic Society of Bengal*: 17-8.

682. **Buragohain, Jaya** : 1987 : Aitons : Some aspects of their life and culture. *North-East India Historical Association*, 8: 539-46.

683. ———— : 1989 : Some devices employed by the Aitons in fixing auspicious and inauspicious moment. *NEIHA*, 10: 155-58.

684. ———— : 1991 : Some traditional beliefs and rituals connected with construction of new houses by the Aitons *NEIHA*, 12: 202-07.

685. ———— : 1992 : *The Aitons in transition*: A study. Unpub. Ph.D. Thesis, Gau. Univ.

686. **Buragohain, Jaya et al** : 1993 : *Socio-economic conditions and cultural aspects of the tribal villagers: (Balijan Adarsha Missing Gaon of Bokakhat region).* Golaghat, Hemo Prava Borbora Girls' College, Sociology Deptt., Feb. 21.

687. **Buragohain, R.** : 1985 : Myths, rituals and traditions: Some aspects in State formation in the early Tai-Ahom State. *NEIHA*, 6: 137-45.

688. **Buragohain, R.** : 1986 : Social stratification in the Ahom State. *NEIHA*, 7: 125-30.

689. ———— : 1987 : On Brahmanical Influence in the formation of the Ahom State. *NEIHA*, 8: 170-82.

690. **Buragohain, S.N.** : 1983 : The Mishings of the Brahmaputra Valley. *Himalaya: Man and Nature*, VII(5), Oct.

691. **Buragohain, Sukapha** : 1988 : Letters to the Editor: Ahoms. *Assam Tribune*, Feb. 6: 4(6).

692. **Burhabhakat, Kantiram** : 1927 : *Phakara* (2nd edition). Barpeta (About Folklore).

693. **Burling, Robins** : 1967 : Tribesmen and lowlanders of Assam. *(In) South East Asian Tribes, Minorities and Nations. (Ed.)* by Peter Kunstadter. Princeton, New Jersey, Princeton University Press: 215-29.

694. **Butler, John** : 1847 : *Sketch of Assam with some account of the hill tribes*. London.

695. ———— : 1855 : *Travel and adventures in the Province of Assam.* London.

696. **Buzarbarua, P.M.** *and* **R.P. Athparia** : 1990 : Social and cultural life of the Mishing of Assam. *Social Research*, 10 (2-3), Aug.-Dec.: 6-11.

697. **Buzarbaruah, P.M.; R.K. Chiring; N. Ojah; P. Acharya** *and* **S. Devi** : 1977 : *A study on some aspects of socio-cultural life of the Mishing of Mainapara village, North Lakhimpur*. Unpub. M.Sc. Disser., Anthropology Deptt., Dib. Univ.

698. **Campbell, George** : 1866 : The Ethnology of India. *Jl. Roy. As. Soc. of Beng.*, 35, Pt. 2: 1-152.

699. **Cantlie, Audrey** : 1984 : *The Assamese: Religion, caste and sect in an Indian village*. London School of Oriental and African Studies, Univ. of London, Curzon Press, 322p.

700. **Chakraborti, Arun Kr.** : 1989 : Kherai: A part of Bodo heritage and culture. *Man and Life*, 16(1-2), Jan.-June: 87-98.

701. **Chakraborty, B.** : 1894 : *Saka*: Goalpara loka utsab. (*in Assamese*) *Bandana*, Kati.

702. **Chakraborty, S.B.** : 1994 : *Tribal Land and Forest Rights in Assam.* Mussourie, LBS National Academy of Administration, 37p.

703. **Chakravarti, Tapo Nath** : 1955 : Some manners and customs in the light of the early inscriptions of Bengal and Assam. *Calcutta Review*, 135: 244-58.

704. **Chakravorty, Jadav** : 1988 : Letters to the Editor: Assamese dress. *Assam Tribune*, Jan. 30: 4(4-5) (Miching).

705. **Chakravarty, Manoj M.** : 1980 : The myth that rocks Assam. *Lokayata* (Karimganj), Aug.: 29-30.

706. **Chakravartty, D.N.** : 1986 : Hills and the hill tribes in Bihu songs. *Assam Tribune*, April 14: 4(3-6), 7(4) (Mikir, Karbi, etc.).

707. **Chakravartty, D.N.** : 1986 ; Hill and hill tribes in Assamese literature. *Assam Tribune*, Feb. 22: 4(3-6).

708. ———— : 1987 : World's unique festival. *Assam Tribune*, April 14: 4(3-6), 9(3-4).

709. ———— : 1988 : Bihu: A unique festival. *Statesman*, April 16: 6(3-4); 7(5).

710. ———— : 1990 : Preservation and Enrichment of Folk culture of North-Eastern Region. *Assam Information*, XXXXII, April-May: 11-8.

711. **Chaliha, Bhaba Prasad** : 1987 : North-East India: A Cultural Panorama. *Assam Tribune*, Dec. 6: 4(3-6), 6(4-5).

712. ———— : 1990 : The Heritage of Assam. *Assam Tribune (Sunday Reading)* Dec. 2: I(1-8).

713. ———— : 1991 : Folklore studies in North-East. *Assam Tribune*, Nov. 17: 4(7-8).

714. **Chaliha, Parag Dhar** : 1994 : *Aspects of Assamese Culture*. Guwahati. Assam Pub. Board.

715. **Chaliha, Pradeep** : 1989 : Letters to the Editor: Folk songs. *Assam Tribune*, March 1: 4(4-5) (Goalpara, Kamrupi).

716. **Chaliha, Purna** : 1980 : *An account of the Sonowal Kachari of Lepetkatta village with reference to the agriculture, birth and pregnancy and economic organisation*. M.Sc. Unpub. Disser. Anthropology Deptt., Dib. Univ.

717. **Chandra, Bhushan** : 1991 : Anekata men ekata ke rang: Ahom ke nritya (*in Hindi*). *Pur. Pra. (Lohit Bharati)*, March 3: 2(1-4) (Mishing or Miri, Karbi, etc. Bihu dance).

718. **Chatterjee, S.** : 1988 : Socio-economic condition in a Lalung village. *Himalaya: Man and Nature*, XII(1-2), June-July: 9-11.

719. **Chatterjee, S.K.** : 1959 : Assam and India. *(In) Souvenir on aspects of the heritage of Assam. (Ed.)* by K.N. Dutt. Gauhati, 22nd session of Indian History Congress, December: 1-7

720. ———— : 1973 : Foreword. *(In) The Meches and the Totos* by C.C. Sanyal. Darjeeling, University of North Bengal.

721. **Chatterjee, S.K.** : 1973 : Foreword. *(In) The Meches and the Totos* by C.C. Sanyal. Darjeeling, Univ. of North Bengal.

722. **Chatterji, Suniti Kumar** : 1951 : *Kirata-Jana-Kriti: The Indo-Mongoloide, their contribution to the history and culture of India.* Calcutta, Royal Asiatic Society of Bengal: 27-8, 30, 55-6, 57-68 (Bodo, Ahom, Koch, Chutiya, Dimasa, Kachari, etc.).

723. ———— : 1968 : The name Assam Ahom. *Jour. Asiatic Society of Bengal,* 28(3): 47-56.

724. **Chattopadhaya, Kamala Devi** : 1978 : *Tribalism in India.* New Delhi, Vikas Publishing House.

725. **Chattopadhyay, B.M.** : 1967 : Folksong of Cachar—Rak-hal-AAI. *Folklore,* VIII(10), Oct.: 350-69.

726. **Chaube, S.K.** : 1980 : *Caste status and power: Social stratification in Assam.* New Delhi, Classical Publications.

727. **Chaudhuri, Buddhadeb** *(Ed.)* : 1982 : *Tribal development in India: Problem and Prospects.* Delhi, Inter India Pubs.; 42, 49, 58, 92, 129-31, 137, 145, 146, 159, 216-20, 224, 226-29, 231, 242, 243, 313, 314, 330, 335, 354, 356, 392, 447, 455, 505.

728. **Chaudhury, B.N.** : 1960 : Judicial Administration of Assam, 1845-58. *Jr. Univ. of Gau.,* XI(I): 1-16.

729. **Chaudhury, M.M.** : 1980 : *Tribes of Assam Plains.* Gauhati.

730. **Chaudhury, P.D.** : 1967 : Arts and Crafts. *Illus. Weekly of India,* 88(17), May 28: 44-6.

731. **Chauhan, Ram Prasad** : 1990 : Asom men Ram Katha janashruti ke rup men lokpriya (*in Hindi*). *Pur. Pra,* June 9: 4(3-8) (Karbi).

732. ———— : Dimasa janajiban aur puja paddhati (*in Hindi*) *Pur. Pra.,* June 19: 5(3-8) (Kachari).

733. **Chauhan, S.K.** : 1970 : Structure of family, role differentiation and decision-making in the villages of Assam. *North Eastern Research Bulletin,* I, Summer: 54-62.

734. ———— : 1972 : Caste hierarchy in three villages of Upper Assam. *Man in India,* 52(1), Jan.-March: 39-45.

735. ———— : Caste, class and power: An analysis of the stratification system in rural Upper Assam. *Eastern Anthropology,* XXV(2), May-Aug.: 149-60.

736. ———— : Social mobility in Upper Assam: A note on Sanskritisation. *Social Action,* 22(3), July-Sept.: 231-36.

737. ———— : Status, power and institutions—A test convergence hypothesis. *Interdiscipline,* 9(4), Winter: 27-41.

738. **Chauhan, S.K.** : 1975 : Changing patterns of stratification in Assam. *Proceedings of a Seminar on Sociological Perspective on North-East India and the Second Annual Conference of North-East India Sociological Association*, Dib. Univ. Deptt. of Sociology, March 10-12, 1975 (*Mimeo*).

739. ———— : 1980 : *Caste, status and Power: Social stratification in Assam*. New Delhi, Classical Publishing Company, 168p.

740. ———— : Caste structure in Assam. *East. Anthropology*, 33(2), April-June: 123-32.

741. ———— : 1984 : Caste and status groups in Assam: Some questions and queries on Weber's concept of 'status group'. *East. Anthropology*, 37(4), Oct.-Dec.: 339-52.

742. **Chetia, Nakul Chandra** : 1981 : Mayamara Dinjay satrar itibritta. *(In) Mayamara Satra Samaj: Bhasau aru Pravandha. (Ed.)* by Sushil Kr. Gogoi. Chabua(Assam), Mayamara Kala Kristi Anusandhan Aru Prachar Samity: 37-53 (*in Assamese*).

743. ———— : Mayamara sampradayar dharma mat. *(In) Mayamara Satra Samaj: Bhasa aru Pravandha. (Ed.)* by Sushil Kr. Gogoi. Chabua(Assam), Mayamara Kala Kristi Anusandhan Aru Prachar Samity: 54-66 *(in Assamese)*.

744. **Chetri, Manbahadur** : 1983 : *Asamiya Nepali Samaj aru Samskritir ruprekha*. Jorhat, *Asam Sahitya Sabha*, 135p (In A.).

745. **Chib, Sukhdev Singh** : 1984 : *Caste, Tribe and Culture of India, Vol. 8: North Eastern India*. New Delhi, Ess Ess Pubns., 384p.

746. **Choudhuri, Alak R.** : 1980 : Short note on Mirijim tribal craft of Deshangmukh, Sibsagar District, Assam. *Bulletin of the Cultural Research Institute*, 14(3-4), 59-61.

747. **Choudhuri, Kalyani** : 1993 : Bihu Bihu lagibo gat (*in Hindi*). *Pur. Pra. (Lohit Bharati)*, April 13: 1(1-2).

748. **Choudhuri, P.C.** : 1981-82 : Ketekibari Satra: A Vaisnava Institution at Gauhati. *Jour. Assam Research Society*, 26: 68-72.

749. **Choudhury, Ambikacharan** : 1992 : *The Koches around the world*. Bongaigaon, Ratnapith Prakashan.

750. **Choudhury, B.N.** : 1982 : *Smriti O Pratiti*. Calcutta, Pub. by the author, 207p. (in B., *Jhumur* folk song of Barak Valley).

751. **Choudhury, J.N.; Sunirmal Dutta Choudhury; Amalendu Bhattacharjee** *and* **Manobendra Bhattacharjee (Eds.)** : 1996: *Srihatta Cacharer Prachin Itihash O Sanskritir Ruprekha.*

Calcutta, Jitraj Offset for Bangiya Sahitya Parishad and Rabindra Smriti Granthagar (*in Bengali*).

752. **Choudhury, M.M.** : 1980 : *Tribes of Assam Plains*. Guwahati.

753. **Choudhury, Medini** : 1991 : Musing over Bohag Bihu. *Assam Tribune* (*Sunday Readings*) April 14: II(1-8).

754. ———— : 1994 : Asamar Atitar Jana Prabrajan (*in Assamese*). *Gariyoshi*, June: 23-4.

755. **Choudhury, Nalini** : 1996 : Bihu ki sarthakata (*in Hindi*) *Pur. Pra., Lohit Bharati*, April 14: 1(3-6).

756. **Choudhury, P.C.** : 1959 : Kamarupi systems of Ayurveda, Astrology and Almanac. *(In) A Souvenir: Aspects of the Heritage of Assam. (Ed.)* by K.N. Dutt. Gauhati, Indian History Congress 22nd Session, December: 22-30.

757. ———— : 1969 : Ketekibari Satra: A Vaisnava Institution at Gauhati. *Assam Tribune*, August 31.

758. **Choudhury, P.D.** : 1967 : Arts and Crafts. *Illustrated Weekly of India*, 88(17), May 28: 44-6.

759. **Choudhury, R.D.** : 1976 : Cultural Heritage of Assam, a Survey. *North Eastern Spectrum*, 1(6), Dec.: 25-30.

760. **Choudhury, Rabijit** : 1995 : S.T. Status planned for Assam communities. *St.*, Feb. 9: 9(1-5) (Koch Rajbongshi, Ahom, Motok, Moran, Chutia, Tea-Tribes; Koch-Rajbanshi are Sch. Tribe in Meghalaya and O.B.C. in West Bengal).

761. **Choudhury, Ranjit** : 1995 : An Assamese sans Bhogali Bihu. *Sentinel, Saturday Fare*, Jan. 14; 1(1-8).

762. **Choudhury, S.** : 1994 : Lalung. *(In) People of India: Meghalaya (Gen. Ed.)* by K.S. Singh. Calcutta, Seagull Books for *An. S.I.*: 219-27.

763. **Choudhury, Sujit** : 1977 : Kartik worship in the Cachar District of Assam. *Folklore*, 18(11), Nov.: 341-47.

764. ———— : 1980 : Ranachandi's transformation of a Dimasa deity. *(In) Religion and Society of North-East India. (Ed.)* by Sujata Miri. New Delhi, Vikas Pub. House: 104-07.

765. **Choudhury, Satyendra Narayan** : n.d. : Eri, Muga, Pat. Guwahati, *Assam Sc.Soc.* (*in Assamese*) (Description about the material of the clothes).

766. **Choudhury Thakuria, Rita** : 1987 : Cultural exchange through Museum. *Assam Tribune*, May 10: 4(3-6), 5(3-4).

767. ———— : 1988 : Cultural Heritage and Planning Commission. *Assam Tribune*, Jan. 24: 4(3-6), 5(7-8) (Kachari).

768. **Choudhury Thakuria, Rita** : 1992 : Legal status of women in non-tribal societies of Assam. *(In) Status of women in Assam. (Ed.)* by S.L. Baruah. New Delhi, Omsons Pubs.: 133-45.

769. **Chowdhury, Nalini** : 1996 : Bhogali Bihu Asam ka pramukh toihar. (*in Hindi*). *Pur. Pra.*, Jan. 14: 5(4-6).

770. **Chowdhury, Prosenjit** : 1994 : *Socio-Cultural aspects of Assam.* New Delhi, Vikas Publishing House, 96p.

771. **Chowdhury, Sudhangsu** : 1952 : Traditional Arts and Crafts of Tripura, Manipur and Assam. *Art in Industry*, III(3).

772. **Chutia, M.** : 1986 : *Continuity and change among the Chaudangs of Assam: A Study in ethnicity and social stratification.* Unpub. Ph.D. Thesis, Anthropology Deptt., Dib. Univ.

773. **Cochrane, W.W.** : 1911 : An Ahom (Shan) legend of creation (from an old Mss). *Jr. of the Royal Asiatic Society of Great Britain and Ireland*: 1132-42.

774. **Committee** : 1978 : *Tribal Women in India*. Calcutta, Indian Anthropology Society, 199p.

775. **Cotton College Planning Forum** : 1977 : Brassmetal industry of Hajo: (A Survey Report). *North Eastern Economic Review*, 1(1), Jan.-March: 45-52.

776. **Crace, J.H.** *and* **J.H. Hutton** : 1960 : Animal tales from Assam. *Folklore*, Sept.: 180-83.

777. **Crawford, T.O.** : 1924 : *Handbook of Castes and Tribes employed on the tea-estates in North-East India*. Calcutta, Indian Tea Association.

778. **Crooke, W.** : 1896 : *The Tribes and Castes of North Western Province and Oudh*, Vol. III. Calcutta, Govt. Press: 153-59, 217-20 (Jogi, Keot).

779. **Crooke, W.** : 1907 : *The Natives of Northern India (Punjab, Bengal, United Provinces, Assam)*. London Archibald Constable (Native Races of the British Empire).

780. **Cumming, R.C.R.** : 1921 : *Census of India 1921, Vol. III*, Pt. I, Appendix-B, Assam: Notes on certain frontier tribes: XIII.

781. **Daimary, Bijoy** : 1987 : Bore and Bodo. *North-East India History Association*, 8: 528-32.

782. **Daimary, Girindra Brahma** : 1976 : A short account of the Bodo Music and Culture. *Khamrup-Bisombi. (Eds.)* Ram Charan Brahma and Bimal Brahma Gayary. Barama (Kamrup, Assam), *Souvenir 17th Conference, All Bodo Sahitya Sabha* (4-7 March): 18-21.

783. **Dalton, Edward Tuite** : 1851 : Notes on the Mahapurushyas: A sect of Vaishnavas in Assam. *Jr. Royal Asiatic Society of Bengal*, 20: 455-69.

784. ———— : 1872 : *Descriptive Ethnology of Bengal*. Calcutta, Supdt. Govt. Printing (Reprinted in 1960 by Indian Studies: Past and Present, Calcutta) : 81-92(Kachari/Bodo, Mech, Koch, etc.).

785. ———— : 1895 : Notes on the Chutiyas of Upper Assam *(In) An Outline Grammar of Deuri Chutiya language spoken in Upper Assam. (Ed.)* by W.B. Brown. Calcutta, Govt. Press.

786. ———— : 1973 : *Tribal History of Eastern India*. Delhi, Cosmo Pubs. (This is the Reprint of the book entitled *Descriptive Ethnology of Bengal*)..

787. **Damant, G.H.** : 1875 : Sword worship in Cachar. *Indian Antiquary*, 4: 114-15.

788. ———— : The North Cachar Hills and their inhabitants. *Calcutta Review*, 61: 97-9.

789. ———— : 1879 : Succession of the sister's son. *Indian Antiquary*, 8: 205-06.

790. ———— : 1880 : Notes on the locality and population of the tribes dwelling between the Brahmaputra and Ningthi rivers. *JRAI (N.S)*, 12: 228-58 (Cachar, Mikir, Sham, etc.).

791. **Danda, Ajit K.** : 1983 : Book Review: *Chomangkan: The death ceremony performed by the Karbis* by B.N. Bordoloi, Guwahati, Tribal Research Institute, Assam, 1982 pp. VI+54, *Human Science*, 32(2), June: 138-40.

792. ———— : 1986 : Development perspectives and the rural poor. *Human Science*, 35(3), Sept.: 169-70.

793. ———— : 1988 : Processes of ethnic integration. Some theoretical and methodological problems. *Human Science*, 37.

794. ———— : Ethnicity and nationality in India: Some theoretical issues. *Human Science*, 37.

795. ———— : Ethnicity in plural-cultural society. *Jr. Ind. Anthropology Society*, 23.

796. ———— : Tribes in India. *Man in India*, 68.

797. ———— : 1989 : On ethnicity and political mobility. *Jr. Ind. Anthropology Society*, 24(3), Nov.: 210-11 (Udayachal by the Bodo-Kachari tribe).

798. ———— : 1990 : *Ethnicity in India*. New Delhi, Inter-India Publications.

799. **Danda, Ajit K.** : 1992 : Ethnicity and social transformation in North-East India. *Man in India*, 72(2), June: 131-40 (Bodoland. etc.).

800. ———— : 1994 : Ethnicity and social transformation in North-East India. *(In) Tribal Situation in North-East India. (Ed.)* by Sarthak Sengupta. New Delhi, Inter-India Pub. 38-50.

801. ———— : *Weaker sections in Indian villages (in 2 vols).* New Delhi, Inter-India Pubn.

802. ———— : 1996 : Shifting cultivation in North-East India. *Jr. Ind. Anthropology Society*, 29(1-2), March-July; 59-74(Assam).

803. **Danda, Dipali G.** : 1994 : Analysis of family structure in double descent system. *(In) The Indian Family. (Ed.)* by Kalyan Kr. Chakravarty, Bhopal, Indira Gandhi Rashtriya Manav Sangrahalaya: 159-64 (Diamsa).

804. ———— : Eco-Cultural Adaptataion of the Semsa. *(In) Tribal Situation in North-East India. (Ed.)* by Sarthak Sengupta, Inter-India Pub.: 206-14.

805. ———— : Method of Hinduization in North Cachar. *Jr.Ind. Anth. Society*. 29 (1-2), March-July: 143-50.

806. ———— : 1996 : Kinship and descent among the Dimasa. *(In) Kinship and Family in North-East India. (Ed.)* by J.S. Bhandari. New Delhi, Cosmo Pubns.: 225-46.

807. **Danda, Dipali Ghosh** : 1964 : Post funeral ritual in a Dimasa Kachari village. *Man in India*, 44(3): 247-51.

808. ———— : 1965 : Notes on family among the Dimasa Kachari. *Man in India*, 45(1), Jan.: 17-26.

809. ———— : Descent and clan among the Dimasa. *Man in India*, 45(3): 185-94.

810. **Danda, Dipali Ghosh** : 1966 : *Life-way of the Dimasa Kachari (An Album)*. Cal., Anthropology Surv. of India.

811. ———— : 1967 : The economy of the Dimasa Kachari of United Mikir and North Cachar Hills. *(In) A Common Perspective for North-East India. (Eds.)* by Rathin Mitra and B. Das Gupta. Calcutta, Pub. by Pannalal Das Gupta: 213-17.

812. ———— : 1978 : *Among the Dimasa of Assam: An Ethnographic Study*. New Delhi, Sterling Pubs., 192p.

813. ———— : Position of women in a bilineal society: The Dimasa case. *(In) Tribal Women in India. (Ed.)* by Committee. Calcutta, Indian Anthropological Society: 181-85.

814. **Danda, Dipali Ghosh** : 1980 : On Dimasa descent system. *(In) Glimpses of Tribal Life in North-East India* by J.K. Bose. Calcutta, Institute of Social Research and Applied Anthropology: 241-56.

815. ———— : 1981 : The Semsa economy. *Jr. Ind. Anthropology Society*, 16(2), July: 95-106.

816. ———— : 1984 : A Note on the Semsa : A Selection of the Dimasa. *(In) The Tribes of North-East India. (Ed.)* by S.Karotemprel. Calcutta, Firma KLM: 414-21.

817. ———— : Dimasa. *(In) Tribal Education in India. (Eds.)* by Biman K. Das Gupta and Ajit K. Danda. Calcutta, Anthropology Survey of India: 7-9.

818. ———— : The Semsa Economy. *Jr. Ind. Anthropology Society*, 19 (1), March: 95-106.

819. ———— : 1988 : Village endogamy and marriage rules among the Semsa. *(In) Marriage in India. (Eds.)* by B.B. Goswami, J. Sarkar and D. Danda. Calcutta, Anthropology Surv. of India: 115-20.

820. ———— : 1991 : Some observations on the Dimasa ethnic identity. *(In) Stratification, Hierarchy and Ethnicity in North-East India. (Eds.)* by R.K. Bhadra and S.R. Mandal. Delhi, Daya Pubg. House.

821. **Danda, Dipali G.** *and* **Ajit K. Danda** : 1980 : On Dimasa descent system. *(In) Glimpses of Tribal life in North-East India* by J.K. Bose. Calcutta, Inst. of Soc. Res. & App. Anthropology: 241-56.

822. **Danda, Dipali G.** *and* **Sanchita Ghatak** : 1985 : *The Semsa and their habitat (Memoir No. 64)*. Cal., Anthropology Survey of India, 87p.

823. **Das, A.C.** : 1969 : Barpetar Tini Satrar Chamu Itibritta (*in Assamese*) *Souvenir: Asam Sahitya Sabha*, Barpeta.

824. **Das, A.K.** : 1971 : The Gamocha in Assam (Society and Culture). *Pine* (Shillong), I(I): 9-14.

825. ———— : 1979 : *Comparison between the Hills and Plains Mikir of Assam in respect of certain anthropogenetic traits and their ethnic position*. Unpub, Ph.D. Thesis, Dib. Univ.

826. **Das, Abhijit** : 1994 : Letters to the Editor: Rongali Bihu. *Assam Tribune*, April 11: 4(3-4).

827. **Das, A.K., M.K. Raha** *and* **S.K. De** : 1990 : *Tribal Situation in West Bengal*. Calcutta, Firma KLM (Rabha etc.).

828. **Das, A.R.** : 1995 : Mikir. *(In) People of India: Arunachal Pradesh.* (Gen. Ed.) by K.S. Singh, Calcutta, Seagull Books for *An. S.I.*: 206-10.

829. **Das, Amal Kr.** : 1994 : Sankradeva: Apostle of Bhaktibad. *Assam Tribune*, Oct. 13: 4 (3-8).

830. **Das, Amal Kumar** : 1964 : *The Koras and some little known communities of West Bengal.* Calcutta, Cultural Research Institute (Mech: 07-102).

831. ———— : 1993 : Tribal Polity in West Bengal: An overview. *(In) Polity, Political Process and Social Control in South Asia: The Tribal and Rural Prospectives. (Eds.)* by Manis Kumar Raha and Iar Ali Khan. New Delhi, Gyan Publishing House: 223-39 (Rabha: 236-37).

832. **Das, Amal Kumar** *and* **Manis Kumar Raha** : 1967 : *Rabhas of West Bengal.* Calcutta, Cultural Research Institute, 176p.

833. ———— : 1968 : Book Review: The Rabhas of West Bengal, Calcutta, Cultural Research Institute, (1967), 176p. *Indian Jr. Social Work* (Bombay), 29(2), July: 220-21 and also in *Man in India*, 48(4), Oct.-Dec.: 373.

834. **Das, Amal Kumar, M.K. Chaudhuri** *and* **S. Basu** : 1982: Anthropology of development: Socio-economic condition of the Scheduled Tribes and Scheduled Castes of Eastern India. *(In) Tribal Development in India: Problem and Prospects. (Ed.)* by Buddhadeb Chaudhuri. Delhi, Inter India Pubs.: 353-70.

835. **Das, Arjun Chandra** : 1962 : *Asamiya Sadhu* (*in Assamese*), (2nd edition). Barpeta.

836. **Das, B.M.** : 1950 : Some aspects of tribal art in Assam. *(In) Souvenir on some aspects of the heritage of Assam. (Ed.)* by K.N. Dutt. Gauhati, 22nd Session of Indian History Congress, December: 82-8.

837. **Das, B.M.** : 1955 : Rabha kinship terms. *Man in India*, 35(1), Jan.-March: 52-6.

838. ———— : 1956 : A note on the Hira potters of Assam. *Man in India*, 36(3), July-Sept.: 199-202.

839. ———— : 1957 : Family structure of the Rabhas of Assam. *Man in India*, 37(2), April-June: 119-23.

840. ———— : 1960 : Ethnic elements in some Bodo populations. *Jr. Assam Research Society* (Gauhati). 14 : 36-42.

841. ———— : *Ethnic Affinities of the Rabha*. Gau. Univ., Deptt. of Tribal Cul. and Folklore, Research, Pub. No. 6. (Arleng, Rabha, Bodo, Kachari).

842. **Das, B.M.** : 1962 : Rabha. *(In) Asamar Janajati. (Ed.)* by Pramod Ch. Bhattacharya. Jorhat, Asam Sahitya Sabha: 163-72 (*in Assamese*).

843. ———— : 1963 : A note on the Khamyang. *Jr. Assam Research Soc.*, 17: 85-8.

844. ———— : 1964 : *Kaharpara: A report on Socio-cultural survey*. Gauhati, Deptt. of Tribal Cul. and Folklore, Res., Univ. of Gau., 69p. (Rajbanshi).

845. ———— : 1967 : Assamese culture and the Hill People of North-East India. *(In) A Common Perspective for North-East India. (Eds.)* by Rathin Mitra and Barun Das Gupta. Calcutta, Pub by Pannalal Das Gupta: 9-14.

846. —— **(Ed.)** : 1974 : *Contemporary Anthropological Research in North-East India*. Dib. Univ., Deptt. of Anthropology, 172p.

847. ———— : 1975 : Ethnic element and castes of Assam. *Jr. Hist. Res.*, Dib. Univ., 1: 8-13.

848. ———— : 1978 : Asomar Samaj Babastha: Keitaman disha. *(In) Asam Gaurav. (Ed.)* by Committee. Gauhati, Dept. of Assamese, Cotton College (In A.).

849. ———— : 1980 : The People of Assam. *The Assam Mirror* (Gauhati), Mani Manik Press: 1-4.

850. ———— : 1985 : *People of Assam: Their Ethnic Composition* (A Textbook of Foundation Course). Gau. Univ., Guwahati.

851. —————— : Assam, its people. *(In) Modern Assamese life and culture. (Eds.)* B. Dutta and A. Choudhury. Guwahati, Assam Academy for Cultural Relations: 7-18.

852. **Das, B.M. (Ed.)** : 1986 : *Asamar Manuh* (*in Assamese*). Jorhat, Asam Sahitya Sabha, 143p.

853. —————— : *Asamar Manuh, Prajati aru Sanskriti: Eti dristipat* (*in Assamese*). Dibrugarh, Assam College Teachers Association, DHSK College Unit.

854. ———— : 1987 : A note on marriage among rural Assamese people. *Bull. Deptt. of Anthropology, Dib. Univ.*, 11-12 (1982-83): 21-4.

855. —————— : Somaj babastha. *(In) Asamiya Viswakosh*, Pt. I. *(Ed.)* by Rajani Kanta Dev Sharma (*in Assamese*). Guawahati, Asam Prakashan Parishad: 283-92.

856. —————— : *People of Assam*. Delhi, Gian Publishing House, 98p.

857. **Das, B.M. (Ed.)** : 1990 : *North-East India: Its people, culture.* D.N. Majumdar Lecture, Ethnographic and Folk Culture Society, Lucknow.

858. ————— : 1991 : Rabha. *(In) Asamar Janajati. (Ed.)* by Pramod Ch. Bhattacharya. Guwahati, Asam Sahitya Sabha: 163-72 (in A., 2nd edition).

859. ————— : 1996 : Ethnic elements in North-East India. *(In) Peoples of North-East India: Anthropological Perspectives. (Ed.)* by Sarthak Sengupta. New Delhi, Gyan Publishing House: 1-12.

860. **Das, B.M.** *and* **Abu Nishar Md. Irshad Ali** : 1974 : Assamese (Muslim) in Muslim people. *(In) A World Ethnographic Survey. (Ed.)* by R.V. Weeks. Washington (USA).

861. ————— : 1985 : Child labour in Guwahati. *(In) Children in North-East India. (Ed.)* by B.M. Das. Calcutta, Anthropology Surv. of India: 43-54.

862. **Das, B.M. (Jt. Auth.)** : 1962 : A Sociological study of post-graduate students of Gauhati University, 1st part. *Jr. Gau Univ.*, XIII(1), 2nd part *(In) Jr. Gau. Univ.*, XIV(1), 1063.

863. **Das, B.M.; I. Ali; D.N. Majumdar** *and* **B. Choudhury** : 1985: Children in need of care and protection in Assam: An assessment. (In) *Children in North-East India. (Ed.)* by B.M. Das. Calcutta, Anthropology Surv. of India (It is also *Bull. Anthropology Surv. of India,* XXXI, 3-4, 1982): 55-73.

864. **Das, Bandana** : 1991 : *Small Units. Seminar on pattern and problems of population growth in India with special reference to North-East India,* held on Oct. 4 by Population Education Club, Women College, Shillong (*Mimeo.*).

865. **Das, Bandana** : 1994 : Assamese. *(In) People of India: Meghalaya. (Gen. Ed.)* K.S. Singh. Calcutta, Seagull Books for An. S.I.: 203-11.

866. **Das, Bhabesh** : 1987 : Kharai song and dance of the Bodos of Assam: A festival of farewell and welcoming a New Year. *Folklore,* 28(1), Jan.: 11-3.

867. ——————— : Love song of North-East India: An Account of some aspects of social gathering. *Folklore,*. 28(10), Oct. 241-43 (Karbi).

868. ————— : 1988 : The Gods and Goddesses of the Karbis: A short note about religion of an Assamese tribe. *Folklore,* 29(10), Oct.: 234-35.

869. **Das, Bhabesh** : 1989 : Botor Kikur: A folk festival of the Karbis for rain. *Folklore,* 30(8), Aug.: 181-83.

870. ———— : n.d. : Khuksi: The folk festival of the Rabhas, an outline of the worship pattern. *Folklore,* (?): 67-8.

871. **Das, Bhakta** : 1986 : *A Glimpse of the Scheduled Castes and their Socio-Economic development in Assam.* New Delhi, Omsons Pubs., 144p.

872. **Das, Bidyut K.** : 1978 : The Hajong Peasants: A study on some agrarian relations. *Jr. NEICSSR,* 2 (1): 6-9.

873. **Das, Birendra Kr.** : 1977 : *Boro Sadhu.* Jorhat, Asam Sahitya Sabha.

874. **Das, Biswajyoti** : 1990 : Assamese folk songs: Dwindling or Ameliorating? *Assam Tribune, (Sunday Reading),* July 29: I(1-8).

875. **Das, D.** : 1972, 1974, 1976 : *Goalpariya loka git, Vol. I(1972); Vol. II(1974); Vol. III(1976).* Gauripur (Assam), Pub. by the author.

876. ———— : 1983 : *Tribal population in Kamrup district.* Unpub. Ph.D. Thesis, Geog. Deptt., G.U.

877. **Das, Dambaru** : 1987 : Kherai Puja aru Kherai nach (*in Assamese*). *Ajir Asom* (Guwahati), Oct. 4 (Bodo).

878. **Das, Debendra Prasad** : 1987 : Letters to the Editor: Recognition as ST. *Assam Tribune,* Dec. 9: 4(5) (Boro-Kachari, Rabha, Koch, Rajbansi).

879. **Das, Dipak** : 1990 : Asamar Janajati Samashya—Year samadhan (*in Assamese*). *Sadin* (Guwahati), Nov. 2: 6(1-5), 12(2-5); Nov. 9.

880. **Das, Farida Ahmed and Indira Barua (Eds.)** : 1996 : *Communities of North-East India: An Anthropological Perspective.* Delhi, Mittal Pubn., 228p.

881. **Das, G.N.** : 1992 : A Glimpse into the Institution of Karbi kinship and its functionaries. *Bull. of Assam Inst. of Research for Tribals and Scheduled Castes* (Guwahati, TRI), Vol. I(VIII): 24-30.

882. **Das, Gopal Chandra** : 1962 : Laloong. *(In) Asamar Janajati. (Ed.)* by Pramod Ch. Bhattacharjee. Jorhat, Asam Sahitya Sabha: 173-81 (*in Assamese*), reprinted in 1991).

883. **Das Gupta, B.K.** : 1963 : Pot making in and around Tinsukia district Lakhimpur, Assam. *Bull. Anthropology Surv. of India,* XII(1-2), Jan.-June: 43-6.

884. **Das Gupta, B.K.** : 1963 : Report of the pottery survey : Assam. *Bull. Anthropology Surv. of India*, XII(1-2), Jan.-June: 109-26.

885. ———— : 1973 : A Note on the Rajbanshi of Eastern India with special reference to social movement. *Bull. Anthropology Survey of India*, XVIII(1), Jan. (1969): 1-44.

886. **Das Gupta, Biman K.** *and* **Ajit K. Danda (Eds.)** : 1984 : *Tribal Education in India (Memoir No. 61)*. Calcutta, Anthropology Survey of India. 203p.

887. **Das Gupta, Rajatananda** : 1965 : The institution of Devdasis in Assam. IHQ, XLIII, Part III, Aug. serial no. 128: 555-76.

888. **Das, Guneswar** : 1995 : The Hira Pottery Industry of Assam facing difficulties in improvement and upgradation. *(In) Core Problems of the Scheduled Castes of Assam. (Ed.)* by Bimal Kr. Hazarika. Guwahati, AIRTSC: 78-82.

889. **Das, Haren** : 1988 : Bihu: The Culture and the anarchy. *Assam Tribune*, April 13: 4(3-6).

890. ———— : 1989 : Bihu : Its present and future. *Assam Tribune*, April 13: 5(3-6), 7(3-5).

891. ———— : A Part of our Heritage. *Assam Tribune*, Sept. 30: 4(7-8).

892. **Das, H.C.** : 1995 : Impact of the Scheduled Caste component schemes among the Scheduled Castes of Assam. *(In) ibid*; 59-69.

893. **Das, H.P., D.K. Singh** *and* **M.N. Sharma** : 1971 : Meghalaya-Mikir Region. *(In) India: A regional study. (Ed.)* by R.L. Singh. Varanasi, NGUI.

894. **Das, J.** : 1968 : *Asomar Loka Kala*. Guwahati, Pub. by the author (In A.).

895. **Das, J.N.** : 1976 : Social changes in an orderly way. *Times of India*, Nov. 20: 10(5-8).

896. **Das, Jayshree** : 1985 : *Spatial structure of urban influence in the neighbouring areas of Gauhati city*. Ph.D. Thesis, Gau. Univ.

897. **Das, Jogesh** : 1972 : Asamer Loksanskriti (*tr. into Beng.*) by Khitish Roy, New Delhi, N.B.T. (Reprinted in 1983, 1986).

898. ———— : *Folklore of Assam*. New Delhi, National Book Trust, 142p. (Ahom, Koch, Lalung, Bodo, Mech, Mikir, Mishing).

899. ———— : 1992 : Rongali Bihu: A Festival of merriment. *North-East Times (Rongali Bihu Supplement)*, April 14: II(1-8).

900. **Das, Jugal** : 1988 : *Gahana Gathari*. Guwahati, Asam Prakashan Parishad, 57p (In A.).

901. ———— : 1982 : *A Study of the Land Systems of North Eastern Region,* Vol. I: Assam. Gauhati, Law Res. Inst., Eastern Region, Gau. High Court (*Mimeo.*).

902. ———— : 1987 : *A Study of Administration of Justice among the Tribes and Races of North Eastern Region*. Guwahati Law Res. Inst., Eastern Region, Gau. High Court.

903. ———— : 1990 : Satra Institution and Namghars. *Assam Tribune*, May 9: 6(3-5).

904. ———— : *A Study of Administration of Justice among the Tribes and Races of North-Eastern Region (excluding Nagaland and Meghalaya).* Guwahati, Law Res. Inst. Eastern Region, 687p.

905. ———— : 1973 : *An Introduction to the Land Laws of Assam*. Guwahati, Lawyers Book Stall.

906. **Das, K.** : 1971 : *A Study of Rituals and Ceremonies among the Mikirs of North Cachar*. Unpub. M.Sc. Disser. Anthropology Deptt., Dib. Univ.

907. **Das, Kamini (Ed.)** : 1981 : *Karbi Loka Sadhu*. Diphu, Diphu Sahitya Sabha.

908. **Das Kashyap, Depankar** : 1983 : *An ethnographic account of the Deuris of Kolowlowa Deuri gaon of Dibrugarh dist. with special reference to their house type, family, clan, marriage and political organisation*. Unpub. M.Sc. Disser., Anthropology Deptt., Dib. Univ.

909. **Das, Laksmi** : 1990 : Kamrupi Lokagit: Pradushan ka sankat. (*in Hindi*) *Pur. Pra.*, Dec. 30: 5(3-8).

910. **Das, M.M.** : 1985 : Kaibarta communities of Assam. *Proceedings of People of India* (Pre-Test Seminar), Anthropology Survey of India, Shillong on Dec. 5.

911. **Das, M.M.** : 1987 : Choudang of Sibsagar, Assam. *People of Assam, Seminar* on May 27, Anthropology Survey of India, Shillong.

912. **Das, M.N.** : 1972 : The place of Namghar in the village community in Assam. *North-East Research Bull.* 3, Summer: 13-9.

913. **Das, Madhav** : 1990 : Sanskriti ki ankh hai Asom. (*in Hndi*) *Pur. Pra. (Lohit Bharati)*, Dec. 16: 2(1-4).

914. **Das, Mrigen** : 1972 : The place of Namghar in the village community in Assam. *North Eastern Research Bull.*, I, Summer: 73-9.

915. ———— : 1978 : The place of Namghar in the village community in Assam. *(In) North-East India: A Sociological Study. (ed.)* by S.M. Dubey. Delhi, Concept Publishing Corp.: 181-88.

916. **Das, Murari Charan** : 1989 : Barpeta Satra: Its origin and development. *Assam Tribune.(Sunday Reading),* May 14: I(1-8).

917. **Das, N.C.** : 1986 : Urbanisation trends in North-East India with special reference to Assam. *(In) Pattern and Problems of Population in North-East India. (Ed.)* by B. Dutta Ray. New Delhi, Uppal Publishing House.

918. **Das, N.K.** : 1982 : Review of the works on social structures of some matrilineal tribes of North-East India and observations therein. *Jr. Ind. Anth. Society,* 17(3), Nov.: 199-214 (Koch, Lalung etc.).

919. ———— : 1989 : *Ethnic identity, ethnicity and social stratification in North-East India*. New Delhi, Inter India Pubn., 329p.

920. ———— : 1994 : Mikir. *(In) People of India: Nagaland.* Vol. xxxiv by K.S. Singh. Calcutta, Seagull Books: 207-12.

921. **Das, N.K.** *and* **P. Gupta** : 1982 : The Ahom movement. *(In) Tribal Movements in India,* Vol. I. *(Ed.)* by K.S. Singh. New Delhi, Manohar Pubn.: 307-15.

922. **Das, N.K** *and* **P.B.S.V. Padmanabham** : 1983 : *The Karbis of Assam Tribes in Contemporary India.* Shillong, Anthropology Surv. of India (Report, *Mimeo.*).

923. **Das, Nakul** : 1957 : Cultural progress of Assam tribes. *All India Congress Committee Economic Review,* Vol. 8, No. 17, Jan. 5: 72.

924. **Das, P.** : 1985 : Kamrupar Dhuliya Anusthan. (*in Assamese*) *Assam Bani (Rangali Bihu issue)*, April 14.

925. **Das, P.K.** : 1988 : Chah-bagichar Asomiya. *Prantik*, 7(28): 17-30 (*in Assamese*).

926. **Das, Prabin Ch.** : 1973 : Hajo Daul Aru Madanotsav. (*in Assamese*) *Dainik Asom*, March 13.

927. ———— : 1979-82 : Madana worship in Assam. *Gau. Univ. Jr. (Arts)*: 30-3.

928. ———— : 1983 : For religious-cultural link of Hajo with

Tibet and the rest of the Buddhist world. *Punya Bhumi Hajo (Hajo).*

929. **Das, Prabin Ch.** : 1983 : A Note on Bulbul-Fight of Hajo. *Folklore,* 24(2), Feb.: 43-5.

930. ———— : 1985 : Magic and supernaturalism in Hajo. *(In) Folklore, in North-East India. (Ed.)* by Soumen Sen. New Delhi, Omsons Pubs.: 85-92.

931. ———— : n.d. : *Punya bhumi Hajo* (In A.).

932. ———— : 1987 : Mare Puja and Deodha dance of Assam: A Note on a type of serpent worship. *Folklore,* 28 (9), Sept.: 216-19.

933. ———— : 1990 : The Sun Beams are there. *Assam Tribune,* Nov. 4: 4(3-6), 5(2-3) (Hajo in Kamrup district).

934. ———— : 1992 : Ambubachi and Satha Vrat of Assam. *Assam Tribune,* June 21: 4(3-6) (Kamakhya etc.).

935. ———— : 1993 : Durgavari : An Assamese version of the Ramayana. *(In) Rama Katha in tribal and folk traditions of India: Proceedings of a Seminar. (Ed.)* by K.S. Singh and Birendranath Datta. Calcutta, Seagull Pub. for Anthropology Survey of India, Calcutta: 139-52.

936. **Das, Prangopal Ch.** : 1989 : Mathura Das Burha Ata of Barpeta Satra. *Assam Tribune,* Sept. 19: 4(3-6), 5(3-5).

937. **Das, R. C.** : 1995 : Environmental awareness among Scheduled Caste population of Assam. *(In) Core Problems of the Scheduled Castes of Assam. (Ed.)* by Bimal Kr. Hazarika. Guwahati, AIRTSC: 29-33.

938. **Das, R.K.** : 1931 : *Plantation labour in India.* Calcutta.

939. **Das, Rajani Kanta** *and* **Ram Charan Brahma** : 1972 : *Sarania sakal kon jatir manuha.* (*in Assamese*) Nalbari.

940. **Das, Ramcharan** : 1955 : Report of the activities of Assam Sewa Samiti. *Vanyajati,* 3 July: 131.

941. **Das, S.** : 1969 : Barpetar utsav aru tithi parva samuh. *Souvenir: Assam Sahitya Sabha* (Barpeta) (*in Assamese*).

942. ———— : 1987 : Naganam. *Prakas,* 10(6), April.

943. **Das, S.K.** : 1940 : The Hindus of Assam: Are they a combination of warring groups? *Assam Tribune,* May 3.

944. ———— : 1972-73 : Disposal of the dead among the Ahoms. *Quart. Rev. of Hist. Stud.,* 12(2): 111-16.

945. **Das, S.T.** : 1980 : *The People of the Eastern Himalayas.* Delhi, Sagar Pubn.

946. ———— : 1982 : *The Indian Islands.* Delhi, Cosmo Pubn.

947. ———— : n.d. : *Our Seven Sisters in the North Eastern India.* Kanya Kumari, Vivekananda Kendra.

948. ———— : 1986 : *Nomads of the Bay of Bengal.* Delhi, National Publishing House.

949. ———— : *Tribal Life of North Eastern India : Habitat, Economy, Customs, Traditions.* Delhi, Gian Publishing House, 320p.

950. ———— : 1987 : *Lifestyle of Indian tribes (Locational Practice), Vol. I.* Delhi, Gian Publishing House : 65-132 (Mikir etc.).

951. ———— : 1993 : *Tribal development and Socio-cultural Matrix.* Delhi, Kanishka Pub. Dist., 272p.

952. **Das, Sankar Ch.** : 1995 : Garokhiya Gosain Than: Popular with pilgrims. *Sentinal, Saturday Fare,* Jan. 14: I (1-8) (Assam Religion).

953. **Das Sharma, P.** : 1971 : Census of India 1961: *Ethnographic study, Monograph series no. 7, Dimasa Kachari of Assam.* New Delhi, Office of the Registrar General of India.

954. **Das, Snigdha Jyoti** : 1995 : *Tamol*: The world's oldest chew. *Sentinel, Saturday Fare,* Sept. 16: I(1-8) (*Tamul*=Assam; *Kowai*= Meghalaya; *Kwa*=Manipur).

955. **Das, Sriramchandra** : 1949 : *Chandan.* Barpeta, Pub. by the author (*Folklore,*).

956. ———— : 1961 : *Mor deshar sadhu katha.* Mangaldai, Pub. by the author (*in Assamese,* 2nd edition).

957. **Das, T.C.** : 1937 : Some notes on the economic and agricultural life of a little known tribe on the Eastern Frontier of India. *Anthropos.,* 32: 440-49.

958. **Das, T.C.** : 1953 : Land tenure among the tribal populations of Assam. *Vanyajati,* I(1): 12-9.

959. ———— : 1955 : Social organisation. *(In) The Adivasis by Publication Division.* Delhi, Ministry of Information and Broadcasting, Pub. Div.: 99-117 (Assam etc.).

960. ———— : 1963 : Aspects of tribal culture under modern impact in Eastern India. *(In) Anthropology on the March. (Ed.)* by Bala Ratnam. Madras, The Book Centre: 137-54 (Assam etc.).

961. **Dasgupta, Barun** : 1975 : The temple of Kamakhya. *Link*, 17(21), Jan. 5: 34-5.

962. **Dasgupta, Biman Kr.** : 1978 : Social mobility movements among the tribes of Eastern and Cultural India. *Jr. Ind. Anth. Society*, 13(1), March : 11-7 (i.e. Goalpara, Nowgong).

963. ———— : 1990 : Book Review: *Ethnicity and Social stratification in North-East India* by N.K. Das, Inter India Publications, New Delhi, 1989: p. 323, *Jr. Ind. Anth. Soc.*, 25(2), July: 197-98.

964. **Dasgupta, P.** : 1941 : *Sedantary games of Rajbanshis*. Anthropological Papers, No. 6, Cal. Univ.: 151-58.

965. **Datta, B.** : 1982 :Bihu in lower Assam. *Assam Academic Review*, Spl. Issue.

966. ———— : 1983 : The study of the folklore material of NE India: The case for taking an integrated and multi-dimensional approach. *Assam Academy Review*, Spl. No. 1.

967. **Datta, B.N.** : 1938 : Anthropological notes on some Assam castes. *Anthropological Papers* (N.S.), No. 5: 1-26 (Cal. Univ.).

968. **Datta, Bhupendra Nath** : 1933 : Traces of totemism in some tribes and castes of North-Eastern India. *Man in India*, 13(2-3), April-Sept.: 97-114 (Cachar tribes).

969. **Datta, Birendranath** : 1973 : *A study of the folk culture of the Goalpara District of Assam*. Unpub. Ph.D. Thesis, Gau. Univ: 390.

970. **Datta, Birendranath (Comp)** : 1974 : *Goalpariya lokagit sangraha*. Guwahati, Barua Book Agency.

971. ———— : 1977 : *Asamiya sangitar aitihya*. Jorhat (*in Assamese*).

972. ———— : 1978 : *A Bibliography of folklore material of Assam and adjoining areas*. Gauhati. *Folklore*, Society of Assam, Gau. Univ.

973. ———— : 1979-82 : Ramakatha in Assam and its neighbourhood. *Jour. of Gau. Univ.* (Arts): 30-33.

974. ———— : 1980 : The Assamese folk-mind. *(In) Assam and the Assamese mind*. Jorhat, Asam Sahitya Sabha.

975. ———— : Assamese folk toys. *Illustrated Weekly of India*, 101(22), June 1: 16.

976. ———— : 1981 : The beliefs and rituals connected with finger. Jorhat, Asam Sahitya Sabha.

977. **Datta, Birendranath (Comp)** : 1981 : The tribal and the non-tribal in the context of Assamese society and culture. *Jour. NEICSSR*, V(II), Oct.: 8-12.

978. ———— : 1982 : Bangits of Assam: An Introduction. *Jour. NEICSSR*, VI(II), Oct.: 23-5.

979. ———— : Non-standard forms of Assamese: Their socio-cultural role. *(In) Linguistic situation in North-East India (Ed.)* by Mrinal Miri. Shillong, North-East Indian Council of Social Science Research: 61-8.

980. ———— : The Karbi Ramayana: An overview. *Assam Tribune*, April 25: 4.

981. ———— : Asamat Ramakatha aru tat Kandali Ramayanar sthan (*in Assamese*). *Bihalangani Sahitya Sankhya*, April.

982. ———— : Assam's Folk Literature needs scientific study. *Assam Tribune*, April 26: 8(7-8).

983. ———— : 1982-83 : Contact togetherness and commonness among tribal and non-tribal populations in North-East India: As reflected in folklore. *Bull. Deptt. of Anthropology, Dib. Univ.* (1987): 229-46.

984. ———— : 1983 : Sabin Alun: The Karbi Ramayana. *Jour. of Assam Research Society.*

985. ———— : The North-East Indian Milieu: Its distinctive character. *(In) Souvenir: Anthropological Society of North-East India. (Eds.)* by H.C. Sharma and B. Choudhury. Gau. Univ., Anthropology Deptt.: 46-50.

986. **Datta, Birendranath (Ed.)** : 1985 : Focus on folklore on North-East India. Special Volume (No. 1, 1983-84: 1-84 and No. 2, 1984-85: 1-78). Guwahati, Assam Academy Review, 162p. (About Dimasa, Karbi, Rabha, Assamese, etc.).

987. ———— : Karbi folklore: Some outstanding features. *Assam Academy Review*, Special Volume No. 2, Guwahati.

988. ———— : Re-Emergence of folklore: The North-East Indian scene. *Man and Life*, 11 (1-2), Jan.-June: 77-88.

989. ———— : The Mishings and their folklore: *An introductory survey Murong* (Dibrugarh).

990. ———— : 1986 : Folk songs of Assam: A survey of the Historical content and methods. *(In) Studies in the History of North-East India: Essays in honour of Professor H.K. Barpujari.*

(Ed.) by J.B. Bhattacharjee. Shillong, North-East Hill Univ. Pubn.: 10-37.

991. **Datta, Birendranath** : 1986 : Changing contours of tribal folklore: Through the North-East Indian window. *Bull. Deptt. of Anthropology, Dib. Univ.*, Vol. 15 (1990): 12-27.

992. ———— : 1987 : Contact, togetherness and Commonness among tribal and non-tribal population in North-East India: As reflected in folklore. *Bull. Anth. Deptt. Dibrugarh University*, XI-XII (1982-83): 29-46 (7 states).

993. ———— : Ramakathà in Assam and folk traditions. *Jour. of Gau. Univ. (Arts)*, XXX-XXXII.

994. ———— : Image of the cultures of the future. *(In) North-East India 2000 AD: Perspective for futurology. (Ed.)* by B. Datta Ray. New Delhi, Deep and Deep Pubn.: 222-29.

995. ———— : n.d. : Anthropological notes on some Assam castes. *Asiatic Soc. of Beng.* (Calcutta), 26p.

996. ———— : 1990 : Metafolklore, ethnic genres and analytical categories: Observations with examples. *Folklore,* 31(357-358), March-April: 63-8.

997. ———— : 1993 : Folklore, studies and the North-East. *Jour. NEICSSR,* 17(1), April: 6-12.

998. ———— : n.d. : Goalparar Loka-Nritya (*in Assamese*). *Santap* (Guwahati).

999. ———— : Tradition and innovation: Bargits, the Vaisnava Raga music of Assam. *Souvenir of International Congress of Youth Festival*, Gau. Univ., 1958.

1000. ———— : 1993 : Rama-katha in Assam and its neighbourhood: Popular and Folk Traditions. *(In) Rama-katha in tribal and folk traditions of India: Proceedings of a Seminar. (Eds.)* by K.S. Singh and Birendranath Datta. Calcutta, Seagull Pubn. for Anthropology S.I.: 119-30.

1001. ———— **(Ed.)** : *Anandam: Jour. of Anundoram Borooah Institute of Language, Art & Cul.* Assam. Vol. I and II, Guwahati.

1002. ———— *et. al* : 1994 : *A Handbook of Folklore Material of North-East India.* Gau. Univ., Folklore Research Deptt.

1003 ———— : Changing contours of tribal folklore in India. Through the North-East Indian window. *(In) Tribal Situation in North-East India. (Ed.)* by Sarthak Sengupta. New Delhi, Inter-India Pub.: 184-98.

1004. **Datta, Birendranath; Nabin Ch. Sarma and Prabin Ch. Das**: 1994 : *A Handbook of folklore material of North-East India*. Guwahati, ABILAC.

1005. ——————— : *A Handbook of folklore material of North-East India*. Guwahati, Anundoram Borooah Inst. of Language, Art & Cul. Assam. 428p.

1006. **Datta, Dandiram** : 1948 : *Kautuk (II)*. Barpeta, Pub. by the author (*in Assamese*). (*Folklore,*).

1007. ————— : 1954 : *Nimati Kanya* (*in Assamese*). Gauhati, Pub. by the author (*Folklore,*).

1008. **Datta, Madhu S.** : 1970 : *Projects on: Bihu festival of Assam: Sabia : A Vaisnavite Institution of Assam; Namghar: A community Vaisnavite in Assam and, pottery, silver ornaments and bellmetal crafts in Bombay, Jodhpur and Assam respectively*. Calcutta.

1009. **Datta-Majumder, Nabendu** : 1957 : The Colonisation of the Earth. Indian *Folklore,* 1(4), Oct.-Dec.: 3-4 (*Folklore,*).

1010. ————— : 1958 : The legend of Synriang. *Indian Folklore,* 2(1), Jan.-March: 35-40 (*Folklore,*).

1011. **Dattabarua, Parvati** : 1955 : *Kailasar Sadhu* (In A.). Nalbari, Datta Barua Pubn. (*Folklore*).

1012. **Datta Ray, B.** : 1996 : Book Review : *Phakials and other minor Thai communities of Assam* by S.K. Agnihotri, published by S. Kumar & Associates, Macholganj, Lucknow-226018, U.P. *Jour. NEICSSR,* 20(1), April: 60-1.

1013. **Datta Ray, B.** *and* **S.K. Agnihotri (Eds.)** : 1993 : *Dynamics of a tribal Society*. New Delhi, Uppal Publishing House, 315p.

1014. **Datta Ray, B.; D.N. Majumdar** *and* **D. Doley (Eds.)** : 1986 : *Crime perspective in North-East India*. New Delhi. Omsons Publishing 111p.

1015. **Daulatram, Jairamdas** : 1951 : The tribal faith in God. *Assam Tribune*, Jan. 26.

1016. **Dawka, Nivedita** : 1994 : Amar Bihu shesh nai: Bihu par vishesh. *Pur. Pra.*, April 9: I(3-6) (*in Hindi*)

1017. **Deb Bharati, Tarak** : 1973 : Eastern Indian Handicrafts: A preliminary survey. *Folklore,* XIV(9), Sept: 354-59.

1018. **Debi, Premalata** : 1993 : *Religious philosophy of the Boros of the Brahmaputra valley*. Unpub., Ph.D. Thesis, Gau. Univ.

1019. **Debi, Renu** : 1994 : *Women of Assam*. New Delhi, Omsons Pubn., 152p.

1020. **Dehingia, N.** : 1978 : *A Kacharis of Lezai Boruah Gaon: Their marriage system*. Unpub. M.Sc. Dissertation. Anthropology Deptt., Dib. Univ.

1021. **Dehotia, Kumar** : n.d. : *Maran Jatir Ruprekha*. Gauhati, Pub. by the author (*in Assamese*).

1022. **Deka, Bijita** : 1996 : Magh Bihu. *Assam Tribune (Sunday Reading)*, Jan. 14: III (3-6).

1023. **Deka, Bishnukamal** : 1996 : Rangalee Bihu Katha. *Pur. Pra. Lohit Bharat*, April 14: 1(3-6) *(in Bhojpuri)*.

1024. **Deka, Dinesh Ch.** : 1987 : *The Bodos of Kamrup: A Sociological Study*. Unpub. Ph.D. Thesis, Gau. Univ.

1025. **Deka, Guneswar** : 1995 : *Mantra prasiddha Mayong aru pobitrar itihas* (*in Assamese*). Pub-Guwahati, Mayong Anchalik College, February.

1026. **Deka, Hazarika, Karabi** : 1992 : Status of Assamese women in family and society as reflected in Assamese literature. *(In) Status of Women in Assam. (Ed.)* by S.L. Baruah. New Delhi, Omsons Pubn.: 64-8.

1027. **Deka, K.** : 1973 : Assamese Society: Structural change during the British regime. *North-Eastern Research Bulletin*, IV, Summer: 73-8.

1028. ———— : 1978 : Assamese society during the early British Period. *(In) North-East India: A Sociological study. (Ed.)* by S.M. Dubey. Delhi, Concept Publishing Compy.: 27-33.

1029. **Deka, K.B.** : 1992 : The Bhaumas in Assamese culture. *Assam Tribune(Sunday Reading)*, Feb. 23: I(1-8) (About Ahom History).

1030. **Deka, Kanak Ch.** : 1988 : The State Museum of Assam. *Assam Tribune*, Feb. 11: 4(3-8).

1031. **Deka, Krishnarajan** : 1990 : Asom men Kumari Puja (*in Hindi*). *Pur. Pra. (Lohit Bharati)*, Sept. 28: I(7-8).

1032. **Deka, Lakshi Singha** : 1894 Shaka: Lalung jatir chamu abhas (*in Assamese*). *Ringchang*, Vol. I, Falguna 27.

1033. **Deka (Medhi), Bandita** : 1993 : *The potters and pottery of Nalbari district, Assam: A Study in Ethno-history and Ethno-archaeology*. Unpub. Ph.D. Thesis. Anthropology Deptt., Gau. Univ.

1034. **Deka, Nirmali** : 1991 : *A Sociological study of the welfare of Harijans of Assam with special reference to Gauhati*. Unpub. Ph.D. Thesis. Gau. Univ.

1035. **Deka, Prasanna Kr.** : 1949 : *Sadhu Kathar Puthi* (*in Assamese*). Sarthebari (Assam), Pub. by the author (*Folklore,*).

1036. **Deka, Suresh Kr.** : 1993 Boro, Kachari janajatiyon par ek najar (*in Hindi*). *Pur. Pra.*, Oct. 5: 5(1-6).

1037. **Denneby, H.G.** : 1927 : The Kani (opium) puja of the Mikirs of Assam. *Man in India*, 7(2-3), March-June : 208-09.

1038. **Deori, Dambarudhar** : 1964 : *Deori sanskriti*. Sibsagar, Assam Pubn. Board (*in Assamese*).

1039. **Deori, R.K.** : 1988 : Birth and death rites of the Deoris. *Resarun*, XIV(1-2), Spring-Winter: 21-4.

1040. **Deptt. of Economics** : 1963 : *A report on the Socio-Economic Survey of the Chaudang Community in Jorhat sub-division, 1962*. Shillong, Assam Govt. Press, Deptt. of Economics and Statistics, 43p.

1041. **Deuri, Basanta Kr.** *and* **Lilakanta Deuri** : 1846 *Saka*: Deuribilakar bishayedu ashar (*in Assamese*). *Chetana*, 6(8), Choit (March-April).

1042. **Deuri, Bitopan** : 1975 : Tiwa samajar bibaha paddhati. *(In) Tiwa Sampradayar Parichaya. (Eds.)* by All Assam Tiwa Yuba Chatra Sanmilan. Jorhat, Asam Sahitya Sabha: 27-40 (*in Assamese*).

1043. **Deuri, Dambaru Dhar** : 1964 : *Deuri Sanskriti*. Sibsagar, Pub. by D.D. Deuri, 58p (*in Assamese*).

1044. **Deuri, Ganak Ch.** : 1962 : Deuri sakalar atit aru bartaman. *(In) Asomar Janajati. (Ed.)* by Pramod Ch. Bhattacharya. Jorhat, Asam Sahitya Sabha: 99-107 (*in Assamese*).

1045. **Deuri, Maneswar** : 1975 : Tiwa Samajar Karam Paddhati. *(In) Tiwa Sampradayar Parichaya. (Eds.)* by All Assam Tiwa Yuba Chatra Sanmilan. Jorhat, Asam Sahitya Sabha: 79-92 (*in Assamese*).

1046. **Deuri, Manojit** : 1994 : *Marigaon's Loka Sanskriti*. Jorhat, Asom Sahitya Sabha (*in Assamese*).

1047. ———— : 1983 : *Tiwa-Samaj*. Jorhat, Asam Sahitya Sabha, 108p. (*in Assamese*).

1048. **Deuri, Rameswar** : 1963 : Deuri Bihur Bangit. *Magazine of B. Barooah College*, Vol. II.

1049. **Dev, B.J.** *and* **D.K. Lahiri** : 1980 : Caste in Assam: A Sociological Study. *Indian Jour. of Politics*, XIV(1-3).

1050. **Dev, Bimal J.** *and* **Dilip K. Lahiri** : 1981 : The Naths of

Assam: The dilemma of Social Mobility. *Social Action*, 31(3), July-Sept.: 311-24.

1051. **Dev, Bimal J.** *and* **Dilip K. Lahiri** : 1984 : *Cosmogony of caste and social mobility in Assam*. Delhi, Mittal Pubn., 183p.

1052. ———— : 1985 : *Assam Muslims: Politics and Cohesion*. Delhi, Mittal Pubn., 220p.

1053. **Dev, Dina Nath** : 1975 : Purbottar Bharat me Samajik Vikas ki Samasya (*in Hindi*). *Vanyajati*, XXIII(4), Oct.: 33-6.

1054. **Dev, Goswami, Keshabanand** : n.d. : *Satra sangitar swar rekha* (*in Assamese*). Guwahati, Asam Prakashan Parishad.

1055. **Dev, Sharma, Rajanikanta** : 1987 : *Asamiya Viswakosha, 1st part* (*in Assamese*). Guwahati, Asam Prakashan Parishad: 1, 3, 260-66.

1056. **Devi, Amiya** : 1988 : Rongali Bihu in olden years. *Assam Tribune*, April 13: 4(3-6).

1057. **Devi, Aruna** : 1954 : *Transcription of Lakshminath Bezbarua's Tales of a Grandfather from Assam*. Indian Institute of Culture (Bangalore).

1058. **Devi, C. Geeta** : 1983 : *Anthropological field report on the people of Kolowlowa Deuri gaon with special reference to clan, family, dress and ornaments, birth and pregnancy and marriage*. Unpub. M.Sc. Dissertation, Anthropology Deptt., Dib. Univ.

1059. **Devi, L.** : 1968 : *Ahom-Tribal Relations (A Political Study)*. Gauhati. Pub. by L. Devi, 275p.

1060. ———— : 1971 : Ahom Khamti relations. *(In) The Tai Khamtis (Comp.)* by Lila Gogoi. Chowkham (NEFA), Chowkhamoon Gohain (Namsoon): 137-41.

1061. **Devi, Lakshmi** : 1968 : The Socio-Economic Life of the Miri Tribe. *North-Eastern Research Bulletin*, IV, Summer.

1062. **Devi, Lanu** : 1986 : *Family and kinship among the Karbi of Hamren(Karbi Anglong) and Narakasur (Kamrup)*. Unpub. Ph.D. Thesis, Gau. Univ.

1063. **Devi, Manju** : 1970 : *A Study of a Sonowal (Kachari) Society with special reference to its political organization in Tepargaon, Mancotta Mouza, Lakhimpur Dist.* Unpub. M.Sc. Dissertation, Anthropology Deptt., Dib. Univ.

1064. **Devi, Premalata** : 1990 : Christianity and its impact among the Boros of the Brahmaputra valley of Assam. *Proceedings of a Seminar on Status of Religion in Tribal Areas in NEI*, sponsored by NEICSSR, Shillong held on 15-16 Feb. (*Mimeo.*).

1065. **Devi, Premalata** : 1996 : Christianity among the Bodos of the Brahmaputra Valley of Assam. *Jour. NEICSSR,* 20(1), April: 43-7.

1066. **Devi, Radhika Bala** : 1991 : *The Kaibartas of the Darrang district of Assam: A Sociological Study.* Unpub. Ph.D. Thesis, Gau. Univ.

1067. **Devi, Rita** : 1967 : Dance heritage. *Illustrated Weekly of India,* 88(16), May 21: 26-7.

1068. **Devi, S.V.; M. Tamuli; M. Kharghoria** *and* **L. Baruah**: 1978: *A Study of some aspects of socio-cultural life of Bodo Kacharis community of Kokrajhar, Assam.* Unpub. M.Sc. Disser., Anthropology Deptt., Dib. Univ.

1069. **Devi, Troilokeswari** : 1937 : *Sandhiyar Sadhu.* Jorhat, Pub. by the authoress (*Folklore, in Assamese*).

1070. ———— : 1950 : *Sadhu katha* (*In* A. 3rd ed.). Gauhati, Pub. by the authoress (*Folklore,*).

1071. **Dey, Ratna** : 1989 : Brief survey of oral sources on the Goalas of Cachar. *Proceedings of NEIHA,* 10: 79-81.

1072. ———— : 1995 : Focus on oral source : Case studies in the Chatla village. *Paper in NEIHA, 16th Session,* 4-6 Dec. 1995, Silchar.

1073. **Dhajanarayan, Govinda Ch.** : 1955 : *Sri Maharashotsava gitamala* (In B.) Silchar, A.K. Burman, Nikhil Kachar Hairimba Barman Samiti.

1074. **Dhar, Bibhash** : 1976 : Tribesmen as townsmen: A case study in Assam. *Bull. Deptt. of Anthropology, Dib. Univ.,* 5.

1075. ———— : 1995 : Mishing. *(In) People of India: Arunachal Pradesh. (Gen. Ed.)* by K.S. Singh. Calcutta, Seagull Books: 211-15.

1076. **Dhar, Gouri** : n.d. : *Alienation and conformity among the University students in Assam.* Unpub. Ph.D. Thesis, Soc. Deptt., Dib. Univ.

1077. ———— : 1970 : Changing pattern of family in a suburb. *North-East Research Bulletin,* I, Summer: 90-5.

1078. **Dhavlikar, M.K.** : 1979 : Boat burial of eastern India. *Paper read at the Seminar on the History and Culture of North-East India.* Shillong, NEHU, History Deptt., (*Mimeo.*).

1079. **Dibrugarh University** : 1975 : *Seminar on Sociological perspective on North-East India and the Second Annual*

Conference of the North-East India, Sociological Association. Dib. Univ., Sociology Deptt., 55p.

1080. **Dibrugarh University** : 1984 : *Seminar on Anthropology and Development with special reference to N-E India*, organised by Anthropology Deptt., Dib. Univ., held on 16-18 Feb. (*Mimeo.*).

1081. ———— : 1990 : *Assam in 2001AD : Silver Jubilee of Dibrugarh University*. Dibrugarh, D.U., Dec. 17 (Golaghat).

1082. **Diphu Sahitya Sabha** : 1971 : *Karbi Prasanga* (*in Assamese*). *Diphu, Diphu Sahitya Sabha* (information about the Karbis).

1083. ———— : 1976 : Sabin Alun. Diphu, *Diphu Sahitya Sabha* (*in K.*).

1084. **DIPR** : 1989 : *Assam Land and People*. Guwahati, Director Information and Public Relations.

1085. ———— : 1975 : *Proceedings of a Seminar on Sociological Perspective on North-East India and the Second Annual Conference of the North-East India Sociological Association*, Dib. Univ., March 10-12, Deptt. of Soc. *(Mimeo)*.

1086. ———— : n.d. : Transformation in tribal societies: Issues and Policies. *Seminar Paper submitted to the 14th All India Sociological Conference*, Jabalpur Univ., M.P.

1087. ———— : 1976 : Modernization among the tribes of the North-Eastern India (Assam). *(In) Tradition and Modernization. (Ed.)* by S.K. Srivastava. Allahabad, Indian International Pubn. (1972).

1088. **DIPR (Ed.)** : 1978 : *North-East India: A Sociological Study*. Delhi, Concept Publishing Company, 426p.

1089. **Director** : 1963 : Bibliography of Prof. K.P. Chattopadhyay. *Bulletin Cultural Research Institute* (Tribal Welfare), 2(1): 8-11.

1090. **Director** : n.d. : *Tribals on the March*. Directorate of Information & Public Relations, Govt. of Assam.

1091. **Dodd, W.C.** : 1923 : The Tai Races. *Iowa*: 26-7.

1092. **Dogra, Neera** : 1958 : Progress of social welfare in Assam. *Social Welfare*, 5(7), Oct.: 13.

1093. **Dohotia, Lilambar (Ed.)** : 1985 : Mayamora. *Souvenir* (Sadau Asom Mayamora Samaj Abhibartan).

1094. **Dohotia, Srikumar** : 1981 : *Moran, Matak, Mayamora*. Tinsukia, Doomdooma Book Stall.

1095. **Doley, Birochan** : 1986 : Law of tribal belts and blocks. *Assam Tribune*, June 28: 5-7.

1096. **Doley, Birochan** : 1987 : Letters to the Editor : Eviction in tribal belts, blocks. *Assam Tribune,* June 9: 4(3-4).

1097. ———— : 1990 : Letters to the Editor: Tribal problems. *Assam Tribune,* Nov. 13: 4(3-5).

1098. **Doley, D.** : 1973 : The Socio-Economic life of the Miri tribe. *North-East, Research Bull.,* Dib. Univ., IV, Summer: 49-61.

1099. ———— : 1984 : The religious beliefs and practices among the Mishing of Assam. *(In) The Tribes of North-East India. (Ed.)* by S.Karotemprel. Calcutta, Firma K.L.M.: 87-94.

1100. ———— : 1987 : Patterns of crime in Assam. *(In) North-East India: A Sociological Study. (Ed.)* by S.M. Dubey. New Delhi, Concept Pub.: 195-210.

1101. **Doley, D.** *and* **Prafulla Medhi** : 1990 : Religion among the Sonowal Kacharis of Assam. *Proceedings of a Seminar on Status of religion in tribal areas in NEI* organised by NEICSSR, Shillong, held on 15-16 Feb. (*Mimeo.*).

1102. **Doley, Dimbeswar** : 1975 : Arunachal tribes and the Ahoms. *North-Eastern Affairs,* 3(4), Jan.-March: 38-48.

1103. ———— : 1991 : *The Mishings: A Socio-Economic Study.* Ph.D. Thesis, Dib. Univ., Soc. Deptt.,

1104. **Doley, Durgeswar** : 1980 : Assamese liberalism. *(In) Assam and the Assamese mind. (Ed.)* by Durgeswar Doley. Jorhat, *Asam Sahitya Sabha*: 35-6.

1105. ———— : 1986 : Samajik paribartan, Asamiya jati aru sanskriti gathan. *(In) Asamar Manuh. (Ed.)* by B.M. Das. Jorhat, Asom Sahitya Sabha: 107-115. (*in Assamese*).

1106. **Donald** : 1900 : *Ivory carving in Assam.*

1107. **Dowarah, Tara Nath** : 1994 : Beliefs and practices related to house-making among the Ahoms. *Bull. Deptt. of Anthropology, Dib. Univ.,* 22: 136-41.

1108. ————: 1996 : Influence of socio-economic factors on traditional rituals and ceremonies among the Mishings of Bormukali Kuli gaon in the district of Dhemaji (Assam). *(In) Communities of North-East India: An Anthropological perspective. (Eds.)* by Farida Ahmed Das and Indira Barua. Delhi, Mittal Pubn.: 212-22.

1109. **Dribeng, J.J.S.** : 1894 : Historical account of the administration of opium in Assam. *(In) Royal Commission on Opium 1893,* Vol. III, Appendix XXX, 454p.

1110. **Duara, Sraddhananda** : 1973 : Ekhan Tiwa Gaor Samaj Byabasthar Eti Dik (*in Assamese*). *Ringchang,* Vol. I(1).

1111. ———— : 1974 : Panchorajia Lalungar Dharmiya Anusthanor oparat Samanya Alokpat (*in Assamese*). *Ringchang,* Vol. II.

1112. **Duara, Thaneswar** : n.d. : *Uttar Kachar Paharar Lok Sanskriti* (*in Assamese*). Haflong, Pub. by the author.

1113. **Duarah, Dharmeswar** : 1996 : Dimasa *(In) Encyclopaedic Profile of Indian Tribes. (Eds.)* by Sachchidananda and R.R. Prasad. New Delhi, Discovery Publishing House: 236-38.

1114. **Dubey, S.M.** : 1966 : Modernization among the tribes of the North Eastern India. *(In) Traditions and Modernization. (Ed.)* by S.K. Srivastava. Allahabad, Indian International.

1115. ———— : 1970 : *Comparative study of modernisation among the Khasis and the Mikirs.* Research Project, Deptt. of Sociology, Dib. Univ. (*Mimeo*).

1116. ———— : 1972 : Tradition, transition and change in Assamese society. *(In) Silver Jubilee Commemoration Volume. (Eds.)* by N.H. Hazarika, D. Kakoty, I. Shah and M.N. Barman. Joysagar, Sibsagar College.

1117. ———————— : Education, social change and political consciousness among the tribes of the North-East India. *(In) Tribal Situation in India. (Ed.)* by K. Suresh Singh. Simla, IIAS: 280-93 (Mikir etc.).

1118. ———— : 1973 : *Social mobility among the professions.* Bombay, Popular Prakashan.

1119. ———— : 1991 : Bihu celebration in Ahom palace. *Assam Tribune (Sunday Reading)*, April 14: I(1-4).

1120. **Dubey, S.M.; P.K. Bordoloi and B.N. Borthakur (Eds.)** : 1980: *Family, Marriage and Social Change.* New Delhi, Cosmo Pubn., 283p.

1121. **Dukpe, Tarin** : 1980 : The Bori Boot Festival. *Arunachal News,* 9(1), Feb.-March: 29-31 (Hill Miri).

1122. **Dumant, G.H.** : 1875 : Sword worship in Kachar. *Indian Antiquary*, 4: 114-15.

1123. **Dunbar, George** : 1915 : Tribes of the Brahmaputra valley. *JRAS (Arts)*, London, LXIII: 189-203.

1124. ———— : 1938 : *Other men's lives: A Study of Primitive People.* London.

1125. **Duncan, W.A.M.** : 1896 : *Monograph on Dyes and Dyeing in Assam*. Shillong, Secretariat Press, 61p.

1126. **Durong, P. Handreas Honse** : 1968 : *Arleng Atam (In K.)*. Diphu, Pub. by the author. (About a Karbi Primer).

1127. **Dutt, K.N.** : 1958 : *Culture and civilization of Assam: An aspect*. Gauhati, Lawyer's Book Stall. 29p.

1128. ——————— : *An aspect of the culture and civilization of Assam*. Gauhati, Srimanta Sankar Kristi Bikash Samiti, 29p.

1129. ———— : 1959 : Tribal contributions in Assam's set up. *(In) Souvenir on aspects of the heritage of Assam. (Ed.)* by K.N. Dutt. Gauhati, 22nd Session of Indian History Congress, December: 96-104.

1130. ——————— **(Ed.)** : *A Souvenir on aspects of the heritage of Assam*. Gauhati, Dr. H.K. Barpujari 22nd Session of Indian History Congress, December, 104p.

1131. **Dutta, Ajit Kr.** : 1988 : *Maniram Dewan and the Politico-economic, socio-cultural history of Assam* (1824-58). Ph.D. Thesis, Gau. Univ.

1132. ———— : 1990 : *Maniram Dewan and the contemporary Assamese society*. Guwahati, Pub. by the author, distributed by Jyoti Prakash and Bidya Mandir.

1133. **Dutta, Aneeta** : 1995 : Hirapara: A potter's village. *Sentinel (Sat. Fare)*, Nov. 4: I(1-8).

1134. **Dutta, Anima** : n.d. : *Assam Vaishnavism: Its twentieth century voice—Lakshminath Bezbaroa*. New Delhi, B.R. Publishing House; distributed by D.K. Pubg.

1135. **Dutta, B.** : 1983 : *The study of the folklore material of North-East India: The case for taking an integrated and multidimensional approach*. Gauhati, Assam Academy Review.

1136. ———— : 1985 : Re-emergence of folklore : North-East India scene. *Man and Life*, 22(1-2).

1137. ——————— : Karbi folklore: Some outstanding features. *(In) Focus on Folklore of North-East India. (Ed.)* by B. Dutta. Guwahati.

1138. ———— : 1987 : Rama Katha in Assam and its neighbourhood: Popular and Folk Traditions. *Gau. Univ. Jr. (Art)*: 30-2.

1139. **Dutta Barua, B.N.** : 1955 : *Rukmini haran natak*. Gauhati, Lawyers' Book Stall, 68p. (*in Assamese*)

1140. **Dutta Barua, B.N.** : 1957 : *Asamar Parbat Vaiamar Bhaisakal.* Gauhati, Lawyers' Book Stall, 60p. (*in Assamese*).

1141. **Dutta Barua, Harinarayan** : 1951 : *Prachin Kamrupar kayastha samajar Itibrittya.* Gauhati, Lawyers' Book Stall (*in Assamese*).

1142. ———— : 1957 : *Kamruiya tantra Mantra.* Nalbari, Datta Barua, 63p. (*in Assamese*).

1143. **Dutta Choudhury, Sunirmal** : 1971 : The Ahom and the Northern tribes of NEFA. *NEFA Information*, VI(4), Nov.: 15-8.

1144. ———— : 1973 : Arunachal tribes and the Ahoms: A history of friction and friendship. *North-Eastern Affairs*, 2(1), Annual Issue: 17-23.

1145. **Dutta, Gokul** : 1992 : Letters to the Editor: Koch Rajbanshis. *Assam Tribune*, April 9: 4(5-6).

1146. **Dutta, Hiren** : 1963 : Afflictions of the deserted daughter-in-law: A Folk-song. *Assam Quarterly* (Gauhati), 3 July: 45-6.

1147. **Dutta, Jharna** : n.d. : *Social change in South Cachar* (1800-1900). M.Phil. Dissertation, History Deptt., NEHU.

1148. **Dutta, Keshab Ch.** : 1995 : Spring dance of the Bodos: A rich heritage. *Sentinel*, May 20: 4(6-8).

1149. **Dutta, Manoranjan** : 1985 : Myth and Reality: A study on the development of kinship in early Assam. *Proceedings NEIHA*, 6: 126-36.

1150. **Dutta, M.N.; J.L. Sharma** *and* **S. Sengupta** : 1994 : A note on main line index and transversality in three Mongoloid population of North-East India. *Bull. Deptt. of Anthropology, Dib. Univ.*, 22: 131-35 (Ahom, Deuri etc.).

1151. **Dutta, M.S.** : 1979 : Some changes in observation of Bihu festival: A preliminary note. *Proceedings of a Seminar on Bio-cultural Profile of North-East India* organised in Silver Jubilee of Anthropology, S.I., Shillong on April 26 (*Mimeo*).

1152. **Dutta, N.L.** : 1992 : Political status of women in Assam since Independence. *(In) Status of Women: Assam. (Ed.)* by S.L. Baruah. New Delhi, Omsons Pubn.: 118-26.

1153. **Dutta, Narendra Nath** : n.d. : *Obscure religious practices among some Vaisnavas of Assam.* New Delhi.

1154. **Dutta, Prafulla Ch.** : 1986 : Assamese Bihu culture: Heritage of handloom industry. *Assam Tribune*, April 14: 4(3-6).

1155. ———— : 1987 : Kati Bihu : Festival of Austerity. *Assam Tribune*, Oct. 18: 6(3-7).

1156. **Dutta, Prafulla Ch.** : 1988 : Bhogali Bihu: Its significance. *Assam Tribune*, Jan. 14: 4(3-6).

1157. ———— : 1989 : Holi festival at Barpeta Satra. *Assam Tribune*, March 22: 4(7-8).

1158. ———— : Worshipping nature: The Bodo culture and Bihu. *Assam Tribune*, April 13: 5(1-4).

1159. ———— : 1990 : Spirit of Bhogali Bihu and the food front. *Assam Tribune*, Jan. 13: 4(7-8).

1160. ———— : Mother earth and Sakti Peeth Kamakhya. *Assam Tribune*, June 22: 4(7-8).

1161. ———— : 1991 : Bhogali Bihu and Agni Puja. *Assam Tribune*, Jan. 13: 4(3-6).

1162. ———— : Bihu: Heritage of handloom industry. *Assam Tribune (Sunday Reading)*, April 14: 1(1-8).

1163. **Dutta, Pulakesh** : 1987 : Socio-Economic problem of Assam: A diagnostic appraisal. *National Geographic*, 22(1), June: 29-36.

1164. **Dutta, S.** : 1983 : Morans. *Proceedings NEIHA*, 4: 96-106.

1165. ———— : 1985 : *The Mataks and their kingdom*. Allahabad, Chugh Pubn., 279p.

1166. ———— : The Mishing and their folklore. *(In) Murong. (Ed.)* by J. Kuli. Dibrugarh: 13-9.

1167. ———— : 1990 : The Sikhs and the Mataks: A comparative study. *Procdg. NEIHA*, 11: 96-99 (Shillong, Hist. Deptt., NEHU).

1168. ———— : 1994 : The Matak Kingdom and the frontier policy in the North-East. *(In) Essays on North-East India. (Ed.)* by Milton S. Sangma. New Delhi, Indus Pub. Comp. 165-82.

1169. **Dutt, S.C.** : 1884 : *The Wild Tribes of India*. London, Gilbert and Revington Ltd., 189p (Reprinted in 1984 by Cosmo Pubn., New Delhi); Meekir: 155-56, Cachare : 153-55).

1170. **Dutta, S.K.** : 1976 : The 'Rascal' in tribal folklore. *N.E. Spectrum*, 1(1), July: 23-6.

1171. **Dutt, Srikant** : 1981 : Migration and development: The Nepalese in North-East. *Eco. and Pol. Weekly*, XVI (28), June 13.

1172. **Duwara, Dibakar** : 1948 : *Namati Ai*. Gauhati, Pub. by the author (It is a collection of marriage songs of the Dibrugarh Sub-division of the North Lakhimpur district) (*in Assamese*).

1173. **Eco. and Pol. Weekly** : 1974 : Bodos., Dec. 21.

1174. **Edwards, Walter N.** *and* **Harold H. Mann** : 1904 : An ancient Assamese fortification and the legends relating thereto. *Jour. R.A.S.B.*, 73, Pt. I: 254-61.

1175. **Eliot, C.** : 1910 : Hinduism in Assam. *Jour. R.A.S. of G.B.* and I., Pt. II: 1155-86.

1176. **Elliot, H.M.** : 1869 : Kewat. *(In) The Races of the North-West Provinces of India*, Vol. I London: 156, 182.

1177. **Elwin, V.** : 1943 : Conception, pregnancy and birth among the tribesmen of the Mikir Hills. *Jour. R.A.S. of Bengal*, 9: 99-147.

1178. ———— : 1946 : Kewat. *(In) Myths of Middle India.* Bombay, 497p.

1179. ———— : 1958 : Tribal Art of Assam. *Akashvani*, 23(18), May 4: 6-8.

1180. ———— : 1960 : *The Hill people of North-East India*. London Oxford University Press.

1181. ———— : 1961 : The beauty of tribal Assam. *Folklore*, II(4), July-Aug.: 209-12.

1182. ———— : 1964 : *Tribal world of Verrier Elwin.* London, Oxford University Press.

1183. ————: 1965 : *Democracy in NEFA*. Shillong, Research Deptt., (This has mentioned about Assam).

1184. **Endle, Sidney** : 1911 : *The Kacharis*. London, Macmillan and Co., 128p. (Reprinted in 1975 by Cosmo Pubn. Delhi, 121p.)

1185. **Enthoven, R.E.** : 1920 : Bharth""aris or Naths. *(In) Tribes and Castes of Bombay*, Vol. I. Bombay: 117-18.

1186. **Enthoven, R.E.** : 1922 : Nath. *(In) Tribes and Castes of Bombay*, Vol. III. Bombay: 127.

1187. **Ering, Oshong** : 1971 : The Tanis and the Donyi-Polo cult. *NEFA Information*. VI(4), Nov.: 22-5 (Mishing (Miri) of Upper Assam are *Tanis*).

1188. **Fick, Richard** : 1897 : *Die sociale Gliederung im nordostlichen Indien zu Buddha's Ziet, mit besonderer Berucksichtigung der Kastenfrage, vornehmlich auf Grund der Jataka dargestellt.* Kiel, C.F. Haeseler Verlag fur Orientalische Literatur (*In G.*).

1189. **Flex, Oscar** : 1873 : Pflanzerleben in Indien, Kulturgeschichtliche Bilder aus Assam. Berlin, Catalogue of the Indian Office Library (*In G.*).

1190. **Flwin, V.** : 1976 : Tribal woman. *(In) Women in India. (Ed.)* by Devaki Jain. Delhi, 203 p. (Reprinted).

1191. **Foy, W.** : 1913 : Fadenstern und fadenkreaz. *Ethnologica* (Leipzing) vol. II: 67-109.

1192. **Francis, W.** : 1902 : Koibarto. *(In) Census of India 1901,* Vol. XVI: Madras, Pt. I, Report. Madras, Govt. of India: 162.

1193. **Friend Pareira, J.E.** : 1911 : The Rabhas. *(In) Census of India 1911,* Assam. Vol. III, Pt. I Simla, Central Govt. Press.

1194. **Fryer, G.B.** : 1875 : Note on the Khyeng people of the Sandoway District, Aracan. *Jour. A.S.B., I(I).*

1195. **Fuch, Stephen** : 1973 : *The aboriginal tribes of India.* Delhi, Macmillan Company. (Rabha, Kachari, Koch, Lalung, Dimasa, etc.).

1196. **Furer Haimendorf, C. von** : 1929 : Zur frage der kultur-beziehungen zwischen Assam und Sudsee *Anthropos.*, 24: 1100-03.

1197. ———— : 1930 : Das Junggesellenhaus in Westlichen Hinterindien *Wiener Beitrage zur Kulturgeschichte und Linguistik,* Vol. I: 333-47.

1198. ———— : 1932 : Gibt es in Hinterindien "Totemistische" Kultur? *Mitteilungen der Anthropologischen Gesellschaft in Wien,* Vol. 62: 328-37.

1199. ———— : 1934 : Volker-und Kultur-gruppen im Westlichen Hinter indien dargestellt mit hilfe des statistischen Verfahrens. *Anthropos,* Vol. 29: 424-40.

1200. ———— : 1936 : Zur Religion einiger Hinterindischer Bergvolker. *(In) Custom is King: Essays Presented to R.H. Marrett.* London, Hutchinsons : 273-88.

1201. **Furer Haimendorf, C. von** : 1938 : Through the unexplored mountains of the Assam Burma border. *Geographical Journal,* 91: 201-19.

1202. ———— : 1946 : Culture types in Assam Himalayas. *Indian Geographical Jour.*(Madras), April 1.

1203. ———— : 1953 : The after life in Indian tribal belief. (The Frazer lecture in Social Anthropology, Cambridge University, 1951). *Jour. R.A.I. of G.B. and I.*, 83, Pt. I: 37-49.

1204. ———— : 1968 : *Fundamental Research in Indian Anthropology.* Simla, IIAS.

1205. ———— : 1982 : *Tribes of India: The struggle for survival.* Delhi, Oxford Univ. Press : 313-22.

1206. **Gait, Edward A.** : 1896 : Manufacture of pottery in Assam. *Jour. of Indian Art,* 7(54), April: 5-8.

1207. **Gait, Edward A.** : Brass and copper wares in Assam. *(In) Notes on some industries of Assam from 1884-1895.* Shillong, Govt. Press.

1208. —————— : The manufacture of brass and copper wares in Assam. *Jour. of Indian Art and Industry,* 7(54): 1-4.

1209. ————— : 1898 : Human sacrifices in ancient Assam. *Jour. R.A.S.B.,* 67, Pt. III: 56-65.

1210. ————— : 1902 : Chasi Kaibarta. *(In) Census of India 1901, Vol. V: The Lower Provinces of Bengal and their feudatories,* Pt. I: *Report.* Calcutta, Govt. Press; 380, 391, LIII.

1211. ————— : 1926 : *History of Assam.* Calcutta, Thacker Spink, 366p (Reprinted in 1981 by LBS Pubn., Guwahati).

1212. **Ganguly, N.** : 1944 : *Namasudras.* Unpub. M.Sc. Disser., Anthropology Deptt., Cal. Univ.

1213. **Ganguly, P.** : 1974 : Book Review: Ethnic affinities of the Rajbanshis of North Bengal by G.D. Kumar and (Ed.) by Henry Field. Field Research Projects, Miami, 1973, VIII+56p, Illus, *Jr. Indian Anthropology Soc.,* 9(1), April: 110-11.

1214. **Garai, P.R.** : 1985 : Kabui Naga of Assam. *Proceedings of People of India,* Pre-Test Seminar of Anthropology, S.I., Shillong on Dec. 5.

1215. **Gharfalia, Sayambar** : 1981 : Matakar atiguri bichari. *(In) Mayanmara Satra Samaj: Bhasan aru Pravandha. (ed.)* by S.K. Gogoi. Chabua (Assam), Mayamara Kala Kristi Anusandhan Aru Prachar Samity: 103-14 (*in Assamese*).

1216. **Ghatowar, N.** : 1975 : *Banuar sanskritik jiwanar ebhumuki.* (*in Assamese*). Jorhat, Asam Sahitya Sabha.

1217. ————— : 1984 : Asamar Sanskritic Jiwanat Chah Mazdurar Avadan (*in Assamese*). *(In) Bihuwan (Ed.)* by T. Bora. Doom Dooma, Doom Dooma Rangali Bihu Udyapan Samity: 26-9.

1218. ————— : 1985 : *Hansali.* Gauhati, Assam Tea Ex-Tea Garden Tribes' Youth Association (*in Assamese*).

1219. **Ghosh, A.K.** : 1978 : What happens when cultural and biological adaptability of man fails, etc. *(In) Cultural and Biological Adaptability of Man with special reference to NE India.* Dib. Univ., Anthropology Deptt.,

1220. ————— : 1979 : Tribal development. *Himalaya: Man and Nature,* 2(8), Jan.: 18-24.

1221. **Ghosh, Aloke Kr.** : 1990 : Book Review: Verrier Elwin and

India's North Eastern Borderlands—Nari K. Rustomji, North Eastern Hill University, Published in 1988, Rs. 45/- 82p (foreword by R.K. Mishra). *Jr. Ind. Anthropology Soc.*, 25(1), March: 96.

1222. **Ghosh Choudhury, B.B.** : 1344BS : *Asam O Bangadesher Bibaha Padhati*. Calcutta, Pub. by the author (*In B.*, 1931).

1223. **Ghosh, Dipali** : 1964 : Post funeral ritual in a Dimasa Kachari village. *Man in India*, 44(3), July-Sept.; 247-51.

1224. ———— : 1965 : Notes on the family among the Dimasa Kachari. *Man in India*, 45(1), Jan.-March: 17-26.

1225. ———— : Descent and clan among the Dimasa. *Man in India*, 45(3), July-Sept.: 185-94.

1226. ———— : 1967 : The Economy of the Dimasa Kachari of United Mikir and North Cachar Hills. *(In) A common perspective for North-East India. (Eds.)* by Rathin Mitra and B. Das Gupta. Calcutta, Pannalal Das Gupta: 213-17.

1227. ———— : 1967-70 : *Life in a Kachari village: Dimasa Kachari life way, an anthropological study.* Ph.D. Thesis, Anthropology Deptt., Cal. Univ.

1228. **Ghosh, G.K.** : 1992 : *Tribals and their culture: Assam, Meghalaya and Mizoram*, Vol. I. New Delhi, Ashish Publishing House: 1-69.

1229. **Ghosh, M.N.** : 1896 : *A brief sketch of the religious beliefs of the Assamese people*. Calcutta, Methodist Publishing House, 61p.

1230. **Ghosh, S.K** : 1977 : *A socio-cultural study of Cachar*. Unpub. Ph.D. Thesis, Gau. Univ., 79p.

1231. **Ghosh, S.K** *and* **Prabha Chopra** : 1980 : *Echoes from North-Eastern India*. New Delhi, S. Chand and Co., 121p. (Assam: 18-70).

1232. **Ghosh, Sunanda** : 1986 : *A study of the Baramahi songs of Assam and Bengal.* Unpub. Ph.D. Thesis, Gau. Univ.

1233. **Gihodes, C.** : 1922 : *Kacharis : Religion and Custom.* Calcutta, Catholic Orphan Press.

1234. **Giri, Swami Yogananda** : 1950 : Rajbanshis. *(In) Tribes of India*. Delhi, Bharatiya Adimjati Sevak Sangh, Vol. I : 21-4.

1235. **Goduka, Suresh Ranjan** : 1993 : Magh Bihu Makar-Sankranti-sathi. *Pur. Pra.*, Jan 13: 5(3-6) *(in H.)*.

1236. **Gogoi, A., T. Sonowal, N. Hussain, J.L. Sharma, M.L. Devi, N. Dehingia, G. Hatibarua** *and* **I. Das** : 1977 : *A Study on some* *aspect of socio-cultural life of the Mishing of Tazik gaon, North Lakhimpur*. Unpub. M.Sc. Dissertation, Anthropology Deptt., Dib. Univ.

1237. **Gogoi, Amar** : 1988 : Letters to the Editor: The Ahoms. *Assam Tribune*, Feb. 29: 4(4-6).

1238. **Gogoi, Anjali** : 1978 : *A Study of family structure and attitude towards family planning.* Unpub. M.Sc. Disser. Anthropology Deptt., Dib. Univ.

1239. **Gogoi, Arun Chandra** : 1988 : Letters to the Editor: Ahom. *Assam Tribune*, Feb. 19: 4(6).

1240. **Gogoi, Ashim Kr.** : 1980 : *An Account of the Sonowal Kachari of Lepetkata with special reference to village organization, agriculture and death and disposal.* Unpub. M.Sc. Disser. Anthropology Deptt., Dib. Univ.

1241. ———— : 1982 : *Impact of welfare activities in a Scheduled Tribe community of Assam.* Unpub. M.Sc. Disser. Anthropology Deptt., Dib. Univ.

1242. **Gogoi, B.** : 1986 : Letters to the Editor: Barak Valley. *Assam Tribune*, Dec. 20: 4(5-6).

1243. **Gogoi, Bonti Rani** : 1990 : The migration and settlement of the Turungs: A Tai community in Assam. *Proceedings of NEIHA, Session 11th* (Imphal). Shillong, Hist. Deptt., NEHU: 117-19.

1244. **Gogoi, Chou Nomal** : 1989 : Me-dam-me-phi: The cult of ancestor worship. *Assam Tribune*, Jan. 31: 4(7-8) (Tai-Ahom, religion).

1245. **Gogoi, Damayanti** : 1981 : *A Study on economic life of the Ahom of Borpather Konwar Gaon, Dibrugarh.* Unpub. M.Sc. disser. Anthropology Deptt., Dib. Univ.

1246. **Gogoi, Deven (Ed.)** : 1971 : *Karbi Prasanga (In A.).* Diphu, Diphu Sahitya Sabha.

1247. **Gogoi, Dimbeswar** : 1988 : 'Me-dam-me-fi': An Ahom religious ceremony. *Assam Tribune*, Jan. 31: 4(7-8) 6(4).

1248. ———————— : Letters to the Editor: The Ahoms. *Assam Tribune*, March 3: 4(6).

1249. **Gogoi, G.** : 1986 : *Urbanisation in Assam: 1901-1971.* Unpub. Ph.D. Thesis, Dib. Univ.

1250. **Gogoi, Hari Chandra** : 1960 : Lokageetit Buranjir Achor *(in Assamese). Amar Pratinidhi*, September.

1251. **Gogoi, Jaggoram** : 1962 : Mikir. *(In) Asamar Janajati. (Ed.)* by

Pramod Ch. Bhattacharya. Jorhat, Asom Sahitya Sabha: 118-40 (*in Assamese*).

1252. **Gogoi, Jotin** : 1972 : *A Study on religion, belief and practices of the Mikirs*. Unpub. M.Sc. Disser. Anthropology Deptt., Dib. Univ.

1253. **Gogoi, K.** : 1983 : Ex-Tea Garden women labour, in Assam. *Social Welfare*, XXIX(10), Feb.-March.

1254. **Gogoi, Kalpana** : 1980 : *An Account of the Sonowal Kachari of Lepetkata village with special reference to agriculture, marriage and economic organization*. Unpub. M.Sc. Disser. Anthropology Deptt., Dib. Univ.

1255. **Gogoi, Kalyanee** : 1996 : Issue facing voluntary bodies in the North-East. *Sentinel (Saturday Fare),* Sept. 14: 1(5-8), 2(3-8) (Mizo, Bodo, A.P.).

1256. **Gogoi, Kiran Kumar** : 1992 : Origin of the Me-Dam-Me-Fie of Tai Ahoms. *Assam Tribune*, Jan. 31: @(3-6) 7(2-5).

1257. **Gogoi, Leela** : 1985 : *Tai Sanskriti rooplekha* (*in Assamese*). Calcutta.

1258. ———— : 1986 : Asomor Sanskriti (*in Assamese*). Guwahati.

1259. ———— : Asamar Manuh : Sanskritik Samannya. *(In) Asamr Manuh. (Ed.)* by B.M. Das. Jorhat, Asam Sahitya Sabha: 31-48 (*in Assamese*).

1260. **Gogoi, Lila** : 1957 : *Asamiya Lokagita* (*in Assamese*). Gauhati, Gauhati Univ., 98p.

1261. ———— : 1958 : The age-old amity of the hills and the plains *(In) The Outlook on NEFA. (*Comp*)* by Parag Chaliha. Jorhat, Asam Sahitya Sabha: 12-7 (Ahom, Mikir etc).

1262. **Gogoi, Lila** : 1961 : *Bihu Geet Aru Bonghosa*. Gauhati, Lawyers' Book Stall. 297p. (*in Assamese*) (Reprinted in 1979, 1981).

1263. ———— : *Ahom Jati Aru Asamiya Sanskriti* (*in Assamese*). Sibsagar, Jeuti Prakash, 205p.

1264. ———— : *Smantar Mati Aru Manuha* (*in Assamese*). Gauhati, Lawyers' Book Stall (Reprinted in 1963), 98p.

1265. ———— : 1964 : *The Assamese Mantra Literature. Proceedings of an Oriental Conference*, Gauhati Session.

1266. ———— : 1966 : *Asamiya Sanskriti (in Assamese)*. Jorhat, Asom Sahitya Sabha, 388p.

1267. ———— : 1967 : *The Art of manuscript preparation and*

preservation in Assam. Proceedings of a Seminar of Gau. Univ., sponsored by U.G.C.

1268. **Gogoi, Lila** : 1968 : *Asamiya Lok-Sahityar Rup Rekha (in Assamese)*. Golaghat, Nabin Pustak Bhandar, 304p.

1269. ——— : 1969 : *Bihu: Eti Samikhya (in Assamese)*. Dibrugarh, Pub. by the author, 128p.

1270. ——— : 1971 : *Tai Sanskritir Ruprekha (in Assamese)*. Calcutta, Sribhumi Pub. Co., 226p.

1271. ——— **(Comp)** : The Tai Khamtis. Chowkham (NEFA), Chowkhamoon Gohain (Namsoon), 210p.

1272. ——— : 1975 : *Fairs and Festival of Eastern India. Jour. Deptt. of Assamese*, Dib. Univ.

1273. ——— : 1982 : Asamar Sanskriti (*in Assamese*). Jorhat, Bharati Prakashan.

1274. ——— : 1993 : *The History of the System of Ahom Administration*. Distributed by United Pub., Guwahati.

1275. **Gogoi, Lokeswar** : 1986 : *Tiwa sanskritir ruprekha (Ist pt.)*. Dewaguri, Raha, Hari Har Mandir.

1276. **Gogoi, Manjoo** : 1980 : *A Study of socio-cultural life of Bodo-Kachari*, Assam. Unpub. M.Sc. Disser. Anthropology Deptt., Dib. Univ.

1277. **Gogoi, Nomal** : 1981 : Mayamara Dharma Sanskritir parampara. *(In) Mayamara Satra Samaj: Bhasan aru Pravandha. (Ed.)* by Sushil Kr. Gogoi. Chabua(Assam), Mayamara Kala Kristi Anusandhan aru Prachar Samity: 170-78 (*in Assamese*).

1278. ——— : *Mayamora Sampraday(in Assamse)*. Tinsukia, Pub. by the author.

1279. **Gogoi, P.** : 1966 : The Tai people of Assam. *Lik Phan Tai (Jour. Tai Historical and Cultural Society of Assam)*, I: 23-51.

1280. ——— : 1974 : Tai-Ahom religion and customs. *Jour. Assam Research Society*, 22: 12-24.

1281. **Gogoi, P.D.** : 1986 : *The Tai and the Tai Kingdom*. Guwahati, Gau. Univ.

1282. **Gogoi, Padmeswar** : 1968 : The Tai Ahom religion and customs, Ahom deities. *Jour. Assam Research Society*, 18: 1-7.

1283. ——— : 1971 : The Tai: Their origin and branches *(In) The Tai Khamtis. (Comp)* by Lila Gogoi. Chowkham(NEFA), Chowkhamoon Gohain (Namsoon): 1-12.

1284. **Gogoi, Padmeswar** : 1976 : *Tai-Ahom religion and customs.* Gauhati, Publication Board, Assam, 117p. (*Reprinted* in 1986).

1285. ————: 1986 : *Tai Ahom religion and Culture.* Guwahati, Publication Board, Assam.

1286. **Gogoi, Puspa** : 1986 : Some aspects of the Tais of North-Eastern India. *Jour. Assam Research Society* (Guwahati), XXVIII, 1984-85 (1984): 79-82.

1287. **Gogoi, Sushil Kr.** : 1977 : Asamar satriya nritya kala aru Mayamara samaj. *Smriti Grantha,* Matak Sanmilan (*in Assamese*).

1288. ———— : 1981 : Mayamara Thular Git-Rag-Tal aru Nritya Prasanga. *(In) Mayamara Satra Samaj: Bhasan aru Pravandha. (Ed.)* by Sushil Kr. Gogoi. Chabua (Assam), M.K.K.A.P.S.: 128-36 (*in Assamese*).

1289. ———— **(Ed.)** : *Mayamara satra samaj*: Bhasan aru Pravandha. Chabua (Assam), Mayamara Kala Kristi Anusandhan Aru Prachar Samity, 179p (*in Assamese*).

1290. **Gogoi, T., T. Barooah, J. Buragohain** *and* **B. Boruah** : 1995: Letters to the Editor: S.T. Status to Ahoms. *Sentinel,* March 2: 4(3-4).

1291. **Gogoi, Tapan** : 1988 : Letters to the Editor: The Ahoms. *Assam Tribune,* March 24: 4(6).

1292. ————: 1989 : Letters to the Editor: Bihu and the New Generation. *Assam Tribune,* May 17: 4(3).

1293. **Gogoi, Thanuram** : 1984 : *Tai jatir prachin dharma aru samajniti. Che-Rai-Doi.* Guwahati, Hemkosh Printers.

1294. **Gohai, Dalim Ch.** *and* **Bhaktibar Gogai** : 1981 : "Chutki Chandra Bansha balit" Matak Raja Sarbananda Singha. *(In) Mayamara Satra Samaj: Bhasan aru Pravandha. (Ed.)* by Sushil Kr. Gogoi. Chabua (Assam), Mayamara Kala Kristi Anusandhan Aru Prachar Samity: 115-27 (*in Assamese*).

1295. **Gohain, A.K.** : 1993 : Rama katha in Tai-Phake cultural tradition *(In) Rama Katha in tribal and folk traditions of India: Proceedings of a Seminar. (Eds.)* by K.S. Singh and Birendranath Datta. Calcutta, Seagull Pub. for Anthropology S.I.: 231-45.

1296. **Gohain, B.** : 1937 : *Human sacrifice and head hunting in Assam.* Ph.D. Dissertation, London University.

1297. **Gohain, B.K.** : 1983 : *Hill Lalungs.* Guwahati, Anundoram Borooah Institute of Language, 65p.

1298. ———— : 1984 : *The Hill Karbis: A Sociological study of the tribe.* Diphu, Pub. by Arunima Gohain.

1299. **Gohain, B.K.** : 1989 : *A study of continuity and change in three Hill Lalung villages of Karbi Anglong District, Assam.*

1300. ———— : 1993 : *The Hill Lalungs.* Guwahati, Anundoram Borooah Institute of Language, Art & Culture, Assam, 110p.

1301. ———— : 1995 : *Continuity and change in the Hills of Assam (Karbi Anglong District).* New Delhi, Omsons Pub., 295p.

1302. ———— : n.d. : *Tai Ramayana.* Guwahati Anundoram Borooah Inst. of Lang., Art & Cul., Assam.

1303. **Gohain, Bikash Ch.** : 1977 : *Human sacrifice and head-hunting in North-Eastern India. Gauhati,* Lawyers' Book Stall, 102p. (Kachari, Koch, Chutya etc.).

1304. **Gohain, Birendra Kr.** : 1990 : *A Study of continuity and change in three Hill Lalung villages of Karbi Anglong District, Assam.* Unpub. Ph.D. Thesis, Gau. Univ.

1305. ———— : 1982 : What is in a name? *Assam Tribune,* April 23: 4 and 5.

1306. **Gohain, Debashish** : 1967 : *Mawtnum.* Jorhat, Agro Economic Research Centre.

1307. **Gohain, Hiren** : 1987 : Discussion: "Tradition and continuity". *North-East Quarterly* (Gau. Univ.), 2(4), Nov.-Dec.: 62-4(Vaisnava faith).

1308. ———— : 1988 : Indianness and alienation in North-East. *A.B.P.,* Feb. 6: 6(3-6).

1309. **Gohain, R.** : 1974 : *Karampuja aru jhumur geet (In Assamese).* Jorhat, Asam Sahitya Sabha.

1310. **Gohain, Rama Kanta** : 1988 : Letters to the Editor: The Ahoms. *Assam Tribune,* Feb. 13: 4(6).

1311. **Gohain, Rukmadhar** : 1974 : *Karam Puja aru Jhumur Geet (in Assamese).* Jorhat, Asam Sahitya Sabha.

1312. **Gohain, Thaneswar** : 1989 : Letters to the Editor: Ethnic aspirations in Assam. *Assam Tribune,* May 6: 4(3-4).

1313. **Gohain, U.N.** : 1950 : *A short note on the Thai.* Guwahati, 30p.

1314. ———— : 1958 : Ahom relations with the neighbouring hill tribes and the tributary chiefs. *(In) The outlook on NEFA.* (Comp) by Parag Chaliha. Jorhat, Asam Sahitya Sabha: 5-11 (Mikir etc., from 'Assam under the Ahoms').

1315. ———— : 1971 : The Tai characteristics and their arts and culture. *(In) The Tai Khamtis.* (Comp) by Lila Gogoi. Chowkham (NEFA), Chowkhamoon Gohain (Namsoon): 97-106.

1316. **Gokulnathan, P.P.** : 1972 : Book Review : Comparative study of modernisation among the Khasis and the Mikirs (*Mimeo.*). Deptt. of Sociology, Dib. Univ. (1970). *North-Eastern Research Bulletin* (Dib. Univ.), III, Summer: 95-7.

1317. **Gokulnathan, P.P. and Prayag Mehta** : 1972 : Achievement motive in tribal and non-tribal Assamese Secondary School adolescents. *Indian Educational Review*, 7(1), Jan: 67-90.

1318. **Gopalakrishnan, R.** : 1991 : *Political Geography of India's North-East.* New Delhi, Vikas Pub. House.

1319. **Goswami, Ananda Ch.** : 1994 : Sivasagar where the Gods still live. *Assam Tribune, Sunday Reading,* March 27: I(1-8).

1320. **Goswami, Atul** : 1990 : Tribal development in India with special reference to Assam. *Bulletin Assam Inst. of Research for Tribals and Sch. Castes* (T.R.I.), Guwahati, 7th Annual Issue: 16-20.

1321. ———————— : Tribal development : Some conceptual issue. *(In) Constraints of Tribal Development in North-East India. (Ed.)* by B.N. Bordoloi. Guwahati, T.R.I.: 83-91.

1322. **Goswami, Atul and Homeswar Goswami** : 1991 : Some quietning trends of urbanization in Assam. *Assam Economic Jour.*, 8: 95-9.

1323. **Goswami, B.B.** : 1964 : Spinning and weaving in Assam. *Folklore,* V(12), Dec.: 441-45.

1324. ———————— : 1972 : The Tribes of Assam: A Few Comments on their Social and Cultural ties with the non-tribes. *(In) Tribal Situation in India. (Ed.)* by K. Suresh Singh. Simla, Indian Institute of Advanced Studies: 271-79.

1325. ———————— : 1973 : The Tribes of North-East India: A Few Comments on their Social and Cultural ties with the non-tribes, *North Eastern Research Bulletin,* IV, Summer: 41-8.

1326. ———————— : 1974 : A Few Propositions for the study of tribes in North-Eastern India. *North Eastern Affairs,* 2(4): 31-2.

1327. ———————— : 1976 : An Anthropo-historical perspective of the Ahom movement. *Newsletter of Indian Inst. of Adv. Study* (Simla), December.

1328. ———————— : 1978 : Cultural nationalism of the Ahoms: An anthro-historical appraisal. *(In) Behavioural Scientist: Essays in honour of Prof. Sachidananda.* Patna, Bihar Council of Young Behavioural Scientists: 29-46.

1329. ———————— : Hill tribes plainsmen relations in an area of North-East India. *Samatat* (Calcutta), No. 4.

1330. **Goswami, B.B.** : 1982 : Hill Tribes-plainsmen relations in an area of North-East India. *(In) Tribal Development in India: Problems and Prospects. (Ed.)* by Buddhadeb Chaudhuri. Delhi, Inter India Pubs.: 129-36.

1331. ———— : 1991 : Ethnic cognition in North-East India. *(In) Ethnonationalism: Indian Experience*. Calcutta, Chatterjee Pub.

1332. ———— : 1993 : Prospects for ethnic re-organisation. Proceedings of a Seminar on *Reorganisation of North-East India since 1947*, 22-23 Feb. 1993 organised by NEICSSR Shillong.

1333. **Goswami, B.B., J. Sarkar** *and* **D. Danda (Eds.)** : 1988 : *Marriage in India (Tribes, Muslims and Anglo Indians)*. Calcutta, An. S.I., 294p.

1334. **Goswami, Basanta Kr. Deva** : 1987 : *A Critical study of the Ramayana tradition of Assam (upto AD 1826)*. Unpub. Ph.D. Thesis, Gau. Univ.

1335. ———— : 1993 : Rama-katha among the Bodo Kacharis of Nalbari district with special reference to Basko bloc. *(In) Rama-katha in tribal and folk traditions of India: Proceedings of a Seminar. (Eds.)* by K.S. Singh and Birendranath Datta. Calcutta, Seagull Pub. for Anthropology S.I.: 166-74.

1336. **Goswami, Bhrigu Mohan** : 1986 : *A Study of the Ojapali Art forms of Assam*. Unpub. Ph.D. Thesis, Gau. Univ.

1337. **Goswami, Bhrigu Mohan** : 1993 : The Ramayana based Ojapalis of Assam *(In) Rama Katha in tribal and Folk traditions of India: Proceedings of a Seminar. (Eds.)* by K.S. Singh and Birendranath Datta. Calcutta, Seagull Pub. for Anthropology S.I.: 153-60.

1338. **Goswami, D.K.** : 1978 : Social backgrounds of the political Elites in North-East India. *(In) North-East India: A Sociological Study. (Ed.)* by S.M. Dubey. Delhi, Concept Pub. Comp.: 305-18.

1339. **Goswami, Dinesh** : 1992 : Book Review: Boat races in Assam's cultural perspective. *North Eastern India*, Feb. 25: 5(1-3).

1340. **Goswami, G.C.** : 1990 : *Mangaldai Rabhas*. Ph.D. Thesis, Gau. Univ.

1341. **Goswami, Hemchandra and Padmanath Gohain Boruah** : 1907: A Note on Assamese language and literature. *(In) Pandit Hemchandra Goswami Rachanabali. (Ed.)* by Benudhar Sarma. Jorhat, Asom Sahitya Sabha.

1342. **Goswami, Hirendra Kr.** : 1985 : *Rabhas: A Sociological study*. Unpub. Ph.D. Thesis, Pol. Sc. Deptt., Gau. Univ.

1343. **Goswami, Hirendra Kr.** : 1988 : Rabhas: A Plains Tribe of Assam. *Assam Tribune*, April 3: 4(3-6), 7(2).

1344. ——————— : Schemes for Scheduled Castes. *Assam Tribune*, April 22: 4(3-6).

1345. ——————— : Music, folk-songs and dances of Rabhas. *Assam Tribune*, July 17: 4(3-6).

1346. **Goswami, Indira** : 1986 : *Shàdow of dark god and the sin* (*Tr.* from Assamese by Prafulla Kotoky). New Delhi, Sundeep Prak.

1347. ——————— : 1993 : *A Saga of South Kamrup*. New Delhi, Sahitya Academi (Satra), 316p.

1348. **Goswami, Jibanananda** : 1974 : Bibartanar Pathedi. Mayamara Samaj. *Ajali* (*in Assamese*).

1349. **Goswami, Jibananda Ch.** : 1981 : Bibartanar Pathedi Mayamara Samaj. *(In) Mayamara Satra Samaj: Bhasan aru Pravandha. (Ed.)* by Sushil Kr. Gogoi. Chabua (Assam), Mayamara Kala Kristi Anusandhan Aru Prachar Samity: 92-102 (*in Assamese*).

1350. **Goswami, K.D.** : 1971 : The Satra and its contributions to Assamese culture. *North-Eastern Research Bulletin*, II, Summer: 68-75.

1351. **Goswami, Kameswar** : 1985 : Hathasuni, a primitive system of marriage of the Bodos. *Jour. NEICSSR*, 9(1), April: 44-7.

1352. **Goswami, Kesavananda Dev** : 1973 : A peculiar prayer service of Assamese Vaisnavas. *Jour. Music Academy*, 44(1-4): 227-33 (dancing).

1353. ——————— : 1985 : The Jhumuras in Assamese. *Sangeet Natak*, 76, April-June: 5-8.

1354. **Goswami, M.C.** : 1954 : *Mongoloid and their contribution towards the growth and development of Assamese culture*. Unpub. M. Litt. Desertation, Cambridge Univ.

1355. ——————— : 1954 : The Social Structure of an Assamese Village (Summary of a Communication to the Royal Anthropological Institute 22nd Oct., 1953). *Man*, 54 (22).

1356. ——————— : 1960 : An annual shamanistic dance (Deodha nach) at Kamakhya, Assam. *Jour. Univ. of Gau. (Sc.),* XI(1): 38-9.

1357. ——————— : 1961 : A note on the magico-medicinal uses of *cult* in Assam. *Jour. Univ. of Gau.*, XII(2): 17-24.

1358. ——————— : 1967 : Tribe-Peasant relationship in Assam. *(In) A Common Perspective for North-East India. (Eds.)* by Rathin Mitra and B. Das Gupta. Calcutta, Pannalal Das Gupta: 72-9.

1359. **Goswami, M.C.** : 1969-71 : Tribe-caste relations in N-E India. Presidential Address, Fifty-eighth Session of Indian Science Congress, Bangalore, 1971, Section of Anthropology, and Archaeo. *Jour. Univ. of Gau.*, XX-XXII(2), Science: 2-14.

1360. ———— : 1970 : Area study in social changes and intercommunity relations. *ICSSR Project,* Deptt. of Anthropology, Gau. Univ.

1361. ———— : 1971 : Kamakhya: Socio-cultural aspects of a temple site. *(In) Souvenir: Assam Sc. Soc.* Gauhati.

1362. ———— : 1972 : The role of *Samadi* in a changing Lalung society. *Bull. Deptt. of Anthropology,* Gau. Univ., I, December: 1-16.

1363. ———— : 1973 : Bell-metal workers of Sarthebari, Assam. *Bull. Deptt. of Anthropology,* Gau. Univ., II. December: 1-12.

1364. ———— : 1975 : Shamans and Shamanism at Kamakhaya Dham, Assam. *Bull. Deptt., Anthropology, Gau. Univ.*, 4: 1-18.

1365. ———— : Structure and functions of a satra in Assam. Proceedings of a Seminar on Sociological Perspective on North-East India and the Second Annual Conference of North-East India Sociological Association, *Dib. Univ. Deptt. of Sociology,* March 10-12, 1975 (Mimeo.).

1366. ———— : 1977 : Tribal Political Organisation of the Karbis: A case of resilient adoption. *Jour. NEICSSR,* 1(1), April.

1367. ———— : Social and Political Institutions of the Karbis (*Mimeo.*).

1368. ———— : 1978 : The Institution of Satras in Assam. *(In) North-East India: A Sociological Study. (Ed.)* by S.M. Dubey. Delhi, Concept Pub.: 189-94.

1369. ———— : 1980 : Tribal unrest and inter-ethnic tensions in North-East India. *Bull. Anthropology S.I.,* XXVII (3-4), July-Dec.: 1-24 (1978) (Bodo of Udalguri, etc).

1370. ——— **(Ed.)** : 1982 : *The Customary laws and practices of the Pati Rabha of Assam.* Gauhati, Law Research Institute, Eastern Region, 139p. (Sponsored by North-Eastern Council, Shillong).

1371. ———— : 1983 : Peasants and Neo-peasants in North-East India and their new dimension. *(In) Social Anthropology of Peasantry. (Ed.)* by Joan P. Mencher. Bombay, Somaiya Pub.

1372. ———— : 1990 : Karbi Jirkedam (Bachelor's Dormitory) *(In) Social and Political Institutions of the hill people of North-East*

India (Eds.) by Jayanta Sarkar and B. Datta Ray. Calcutta, Anthropology S.I.: 14-28.

1373. **Goswami, M.C.** : 1992 : Peoples and Cultures in N-E India: The changing trends. *Bull. Deptt. of Anthropology*, Gau. Univ., VI, March: 1-8.

1374. **Goswami, M.C.** *and* **K.C. Mahanta** : 1974 : The concept of soul, sin and religious merit among the Kaibartas of Monpur: A fishing community of Assam. *Bull. Deptt. of Anthropology*, III, Dec.: 27-36 (It is 18 kms to the west of Guwahati).

1375. **Goswami, M.C.** *and* **P.C. Saikia** : 1968 : Some rituals of the Deuri-Chutiya *Jour. Assam Sc. Soc.*, XI.

1376. ———— : 1969-71 : Bahagiyo-bisu : A festival of the Dibongiya. *Jour. Univ. of Gau.* XX-XXII(2).

1377. ———— : 1970 : Magiyo-bisu: A festival of the Deuri-Chutiya. *Jour. Univ. of Gau.*, XVIII-XIX(2), Science: 133.

1378. **Goswami, M.C., S.N. Ratha** *and* **F. Nesha** : 1966 : Caste and occupation in an Assamese village. *Man in India*, 46(3), July-Sept.: 191-97.

1379. **Goswami, Mira Rani** : 1983 : *A study of socio-economic change and urban impact in a fishermen community, Tulasigaon*, Dibrugarh. Unpub. M.Sc. Disser. Anthropology Deptt., Dib. Univ.

1380. **Goswami, Narayan Ch.** : 1984 : *Satriya Sanskritir Swamarekha.* Jorhat, Purvasri Printers (*in Assamese*).

1381. **Goswami, P.** : n.d. : The Namghar: An Assamese Institution. *Educational Review* (Madras), LVI(11): 229-30.

1382. **Goswami, Pramod** : 1994 : Shifting cultivation of the hill tribes of Assam. *Bull. AIRTSC*, I(IX): 8-10.

1383. **Goswami, Pranay Jyoti** : 1989 : *Socio-economic life of plains tribal communities in the Barak valley: The extent of transition.* Unpub. Ph.D. Thesis, Gau Univ.

1384. **Goswami, Praphulladatta** : 1943 : Assamese Ballads. *Triveni Quarterly*, 15: 164-69.

1385. ———— : 1947 : The Cinderella motif in Assamese folk tales. *The Indian Historical Quarterly*, 23: 311-19.

1386. ———— : 1949 : Assamese proverbs and aphorisms. *MII*, 29(2), April-June: 92-7.

1387. ———— : The Folk tales of Assam. *E.A.*, II(4), June: 175-81.

1388. **Goswami, Praphulladatta** : 1949 : The Bihu girl. *I.H.Q.*, March.

1389. ———— : 1949-50 : The Bihu songs of Assam. *E.A.*, III(2-3), Dec.-March: 57-100.

1390. ———— : 1950 : Music in Assam : Its divine origin. *MII*, XXX(1), Jan.-March : 13-6.

1391. ———— : 1951 : Assamese marriage customs: Prenuptial. *E.A.*, 4(3-4), Dec.-Feb.: 133-49.

1392. ———— : 1952 : Assam's folksongs: A general survey. *Triveni*, April.

1393. ———— : 1953 : *A study of the folklore of Assam: The ballads of magic*. Unpub. Ph.D. Thesis, Gau. Univ.

1394. ———— : Riddles in Assamese. *E.A.*, 6(2), Dec.-Feb.: 110-15.

1395. ———— : 1954 : *Folk-literature of Assam: An introductory survey with foreword by Suryya Kumar Bhuyan*. Gauhati, Deptt. of Historical and Antiquarian Studies in Assam, vii+91p *(Reprinted in 1965)*.

1396. ———— : 1955 : Folk literature in Assam. *E.A.*, 8(2), Dec.-Feb.: 122.

1397. ———— : 1958 : An Assamese ballad of Magic. *Indian Folklore*, 1(2), Sept.-Dec. : 13-9.

1398. ———— : 1957 : *Bihu songs of Assam*. Gauhati, Lawyers' Book Stall, viii+174p.

1399. ———— : 1958 : Ultimate literary source of Assamese folk tales. *Indian Folk Lore*, 1(1), Jan.-March: 57-63 (It was first submitted at All India Oriental Conference, Delhi in 1957 and it appeared also in the book: *Studies in Indian Folk Culture*, Calcutta, 1964).

1400. ———— : 1959 : Miri folk songs. *Folklore*, 2(II), April-June: 103-06.

1401. ———— : 1959 : Folk literature of Assam. *(In) Souvenir on aspects of the heritage of Assam. (ed.)* by K.N. Dutt. Guwahati, 22nd Session of Indian History Congress, December: 70-81.

1402. ———— : 1960 : Folk drama in Assam. *Folklore*, 1(3), May-June: 148-50.

1403. ———— : *Assamese drama: An outline*. Calcutta, Srilekha Pub., 34p.

1404. ———— : *Ballads and tales of Assam*. Gauhati, Deptt.

of Tribal Culture and Folklore, Research, Gau. Univ., 252p. (*Reprinted* in 1970 by Lawyer's Book Stall, Guwahati; it is D. Phil Thesis forwarded by B.K. Barua).

1405. **Goswami, Praphulladatta** : 1961 : Recent ballads in Assamese. *Folklore,* 2(1), Jan.-Feb.,: 15-6.

1406. ———— : 1962 : Assam's folk tale. *Folklore,* III(I), Jan.: 30-6.

1407. ———— : *Folklore* of the Assam Plains. *The Assam Quarterly,* II(I), Jan.: 51-6. (Written in the name of "G.P.").

1408. ———— : Rain compelling ceremonies in Assam. Folklore, III(10), Oct.: 459-61.

1409. ———— : *Baro Mahar Tero Geet (In Assamese).* New Delhi, Sahitya Akademi.

1410. ———— : *Asam Deshar Sadhu (In Assamese,* 2nd ed.). Calcutta, Srilekha Pub. (about folklore).

1411. ———— : 1964 : The milk-pouring cow: A new motif? *Folklore,* 5: 46-9.

1412. ———— : Spinning and weaving in Assam. *Folklore,* V(12), Dec.: 441-45.

1413. ———— : 1966 : *The Spring time Bihu of Assam: A Socio-cultural study.* Gauhati, Lawyers' Book Stall, 114p (Assamese, Deuri, Kachari, Miri, Rabha, Lalung etc.).

1414. ———— : 1967 : Assamese folk songs: A general survey. *(In) Folk Music and Folklore, Anthropology. (Ed.)* by Hemanga Biswas. Calcutta, Folklore, Research Institute, Vol. I: 106-17.

1415. ———— : 1967 : The Hill Tribes of Assam and Christianity. *(In) A Common Perspective for North-East India. (Eds.)* by R.Mitra and B.Das Gupta. Calcutta, Pannalal Das Gupta: 232-34.

1416. ———— : Hindu and tribal folklore in Assam, *A.F.S.,* 26(1): 19-27.

1417. ———— : 1968 : Women in Assam's folklore. *Folklore,* IX(2), Feb.: 39-45.

1418. ———— : The Dakshinpat Satra of Assam. *Jour. Assam Res. Soc.,* 18: 64-7.

1419. ———— : Secret knowledge of animal languages. *Jour. Assam Research Society,* 18: 41-5.

1420. ———— : Folktales of the Miris. *Folklore,* 10(10), Oct.: 390-92.

1421. **Goswami, Praphulladatta** : 1969 : Folk tales of the Miris. *Folklore,* X(10), Oct.: 390-92.

1422. ———— : 1972 : The clever old man (Folk tale Assamese: Kachari). *Folklore,* XIII(12), Dec.: 489-91; XIV(5), May: 178-81.

1423. ———— : 1976 : *Songs and tales of North-Eastern India.* Gauhati.

1424. ———— : The overinquisitive wife (Folk Tale). *North-Eastern Spectrum,* I(3-4), Sept-Oct.: 34-7, 42.

1425. ———— : 1977 : Beliefs associated with music: From Assam's folklore. *Jour. NEICSSR,* I(II), Oct.: 1-2.

1426. ———— : 1978 : Assam's cultural role in the context of India. *(In) Social and Economic Profile of North-East India. (Ed.)* by B. Datta Ray. Delhi, B.R. Pub. : 239-47.

1427. ———— : 1979 : Assam's contribution to country's culture and well-being. *Times of India,* Dec. 3: 8 (1-4).

1428. ———— : 1980 : *Tales of Assam.* Gauhati, Publication Board, 323p.

1429. ———— : 1981 : A Karbi myth: Rangsina. *Jour. NEICSSR,* V(II), Oct.: 6-7.

1430. ———— : Rain compelling ceremonies in Assam. *Folklore,* 22(1), Nov.: 221-23.

1431. ———— : 1982 : *Essays on the Folklore, and Culture of North Eastern India.* Gauhati, Spectrum Pub., 174p. (about Kachari, Mikir, etc.).

1432. ———— : *Folklore*: The North-Eastern Scene. *(In) India's North-East. (Ed.)* by Pankaj Thakur. Tinsukia, Prakash Pub.: 95-107.

1433. ———— : 1983 : Folkore in North-Eastern India. *The Assam Academy Review,* Special Volume, No. 1.

1434. ———— : 1984 : Land and land relations: A note based on proverbs. *Jour. NEICSSR,* 8(1), April: 38-40.

1435. ———— : 1985 : Social criticism in Assamese tales *(In) Folklore, in North-East India. (Ed.)* by Soumen Sen. Delhi, Omsons Pub.: 62-9.

1436. ———— : Guwahati in the folksong of Assam. *Jour. NEICSSR,* 9(1), April: 37-40.

1437. ———— : *Folklore,* in North-Eastern India. *(In) Focus on Folklore, of North-East India. (Ed.)* by B. Datta. Guwahati, Assam Academy Review: 1-14.

1438. **Goswami, Praphulladatta** : 1987 : The spring time festival of Assam: Bohag Bihu. *Pratibha India*, VI(3), April-June : 3-8.

1439. ——————— : 1988 : *Bohag Bihu of Assam and Bihu songs.* Guwahati, Asam Prakashan Parishad, 172p.

1440. ——————— : 1990 : Problems of tribal areas. *(In) Constraints of tribal development in North-East India. (Ed.)* by B.N.Bordoloi. Guwahati, Tribal Research Inst.: 92-4.

1441. ——————— : 1992 : Folksongs in Assam. *(In) India through ages, Vol. V: Folklore of India. (Ed.)* by T.R. Sareen and S.R. Bakshi. New Delhi, Anmol Pub.: 1-35.

1442. ——————— : 1993 : *Tales of Assam.* Guwahati, Assam Prakashan Parishad.

1443. ——————— : 1994 : *Festivals of Assam.* Guwahati, Anundoram Borooah Institute of Language, Art & Cul., Assam.

1444. ——————————— : n.d. : *Bohag Bihu of Assam and Bihu songs.* Guwahati, Asam Prakashan Parishad.

1445. ——————— : n.d. : *Psychological treatment of Bihu songs.*

1446. ——————————— : Asamiya jana sahitya *(In Assamese)*. Guwahati, Bani Prakash (about folk literature).

1447. ——————— : n.d. : *Phulkonwar and Manikonwar.* Gau. Univ. Publication.

1448. ——— **(Ed.)** : 1972 : *Boro: Kachari Solo.* Univ. of Gauhati, Publication Division.

1449. ——— **(Ed.)** : 1973 : *Assamese popular superstitions and Assamese Demonology* by Benudhar Rajkhowa. Gau. Univ., Folklore, Research. 163p.

1450. **Goswami, Praphulladatta** *and* **Birendranath Datta** : 1974 : Folksongs of Assam. *Sangeet Natak*, 31, Jan.-March: 60-9.

1451. **Goswami, S.** : 1979 : British opium policy in Assam. Proceedings of a Seminar on *The History and Culture of North-East India*, Deptt. of History, NEHU held on 26-28 April, 1979.

1452. **Goswami, S.C.** : 1920 : *The night worshippers or Rati-Khowa sect of Assam.* Gauhati, Kamarupa Anusandhan Samiti.

1453. **Goswami, S.N.** : 1971 : Bhatheli: A Spring time festival of lower Assam. *Folklore*, XII(2), Feb.: 57-61.

1454. ——————— : 1972 : Snake worship and Manasa cult in Assam. *The North-Eastern Research Bulletin*, I, Summer: 52-7.

1455. **Goswami, S.N.** : 1982 : Saka : Namani Asamar thaluwa utsab: Mahoho aru Euri. *(In Assamese) Asam Bani*, Aghon, 27.

1456. **Goswami, Sarat Chandra** : 1943 : The Bhatheli festival. *Jour. Assam Res. Soc.*, 10: 27-33.

1457. **Goswami, Shashwati** : 1993 : Children's homes in Guwahati: An overview. *Assam Tribune (Sunday Reading)*, Feb. 28: I(1-8).

1458. **Goswami, Shrutidev** : 1982 : The opium evil in nineteenth century Assam. *The Indian Economic and Social History Review*, XIX (3-4): 365-76.

1459. ———— : 1986 : The Nature and effects of opium monopoly in Assam, 1860-1919. *Paper read in Indian History Congress* at Srinagar on 7-9 Oct.

1460. **Goswami, Tarun** : 1985 : Rendezvous with a Dimasa folk melody and a few observations on folk music. *(In) Folklore, in North-East India. (Ed.)* by Soumen Sen. Delhi, Omsons Pub.: 97-107.

1461. ———— : *Kuki life and lore.* Haflong (Assam), North Cachar Hills Dist. Council, 580p. (about North Cachar Hills, Karbi Anglong, etc.).

1462. ———— : 1989 : Folk songs spring from society. *Assam Tribune*, May 14: 4(3-6), 7(3-4).

1463. **Goswami, Triveni** : 1989 : Assam's spring festival. *Assam Tribune*, April 13: 5(5-8).

1464. **Goswami, Upendra Nath** : 1962 : Deuri-Chutiar sadharan parichaya (*In Assamese*). *(In) Asamar Janajati. (Ed.)* by Pramod Ch. Bhattacharya. Jorhat, Asom Sahitya Sabha: 87-98.

1465. **Goswami, Vandana** : 1994 : *Potent Words, Potent Objects; Doing Mantras' in Assamese everyday life*, Unpub. Ph.D. Thesis, Anthropology Deptt., Michigan State Univ., USA.

1466. **Govt. of Assam** : 1974 : *Draft outline 5th Five Year Sub-Plan for Scheduled Tribes (Plain), Scheduled Castes and Other Backward Classes.* Gauhati, Deptt. of Planning and Development.

1467. ———— : 1976 : *Report of the Sub-Committee of Advisory Council for Welfare of Sch. Tribes (Plains) on settlement of land in tribal belts and blocks and of forest land, 1976.* Gauhati, Deptt. for Welfare of Plains Tribes and Backward Classes.

1468. ———— : 1978 : *Report on bench mark survey (universal) in the tribal sub-plan of Assam 1978.* Guwahati, Assam Tribal Development Authority.

1469. **Govt. of Assam** : 1978 : *Tribals on the March*. Guwahati, Directorate of Information and Public Relations.

1470. ―――――― : 1979 : *Welfare measures for the backward classes in the Plain districts of Assam.* Guwahati, Deptt. for Welfare of Plains Tribes and Backward Classes.

1471. ―――――――― : *Report of the Committee on Welfare of Sch. Castes and Sch. Tribes relating to Land and Revenue.* Guwahati, Deptt. of Planning and Development.

1472. ―――――― : 1979-81 : *Integrated tribal development project reports* (year of preparation of the project reports are shown in brackets): Gauhati I (1979), Gauhati II (1979), Marigaon (1979), Goalpara (1980), Dhemaji (1980), Dhubri (1980), Tezpur (1980), Mangaldoi (1980), Sibsagar (1980), Dibrugarh (1980), Jorhat (1981), Golaghat (1981), Majuli (1981), Silchar (1981), Barpeta (1981), Kokrajhar (1981), Tinsukia (1981), North Lakhimpur (1981). Gauhati, Direct. of Res. and Statistics.

1473. ―――――― : 1980 : *Tribes of Assam Plains.* Gauhati, Deptt. of Planning and Development (Direc. of Welfare of Plains and Backward Classes).

1474. ―――――― : 1984 : *Indicators of development of tribals and tribal Sub-Plan areas of Assam, 1984.* Guwahati, Assam Tribal Development Authority.

1475. ―――――― : 1987 : *Annual Report (1986-87) of the Assam Tribals Development Authority*, 1987. Guwahati, Tribal Research Institute.

1476. **Govt. of Assam** : 1990 : *Report on the study of the problems of forest villages inhabited by tribals in Assam, 1990.* Guwahati, Assam Tribal Development Authority.

1477. **Grace, J.R.** : 1935 : The Hill Kacharis... *(In) Census of India 1931, Vol. I: India, Part III : Ethnographical. (Ed.)* by J.H. Hutton. Simla, Govt. Press: 132 and *Census of India 1931, Vol. III: Assam, part I, Report. (Ed.)* by C.S. Mullan. Shillong, Govt. Press (1932): vii-viii.

1478. **Graw, T.C.** : 1924 : *Handbook of Castes and Tribes employed in the Tea Estates in North-East India.* Calcutta, Indian Tea Association.

1479. **Grierson, George Abraham** : 1902 : Notes on Ahom. London, Luzac *(Reproduced from Zeitschrift den Deutschen Morgenlandischen Gesellschaft)*, Vol. 56: 1-59.

1480. ―――――― : 1904 : An Ahom cosmogony, with a translation and a vocabulary of the Ahom language. *JRAS*: 181-232.

1481. **Growse, F.S.** : 1879 : The sect of the Pran-nathis. JRASB (Calcutta), Vol. 48: 171-80.

1482. **Guha, Amalendu** : 1979 : Tribal State Formation. *Proceedings of a Seminar on The History and Culture of North-East India*, Deptt. of History, NEHU held on 26-28 April.

1483. ———— : 1989 : The ethnic process in India with a special reference to Assam (An Abstract). *Proceedings of NEIHA*, 10: 87-8.

1484. **Guha, Anima** : 1988 : Kherai: The National Festival of the Boro Kachari. *Jour. Ind. Anthropology Society*, 23(1), March: 95-8.

1485. **Guha, B.S.** : 1935 : The racial affinities of the peoples of India. *Census of India 1931, Vol. I (iii)*. Simla, Govt. Press: 10-22.

1486. **Guha, K.** 1960 : Tribal handicrafts in India. *Vanyajati*, VIII (3), July: 117-23 (Kachari etc).

1487. **Guha, Kamalesh** : 1971 : The plough of Upper Assam: A technological innovation in a marginal culture. *Ethnos*, 36(1-4): 105-14.

1488. **Guha, P.K.** : 1985 : Nath Community of Assam. *Proceedings of People of India*. Pre-Test Seminar of Anthropology, S.I., Shillong on Dec. 5.

1489. ———— : 1992 : Sacred complex of Hajo. *Jr. Ind. Anthropology Soc.*, 27(2), July: 197-200a.

1490. **Gupta, K.M.** : 1932 : Kaivartta or Jalika or Jalua-dasa. *(In) Census of India 1931, Vol. III: Assam, Pt. I: Report.* Shillong, Govt. Press: App. XXVI.

1491. ———— : 1932 : Casi-Kaivarthas or Mahisyas or Halika or Haluadasa... *(In) Census of India 1931, Vol. III: Assam, Pt. I: Report.* Shillong, Govt. Press: App. XXV.

1492. **Gupta, P.K.** : 1979 : *Stratification and religion in the Rabha society*. Unpub. Ph.D. Thesis, Calcutta Univ.

1493. **Gupta, Pabitra Kr.**: 1977 : Religion of the Hajongs of Garo Hills. *Man and Life*, 3(1-2), Jan.-June: 105-12.

1494. **Gupta, Sangita** : 1995 : Asam ka mahaparba: Bhogali Bihu. *Pur. Pra., Lohit Bha.*, Jan. 14: 14: I (3-5) (*In Hindi*).

1495. **Gupta, Srilal** : 1990 : Rup-Prakriti ka pratik parva Rangali Bihu. *Pur. Pra.*, April 14: 5(1-8) (*in Hindi*).

1496. **Gurdon, P.R.T.** Comp : 1904 : The Morans. *JASB* (Cal.), 73, Pt. I: 36-48.

1497. **Gurdon, P.R.T.** : 1908 : Ahom.. *(In) Hasting's Encyclopaedia of Religion and Ethics, Vol. I.* Edinburg, T.&T. Clark: 234-37.

1498. ———— : 1913 : On the origin of the Ahoms. *JRASGBI* (London): 283-87.

1499. **Hagjar, Nirupama** : 1974 : *Dimasa*. Jorhat, Asom Sahitya Sabha *(In Assamese)*, 52p.

1500. **Hajong, Abani Kr.** : 1977 : The Hajongs. *North-Eastern Spectrum* (Gauhati), 2 (1), July: 16-8.

1501. **Hajong, Biresh Ch.** : 1989 : Uttar purbanchal at Hajong Janagosthir Abhumuki. *(In Assamese). Souvenir, 3rd Annual session of All Assam Hills Tribal Council,* Guwahati: 5.

1502. **Hajong, Kanu Ram** : 1994 : The Hajongs: Through the mists of time. *Assam Tribune(Sunday Reading)*, March 13: I(1-8).

1503. **Hajong, Paresh** : n.d. : Hajong janajatir janma rahashya. *(In Assamese). Janaskikhya*: 11-2.

1504. **Hajong, Paresh Ch.** : 1985 : Hajong Bia aru Bibah Padhati *(In Assamese). Dainik Asom*, 21st July.

1505. ———— : 1987 : Gotra Ba Nikni (in Hajong language). *Smritigrantha, Uttar Pub Bharat Hajong Unnayan Samity*, Lakhimpur: 5.

1506. **Haldar, A.K.** : 1973 : Book Review: Census of India 1961: Dimasa Kachari of Assam. *(Ed.)* by B.K. Roy Burman. New Delhi, Office of the Registrar General of India, VII+34. *Man in India*, 53 (1), Jan.-March: 114.

1507. **Haldar, A.K.** : 1995 : Book Review: Tribal Development and Socio-Cultural Matrix by S.T.Das, 272p, 1993. Kanishka Publishers Distributors, Delhi, *South Asian Anthropologist* (Ranchi), 16(2): 110.

1508. **Haldar, Rakhal Das** : 1925 : A Kurmi marriage. *MII*, 5: 255-58 (Tea Garden's People).

1509. **Haldipur, R.N.** : 1979 : Problems of administration of tribals of North-East India. *Vanyajati*, XXVII (2), April: 15-24.

1510. **Hannay, Major** : n.d. : *Notes on the Twangs and Turungs.*

1511. **Hannay, S.F.** : 1838 : A short Account of the Moa Morah Sect, and of the Country at Present Occupied by the Bor Senaputtee. *JRASB*, vol.7, Pt. 2: 671-79.

1512. **Hanse, S.** : 1985 : Bare Baronia Bhasha Sanskritir Milan Bhumi Asom *(In Assamese). Asam Sahitya Sabha Patrika* (41st year, No. 2).

1513. **Hanse, Samsing** : 1926 : *Sabin Alun*. Jorhat, Asam Sahitya Sabha (*In Assamese*).

1514. ———— : 1972 : *Kumlin* (In Karbi). Diphu, Durga Press.

1515. ———— : 1973 : *Romir* (In Karbi). Diphu, Diphu Press.

1516. ———— : 1974 : *Name Tair Haimu* (*In Karbi*). Diphu, Diphu Press (It is a story book on love of Haima).

1517. ———— : 1979 : *Edited Lamet Acheng* (*In Karbi*). (A collection of Karbi short stories).

1518. ———— : 1981 : Rangsinar Itibritta. *Agradut*, July 5 (About folklore).

1519. ———— : *(Tr and Ed.)* : 1986 : *Sabin Alun*. Diphu, Asam Sahitya Sabha (*In Karbi*).

1520. —— **(Ed.)** : 1975-76 : *Ovekimi: Karbi-Riso-Darbar* (*In Karbi*). Diphu, Diphu Press.

1521. **Haq, Rafikul** : 1995 : Asamiya Lok parampara— Sanskriti men Janama, janani aur panchamrita. *Pur. Pra.*, March 14: 5(1-6) (*In Hindi*)

1522. ———— : Asom ki Hira jati aur inki kalakritiya (*In Hindi*). *Pur. Pra.*, June 27: 5(7-8).

1523. **Hardinge, F.W.** : 1939 : *Indigenous Christianity in Assam*. Gauhati, Assam Christian Council, 12p.

1524. **Harlalka, S.S.** : 1975 : *Tea garden labour in Assam*. Dhubri, Peoples' Pub. House.

1525. ———— : 1995 : Women enterprise in North-East. *Eastern Panorama*, III (5), March: 45-6 (Assamese weave cloth of Muga, Silk).

1526. **Hassan, Mahmood** : 1992 : Neglect of tribal history. *Assam Tribune*, Feb. 18: 4(3-6), 7(5-8) (About Ahom).

1527. ———— : Neglect of tribal culture-I. *North Eastern Times*, April 11: 4(3-8) (Ahom).

1528. ———— : Neglect of tribal culture-II. *North-Eastern Times*, April 12: 4(1-6) (Ahom).

1529. **Hati Barua, Gobin** : 1978 : *A Study on marriage system among the Bodos of Chota Adabari village of Kokrajhar*. Unpub. M.Sc. Disser. Anthropology Deptt., Dib. Univ.

1530. **Hatikakoty, Makhan** : 1985 : Cultural Heritage of Assam. *A.T.*, April 14: 4.

1531. **Hazarika, Annie** : 1996 : *Aniruddhadeva and Mayamorya sect of Assam Vaishnavas*. Unpub. Ph.D. Thesis, Gau. Univ.

1532. **Hazarika, Atul Ch.** : 1968 : *Aitar Sadhu*. Gauhati (*In Assamese*).

1533. ————: 1973 : *Utshovor rongsora* (*In Assamese*). Gauhati.

1534. **Hazarika, B.K.** : 1995 : An insight into the core problems of the Scheduled Castes of Assam *(In) ibid* : 101-06.

1535. **Hazarika, Bimal Kr. (Ed.)** : 1995 : *Core Problems of the Scheduled Castes of Assam.* Guwahati, AIRTSC (TRI), 159p.

1536. **Hazarika, Bisweswar** : 1992 : A Secular festival. *North-East Times (Rongali Bihu Supplement)*, April 14: I(1-8), IV(1-8).

1537. **Hazarika, Chandan** : 1990 : Dimasa Kacharis of N.C. Hill. *Assam Information*, XXXXII, April-May: 9-10.

1538. **Hazarika, Deben Ch.** : 1977 : Matak sampradai ketia aru kiya bechi pich pora srenir talikabhukta h'al (In A.). *Smriti Grantha,* Matak Sanmilan: 2.

1539. **Hazarika, Haren Kr.** : 1990 : The Socio-religious aspects of Bodos: A plain tribes in Assam. *Proceedings of a Seminar on Status of Religion in Tribal Areas in NEI* organised by NEICSSR, Shillong on 15-16 Feb. (*Mimeo.*).

1540. **Hazarika, J.** : 1978 : *A Study on some aspect of socio-cultural life of the Bodo-Kachari of Kokrajhar.* Unpub. M.Sc. Dissert. Anthropology Deptt., Dib. Univ.

1541. **Hazarika, K.** : 1978 : Traditional administrative set-up and social contact in Karbi society. *Resarun*, IV(2), Aut. and Winter: 30-40.

1542. **Hazarika, M.P.** : 1991 : NEC and the tribal areas. *Shillong Times*, Nov. 26: 2(3-6).

1543. **Hazarika, Munindra Prasad** : 1989 : Hill-Folk culture of the North-East. *Assam Tribune, Sunday Reading,* April 16: I(1-8).

1544. **Hazarika, Nagen** : 1990 : Ban Ok pup lik Mioung Tai: A short History. *Assam Tribune*, Feb. 17: 4(7-8) (Tai of Assam).

1545. ———— : 1994 : Me-dam-me-Fie. *Assam Tribune*, Jan. 31: 4(7-8).

1546. ———————— : Ahomon ka varshik shradha: Me-dam-me-Fi (*Translated* by Arvind Kr. Sharma). *Pur. Pra.*, Jan. 31: 5(1-4) (*In Hindi*).

1547. **Hazarika, Niru** : 1995-96 : *Ethnicity and Socio-political Change in Assam.* Unpub. Report of a Research Project of Planning & Development, Deptt. of Pol. Sc., G.U.

1548. **Hazarika, P.** : 1995 : Impact of special component plan among the Scheduled Castes of Assam. *(In) ibid.*: 129-33.

1549. **Hazarika, Pratap** : 1981 : Matak: Govinda Ram. *(In) Mayamara Satra Samaj: Bhasan aru Pravandha. (Ed.)* by Sushil Kr. Gogoi. Chabua, Mayamara Kala Kristi Anusandhan: 87-91 (*In Assamese*).

1550. **Hazarika, Rajani** : 1990 : Prachin Kachari Itihasat Haidang gitar prabhab (*In Assamese*). *Social Sc.* (Silchar), 3(1-2): 201-13.

1551. **Hazarika, Rani** : 1992 : *Urbanization and social change: A Study in Assamese culture with reference to Guwahati*. Unpub. Ph.D. Thesis Anthropology Deptt., Gau. Univ.

1552. **Heine-Geldern, Robert von** : 1917 : Kopfjagd und Menschenopfer in Assam und Birma und ihre Ausstrahlungen nach Vorderindien. *Mitteilungen der Anthropologischen Gesellschaft in Wien*, 47: 1-165.

1553. ———— : 1921 : Mutterrecht und Kopfjagd im Westlichen Hinterindier *Mitteilungen der Anthropologischen Gesellschaft in Wien*, 51: 105-40.

1554. ———— : 1923 : Sudostasien *(Ed.)* by G. Buschan. *Illustrierte volkerkunde* (Stuttgart), 2, Pt. I: 689-968.

1555. ———— : 1927 : Die Sammlungen aus Hinterindien und Assam im Besitze des Museums fur volkenkunde in Munchen. *Mitteilungen der Anthropologischen Gesellschaft in Wien*, 57: 114-25.

1556. ———— : 1932 : Bedeutung und Herkunft der seltesten hinterindischen Metalltrommeln (Kesselgongs). *Asia Major*, 8: 519-37.

1557. **Henniker, Frederick Chanclos** : 1905 : *Gold and silver wares of Assam*. Shillong. Govt. Press.

1558. **Hermanns, Matthias** : 1954 : *The Indo-Tibetans: The Indo-Tibetan and Mongoloid Problem in the Southern Himalaya and North, North-Eastern India*. Bombay, K.L. Fernandes, 159p (About Bodo, Kachari, Koch, Dimasa, Rabha, Mech, Lalung Hajong, etc.)

1559. **Hesselmeyer, C.H.** : 1868 : The hill tribes of the northern frontier of Assam. *Jour. Asiatic Society of Bengal*, 37, pt. II: 192-208.

1560. **Hindustan Times** : 1993 : Assamese titles betray feudal status. *H.T.*, June 9: 3(1-4) (Title/Surnames of Assamese people).

1561. **Hmar Sikpui** : 1995 : Hmar Sikpui ruoi festival, 94 celebrated. *Eastern Panorama*, III (3), Jan.: 45-6 (Haflong: Hmar).

1562. **Hocart, A.M.** : 1927 : The dual organisation (Assam). Man, 27(104): 231-32.

1563. **Hodgson, Brian H.** : 1849 : On the origin, location, numbers, creed, customs, character and condition of the Koch, Bodo and Dhimal people with a general description of the climate they dwell in. *Jour. Roy. As. Soc. Bengal*, 18, Pt. II: 702-47.

1564. ——————: 1880 : *Miscellaneous essays relating to Indian subject* (Section I: On the Kooch, Bodo and Dhimal tribes). London, Trubners' Oriental Services.

1565. **Hodgson, Brian Houghton** : 1847 : *Essay the First: On the Koch, Bodo and Dhimal tribes.* Calcutta, Baptist Mission Press.

1566. **Hodson, T.C.** : 1905 : *The Assam Hills.* Liverpool, C.Trinding and Co.

1567. ——————: 1906 : The "Genna" amongst the tribes of Assam. *Jour. of the Anthropology Inst.*, 36 : 92-103.

1568. ——————: 1908 : *Funerary customs and eschatological beliefs among hill tribes of Assam.* Transactions of the 3rd Int. Cong. of the Religion, Oxford.

1569. ——————: 1909 : Mortuary ritual and eschatological beliefs among the hill tribes of Assam. *Archiv fur Religious wissenschaft.* 12: 447-59.

1570. —————— : 1960 : *The Adivasis.* Delhi, Pub. Div. (*Revised ed.*).

1571. **Horam, M.** : 1975 : *Naga Polity.* Delhi, B.R. Pub. (A little mentioned about Ahoms).

1572. **Houghton, Brian Hodgaon** : 1909 : Mortuary ritual and astrological beliefs among the hill tribes of Assam. *Archive fur Religiouswis Wissen Acharf,* 12: 447-59.

1573. ——————: 1990 : *North-East India: A Profile.* Delhi, 223p.

1574. **Hunda, M.** : 1975 : *Sibsagar town: A study of urbanisation.* Unpub. Ph.D. Thesis, Dib. Univ.

1575. **Hunter, Grey** : 1966 : *South-East Asia: Race, Culture* and Nation. London, OUP, 190p.

1576. **Hussain, Md. Mahmood** : 1995 : Is it 'the time of the Assassins'? *Sentinel (Sunday)*, Sept. 3: I(1-8) (Fast changing Socio-Cultural Process in the contemporary.

1577. **Hussain, Monirul** : 1986 : Interaction between caste and politics. *Indian Jour. of Politics,* XX(3-4), July-Dec.

1578. —————— : 1987 : Caste, among the Assamese Muslims: An essay in social stratification, *Proc. of a Seminar on Stratification, Hierarchy and Ethnicity in North-East India, organised by the*

Deptt. of Sociology and Social Anthropology, North Bengal Univ., Darjeeling, March (*Mimeo*).

1579. **Hussain, Monirul** : 1987 : Muslims of contemporary Assam: A Sociological Introduction. *Jour. NEICSSR*, 11(2).

1580. ———— : 1988 : Caste among non-Hindu Indians: An exploratory study of Assamese Muslims. *E.A.*, 41(4), Oct.-Dec.: 273-85.

1581. ———— : 1992 : Tribal question in Assam. *EPW*, XXVII(20-21), May 16-23: 1047-1050.

1582. ———— : 1994 : The tribal ; question in Assam: A sociological appraisal. *(In) Essays on North East India (Ed.)* by Milton S. Sangma. New Delhi, Indus Pub. Com.: 278-93.

1583. **Hutton, J.H.** : 1925 : Some astronomical beliefs in Assam. *Folklore*, 36, June: 113-31(various tribes of Assam).

1584. ———— : 1929 : Oraon religion and customs: cultural Affinities of the Oraons with the Hill Tribes of Assam. *MII*, 9: 1-16.

1585. ———— : 1932 : Races of further Asia. *MII*, XII(1), Jan.-March: 1-6 (Mikir, Kachari, Bodo etc.).

1586. **Hutton, J.H.** : 1939 : Clan monopoly of personal names. *Man*, 39(61): 64.

1587. ———— : 1946 : *Caste in India*. Cambridge, Camb. Univ. Press.(Reprinted in 1951 from Bombay, Asia Pub. House; Koch: 30, 112, 216; Namasudra: 30, 31, 86, 112, 205, 207, 211, 213; Rabha: 116; Rajbangsi: 30,116).

1588. **ICSSR** : 1974 : *A Survey of research in Sociology and Social Anthropology*, Vol. II. Bombay, Popular Prakashan.

1589. **Idrish, A.S.M.** : 1993 : In quest of the Lalung Ramayana. *(In) Rama Katha in tribal and folk traditions of India: Proceedings of a Seminar. (Eds.)* by K.S. Singh and Birendranath Datta. Calcutta, Seagull Pub. for Anthropology S.I.: 213-18.

1590. **Indian Anthropologist** : 1988 : Book Review: Matriliny to Patriliny: A Study of Rabha Society—Manis Kumar Raha, pp. X+373. Gian Publishing House, New Delhi. *Indian Anthropologist*, 18(2), Dec.: 71-3.

1591. **Indian** *and* **Foreign Review** : 1973 : Assam. Delhi, Pub. Div., 67p., 10(10), March 1: 22.

1592. **Indian Law Research Institute** : 1986 : *The Customary Laws of the Dimasa of Assam*. Guwahati, Law Res. Inst., Eastern Region (sponsored by NEC, Shillong), *Mimeo*.

1593. **Indian Law Research Institute** : n.d. : *The customary laws and practices of the Pati Rabha of Assam. ibid, Mimeo.*

1594. **Institute of Research** : 1994 : Seminar on *Core group of tribal population of Assam,* held on 5-7 Oct. 1994, organised by TRI, Assam Inst. of Res. for Tribals and Sch. Castes (*Mimeo*).

1595. **Itagi, N.H. et al** : 1986 : *Communication potential in the tribal Population of Assam and Madhya Pradesh*. Mysore, Central Inst. of Indian Languages.

1596. **Iyer, E.V. Ganapati** : 1960 : Assam. *Modern Review*, 107(1), Jan.: 52-8.

1597. **Iyer, L.A. Krishna** *and* **Ratnam, L.K. Bala** : 1961 : *Anthropology in India*. Bombay, Bharatiya Vidya Bhavan; 3, 6, 7, 10, 43, 48, 49, 51, 59, 63, 76.

1598. **Jagidar, M.P.** : 1986 : Status of women: A case study with special reference to North-Eastern Region. *(In) Proceedings of the National Conference on Tribal women and development; Problems and perspectives.* Udaipur.

1599. **Jain, Rajkumar (Jhanjari)** : 1990 : Palashbari rasotsov ke sath jura hai sangharshamoy Itihas (*In Hindi*) *Pur. Pra.*, Nov. 1: 7(4-8).

1600. **Jain, S.K. (Ed.)** : 1981 : *Glimpses of Indian Ethno-botany.* New Delhi, Oxford and IBH., Pub.

1601. **Jain, Shobhita** : 1991 : Acculturation processes on an Assam Tea Garden. *E.A.*, 44(1), Jan.-March : 13-43.

1602. **Jalil, A.** : 1961 : Bihu as descrbed in an old Persian book. *Assam Tribune*, April: 15.

1603. **Jana, Sunil (Ed.)** : 1993 : *The Tribals of India*. Delhi, Mittal Pub., 144p(Miris of Brahmaputra Valley, the Kacharis, the Mikirs, etc.).

1604. **Jenkins, Colonel** : 1854 : An Account of the Assam Tribes. *(In) Report on the Province of Assam* by A.J. Maffatt Mills. (Reprinted in 1980 by Gian Pub., Delhi).

1605. **Jenkins, F.** : 1942 : *Selection of papers regarding the hill-tract between Assam and Burma and on the Upper Brahmaputra.* Calcutta (*Reprinted*).

1606. **Jethani, Urmila** : 1994 (n.d.) : *Single Woman*. Jaipur, Rawat Pubn.

1607. **Jha, M.** : 1988 : Myths, history and social organisation of Kamakhya temple. *Man in Asia*, I(I), June : 68-77.

1608. **Jha, Prem Shankar** : 1967 : Assam the alienation of the tribes. *H.T. (Weekend Review)*, Dec. 16, II(2): 6-11 *(Ed.)* by S. Mulgaonkar.

1609. **Jha, Srinand** : 1988 : Drug smuggling through North-East : New threat from 'Golden Triangle'. *Shg. T.*, Dec. 24 : 2 (3-6), 3 (4-5) (Assam).

1610. **Jha, Tarakanta** : 1991 : Bihu men jab pura Asom khil-khil jata hai (*In Hindi*) *Pur. Pra.*, Jan. 13: 5 (1-3).

1611. ————: 1991 : Asom: Ek jhalak (*In Hindi*) *Pur. Pra* (*Lohit Bharati*), Feb. 17 : I (1-8).

1612. ———— : Asom ke Satra ebang Uttar Bharat ke Mahanthan Mandir (*In Hindi*) *Pur. Pra.* (*Lohit Bha.*) May 12: 2 (5-8).

1613. ———— : Asom ke Satra-sa hi hai Mahanthan Mandir (*In Hindi*) *Pur. Pra. (Loh. Bha.)*, May 19 : II (1-4).

1614. ———— : Asom tatha Mithila ka Sanskritik samagam (*In Hindi*) *Pur. Pra. (Loh. Bha.)*, Aug. 4 : 2 (1-4).

1615. **Jha, Tarakanta** : 1993 : Hindi, Moithili ebang Asamiya nattya sahitya ki pristha bhumi (*In Hindi*) *Pur. Pra.*, Nov. 1: 5 (3-6).

1616. ———— : Maithili ebang Asamiya natya sahitya ki pristha bhumi. *Pur. Pra.*, Nov. 22: 5 (3-6) (*In Hindi*).

1617. **Jhanjri, Raj Kumar** : 1993 : Purbanchal ka Jain tirtha Surya pahar (*In Hindi*) *Pur. Pra.*, March 16: 5 (1-8) (Goalpara).

1618. **John, Ashish** : 1992 : Glimpses of a tribe in the north east India. *Shg. T. (Sunday Special)*, March 8: I (1-4) (Karbi) etc.

1619. ————: 1994 : Karbis: An idyllic life. *Assam Tribune, Sunday Reading*. July 10: I (1-8).

1620. **Joshi, Vibha** : 1991 : Book Review: *Matriliny to patriliny: A Study of the Rabha Society* by M.K. Raha. Delhi, Gian Publishing House, 1989, pp. 373, *E.A.*, 44 (3), July-Sept.: 298-99.

1621. ———— : n.d. : Journal: Kochi Bihar and Assam: *Jour. Asiatic Society of Bengal*, I.

1622. **Jyrwa, E.** : 1996 : Formation of the District Council in the Hill areas of Assam. *Jour. NEICSSR*, 20(1), April: 22-7.

1623. **Kabui, G.** : 1977 : Nagas and the Ahoms: A Study in their relationship. *Thinker* (Kohima), 5 (4), Nov.: 28-50.

1624. **Kagyung, Bhrigumuni (Ed.)** : 1970 : *Mishing sanskritir alekhya* (*In Assamese*) Gauhati, Lawyers' Book Stall (*Reprinted* in 1989).

1625. **Kaith, D.C.** : 1939 : Hill tribes of Assam. *Modern Review*, 66, Oct.: 409.

1626. **Kakati, Ajoy** : 1972 : *A Study of family structure and functions of Mikirs.* Unpub. M.Sc. Disser. Anthropology Deptt., Dib. Univ.

1627. **Kakati, B.** : 1939-40 : The Kalita caste of Assam. *New India Antiquary*, 2: 332-39.

1628. **Kakati, Banikanta** : 1941 : *Assamese, its formation and development.* Gauhati, Deptt. of Hist. & Antiquarian Studies, Narayani Handique Hist. Inst.

1629. ————: 1941-42 : Place and personal names in the early land grants of Assam. *New Indian Antiquary*, 4: 388-94.

1630. ———— : 1948 : *The Mother Goddess Kamakhya, or studies in the fusion of Aryan and primitive beliefs of Assam.* Gauhati, Punya Prasad Duara for Assam Pub. Cor, 91p.

1631. ———— : 1949 : The Kalita caste in Assam. *A volume of Indian & Iranian Studies,* presented to Sir E. Denison Ross on his 68th birthday 6th June, 1949. Bombay, Karnatak Pub. House, N.D.: 171-78.

1632. **Kakati, Banikanta** : 1951 : Place and personal names in the early land grants of Assam. *(In) A Cultural History of Assam: Early Period, Vol. I (Ed.)* by B.K. Barua. Nowgong, Pub. by K.K. Barooah : 202-07.

1633. ———— : 1952 : *Visnuite myths and legends, in folklore setting.* Gauhati, Sadhana Sahitya Mandir, 140p.

1634. ———— : 1955 : *Purani Kamrupar dharma dhara.* Gauhati, Bani Prakash Mandir, 139p.

1635. ———— : 1962 : *Kalita jatir itibrittya* (*In Assamese*) (Reprinted) Gauhati, Lawyers' Book Stall, 66p (1st Published in 1943).

1636. ———— : *Assamese, its Formation and Development.* Gauhati, Lawyers' Book Stall, 432p.

1637. ————: 1987 : *Assamese, its Formation and Development (Revised & Reprinted).* Guwahati, LBS Pub., 86p (1st Pub. in 1941).

1638. **Kakati, D.** : 1985 : Baishyas of Kamrup district of Assam. *Procg. of People of India.* Pre-Test Seminar of Anthropology, S.I., Shillong on Dec. 5.

1639. **Kakati, Devakanta** : 1991 : Letters to the Editor: Madhupur Satra. *Assam Tribune*, Dec. 30: 4(5-6) (Cooch Behar + Assam).

1640. **Kakati, Dwijen** : 1988 : Demographic & Ethnographic Profile of Assam. *Assam Tribune*, July 3: 4 (3-6), 6(3-4).

1641. **Kakati, Haladhar** : 1951 : *Bhedeli Bharal*. Nowgong (About Folklore).

1642. **Kakati, Siba Ch.** : 1993 : Biswanath: Kashi of the North-East. *Assam Tribune, Sunday Reading*, Jan. 3: 1(1-4).

1643. **Kakoty, Chikon** : 1994 : Bhogali Bihu, Harvest festival of Assam. *Shg. T.*,Jan. 14 : 4(3-6).

1644. ————— : 1996 : Sankardeva: A remarkable Vaishnavite saint *Sentinel* (Sunday), April 14: 4(1-8).

1645. **Kakoty, Sanjeeb** : 1994 : A beacon of hope. *Assam Tribune (Sunday Reading)*, Aug. 7: I(1-8) (Karbi culture and heritage).

1646. **Kakoty, Tridib** : 1993 : Celebration of Bihu. *Assam Tribune Sunday Reading*, April 11: 1(1-4).

1647. ————— : 1995 : Semkhor : Where time stands still. *Sentinel (Sunday)*, May 21 : I(1-8) (Semsa, Dimasa, N. Cachar Hills).

1648. **Kali, J.** : 1985 : Murong, Dibrugarh, Taun Bangke Agom Kebang.

1649. **Kalita, Bakul (Ed.)** : 1991 : *Banshi (In Assamese)*. Souvenir Nikhil Jatiya Parishad. Beltola (Amsoi) Nowgong, Reception Committee 29th session Nikhil Jatiya Parishad.

1650. **Kalita, Dhaneswar** : 1991 : *Traditional performances of South Kamrup*. Delhi, Gian Pub. House, 82p (Folklore & Art).

1651. **Kalita, Dilip** : 1982 : The status of women in Karbi society. *Assam Tribune*, April 24 : 4.

1652. ————— : 1987 : Chhayagaon Anchalar Loka Sanskriti. *Champakjyoti*: 7.

1653. **Kalita, Dilip Kr.** : 1982 : *Rangsina Sapo aru Karbi Samaj*. Diphu, Asam Sahitya Sabha *(in Assamese)*.

1654. ————— : 1994 : The charmed arrow : A concept common in the field of Indian Magic. *Man and Life*, 20(3-4). July-Dec.: 251-57 (Mayong area in Nagaon Dist. Assam).

1655. ————— : 1996 : Karbi Folklore and Sabin Alun. *Seminar paper on Traditional Culture and Folklore in North-East India*, 18-19 Nov., Shillong, NEICSSR.

1656. **Kalita, J.C.** : 1990-91 : *Verbal art of Dimoria : An introductory survey*. Gauhati University, M.Phil Dissertation.

1657. **Kalita, Jagadish** : 1992 : Tribal problems. *Assam Tribune*, Dec. 16: 4 (7-8) (Bodo, Karbi, Mishing, Sonowal, Rabha).

1658. **Kalita, Krisna** : 1990 : Asom ka Bhogali Bihu : Ek Sanskritik yoihar. (*In Hindi*) *Pur. Pra (Saptahik Parishist)*, Jan. 14: 1(7-8).

1659. **Kalita, Naren** : 1982 : Painting of Assam : A Note *(In) India's North East. (Ed.)* by Pankaj Thakur. Tinsukia, Prakash Pub. House : 51-68.

1660. **Kalita, Ramesh Ch.** : 1992 : Evils of British imperialism in Assam: Opium trade. *Assam Tribune*, Nov. 17: 4(3-6), 7(4-5).

1661. **Kalita, Srikanta** : 1963 : *Mani Lanir Sadhu* (*In Assamese*) Gauhati (on Folklore).

1662. **Kalita, Thaneswar** : 1939 : *Tikani Atar Katha*. Gauhati (on Folklore).

1663. **Kalla, A.K.** *and* **K.S. Singh (Eds)** : 1987 : *Anthropology, development and nation-building*. New Delhi, Concept Pub.

1664. **Kanu, Babul Narayan** : 1987 : Barak upatyakar *cha* banuar loka sanskritir eti abhas. *Ashom Sahitya Sabha Journal* (Silchar), 1986-87: 78 (*In Assamese*).

1665. **Kannittanan, Willaiwan** : 1981 : Khwan, an ancient Tai belief. Proceedings of the *International Conference on Tai Studies*, New Delhi.

1666. **Kapoor, D.** : n.d. : The Bishu festival and its role. *Folklore*, Nov.-Dec.: 393-98.

1667. **Kapuria, R.S.** : 1979 : The Bell metal industry of Assam. *Indian Co-operative Review*, 16(3), April : 227-35.

1668. **Kar, B.** : 1985 : Ex-tea garden labourers of Assam valley— An appeal for socio-metric study. Paper presented in *NEICSSR Seminar*.

1669. **Kar, Biman** : 1991 : Rural working women: A study of a few villages. *Proceedings of a Seminar on Women and Economic Development* held on Dec. 1, 1991, organised by Economics Deptt., Gau. Univ. (*Mimeo.*).

1670. **Kar Choudhury, Amalendu Bikash** : 1984 : *Tribal songs of North-East India*. Calcutta, Firma KLM.

1671. **Kar, Parimal Chandra** : 1980 : *Chathar* songs of the Rabha of Meghalaya. *Jour. NEICSSR*, IV (11), Oct. : 9-15.

1672. **Kar, R.K.** : 1972 : Rites and customs associated with the marriage of the Assamese Hindus. *Bull. Deptt., Anthropology*, Dib. Univ., 1:53-62.

1673. ———————— : 1973 : Student versus the traditional joint family system. *Bull. Deptt. of Anthropology, Dib. Univ.* II: 10-5.

1674. **Kar, R.K.** : 1977 : A tribe in the context of a tea industry: Some preliminary observations. *Anthropologyropos*, 71: 868-77.

1675. ———— : 1974 : The Savara kinship terminology : A taxonomic profile *(In) Contemporary Anthropological Research in North-East India (Ed.)* by B.M. Das. Dib. Univ. : 86-92 (This is also Bull. Anthropology Deptt., Dib. Univ., III, 1974).

1676. ———— : 1975 : Attitudes of the educated youth towards divorce and widow remarriage. *North-Eastern Research Bulletin*, VI, Summer: 51-5.

1677. ———— : Some aspects of marriage in a tea garden tribe. *Proceedings of a Seminar on Sociological Perspective on North-East India and the Second Annual Conference of North-East India Sociological Association*, Dib. Univ., Deptt. of Sociology, March 10-12, 1975.

1678. ———— : Selection of spouse: Past and present views. *Eastern Anth.*, 28(3), July-Sept.: 241-54.

1679. ———— : 1976 : Unity in diversity: A note on the process of adaptation in the tea industry. *Bull Deptt. of Anthropology*, Dib. Univ., IV: 11-5 (1975).

1680. ———— : *The Savaras of Mancotta: A study on the effects of tea industry on tribal life*. Ph. D. Thesis, Dib. Univ., Anthropology Deptt.

1681. ———— : Some aspects of social life of a tea garden tribe in Assam, India. *Proceedings of a Seminar on Social Change in North-East India*, organised by the Deptt. of Anthropology, Dib. Univ., March 26-27.

1682. ———— : A migrant tribe in a tea plantation in India: Economic profile. *Anthropos*, 74(5/6) : 770-84.

1683. ———— : Tribe in the context of a tea industry in India: Some preliminary considerations and observations. *Anthropos*, 71(5/6) : 868-77.

1684. ———— : 1977 : Marriage and Family : An opinion survey among the educated youths of Assam. *Bull. Deptt. of Anthropology, Dib. Univ.* 5(1976): 40-52.

1685. ———— : 1978 : The Savaras of Mancotta : Effects of wage labour in tea on tribal life (Research conclusion). *Current Anthropology*, XIX (I): 211-12.

1686. ———— : Kinship profile of a tea garden tribe *(In) Cultural and Biological Adaptability of Man with Special Reference to North-East India. (Eds.)* by A.C Bhagabati and R.K.

Kar (This is also *Bull. Deptt. of Anthropology, Dib. Univ.*, VI, 1977), pp. 73-85.

1687. **Kar, R.K.** : 1978 : Some aspects of marriage in a tea garden tribe: A case study. *(In) North-East India: A Sociological Study (Ed.)* by S.M. Dubey. Delhi, Concept Pub.: 125-34.

1688. ———— : 1979 : A migrant tribe in a tea garden in India : Economic profile. Anthropos, 74: 778-81.

1689. ———— : 1980 : Tea labour in Assam: A note on social relations. *Bull. Deptt. of Anthropology, Dib. Univ.*, IX: 25-39.

1690. ———— : Some aspects of marriage: Traditionalism vs. Modern Education. *(In) Family, Marriage and Social Change. (Eds.)* by S. M. Dubey, P.K. Bordoloi and B.N. Borthakur. New Delhi, Cosmo Pub.: 128-36.

1691. ———— : 1981 : *The Savaras of Mancotta: A study on the effects of tea industry on the tribal life*. New Delhi, Cosmo Pub., 256p.

1692. ———— : Social change in a tea plantation tribe in Assam, India. *Acta Ethnographica*, XXX (3-4).

1693. ———— : Bodo relationship terms. *E.A.*, 34(1), Jan.-March: 37-46.

1694. ———— : Tea industry in Assam: A chronological account. *Man and Life*, 7: 131-50.

1695. ———— : 1982 : Tea Labour in Assam: A note on social relations. *Bull. Deptt. of Anthropology, Dib. Univ.*, IX(1980): 25-39.

1696. ———— : Community life of a tea garden tribe: A case study in Assam. *(In) Tribal Development in India: Problem and Prospects. (Ed.)* by Buddhadeb Chaudhuri. Delhi, Inter-India Pub.: 447-59 (Ahoom, Kachari etc.)

1697. ———— : 1982-83 : A note on child labour in tea plantations in Assam. *Bull. Deptt. of Anthropology, Dib. Univ.*, XI-XII (1987): 51-66.

1698. ———— : 1984 : Labour pattern and absenteeism: Case study in tea plantation in Assam. *Anthropologyropos*, 79: 13-24.

1699. ———— : 1985 : Tea labour in Assam: A note on the problem of identity. *Paper presented in a Seminar on Tea Garden Labourer in North-East India: A Multi-Dimensional Study held* on 25-27 Feb., organised by NEICSSR, Shillong in collaboration with Sacred Heart Theological College, Shillong.

1700. **Kar, R.K.** : 1986 : Absenteeism among tea labour: A case study in cultural ecology. *Man and Life*, 12(3-4), July-Dec.: 143-58.

1701. ———————— : A note on health sanitation among the tea labour in Assam. *Vanyajati*, XXXIV (2), April: 12-20 (This paper was presented to the Seminar of Anthropology and Development with Special Reference to N.E. India, held in the Deptt. of Anthropology, Dib. Univ. in Feb. 16-18, 1984).

1702. ———————— : The People of North-East India: An appraisal. *Bull. Deptt. of Anthropology, Dib. Univ.*, 15 (1990): 128-39.

1703. ———————— : Tea plantation labour in Assam: Some Anthropological observations. *Paper read in the Thirty-second International Congress for Asian and North African Studies*, held at Hamburg during 25-30 August, 1986.

1704. ———————— : 1988 : A small tribe in the Eastern Himalayas: An appraisal of its problems and development. *Paper presented in a Seminar on Problems and Strategies of Development in the Eastern Himalayas* organised by Centre for Himalayan Studies, North Bengal Univ.

1705. ———————— : 1989 : The Savaras of Assam. Vanyajati, 37(2), April: 5-11.

1706. ———————— : 1990 : The People of North-East India: An appraisal. *Vanyajati*, 38(1), Jan.: 11-9.

1707. ———————— : Tea labour in Assam: A note on the problem of identity. *(In) Tea garden labourers in North-East India. (Ed.)* by S. Karotemprel and B.Datta Roy. Shillong. Vendrame Inst.: 118-30.

1708. ———————— : 1992 : Migration and acculturation : A case study among tea labour in Assam. Bull. Deptt. of Anthropology, Dib. Univ. 18-19 (1989-90): 165-83.

1709. ———————— : Plantation workers and heteroethnicity: An appraisal of the Tea labour in Assam. *(In) Political Development of North East, Pt. II. (Ed.)* by B.C. Bhuyan. New Delhi, Omsons Pubs.: 80-95.

1710. ———————— : 1993 : Socio-Economic life of tea and ex-tea labour Assam : An appraisal. *Bull. Deptt. of Anthropology, Dib. Univ.* 20-21(1991-92): 110-20.

1711. ———————— : 1994 : The Tribes of North-East India: An overview *(In) Tribes of North East India. (Ed.)* by Sarthak Sengupta. New Delhi, Gyan Pubg. House: 1-20.

1712. ———————— : 1995 : Some Basic facts of child rearing and the tea labour of Assam: A preliminary appraisal. *Bull. Deptt., Anthropology, Dib. Univ.*, 23: 76-85.

1713. **Kar, R.K.** : 1996 : Ethnic groups and ethnicity in North-East India: A case study among the tea labourers in Assam. *Paper presented in Golden Jubilee Celebration of An.S.I.*, Shillong, 13-14 Sept. 1996 for *Ethnic Situation in North-East India: Field and Frontier* (*Mimeo.*).

1714. **Kar, R.K.** *and* **Geetanjali Baruah** : 1979 : Tea labour: Preliminary appraisals of common identity in a multi-ethnic community in Assam. *Man in India*, 59 (1), Jan.-March: 33-42.

1715. **Kar, R.K.** *and* **J.L. Sharma** : 1990 : The Oraons of Assam. *Vanyajati*, XXXVIII (2), April: 22-32.

1716. —————— : Ethnic Identity of Tea Labour: A case study in Assam. *(In) Nationality, Ethnicity and Cultural Identity in North-East India. (Ed.)* by B. Pakem. New Delhi, Omsons Pub.: 147-64.

1717. **Kar, R.K.** *and* **Juri Konwar (Gogoi)** : 1996 : Mishing. *(In) Encyclopaedic Profile of Indian Tribes. (Eds.)* by Sachidanand and R.R. Prasad. New Delhi, Discovery Pubg. House : 694-97.

1718. **Kar, Subir** : 1990 : *Jangier geet : A heroic tale of Surma Barak Valley*. Unpub. Ph.D. Thesis, Gau. Univ.

1719. **Karan, Kashi Kumar** : 1988 : Bargeets : A musicological study. *Assam Tribune*, July 3 : 4(3-6), 6(1-2).

1720. **Karmakar, M.** : 1983 : *Sohrai Parab*. Dibrugarh, Bhattacharya Agency (*In Assamese*).

1721. **Karmakar, Meghraj** : 1985 : Cha mazdoor samaj aru sanskriti. *(In) Hansali. (Ed.)* by N. Ghatowar. Dibrugarh, Assam Tea & Ex-Tea Garden Tribes Youth Association (*In Assamese*).

1722. **Karmakar, Rahul** : 1992 : Sports, dance and fun. *North-East Times (High point supplement)*, April 26: I(1-8) (Boko Anchalik Suwori Utsav Committee, 7th day of Bohag Bihu).

1723. **Karnick, C.R., K.C. Tiwari, R. Majumder** *and* **S. Bhattacharjee**: 1981: Newer ethno-botanical and folklore studies of some medicinal plants of Guwahati and surrounding areas. *Nagarjun* (Calcutta), XXIV (1): 240-45.

1724. **Karotemprel, S.** : 1981 : *A brief history of the Catholic Church among the Tiwa (Lalungs)*. Shillong.

1725. ———— **(Ed.)** : 1984 : *Tribes of North-East India*. Calcutta, Firma K. L. Mukherjee, 430p.

1726. ———— : 1985 : The future of the Adivasi community in Assam. *Indian Missiological Review*, 7(2).

1727. **Kathar, Dayaram** : 1994 : Letters to the Editor: The Karbis. *Assam Tribune*, Aug. 19: 4(5-6).

1728. **Kauffmann, H.E.** : 1934 : Landwirtschaft bei den Bergvolkern von Assam und Nord-Burma. *Zeitchrift fur Ethnologie*, Vol. 66: 15-111.

1729. ———— : 1939 : Das Fadenkreuz in Hinterindien. *Forschungen und Fortschritte*, Vol. 16 (15); 193-95.

1730. **Kaur, Darsan** : 1980 : *An account of the Sonowal Kacharis of Lepetkata village Dibrugarh with special reference to the fishing, marriage and economy*. Unpub. M.Sc. Disser. Anthropology Deptt., Dib., Univ.

1731. **Kejrhival, Kumar Rakesh** : 1995 : Hojai ka shantivan smashan: Manav jivan ka aina (*In Hindi*). *Pur. Pra.*, Dec. 19: 5 (1-8) (about Cremation ground).

1732. **Kellner, H.F.D.** : 1895 : Remarks on Dalton's Note on the Chutiyas of Upper Assam. *(In) An Outline Grammar of Deuri-Chutiya Language spoken in Upper Assam. (Ed.)* by W.B. Brown.

1733. **Kha Rarish, Alauddin** : 1991 : Kitna nirapad : Kitna surakshit: Guwahati ka pahari jivan (*In Hindi*). *Pur. Pra.* (*Lohit Bharati*), Oct. 20: 2(1-8)

1734. **Khandpur, Swarn** : 1971 : Our Country Series, India: The Land and its People. Bombay, Ratnabharati: 136-41.

1735. **Khatun, I.S. Mumtaz** : 1981 : Marriage relations of the Ahom rulers with the neighbouring ruling families. *Proceedings of NEIHA*, 2: 89-96.

1736. ———— : 1985 : Nature of the Ahom-Kachari relations. *Proc. of NEIHA*, 6: 163-69.

1737. **Khound, Chinmayi** : 1996 : Bihu. *Sentinel* (Sunday), April 14: 3(7-8).

1738. **Khound, G.** : 1967 : *Cha bagichar Asomiya*. Jorhat, Asom Sahitya Sabha (*In Assamese*).

1739. **Koch, Bimal (Ed.)** : 1980 : *Rashan*: 17-19 (*In Assamese*)

1740. **Koch, J.** : 1985 : *Sambhabayapurna ajan Asamiyar apamrityu* (*In Assamese*).

1741. **Koch, S.N.** : 1981 : The Koches: Their migration and settlement. I.S, 3.

1742. ———— : *Mongoloid Speech*. Jorhat. Asam Sahitya Sabha.

1743. **Koch, S.N.** : 1983 : Eta sangketik chin'dash' (—), eta jati aru ejan panditor janma: Eti parjalochona. *Rasan*, March: 18-24 (*In Assamese*).

1744. ——————— : 1984 : The Koches: Their migration and settlement, 1-IV. *New Star*, April 29-30 and May 1-3, 1984.

1745. ——————— : The Koch of Garo Hills. *(In) Garo Hills Land and the People. (Ed.)* by L.S. Gassah. Gauhati, Omson Pub.: 173-95.

1746. ——————— : Koch jatir chamu parichay. *Ganachabuk*, 2nd May: 3-4 (*In Assamese*).

1747. ——————— : Bodo: A much misused term, I and II. *New Star* (Eng. daily of N.E. India), June 12 and 13.

1748. **Koch, S.N.** : 1986 : The Assam Mongoloid. *Souvenir, Silver Jubilee, All Assam Tribal Sangha* (Tipkai): 10-5.

1749. **Koch, Sibendra Narayana** : 1986 : The role of the Koches in shaping the history and culture of North-East India. *Jour. Assam Research Society* (Guwahati), XXVIII, 1984-85 (1984): 83-93.

1750. **Kohli, D.C.** : 1955 : Assam Today. *March of India*, 7(6), April: 34-7.

1751. **Kokoty Tridib** : 1996 : Mirroring the mosaic of Assamese culture *Sentinel Sunday,* April 14: 1(4-8), 2(3-6) (Earlier and modern culture).

1752. **Kopped, K.B.** : 1971 : Bhatheli: A spring time festival of lower Assam. *Folklore*, XII (2), Feb.: 49-56.

1753. **Kotoky, P.** : 1987 : Book Review: Tantra and Tantrism of Ancient Assam by Nirmalprabha Bordoloi, Sahitya Prakash, Guwahati, 1986, 36+522p. *Assam Tribune*, March 29: 4(7-8).

1754. **Koundinya, Bhikshu** : 1975 : Asom rajya ki Misid janjati ki bibaha padhyati ebong samaj me nari ka sthan (*In Hindi*). *Vanyajati* XXIII (2-3), April-July: 16-7.

1755. ——————— : 1982 : *Mishing janajati*. New Delhi.

1756. **Kour, Harabhanjan** : 1990 : Mishing samaj: Kal aur Aaj (*In Hindi*). *Pur. Pra.*, Sept. 3: 5(1-8).

1757. **Kuli, J.** : 1992 : *Folk literatures of Mishings*. Dibrugarh, Tasen Bangke Agon Kebang.

1758. **Kuli, Jawahar Jyoti** : 1988 : Mishing Ali Aye Ligang. *Assam Tribune*, Feb. 17: 4(7-8) 5(4) (Sibsagar, Darrang, Golaghat district's tribe).

1759. **Kumar, Anupam** : 1989 : Koch Bihar Ka Madhupur Satra aur Sri Sri Shankar Dev. *Pur. Pra. (Lohit Bha.)*, Dec. 31: I (7-8) (*In Hindi*)

1760. **Kumar, D.P.** : 1988 : Restive tribes-I : Still nibbling at Assam. *St.*, Oct. 12 : 8(4-6) (ABSU, Bodo, Karbi, Dimasa).

1761. **Kumar, Jamini** : 1950 : *Tribes of India*. New Delhi, Bharatiya Adimjati Sevak Sangh. (*Ed.*) by V. Raghaviah (Rabha: 35).

1762. **Kumar, N.** : 1984 : Are the Koch Rabha Scheduled Tribe? *News Star*, Nov. 24.

1763. **Kungkhra** : 1982 : *Introduction of the Mishings and the Bodos, Vol. I.* Kokrajhar, Pub. by Padma Lochan Bora, 52p.

1764. **Kunstadter, Peter (Ed.)** : 1967 : India : Introduction. *(In) South-East Asian Tribes Minorities and Nations, Vol. 1. (Ed.)* by Peter Kunstadter. Princeton New Jersey, Prinecton University Press : 205-14.

1765. **Kurmi, Susheel** : 1977 : *Tushu gitar maje maje* (*In Assamese*) Dibrugarh, Asom Chah Mazdoor Sangha.

1766. ———— : 1981 : *Cha bagichar Asamiya sampradaya* (*In Assamese*) Jorhat, Asam Sahitya Sabha.

1767. ———— : 1983 : *Cha bagichar Kotha* (*In Assamese*). Jorhat, Asam Sahitya Sabha.

1768. **Kutty, N. Madhavan** : 1982 : Social Parameters of Assam. *Link*, Aug. 22.

1769. **Lachan, Chandra Kanta** : n.d. : *Mishing Agom Kebangar Chamu Abhash*. Unpub. 1455.

1770. **Lahiri, Dilip Kr.** : 1979 : The folklore study in India in early period and a note on two works in N-E Region. *Folkore*, 20(7), July : 277-80.

1771. **Lahiri, Dilip K.** *and* **Bimal J. Dev** : 1983 : Origin and development of the Ahoms: An explanatory note of the folk-customs. *Folklore,* 24 (3), March: 49-53.

1772. ———— : 1984 : Ahom concept of war and peace. *Folklore*, 25 (9), Sept. 165-68.

1773. **Lahiri, M.R.** : 1982 : Boro Mahariao Bad. *Souvenir, Bodo Sahitya Sabha*, 23rd Conference, Goreswar (*in Bodo*).

1774. **Lahkar, A.** : 1990 : Social status of the Koch in an Assam village in the local social hierarchy: A case study. *Social Sc.* (Silchar), 3(1-2): 165-70.

1775. **Lais, Abul** : 1961 : The One Act Play in Assam : A Note. *Assam Quarterly*, 1(2), April: 28-31.

1776. **Lakhar, B.C.** : 1976 : *Socio-Economic profile of a tribal community in an urban fringe*. Unpub. Ph.D. Thesis, Anthropology Deptt., Dib. Univ.

1777. ——————— : Changing pattern of occupation of a tribal community. *Proceedings of a Seminar on Social change in North-East India*, organised by the Deptt. of Anthropology, Dib. Univ., March 26-27.

1778. **Lambert, E.T.D.** : 1938 : Human sacrifices in Assam. *Jour. Assam Research Society*, 6: 65-7.

1779. **Lambert, E.T.D.** : 1946 : Three Ahom folk tales. *Man in India*. XXVI (3-4), Sept.-Dec.; 196-201.

1780. ————— : 1952 : A short account of the Ahom people. *Jour. Siam Society*, 40: 39-65.

1781. **Land, C. Op't** : 1961 : Kin terms of the Mikir. *E.A.*, XIV(2), May-Aug.: 161-68.

1782. **Laskar, A.A.** : 1983 : *Ethnography : Structure and process among the Burman Kachari of Cachar district of Assam*. Report submitted to Anthropology S.I., Calcutta. (*Mimeo.*)

1783. **Laskar, G.K.** : 1991 : Letters to the Editor: Assamese and Census '91. *Assam Tribune*, Feb. 14: 4(4-5).

1784. **Laskar, Nitish Rajan** : 1985 : Mahishya Das of Cachar and their social background. *Proceeding of NEIHA*, 6: 454-62.

1785. **Leach, E.R.** : 1947 : *Cultural change with special reference to the Hill Tribes of Burma and Assam.* Ph.D. Dissertation, Univ. of London (Subsequently revised and Published as Political Systems of Highland Burma: A Study of Kachin Social Structure). Cambridge,. Harvard Univ. Press, 324p.

1786. —————: 1949 : Tree ern sago. *Man*, 49 (60).

1787. —————: 1961 : *Rethinking in Anthropology*. London, Athlone Press, 143p.

1788. **Lekharu, Upendrachandra** : 1952 : *Kathaguruchari*t. Gauhati, Pub. by the author *(Folklore)*.

1789. **Lekhika** : 1981 : Nari nirjatan samashyas bhitit jugut kora (*In Assamese*). *Lekhika*, 12.

1790. **Lewin, T.H.** : 1984 : *Wild Races of the Eastern Frontier of India*. Delhi, Mittal Pub. (*Reprinted*, 1st Pub. in 1870).

1791. **Lewison, R. Grace** : 1939 : Folklore of the Assamese. *Jour. Roy. As. Soc. Bengal*, Letter 5: 341-95.

1792. **Lloyd, G.T.** : 1923 : Assam *(In) Census of India 1921,* Vol. III. Assam, Pt. 1, Report, 2 Vols. Shillong, Govt. Press (Appendices: 144, 145, 147-48, 149 about Koch, Hira, Kachari, Kaibartta, Namasudra).

1793. **Logan, J.R.** : 1848 : Customs common to the Hill Tribes bordering Assam and those of the Indian Archipelago. *Jour. Indian Archipelago and Eastern Asia,* 2 : 229-36.

1794. ———— : 1858 : The West Himalayan or Tibetan tribes of Assám, Burma and Pegu. *Jour. Ind. Arch. & East. Asia,* 2: 68-114; 230-36.

1795. **Loing, Tankeswar** : 1970 : Mishing bhasa nokowa Miching. *(In) Mishing Sanskritir Alekhya, 1st pt. (Ed.)* by Bhrigumuni Kagyung. Gauhati, Lawyers' Book Stall : 30-1 *(In Assamese).*

1796. **Luthra, P.N.** : 1971 : North-East Frontier Agency Tribes: Impact of Ahom and British Policy. *E.P.W.,* VI (23), June 5 : 1143-49.

1797. **Lyall, Charles J.** : 1883 : Note on the geographical distribution and ethnological affinities of the Mikir.. *(In) Census of India 1881, Assam.* Calcutta, Govt. Press : 78 (Reprinted in Census of India 1891).

1798. ———— : 1908 : *The Mikirs.* London, David Nutt, 183p. (*Reprinted* n.d., by United Pub., Gauhati).

1799. ———— : 1915 : Mikirs *(In) Encyclopaedia of Religion and Ethics, Vol. 8 (Ed.)* by James Hastings. Edinburg, T. & T Clark: 628-31 (*Reprinted* in 1921 from London, again in 1973 from New York).

1800. **Lyngdoh, F.B.** *and* **B.K. Roy Burman (Eds.)** : 1972 : *Census of India 1961,* Vol.I, *Monograph series,* Pt. V-B "Mikirs of Assam". Delhi, Manager of Pub., 34p.

1801. **Mackenzie, Alexander** : 1884 : *History of the relations of the Govt. with the Hill Tribes in the North-East Frontier of Bengal.* Calcutta, Home Deptt., Press, 586p.

1802. ———— : 1979 : *The North-East Frontier of India.* Delhi, Mittal Pub., 586p (*Reprinted* and again reprinted with a new Introduction by B.K. Roy Burman in 1989).

1803. **Mahanta, Aparna** : 1988 : Emergence of new women's groups in Assam. *(In) A decade of women's movement in India. (Ed.)* by Neera Desai. Delhi, Himalaya Pubg. House: 130-47.

1804. ———— : 1992 : Women, religion and science in Non-Tribal societies of Assam. *(In) Status of women in Assam (with special reference to non-tribal societies). (Ed.)* by S.L. Baruah. New Delhi, Omsons Pub.: 93-101.

1805. **Mahanta, Aparna** : 1994 : The women's movement in Assam and North East India: An Assessment. *Seminar on social Movements in North East India with special reference to women, youth and religion*, Organised by NEICSSR, Shillong on 26-27 August, 1994 (*Mimeo.*).

1806. **Mahanta, Aparna** : 1990 : Problems of the women's movement in Assam. *North-East Politics*, 1(2), Feb.: 11-6.

1807. **Mahanta, Bandana** : 1980 : *An account of the Sonowal Kacharis of Lepetkata village with special reference to the agriculture, birth, and pregnancy and kinship organization*. Unpub. M.Sc. Disser., Anthropology Deptt., Dib. Univ.

1808. **Mahanta, Bandana** : 1981 : *Modernization of Karbis in Diphu, Karbi Anglong*. Unpub. M.Sc. Disser. Anthropology Deptt., Dib. Univ.

1809. ———— : 1982-83 : A note on the initiation ceremony of the Matak. *Bull. Deptt. of Anthropology, Dib. Univ.*, 11-12 (1987): 91-7.

1810. ———— : 1988 : *The Mataks of Upper Assam : A case study in social network*. Unpub. Ph.D. Thesis, Anthropology, Deptt., Dib., Univ.

1811. **Mahanta, D.** : 1973 : *Society and religion among the Duonias of Ketetong: Margherita*. Unpub. M.Sc. Disser. Anthropology Deptt., Gau. Univ.

1812. ———— : 1989 : To the Editor: Should Assam be a tribal State? *Shillong T.*, Sept. 7: 2 (3-6).

1813. **Mahanta, Dipjyoti** *and* **M.C. Goswami** : 1974 : Ritual and secular role of a Duonia Monastery. *Bull. Deptt. of Anthropology, Gau. Univ.*, III, Dec.: 32-40 (Margherita, Assam).

1814. **Mahanta, K.C.** : 1972 : Occupational pattern in a fishing community. *Bull. Deptt. of Anthropology, Dib. Univ.*, I: 42-9.

1815. ———— : 1973 : Features of Kaibarta kinship system. *Bull. Deptt. of Anthropology, Dib. Univ.*, II: 27-34.

1816. ———— : 1976 : *Socio-Economic structure of Monpur: A scheduled caste village of Kamrup, Assam*. Unpub. Ph.D. Thesis, Anthropology Deptt., Dib. Univ.

1817. ———— : Gift giving, reciprocity and the Institution of *Bhal-Manuh* in a Scheduled Caste Community of Assam. *Bull. Deptt. of Anthropology, Dib. Univ.*, 4 (1975): 1-5.

1818. ———— : Occupational mobility among the Kaibarta

of Kamrup of Assam, and the structural changes. *Proceedings of a Seminar on Social Change in North-East India* organised by the Deptt. of Anthropology, Dib. Univ., March 26-27.

1819. **Mahanta, K.C.** : 1982-83 : Man-land relationship in a Scheduled Caste community of Assam: A case study. *Bull. Deptt. of Anthropology, Dib. Univ.*, 11-12 (1987): 81-90.

1820. ———— : 1989 : Asamar bivinna janagosthi: Abayabik Bishleshan. *(In) Asamar Manuh. (Ed.)* by B.M. Das. Jorhat, Asam Sahitya Sabha : 57-72 (*In Assamese*).

1821. ———— : Barter system in a fishing community of Assam. *Bull. Deptt. of Anthropology, Dib. Univ.*, 13-14 (1984-85): 46-52.

1822. ———— : A town of Assam and its impact on the hinterland. *MII*, 69 (2), June: 159-78.

1823. ———— : 1991 : Cultural interaction between Assam and the rest of India. *(In) Nation Building and Development in North-East India(Ed.)* by Udayan Misra. Guwahati, Purbanchal Prakash: 150-60.

1824. ———— : 1992 : Mailbag : Stereo-typed view. *North-East Times*, March 28 : 4(3-7) (Bodo, Rabha, Lalung, Chutiya, Moran, Deuri, Sonowal, Dimasa, Karbi, Mishing).

1825. ———— : Assamese culture and youth. *North-East Times*, April 5: 4 (1-6).

1826. ———— : 1993 : Socio-Economic status of the aged: A case study. *MII*, 73 (3), Sept.: 201-13.

1827. ———— : Over exploitation of North Sub-Himalayan vegetable resources: Its impact on the Brahmaputra valley of Assam. *Jour. Human Ecology*, 4 (4), Oct.: 261-66.

1828. ———— : 1994 : Change and mobility in caste occupations: A development sequel in Assam. *Bull. Deptt. of Anthropology, Dib. Univ.*, 22 : 19-28 (Kaibarta).

1829. ———— : 1995 : A diachronic study of change and development in three Kaibarta villages of Assam. *(In) Core Problems of the Scheduled Castes of Assam. (Ed.)* by Bimal Kr. Hazarika. Guwahati, AIRTSC (TRI): 34-7.

1830. ———— : 1996 : Bodo Kachari. *(In) Encyclopaedic Profile of Indian Tribes. (Eds.)* by Sachchidananda and R.R. Prasad. New Delhi, Discovery Pubg. House: 148.

1831. ———— : Karbi. *(In) ibid*: 394-95.

1832. ———— : Lalung/Tiwa. *(In) ibid*: 556-57.

1833. **Mahanta, K.C.** : 1996 : Of tribal tradition and identity crisis. *Sentinel*, Nov. 2: 3 (1-8), 4(4-8).

1834. ———— **(Ed.)** : 1997 : Assam and North-East India. *Jour. of Human Ecology*, vol. 8.

1835. **Mahanta, K.C.** *and* **T. Barua** : 1982-83 : Growth of sub-cultural identity in Assam. *Bull. Deptt. of Anthropology, Dib. Univ.*, 11-12 (1987): 98-106.

1836. **Mahanta, Khagen Ch.** : 1986 : Asamar bibhinna janagosthi: Abayabik bisleshan. *(In) Assmar Manuha. (Ed.)* by Bhuban Mohan Das. Jorhat, Asam Sahitya Sabha: 57-72 (*In Assamese*).

1837. ———— : 1988 : Vaishnavism in Assam and its impact on the Noctes of Arunachal Pradesh. *MII*. 68(1): 70-83.

1838. **Mahanta, Nila Kanta** : 1992 : *The influence of Neo-Vaisnavism on the Bodo Kacharis of Kamrup with special reference to socio-cultural aspects*. Unpub. Ph.D. Thesis, Gau. Univ.

1839. **Mahanta, P.K.** : 1993 : Karbi Ramayan sabin alun. *Prakash*, 9 (1).

1840. **Mahanta, Pona** : 1985 : *Western influence on modern Assamese drama: From 1857 to the present time*. New Delhi, Mittal Pub.

1841. **Mahanta, Pradip Jyoti** : 1987 : *The role of Assam Vaisnavism in the making of Assamese life and culture: A study in an enduring tradition*. Unpub. Ph.D. Thesis, Gau. Univ.

1842. ———— : 1993 : Folk classical continuum in the Assamese neo-Vaishnava dramatic tradition, exemplified in a Rama-Katha-based play. *(In) Rama-Katha in tribal and Folk traditions of India: Proceedings of a Seminar. (Eds.)* by K.S. Singh and Birendranath Datta. Calcutta, Anthropology S.I.: 131-38.

1843. **Mahanta, Renu** : 1989 : The role of Satras in the history of Medieval Assam. *Proceeding of NEIHA*, 10: 200-02.

1844. **Mahanta, Rohini Kr.** : 1975-76 : The category of cash in Assamese: A Phonological study. *Jour. Univ. Gau. (Arts)*, 26-27(1): 79-94.

1845. **Mahapatra, L.K.** : 1959 : *A Hill Bhuyan village*. D. Phil Thesis, Hamburg Hectography.

1846. ———— : 1981 : Economic interdependence and Jajmani relations in tribal areas. *(In) Economies of the tribes and their transformation. (Ed.)* by K.S. Singh. New Delhi, Concept Pub.: 108-19 (Kachari, Miri, Lalung, Rabha etc.).

1847. **Mahato, P.P.** : 1983 : Uttar Bango, Assamer lok sanskriti O Tripurar Ganotantra (Review). *Desh*. Dec. 17 (*in B.*)

1848. **Maitra, Asim** : 1995 : Deori; Sonowal Kachari. *(In) People of India: Arunachal Pradesh. (Ed.)* by K.S. Singh. Calcutta, Seagull Books: 156-60; 298-302.

1849. **Maitra, Sunil Ranjan** : 1976 : Bachelor's dormitories of the tribes of Eastern India. *Bull. Anthropology S.I.* XIX (2), April (1970): 61-5 (Mikir etc.).

1850. **Maity, P.K.** : 1966 : *Historical studies in the cult of the Goddess Manasa.* Calcutta, Pub. by the author, 295p.

1851. **Majhi, Prithibi** : 1986 : Letters to the Editor : Chah Mazdoor tribe. *Assam Tribune*, Sept. 26: 4 (3-4) (Cachar).

1852. **Majumdar** *and* **Choudhury** : 1994 : *Land laws of Assam,* Vol.I. Guwahati, Distributed by United Pubn.

1853. **Majumdar, D.N.** : 1967 : Social organization of the Koch of Garo Hills, Assam *(In) Common Perspective for North-East India. (Eds.)* by R. Mitra and B. Das Gupta. Calcutta, Pannalal Das Gupta: 67-71 (Koch, Rajbansi etc.).

1854. ———— : 1968 : A note on Hajong marriage customs. *Bull. Anthropology S.I.*, XVII (2): 79-82 (1971).

1855. ———— : 1969 : A study of sanskritisation among the Bodo speaking tribes of Garo Hills. Paper read in a Seminar on *Tribal Situation in India*, Simla, Indian Inst. of Adv. Study.

1856. ———— : A comparative study of three kinship systems of Assam. *Proceedings of the All India Sociological Conference*, Delhi (only *Abstract* Published).

1857. ———— : 1971 : An account of magico-religious rites and beliefs of the Rongdani Rabha. *Bull. Anthropology S.I.*, XVII (3), July (1968): 245-56.

1858. ———— : A study of the clan organization of the Rabha. *Bull. Anthropology S.I.*, XVII (3), July (1968): 316-24.

1859. ———— : A study of religious practices among the Song Koch of Garo Hills. *Bull. Anthropology S.I.*, XVII (3) July (1968): 325-35.

1860. ———— : 1972 : Acculturation among the Hajong of Meghalaya. *MII*, 52(1), Jan.: 46-63.

1861. ———— : A study of Tribe-caste continuum and the process of sanskritization among the Bodo speaking tribes of the Garo Hills. *(In) Tribal Situation in India. (Ed.)* by K. Suresh Singh. Simla, Indian Institute of Adv. Study: 263-70.

1862. ———— : A comparative analysis of Boro and Koch

Kinship terminologies. *Bull. Deptt. of Anthropology, Gau. Univ.*, I, Dec.: 58-68.

1863. **Majumdar, D.N.** : 1972 : A study of the kinship terminology of the Koch of Garo Hills. *Proceedings of 58th Indian Science Congress*, Bangalore.

1864. ———— : 1978 : Asomiya jati aru Sanskriti. *(In) Asam Gaurav. (Ed.)* by Committee. Gauhati, Deptt. of Assamese, Cotton College (*In Assamese*).

1865. ———— : 1980 : North-East India: A profile. *(In) Eastern Himalaya (Eds.)* by T.C. Sharma and D.N. Majumdar. New Delhi, Cosmo Pub.: 32-6.

1866. ———— : Growth of ethnological studies in North-Eastern India. *(In) Eastern Himalayas. (Eds.)* by T.C. Sharma and D.N. Majumdar. New Delhi, Cosmo Pub.: 136-46.

1867. ———— : 1982 : An appraisal of the tribal situation in North-East India *(In) India's North-East India (Ed.)* by Pankaj Thakur. Tinsukia, Prakash Pub. : 126-29.

1868. ———— : 1983 : The Tribes and their problems in North-East India (In) *Souvenir* : Anthropological Society of North-East India (Eds.) by H.C. Sharma and B. Choudhury. Gau. Univ., Anthropology Deptt : 12-7.

1869. ———— : *Development and planning in the tribal areas of Assam in the cultural context.* Shillong, NEICSSR, 12p. (*Mimeo.*).

1870. ———— : 1984 : Tea garden communities and the Assamese society. *Proc. of a Seminar on Tea Plantation labour in Eastern India*, organised by the Deptt. of Sociology and Social Anthropology, North Bengal Univ., Nov. (*Mimeo.*).

1871. ———— : 1985 : The story about the origin of the Koches and their migration to Garo *Hills. (In) Folklore in North-East India. (Ed.)* by Soumen Sen. New Delhi, Omsons Pub.: 183-90.

1872. ———— : 1986 : Asamar Janagosthi. *(In) Asamar Manuh (Ed.)* by B.M. Das. Jorhat, Asam Sahitya Sabha: 15-30 (*In Assamese*).

1873. ———— : 1988 : Development of Scheduled Tribes in Assam: Retrospect and prospects. *The Thinker: Jour. of Thinker's Forum* (Kohima), X (1-2).

1874. ———— : Contribution of the Boros in the History and Culture of Assam. *Charuchandra Sanyal Memorial Vol.*, Jalpaiguri.

1875. **Majumdar, D.N.** : 1989 : Some basic points for considering the Status of women particularly among plain tribal societies of Assam. Seminar paper on *Status of women in plain tribal societies of Assam*, 19-20 Jan. organised by the Deptt. of Folklore Research, Gau. Univ.

1876. —————————— : Tribal development in retrospect. *(In) Sequences of development in North-East India. (Ed.)* by J.B. Bhattacharya. New Delhi, Omsons Pub.: 71-80.

1877. ————— : 1990 : Tai migration to North-East India. (*T.V. Interview*).

1878. ————— : 1993 : Ethnicity and regionalism in North-East India *(In) Tribal Transformation in India,* Vol. III, pt. VI. *(Ed.)* by Buddhadeb Chaudhuri. New Delhi, Inter India.

1879. ————— : n.d. : *Dresses and ornaments of South-East Asia (Research Project)*. Tokyo, National Museum of Ethnology, Japan.

1880. **Majumdar, D.N.** *and* **B. Datta Roy** : 1984 : *Tribal occupational mobility*. Calcutta, Research India Pub., 204p.

1881. **Majumdar, D.N.** *and* **C.R. Rao** : 1960 : *Race elements in Bengal*. Bombay, Asia Pub. House and Calcutta, Statistical Pub. Society (Assam also mentioned).

1882. **Majumdar, S.K.** : 1984-85 : Hanaghora : Rabha sanskritir eti dis. *Dokhin Kol, Palashbari Sahitya Sabha 7th Issue,* Mirza (*In Assamese*).

1883. ————— : 1985-86 : Rabha kristi: Bagejari. *Dakhin Kol, 8th Issue. (Eds.)* by Paresh Kalita and Jogen Kumar. Mirza, *Annual Magazine*, Palashbari Sahitya Sabha: 85-6 (*In Assamese*).

1884. **Malik, Syed Abdul (Ed.)** : 1958 : *Asamiya Zikir aru Jari*. Gau. Univ. (*In Assamese*).

1885. **Mallick, K.** : 1950 : Nath Sampradayer Itihash Sadhana *O Darsan* (*in B.*). Calcutta University.

1886. **Maloney, Clarence** : 1974 : *Peoples of South Asia*. New York, Holt Rinehart & Winston Inc.: 422-24.

1887. **Man** : 1954 : The social structure of an Assamese village. *Man.* IV.

1888. **Man in India** : 1936 : Indian ethnology in current periodical literature: "Origin of Levirate in Assam" by J.K. Bose in *Nature* for 6th June, 1936. XVI (2-3), April: 205.

1889. ————— : 1937 : Notices of books: The Advancement of Science, 1937, London, British Association, pp. 264, 3s 6d., XVII (4), Oct.: 263-64.

1890. **Man and Life** : 1986 : Book Review: *Focus on Folklore of North-East India. (Ed.)* by Birendranath Datta, Special Vol., No. 1-2 (1983-84 & 1984-85) of Assam Academy Review, Guwahati, 1985, Part I & II: 1-84 & 1-78, 12 (3-4), July-Dec.: 221-22.

1891. **Mandal, Pralibha** *and* **Debal Deb** : 1994 : Structural generalities in folktales from three states of North-East India. *Jr. India. Anth. Society,* 29 (1-2), March-July: 105-12 (Assam-Dimsa etc.).

1892. **Mandal, Sekh Rahim** : 1991 : Book Review: *Caste and Class: Social stratification in Assam* by Ranjit K. Bhadra. Delhi, Hindustan Publishing Corporation (India), 1991, pp. XII+172, *Man in India,* 71(2-3), June-Sept.: 539-41.

1893. **Mann, R.S.** : 1984 : Research ventures and trends : Case of tribal North-East India. *Paper presented in the Seminar on Tribal Research in North-Eastern Region.* Organised by North Eastern Council Secretariat, Shillong (*Mimeo.*).

1894. ———— : 1985 : Protective legislations in British tribal India. *Paper presented in the Seminar on Various aspects of socio-cultural development of the plain tribes of Assam.* Organised by Tribal Research Institute, Guwahati. (*Mimeo.*).

1895. ———— : 1994 : *Culture and integration of Indian tribes.* New Delhi, M.D. Pubn., 193p.

1896. ———— **(Ed.)** : 1996 : *Tribes of India: Ongoing challenges.* New Delhi, M.D. Pubn.

1897. **Mann, R.S. and K. Mann** : 1989 : Nehru and tribal integration. *Human Sc.,* 38 (2), June: 115-20 (NEI, Dimasa, Kachari, Karbi etc.).

1898. **Marak, Manoranjan** : 1992 : Comparative Study of Garo, Boso, Rava, Dimasa, Mising, Tiwa, Deuri. *Proceedings of a workshop on North East Language,* Shillong, NEHU. *Shillong T.,* June 5: 3 (4-5).

1899. **Marar, K.W.P.** : 1942 : *Assam. Census of India 1941,* Vol. IX. Delhi, Manager of Pub. (Part I & II, Report and Tables), 64p.

1900. **Maretina, Sofia A.** : 1964 : Obscina o Malykh Narodov Assama (i.e. The Community of the Hill Tribes in Assam). *Mezdunarodnyj Kongress Anthropologiceskikh i Etnographiceskikh Nauk* (Moscow), VII: 11p.

1901. ———— : 1966 : Community of the hill people of Assam. *Jr. Soc. Res.,* IX(1), March: 89-98.

1902. ———— : 1972 : Formation of estates and classes among the mountain peoples of North-Eastern India (on the problem of class formation). *Stranyi narody Vastaka,* (Moscow), XIV.

1903. **Maretina, Sofia A.** : 1978 : The Kachari state: The character of early state-like formation in the hill districts of North East India. *(In) The Early State. (Eds.) by Claessen*, H.J.M. and P. Skalnik. The Hague, Mouton Pubs.

1904. **Mark, G. P.** : 1984 : The Koch-Rabha. *Assam Tribune*, Nov. 15.

1905. **Mattumana, Mathew** : 1988 : *Christianity in Assam and Inter-Faith, Faith*. Indore, Satprakashan Sanchar Kendra.

1906. **Maury, L.F.A.** : 1854 : Les populations primitives du nord de l'hindoustan. *Bulletin de la Societe de Geog.*, VII: 173-210.

1907. **Mayamara** : 1981 : *Mayamara Satra Samaj Bhashan aru prabandha (In Assamese)*. Chabua, Mayamara Katha Krishi Anusandhan aru Prachar Samiti,

1908. **Mazumdar, B.C.** : 1932 : Note on the Bhuiyas of Utkals and Jharkhanda. *Man in India*, 12(4), Dec.: 320-30 (They are also inhabited in Assam).

1909. **Mazumdar, B.P.** : 1960 : Kaivartas. *(In) Socio-economic History of Northern India* (1030-1194 A.D.). Calcutta, 111p.

1910. **Mazumdar (Baruah), Labanya** : 1988 : *Traditional textiles of Assam: A study of an indigenous craft with reference to continuity and change*. Unpub. Ph.D. Thesis, Jorhat, Assam Agricultural University.

1911. **Mazumdar, Surya Kr.** : 1989 : *Dakshin Kamrupar Rabha Sanskritit a bhumuki* (i.e. Glimpses of Rabha Culture in South Kamrup). Guwahati (*in Assamese*).

1912. **Mc Cosh, J.** : 1836 : Account of the mountain tribes on the extreme north-east frontier of Bengal (*Compiled* from original manuscripts by Captain Jenkins, Major White and Mr. Bruce). *Jour. Asiatic Society of Bengal*, V: 192-208.

1913. **Mc. Swiney, J.** : 1912 : *Assam Census of India 1911*, Vol. III. Shillong, Assam Secretariat Printing Office (2 Vols).

1914. **Mccormack, A.P.** : 1965 : Research among Assam tribes. *Bull. Inter. Committee for Urgent Anthropology & Eth. Research*, No. VII: 17-21.

1915. **Md. Khairozzaman, A.E.** : 1987 : Bihu: Origin and heritage. *Assam Tribune*, April 12: 4(3-6).

1916. **Medhi, Birinchi Kr.** : 1980 : *Ekhan desh, alekh manuh (A collection of life and culture of a few selected Indian tribes with a brief description of cultural evolution of man)*. Mangaldai, J.N. Chakrabarti (in A.: Karbi, Dimasa, Kachari, etc.).

1917. **Medhi, Birinchi Kr.** : 1981 : Concept of malevolent spirits among the Pati Rabha of Assam. *Bull. Deptt. of Anthropology, Dib. Univ.,* X: 135-43.

1918. ———— : 1982 : Beliefs, rituals and ceremonies connected with principal events of the life of the Pati Rabhas of Assam. *Bull. Deptt. of Anthropology, Dib. Univ.,* IX: 40-53 (1980).

1919. ———— : Some aspects of beliefs in Pati Rabhas Society. *Jour. Gau. Univ. (Sc.),* XXVIII: 6-12.

1920. ———— : 1983 : Langa : The tutelary God of the Pati Rabhas of Assam. *Jour. of NEICSSR,* VII (1): 31-3.

1921. ———— : 1984 : Snake goddess Marai of the Pati Rabhas of Assam. *E.A.,* XXXVII (2), April-June: 159-64.

1922. ———— : 1985 : Concept of supernaturals among the Pati Rabhas of Assam. *Jr. NEICSSR,* IX (1), April : 41-3.

1923. ———— : Concept of malevolent spirits among the Pati Rabhas of Assam. *(In) Anthropological Perspectives on North-East India (Bull. Deptt. of Anthropology, Dib. Univ.,* X, 1981): 35-43.

1924. ———— : 1986 : A few female malevolent spirits of the Pati Rabhas of Assam. *Jr. NEICSSR,* X (1), April: 53-6.

1925. ———— : 1988 : Concept of benevolent spirits among the Pati Rabhas of Assam. *Man and Life,* XIV (3-4), July-Dec.: 187-94.

1926. ———— : 1990 : *The Assamese Sikhs: A study on their social relations in a rural situation.* Unpub. Ph.D. Thesis, Anthropology Deptt., Gau. Univ.

1927. ———— : 1991 : Glimpses of village and house type of the Karbis. *Jr. NEICSSR,* XV(2) , Oct.: 8-10.

1928. ———— : 1996 : The Assamese Sikh: The Samurais of Assam. *(In) Peoples of North-East India: Anthropological Perspectives (Ed.)* by Sarthak Sengupta. New Delhi, Gyan Pubg. House: 191-98.

1929. **Medhi, Birinchi Kr.** *and* **Mrinal Sharma** : 1990 : Marriage among the Rongdani Rabhas of Assam: An Appraisal. *Jr. NEICSSR,* XIV (1), April: 64-7.

1930. **Medhi D.N.** : 1957 : *Handloom weaving and designing.* Shillong, Pub. by the author.

1931. **Medhi, Dilip Kr.** : 1978 : The changing community pattern of Bhakatpara. *(In) Cultural and Biological Adaptability of Man with special reference to North-East India (Eds)* by A.C. Bhagabati and R.K. Kar (*Bull. Deptt. of Anthropology, Dib. Univ., VI, 1977*): 149-55 (Barpeta).

1932. **Medhi, Gopal** : 1974 : Jirkedam, an ancient educational institution of the Karbis of Assam. *Ind. Jou. of Social Work*, XXXIV (4), Jan.: 307-14.

1933. **Medhi, Gopal Ch.** : 1976 : The route of Karbi migration to Assam. *North-Eastern Spectrum*, 1(3-4), Sept.-Oct.: 9-13.

1934. ———— : 1977 : Traditional administration of the Karbis. North-Eastern Spectrum, II (I), July: 26-8 (Mikir).

1935. **Medhi, Indrani Rai** : 1994 : Where have all the dancers gone? *Assam Tribune, Sunday Reading*, April 10: I(1-8) (Bihu).

1936. **Medhi, Prafulla** : 1990 : Baitha Puja of the Kacharis (Sonowal). *Assam Tribune*, March 5: 4(7-8), 5(3-4).

1937. ———— : Saragdeo Puja of Kacharis (Sonowals). *Assam Tribune*, May 24: 4(7-8).

1938. ———— : 1991 : *Religion among the Sonowal Kacharis of Assam*. Unpub. Ph.D. Thesis, Dib. Univ.

1939. ———— : 1993 : Religion of the Sonowal Kacharis of Assam. *(In) Religion in North-East India. (Ed.)* by Soumen Sen. New Delhi, Uppal Pub. House: 135-47.

1940. **Meerworth, A.M.** : 1919 : Monograph on Khasis: *The Andamanese and Hill tribes of Assam*. Calcutta, Indian Museum.

1941. ———— : 1980 : *The Andamanese, Nicobares and Hill Tribes of Assam* (Reprinted with a new introduction by N.N. Acharyya). Gauhati, Spectrum Pub., 51p.

1942. **Mehra, Jai Dayal** : 1954 : Effects of acculturation among the Garos of Boko (Assam). *Vanyajati*, II(I), Jan.: 10-3.

1943. **Mikir (Phangsho), Phukan Chandra** : 1990 : *The Karbis: A spatio-temporal analysis in tribal geography*. Unpub. Ph.D. Thesis, Gau. Univ.

1944. **Mili, Gayatri** *and* **Peter Pegu** : 1996 : The spring festival of the Mishings. *Sentinel*, Feb. 17 : 3(1-8) (Ali-ayeligang festival).

1945. **Mills, J.P.** : 1926 : The head hunters of Assam. *Illustrated London News*, 168: 262-65.

1946. ———— : 1928 : The Hill Tribes of Assam. *Assam Review*, I(1-8), 10.

1947. ———— : 1932 : Assam as a field for research. *Jr. Assam Res. Soc.*, I(I): 3-6.

1948. **Mills, J.P.** : 1948 : The sacred chiefs of Assam. *Man in India,* XXVIII (3): 149-51.

1949. ———— : n.d. : *A Note on the future of the Hill tribes of Assam and the adjoining hills in a self-governing India. (Secret Mss.).*

1950. **Mills, J.P. et al** : 1932 : Notes on certain Hill tribes of Assam,. *(In) census of India 1931,* Vol. III, *Assam.* Calcutta, Govt. of India, Central Pub. Branch, Pt. I, Report, Appendix-B: VI: XXI (*Reprinted* in Census of India, Vol. I, India, Ed. by J.H. Hutton, Simla, Govt. of India Press, Pt. III-B, Ethnographic Notes by various hands).

1951. **Minda, Shakuntala** : 1996 : Letters to the Editor: Log aundha viswas ke karan jiv hattya na karen (*In Hindi*). *Pur. Pra.,* Feb. 8: 4 (3-4) (Kamakhya).

1952. **Mipin, Jatin** : 1992 : *The Mishings (Miris) of Assam: Development of a new lifestyles.* New Delhi, Gyan Books, 160p.

1953. **Mipun, B.S.** *and* **D.K. Nayak** : 1993 : Socio-cultural transformation among the Miris of the Brahmaputra valley. *Proceedings of a Seminar on Literature & Social Reality in Tribal Societies of North-East India* (1968-93) held on 24-25 Nov. 1993 in NEHU, organised by Centre for Literary & Cultural Studies, NEHU, NERC, ICSSR, Shillong.

1954. **Mipun, J.** : 1976 : Acculturation, communication and development among the Dimasa Kacharis of the North Kachar Hill District in Assam. North Eastern Res. *Bull., Dib. Univ.,* VII, Summer: 63-75.

1955. ———— : 1978 : Acculturation, communication and development in a Mishing village. *(In) North-East India: A Sociological Study. (Ed.)* by S.M. Dubey. Delhi, Concept Pub.: 165-79.

1956. ———— : 1980 : Clan and kinship organisation among the Mishings in Assam. *(In) Family, Marriage and Social Change. (Eds.)* by S.M. Dubey, P.K. Bordoloi and B.N. Borthakur. New Delhi, Cosmo Pub.: 115-27.

1957. **Miri, Mrinal (Ed.)** : 1993 : *Continuity and change in tribal society.* Simla, Ind. Inst. of Adv. Study, 575p.

1958. **Miri, Sujata (Ed.)** : 1980 : *Religion and Society of North-East India.* Delhi, Vikas Pub., 122p.

1959. **Mishra, S.S.** : 1991 : Socio-cultural life of the Man of Assam. *Social Sc.,* IV (1-2), June-Dec.: 237-40.

1960. **Mishra, S.S.** *and* **R.P. Athparia** : 1991 : The process of urbanisation among the Karbis of Karbi Anglong District, Assam. *Proc. of a Seminar on Pattern Problems and Prospects of Urbanisation in North-East India,* held on 22-23 Nov., 1991, organised by NEICSSR, Shillong (*Mimeo.*).

1961. **Mishra, S.S.** *and* **R.P. Athparia** : 1993 : Karbi folktales: The study of marriage prohibition, restriction and prescription. *Jr. NEICSSR*, XVII (1), April: 13-5.

1962. ———— : 1995 : Impact of urbanisation on the Karbis of Assam. *(In) Urbanization and development in North-East India: Trends and Policy Indications. (Ed.)* by J.B. Ganguly. New Delhi, Deep & Deep Pubs.: 199-205.

1963. **Misra, Bani Prasanna** : 1979 : Kirata-Karyo Kiness : Modes of production in tribal societies in North-East India. *(In) Agrarian Relations in India. (Ed.)* by Arvind N. Das and V. Nilakant. Delhi, Manohar Pub.

1964. ———— : 1980 : The spread of Christianity in North-East India: An exchange theory of conversion. *(In) Religion and Society of North-East India. (Ed.)* by Sujata Miri. New Delhi, Vikas Publishing House: 83-128.

1965. **Misra, Partha Sarathi** : 1985 : Dimasa-Kacharis in transition. *Proceedings of a Seminar on Sequences in Development in North-East India (A Study of Tradition, Continuity and Change)*, organised by NEICSSR, Shillong on 9-10 Dec.

1966. ———— : Myths and Rituals of Dimasa-Kacharis of Assam. *(In) Folklore in North-East India. (Ed.)* by Soumen Sen. Delhi, Omsons Pub. : 108-12.

1967. ———— : 1986 : Identity consciousness among the Dimasa as of Assam. *Proceedings of a Seminar on the question of Nationality, Ethnicity and Cultural Identity in the context of North-East India*, organised by NEICSSR on 5-6 Dec., Shillong.

1968. ———— : 1989 : Dimasa-Kacharis in transition. *(In) sequences of development in North-East India. (Ed.)* by J.B. Bhattacharya. New Delhi, Omsons Pub.: 141-48.

1969. ———— : 1990 : Identity consciousness among the Dimasas of Assam. *(In) Nationality, Ethnicity and Cultural Identity in North-East India. (Ed.)* by B. Pakem. New Delhi, Omsons Pub. 191-98.

1970. **Misra, Promod Kr.** : 1977 : Patterns of Inter-Tribal Relations *(In) Tribal Heritage of India, Vol. I: Ethnicity, Identity and Interaction (Ed.)* by S.C. Dube. New Delhi, Vikas Pub.: 88-95 (Koch, Mech etc.).

1971. **Misra, Rashmi** : 1993 : Asom ka indra dhanush 'Bihu'. *Saptasetu (In Hindi)*, Jan. 14.

1972. ———— : 1994 : Purbottar ki janajatiya : Rochak bibaha (*In Hindi*). *Pur. Pra. (Lohit Bharati)*, Sept. 4: I(3-8) (Mikir)

1973. **Misra, Tilottama** : 1987 : *Literature and Society in Assam*. New Delhi.

1974. **Mitra, A.** : 1953 : *Census of India 1951, West Bengal: Land and Land Revenue department, the tribes and castes of West-Bengal.* Alipore, Supdt. Govt. Ptg.: 251-52 (Koch), 245-46 (Jugi), 238-45 (Kayastha, Kaet, Kait), 224-26 (Mech, Koch).

1975. **Mitra, Kalipada** : 1928 : A Mikir tale and its Santali parallels. *JBORS*, Pt. IV, March.

1976. **Mitra, R.** *and* **P. Das Gupta (Eds)** : 1967 : *A Common Perspective for North-East India.* Calcutta, Pub. by P. Das Gupta.

1977. **Mitra, S.** : 1970 : Bachelor's dormitories of the tribes of Eastern India. *Bull. Anthropology S. I.* XIX. (2), April: 61-5.

1978. **Mitra, S.C.** : 1846 : Nath sect and Yogi caste. *Jr. Anthropology Soc. of Bombay*, XV(6): 577.

1979. ———— : 1924-28 : On five recent instances of the folk belief in witchcraft, sorcery and charming from Southern Bengal and Assam. *Jr. Anthropology Soc. of Bombay*, XIII: 370-80.

1980. ———— : 1928 : The caterpillar boy and the caterpillar husband in Santali and Lhota Naga folklore. *Jr. Bihar & Orissa Res. Soc.*, XIV: 428 (Santali Tea Garden Labourer in Assam).

1981. ———— : 1933 : Notes on the Gooling Mahakola worshipped by the Rajbanshis of Jalpaiguri District in North Bengal. *Jr. Anthropology Soc. of Bombay*, XV: 425-29 (Rajbanshis are also inhabited in Assam).

1982. **Mitra, Sevati** : 1976 : Growth, distribution and occupational pattern of tribal population of India. *Jr. Ind. Anthropology Soc.*, XI (3), Nov. : 257-71 (North East Zone: 259-61).

1983. **Modal, Sekh Rahim** : 1991 : Book Review: *Caste and Class, social stratification in Assam* by Ranjit K. Bhadra. Delhi, Hindustan Publishing Corporation (India), 1991, pp. xii+172, *MII*, 71 (2-3), June-Sept.: 539-54.

1984. **Mohanty, Banshidhar** : 1966 : Cultural relation of Assam and Orissa *(In) Professor S. K. Bhuyan Commemoration volume (Eds)* by Maheshwar Neog and H.K. Barpujari. Gauhati, All India Oriental Conference: 162-67.

1985. **Mookherji, Raj** : 1940 : Combined pottery and basket specimens from Upper Assam. *Man*, 40 (157).

1986. **Mooshahary, R.S.** : 1987 : Marriage and morals: Contents of the tribal customs. *Assam Tribune*, Dec. 6: 4(3-6), 6(3-5) (Assam).

1987. **Moral, Star Mamoni** : 1989 : Handloom : Bridging culture and generations. *Assam Tribune, Sunday Reading*, Sept. 10: I(1-8) (Mishing, Bodo, Karbi).

1988. **Moran, Girish** : 1993 : Letters to the Editor : Mattaks and Morans. *Assam Tribune*, July 2: 4(3-4).

1989. **Mosahary, Ananda** (*Comp*) : n.d. : *Takimari*. Goalpara, Kokrajhar.

1990. **Mosahary, R.N.** : 1983 : Boros: Their origin, migration and settlement in Assam. *Proc. NEIHA, 4th (Ed.)* by J.B. Bhattacharjee. Shillong, Hist. Deptt., NEHU: 42-70.

1991. ———— : 1985 : Brahma religion and social change among the Boros. *Proc. NEIHA, 6th (Ed.)* by J.B. Bhattacharjee. Shillong, Hist. Deptt., NEHU: 347-52.

1992. ———— : 1986 : Origin and growth of Christianity among the Boros of Assam. *Proc. NEIHA, 7th*: 273-82.

1993. ———— : Social History of Bodos of Assam: A study of oral history. *NEHU Jour. Soc. Sc. and Humanities (Shillong)*, IV (1), Jan.-March.

1994. ———— : 1987 : Traditional religion of the Boros of Assam. *Proc. NEIHA, 8th*: 510-27.

1995. ———— : 1988 : Social History of Boros of Assam : A study of oral history. *NEHU Jr. of Soc. Sc. & Humanities*, IV (1), Jan.-March : 79.

1996. ———— : Legendary origin of the Boro clans. *Proc. NEIHA, 9th*: 84-94.

1997. ———— : 1989 : Aryanisation and Hinduisation of the Boros. *Proc. NEIHA, 10th*: 165-75.

1998. ———— : 1990 : Tripartite Bodo Talks: Circumstances, Proceedings and Observations. *Proc. NEIHA, 11th*: 316-30.

1999. ———— : 1991 : Kherai : A Traditional Boro festival. *Proc. HEIHA, 12th*: 215-22.

2000. ———— : 1994 : Boro folk-songs: A few examples with their contents. *(In) Essays on North-East India. (Ed.)* by Milton S. Sangma. New Delhi, Indus Pub. Com. : 124-46.

2001. **Mosahary, R.N.** : n.d. : *Social History of the Boros of Assam.* Ph.D. Thesis, History Deptt., NEHU.

2002. **Mudiar, K.K.** *and* **M.M. Das** : 1978 : Spatio-temporal change in the socio cultural level in Assam. *North-Eastern Geography,* X(1-2): 33-43.

2003. **Muhibul, Alhaji** : n.d. : *Asamat Musalman.* Gauhati, (*In Assamese*).

2004. **Mukherjee, Aruna Devi** : 1955 : *Tales of a grand-father from Assam.* Bangalore (about folklore).

2005. **Mukherjee, B. M.** : 1992 : Book Review: Stratification, hierarchy and ethnicity in North-East India. *(Ed.)* by R.K. Bhadra and S.R. Mandal. *Bull. Deptt. of Anthropology, Dib. Univ.,* 18-19 (1989-90): 185.

2006. **Mukherjee, Bhabananda** : 1958 : Tales of orphan boys. *Indian Folklore,* 1(4): 13-7.

2007. ————— : 1962 : Rajbanshi kinship system. *Bull. Anthropology S.I.,* XI(1): 47-56.

2008. ————— : 1963 : Socio-economic and religious organisation of Rajbanshi. *Bull. Anthropology S.I.,* XII (1-2): 65-80.

2009. ——————— : Caste ranking among Rajbanshis in North Bengal. *(In) Anthropology on the March. (Ed.)* by Bala Ratnam. Madras, The Book Centre: 206-12.

2010. ————— : 1968 : Trends of Social mobility movement. *Jr. Ind. Anthropology Soc.,* III (1-2), March-Sept.: 23-9 (Rabha, Rajbanshi: 123-26).

2011. **Mukherjee, D.P.** *and* **S.K. Mukherjee** : 1982 : Contemporary cultural and political movements among the Bodos of Assam. *(In) Tribal Movements in India,* Vol. I. *(Ed.)* by K.S. Singh. New Delhi, Manohar Pub.: 253-80.

2012. **Mukherjee, Najma** : 1993 : Book Review: Asamiya Lok-Sanskritir Safura by Jogendra Nath Talukdar, Ist Published November/92, *Dainik Assam,* Sept. 27: 5(3-7) (*In Assamese*).

2013. **Mukherjee, S.K.** : 1979 : Social mobility movement among the Hiras of Assam. *Proc. of a Seminar on Bio-cultural Profile of North-East-India,* organised in Silver Jubilee of Anthropology, S.I., Shillong on April 26 (*Mimeo.*).

2014. ————— : 1980 : Culture trait and culture area survey in the plains of Assam. *Paper submitted in a Seminar organised by Anthropology* S.I., Calcutta.

2015. **Mukherjee, S.K.** : 1983 : Marriage system among the Bodo Kacharis of Assam: A Study of Change. *Proc. of a Seminar on Marriage in India* held on 11-12 Feb. 1983, organised by Anthropology S.I., Nagpur Stn., 5p (*Mimeo.*).

2016. ———— : 1989 : Marriage system among the Bodo Kacharis of Assam: A Study of Change. *Social Research* (Shillong), IX (1-2), Jan.-July: 16-9.

2017. ———— : 1990 : Religion among the Boro-Kachari of Assam. *Proc. of a Seminar on Status of Religion in Tribal Areas in North-East India*, organised by NEICSSR, Shillong on 15-16 Feb. (*Mimeo.*).

2018. ———— : Social mobility movement among the Hiras of Assam. *Jr. NEICSSR*, 14(1), April : 62-3.

2019. ———— : 1993 : Religion among the Boro-Kacharis of Assam. *(In) Religion in North-East India. (Ed.)* by Soumen Sen. New Delhi, Uppal Pub. House: 130-34.

2020. ———— : Bamuna: A village in Assam. *(In) Anthropology of Weaker Sections. (Ed.)* by Surajit Ch. Sinha. New Delhi, Concept Pub. Co.: 31-47 (Kayastha, Kalita, Keot, Napit, Hira, Namasudra).

2021. **Mukherjee, Sibsankar** : 1994 : The early history of the Koches of North Bengal. *(In) Essays on North-East India. (Ed.)* by Milton S. Sangma. New Delhi, Indus Pub. Com. 108-23.

2022. **Mukhopadhya, Kanchan** : 1985 : Bishnupriya Manipuris of Assam. *Proceedings of People of India: Pre-Test Seminar of Anthropology, S.I.*, Shillong on Dec. 5.

2023. **Mukhopadhyay, K.** : 1989 : Ethnicity & Politics: Study of some ethnic associations in Barak Valley. *Social Sc.*, II (I), June: 65-74.

2024. **Mullan, C.S.** : 1932 : The Depressed and Backward Classes of Assam. *Census of India 1931, Vol. III, Assam*. Calcutta, Govt. of India Central Pub. Branch, Pt. I: Report, Appendix-1 to Chapter 12: 209-24.

2025. **Muller, D.S.G.** : n.d. : *Short stories from North-East India.*

2026. **Murthy, H.V.S.** : 1958 : The Role of the Satra Institutions in Assam. Indian Historical Quarterly, 34 : 66-9.

2027. **Mushahari, Megh Nath** : 1987 : *Bathow, 29th Annual Conference of Bathow Dharma Sangha Kendriya Committee*. Kokrajhar, Bathow Dharma Sangha (*in Bodo*).

2028. **Nag, A.K.** : 1966 : *Tribal Mirror, Vol. II*, Winter. Silchar: 29, 31-5.

2029. **Nag, Amit Kr.** : 1977 : The Bodo-Kacharis. *North-Eastern Spectrum*, II(3-4), Sept.-Oct.: 7-11.

2030. **Nandi, S.B.; R.P. Athparia; M.M. Das** *and* **S.K. Mukherjee** :1993 : Tribal customary law in North-East India. *(In) Tribal Ethnography, Customary Law and Change. (Ed.)* by K.S. Singh. New Delhi, Concept Pub.: 23-8 (Boro Kachari, Karbi, etc.)

2031. **Narayan, Kamal** : 1990 : Kamrup ki kingbadanti (*In Hindi*). *Pur. Pra* (Lohit Bha.), Dec. 16: 1(4-7).

2032. **Narimattam, M.** : 1988 : *The valley in blossom: Neo-vaishnavism and the peoples of the Brahmaputra valley*. Guwahati, Spectrum Pub., 187p (Mishing, Rabha, Mech, Bodo, Kachari, Moran, Tai, Ahom, Chutiya, Koch, Kaivarta, Brahmin, Keot, Kalita).

2033. **Narjinari, H.C.** : 1985 : *In search of identity: The Mech*. Calcutta, B.B. Prakashan.

2034. **Narzary, Charan** : 1976 : The Bodos: Their plight and aspirations. *Khamrub Bisombi*, Boro Sahitya Sabha.

2035. **Narzary, Giridhar** : 1978 : A study of religion and society in a Boro village. Unpub. Ph.D. Thesis, Gau. Univ.

2036. **Narzi, Bhaben** : 1957 : *Bodo-Kacharir Jana-Sahitya*, Guwahati.

2037. **Narzi, Bhabendra** : 1962 : Boro Kachari. *(In) Asamar Janajati. (Ed.)* by Pramod Ch. Bhattacharya. Jorhat, Asam Sahitya Sabha: 54-69 (*In Assamese*).

2038. ———— : 1966 : *Boro Kacharir Samaj Aru Sanskriti* (*In Assamese*). Gauhati, Lawyers' Book Stall, 326p.

2039. ———— : n.d. : *Boro Kacharir git mat* (*In Assamese*). Gauhati, Asom Prakasan Parisad.

2040. **Nath, A.C.** : 1994 : A micro-level study of the process of Christianisation: Its impact, problems and prospects among the Karbis. *TUI: Research Jour. on Tribal life and culture, Agartala*, II (4): 112-27.

2041. **Nath, A.C.** *and* **B. Das (Nath)** : 1900 : The impact of Christianity on the Karbis of Guriaghuli village. *Proc. of a Seminar on Status of Religion in Tribal Areas in North-East India* organised by NEICSSR, Shillong on 15-16 Feb. (*Mimeo.*).

2042. **Nath, Alakananda** : 1986 : Demographic changes among Scheduled Tribes: 1961-1981. *(In) The Pattern and Problems of Population in North-East India. (Ed.)* by B. Datta Ray. New Delhi, Uppal Pub.

2043. **Nath, Alakananda** : 1987 : Women in folklore of North-East India: Some focus on the position and status. *Folklore*, 28 (6), June: 120-26 (Karbi etc.).

2044. ———— : 1988 : Tribal woman of North East India in the perspective of change and continuity. *(In) Tribal women and development. (Ed.)* by J.P. Singh *et al.* Jaipur, Rawat Pub.: 143-69.

2045. **Nath, Alokananda** *and* **D.N. Majumdar** : 1985 : Tribal Women of North-East India in the perspective of change and continuity. *(In) Tribal Women and Development. (Ed.)* by J.P. Singh, N.N. Vyas, R.S. Mann. Udaipur, MLV Tribal Res. & Trai. Inst. Tribal Area Dev. Deptt.,: 149-68.

2046. ———— : 1987 : Tribal youth of North-East India, at cross road. *Bull. Deptt. of Anthropology, Dib. Univ.*, 11-12 (1982-83): 107-20.

2047. ———— : 1989 : An examination of the concept of status in the context of male-female relation in the tribal societies of the Brahmaputra valley. *Jr. NEICSSR*, 13(2), Oct.: 9-14.

2048. **Nath, Amar** : 1990 : Boro Sanskriti par sankat (*In Hindi*). *Pur. Pra*, (Loh. Bha.), July 8: 1(1-8).

2049. **Nath, Ananda Chandra** : 1994 : A short study of basketry techniques among selected tribes of Assam. *Bull. AIRTSC*, I (IX): 35-44 (Kachari).

2050. **Nath, Ananda Ch.** *and* **Bandana Devi** : 1994 : The impact of Christianity of the Karbi: Tribe of Kamrup district (Assam). *Vanyajati*, XLII (2), April: 16-21.

2051. **Nath, A.N.** *and* **D.N. Majumdar** : 1986 : Tribal women of North-East India: In the perspective of Change and Continuity. *(In) proceedings of the National Conference on Tribal Women and Development : Problems and perspective.* Udaipur.

2052. **Nath, Aruna** : 1988 : *A Study of the Social changes in Assam*, 1825-1900. Unpub. Ph.D. Thesis, Gau. Univ.

2053. **Nath, D.** : 1977 : *Goalparar loka sahityat dristipot (In Assamese*). Guwahati.

2054. ———— : 1986 : Early Hinduisation of the ruling tribes of North-East India. *Proc. NEIHA, 7th. (Ed.)* by J.B. Bhattacharjee Shillong, Hist. Deptt., NEHU : 253-58.

2055. ———— : 1989 : *History of the Koch kingdom* (c. 1515-1615). Delhi, Mittal Pub.

2056. **Nath, Dambarudhar** : 1988 : Mishing society in transition. *Proc. NEIHA*, 9th.: 262-71.

2057. **Nath, Dambarudhar** : 1994 : Asamar Kaibarta (*In Assamese*). *Natun Dainik*, June 30 *(Spl. Supp.)*.

2058. **Nath, Jahnabi Gogoi** : 1992 : Social attitude towards women in Medieval Assam. *(In) Status of Women in Assam. (Ed.)* by S.L. Baruah. New Delhi, Omsons Pubs.: 9-15.

2059. **Nath, Nareswar** : 1949 : *Bhaiyamar Sadhu* (*In Assamese*). Tangla, Pub. by the author (about folklore).

2060. **Nath, R.M.** : 1948 : *The Background of Assamese culture*. Shillong, Pub. by A.K.Nath,158p (Ahom, Lalung, Mikir, Kachari, Chutia, Kalita, Moran, Koch, Bhuyan, Bodo, etc.).

2061. ———— : 1959 : The background of Assamese architecture. *(In) Souvenir on aspects of the heritage of Assam. (Ed.)* by K.N.Dutt. Gauhati, 22nd Session of Indian History Congress, December: 8-17.

2062. **Nath, S.C.** *and* **D.N. Bordoloi** : 1988 : North-East India: An ethnobotanic survey. *Himalaya : Man and Nature*, XI (8-9), Jan.-Feb.: 2-6 (Ahom, Chutiya, Koch, etc).

2063. **Nath, T.K.** : 1996 : Bamboo and cane work: King of crafts. *Sentinel* (Sunday), March 31: 1(1-8), April 7: 1.

2064. **Nath, Uday** : 1992 : *Barpeta as a Centre of Assamese culture: A study in tradition and change with special reference to the Satra Institution*. Unpub. Ph.D. Thesis, Gau. Univ.

2065. **Neel Kamal** : 1954 : Assamiya Lok Kathayen (*In Hindi*). *Ajkal*, May.

2066. **Negi, Balbir Singh** : 1964 : Tribes of the North-East Frontier Region. *(In) Anthropologyropogeography: A study of races and peoples of the world (Geog. series N.1)*. Allahabad, Kitab Mahal: 237-69.

2067. ———— : 1979-80 : *Human Geography: An Ecological Approach*. Meerut, Kedar Nath Ram Nath: 355-61 (Mikir, etc.).

2068. **NEHU** : 1996 : *Seminar on North East Folk Literature*, organised by Centre for Creative Arts, NEHU, Shillong on 9-10 May, 1996 (*Mimeo.*).

2069. **NEICSSR** : 1996 : *Seminar on Traditional Culture and Folklore in North-East India*, 18-19 Nov., organised by NEICSSR, Shillong (*Mimeo.*).

2070. **Neog, A.K.** : 1995 : Problems of the Scheduled Castes of Assam and plans for development. *(In) Core Problems of the Scheduled Castes of Assam. (Ed.)* by Bimal Kr. Hazarika. Guwahati, AIRTSC (TRI): 1-8.

2071. **Neog, H. and L. Gogoi (Eds)** : n.d. : Asamiya Sanskriti *(in Assamese, Translated version of* Art of North-East Frontier of India by Verrier Elwin). Guwahati. Pub. by the editors.

2072. **Neog, Hariprasad** *and* **Lila Gogoi (Eds)** : 1966 : Asamiya sanskriti. Jorhat, Asom Sahitya Sabha (*Reprinted* in 1975).

2073. **Neog, M.** : 1959 : The Vaisnava renaissance in Assam. *(In) A Souvenir: Aspects of the Heritage of Assam. (Ed.)* by K.N. Dutt. Gauhati, Indian Congress, 22nd Session, December: 31-49.

2074. ———— : 1960 : The role of *tambul* in Assam's social life. *(In) Professor P.K. Gode commemoration volume (Poona Oriental series No. 93).. (Ed.)* by H.L. Hariyappa and M.M. Patkar. Poona, Oriental Book Agency : 270-81.

2075. ———— : Three dance styles of Assam. *Jr. Music Academy*, (Madras), 31(1-4): 138-45.

2076. ———— : 1962 :Parbatar Miri. *(In) Asamar Janajati. (Ed.)* by Pramod Ch. Bhattacharya. Jorhat, Asam Sahitya Sabha: 294-98.

2077. ———— : *Simantar shikhya aru sanskritik niti* (*In Assamese*). Jorhat, Asam Sahitya Sabha.

2078. ———— : 1980 : *Religions of the North-East*. New Delhi, Munshiram Manoharlal, 176p (Neo-Vaisnavism, Satra, Namghar, Vaisnava sect, Mayamariya, etc.).

2079. —— **(Ed.)** : 1975 : *Satriya dances of Assam and their rhythms*. Gauhati, Pub. by the author.

2080. **Neog, M.N.** : 1969 : Tradition of classical music and dance. *(In) The Land and People: Assam (Comp)* by S. Barkataki. New Delhi, N.B.T.: 81-95.

2081. **Neog, Maheshwar** : 1951 : Ai, the smallpox Goddess of Assam. *MII*, XXXI (2), April-June: 72-83.

2082. ———— : Serpent-lore and serpent-worship in Assam. *EA*., IV(3-4), March-May, June-Aug.: 150-59.

2083. ———— : Phul Kowar and Jana Gabharu. *Jr. Univ. of Gau*., 2: 123-43.

2084. ———— : 1957 : *Purani Asamiya Samaj aru Sanskriti*. Gauhati, New Book Stall (*Reprinted* in 1971).

2085. ———— : 1958 : The art of painting in Assam. *Jr. Gau. Univ*., IX(1), Arts: 173-85.

2086. ———— : 1959-'60 : Folk dances of Assam. *Marg*, XIII (1): 9-20.

2087. **Neog, Maheshwar** : 1985 : *Early history of the Vaishnava faith and movement in Assam.* Delhi, Motilal Banarasidas, 400p.

2088. ———— : 1986 :. Early history of the Vaisnava faith and movement in Assam: Sankaradeva and his time. *Darshana International,* 26(1), Jan.: 85-6.

2089. **Neog, Maheshwar** : 1987 : Bhaona: *Ritual Play of Assam.* Guwahati, Sangeet Natak Akademi.

2090. **Neog, Shila** : 1981 : *A study on occupational changes among the Ahoms of Jopara gaon in the district of Dibrugarh, Assam.* M.Sc. disser., Anthropology Deptt., Dib. Univ. (Unpub).

2091. **NERC** : 1988 : *Seminar on Status of women in non-tribal societies of Assam.* Sponsored jointly by the North Eastern Regional Centre, Shillong, ICSSR, New Delhi and Dibrugarh Univ. held in the Deptt. of History, Dib. Univ. on 4-5 Oct. 1988 *(Mimeo.).*

2092. **Nessa, Saifun** : 1990 : *The Assamese Muslim social structure: Study in a Goalpara village.* Unpub. Ph.D. Thesis, *Sociology Deptt.,* NEHU, Shillong.

2093. ———— : The Muslims of Assam: Their Historical Background. *Social Research,* X(2-3), Aug.-Dec. : 15-9.

2094. ———— : 1991 : The Muslims of Assam: An observation. *Jr. NEICSSR,* 15(1), April: 31-9.

2095. ———— : Book Review: *Muslims in Assam politics* by M.Kar, Omsons Publications, T-7, Delhi, pp. 390, *Jr. NEICSSR,* 15(2), Oct.: 55-7.

2096. **Nevill, G.A.,T.P.M.O' Callaghan, R.C.R. Cumming** *and* **G.C. Bardaloi** : 1923 : Notes on Certain Frontier Tribes. *Census of India 1921,* Vol. III, *Assam.* Shillong, Govt. Press (Pt.I, Report, Appendix-B): 10-6.

2097. **Nicholas, R.N.** *and* **R.B. Inden** : 1976 : *Kinship in Bengali culture.* Chicago, Univ. of Chicago Press.

2098. **North East Times** : 1995 : Rabha, Bodo Folk Theatre Dominates Discussions. Dec. 3: 1(2-6).

2099. ———— : 1996 : Bihu of Assam. April 14.

2100. **North Eastern Institute** : 1988 : *Proceedings of a Seminar on Status of Women in Barak Valley,* organised by North Eastern Institute of Anthropology, Research, Silchar, on Nov. 26 at Karimganj (*Mimeo.*).

2101. **North Eastern Spectrum** : 1976 : Sattriya dance of Assam. *North Eastern Spectrum* (Gauhati), I(I), July: 35.

2102. **Nuhurshi, B.** : 1991 : Letters to the Editor : Boro not Bodo. *Assam Tribune,* Sept. 24: 4(6).

2103. **O'Donel, J.H.** : 1863 : Notes on the tribes of the eastern frontier Nos. I & II. *Jr. Asiatic Society of Bengal,* 32: 400-07.

2104. **Ojah, G.C.** : 1985 : Mukhi caste group. Proc. of *People of India pre-test Seminar of Anthropology,* S.I., Shillong on Dec. 5 *(Mimeo.).*

2105. ———— : 1987 : Dhobi of Assam. Proc. of *People of India.* Seminar on 27th May in Anthropology S.I., Shillong.

2106. **Ojah, G.C.** *and* **P.M. Buzar Baruah** : 1994 : The Zemi Nagas of Assam : Some aspects of cultural life. *Jr. NEICSSR,* 18(1).

2107. **Oldham, C.F.** : 1891 : Serpent worship in India. *Jr.Royal Asiatic Soc. of Great Britain & Ireland:* 361-92.

2108. **O' Malley, L.S.S.** : 1913 : *Census of India 1911, Vol. V: Bengal, Bihar, Orissa and Sikkim,* Pt. I, *Report.* Calcutta, Govt. Press: 483, 498-99, 511, 513-14 (Kaibartta, Koch, Rajbansi).

2109. **Omsons Publications** : n.d. : *The Tai-Khamtis of North-East India.* New Delhi, Omsons Pub. by L. Gogoi: 374.

2110. **Onker** : 1990 : Karbi-Anglong: Ek Parichaya (*In Hindi*). *Pur. Pra.,* May 7: 5(1-5).

2111. **Op't Land, C.** : 1961 : Kin terms of the Mikirs. *E.A.,* XIV (2), May-Aug.: 161-68.

2112. **Padmanabha, P.** : 1981 : *Census of India 1981: List of Scheduled Castes and Scheduled Tribes.* New Delhi, Office of the Ministry of Home Affairs.

2113. **Padun, Mahendra** : 1972 : Mishing Gutra Bishar. *(In) Mishing Sanskritir Alekhya. (Ed.)* by B Kagyung. Birubari (Gauhati) : 285-86. (*In Assamese*).

2114. ———— : Mishing sakalar baibahik niti.... *(In) ibid.*

2115. ———— : Mishing Bhasa.... *(In) ibid.*

2116. ———— : Mishing Loka Sahitya.... *(In) ibid.*

2117. ———— : Mishing Janajatir Parichay.... *(In) ibid.*

2118. ———— : 1973 : Mishing samaj paddhoti (*In Assamese*). *Pragati* (Pathsala, Assam), Bajali Pragati Sangh: 23-31.

2119. ———— : Saka 1880 : Ai-Nitamat samayar prabhab. (*In Assamese*) *Ramdhenu,* Ahin (Aug./Sept.).

2120. ———— : 1993 : *Asamiya Sanskritiloi Janajatia Barangani* (*In A.*). Guwahati, L.B.S.

2121. **Pakem, B.** : 1991 : Polity formation in Pre-Colonial Karbi chieftaincy. *(In) Proceedings NEIHA, 12th. (Ed.)* by J.B. Bhattacharjee. Shillong, History Deptt., NEHU. :185-95.

2122. ———— : 1994 : Twenty years of Social Science Research in North-East India (1974-1994). *(In) Bi-Decennial Celebration of North-East India Council for Social Science Research. (Eds.)* by B. Pakem *et al.* Shillong, Jr. NEICSSR: 1-7.

2123. ———— : 1995 : Ethnicity and ethnic processes in North-East India. *Shillong Times,* Nov. 2 : 4(3-6), 6(4-6) (Assamese, Kamrup, Meghalaya, etc.).

2124. ———— **(Ed.)** : 1990 : Nationality, Ethnicity and cultural identiy in North-East India. New Delhi, Omsons Pub., 388p.

2125. **Pakrasi, K.**: 1953 : A Note on the Kurs and Sub-Kurs of the Arlengs (Mikirs). *MII,* 33(4), Oct.-Dec.: 307-14.

2126. ———— : 1954 : The traditional story of Arleng (Mikir) migration. *MII,* 34(3), July-Sept.: 211-19.

2127. ———— : A problem in tribal welfare. *Calcutta Review,* 132(2).

2128. ———— : 1955 :Jambili Athon (Mikir clan mast). *JAS (Sc.),* XXI.

2129. ———— : A study of Arleng (Mikir) kinship terminology. *MII,* 35(2), April-June :119-26.

2130. ———— : 1957 : Organisation of social education among the tribals (Report). *First Seminar on Social Education* organised by the Govt. of Bihar.

2131. ———— : 1959 : Notes on Lalungs and their deka-chang. *Jr. Gau. Univ. (Sc.),* XIX(2).

2132. **Pakyntein, E.H.** : 1964 : *Census of India 1961, Vol. III, Assam, Pt. V-(A) : Scheduled Tribes and Scheduled Castes (Reprints from Old Census Reports and Special Tables).* Delhi, Manager of Publications, 148p. (Census since 1881-1921).

2133. ———— **(Ed.)** : *Census of India 1961, Vol. III, Assam, Village Survey Monographs : Resubakrapara.* Delhi, Registrar General of India, 77p.

2134. —— **(Ed.)** : 1966 : *Census of India 1961, Vol. III, Assam, Pt. VI, Village Survey Monograph of Nasatra (Police Station Barpeta, District Kamrup).* Delhi, Manager of Pub., 107p.

2135. ---- **(Ed.)** : 1967 : *ibid, Village Survey Monograph of Laisong (Haflong Police Station, United Mikir and North Cachar Hills).* Ibid.

2136. **Pal, Indu Bhusan** : 1989 : *On Hindu influence in the Ahom court. Proc. NEIHA, 10th(Ed.)* by J.B. Bhattacharjee. Shillong, Hist. Deptt., NEHU : 147-54.

2137. **Pal, S.K.** : 1990 : The Koch : Some issues on their identity crisis. (In) *Nationality, Ethnicity and Cultural Identity in North-East India. (Ed.)* by B. Pakem. Delhi, Omsons Pubn.

2138. ———— : 1993 : Agrarian relations in a Rabha village of Assam. *Jr. Anthropology* S.I., 42 (2), June: 91-103.

2139. ———— : The Rabha customary law in transition: From Matriliny to Patriliny. *(In) Tribal Ethnography, customary law and change. (Ed.)* by K.S. Singh. New Delhi, Concept Pub.: 49-55.

2140. ———— : 1995 : Book Review : Ethnic identity, ethnicity and social stratification in North-East India by N.K. Das. Inter India Publications. New Delhi. 1989. 320p. *Man and Life*, 21 (1-2), Jan. June: 87-9.

2141. **Pal, Sunil Kr.** *and* **Manis Kr. Raha** : 1967 : Riddles from North Bengal. *Bull. Cul. Res. Inst.* (Cal.), VI(1-2): 51-6 (Rajbanshi, Rabha of West Bengal).

2142. **Pal, Surajit Kr.** : 1982 : Effect of religious movement among the Rabha of West Bengal: An assessment. *Proc. of a Seminar on Social Change in India*, held in Calcutta on Dec. 22-24 under the auspices of Anthropology, S.I., Calcutta.

2143. ———— : 1984 : Tribal Council of the Rongdani Rabha: An Autonomous socio-political Institution. *(In) The Tribe of North-East India. (Ed.)* by S. Karotemprel. Calcutta, Firma K.L.M.: 376-90.

2144. ———— : *The Rabha: A changing matrilineal tribe of West Bengal.* Report submitted to Anthropology S.I., Calcutta.

2145. ———— : 1987 : Emergence of conflict between the non-Christian and Christian Koch Rabhas of Assam. *Bull. Cul. Res. Inst.*, XVII(1-2).

2146. ———— : 1988 : Changing marriage practices among the Rabha. *(In) Marriage in India. (Eds.)* by B.B. Goswami, J. Sarkar and D. Danda. Calcutta, Anthropology S.I.: 273-78.

2147. ———— : 1989 : Effect of religious movement on the Rabha of West Bengal: An assessment. *(In) Acculturation and social change in India: An interdisciplinary appraisal. (Ed.)* by S.C. Panchbhai and M.K.A. Siddiqui. Calcutta, Anthropology S.I.: 401-09.

2148. **Pamegam, Nandeswar** : 1970 : Mishing samajat narir sthan (*In Assamese*). *(In) Mising Sanskritir Alekhay. (Ed.)* by Bhrigumuni. Gauhati.

2149. **Pamegam, T.C.** : 1977 : *Mishing Sadhu*. Jorhat, Asam Sahitya Sabha.

2150. **Pamegam, Tarun Ch.** : 1962 : Miri or Miching. *(In) Asamar Janajati. (Ed.)* by Pramod Ch. Bhattacharya. Jorhat, Asam Sahitya Sabha: 155-62 (*In Assamese*).

2151. ———— : 1972 : Miri ba Mishing. *(In) Mishing Sanskritir Alekhya. (Ed.)* by B. Kagyung. Birubari (Gauhati) (*In Assamese*).

2152. **Pandey, Ajit Kr.** : 1993 : Book Review : Kinship affinity and domestic group : A study among the Mishing of the Brahmaputra Valley by J.B. Bhandari. *E.A.*, 46(2), April-June : 223-25.

2153. **Pandey, B.B.** : n.d. : *The Hill Miris*. Dir. of Inf. & Pub. Rel., 176p.

2154. **Pandey, D.N.** : 1979 : From Tribal Kebang to national democracy. *Jr. NEICSSR*, III (I), April: 13-5.

2155. **Pandey, Gyaneswar** : 1990 : Asom men vartaman Sikh samaj: Kal aur aj (*In Hindi*). *Pur. Pra.*, April 13: 5(1-8) (Dhubri Sikh Gurudwara).

2156. **Pandey, Nutan** : 1994 : Rangali Bihu ka Sringer : Nrittya ebang Geet. *Pur. Pra.*, April 14: 5(7-8) (*In Hindi*).

2157. **Pandit, Manoranjan** : 1991 : *Caste system and its impact in politics in the Lakhimpur district of Assam*. Unpub. Ph.D. Thesis, Gau. Univ.

2158. **Pandit, T.N.** *and* **N.K. Das (Eds.)** : 1993 : *The Pre-agricultural Communities of Assam*. Cal., An. S.I., 163p.

2159. **Panigrahi, G.** *and* **S.K. Kar** : 1966 : *The family composition in Assam and North-East Frontier Agency*.

2160. **Pappu, Shyamala** : 1975 : Legal Provisions: An Assamese. *(In) Indian Women. (Ed.)* by D. Jain. Delhi, Pubn. Division, Govt. of India: 113-24.

2161. **Pardesi, Ghanshyam** : 1987 : Assam changes policy on tribals. *Statesman*, May 6: 9(2-3).

2162. ———— : Karbis: Assam's 'native' children. *ST.*, June 11: 1(2-5) 9(4-5).

2163. ————: 1988 : Woes of a North-East Tribe. *Shillong T.*, May 16 : 2(3-6) 3 (3) (Assam, Manipur, Nagaland).

2164. **Parichalan, Samiti** : 1981 : *Koch Samaj Nitimala* (*In Assamese*). Lakhimpur, Anchalik Board Koch Samaj Samiti.

2165. **Parry, N.E.; J.P. Mills; J.H. Crace** *and* **G.D. Walker** : 1935: Notes on some Assam Hill Tribes. *Census of India, Vol. I, India. (Ed.)* by J.H. Hutton. Simla, Govt. of India Press (Part-III B, Ethno. Notes): 126-46.

2166. **Passah, P.M.** : 1994 : Book Review : India's North-East : The Process of Change and Development, *Ed.* by R.K. Samanta, Delhi, B.R. Publishing Corporation (1994), pp. ix+198. *Jr. NEICSSR*, 18 (2), Oct.: 67-71.

2167. **Patgiri, Gagannath** : n.d. : *Satra aru Math Mandirar itibritta* (*In Assamese*). Guwahati.

2168. **Patgiri, Jagadish** : 1990 : The status of religion in the Karbi society. *Proc. of a Seminar on Status of Religion in tribal areas in NEI*, organised by NEICSSR, Shillong on 15-16 Feb. (*Mimeo.*).

2169. **Pathak, B.C.** : 1962 : Tribal welfare in Assam. *March of India*, XIV(8), Aug.: 27-8.

2170. **Pathak, G.** : 1969 : Barpeta satrar itihas. *Souvenir Asam Sahitya Sabha*, Barpeta (*In Assamese*).

2171. **Pathak, Janardan** : 1950 : *Tribes of India*. Delhi, Bharatiya Adimjati Sevak Sangh, Vol. I: 16-21 (Mikir).

2172. **Pathak, Jiban Ch.** : 1987 : *The Krishna cult in Assam: A study in its antiquity literature and philosophy.* Unpub. Ph.D. Thesis, Gau. Univ.

2173. **Pathak, R. D.** *and* **N. Saha** : 1982 : Political development in North Cachar Hills district. *(In) Tribal Movements in India, Vol. I. (Ed.)* by K.S. Singh. New Delhi, Manohar Pub.: 281-85.

2174. ———————— : Political dynamics of the Karbi-A-Darbar. *(In) Ibid.*: 287-93.

2175. **Pathak, Ram Deo** : 1978 : Some social psychological aspects of Jaintias and Assamese. *Workshop on Social Psychological Aspects of Indian Council*, sponsored by the Anthropology S.I., Calcutta.

2176. **Patra, Jiban Krishna** : 1994 : English April brings Assamese New Year. *Assam Tribune*, April 14: 4 (3-6).

2177. **Paul Choudhury, Dipshikha** : 1990 : The status of religion among the semi Nagas of Boro Haflong in North Cachar Hills. *Proc. of a Seminar on Status of Religion in Tribal Areas in NEI*, organised by NEICSSR, Shillong on 15-16 Feb. (*Mimeo.*).

2178. **Paul, Gemini** : 1957 : Anthropology and tribal administration. *Vanyajati*, V (1), Jan.: 4-11 (Assam etc.).

2179. **Paul, M.C.** : 1980 : Bodo-Kacharis of the Brahmaputra valley. *Himalaya: Man & Nature*, 4 (2), July: 3-5.

2180. **Paul, M.C.** : 1991 : Movements, plains tribals and social structure in Assam valley: A sociological exploration. *Social Change,* 21(2).

2181. **Payeng, Punyeswar** : 1989 : Status of Mishing (Miri) Women. *Assam Tribune, (Sunday Reading)*, Feb. 19: I (6-8).

2182. ———— : 1990 : Strategy for Socio-Economic Upliftment of Plains Tribes of Assam. *Assam Information* (Guwahati), XXXXI, Feb.: 32-4.

2183. ———— : Marriage system in Mishing society. *Assam Inf.*, XXXXII, Oct.: 13-4.

2184. ———— : A synopsis of Mishing folk dance. *Assam Tribune, (Sunday Reading)*, Dec. 30 : 1 (1-8).

2185. ———— : 1992 : Origin and migration of the Mishings (Miris). *Assam Tribune, (Sunday Reading)*, Nov. 15: I(1-8).

2186. ———— : Traditional Socio-Political Institutions of Mishing. *Assam Inf.*, XXXXIII, April 91-March 92 : 55-6.

2187. ———— : Origin and migration of the Mishings. *Assam Inf.*, XXXXIV, Nov.: 32-6.

2188. **Payengkataki, S.** : 1935 : *Miri Jatir Buranji*. Dhemaji, Marnoi Bebejia (*In Assamese*).

2189. **Payne, Ernest A.** : 1933 : *The Saktas, an introductory and comparative study (Bengal and Assam)*. Calcutta, YMCA Pub. House and London, Oxford Univ. Press, (Religious Life of India Series).

2190. **Peal, S.E.** : 1872 : Notes on a visit to the tribes inhabiting the hills south of Sibsagar, Assam. *Jr. Asiatic Soc. of Bengal*, 41, Pt. I: 9-29.

2191. ———— : 1882 : Note on platform dwellings in Assam. *Jr. Anthropology Inst.*, XI : 53-5.

2192. ———— : 1892 : The communal barracks of primitive races. *Jr. Asia. Soc. of Beng.*, 61, Pt. II : 246-69.

2193. ———— : 1897 : Identical customs of the Dyaks and the Races around Assam. *Nature*, 56: 53-4.

2194. ———— : The pre-Aryan races of India, Assam and Burma. *Jr. Asiatic Soc. of Beng.*, 65, Pt. III : 59-63.

2195. ———— : 1898 : Ein Ausflug nach Banparra. *Zeitschrift fur Ethnologie*, 30: 231-71.

2196. **Peal, S.E.** : 1898 : Selections of papers regarding the hill tracts between Assam and Burma and on the Upper Brahmaputra. *Z. Ethnol.*, 30: 281-371 (earlier Pub. in 1873 from Calcutta, no. 10).

2197. **Pegu, Ganesh** : 1960 : Ali-ai-ligang. Asam Bani, Feb. 19 and also. *(In) Uchhabar Rangchora, Chap. 7 (in Assamese).*

2198. **Pegu, H.K.** : 1980 : *A study of some aspect of family life among the Sonowal Kachari of Tepor gaon, Dibrugarh. (In Assamese)* M.Sc. Disser., Anthropology Deptt., Dib. Univ.

2199. **Pegu, I.** : 1970 : Mishing Dharma. *(In) Mishing Sanskritir Alekhya. (Ed.)* by Bhrigumuni Kagyung. Gauhati, Lawyers' Book Stall.

2200. **Pegu, M.** : 1981 : *The Mishings of the Brahmaputra Valley.* Dhemaji, Pub. by Manumati Pegu.

2201. **Pegu, N.C.** : 1956 : *The Miris or the Mishings of the Brahmaputra Valley.* Kumarbari, Majuli (Assam), Pub by Dasiram Pegu, 63p.

2202. ———— : 1972 : Miri ba Mishing. *(In) Mishing Sanskritir Alekhya. (Ed.)* by Bhrigumuni Kagyung. Birubari (Gauhati).

2203. **Pegu, S.S.** : 1970 : Marriage and Kinship among the Mikirs. *Paper presented in the 3rd Summer school in the Sociology,* organised by the Centre for Advanced Study in Sociology, Delhi University at Kohima on 7-14 April *(Mimeo.).*

2204. ———— : 1980 : Diphu; A study in urban growth. *(In) Family, Marriage and Social Change. (Eds.)* by S.M. Dubey, P.K. Bordoloi and B.N. Borthakur. New Delhi, Cosmo Pubs.: 196-206.

2205. **Perelia, C.** : 1903 : Prayer cure amongst the Kaibarttas of West Bengal. *Jr. Asiatic Soc. of Beng.*, 72(3): 39.

2206. **Perry, W.J.** : 1927 : The children of the Sun. *Man*, 27 (147) : 215-16.

2207. **Phangsho, P.C.** : 1984 : Traces of Austric and Aryan influences on the Karbis. *Jr. NEICSSR*, VIII (2), Oct.: 32-5.

2208. **Philip, N.** : 1968 : *Census of India 1961, Vol. III, Assam, Village Survey Monograph: Batasipur.* Delhi, Registrar General, 45p.

2209. ——— **(Ed.)** : 1970 : *ibid, Village Survey Monograph: Gonjung (United Mikir & North Cachar Hill District).* Delhi, Manager of Pub., 42p.

2210. **Phookan, Biju** : 1994 : Santras ke chakra bhuha men vi 'Bihuvan' BA bahut payara hai *(In Hindi). Pur. Pra.,* April 9:1.

2211. **Phookan, Manabendra** : 1986 : Asamiya jati: Abayabik sangmishran. *(In) Asamar Manuh. (Ed.)* by B.M. Das. Jorhat, Asam Sahitya Sabha: 49-56 (*In Assamese*)

2212. **Phukan, Anurag** : 1996 : Bihu : Transition through the ages. *Sentinel (Saturday Fare)*, April 13 : 1(1-8).

2213. **Phukan, Bipin** : 1991 : Letters to the Editors : Bihu dance. *Assam Tribune*, April 15 : 4(4-5).

2214. **Phukan, Biren** : 1982 : Music of Assam. *(In) India's North-East. (Ed.)* by Pankaj Thakur. Tinsukia, Prakash Pub. House: 143-50.

2215. **Phukan, Girin** : 1990 : Search for Tai-Ahom identity in Assam. *Proceedings of NEIHA, 11th*: 304-11.

2216. **Phukan, Gunjalal** : 1970 : *Kinship system of chutiya of Moran. Abhoypuri village of Dibrugarh.* Unpub. M.Sc. Disser. Anthropology Deptt., Dib. Univ.

2217. **Phukan, G.K.** : 1988 : Letters to the Editor : The Ahoms. *Assam Tribune*, March 22 : 4 (4-5).

2218. **Phukan, J.N.** : 1963 : The Khamjang valley and the Ahoms. *Jr. Gau. Univ.* XIV (1) : 13-20.

2219. ———— : 1990 : In search of ancient religion of the Tai. *Lik Tai Khwam Tai* (Guwahati, Chukafa Bhawan).

2220. **Phukan, Minoti** : 1992 : Status of labour women in the Tea Gardens of Assam. *(In) Status of Women in Assam. (Ed.)* by S.L. Baruah. New Delhi, Omsons Pubs.: 69-81.

2221. **Phukan, Mitra** : 1995 : Culture: An Assamese wedding, Ridiculous Rigmarole. *Sentinel*, Feb. 18: 1 (1-8), 2 (3-8).

2222. **Phukan, U.** : 1972 : *Tegheriartari: A village re-survey in Kamrup district of Assam (1957-1968).* Jorhat, AERCNEI, AAU.

2223. **Phukan, Umananda** : 1972 : Economic consequence of a traditional habit : A case study of Miri society in Assam. *(In) Socio-Economic Research in Tribal Areas. (Ed.)* by P.C. Goswami. Jorhat, AERCNEI : 41-4.

2224. ———— : 1974 : Research in rural communities of North-East India: A need for an inter-disciplinary approach. *(In) Contemporary Anthropological Research in North-East India. (Ed.) by B.M. Das (Bull. Anthropology Deptt., Dib. Univ.,* III): 101-04.

2225. **Phukan, Umananda** : 1975 : Class structure of a village in Kamrup district in Assam. *Proc. of a Seminar on Sociological* *perspective on North-East India and the second Annual conference of North-East India Soc. Asso.* Dib. Univ., March 10-12 (*Mimeo.*).

2226. ———— : 1978 : Class structure of a village in Kamrup district of Assam. *(In) North-East India: A Sociological Study. (Ed.)* by S.M. Dubey. Delhi, Concept Pub. Comp.: 77-88.

2227. **Piddington, H.** : 1847 : Notice of the Deomones, or Sacred Beads of Assam. *Jr. Asiatic Soc. of Beng.*, XVI: 713-15.

2228. **Plowden, W.** : 1883 : *Report on the Census of British India 1881, Vol. I, Assam*. London: 94-5, 283-84, 288, 291 (Kaibarta, Kewat, Koch, Kachari).

2229. **Pollok, Fitz; William Thomas** *and* **W.S. Thom** : 1900: *Wild sports of Burma and Assam*. London,. Hurst & Blocket, 507p.

2230. **Poter, A.E...** *(Ed.)* : 1933 : *Census of India 1931*, Vol. V: *Bengal and Sikkim, Pt.I, Report*. Calcutta, Govt. Press: 524-28 (Namasudra, Baidya, Brahmin, Kaivarta, etc.), 473-75 (Koch, Rajbansi, etc.).

2231. **Prakash** : 1982 : Maria musalman (*In Assamese*). *Prakash*, 7 (12), Sept.: 76-89.

2232. **Pur. Pra.** : 1989 : Koch Bihar ka Madhupur Satra aur Sri Sri Shankar Dev. *(Sunday Supp.)*, Dec. 31: I (7-8) (*In Hindi*).

2233. ———— : 1990 : Peyar ka swapna dikhakar is tarah masali jati hai masum kaliya, Feb. 4: 7(2-7) (Daranga Mela).

2234. ———— : Kamakhya ke deodha aur deodhani, Aug. 22: 4(3-8).

2235. ———— : Mishing Samaj:. Kal aur Aaj, Sept. 3: 5(1-8)

2236. ———— : 1991 : Koch, Rajbanshiyaon ko anusuchit janajati men shamil karne ki mang, Aug. 15: 7(6-8).

2237. ———— : Aha bhi ek Kamakhya Mandir hai, Nov. 4: 7(6-8) (Another kamakhya Mandir is on *Gao* Hill near Mancachar, Assam).

2238. ———— : 1994 : Uttar Purbanchal ka Bihu. *(Lok. Bha.)*. April 17: (1-8)

2239. ———— : Sanskritik mulloyon ka prati ham sachetan to hai magar........... *(Loh. Bha.)*, April 17: 1 (1-8).

2240. **Pur. Pra.** : 1995 : Rabha samaj ki vishista kala 'Kayrang Bunai' ka bhavisha samapti ki aur, March 20: 7 (3-7) (*In Hindi*).

2241. ———— : Koch-Rajbangshiyon se kia gaya vada pura: Saikia (*In Hindi*), Nov. 6: 1(6-7) (Sch. Caste).

2242. **Pur. Pra.** : 1996 : Visnupriya Manipuri vi OBC ki suchi men shamil, March 20: 1(3) (Assam, *in Hindi*).

2243. **Purbanchal News Network** : 1995 : Ojapali: A vibrant folk art. *Sentinel (Saturday Fare)*, May 27: 1(1-8).

2244. **Purbanchal Prahari** : 1996 : Hanuman Nouka Mahotsav Paramparagat Dhang se mana (*In Hindi*), Aug. 25: 3(4-5).

2245. **Puri, R.K.** : 1980 : Trends of urbanization in Assam. *(In) Family, Marriage and Social Change. (Eds.)* by S.M. Dubey, P.K. Bordoloi and B.N. Borthakur. New Delhi, Cosmo Pub.: 147-61.

2246. **Queah, Milton** : 1991 (n.d.) : Assam: A tryst with destiny. *Assam Tribune*, July 31; 4(3-6), 5(1-3).

2247. **Rabha, Biren** : 1982 : Marai gitar antaratat Rabha sanskriti (*In Assamese*). *Souvenir, Nikhil Rabha Jatiya Parisad, 26th conference* (Kulsi), 2p.

2248. **Rabha, Bishnu** : 1947 : *Assamiya Kristi*. 10p.

2249. **Rabha, Bishnuprasad** : Saka 1869 : Chiphung Banhir Sur (*In Assamese*). *Nayak*, Kati (Sept./Oct.).

2250. ———— : 1984 : *Asamiya kristir chamu abhash*. Gauhati, Pragjyotish Bhavan (Reprinted).

2251. **Rabha, Dhirendra Kr.** : n.d. : *Satra Sabhar Sadhu* (*In Assamese*) Guwahati, Asom Prakashan Parishad.

2252. **Rabha, H.K.** : 1984 : Are the Koch-Rabha Scheduled Tribe? *News Star*, Dec. 3.

2253. **Rabha, M.** : n.d. : *Rabha sanskritir dhara*. Tikrikilla, Pub. by the author (*In Assamese*).

2254. **Rabha, Mani** : 1963 : Baikhu Nritya Aru Git. *Asom Bani*. April 19 (*In Assamese*).

2255. **Rabha, Mukul** : 1992 : Rabha: Rapport with nature. *Assam Tribune, Sunday Reading*, July 12: I (1-8).

2256. **Rabha, Rajen** : 1974 : *Rabha janajati* (*In Assamese*). Jorhat, Asom Sahitya Sabha: 28-32.

2257. ———— : n.d. : Rabha sakolar loka-git. *(In) Ciphung gunggang. (Ed.)* by B. Datta. Gauhati. (*In Assamese*)

2258. ———— : 1993 : Rabha jatir prabajan. *(In) Bahurangi. (Ed.)* by P. Rabha. Jorhat, Asom Sahitya Sabha (*In Assamese*).

2259. **Rabha, Samar Singh** : 1982 : Rabhar bhaluk nachowa git. *Souvenir, Nikhil Rabha Jatiya Parisad*. (*In Assamese*).

2260. **Rabha, Satish** : n.d. : *Totla Rabhar Sadhu*. Tangla (Darrang), Sunny Pub. (*In Assamese*).

2261. **Rabha, Uma Kanta** : 1982 : Pati-Rabha sakalar samajik riti-nitit ebhumuki. *Souvenir, Nikhil Rabha Jatiya Parisad*, 26th Conference (Kulsi), 10p (*In Assamese*).

2262. **Raghaviah, V.** *(Ed.)* : 1950 : *Tribes of India*. New Delhi, Bharatiya Adimjati Sevak Sangh.

2263. ———— : 1951 : The Mishings. *(In) The Tribes of India*. Delhi, Bharatiya Adimjati, II: 30-4.

2264. **Raha, Manis Kr.** : 1963 : The Rabhas of West Bengal. *Bull. Cul. Res. Inst.*, I (3): 24-9.

2265. ———— : 1967 : Ceremonial friendship among the Rajbanshis of Jalpaiguri district, West Bengal. *Science and Culture* (Calcutta), II(3).

2266. ———— : 1970 : *Social organisation of the Rabha of Jalpaiguri, West Bengal.* Unpub. Ph.D. Thesis, Cal. Univ., 55p.

2267. ———— : 1972 : A note on the youth dormitory among the Rabhas. *Bull. Cul. Res. Inst.*, IX: 91-3.

2268. ———— : Paschim Banger Rabha O Tader Samajer dhara *(in B.) Bull. Academy of Folklore*, I (3-4).

2269. ———— : 1973 : Rabha Kinship terms: An analysis. *Jr. Ind. Anthropology Soc.*, VIII (2), Oct.: 9a.

2270. ———— : 1974 : The Rabhas of Western Duars: A structural analysis of a changing matrilineal society. *Bull. Cul. Res. Inst.*, 10(1-2): 70-9.

2271. ———— : 1985 : Book Review: *Chomangkan* by B.N. Bordoloi, Tribal Research Institute, Assam, Guwahati, 1982, pp. 184. *Man and Life*, XI (1-2), Jan.-June: 121.

2272. ———— : 1986 : Book Review: *Focus on folklore of North-East India*, Special Volume, No. 1 &.. *(Ed.)* by Birendranath Dutta, Guwahati, Assam Academy Review, *Man and Life*, XII (3-4), July-Dec.: 221-22.

2273. ———— : 1988 : Book Review: *Life Style Indian Tribes* by S.T. Das, Delhi, Gian Pubg. House, 1987, pp. XI+309, *Man and Life*, XIV (3-4), July-Dec.: 195-96.

2274. **Raha, Manis Kr.** : 1989 : *Matriliny to Patriliny: A study of the Rabha society*. New Delhi, Gian Pubg. House, 373p.

2275. **Raha, M.K.; J. C. Das** *and* **S.C. Mandal** : 1979 : Socio-political movement among the Rabha of North Bengal. *Bull. Cul. Res. Inst.*, XX(3-4): 50-5.

2276. **Raha, M.K.; J. C. Das** *and* **S.C. Mandal** : 1993 : Socio-Political Movement among the Rabhas of North Bengal. *(In) Tribal transformation in India, Vol. III, Pt. IV. (Ed.)* by Buddhadeb Chaudhuri. New Delhi, Inter India Pub.

2277. **Raha, Manis Kr.** *and* **Iar Ali Khan (Eds)** : 1993 : *Polity political process and social control* in *South Asia: The tribal and rural perspectives. New Delhi, Gyan Pub.*, 374p.

2278. **Raha, Manish Kr.** *and* **Palash Ch. Coomar** : 1992 : Himalayas and the Himalayans. Calcutta, *An. S.I.*

2279. **Rahaman, Aminur** : 1994 : Asamer Muslimder Bouddhic deulepnai prakatit kare. *Samai Prabaha* (Guwahati), March 12: 4 (3-8) (*in B.*).

2280. **Rahman, F.** : 1980 : *A study of kinship system among the Muslims of Dibrujan vIllage, Dibrugarh*. Unpub. M.Sc. Disser. Anthropology Deptt., Dib. Univ.

2281. **Rahman, M.** : 1975 : *The Kacharis of Tengakhat: Their economic activities*. Unpub. M.Sc. Disser. Anthropology Deptt., Dib. Univ.

2282. **Rahmann, R.** : 1936 : Gottheiten der Primitivstamme in nordostlichen Vorderindien. *Anthropos*, 31: 37-96.

2283. **Rahmann, Rudolf** : 1952 : The ritual spring hunt in north-eastern and middle India. *Anthropologyropos*, 47: 871-90.

2284. **Rai Hajong, Ratan Kr.** : 1982 : Hajong Samaj ati Samikhya (*In Assamese*). *Payobhara* (New Delhi), 13 (20), Dec.: 16-31.

2285. **Raimedhi, Indrani** : 1992 : Sattriya dance as classical form. *Assam Tribune, Sunday Reading*, May 17: I (1-8).

2286. **Rajadhon, Phya Anuman** : 1968 : *Essays on Thai Folklore*. Bangkok, Social Science Association Press, 202p.

2287. **Rajguru, Sarbeswar** : 1988 : *Medieval Assamese Society: 1223-1826*. Haibargaon (Nagaon, Assam), Assami Publications, 521p.

2288. ———— : 1989 : Letters to the Editor: Cremation of Ahom kings. *Assam Tribune*, Sept. 16: 4 (3-4), Oct. 24: 4(3-5), Nov. 16: 4(3-4)

2289. **Rajkhowa, A.** : 1980 : *An account of the Sonowal Kacharis of Lepetkata village with special reference to death and disposal, agriculture and economic organization*. Unpub. M.Sc. Disser. Anthropology Deptt., Dib. Univ.

2290. **Rajkhowa, Ashok** : 1981 : *A study on economic lifestyle of Mura and Manjhi (Santal) of Azizhash Tea Estate (Assam)*. Unpub. M.Sc. Disser. Anthropology Deptt., Dib. Univ.

2291. **Rajkhowa, Benudhar** : 1905 : *Assamese demonology*. Gauhati.

2292. ———— : 1973 : *Assamese Popular Superstitions and Assamese Demonology. (Ed.)* by Praphulla- datta Goswami. Gauhati University, Folklore Research Deptt., *(Reprinted)*, 163p. (Folk-belief).

2293. **Rajkhowa, B. Baruah** : 1996 : The 'Ret-ki-nang' or Jhum cultivation among the Hill Karbis of Dimoria. *Seminar paper on Traditional Culture and Folklore in North-East India*, 18-19 Nov., Shillong, NEICSSR.

2294. **Rajkhowa, Bijoya Baruah** : 1991 : Costume, coiffure and ornaments in the Medieval Assamese Society. *Folklore*, 32 (4), April: 57-61.

2295. **Rajkhowa, Chandar** : 1990 : *Studies on Schistosomiasis in domestic animals in Assam with special reference to schitosomaindiceun*. Unpub. Ph.D. Thesis, Assam Agri. Univ.

2296. **Rajkhowa, N.C.** : 1970 : Decentralization of administration in Mikir and North Cachar Hills. *St.*, Jan. 18: 3(4).

2297. **Rajkhowa, S.C.** : 1942 : Ahom Kinship. *Jr. Assam Res. Soc.*, IX: 31-40.

2298. **Rajkumar, Sarbananda** : 1962 : Dobania. *(In) Asamar Janajati. (Ed.)* by Pramod Ch. Bhattacharya. Jorhat, Asam Sahitya Sabha: 108-11 (*In Assamese*).

2299. ———————— : Fakiyal. *(In) ibid*: 112-17 (*In Assamese*).

2300. ————— : 1965 : *Chutiya, Bhuyan aru Matak Rajya*. Gauhati, 90p. (In Assamese).

2301. ————— : 1980 : Khel/Mel System. *(In) Itihashe Soaura Chashata Bachan*. Jorhat, Pub. by A. Rajkumari, 81p.

2302. ————— : 1982 : *Singfau janagoshthi (A study on the Singfau tribe of Assam)*. Jorhat, Asam Sahitya Sabha, 64p (*In Assamese*).

2303. ————— : 1991 : Tara-Turung-Aitoniya. *(In) Asamar Janajati. (Ed.)* by Pramod Ch. Bhattacharya. Guwahati, Asam Sahitya Sabha: 233-35 (*in Assamese, Reprinted*).

2304. **Rakshit, Birendranath** : 1977-78 : Inheritance of old tradition in Assamese verification. *Jr. Univ. Gau. (Arts)*, 28-29 : 182-94.

2305. **Ramachandran, A.** : 1993 : A Survey of Nishi-Ahom relationship (1562-1810 A.D.). *Jr. NEICSSR*, XVII (2), Oct. : 8-12.

2306. **Raman, Vasanthi** : ? : *The Nari Mukti Movement in Assam.* Calcutta, Santosh Rana Published from 8B, Palam Place.

2307. **Ramchiari, Balicharan** : 1977 : *Bathou Kherai Puja Aru Boro Jati (In Assamese).* Nalbari.

2308. **Ramdia Sahitya Sabha** : 1993 : *Folk Culture of Assam.* (It was held at Ramdia in Feb. '93 organised by Ramdia Sahitya Sabha).

2309. **Ranchi University** : 1986 : *The sacred complex of Kamakhya: An Anthropological approach to study, the Sakti Cult in India.* Ranchi University, Anthropology Deptt., (*in Press*).

2310. **Ranjit, Mrinmoy** : 1995 : The festival of plenty. *Assam Tribune (Sunday)*, Jan. 22: 1(1-4) (Bhogali Bihu).

2311. **Rao, V.V.** : 1979 : Slavery in North-East India. *Proc. of a Seminar on The History and Culture of North-East India*, Deptt. of History, NEHU held on 26-28 April.

2312. **Rastogi, T.C.** : 1981 : Performing arts in Assam. *Sangeet Natak*, 60, April-June: 41-52.

2313. ———— : 1996 : *Assam Vaisnavism.* New Delhi, Omsons Pubs., 91p.

2314. **Ratha, S.N.** : 1968 : Caste and occupation in two peri-urban Assamese villages. *EA*, XXI (2), May-Aug.: 155-66.

2315. ———— : 1969 : Madarbari: A Bodo Kachari village in North Kamrup Assam. *Jr. Gau. Univ. (Sc.)*, 20 (1): 102-08.

2316. ———— : 1970 : Religion and occupational differentiation. *Man in India*, 50 (3), July-Sept.: 248-56.

2317. ———— : 1976 : Changing trends in inter-caste attitude and behaviour in a multi-caste Kamrupi village. *Proc. of a Seminar on Social Change in North-East India*, organised by the Deptt. of Anthropology, Dib. Univ., March 26-27.

2318. ———— : Observations on some economic activities of the Boro-Kachari: Data from a North Kamrup village. *Proc. of a seminar on Tribal Economy. (Ed.)* by T. Mathew. Shillong, NEHU: 439-48.

2319. ———— : 1984 : Matrilateral cross-cousin marriage and the kinship terminology: *The Arleng case. (In) The Tribes in North-East India. (Ed.)* by S. Karotemprel. Calcutta, Firma K.L.M.: 224-30.

2320. **Ratha, S.N.** : 1985 : Land use of human relations: A case study of a Bodo Kachari village. *Jr. Social Research* (Ranchi), XXVIII (1), Oct.: 55-65.

2321. **Ratha, S.N.** : 1986 : Land use and human relations : Data from Bodo Kachari village. *(In) Land Use Pattern in North-East India. (Ed.)* by B.B. Dutta. Ludhiana, Gagan Pub. : 156-64.

2322. ———— : 1994 : Notes on ecology, economy and religion : Data from a Bodo Kachari village. *Bull. Anthropology Deptt.*, Dib. Univ., 22: 96-105.

2323. **Ratha, S.N.** *and* **M.C. Goswami** : 1966 : Caste and occupation in an Assamese village. *MII*, 46(3).

2324. **Rattan, Kamaljit** : 1989 : Assam: Striking a separatist stance. *India Today*, 14 (6), March 16: 53-4.

2325. **Rava, Mukul** : 1983 : Rava sangeet banam Bisnu sangeet (In A.). *Agradut*, Feb. 27: 7(1-5).

2326. **Ray, Debidas** : 1962 : *Kanther Terang: Report on Socio-Economic Survey of a Mikir village in Assam*. Jorhat, AERC.

2327. ———— : 1969 : Kanther Terang (A Mikir village), Pt. II: *The Socio- Economic Survey of Kanther Terang*, 1960. *(In) Rural Life in Assam Hills. (Ed.)* by P.C. Goswami, Jorhat, AERC for NEI: 11-78.

2328. **Ray, Manmohan** : 1902 : Some notes on the Rajvansi caste. *Jr. Asiatic Society of Bengal*, 71, Pt. III: 50-61.

2329. **Ray, Sukumar** : 1967 : Music of the Hill People of North-Eastern India. *(In) A Common Perspective for North-East India. (Eds.)* by Rathin Mitra and Barun Das Gupta. Calcutta, Pannalal Das Gupta: 29-40.

2330. **Raychaudhuri, Bikash** : 1970 : Social mobility movement among the Rabha of North Bengal. *MII*, 50 (1), Jan.-March: 87-97.

2331. ———— : 1978 : Dormitory among the tribal women in India. *(In) Tribal Women in India. (Ed.)* by Committee Calcutta. Indian Anthropological Society: 154-65.

2332. **Raza, Moonis** *and* **Aijazuddin Ahmad** : 1990 : *An Atlas of Tribal India*. New Delhi, Concept Pub., 472p.

2333. **Raza, Moonis** *and* **Sudesh Nangia** : 1986 : *Atlas of the child in India*. New Delhi, Concept Pub., 477p.

2334. **Reddy, B.S.N.** *and* **N.V. Rao** : 1988 : Appropriate technology and its transfer strategy for tribal development. *(In) Application of Science and Technology for Tribal Development. (Ed.)* by B.N. Bordoloi. Guwahati, Tribal Research Inst., 69p.

2335. **Registrar General** : 1967 : *Census of India 1961 : Village Survey Monograph, Laisong (Haflong Police station, United Mikir & North Cachar Hills)*. Delhi. Manager of Pub

2336. **Registrar General** : 1968 : *Census of India 1961, Assam: Village Survey Monograph, Bilasipara (Dhekiajuli Police Station, Darrang District)*. Delhi, Manager of Pub., 45p.

2337. **Regon, D.** : 1972 : Mishing Bibah Paddhati. *(In) Mishing Sanskritir Alekhya. (Ed.)* by B. Kagyung. Birubari, Gauhati.

2338. **Reid, Robert** : 1944 : Assam. *Jr. Royal Soc. of Arts*, 92: 241-47.

2339. ———— : 1944 : The excluded areas of Assam. *Geographical Jr.*, 103 (1-2), Jan.-Feb.: 18-29.

2340. ———— : 1963 : *Years of change in Bengal and Assam. Mas. Eur. E. 278/22*. (India Office Library & Record, London).

2341. ———— : 1966 : *Years of change in Bengal and Assam*. London, Ernest Benn Ltd.: 118, 137, 154-5, 93, 105, 113, 116, 126, 137, 151, 117-8, 136.

2342. **Report** : 1959 : *Study team on Social Welfare and Welfare of Backward Classes*, Report, 2 Vols. Delhi.

2343. ———— : 1963 : *Morangaon: A plain village of Sibsagar district*. Jorhat, AERC (*Survey No. 3*).

2344. ———— : 1964 : *Chalihagaon: A plain village in Sibsagar, Assam*. Jorhat, AERC (*Survey No. 6*).

2345. ———— : *Report on socio-economic survey in United Mikir and North Cachar Hills*. Jorhat, AERC.

2346. ———— : 1964 & 1966 : *Co-operative farming in Assam Ist and 2nd round*. Jorhat, AERC (*Study Nos. 4 & 5*).

2347. ———— : 1965 : *Chotahaibor: A plain village in Nowgaon, Assam*. Jorhat, AERC (*Resurvey Report No. 2*).

2348. ———— : 1967 : *Dispur: A plain village near Gauhati, Assam. Jorhat*, AERC (*Resurvey Report No.* 1).

2349. ———— : *Khonajan: A plain village in Lakhimpur district*. Jorhat, AERC (*Survey No. 5*)

2350. ———— : 1970 : *Batgarh, Hudubari and Bhoroli: Darrang, Assam*. Jorhat, AERC (*Survey No. 11*)

2351. ———— : 1971 : *Borkuloi (Nowgaon, Assam)*. Jorhat, AERC (*Survey No. 12*).

2352. ———— : 1972 : *Tegheriartari a plain village in Kamrup, Assam*. Jorhat, AERC (*Resurvey Report No. 5*).

2353. ———— : 1974 : *Khonajan a immigrant village in Lakhimpur district*. Jorhat, AERC (*Resurvey Report No. 6*).

2354. **Report** : 1975 : *Morangaon : A village in Sibsagar district.* Jorhat, AERC (*Resurvey Report No. 7*).

2355. ———— : 1976 : *Habrubari (Goalpara, Assam). Jorhat,* AERC (*Survey No. 14*).

2356. ———— : *Namoni Borpomua a Mishing village in Sibsagar*, Assam. Jorhat, AERC (*Survey No. 15*).

2357. ———— : 1979 : *Khejurbond (N.C. Hills, Assam).* Jorhat, AERC (*Survey No. 17*).

2358. ———— : 1981 : *Nam-Deuri (Sibsagar, Assam).* Jorhat, AERC (*Survey No. 18*).

2359. ———— : 1983 : *Namoni Borpomuai : A Mishing village in Sibsagar district.* Jorhat, AERC (*Resurvey Report No. 10*).

2360. **Rickards, R.** : n.d. : *The character and conditions of the native inhabitants (2 Vols).* New Delhi, Omsons Pubs.

2361. **Risley, H.H.** : 1891 : *The tribes and castes of Bengal, Vol. I.* Calcutta, Bengal Secretariat Press (Koch, Rajbansi: 491-500), Vol. II, Mech : 86-91 (*Reprinted* in 1980 by Firma KL Mukhopadhyay, Calcutta).

2362. ———— : 1903 : *Census of India 1901 , Vol. I: India, Pt. I, Report, Ethnographic Appendices.* Calcutta, Supdt. Govt. Printing,: 28, 188-97 (Koch).

2363. **Rizvi, S.H.M.** *and* **P.M. Buzarbarua** : 1991 : Inbreeding in Garia Muslim of Assam. *Social Sc.*, 4(1-2), June-Dec.: 245-49.

2364. **Robinson, W.** : 1841 : *A descriptive account of Assam to which is added a short account of the neighbouring tribes.* London, Ostell & Lepage, 421p (*Reprinted* in 1975 by Sanskaran Prakashak, Delhi).

2365. **Rose, H.A.** : 1911 : *A Glossary of the Tribes and Castes of Punjab and North West Frontier Province,* Vol. II. Lahore, 552p (A little description about Koch).

2366. **Rowney, H.B.** : 1882 : *The Wild Tribes of India.* London, Thos. De La Rue & Co. (Koch: 146-47, Mech: 143-45, Mikir: 178-79; Reprinted in 1974 by B.R. Pub., New Delhi).

2367. **Roy, Babul** : 1993 : A note on geographical mobility of the Dimasa of Maibong area. *Bull. Anthropology Deptt., Gau. Univ.*, VII:77-82.

2368. ———— : 1994 : Supernatural beliefs among the Dimasa Kacharies. *Bull. Anthropology Deptt., Gau. Univ.*, VIII: 115-19.

2369. **Roy Burman, B.K.** : 1953 : *Synoptic Report on Mech Acclturation.* Submitted to the Govt. of West Bengal (*Mimeo*).

2370. ———— : 1958 : Story of Ramayana as related by a Mech elder. *Indian Folklore*, 1(4), Oct.-Dec. : 67-9.

2371. ——— **(Ed.)** : n.d. : *Preliminary appraisal of Scheduled Caste of India*. New Delhi, Office of the Registrar Gen. India (*Mimeo.*).

2372. ——— **(Ed.)** : n.d. : *Preliminary appraisal Scheduled Tribe of India*. New Delhi, Office of the Reg. Gen. of India (*Mimeo.*).

2373. ———— : 1968 : *Socio-economic process in tea plantation with special reference to tribal labourer*: Census of India, Vol. I, Pt. VII-A. Delhi, Controller of Pub.

2374. ———— : 1970 : Modernization process in the Hills of North-East India. *Jr. Inst. of Defence Study*, January.

2375. ———— **(Ed.)** : *Census of India 1961 : Demographic and Socio-Economic Profiles of the Hill Areas of North-East India*. Delhi, Controller of Pub., 397p.

2376. ——— **(Ed.)** : 1971 : *Census of India 1961, Vol. I, Monograph series, Pt. V-B, Dimasa Kachari of Assam, Ethnographic study*, No. 7. New Delhi, Reg. Gen., 34p.

2377. ———— : 1972 : Tribal Demography: A Preliminary Appraisal. *(In) Tribal Situation in India. (Ed.)* by K. Suresh Singh. Simla, Indian Inst. of Advanced Study: 39-50 (Assam etc.).

2378. ———— : 1973 : Impact of establishment of urban centres and introduction of improved technology in the hills of North-East India. *Highlander: The Bull. of the C.R. & S.M.* (Delhi), 1(1), March: 1-2.

2379. ———— : 1976 : New age in age less North-East India. *Jr. Soc. Res.*, XIX (1), March: 64-7.

2380. ———— : 1977 : Social Process in the Hills of North-East India: An ecological perspective. *(In) Dimensions of social change in India. (Eds.)* by M.N. Srinivas, S. Seshaiah and V.S. Parthasarathy. Bombay, Allied Pub.: 405-08 (North Cachar Hills, United Mikir Hills, etc.).

2381. **Roy Burman, B.K.** : 1978 : Problems and strategies of social work in the Eastern Himalaya. *Himalaya : Man & Nature*, 1(10), March: 22-30.

2382. ———— : 1980 : Problems of Nation Building in North-East India. *Mainstream*, June 14.

2383. ———— : North-East India: An overview. *Mainstream* (Delhi). LXI (14), Dec. 6.

2384. ———— : 1983 : Assam : A case for intellectuals intervention. *Mainstream*, 21 (32), April 9: 6, 32.

2385. ———— : 1984 : Issues in the North-East : An appraisal. *(In) North-East Region: Problems and prospects of development. (Ed.)* by B.L. Abbi. Chandigarh, Centre for Research in Rural & Industrial Development : 174-80.

2386. ———— : 1987 : Foreword. *(In) Demographic Profile of North-East India* by S.C. Srivastava. Delhi, Mittal Pub.: i-iv.

2387. ———— : 1988 : Problems and prospects of tribal development in North-East India. *Paper presented in the Seminar on Constraints of tribal Development in* NEI, organised by the TRI, Assam held in June, 1988.

2388. ———— : 1990 : Tribal population and development. *(In) Tribal Demography and Development in North-East India. (Ed.)* by Ashis Bose, T. Nongbri and N. Kumar. New Delhi, B.R. Pub.: 67-83.

2389. ———— : 1994 : *Tribes in perspective: Encyclopaedia of Scheduled Tribes, Scheduled Castes & Disadvantageous people.* Delhi, Mittal Pubn.

2390. **Roy Choudhury, B.K.** : 1970 : Social mobility movement among the Rabha of North Bengal. *MII*, 50(1): 87-97.

2391. **Roy Choudhury, Bhupendra** : 1990 : Barpeta Satra ki Holi: Range Phagu khele Vanamali (*In Hindi*). *Pur. Pra.*, March 13: 5(1-4).

2392. **Roy Choudhury, T.C.** : 1952 : The racial problem of Bengal. *MII*, 32 (2), March: 52-63 (Namasudra).

2393. **Roy, Debesh** : 1991 : Cha bagichar prekshapate ek Adivasi sampradayer jiban katha (*In B.*). *Lokcharcha* (Jalpaiguri), West Bengal.

2394. **Roy, D.N.** : 1995 : Asom ke atit ke dou Rajbangsha: Chutiya and Bhuyan. (*In Hindi*). *Pur. Pra..*, June 27: 5(1-6).

2395. **Roy (Hajong)** : 1980 : *A Note on the festivals of the Hajongs* (unpub. MSS).

2396. **Roy, Jotirmoy** : 1954 : Economic and social customs of the Rajbanshis. *Modern Review*, 96: 129-38.

2397. ———— : 1992 : Economic and Social Customs of Rajbanshis. *(In) India through ages, Vol. IV: Castes and Tribes of India. (Eds.)* by T.R. Sareen and S.R. Bakshi. New Delhi, Anmol Pubs.: 214-27.

2398. **Roy, Khitish (Tr.)** : 1972 : *Assamer lokasanskriti* by Jogesh Das (*In B.*). New Delhi, Nat. Book Trust (India), 152p.

2399. **Roy, Mrinal** : 1971 : *Kamarupa-Kamakhya Bhagats: A study of a cult in its social perspectives.* Unpub. Ph.D. Thesis, Origon Univ.

2400. **Roy, Niranjan** : 1991 : Bodos : Bathow, Baisagu and Bagrumba. *Assam Tribune, Sunday Reading,* April 21: I (I-6).

2401. ———— : 1993 : Social and cultural life of Hajong tribe. *Assam Tribune, Sunday Reading,* Jan. 3: I(1-8).

2402. **Roy, Nirode Bihari** : 1967 : *On their origin of the Namasudra.* Calcutta, Kirti Pub. Concern.

2403. **Roy, R.C.** : 1902 : Some notes on the Rajvanshi caste. *Jr. Royal Asia. Soc. of Beng.*, III.

2404. ———— : 1937 : Caste,. Race and Religion in India. *MII*, XVII (3), July-Sept.: 147-76; XVII (4), Oct.-Dec.: 212-54 (Mikir, Bodo, Assam etc.).

2405. **Roy, S.B.** *and* **Asok K. Ghosh (Eds)** : 1994 : *People of India.* New Delhi, Inter India Pub. 456p. (People of North to South, East to West).

2406. **Roy, S.C.** : 1935 : *The Hill Bhuiyas of Orissa.* Ranchi, Man in India Office, 320p.

2407. ———— : 1981 : The Nagas, the Kacharis and the Meitheis: Their affinity with the Chotanagpur tribes. *MII*, 61 (3), July: 293-304.

2408. **Roy, S.K.** : 1994 : Textiles of Assam: A cultural spectrum. *Bull. Deptt., Anthropology, Gau. Univ.*, VIII: 46-56.

2409. **Roy, Sankar Kr.** : 1985 : Two indigenous potter communities of Assam and classical codes. *(In) Anthropological perspectives on North-East India (Bull. Anthropology Deptt., Dib. Univ., X,* 1981): 30-49.

2410. ———— : 1992 : Religious Institution and pottery of Assam: An ethno-archaeological study. *Bull. Anthropology Deptt., Gauhati Univ.*, VI, March: 87-98.

2411. **Roy, Sankar Kr.** : 1992 : Two indigenous potter communities of Assam and classical codes. *Bull. Anthropology Deptt., Dib. Univ.*, 18-19 (1989-90).

2412. **Roy, S.K.** *and* **N.K. Choudhury** : 1991 : Some observations on tribal arts from some selected areas of North-East India. *Ethnolab (State Museum, Guwahati).*

2413. **Roy, Shibani et al** : 1984 : *Major Ethnic Groups of North Eastern India (Ethnographic Notes).* Shillong, Anthropology S.I. (*Mimeo.*)

2414. **Roy, Shibani** *and* **S.H.M. Rizvi** : 1990 : *Tribal customary laws of North-East India.* Delhi, B.R. Pub.: 111 (Rabha).

2415. ———— : 1991 : In search of the dream. *The Newsfront* (Guwahati), Sept. 7.

2416. **Roy, Shyamsundar** : 1995 : Witchcraft, ignorance bedevils: Santhal life, *St.*, Nov. 18: 4(4-8) (Santhal community).

2417. **Ruhemann, Barbara** : 1948 : The Relationship terms of some Hill Tribes of Burma and Assam. *South-Western Journal of Anthropology*,. 4: 155-98.

2418. **Russell, R.V.** *and* **Hira Lal** : 1916 : *The Tribes and Castes of the Central Provinces of India,* Vol. I: 376 (Glossary); Vol. III: 370, 374, 422 (Kewat, Khewat, Kaibartta). London, Macmillan & Co. Ltd.

2419. **Sachchidananda** : 1992 : *Tribal India : Past and Present.* Calcutta, Inst. of Soc. Res. & App. Anth. (Status of women etc.).

2420. **Sachchidananda** *and* **R.R. Prasad (Eds.)** : 1996 : *Encyclopaedic Profile of Indian Tribes*, Vol. I-IV. New Delhi, Discovery Pubg. House.

2421. **Sadashivaiah, K.** : 1979 : Trend in age of marriage, family size and level of education among sterilised cohont in Assam and Kerala. *Jour. Family Welfare,* 35(3), March: 46-56.

2422. **Saggar, Mridal and Indranil Pan** : 1994 : Scheduled Castes and Scheduled Tribes in Eastern India: Inequality and poverty estimates. *EPW*, XXIX, March 5: 567-74.

2423. **Saha, N. (Sr.)** : n.d. : Morangaon socio-economic study in a village. *Jour. of Assam Sc. Society* (Gauhati), 6.

2424. **Saha, N. (Sr.) and M.D. Barkataky** : 1969 : *Banshidua: Rural Life in Assam Hills.* Jorhat, Agro Economic Research Centre.

2425. **Saha, N. (Jr.)** : 1990 : Status of women in Borak Valley: A Brief Seminar Report. *Social Science* (Silchar), III (1-2): 139-49.

2426. **Saha, N. (Jr.) and S.S. Mishra** : 1990 : Dimension of tribal religious movements in India. *Social Sc.*, III (1-2) : 150-64 (Bodo Kachari, etc.).

2427. **Saha, R.M.** : 1983 : *Koch-Rabhader sangkhipta itibritya* (*in B.*). Bilasipara, Pub. by the author.

2428. **Saharia, Ganesh** : 1990 : *Tea-Garden labour.* Unpub. Ph.D. Thesis, Gau. Univ.

2429. **Sahariya, Mahendra** : 1991 : Letters to the Editor : Origin of Bihu. *Assam Tribune*, April 23 : 4(3-4).

2430. **Sahay, K.N.** : 1977 : Tribal self image and identity. *(In) Tribal Heritage of India*, Vol. I, *Ethnicity, Identity and Interaction. (Ed.)* by S.C. Dube. New Delhi, Vikas Pub. House: 8-57.

2431. **Sahay, Vijoy S.** : 1994 : Book Review : Community and village development by B.N. Borthakur, Institute of Social Research and Applied Anthropology, Calcutta, 1993, IX+227, *Man & Life*, XX (1-2), Jan.-June: 134-35.

2432. **Sahitya Sabha** : 1967 : *Eikhan Dimariya*. Dimariya (Assam), Dimariya Sahitya Sabha (*In Assamese*).

2433. **Sahu, Kamakhya Pr.** : 1994 : Asam ke adivasiyon men baibahik pratha (*In Hindi*). *Pur. Pra.*, Oct. 25: 5(1-6) (Dimasa-Kachari, Mikir, Karbi, Lalung, Miri, Mishing).

2434. **Saikia, A.** : 1982 : *Female participation in Agricultural operations in Assam: A study in Sibsagar District (undivided)*. Unpub. Ph.D. Thesis, Gau. Univ.

2435. **Saikia, A.K. (Ed.)** : 1964 : *Census of India 1961, Vol. III Assam, Village Survey Monograph: Katanipara*, Delhi, Registrar General, 52p.

2436. ——— **(Ed.)** : 1969 : *Census of India 1961 : Village Survey Monograph : Kumargaon (Jorhat, Sibsagar)*. Delhi, Manager of Pub., 64p.

2437. ——————— : *Census of India 1961, Village Survey Monograph; Japisajia (Sibsagar District)*. Delhi, Manager of Pub., 36p.

2438. ——— **(Ed.)** : 1970 : *Census of India 1961 : Village Survey Monograph: Khara (Dudhnoi, Goalpara District)*. Delhi, Manager of Pub., 104p.

2439. ——————— : *Census of India 1961, Vol. III, Assam, Pt. VI*: Village Survey Monograph, Gonjung. Delhi, Registrar General, 42p.

2440. **Saikia, A.K. (Ed.)** : 1971 : *Census of India 1971, Vol. III, Assam, Pt. II-C (i) Social and Cultural Tables (Tables-C-VII and C-VIII)*. Gauhati, Directorate of Census Operation of Assam.

2441. ——— **(Ed.)** : 1972 : *Census of India 1971, Series-3, Assam, Pt. X-A: Village and Town Directory, Pt. X-B, Primary Census Abstract: District Census Handbook, Cachar District*. Gauhati, Directorate of Census Operation Assam, 414p.

2442. ——————— : *Census of India 1971 , Series-3, Assam,*

Pt. X-A: Village and Town Directory, Pt. X-B, Primary Census Abstract: District Census Handbook, North Cachar Hill District. Gauhati, Dir. of Census Assam, 92p.

2443. **Saikia, A.K. (Ed.)** : 1972 : *Census of India 1971, Series-3, Assam, District Census Handbook: Mikir Hills District.* Gauhati, Dir. of Census Assam, 254p.

2444. ———————— : *Census of India 1971 , Series-3,Assam, D.C.H.: Nowgong District.* Gauhati, Dir. of Census Operation Assam, 350p.

2445. ————————: *Census of India 1971, Series-3, Assam, DCH: Lakhimpur District.* Gauhati, Dir. of Census Operation Assam, 633p.

2446. ————————: *Census of India 1971, Series-3, Assam, DCH: Goalpara District.* Gauhati, Dir. of Census Operation Assam, 575p.

2447. ———————— : *Census of India 1971, Series-3, Assam, DCH: Sibsagar District.* Gauhati, Dir. of Census Operation Assam, 417p.

2448. ———————— : *Census of India, Series-3, Assam, DCH: Darrang District.* Gauhati, Dir. of Census Oper. Assam, 401p.

2449. ———————— : *Census of India 1971, Assam, Series-3, Pt. II-A, General Population Tables.* Delhi, Manager of Pub. 212p.

2450. ——— **(Ed.)** : 1981 : *Census of India 1971: A Portrait of Population, Assam.* Delhi, Controller of Pub., 143p.

2451. **Saikia, Chandra Pr.** : 1982 : Rongmilir hahi; A human document of Karbi life. *Assam Tribune*, April 24: 4.

2452. **Saikia, Devajani** : 1985 : Some folk songs of a tribal community in the urban fringe of Gauhati. *(In) Folklore in North-East India. (Ed.)* by Soumen Sen. Delhi, Omsons Pubs.: 77-84.

2453. ————— : 1992 : Some folk songs of a tribal community in the urban fringe of Gauhati. *(In) India Through Ages, Vol. V: Folklore of India. (Eds.)* by T.R. Sareen and S.R. Bakshi. New Delhi, Anmol Pubs.: 253-61.

2454. **Saikia, Dharani Kanta** : 1983 : *Religious beliefs and practices among the Deuri based on the field work done in Kolowlowa Deuri Gaon in Dibrugarh District.* Unpub. M.Sc. Dissertation, Anthropology Deptt., Dib. Univ.

2455. **Saikia, Hiteswar** : 1976 : Changes in Socio-Economic Scene. *Link,* 18(48), July 11: 17-9.

2456. **Saikia, J.P.** : 1980 : Bihu : Assam's Spring Festivals. *Illustrated Weekly of India,* 101 (22), June: 18.

2457. **Saikia, K.N.** : 1968 : *Assam Muslim Relations and their Cultural Significance.* Unpub. Ph.D. Thesis, Gau. Univ.

2458. **Saikia, Labhit Kr.** : 1981 : *Sonowal Kachari Sanskriti.* Saikhowa (Dibrugarh), Pub. by. L.K. Saikia.

2459. **Saikia, M.** : 1967 : *Assam Muslim relations and its cultural significance.* Unpub. Ph.D. Thesis, Anthropology Deptt., Gau. Univ.

2460. **Saikia, Menoka** : 1991 : *Development of primary education in the Karbi Anglong District.* Unpub. Ph.D. Thesis, Gau. Univ.

2461. **Saikia, M.C.** : 1987 : "Bodo-Kacharis", "Rabhas". *(In) Tribes of Assam,* Pt. I by B.N. Bordoloi, G.C. Sharma Thakur and M.C. Saikia. Guwahati, Tribal Research Institute (Assam): 1-21; 119-39.

2462. **Saikia, Mohini Kr.** : 1986 : Asamaloi Islam dharmir agaman aru sangmishran. *(In) Asamar Manuh. (Ed.)* by B.M. Das. Jorhat, Asom Sahitya Sabha: 73-90 (*In Assamese*).

2463. **Saikia, Mohini Kr.** : 1968 : *Early Assam Muslim Relations and its cultural significance.* Unpub. Ph.D. Thesis, Gau. Univ.

2464. ———— : 1978 : *Assam-Muslim Relations and its cultural significance.* Golaghat, Luit Printers.

2465. **Saikia, N. (Ed.)** : 1980 : *Assam and the Assamese mind.* Jorhat, Asam Sahitya Sabha.

2466. ———— : n.d. : Cha Majdoor Asamiya samaj samparke eti sarab chinta. *(In) Nibandha Nirayas. (Ed.)* by N. Ghatowar. Jorhat, Asam Sahitya Sabha: 59-62 (*In Assamese*).

2467. **Saikia, Panchami** : 1980 : *Some aspect of socio-cultural life of Bodo-Kachari, Assam.* Unpub. M.Sc. dissertation, Anthropology Dept., Dib. Univ.

2468. **Saikia, P.C.** : 1967 : Some magico religious beliefs of the Deuri-Chutiyas. *Jour. of Assam Sc. Soc.,* X.

2469. ———— : 1967-68 : Magiye-bisu : A festival of the Deuri-Chutiya *Jour. of Gau. Univ.,* 8-19 (2), *Science.*

2470. ———— : 1968 : *Chutiya Jati aru Kristi (a lecture).* Gauhati, Sadou Asam Chutiya Sanmilan (*In Assamese*).

2471. ———— : 1970 : *Chutiya Biparjoy (a lecture).* Gauhati, Sadou Asam Chutiya Sanmilan (*In Assamese*).

2472. ———— : 1972 : Deuri jatir parichaya. *Janajati* (*In Assamese*).

2473. **Saikia, P.C.** : 1972 : Individual life cycle: A comparison between the urban and the rural Chutiyas of Dibrugarh. *Bull. Deptt. of Anthropology, Dib. Univ.*, I(1): 33-7.

2474. ———— : 1973 : Memo-Hareruba: Ancestor worship in a Dibongiya Village. *Bull. Deptt. of Anthropology, Dib., Univ.*, II: 16-21 (Ahom).

2475. ———— : n.d. : *Socio Ritual structure of a Dibongiya village.* Ph.D. Thesis, Dib. Univ.

2476. ———— : 1974 : *Deuri-Chutiya.* Jorhat, Asam Sahitya Sabha, 88p (*In Assamese*).

2477. ———————— : Importance of Bihu (Bisu) festival in rural life with special reference to the Deuri-Chutiyas of Assam. *(In) Contemporary Anthropological Research in North-East India. (Ed.)* by B.M. Das. Dibrugarh, Dib. Univ.: 127-32 (This is also *Bull. Anthropology Deptt., Dib. Univ.*, III, 1974).

2478. ———— : 1976 : *The Dibongiyas: Social and Religious life of a priestly community.* Delhi, B. R. Pubg. Corn., 109p.

2479. ———————— : Social change with special reference to marriage customs in Chutiya society. *Proceedings of a Seminar on Social Change in North-East India,* organised by the Deptt. of Anthropology, Dib. Univ., March 26-27.

2480. ———— : 1978 : Ancestor worship : Its changing pattern among the Chutiya migrants. *(In) Cultural and Biological Adaptability of Man with special reference to North-East India. (Eds.)* by A.C. Bhagabati and R.K. Kar (*Bull.Deptt. of Anthropology,* VI, 1977, Dib. Univ.): 139-48 (Dibrugarh).

2481. ———— : 1980 : Marriage and family in the Deuri-Chutiya community. *(In) Family, Marriage and Social Change. (Eds.)* by S.M. Dubey, P.K. Bordoloi and B.N. Borthakur. New Delhi, Cosmo Pubs.: 106-14.

2482. **Saikia, P.C.** : 1986 : Some aspects of the history and culture of the Chutiyas of Upper Assam. *Jour. Assam Research Society* (Guwahati), XXVIII, 1984-85 (1984): 51-61.

2483. ———————— : Asamat janajatirpara jatiloi rupantarar prabahit prakria. *(In) Asamar Manuha. (Ed.)* by B.M. Das. Jorhat, Assam XXX Prakasan Parishad; 116-30 (*In Assamese*).

2484. **Saikia, P.C.** *and* **M.C. Goswami** : 1969-71 : Bahagiyo-bisu: A festival of the Dibongiya. *Jour. Univ. of Gau.*, 42 (2), Science.

2485. **Saikia, P.D.** : 1968 : *Changes in Mikir Society (Socio-Economic study of a Hill Tribe of Assam).* Jorhat, Agro Economic Research Centre, 82p.

2486. **Saikia, P.D.** : 1969 : Changes in Mikir Society : A Case Study of Kanther Terang village, Mikir Hills, Assam. *Indian Jour. of Agricultural Economics* (1968). Agro Eco. Res. Cent., Jorhat.

2487. —————— : Kanther Terang (A Mikir Village). *Rural Life in Assam Hills*. Jorhat, Agro. Eco. Res. Cent.: 1-10.

2488. ————— : 1970 : *Mikir Society*. Jorhat, Agro Eco. Res. Cent.

2489. ————— : 1971 : *Betgarh, Hudubari and Bhoroli*. Jorhat, Agro. Eco. Res. Cent.

2490. ————— : 1972 : Village as a unit of study. (In) *Socio-Economic Research in tribal areas. (Ed.)* by P.C. Goswami. Jorhat, Agro. Eco. Res. Cent.: 112-16 (Namghar, Assamese Hindu).

2491. ————— : 1986 : *Indian Rural Women : A Study on Role and Status of Rural Women in Assam*. Delhi. Mittal Pub., 134p.

2492. ————— : 1992 : Economic and Social status of Rural women (non-tribal) in Assam : A case study. *(In) Status of women in Assam. (Ed.)* by S.L. Baruah. New Delhi, Omsons Pubs. : 35-50.

2493. **Saikia, P.D.** *and* **Durgeswar Borah** : 1992 : *Constraints of economic development in North-East India*. Delhi, Omsons Pubs., 159p.

2494. **Saikia, P.D.** *and* **S.N. Buragohain** : 1985 : Some aspects of Socio-Economic changes in a Mishing village of the river island, Majuli. *(In) Anthropological Perspectives on North-East India. (Bull. Deptt. of Anthropology, Dib. Univ.* X, 1981) : 15-25.

2495. ————— : 1989 : Folklore in societal development in relation to arts, culture and belief. *Himalaya : Man and Nature,* XII (4), Sept. : 10-3 (Bodo, Kachari, Rabha etc.).

2496. **Saikia, P.D., K. Gopi** *and* **Anjali Lekharu** : 1986 : *Indian Rural Women: A study on role and status of rural women in Assam*. Delhi, Mittal Pubs., 134p.

2497. **Saikia, P.D., U. Phukan, D. Bora** *and* **C. Kalita** : 1977: *Socio-Economic development in the North-East India with special reference to Scheduled Caste and Scheduled Tribe. Proceedings of an Academic Seminar, North East Zone*, organised by Dhemaji College, Lakhimpur.

2498. **Saikia, T.C.** : 1927 : Anthropological notes and news: The frog marriage in Assam. *Man in India*, VII(1), Jan.-March: 66.

2499. —————— : The frog marriage in Assam (The Pouranic story). *NII*, MI(2-3), April-Sept.: 194-95 also, VII (4): 210-11.

2500. **Samanta, R.K.** : 1980 : Notes on Hill tribes of North-East India. *MII,* 60(1-2), June: 129-34.

2501. ———— **(Ed.)** : 1994 : *India's North-East : The Process of change and development.* Delhi, B.R. Pubs., 198p.

2502. **Samanta, R.K.** *and* **M.M. Adhikary** : 1988 : Marriage systems among tribals of North-East India: An overview. *MII*, 68 (4), Dec.: 401-12 (Deuri-Chutiya, Lalung etc.).

2503. **Sankalia, H.D.** : 1949 : Review : The Mother Goddess Kamakhya by Bani Kanta Kakati, Published by Punya Prasad Duara, Assam Publishing Corporation Uzanbazar, Gauhati, Assam, 1948, pp. ix+91. *E.A.*, II (4), June: 216-17.

2504. **Sanyal, C.C.** : 1956 : Notes on folklore of Rajbanshis of North Bengal. *Folklore*, 7(1): 50-1.

2505. ———— : 1965 : *The Rajbanshis of North Bengal.* Calcutta, Asiatic Society of Bengal, 272p.

2506. ———— : 1973 : *The Meches and the Totos: The Sub-Himalayan tribes of North Bengal.* Darjeeling, Univ. of North Bengal, 198p (Bodo people of West Bengal).

2507. **Sareen, T.R.** *and* **S.R. Bakshi** ***(Eds.)*** : 1992 : *India Through Ages, Vol. IV: Castes and Tribes of India.* New Delhi, Anmol Pubs.: 1-13.

2508. **Sarkar, Ambika Charan** : 1969 : *Koch Rajbanshi jatir itihas aru Sanskriti* (*In Assamese*). Bongaigaon, Pub. by the author, 117p.

2509. **Sarkar, Jayanta** *and* **B. Datta Ray** : 1990 : *Social and Political Institutions of North-East India.* Calcutta, Anthropology Survey of India, 230p.

2510. **Sarkar, Harimohan** : 1989 : *Rabha Samaj Aru Sanskritir abhas* (*In Assamese*). All Rabha Sahitya Sabha.

2511. **Sarkar, Niranjan** : 1962 : Dimasa marriage system. *Bull. Deptt. of Tribal culture and Folklore Research*, Gau. Univ.: 81-90.

2512. **Sarkar, R.M.** : 1992 : Book Review: *Ethnic Identity, Ethnicity and Social Stratification in North-East India* by N.K. Das. Inter-India Publications, D-17 Raja Garden Extension, New Delhi-110015, 1987, pp. 323, *MII*, 72 (2), June: 253-55.

2513. **Sarma, A.C.** : n.d. : *Tai Ahom system of Government.* New Delhi, Distributed by D.K. Pub.

2514. **Sarma, Ananta Kr.** : 1994 : *Asamat Manasa Pujar eti loka sanskritik Adhyayon: A bibhakta kamrup zilar bishesh ullekhan.* Unpub. Ph.D. Thesis, Gau. Univ. (*In Assamese*).

2515. **Sarma Benudhar** : 1974 : Chutiya Sanskriti. *Souvenir Golden Jubilee issue*. All Assam Chutiya Sanmilan.

2516. **Sarma, Bijoy Kr.** : 1990 : *Darrang jilar utsava anusthanar adhyayana*. Unpub. Ph.D. Thesis, Gau. Univ.

2517. **Sarma, Binod** : 1979 : A note on the Assamese Jikir and its philosophy. *Folklore*, XX (12), Dec.: 277-80.

2518. ———— : 1981 : Tree worship in Assam. *Folklore*, XXII (2), Feb.: 34-41.

2519. **Sarma, Debabrat** : 1986 : *Change and continuity in a village community: A case study of Niz Haje village in Kamrup District*. Unpub. Ph.D. Thesis, Gau. Univ.

2520. **Sarma, Dimbeswar** : 1968 : Religious fairs and festivals of Assam. *Jour. Assam Research Society*, XVIII: 22-45.

2521. **Sarma, Dipti** : 1992 : The Women of the Brahmaputra valley in the freedom struggle (1921-47)... *(In) Status of Women, Assam. (Ed.)* by S.L. Baruah. New Delhi. Omsons Pubs.: 110-17.

2522. **Sarma, Gobinda Prasad** : 1982 : Tribal life and Society in the Assamese Novel. *(In) India's North East. (Ed.)* by Pankaj Thakur. Tinsukia, Prakash Publishing House: 76-94 (literature about tribes in story books)

2523. **Sarma, H.** : 1978 : *Kamrupiya Loka Git Sangrah*. Jorhat, Pub. by the author.

2524. **Sarma, Hem Ch.** : 1987 : A study on Rangali Bihu. *Assam Tribune*, April 14; 4 (3-6).

2525. **Sarma, Hemanta Kr.** : 1968 : The Bhatheli festival of Assam. *Jour. Assam Research Society*, XVIII: 17-22.

2526. **Sarma, Hemanta Kr.** : 1987 : A Folk-Festival: "Mahoho". *Assam Tribune*, Dec. 5: 4(7-8) (Assam, Ahom Buranji).

2527. ———— : 1992 : *Socio-religious life of the Assamese Hindus. (A Study of the Fasts and Festivals of Kamrup district)*. Delhi, Daya Pubg. House, 262p.

2528. **Sarma, Jajneswar** : 1996 : Bihu Ramblings. *Sentinel (Sunday)*, April 14: 1(1-3).

2529. **Sarma, Joy Kanta** : 1978 : Cottage Industry: Bell-metal Workers of Assam, *EPW*, XIII (42), Oct. 21: 1764-65.

2530. **Sarma, Jyotirmoyee** : 1993 : Changes in Tribal Culture in India. *Anthropologyropos*, 88(4/6): 506-08.

2531. ———— : 1990 : Woebegone Crumbling Majuli. *Assam Tribune*, April 18: 4(7-8) (Mishing).

2532. **Sarma, Kailash** : 1994 : *Social movements in Assam with special reference to the tribals.* Seminar on *Social Movements in North-East India with special reference to women, youth and religion,* organised by NEICSSR, Shillong on 26-27 August, 1994 *(Mimeo.).*

2533. **Sarma, Kiran Ch.** : 1988 : The first Public Bihu at Guwahati. *Assam Tribune,* April 13: 4(7-8).

2534. **Sarma, Kiran Ch.** : 1986 : The image of the sweetheart in the songs of Bihu. *Assam Tribute,* April 13: 4(3-6).

2535. ———— : 1988 : The Pujas and the Arts in Assam. *Assam Tribune,* Oct. 17: 4(3-6).

2536. ———— : 1992 : The temple of Mangal Chandi. *Assam Tribune,* Oct. 4: 4(3-6). (Assam).

2537. ———— : 1994 : Bihu and the literature of Assam. *Assam Tribune,* April 15: 4(3-6).

2538. ———— : 1995 : The worship of five. *Assam Tribune,* Jan. 13: 4(3-6) (All India based festival).

2539. **Sarma, Minati** : 1987 : Dowry and Assamese society. *Assam Tribune,* Dec. 27: 4 (3-6), 5 (4).

2540. **Sarma, Mohan** : 1973 : *Census of India 1971, Vol. I, Pt. VI-B: A town of Assam, Kamakhya.* New Delhi, Office of the Registrar General, India, 72p.

2541. **Sarma, Mrigen** : 1986 : Letters to the Editor: Goalpara Folk Dance. *Assam Tribune,* Aug. 25: 4(4).

2542. **Sarma, Mrinal** : 1992 : Village level Institutions among the Hill Karbis in Hamren area of Assam: A preliminary note. *Bull. Deptt. of Anthropology, Gau. Univ.,* VI, March: 40-5.

2543. **Sarma, Mrinal** : 1993 : Techniques and workmanship associated with different artifacts used by the Hill Karbis: An account. *Bull. Anthropology Deptt.,* Gau. Univ., VII: 20-4.

2544. ———— : 1996 : *Ritual structure among the pati Rabhas: An Anthropological Folkloristic study in a village of Kamrup District,* Assam. Calcutta, K.K. Pubn.

2545. **Sarma, Mukunda** : 1963 : Bihur geet bahurangi. *Asam Bani,* April 12 (*In A.*).

2546. ———— : n.d. : Bahurangi (*In Assamese*). Shillong, Chakraborty & Co. *(Assam and Aru. Pr.).*

2547. ———— : 1973 : *Bibah-Bichitra (A Socio-Anthropological book)* Shillong, Pub. by Mrs. Minati Sarma, 255p (*In Assamese*) (Boro-Kachari: 130-53; Ahom: 121-29; Rabha: 154-60; Deuri-Chutia: 162-69; Mishing: 176-84; Mikir: 185-98).

2548. **Sarma, N.C.** : 1982 : Origin and development of the Ojapali Institution in Assam and similar Artforms in other Sparts of India. *Folklore*, 23 (12), Dec.

2549. **Sarma, Nabin Ch.** : 1985 : Folk epic and its impact on early Assamese literature. *(In) Folklore in North East India. (Ed.)* by Soumen Sen. New Delhi, Omsons Pubs.: 70-6.

2550. ——————— : Folk- epiç and its impact on early Assamese life. *Folklore*, 26 (9), Sept.: 161-69.

2551. ————— : 1986 : Study of a few Assamese proverbs. *Folklore*, 27 (3), March: 71-7.

2552. ————— : 1987 : Tradition and innovation of Vyasa Sangita of Assam: A Preliminary Study. *Folklore*, 28 (2), Feb.: 25-33.

2553. ——————— : Chhaygaon Manasa Pujar Parampara. *Campakjyoti*: 18 (*In Assamese*).

2554. ————— : 1988 : The Rabhas and their folk literature: An exposition of the life and culture of the people. *Folklore*, 29 (12), Dec.: 264-71.

2555. ——————— : The Mahabharata-based Art form: Ojapali. Seminar in Folklore Deptt., Gau. Univ. in Feb. on *Folk and Tribal Versions of the Ramayana*, organised by Folklore Deptt., Gau. Univ. and Anthropology Survey of India, Calcutta.

2556. **Sarma, Nabin Ch.** : 1989 : Folk Painting of the Lamkakanda: Discussion in Assamese Perspective. *Folklore*, 30 (10), Oct.: 227-29.

2557. ————— : n.d. : *Essays on the Folklore of North-East Asia*. Guwahati, Bani Prakash.

2558. ——————— : *Asamiya lok sanskritir abhas* (*In Assamese*). Guwahati, Bani Prakash (Folk culture).

2559. **Sarma, Nibedita** : 1986 : Rangali Bihu, Gamocha and wild rhythm. *Assam Tribune*, April 15: 4(3-6).

2560. **Sarma, Nilotpal** : 1993 : The Brahma Religion and Bodo Identity Movement. *(In) Religion in North-East India. (Ed.)* by Soumen Sen, New Delhi, Uppal Publishing House: 123-29.

2561. **Sarma, P.C. (Ed.)** : 1990 : *Dimorua* : *Commemorative volume (18th Conference)*. Guwahati, Kamrup Dist. Sahitya Sabha.

2562. **Sarma, S.** : 1955 : An interesting custom in the Holi festival of Assam. *Jour. Univ. of Gau.*, VI : 217-20.

2563. ————— : 1989 : Spatio-temporal distribution of tribes of North-East India with special reference to Assam. *Proceedings of NEIHA*, 10: 106-11.

2564. **Sarma, Shasi** : 1980 : *Adhunik Asamiya Samaj Bibortanot Sahittikar Bhumika (In Assamese)*. Gauhati., Pub. by the author.

2565. **Sarma, Siddheswar** : 1991 : Identification of tribal pockets in Assam for political strategy based on Historical Perspective and Geographical Review. *Jour. NEICSSR*, 15(2), Oct.: 18-22.

2566. **Sarma, Shibanath** : n.d. : *History of Goalpara District*. (Hajong, Koch, Joldha, Tot tribes).

2567. **Sarma, S.N.** : 1951 : A brief survey of the Vaisnavite Satra Institution of Assam. *Jour. Gau. Univ.*, II: 95-122.

2568. ———— : 1954 : *The Neo-Vaisnavite movement and the Satra Institutions of Assam*. Ph.D. Dissertation, Gau. Univ.

2569. ———— : 1959 : The Satra Institution of Assam. *(In) Souvenir on aspects of the Heritage of Assam*. Gauhati, 22nd Session of Indian History Congress, Dec.: 50-5.

2570. ———— : 1960 : A note on the worship of Suvacani in Assam. *Jour. Assam Research Soc.* (Gau.), XIV: 107-09.

2571. ———— : 1966 : *The neo-Vaisnavite movement and the Satra Institution of Assam*. Gau. Univ., Pub., 240p.

2572. ———— : 1968 : Cultural Heritage of Assam. *(In) Assam: An outline. (Ed.)* by M. Borthakur. Gau. Univ., Geography Deptt.: 6-11.

2573. ———— : 1977-78 : Social changes in Assam, 1750-1950. *Jour. Univ. Gau. (Arta)*, 28-29: 109-21.

2574. ———— : 1981 : Social changes in Assam 1750-1950. *Jour. Gau. Univ. (Eds.)* by M. Neog *et al*, Vols. XXVIII-XXIX (1): 109-21.

2575. **Sarma, S.N.** : 1993 : *Folk Versions of Rama-Katha* in early Assamese. *(In) Rama Katha in Tribal and Folk Traditions of India: Proceedings of a Seminar. (Eds.)* by K.S. Singh and Birendranath Dutta. Calcutta, Seagull Pubn. for Anthropology S.I.: 110-18.

2576. **Sarmah, Ananta Kr.** : 1991 : Tea tribe in Assam. *A.T.*, June 12: 4 (3-6), 7(1-3).

2577. **Sarmah, B.** : 1978 : *Clustering and concentration of tribal population in Assam*. Unpub. M. Phil. Thesis, Deptt. of Geography, CRB, JNU (Delhi).

2578. **Sarmah, B.L.** : 1997 : Socio-Demographic and special relationship between large sized villages and urban centres in Assam, Manipur, Tripura and Arunachal Pradesh. Delhi, M.Phil Dissertation, JNU, 118p.

2579. **Sarmah, K.K.** : 1981 : Boro-Kachari kinship terms : A preliminary note. *Bull. Anthropology Deptt.*, Dib. Univ., VII-VIII (1978-79): 123-31.

2580. ———— : 1985 : A note of the Aitonias: A Buddhist Population of Assam. *Jour. NEICSSR*, IX (2), Oct.: 36-8.

2581. ———— : Cultural profile of a Tea Garden Community: A case-study in Karbi Anglong District, Assam. *Paper presented in a Seminar on Tea Garden' Labourers in North-East India: A Multi-Dimensional Study* held on 25-27 Feb., organised by NEICSSR, Shillong in collaboration with Sacred Heart Theological College, Shillong.

2582. ———— : 1990 : Cultural Profile of a Tea Garden Community: A case-study in Karbi Anglong District, Assam. *(In) Tea Garden Labourers of North-East India (Eds)* by S. Karotemprel and B. Datta Ray. Shillong, Vendrame Institute: 373-78.

2583. **Sattar, Abdus** : 1969 : Samajik achar bayabahar khetrat Asamiya Hindu Musalmanar Ghanisthata. *Nilachal* (Gau.), 1(1): 228-30.

2584. ———— : 1972 : *Sangmisranat Asamiya Sanskriti*. Jorhat, Grantha-peeth (Ajan Fakir of Assam).

2585. **Scidenfaden, Erik** : 1958 : *The Tai Peoples*. Bangkok. The Siam Society (Khamti, Singpho, Mishmi, Ahom).

2586. **Scorpion** : 1991 : Marriage, Guwahati style. *Assam Tribune* Feb. 9: 4 (7-8).

2587. **Seminar** : 1984 : *Tea plantation labour in Eastern India*. Seminar organised by Uni. of North Bengal in Nov. (Deptt. of Sociology & Soc. Anth.).

2588. ———— : 1985 : *Seminar on Common Motifs in Indian Folklore*, organised jointly by Central Institute of Indian Languages, Mysore and Deptt. of Manipuri language and literature, Manipur Univ., Imphal, June 1-3, 1985.

2589. ———— : *Seminar on Ethnicity Cooperation and Conflict in Eastern Himalayas* held at Shillong organised by North Eastern Council. (*Mimeo.*).

2590. ———— : 1989 : Status of Women (Report). *Seminar paper of ICSSR*, Guwahati, February.

2591. ———— : 1992 : *National Seminar on Tribal Women and Development organised by Assam Institute of Research for Tribals and Scheduled Castes in Guwahati* from April 4 to 6, 1992.

2592. ———— : 1994 : *Three days Seminar on Vaishnavite Satras of the State Assam at State Museum Guwahati*, Nov. 28-30 by State Directorate of Museums.

2593. **Seminar** : 1996 : *Workshop Seminar on Folklore at Gauhati University* on 12-16 March, 1996 organised by Central Institute of Indian Language (Mysore), Tezpur Univ. and Gau. Univ.

2594. ——————— : *Ethnic Situation in North-East India: Fields and Frontiers*. Shillong, Anth. Survey of India (Golden Jubilee, 13-14 Sept. 1996).

2595. ——————— : *Seminar on Karbi people* by T.R.I. Guwahati on 19-21 Sept. 1996 (*Mimeo.*).

2596. **Sen, Jayotirmoy** : 1992 : Falimari : A socio-economic profile of a rural settlement in Kooch-Bihar district, West Bengal. *Geographical Review of India,* 54 (2), June : 85-90.

2597. **Sen, Sipra** : 1966 : *The Lalungs of Nambar Lalung Gaon (Nowgong District of Assam)*. Unpub. M.Sc. Dissertation, Anthropology, Deptt., Gau. Univ., 201p.

2598. ————— : 1985 : *The Tribes of Meghalaya*. Delhi, Mittal Pubn., 170p.

2599. ————— : 1986 : *Arunachal Pradesh and the tribes*. Delhi, Gian Pub. House, 232p.

2600. ————— : 1987 : *Tribes of Nagaland*. Delhi, Mittal Pubn., 283p.

2601. **Sen, Sipra** : 1992 : *Tribes and Castes of Manipur*. Delhi, Mittal Pubn., 371p.

2602. ——————— : *Tribes of Mizoram*. Delhi, Gian Pub. House, 428p.

2603. ————— : 1993 : *Tribes of Tripura*. Delhi, Gyan Pub. House, 250p.

2604. **Sen, Soumen. (Ed.)** : 1985 : *Folklore in North-East India*. New Delhi, Omsons Pub., 233p.

2605. ——————— : Book Review : Sixth Schedule to the Constitution of India by B.L. Hansaria, Ashok Publishing House, Guwahati-781 001, 1983, pp. viii+75, Appendices pp. 342, *Jour. NEICSSR*, IX (1), April: 63-4.

2606. ————— : 1991 : Status of Folklore studies in North-East India. *(In) Proceedings of North East India History Association: Twelfth Session. (Ed.)* by J. B. Bhattacharjee. Shillong, History Deptt., North Eastern Hill Univ.: 52-9.

2607. ——— **(Ed.)** : 1993 : *Religion in North-East India*. New Delhi, Uppal Pub. House, 187p.

2608. **Sen, Soumen** : 1994 : Preservation of culture with special reference to North-East India. *Jour. North Eastern Council (Shillong)*, XIV (1), Jan.-March: 8-12.

2609. **Sen, Soumen** : 1994 : Folklore and Anthropology, *4th D.N. Majumdar lecture*. Anthropology Deptt., NEHU, 25th July at 2pm.

2610. **Senapati, Balairam** : 1963 : Lalungsakalar Bihu. *(In) Uchhabar Rongchora. (Ed.)* by A.C. Hazarika. Gauhati, Pub. by the editor (*In Assamese*).

2611. **Senapati, Ganesh Ch.** : 1975 : Tiwa Samajar Ashouch Bidhi. *(In) Tiwa Sampradayar parichaya. (Eds.)* by All Assam Tiwa Youba Chatra Sanmilan. Jorhat, Asam Sahitya Sabha: 14-26 (*In Assamese*).

2612. ————— : 1975 : Tiwa jatir mankhar sthapan aru Sha-Daha-Pratha. *(In) Tiwa Sampradayar parichaya. (Eds.)* by All Assam Tiwa Youba Chatra Sanmilan. Jorhat, Asam Sahitya Sabha: 41-78 (*In Assamese*).

2613. **Sengupta, A.K.** *et al* : 1959 : The Kacharis of Assam. *Folklore*, II (2): 226-27.

2614. **Sengupta, Gaurangagopal** : 1958 : The Bihu Festivals of Assam. *Indian Folklore*, I(4), Oct.-Dec.: 52-4.

2615. **Sengupta, Gaurangagopal** : 1959 : The Kacharis of Assam. *Indian Folklore*, II(3), July-Sept.: 226-27.

2616. **Sengupta, S.** : 1972 : Village study as a tool of study in tribal areas. *(In) Socio Economic Research in Tribal Areas. (Ed.)* by P.C. Goswami, Jorhat, Agro Eco. Res. Centre: 106-11.

2617. **Sengupta, S.** : 1981 : Madhupur Satra and Resurrection of Mahapurus Sankardev. *Proceedings of NEIHA*, I: 118-19 (1980).

2618. **Sengupta, Sailendranath** : 1953 : *The Caste system in Bengal. (In) Census of India 1951, West Bengal, Land and Land Revenue Department, The Tribes and Castes of West Bengal* by A. Mitra. Alipure, Govt. Printing: 11-81.

2619. **Sengupta, S.C.** : 1987 : *Social transition in Assam. Proceedings of NEIHA*, 8 : 291-99.

2620. **Sengupta, Santanu** : 1992 : *The status of Assamese women in religion. (In) Status of Women in Assam. (Ed.)* by S.L. Baruah. New Delhi, Omsons Pubs.: 82-92.

2621. ————— : 1994 : *Assam's tryst with federalism: Tale of two Hills*. New Delhi, Vikas Pubg. House.

2622. **Sengupta, Sarthak** : 1985 : *The Sonowal Kachari. Proceedings of People of India pre-test Seminar of An. S.I.* Shillong on Dec. 5.

2623. ——————— : 1994 : Anthropological studies among the Koch population of Goalpara District, Assam. *(In) Tribal Situation in North East India. (Ed.)* by Sarthak Sengupta, New Delhi, Inter India Pub.: 230-40.

2624. ——————— **(Ed.)** : *Tribal situation in North East India.* New Delhi, Inter India Pub., 265p.

2625. ——————— **(Ed.)** : *Tribes of North-East India.* Delhi, Gyan Pub. House, 260p.

2627. ——————— : 1996 : *Sonowal. (In) Encyclopaedic Profile of Indian Tribes (Eds)* by Sachchidananda and R.R. Prasad. New Delhi, Discovery Pubg. House: 944-46.

2626. ——————— **(Ed.)** : *People of North East India.* New Delhi, Gyan Publishing House, 256p.

2628. **Sengupta, Sarthak** *and* **Jagadeeshwar Lal Sharma** : 1990 : Jhumar: Folksongs and dances of tea garden Labourers of Assam. *(In) Tea Garden labourers of North-East India. (Eds.)* by S. Karotemprel and B. Datta Roy. Shillong, Vendrame Institute: 214-26.

2629. **Sensowa, Prafulla Kr.** : 1995 : *Impact of the Scheduled Castes component schemes among the Scheduled Castes of Assam. (In) Core Problems of the Scheduled Castes of Assam. (Ed.)* by Bimal Kr. Hazarika. Guwahati, AIRTSC(TRI): 107-19.

2630. **Sentinel** : 1995 : Koch Rajbonshi team in Delhi demand for S.T. status, March 20: 3(7-8).

2631. ——————— : Ali-Aye-Ligang on Feb. 15, Feb. 10: 3 (1-2) (Dergaon Mising community's agricultural festival in Mirang Ghar).

2632. ——————— : 1995 : Tea tribes meet held, March 7: 3(1-2) (Asam Chah Janajati Samitee, 70 lakh tea tribes of Assam).

2633. ——————— : Elementary physics explains phenomenon, say scientists : People go crazy over 'miracle', Sept. 22: 1(3-6) (Onlookers thronged temples in the city today, 21st Sept. 1995 as reported idols of Lord Ganesha "drinking milk").

2634. ——————— : Missions destroyed tribal culture, felt Elwin, Oct. 11: 1(4-8) (Dr. Daniel (O'Connor in NEHU Oct. 10, 1995).

2635. ——————— : Muttack-Moran seek autonomy, Nov. 20: 3(7-8) (Chabua).

2636. **Sentinel** : 1996 : Land reform day on Aug. 26, Aug. 13: 3(5) (Asam Rajyik Krishok Sabha, peasantry in India etc.).

2637. ——————— : S.T. status demanded, Aug. 20: 3(6) (Mattak and Moran).

2638. ——————— : Editorial : The Sixth Schedule State. *Sentinel*, Jan. 10: 4(1-2) (Ahom, Koch-Rajbonshi, Moran, Matak, OBC).

2639. ——————— : S.T. status granted to Koch-Rajbonshis, Jan. 29: 1(6) (The Centre has included the Koch Rajbonshis in the list of Sch. Tribes of Assam, excluding those in the autonomous districts).

2640. ——————— : Editorial: Premium on Backwardness, Jan. 31: 4(1-2) (Koch Rajbanshi got Sch. Tribe Status on 28th Jan. 1996, Ahom, Moran, Matak too will get soon).

2641. ——————— : Advertisement of Cong-I, Jan. 31: 1(5-8) (Sch. Tribe status, tea garden labourer and ex-tea garden labourer, Tai-Ahom, Matak, Maran, Chutia, Hajang, Tea garden labourer etc.).

2642. ——————— : Letters to the Editor: An alluring appeal by a member of the Kayastha, Feb. 2: 4(3) (Kayasthas are made equal to the rank of Sch. Caste).

2643. ——————— : Ali-Aye-Ligang on Feb. 14, Feb. 13: 3 (3) (2nd Wednesday this festival is observed at the premises of the Murong Ghar; *Liggad* is the main function of this festival).

2644. **Seyie, K.** : 1989 : Letters to the Editor: A Naga Assessment. *Assam Tribune*, Feb. 28: 4(4-5) (Bodo, Karbi, Dimasa).

2645. **Shakespear, J.** : n.d. : *Dancing among the Hill Tribes of Southern Assam*. Shillong, Assam Secretariat Press, 7 p.

2646. ——————— : 1911 : Note on rain stopping. *Folklore*, XXII (3).

2647. ——————— : 1913 : The Pleasing of the God Thangjing. *Man*, 13 (50).

2648. **Shakespear, L.W.** : 1914 : *History of Upper Assam, Upper Burmah and North-Eastern Frontier*. London, Macmillan & Co., 272p.

2649. ——————— : 1929 : *History of the Assam Rifles*. London, Macmillan, 301p.

2650. **Sharma, A.C.** : 1992 : (n.d.) : *Tai Ahom system of Government*. New Delhi, B.R. Pubn., 165p.

2651. **Sharma, A.K.** : 1993 : *Emergence of early culture in North-East India*. New Delhi, Aryan Books International: 3-5, 8, 9, 13, 20, 21, 43, 10, 18, 22, 24, 36.

2652. **Sharma, A.K.** : 1993 : *Emergence of early culture in North-East India*. New Delhi, Gyan Pubg. House.

2653. **Sharma, Ananta Kr.** : 1991 : Tea Tribes in Assam. *Assam Tribune*, June 12.

2654. **Sharma, Arvinda Kr.** : 1990 : Asamiya Lok Katha: Narkasur ki Katha. *Pur.Pra. (Lok Bharati)*, July 22: 3(2-4) (*In Hindi*).

2655. ———— : 1991 : Bhogali Bihu ka tatparya (*In Hindi*). *Pur. Pra.*, Jan. 13: 4(1-6).

2656. ———— : Asam men Holi. *Pur. Pra. (Suppliment)*, Feb. 28: I (1-5) (*In Hindi*).

2657. ———— : Asam ka sanskritik tohar: Bihu (*In Hindi*). *Pur. Pra.*, April 14: 1(1-5).

2658. ———— : 1992 : Apne Asom ka Kangali Bihu (*In Hindi*). *Pur. Pra.*, Oct. 17: 4(3-8) (Kati Bihu is Kangali Bihu).

2659. ———— : 1993 : Bihu : Hamara paitrik dharohar (*In Hindi*). *Pur. Pra.*, Jan. 13: 5(3-6).

2660. ———— : Bihu ki bahar rahe barkarar. *Pur. Pra. (Loh.Bha.)*, April 13, I (1-4) (*In Hindi*).

2661. ———— : Asom me Dipavali. *Pur. Pra. (Loh.Bha.)*, Nov. 14: I (5-8) (*In Hindi*).

2662. **Sharma, Arabinda Nath** : 1979 : Tantric and cult dances of Assam. *Sangeet Natak*, 52, April-June: 27-30.

2663. ———— : 1994 : Aji Bihu Bihu, Kali Bihu, Bihu. *Pur. Pra.*, April 14: 5(1-4) (*In Hindi*).

2664. ———— : Ambubhasi Mela aur Mandir nirman ka mahatma (*In Hindi*) *Pur. Pra.*, June 25: 4(3-7).

2665. **Sharma, Babulal** : 1994 : Asamiya kala sanskriti par 'paschattya' ka kasta shinkaja?: *Pur. Pra.*, April 14: 5(1-6) (*In Hindi*).

2666. **Sharma, Benudhar** : 1969 : Fool Chandan. Gauhati, *Asam Joti*, 146p (In A.) (About Muslim's Garia group).

2667. ———— : 1974 : Chutia kristi. *(In) Smriti Grantha. (Ed.)* by Paban Ch. Saikia. Dibrugarh, Sadou Asam Chutia Sanmilanar Astadash Adhibeshan, Sonali Jayanti (*In Assamese*).

2668. ———— : 1981 : Prachin Matak rajyar itibritta. *(In) Mayamara stra Samaj: Bhasan aru Pravandha. (Ed.)* by Sushil Kr. Gogoi. Chabua (Assam), Mayamara Kala Kristi Anusandhan Aru Prachar Samity: 1-22 (*In Assamese*).

2669. **Sharma, Binod** : 1979 : A note on Assamese Jikir and its philosophy. *Folklore*, Dec.: 277-80.

2670. **Sharma, D.N.** : 1987 : Dimasa Kacharis of Assam. *Amrita Bazar Patrika*, Aug. 31: 7 (2-5).

2671. **Sharma, Hemant** : 1990 : Asomiya mantra sahitya (translated in Hindi by Chitra Mahanta). *Pur. Pra. (Loh. Bha.),* June 24: I(1-8).

2672. —————— : Asamiya Mantra Sahitya (2nd Part). *Pur. Pra. (Loh. Bha.),* July 1: 2(7-8).

2673. —————— : Asamiya Mantra Sahitya. *Pur. Pra.*, July 8: 2(7-8).

2674. —————— : Asamiya Mantra Sahitya. *Pur. Pra. (Loh. Bha.),* July 15: 2(1-4).

2675. **Sharma, Hemanta Kr. (Ed.)** : n.d. : *Asamiya lokagiti Sanchayan: A Collection of Assamese Folk songs.* Gauhati, the author, 304p (Pt. I).

2676. —————— : *Assamiya Lokagit : Sanchayan* (A collection of Assamese Folk songs). Gauhati, Pub. by the author, 304p. (*In A.*).

2677. **Sharma, H.C.** *and* **B. Choudhury (Eds.)** : 1983 : *Souvenir: Anthropological Society of North-East India (19th Annual Session).* Gau.Univ., Deptt. of Anthropology, 76p.

2678. **Sharma, J.L.** : 1987 : *Traditional and changed the migrant Oraons in Assam: A case study.* Unpub. Ph.D. Thesis, Dib. Univ., Anthropology Deptt.

2679. ———— : 1992 : Birth and name giving ceremony among the Oraons of Assam. *Bull. Deptt. of Anthropology, Dib. Univ.*, 18-19 (1989-90): 151-56.

2680. **Sharma, J.L.** *and* **Sarthak Sengupta** : 1985 : Jhumar: Folk songs and dances of Tea Garden Labourers of Assam. *Paper presented in a Seminar on Tea garden labourer in North-East India: A Multi-Dimensional study*, held on 25-27 Feb., organised by NEICSSR, Shillong in collaboration with Sacred Heart Theological College, Shillong.

2681. **Sharma, Manorama** : 1982 : Socio-Economic changes in Assam: 1870-1900. *North-East Quarterly,* I(2), Nov.

2682. ———— : 1990 : *Social and Economic changes in Assam: Middle class hegemony.* New Delhi, Ajanta Pubn.

2683. ———— : 1991 : Class formation in Assam: The Agrarian Sector (1911-1947). *(In) Proceedings of NEIHA, Twelfth Session.* Shillong, Hist. Deptt., NEHU: 376-83.

2684. **Sharma, Naba** : 1988 : Clinging to age-old tradition. *Economic Times (Supplement),* Oct. 7: 7(5-8).

2685. **Sharma, N.C.** : 1988 : Shamanistic dance associated with the worship of the snake Goddess Manasa in Assam. *Folklore,* 29 (7), July: 145-52.

2686. —————— : *Essays on folklore of North Eastern India. Pathsala (Assam),* Bani Prakash.

2687. **Sharma, Nabin Ch. (Ed.)** : 1993 : *Darang Raj Bangsabali* (*In Assamese*). Guwahati, Bani Prakash.

2688. **Sharma, Nalni Ranjan** : 1989 : *The Kamarupa School of Dharmasastra.* Unpub. Ph.D. Thesis, Gau. Univ.

2689. **Sharma, Nalini Ranjan** : 1994 : *The Kamarupa School of Dharma Sastra.* Guwahati, Distributed by United Pubn.

2690. **Sharma, Prema** : 1996 : Janajivan se juri me Makar sanskranti, *Pur. Pra.,* Jan. 14: 5(7-8) (*In Hindi*).

2691. **Sharma, Rajkumar** : 1996 : Sow varsha purane Sri Sri Hanuman Mandir ki pouranik Mahatta *(in Hindi). Pur. Pra.,* March 4: 5 (1-8) (Ulubari, Guwahati).

2692. **Sharma, Ramen** : 1991 : Tejpur: Sanskritik virasat ka amulya dastavej (In Hindi). *Pur. Pra.,* Jan. 30: 5(1-8).

2693. **Sharma, Remesh Ch** : 1994 : Kamakhya: Dakhya Prajapati ke yagya se sangbandhit katha hi jukti sangat hai (*In Hindi*). *Pur. Pra.,* Sept. 20: 5(1-2).

2694. ———— : 1995 : Rabha janajati men "marei" geet-prastuti (*In Hindi*). *Pur. Pra..,* April 4: 5(3-6) ('Marei' worship Shiv, Marei puja or Manasa puja, North Kamrup, Darang dist.).

2695. **Sharma, Surajit** : 1983 : *Anthropological field report on the people of Kolowlowa Deuri Gaon, with special reference to fishing, death and disposals and ritual.* Unpub. M.Sc. Dissert. Anthropology Deptt., Dib. Univ.

2696. **Sharma, T.C.** : 1983 : The Indo-Mongoloid and their contributions to the culture and civilisation of India. *Bull. Tribal Research Institute,* I.

2697. **Sharma, T.C.** *and* **D.N. Majumdar (Eds.)** : 1980 : *Eastern Himalayas (A Study on Anthropology and Tribalism).* New Delhi, Cosmo Pub., 221p.

2698. **Sharma Thakur, Ganesh Ch.** : 1962 : Death and disposal of the dead among the Phakials. *Bull. Gau. Univ.,* Deptt. of Anthropology.

2699. **Sharma Thakur, Ganesh Ch.** : 1972 : *Plain Tribes of Lakhimpur, Dibrugarh, Sibsagar and Nowgong*. Shillong, Tribal Research Institute, 104p. (Mishing, Deori, Chutia, Sonowal Kachari, Phakeal, Khamyang, Aitonia, Turung, Lalung, etc.).

2700. ———— : 1976 : Socio-Economic change in post-independence period in a tribal village in Assam. *North-East Research Bull.*, Dib. Univ., VII, Summer: 40-50.

2701. ———— : *A study on the Socio-Cultural life of the Tai Phakes of Assam*. Unpub. Ph.D. Thesis, Dib. Univ., Anthropology Deptt.

2702. ———— : Changing trends of Phake socio-cultural life. *Proc. of a Seminar on Social change in North-East India* organised by the Deptt. of Anthropology, Dib. Univ., March 26-27.

2703. ———— : 1977 : Salient features of the kinship system of the Tai Phakes of Assam. *Bull. Dib. Univ., Deptt. of Anthropology*, 5 (1976): 27-33.

2704. ———— : Marriage among the Lalungs (Tiwas). *Proc. of a Seminar and 3rd Conference of the NEI Sociological Asso.* held on Feb. 22-24, 1977.

2705. ———— : 1978 : Selective assimilation among the Tai-Phakes: A case study. *(In) Cultural and Biological Adaptability of Man with Special Reference to North-East India. (Eds.)* by A.C. Bhagabati and R.K. Kar (Bull. Deptt. of Anthropology, VI, Dib. Univ., 1977): 54-8.

2706. ———— : 1980 : Marriage among the Lalungs (Tiwas). *(In) Family, Marriage and Social Change. (Eds.)* by S.M. Dubey, P.K. Bordoloi and B.N. Borthakur. New Delhi, Cosmo Pub.: 90-8.

2707. ———— : 1982 : *The Tai Phakes of Assam*. Delhi, B.R. Pub., 292p.

2708. ———— : 1983 : A cultural profile of a lesser known tribe: The Lalungs. *Bull. Tribal Research Inst.*, I(I).

2709. ———— : The Plain Tribes of Assam: Spatial pattern of clustering and concentration. *Bull. Tribal Research Inst.*, I(I).

2710. ———— : 1984 : Problems of marketing among the plain tribes of Assam. *(In) Marketing in North-East India: Problems of Rural Markets. (Ed.)* by J.B. Ganguly. New Delhi, Omsons Pub.: 52-8.

2711. ———— : The Lalungs (Tiwas). *(In) The Tribes of*

North-East India. (Eds.) by S. Karotemprel. Calcutta, Firma KLM.: 138-56.

2712. **Sharma Thakur, G.C.** : 1985 : The Kaibartas of Assam: Some reflections on changing traditional occupation in two Kaibarta villages of Jorhat district of Upper Assam. *Bull. Tribal Researh Inst. Assam* (Guwahati), I (V): 33-44.

2713. ——————— : Pu Son Lan : Folk tradition of the Tai Phakes. *(In) Folklore in North-East India. (Ed.)* by Soumen Sen. Delhi, Omsons Pub.: 121-36.

2714. ——————— : *The Lalung (Tiwas)*. Guwahati, Tribal Research Inst., 127p.

2715. ————— : 1986 : Search for cultural identity among the Chaodangs. *Proc. of a Seminar on question of Nationality, Ethnicity and Cultural Identity in the context of North-East India,* 5-6 Dec., organised by NEICSSR, Shillong.

2716. ——————— : Some demographic aspects of integrated tribal development projects of Assam with special reference to the Marigaon Nagaon I.T.D.P. *(In) The Pattern and Problems of Population in North-East India. (Ed.)* by B. Datta Ray. New Delhi, Uppal Pub.: 335-42.

2717. ——————— : Some reflection on endogenous arrangement of land in traditional tribal societies. *Bull. Deptt. of Anthropology, Dib. Univ.*, XV (1990): 109-15.

2718. ————— : 1987 : 'The Deoris'; "The Lalungs (Tiwas)"; "The Miris (Mishings)"... *(In) Tribes of Assam, Pt. I* by B.N. Bordoloi, G.C. Sharma Thakur and M.C. Saikia. Guwahati, Tribal Res. Inst.: 22-35; 74-98 and 99-112.

2719. ————— : 1988 : Sonowal Kacharis. *(In) Tribes of Assam, Pt. II (Ed.)* by B.N. Bordoloi and G.C. Sharma Thakur. Guwahati, TRI,: 77-93.

2720. ————— : 1990 : The Tai Phakes : Emergence of district identity through affiliation of a World Religion. *Proc. of a Seminar on Status of religion in tribal areas in North-East India* sponsored by NEICSSR, Shillong on 15-16 Feb. (*Mimeo.*).

2721. ——————— : Search for cultural identity among the Chaodangs. *(In) Nationality, Ethnicity and Cultural Identity in North-East India. (Ed.)* by B. Pakem. New Delhi, Omsons Pub.: 173-80.

2722 ——————— : Constraints of tribal development in the plain areas of Assam as reflected in few studies conducted by the

Tribal Research Institute, Assam. *(In) Constraints of tribal development in North-East India. (Ed.)* by B.N. Bordoloi. Guwahati, TRI: 183-201.

2723. **Sharma Thakur, G.C.** : 1992 : A Review Report of the Seminar on Socio-Economic Development of the Scheduled Castes of Assam. *Bull. Assam Inst. of Res. for Tribal and Sch. Castes*, Guwahati, I (VIII): 17-23.

2724. —————— **(Ed.)** : *Socio-Economic Development of the Scheduled castes of Assam*. Guwahati, Ass. Inst. Res. for Tri. & Sch. Castes.

2725. ———— : 1993 : The Tai Phakes : Emergence of a distinct identity through affiliation to a World Religion. *(In) Religion in North-East India. (Ed.)* by Soumen Sen. New Delhi, Uppal Pub.: 116-22.

2726. ———— : 1994 : Socio-cultural dynamics of Scheduled Castes development. *Bull. Assam Inst. Res. for Tri. & Sch. Castes*, I (IX): 5-7.

2727. —————— : Socio-cultural consequences of Tribal Development with Special Reference to the Scheduled Tribes of Assam. *(In) India's North-East: The Process of Change and Development. (Ed.)* by R.K. Samanta. Delhi, B.R. Pub.: 129.

2728. ———— : 1995 : Core problems vis-a-vis Socio-Cultural factors of Scheduled Caste development in Assam. *(In) Core Problems of the Scheduled Castes of Assam. (Ed.)* by Bimal Kr. Hazarika. Guwahati, AIRTSC (TRI): 95-100.

2729. ———— : 1996 : Tai Aitonia. *(In) Encyclopaedic Profile of Indian Tribes. (Eds.)* by Sachchidananda and R.R. Prasad. New Delhi, Discovery Pubg. House: 964-66.

2730. —————— : Tai Khamyang: Tai Phake; Tai Turung. *(In) Ibid* : 967-69; 970; 970-76.

2731. **Sharma Thakur, G.C.** *and* **M.C. Saikia** : 1989 : Report on impact of enforcing liquor prohibition among the Bodo Kacharis in a rural setting : A case study. *Bull.T.R.I.*

2732. **Shashi, S.S.** : 1978 : *Night life of Indian Tribe*. Delhi, Agam Prakashan, 110p.

2733. —————— : *The Tribal Women of India*. Delhi, Sundeep Prakashan, 163p.

2734. ———— **(Ed.)** : 1994 : *Tribes of Assam and Manipur*. New Delhi, Manas Pubn.

2735. **Sharma, Vivek** *and* **Lad Rymbai** : 1990 : To the Editor: Bodo

Labourers in Khliehriat. *Shillong Times*, May 25: 2(5-6) (Bodos of Jaintia Hills, Meghalaya).

2736. **Shastry, B.** : 1958 : History and Culture of Assam. *(In) This is Assam. (Eds.)* by B. Shastry and P.C. Bhattacharya. Gauhati, Assam Sahitya Sabha.

2737. **Shastri, Biswanarayan** : 1962 : *Asamar Janajatiya Sadhu.* Jorhat *(Folklore).*

2738. ———— : 1986 : Tantra: A neglected source of materials for the History of Assam. *Jour. Assam Research Society*, XXVIII, 1984-85(1984): 94-104.

2739. ———— : n.d. : Kamarupa-pithadhikara 14th Patala. *Yoginitantra* (Delhi).

2740. **Shastri, B.N.** : 1989 : Book Review: Essays on Folklore of North Eastern India by N.C. Sharma, Bani Prakash, Pathsala, Assam, 1988, *Folklore*, 30 (8), Aug.: 190.

2741. **Shastri, Bhola Paswan** : 1981 : *Report of the Commission for Scheduled Castes and Scheduled Tribes,* April 1979-March 1980. Delhi, Controller of Pubs. 555p.

2742. **Shastri, B.N.** *and* **P.C. Bhattacharya** : 1958 : *This is Assam.* Jorhat, Asam Sahitya Sabha.

2743. **Sherfuddin, Farida** : 1992 : Status of women in the Assamese Muslim Society. *(In) Status of women in Assam. (Ed.)* by S.L. Baruah. New Delhi, Omsons Pubs.: 1-8.

2744. **Sherring, M.A.** : 1872 : *Hindu Tribes and Castes as represented in Benaras.* Vol. II. Calcutta: 160 (Keot).

2745. **Shillong Times** : 1984 : Tai-Mongoloid and tribal youth festival, April 7: 6(4-5).

2746. ———— : 1988 : Chutiyas demand S.T. status, Aug. 27: 3 (3).

2747. ———— : 1989 : Editorial : The old story back again, Sept. 7: 2 (1-2) (Assam's Manipuri Bisnupriya and Meitei).

2748. ———— : 1992 : A peep, March 12: 4(3-8), 6(5) (Kachari).

2749. ———— : Ethnic stirrings in the North-East, Sept. 5: 5(1-4).

2750. ———— : Looking back (*The Shillong Times*, January 1, 1954). Let the term "scheduled Caste" be a thing of the past, Assam Chief Minister's hope: Lifting up to same level. Sept. 17: 4(1-2).

2751. **Shillong Times** : 1994 : Hajo—An Epitome of composite culture. Jan. 11: 3(3-5).

2752. ————————— : Looking back, *The Shillong Times*, January 10, 1953 "Assam's dance and music". *Shg. T.*, Feb. 21: 4(1-2).

2753. ————————— : Looking Back, The Shillong Times, March 13, 1954: Rajbanshi-Kshatriya convention. Nov. 29: 4(1-2), Dec. 1: 4(1-2).

2754. ————————— : Looking back, November 27, 1954 "Tribal Affairs in New Delhi". March 12: 4(1-2) (Assam, place of Music).

2755. ————————— : Child workers in Assam tea gardens face bleak future. April 1: 3 (3-7).

2756. ——————— : 1996 : Looking back, *The Shillong Times*, March 13, 1954: Rajbangshi Kshatriya convention. Jan. 17: 4(1-2) (All Goalpara Rajbanshi Kshatriya Samaj, Raja Ajit Narayan Deb of Sidli).

2757. **Shimray, R.R.** : 1986 : Relations with Ahom. *(In) Origin and Culture of Nagas* by R.R. Shimray. New Delhi, Somsok Publications: 266-71 (Godapani, Joymati, Lora Raja).

2758. **Shiwakoti, Hari Krishna** : 1983 : *Anthropological field report on the people of Kolowlowa Deuri Gaon, with special reference to kinship system, marriage, fishing, family and clan.* Unpub. M.Sc. Dissert., Anthropology Deptt., Dib. Univ.

2759. **Shukla, Sharad Vidhu** : 1990 Kamakhya ke Deodha aur Deodhani............*(In Hindi)*. *Pur. Pra.*, Aug. 22: 4(3-8).

2760. **Shyam, N.** : 1993 : A Note on the Tai Ramayana. *(In) Rama Katha in tribal and folk traditions of India*: *Proceedings of a Seminar. (Eds.)* by K.S. Singh and Birendranath Datta. Calcutta, Seagull Pub. for Anthropology S.I.: 246.

2761. **Siack, E.** : 1883 : *Census of India 1881 , Assam, Report.* Calcutta, Govt. Press, 96p. (Chandal and Hira castes).

2762. **Siiger, Halfdan** : 1956 : Ethnological field research in Chitral, Sikkim and Assam. *Hidyotidk- Gilolo- gishe* (Middlesex), XXXVI.

2763. **Sills, D.L. (Ed.)** : 1968 : *International Encyclopaedia of Social Science*. The Macmillan Company & the Free Press.

2764. **Singh, Anil Kr. (Ed.)** : 1993 : *Tribes and tribal life, Vol. I: Aspects of Tribal life in India*. New Delhi, Sorup & Sons: 113-33 (some races and tribes of Assam) 339-49 (An account of North Eastern Tribes).

2765. **Singh, B.P.** : 1986 : *The problem of change: A study of North-East India.* New Delhi, Oxford Univ. Press.

2766. **Singh, E. Nilakanta** : 1996 : Tai elements in Manipuri Folklore. *Seminar paper on Traditional culture and folklore in North-East India*, 18-19 Nov., Shillong, NEICSSR.

2767. **Singh, G.P.** : 1990 : *The Kiratas in Ancient India: Spotlight on North East.* Delhi, Gian Pubg. House, 506p. (Kacharis, Chutiyas, Lalung, Miri, Mikir, Dimasa, etc.).

2768. **Singh, Irom Maipak** : 1983 : *Anthropological field report on the people of Kolowlowa Deuri Gaon with special reference to family and clan, agriculture, death and disposal and economic organization.* Unpub. M. Sc. Dissert., Anthropology, Deptt., Dib. Univ.

2769. **Singh, J.P.** : 1994 : On an Assamese Folk view of the British. *NEIHA*, No. 15.

2770. **Singh, Jai Prakash** : 1990 : Source of the wise daughter-in-law from Assam and Birbal. *Proceedings of NEIHA, 11th Session.* Shillong, History Deptt., North Eastern Hill Univ.: 38-42.

2771. **Singh, K Suresh. (Ed.)** : 1972 : *Tribal Situation in India: Proceedings of a Seminar.* Simla, Indian Institute of Advanced Studies, 639p.

2772. **Singh, K.S. (Ed.)** : 1982 : *Tribal Movements in India,* Vol. I. New Delhi, Manohar Pubs., 405p.

2773. ———————— **(Ed.)** : *Economies of the Tribes and their Transformation.* New Delhi, Concept Publishing Comp., 459p.

2774. ——— **(Ed.)** : 1985 : *Tribal Society in India: An Anthropo-Historical Perspective.* New Delhi, Manohar Pubs., 327p.

2775. ————— : 1988 : Land rights of tribal women. *Human Science*, 37(3), Sept. : 260-68 (Koch, Lalung, Dimasa, Semsa, etc.).

2776. ————— : 1993 : *An Anthropological Atlas, Vol. XI, People of India.* Delhi, Oxford Univ. Press.

2777. ———————— **(Ed.)** : *Tribal Ethnography, Customary Law and Change.* Delhi, Concept Pubg. House, 452p.

2778. ———————— **(Ed.)** : *People of India, National Series, Vol. II: The Scheduled Castes.* Madras, Affiliated East-West Press for Anthropology S.I., Calcutta.

2779. ———————— **(Ed.)** : *The Mahabharata in the tribal and* *folk traditions of India*. New Delhi, Anthropology S.I. and Indian Inst. of Advanced Studies (Simla), 266p.

2780. **Singh, K.S. (Ed.)** : 1994 : *People of India, National Series, Vol. III: The Scheduled Tribes*. New Delhi, Affiliated East-West Press for Anthropology S.I., Calcutta, 1266p.

2781. ——— **(Ed.)** : 1996 : *People of India, Vol. XV, State Series: Assam*. New Delhi, Seagull Pub. for Anthropology S.I., Calcutta.

2782. **Singh, K.S.** *and* **Birendranath Datta (Eds.)** : 1993 : *Rama-katha in Tribal and Folk Traditions of India : Proceedings of a Seminar*. Calcutta, Seagull Pub. for Anthropology S.I., 246p.

2783. **Singh, L.G.** : 1972 : *A study of material culture of Mikir*. Unpub. M.Sc. Dissert, Anthropology Deptt., Dib. Univ.

2784. **Singh, L. Tarani Kanta** : 1989 : A look at the Dimasa Kacharis: *Assam Tribune, (Sunday Reading)*, Oct. 15: I(1-8).

2785. **Singh, M. Bokul** : 1980 : *An Account of the Sonowal Kachari of Lepetkata village with special reference to house type, death and disposal and family*. Unpub. M.Sc. Dissert., Anthropology Deptt., Dib. Univ.

2786. **Singh, Niranjan** : 1984 : *Asamiya Sikhar itibritta. Souvenir, Assamese Sikh Association (Assam), Annual Conference, Jan. 21-22, 1984. (Ed.)* by Jiban Singh. Barkola, S. Assamese Sikh Association: 1-10.

2787. **Singh, Sardar Kirpal** : 1982 : Assamese Sikhs, their originality and Assimilation. *(In) Smritigrantha. (Ed.)* by Manjit Singh. Chaparmukh (Assam), Gurdwara Matajir Udbodhani Anusthan: 8-11.

2788. **Singh, Shyama Charan** : 1983 : *Anthropological field report on the people of Kolowlowa Deuri Gaon with special reference to family, clan, house type, marriage, political organization*. Unpub. M.Sc. Dissert. Anthropology Deptt., Dib. Univ.

2789. **Singh, T. Hemant Kr.** : 1983 : *Anthropological field report on the people of Kolowlowa Deuri Gaon with special reference to family, clan, agriculture, death and disposal, marriage*. Unpub. M.Sc. Dissert. Anthropology Deptt., Dib. Univ.

2790. **Singh, T. Shyamacharan** : 1996 : Inter group variability of the Tai people of Assam. *(In) Peoples of North-East India: Anthropological Perspectives. (Ed.)* by Sarthak Sengupta. New Delhi, Gyan Publishing House: 13-30.

2791. **Singh, Yash K.** : 1995 : Marriage system of the Mishings. *Vanyajati*, XLIII (4), Oct.: 6-7.

2792. **Singha, Biren** : 1994 : The Hills are alive (*Translated* by Pradip Acharya). *Assam Tribune, (Sunday Reading)*, April 17: I(1-8) (Dimasa etc.)

2793. **Sinha, A.C.** : 1982 : Nepalese of North-East India : Ethnicity and Resource Appropriation. *(In) Social Tension in North-East India. (Ed.)* by J.B.Bhattacharjee. Shillong, NEICSSR (Calcutta, Research India Pubn.): 84-97.

2794. ——— : 1994 : The North-East India: Perspective of sociological research. *(In) Bi-decennial celebration of North-East India Council for Social Science Research. (Eds.)* by B. Pakem *et al.* Shillong, Jour. NEICSSR : 26-34.

2795. **Sinha, A.C.** : 1986 : *Video penetration in North-East India.* Deptt. of Sociology, NEHU, Shillong.

2796. ———: 1989 : A note on social formation in North-East Frontier Region. *Proceedings of a Seminar on Problems of development and undevelopment in North-East India.* Shillong, Sacred Heart College.

2797. **Sinha, A.K.** : 1991 : Culture conflict and Assam. *A.T., (Sunday Reading)*, April 14: II(1-5).

2798. **Sinha, Amala P.** : 1959 : The Lalung (Member of the Bodo tribe). *Vanyajati* 7(1), Jan.: 11-6.

2799. **Sinha, Harimohan** : 1903 : Notes on the Koch, Poliya and Rajvanshi in Dinajpur. *Jour. Asiatic Society of Bengal*, 72(3): 20-5.

2800. **Sinha, Purna Narayan** : 1986 : Letters to the Editor: Tea Garden Tribe. *Assam Tribune*, Oct. 9: 4(3-4).

2801. ——— : 1987 : Letters to the Editor: Koch-Rajbongshis. *Assam Tribune*, Sept. 11: 4(4).

2802. ——— : 1988 : Unlisted tribes in Assam. *A.T.*, Dec. 28: 4(3-8).

2803. ——— : 1989 : Letters to the Editor: There are many Bodo tribes. *Statesman*, April 12: 8(4-6).

2804. **Sinha, Purna Narayan (Ed.)** : 1993 : *Anthropology of Weaker Sections.* New Delhi, Concept Pub. Com., 632p.

2805. ——— : 1995 : Letters to the Editor: Rajbonshis. *St.*, Feb. 26: 8 (5-6) and Feb. 9: 9(1-5).

2806. **Sinha, Raghuvir** : 1977 : *Religion and culture of North-East India.* New Delhi, Abhinav Pubn.

2807. **Sinha, Samir** : 1995 : Fashion from the land of Bihu. *ST.*, Nov.

4 : 6(1-8) (traditional Mekhla-Chadar of Assam are hand woven on mulberry silk, motifs and pattern, etc.).

2808. **Sinha, S.C. (Ed.)** : 1970 : *Research Programmes on cultural anthropology and allied disciplines.* Calcutta, An. S.I.

2809. **Sinha, Sarat C.** : 1993 : Existing justice system of the ethnic communities. *(In) Criminal Justice System in Assam. (Ed.)* by J. Barooah. Guwahati, Law Res. Inst. High Court.

2810. **Sinha, Sunil** : 1994 : Bihu: Satta aur Sundarata ki gajab ki sakti *(In Hindi). Pur. Pra.*, April 14: 5(1-6).

2811. **Sinha, Surajit** : 1967 : Social integration of the Hill tribes and the plainmen. *(In) A Common Perspective for North-East India. (Eds.)* by Rathin Mitra and B. Das Gupta. Calcutta, Pannalal Das Gupta: XIV-XVI.

2812. ——— **(Ed.)** : 1978 : *Field Studies on the People of India, methods and perspectives in memory of Professor Tarak Chandra Das.* Calcutta, Indian Anthropology Society, 307p.

2813. —— **(Ed.)** : 1987 : *Tribal Polities and State Systems in Pre-Colonial Eastern And North-Eastern India.* Calcutta, K.P. Bagchi, 366p.

2814. **Sircar, A.H.** : 1986 : Letters to the Editor: Goalpara Lokgeet. *Assam Tribune*, Sept. 16: 4 (4-5).

2815. **Snaitang, O.L.** : 1993 : *Christianity and Social change in North-East India.* Calcutta, Firma KLM.

2816. **Social Welfare** : 1975 : Child welfare activities of the Assam Harijan Sevak Sangh. *Social Welfare,* 22(8), Nov.: 23.

2817. **Socio-Economic** : 1962 : *An interim report on the Socio-Economic Survey of the Chaudang Village in Jorhat Sub-Division. Gauhati,* Govt. of Assam.

2818. **Sociology Deptt.,** : 1973 : *Urbanization in Tribal areas in North-East India (with special reference to Pasighat, Dimapur, Diphu, Haflong, Jowai and Aijal)* by the members of the Teaching Staff of Sociology, Dib. Univ. *(Mimeo.).*

2819. ————— : 1975 : *Seminar on Sociological Perspective on North East India And the Second Annual Conference of the North-East India, Sociological Association.* Dib. Univ., Soc. Deptt., March 10-12.

2820. **Sonowal, Barun** : 1980 : *A Study of the Sonowal Kachari of Lepetkata with special reference to agriculture, marriage and kinship.* M.Sc. Unpub. Dissert., Anthropology Deptt., Dib. Univ.

2821. **Sonowal, Chandra Jyoti** : 1992 : Influence of Environmental Factors on a traditional occupation: A case study among the Kumars of Jokai Forest Kumar Gaon, Dibrugarh, Assam. *Bull. Deptt. of Anthropology, Dib. Univ.*, 18-19 (1989-90): 89-97.

2822. ———— : 1993 : Female initiation ceremony among the Deories, a plain tribe of Assam. *Vanyajati*, XLI(4), Oct.: 15-19, 23.

2823. **Sonowal, Chandra Jyoti** : 1995 : Identity crisis and revivalism among Sonowal Kacharis: A plain tribe of Assam. *MII*, 75(1), March: 49-58.

2824. ———— : 1996 : Religious trends and identity crisis: A cross-cultural study among three tribes of Assam. *(In) Peoples of North-East India: Anthropological Perspectives. (Ed.)* by Sarthak Sengupta. New Delhi, Gyan Publishing House: 174-90.

2825. **Sonowal, Gagan Ch.** : 1962 : Sonoyal Kachari. *(In) Asamar Janajati. (Ed.)* by Pramod Ch. Bhattacharya. Jorhat, Asom Sahitya Sabha (*In Assamese*).: 70-8.

2826. **Sonowal, T.** : 1978 : *A Study of kinship system among the Bodos of Chutiya Adabari village of Kokrajhar, Assam*. Unpub. M.Sc. Dissert. Anthropology Deptt., Dib. Univ.

2827. **Soppitt, C.A.** : 1885 : *A Historical and descriptive account of the Kachari tribes in the North Cachar Hills and specimens of Tales and Folklore*. Shillong, Assam Secretariat Printing Press (*Reprinted* in 1901).

2828. **Spectrum** : 1977 : *North-Eastern Spectrum*, Vol. I, 1976-77. Gauhati, Spectrum Publication.

2829. **S.P.C.** : 1992 : Gauhati—The Temple Town of Assam and its Temples. *(In) India Through Ages, Vol. II: Temples of India. (Eds.)* by T.R. Sareen and S.R. Bakshi. New Delhi, Anmol Pubn.: 269-75.

2830. **Srikant, L.M.** : 1957 : Notes: Scheduled Tribes. *Vanyajati*, V(1), Jan.: 1-3, 44-5.

2831. ———— : 1961 : Tribal welfare under Panchayati Raj. *Vanyajati*, IX (4), Oct. : 136-44 (Assam etc.).

2832. ———— : 1962 : *Tenth Report of the Commissioner for Scheduled Caste and Scheduled Tribe.* Delhi, Controller of Pubn.

2833. **Srivastava, L.R.N.** : 1968 : Habitation, origin and migration of North-Eastern Tribe. *Vanyajati*, XVI(4), Oct. : 123-32.

2834. ———— : 1969 : The Problem of Modernization of the Tribes of North-East India. *Bull. Cultural Research Inst.* (Cal.), VIII (1-2): 21-5.

2835. **Srivastava, R.P.** : 1973 : *The impact of community development programme and culture change among the Miris of Assam.* Dibrugarh, Dib. Univ. (Unpub. Report).

2836. **S.S., In Comp.** : 1974 : Book Review : Kamakhya, a town of Assam, Census of India 1971, Vol. I, Part VI-B-Mohan Sarma, Office of the Registrar General, India, New Delhi, 72 pages, *MII*, 54(2), April-June: 175.

2837. **Stack, E.** : 1883 : *Census of India 1881, Assam, Report.* Calcutta, Govt. Press: 73-5, 86-90, 94-5 (Kaibartta, Kewat, Koch, Mikir).

2838. ———— : 1908 : *The Mikirs* (From the Papers of Edward Stack, Edited, Arranged and Supplemented by Sir Charles Lyall). London, David Nutt, 183p.

2839. **Statesman** : 1994 : Tribal Affinity Replaces Ethnic Strife in North Cachar. July 10: 16(1-3).

2840. **Stewart, R.** : 1855 : Notes on Northern Cachar. *Jour. Asiatic Soc. of Bengal*, 24: 582-657 (Cacharee etc.).

2841. **Stonor, C.R.** : 1950 : Foundation legends (Note). *Man*, 50 (27).

2842. **Subba, T.B.** : 1984 : Inter Ethnic Relationship in North-East India and the negative solidarity thesis. *Proceedings of XVII All India Sociological Conference*, Dec. 28-30.

2843. **Subba, T.B.** : 1988 : Interethnic relationship in North-East India and the Negative Solidarity Thesis. *Human Sc.*, 37(4), Dec.: 369-77.

2844. ———— : 1992 : Inter-ethnic relationship in North-East India and the Negative Solidarity Thesis. *MII*, 72(2), June: 153-63.

2845. **Swami Yoganand Giri** : 1950 : *Tribes of India*. New Delhi, Bharatiya Adimjati Sevak Sangh. *(Ed.)* by V. Raghaviah (Rajbanshis: 21).

2846. **Syamchaudhuri, N.K.** : 1966 : Indigenous irrigation in Assam: An eco-cultural trait. *(In) Professor Suryya Kumar Bhauyan Commemoration volume. (Ed.)* by M. Neog and H.K. Barpujari. Gauhati, XXII Session of All India Oriental Conference.

2847. ———— : 1967 : Anthropology and tribes of Assam. *(In) Common Perspective for North-East India. (Eds.)* by Rathin Mitra and B. Das Gupta. Calcutta, Pannalal Das Gupta: 58-63 (Mikir, Kachari, etc.).

2848. **Syamchaudhuri, N.K.** *and* **S.K. Biswas** : 1963 : A trait of making earthenwares in the Mizo District and its cultural evaluation in Assam. *Bull. Anthropology S.I.*, XII (1-2), Jan.-June: 57-64.

2849. **Syamchaudhuri, N.K.** *and* **M.M. Das** : 1973 : *The Lalung Society: A Theme for Analytical Ethnography* (Memoir No. 31). Calcutta, Anthropology S.I., 165p.

2850. **Taher, M.** : 1982 : A glimpse of the population geography of North-East India. *Souvenir: North-East India Geographical Society (NEIGS),* 82p.

2851. **Taher, Md.** : 1977 : Tribes of North-East India: A Diagnostic Survey in special pattern. *North Eastern Geographer* (Gauhati), IX (1-2): 16-26.

2852. **Taid, Tabu** : 1970 : Mishing Samajat Narir Sthan. *(In) Mising Sanskritir Alekhya. (Ed.)* by Bhrigumuni. Gauhati (*In Assamese*).

2853. **Taid, Tabu** : 1993 : On different aspects of Mishing culture. Proceedings of a Seminar cum-workshop on the *Cultural Heritage of the North-East India*, held on 25th Sept. at Gouri Sadan, Guwahati by Vivekananda Kendra Institute of Culture *(Mimeo.).*

2854. **Talents, P.C.** : 1923 : *Census of India 1921, Vol. VII : Bihar and Orissa*, Pt. I, Report. Patna, Govt. Press: 243 (Kewot).

2855. **Talukdar, B.N.** : 1981 : Assamese cultural Institutions of Shillong. *Proceedings of a Seminar in 1981 on Shillong 1971-1981* organised by NEICSSR, Shillong on 11-12 Dec. (It was Published in 1984, Edited by B.Pakem entitled "Shillong 1971-1981" from Shillong, NEICSSR).

2856. **Talukdar, Harendra Mohan** : 1988 : Letters to the Editor: Recognition as Scheduled Tribe. *Assam Tribune*, Jan. 8: 4(3-5) (Koch-Rajbongshi)

2857. **Talukdar, J.** : 1982 : *A socio-cultural study of the Matak people of Upper Assam with special treatment of the Moran.* Unpub. Ph.D. Thesis, Gau. Univ.

2858. **Talukdar, Jitendra Kr.** : 1981 : Matak shabdar utpatti aru tatparjya. *(In) Mayamara Satra Samaj: Bhasan Aru Pravandha. (Ed.)* by Sushil Kr. Gogoi. Chabua (Assam), Mayamara Kala Kristi Anusandhan Aru Prachar Samity: 67-86 (*In Assamese*).

2859. **Talukdar, Jogendra Nath** : 1992 : *Asamiya Lok-Sanskritir Sanfura.* Guwahati, Padma Prakash. (*In Assamese*) (Asamiya Fakra Jojana; Bihu; Kamrupi Lok-Sanskritit Ainam; Bihu Gitat Nari Soundarjya; Kamrupiya Dharmanusthan; Namghoshat 'Harinam': Namghar etc.).

2860. **Talukdar, Kailash Ch.** : 1990 : A peep into the Mishing religious beliefs and practice. *Proceedings of a Seminar on Status of Religion in Tribal Areas in North-East India* sponsored by NEICSSR, Shillong on 15-16 Feb. (It was Pub. in 1993 by Uppal Pub. House, New Delhi, *(Ed.)* by Soumen Sen *Religion in North East-India*.)

2861. **Talukdar, M., N.A. Begum, D. Dutta, R.K. Dutta, I. Ali, S. Saikia, S. Barua, R. Dutta** *and* **Renu Dutta** : 1975 : *A study on some aspects of Socio-Cultural Life of the Ahoms, Tengakhat.* Unpub. M.Sc. Dissert. Anthropology Deptt., Dib. Univ.

2862. **Talukdar, Phani** : 1976 : Barpeta Satra: A Vaishnava Monastery of Assam. *North-Eastern Spectrum,* 1(3-4), Sept.-Oct.: 26-7, 30.

2863. **Talukdar, Sushanta** : 1995 : Ojapali: Jana manoranjan ka anokha rivaj (*In Hindi*). *Pur. Pra. (Lok Bharati),* June 4: 1(2-5), 2(7-8).

2864. **Tamuli, Jogesh Ch.** : 1916 : *Collection of Assamese folk songs and Ballads.* Gauhati.

2865. **Tamuli, Tirthalochan** : 1994 : Sarthebarir Raiz Mel—1894 (*In Assamese*). *Dainik Asam*, Feb. 1: 4(3-6), 5 (Centenary of *Raiz Mel*).

2866. **Tamuly, Laxminath** : 1992 : Pragjyotisapura : Myth or reality. *Assam Tribune*, April 11: 4(3-8), 7(4-6).

2867. **Tasa, Dewram** : 1986 : *Chah Bagichar Jati-Janajati.* Jorhat, Asam Sahitya Sabha (*In Assamese*), 176p. (Tea garden people).

2868. **Tea Districts Labour Association** *(Comp)* : 1924 : *Hand-book of Castes and Tribes: Employed on Tea Estates in North-East India*. Calcutta, printed by A. Rome, Catholic Orphan Press, 360p. (*Reprinted* in 1989 by Vintage Books, Gurgaon) entitled, *Castes and Tribes in the Tea-Estates of North-East India.*

2869. **Teran, Lenkam** : 1974 : Karbi Janagosthi (*In Assamese*)

2870. **Terang, Jay Sing** : 1965 : *Ek dristit Karbi-Mikir*. Satgaon (Assam), Pub. by the author.

2871. **Terang, R.** : 1978 : Sabin Alun, the Karbi Ramayana. *Souvenir, All India Tribal Conference,* Gauhati.

2872. **Terang, Rongbong** : 1982 : Karbi Lullaby : A Petal of Folklore. *Assam Tribune*, April 23: 4.

2873. ———————— : *Karbi Sahitya Aru Sanskritit Ebhumuki* (*In Assamese*). Jorhat, Asam Sahitya Sabha.

2874. ———————— **(Ed.)** : 1982 : *Wojaru Ahir*. Diphu (Karbi Anglang).

2875. **Terang, Rongbong** *and* **Sabin Aeun** : n.d. : *The Karbi Ramayana.*

2876. **Terang, R.B., P.K. Mohonta, B.K. Gohain** *and* **S.B. Parampanthi** : 1993 : Ramakatha in Karbi Folk Tradition. *(In) Ramakatha in Tribal and Folk Traditions of India: Proceedings of a Seminar. (Eds.)* by K.S. Singh and Birendranath Datta. Calcutta, Seagull Pub. for Anthropology S.I., Calcutta : 183-212.

2877. **Teranpi, Lado** : n.d. : *The role of Karbi women in Society: Past and Present.*

2878. **Teron, Langkam** : 1974 : *Karbi Janagosthi.* Jorhat, Chandrakanta Handique Bhaban (Asam Sahitya Sabha) (*In Assamese*).

2879. **Terwiel, B.J.** : 1975 : *Monks and magic : An analysis of Religious ceremonies in Central Thailand.* Scandinavian, Institute of Asian Studies, Monograph. No. 24 (London, Curzon Press), 52p.

2880. **Terwiel, B.J.** : 1980 : The Tais and their belief in Khuwans: Towards establishing an aspect of Proto-Tai culture. *(In) The Tribal world and its transformation. (Eds.)* by Bhupinder Singh *and* J.S. Bhandari. New Delhi, Concept: 151-73.

2881. ———— **(Ed.)** : 1980-1981 : *The Tai of Assam*, and *The Ancient Tai Ritual*, Vol. I (1980); Vol. II (1981). Gaya, Centres for South East Asian Studies.

2882. ———— : 1981 : The Tai of Assam : Sacrifices and Time Reckoning. *South East Asian Review,* 6(1-2), Jan.-Dec.: 1-191 (Ethnology).

2883. **Thakkar, A.V.** : 1941 : Census of Assam Tribals. *MII*, XXI (4), Oct.-Dec.: 243-47.

2884. **Thakkar. Natbar** : 1958 : Chu-chu-imlong (*In Hindi*). *Vanyajati,* VI (1), Jan.: 18-24.

2885. **Thakur, Meera** : 1994 : Bihu Asamiya jati ke rag-rag men basa hai (*In Hindi*). *Pur. Pra.*, April 14: 5(1-6).

2886. **Thakur, Mini Bhattacharyya** : 1993 : Marriage among the Dibongia Deoris. *Bull. Deptt. of Anthropology, Gau. Univ.*, VII: 25-9.

2887. **Thakur, Pankaj (Ed.)** : 1982 : *India's North East: A Multi-faceted View.* Tinsukia, Prakash Pubg. House, 269p.

2888. ——— **(Ed.)** : 1988 : *Profile of a development strategy for India's North East.* Guwahati, Spectrum Pubn., 282p.

2889. **Thakur, Ram Charan** : n.d. : Book Review: *Uttar Cachar Paharer Lok Sanskriti* by Thaneswar Duara. Haflong, Pub. by the author.

2890. **Thakuria, Nava** : 1996 : Nao Khel of Assam. *Eastern Panorama,* Oct.: 46-7 (Barpeta, Sualkuchi Nao-khel, Satra).

2891. **Thaosen, Sonaram** : 1962 : Dimasa Kachari. *(In) Asomar Janajati. (Ed.)* by Pramod Ch. Bhattacharya. Jorhat, Asam Sahitya Sabha: 44-53 (*In Assamese*).

2892. **Thompson, Virginia** : 1941 : *Thailand the New Siam*. New York: 292-93, 313, 546, 675 (Koch and Meitei).

2893. **Thompson, W.H.** : 1923 : *Census of India 1921, Vol. 5: Bengal, Pt. I: Report*. Calcutta, Govt. Press: 354-56 (Kaibartta, Mahisya, Koch).

2894. **Thomson, R.C. Muirhead** : 1948 : *Assam Valley : Beliefs and Customs of Assamese Hindus*. London, Luzac & Co., 96p (Assamese Brahmin; Miri girl; Ahom sports ; Kamakhya Temple; Mech girl; Kachar Fort etc.).

2895. **T'ien Ju-K' ang** : 1949 : Pai cults and social age in the Tai Tribes of the Yunnan Burma Frontier. *Am. Anthropology*, LI.

2896. **Tribal Research Institute** : 1982 : Proceedings of a Seminar on *The Contribution of Assam Tribes to the Cultural Heritage of Assam and India*, held at Boko (Assam) in State level.

2897. **Tunga, Sudhansu S.** : 1975 : Aryanisation in North-East India. *North Eastern Affairs*, 3(4), Jan.-March: 17-33 (Assam: 23-27, Koch, Ahom, Rabha, Lalung, Hajong etc.).

2898. ————— : 1978 : An obscure people of Cachar called Dheyan. *Jour. NEICSSR*, II (II), Oct.: 9-10.

2899. **Tuolor, Lalhmarthang** : 1995 : Hmar Sikpui Ruoi festival '94 celebrated. *Eastern Panorama*, III (3), Jan.: 45-6 (Haflong).

2900. **Turner, A.C.** : 1933 : *Census of India 1931, Vol. XVIII: United Provinces of Agra and Oudh, Pt. I: Report*. Allahabad, Govt. Press: 619, 631 (Kewat).

2901. **Ullah, Emdad** : 1976 : Muslim saints and their tombs in Assam. *North-Eastern Spectrum*, 1(2), Aug.: 31-5.

2902. **Ullah, W.** : 1990 : An appraisal of special component plan for Scheduled Castes: Problems and prospects. *Assam Information*, XXXXII, Nov.-Dec.: 14-24.

2903. **University of Delhi** : 1970 : Sociology of North East Hill Areas. *Proc. IIIrd Summer School, Kohima* (Delhi Univ.).

2904. **Upadhyaya, Baidyanath** : 1996 : Koch Rajbonshi Bill hangs in balance. *East. Pano.*, Oct.: 26.

2905. **Vaisya, Haragovinda** : 1958 : *Ashamiya Kristi*. Gauhati, N.C. Das, 16p.

2906. **Vanyajati** : 1965 : Bharat ki Uttar Purbi Simanta (*In Hindi*). 13 (2), April: 67-9.

2907. ———— : 1971 : Hamare seema nivashi mitra ka shesh bhag (In H.). *Vanyajati*, XIX (2), April-July : 103-17.

2908. ———— : n.d. : *Souvenir, All India Tribal Conference in Assam*. New Delhi, Bharatiya Adimjati Sevak Sangh.

2909. **Vasu, Nagendra Nath** : 1922 : *Social History of Kamrupa*. Calcutta, Thacker and Spink, 60p *(Reprinted* in 1926, 1933, 1986, 1990).

2910. ———— : 1990 : *The Social History of Kamrupa,* Vols. I, II, III. Delhi, Low Price Pubn., *(Reprinted).*

2911. **Vatsyayan, Kapila** : 1981 : *A study of some traditions of performing arts in Eastern India*. Gau. Univ.

2912. **Vickland, Elten Elizabeth** : 1928 : *Women of Assam*. Philadelphia, Judson's Press, 179p.

2913. **Vidyarthi, L.P.** : 1973 : Tribal researches in the Himalayan region. *North-Eastern Affairs*, 2(1): 75-86.

2914. ———— : 1974 : Priorities in Tribal researches in India. *Jour. of Soc. Research* (Ranchi), XVII(II), Sept.: 1-4 (Assam).

2915. ———— : 1978 : *Rise of Anthropology,* Vol. I. Delhi, Concept Pub. Cor.: 48, 66-67, 347-48, 377-79; Vol. II: 31-3.

2916. ———— : 1986 : *Art and Culture of North East India*. New Delhi, Pubn. Divin., 124p.

2917. **Vidyarthi, L.P.** *and* **B.K. Rai** : 1977 : *Tribal Culture of India*. New Delhi, Concept Pubn., 448p.

2918. **Vintage Books** : 1988-89 : *Castes and Tribes on the Tea Estates of North-East India*. Gurgaon (Haryana), Vintage Books (Reprint of 1924).

2919. **Vivekananda Kendra** : 1993 : *Cultural Heritage of North East*. Seminar-cum-Workshop held on 25 Sept. in Gauri Sadan by Vivekananda Kendra Institute of Culture, Guwahati (Papers given by Tarun Goswami; B.N. Bordoloi; Pradip Sarma; B.K. Gohain and many others).

2920. **Vohra, Sahdev** : 1990 : India's North-East and China's claim. *Amrita Bazar Patrika* Jan. 7: 6(3-8) (Ahom).

2921. **Vrigumuni (Ed.)** : 1970 : *Mishing Sanskritir Alekhya.* Guwahati.

2922. **Vyas, Shrikant** : 1952 : *Asam Ki Lok Kathayen (In Hindi).* Delhi, Atmaram & Sons.

2923. **Waddell, L.A.** : 1901 : The Tribes of the Brahmaputra Valley. *JASB,* LXIX, Pt. III (1900) (*Reprinted* in 1975 by Sanskaran Publications, Delhi, 127p).

2924. ———— : 1911 : A note on the derivation of Miri. *Man,* XI (56): 86 (i.e. Miris-Mishing).

2925. **Ward, F. Kingdom** : 1942 : *Assam Adventure.* London, Travel Book Club, 304p.

2926. **Ward, S.R.** : 1884 : *A Glimpse of Assam.* Calcutta, T.S. Smith, City Press Print, 219p. (*Ed.* by Thomas S. Smith).

2927. **Watson & Kaye** : 1987 : *The People of India,* Vol. I, New Delhi, B.R. Pub. Cor. (Santhal, Rajbanshi, Meree, Moamuria or Muttuck, Dooaneah, Kachari or Bodo).

2928. **Wickstrand, R.R.** : 1936 : *After a Century in Assam.* New York, 6p.

2929. **Wight, W.** *and* **P.K. Barua** : 1938 : Custom of the Ahoms to bury an earthen ware vessel of mercury on the site of springs. *Nature.* 142, Oct. 22: 754.

2930. **Wood, R.** : 1953 : The Hill Tribes of Assam. *Jour. of Bombay Branch of the Royal Asiatic Society,* 28: 187-214

2931. **Woodthorpe, R.G.** : 1897 : Some Account of the Shans and Hill Tribes of the States on the Mekong. *Jour of the Inst. of Great Britain & Ireland,* 26: 13-28.

2932. **Wright, M.A.** : 1968 : Some observations on Thai Animism. *Practical Anthropology,* Vol. 15: 5.

2933. **Young, A.W.** : n.d. : The Jew's Harp in Assam. *Jr. Proc., A.S.B.,* IV (N.S.): 233-37 (Musical instrument).

PART-II (B)

FULL BIBLIOGRAPHY OF PHYSICAL ANTHROPOLOGY

2934. **Adak, Dipak Kr.** : 1996 : On some aspects of infant mortality of two Mongoloid population of Assam. *Paper for a Seminar on Nutrition, Health and Growth, etc.* Guwahati, Directorate of AIRTSC (It is a comparison in between Deories and Moran people).

2935. **Adak, Dipak Kr.** *and* **B.M. Das** : 1994 : A study of numerical taxonomy and group divergence in five Mongoloid population groups of Assam. *Jour. of Human Ecology*, 5(3), July: 179-83.

2936. ———————— : 1996 : A Study of numerical Taxonomy and group divergence in seven endogamous groups of Assam, *Jr. Hum. Eco.*, 7(3), July: 181-86.

2937. **Adak, Dipak Kr., Ajoy Lahkar** *and* **Manoj Dutta** : 1992 : Relationship between birth rate and death rate: A study on Assam population (1971-1987). *Bull. Deptt. of Anth., Gau. Univ.*, VI, March: 104-07.

2938. **Adak, Dipak Kr.** *and* **Sarit Kr. Choudhury** : 1993 : Infant mortality in Assam: A strategy for better Government Policy. *Seminar on Social Health, Amity and Development*, organised by NEICSSR, Shillong and Voluntary Health Association, Shillong on 24-25 March.

2939. **Ager, J.A.M.** *and* **H. Lehman** : 1957 : Haemoglobin K in an East Indian family. *British Medical Jour.*, I (1949): 50.

2940. **Ahmed, S.** : 1975 : *The Ahoms of Tenghakhat: Their finger prints, a Mongoloid population of Assam.* Unpub. M.Sc. Dissert. Anth. Deptt., Dib. Univ.

2941. **Ahmed Syed I.** : 1992 : Truck drivers are vulnerable groups in North-East India, Abstract.. *(In) 2nd International Congress on AIDS in Asia and the Pacific.* Randwick, Australia, AIDS Society of Asia and the Pacific: 195.

2942. **Ali, Md. Hasmat** : 1974 : ABO blood groups among the Assamese Muslims and Hindus of Kamrup District, Assam. *(In) Contemporary Anthropological Research in North-East India. (Ed.)* by B.M. Das (It is also *Bull. Deptt. of Anth. Dib. Univ.*, III, 1974). Anth. Deptt., Dib Univ.: 78-9.

2943. **Amrit Bazar Patrika** : 1987 : *High birth, low death among Hajongs,* March 11: 7(5).

2944. **Archer, W.G.** : 1947 : The exposure of buttocks as a mark of contempt. *MII,* 27(2): 173-74.

2945. **Assam Tribune** : 1986 : Folk-Medicine to check population explosion. Nov. 11: 6(4-5).

2946 **Assam Tribune** : 1987 : They are heavier. Jan. 6 : 3(6) (Weight of an Assamese baby is more than a Bengali baby: P.B. Das and B. Bhattacharjee).

2947. ———————— : High fertility rate of Hajongs. March 9: 3(7-8).

2948. ———————— : 1988 : 3,60,000 TB patients in Assam. March 28: 1(1-3).

2949. ———————— : 1989 : Editorial : Drugs and liquor. Feb. 11: 4(1-2) (Assam).

2950. ———————— : The spreading tentacles of the drug menace. *Sunday Reading,* Nov. 19 : 1(1-8) (Assam etc.)

2951. ———————— : 1990 : Incidence of neck cancer highest in North-East. May 30 : 8(5).

2952. ———————— : First AIDS case detected in Assam. Sept. 20: 1(4-6), 8(7).

2953. ———————— : Editorial: AIDS menace. Oct. 13 : 4(1-2) (Guwahati).

2954. ———————— : 1992 : Editorial: Drugs and Youth. Sept. 11: 4(1-2).

2955. ———————— : Assam : Paradise of herbs. Feb. 24: 2(6-8).

2956. ———————— : 1994 : 14 AIDS cases detected in Assam. March 11: 1(2-4), 8(5-6).

2957. ———————— : 156 HIV-positive cases in the State. Dec. 29: 1(6-7).

2958. **Athparia, R.P.** : 1995 : Population trend in a century of the Karbis (1872 to 1971). *Paper presented in a Seminar on Population Growth Trend in NEI and its impact on National Resources and Social Services,* organised by NEICSSR, Shillong, 27th March.

2959. **Balgir, Praveen P.** : 1984 : Sexual diamorphism and age changes of PTC testing ability among Assamese. *Ind. Jour. Phy. Anth. & Hum. Genetics,* X(1), April: 64-7.

2960. **Balgir, R.S.** : 1991 : Genetic diversity among the six Mongoloid populations of North-Eastern India. *Jour. of Hum. Eco.,* 2(2), May: 207-10 (Ahom, Kachari, etc.).

2961. ———————— : Red Cell Genetic Polymorphism in a Non-Mongoloid Scheduled Caste population of Dibrugarh District, Assam. *Ind. Jour. Hematol. Blood Transf.,* IX: 175-84.

2962. **Balgir, R.S.** : 1992 : Sero-Genetic Variations in a Mech-Kachari tribal population. *MII,* 72(3), Sept.: 293-301.

2963. ————— : 1992 : Genetic markers in the tribal health, development and welfare of North Eastern India. *Paper presented in 79th Indian Sc. Cong.* held during 3-8 Jan., Baroda.

2964. ————— : Distribution of serogenetic markers in the tea garden tribal population of Dibrugarh District, Assam. *Bull. Deptt. of Anth., Dib. Univ.*: 29-38.

2965. ————— :Reproductive profile of mothers in relation to haemoglobin E genotype. *Ind. Jour. of Pediatrics,* 59: 449-54.

2966. ————— : 1993 : Menarcheal age in relation to ABO blood group phenotypes and haemoglobin E genotypes. *Jour. Assocn. Phys. India,* 41: 210-11.

2967. ————— : Sero-epidemiological profile of some selected populations in North-East India. *Bull. Deptt. of Anth., Dib. Univ.,* 20-21 (1991-92): 22-9 (Sonowal, Mech, Tiwa, Kaibarta, Ahom, Sut, etc.).

2968. ————— : 1994 : Age at sexual maturity among the eight endogamous populations of North-Eastern India. *Jour. of Hum. Eco.,* 5(2), April: 91-6.

2969. ————— : 1996 : Biomedical anthropological approaches in North-Eastern India : A synthesis of the tea garden population of Assam. *(In) Peoples of North-East India : Anthropological Perspectives. (Ed.)* by Sarthak Sengupta. New Delhi, Gyan Pubg. House : 91-104.

2970. **Balgir, R.S.** *and* **L.P. Dutta** : 1990 : Studies on genetic polymorphism in relation to Malaria in tea gardens of Dibrugarh District, Assam. *Indian Jour. Malarial.,* 27: 237-41.

2971. **Balgir, R.S.** *and* **S.K. Sharma** : 1988 : Distribution of sickle cell haemoglobin in India. *Indian Jour. of Hematology,* VI: 1-14.

2972. **Banerjee, A.R.** : 1974 : Research in Physical Anthropology in North-East India: Problems and Prospects. *(In) Contemporary Anthropological Research in North-East India. (Ed.)* by B.M. Das, *Bull. Anth. Deptt., Dib. Univ.,* III: 156-57.

2973. **Banerjee, A.R.** *and* **D.K. Banerjee** : 1975 : Inter caste distance in dermatoglyphics in some Bengalee caste groups. *Indian Jr. Phy. Anth. & Hum. Genetics,* I: 29-39.

2974. **Banerjee, S.K.** : 1972 : A Short Note on menarcheal age of the Assamese girls. *The Anthropologist,* XIX (1-2), March-Sept. 51-2.

2975. **Barthakur, S.K.** : 1976 : Less known medicinal uses of plants among the tribes of Karbi Anglong (Mikir Hills), Assam. *Bull. Bot. Survey of India,* XVIII: 166-71.

2976. **Barua, A.C.** : 1989 : Pediatric education and care in North East. *A.T.*, March, 5: 4 (3-6), 5(2).

2977. **Barua, G.** : 1974 : *A study on the palm prints of the Khamyang, a Mongoloid population.* Unpub. M.Sc. Dissert. Anth. Deptt., Dib. Univ.

2978. **Barua, Indira** : 1996 : Child rearing practices: A study among the Deuris. *(In) Communities of North-East India: An Anthropological perspective. (Eds.)* by Farida Ahmed Das and Indira Barua. Delhi, Mittal Pubn.: 161-70.

2979. —————— : Menarche in NEI communities. *South Asian Anth.*, 17(2): 65-72.

2980. **Barua, Indira** *and* **Anjali Gogoi** : 1981 : Attitude towards family planning: A case study among the Sonowal Kachari women of Lejai Barua Gaon. *Bull. Anth. Deptt., Dib. Univ.,* VII-VIII (1978-79): 105-10.

2981. **Barua, I.** *and* **Deepanjana Dutt** : 1994 : A Note on earlobe distribution among the Tai Turungs of Assam. *Bull. Deptt. of Anth., Dib. Univ.,* 22; 126-30 (Tai Turungs, Kachari, Suri, Kaibarta, Rajbanshi, Ahom, Miri, Baishya, Kalita, Brahmin, etc.).

2982. **Barua, I., D.D. Das** *and* **P.M. Buzarbarua** : 1987 : A study of some genetic traits among the Turungs of Assam. *Bull. Deptt. of Anth., Dib. Univ., 11-12*: 15-20 (1982-83).

2983. **Barua, N.** : 1972 : *Finger and palmer dermatoglyphics of the Kaibartas of Kamrup, Assam.* Unpub. M.Sc. Dissert. Anth. Deptt., Gau. Univ.

2984. **Barua, Saumitra** : 1979 : Incidence of Red Green colour vision deficiency among the Hajongs of West Garo Hills District of Meghalaya. *Paper of a Seminar on Bio-Cultural Profile of North-East India (Silver Jub. of An. S.I. Shillong).*

2985. —————— : n.d. : Mating system and micro-evolutionary dynamics among the Hajongs of the Garo Hills District of Meghalaya. *Report submitted to An. S.I., Shillong,* 1981.

2986. —————— : 1983 : Bio-demographic factors associated with offspring mortality among the Hajongs of Meghalaya. *Jr. of Ind. Anth. Society.* 17(2), July: 143-46.

2987. **Barua, Saumitra** : 1983 : The Hajongs of Meghalaya: A Bio-demographic Study. *Human Sc.,* 32: 190-200.

2988. **Barua, Saumitra** : 1985 : Red, green colour blindness and earlobe attachment among the Hajongs of Meghalaya. *Hum. Sc.*, 34(2).

2989. **Barua, Saumitra, R. Th. Varte** *and* **N.C. Sarkar** : 1994 : Fertility and mortality differentials among the Khamti of Assam and Arunachal Pradesh : A study on the effect of migration. *Jour. Ind. Anth. Society*, 29(1-2), March-July: 136-42.

2990. **Baruah, Kanaki** : 1983 : *A study on finger and palm prints of the Ahom of Dinjoy Gaon of Chabua, Dibrugarh, Assam.* Unpub. M.Sc. Dissert. Anth. Deptt., Dib. Univ.

2991. **Baruah, Gairika** : 1974 : *Study of growth and body proportion of children of tea garden labourer.* Unpub. M.Sc. Dissert. Anth. Deptt., Dib. Univ.

2992. **Baruah, Geetanjali** : 1977 : A Note on the palm prints of the Khamyang: A Mongoloid population of Assam. *Bull. Deptt. of Anth., Dib. Univ.*, 5: 7-13 (1976).

2993. **Baruah, Satyabati** : 1976 : *A study on menarcheal age in relation to body size among the women of Brahmin and Kaibarta of Dibrugarh, Assam.* Unpub. M.Sc. Dissert. Anth. Deptt., Dib. Univ.

2994. **Baruah, T.** : 1992 : Problems of ear, nose and throat cancer in North-East. *A.T.*, Nov. 27: 4 (3-6), 6(2-4).

2995. **Baruah, Tiluttoma** : 1993 : *A demogenetic study of the Tai Phakes of Assam.* Unpub. Ph.D. Thesis, Anth. Deptt., Gau. Univ.

2996. **Baruah, Tultul** : 1991 : Socio-economic aspects of health in an Assamese village. *Bull. Deptt. of Anth., Dib. Univ.*, 16-17 (1987-88): 94-100.

2997. **Basu, A.** : 1990 : Anthropological approach to tribal health. *(In) Tribal Demography and Development in North-East India. (Eds.)* by Ashish Bose, Tiplut Nangbri & Nikhlesh Kumar. Delhi, B.R. Pub.: 131-42.

2998. **Basu, Amitabha; Partha P. Majumder; Aloke K. Ghosh** *and* **Suhas K. Biswas** : 1980 : Human Biological variations in Asia with special reference to India. *(In) La Diversite Biologique Humaine: Human Biological Diversity (Collection d' Anthropologie Physique)* by J. Hiernaux, A. Basu, J. Benoist, S. Biswas, E. Crognier, J. Friedlaender, A. Ghosh, J. Gomila, P. Majumder. Paris, Masson Pub.: 197-273 (Assam etc.).

2999. **Basu, Arabinda** *and* **Anadi Pal** : 1990 : Blood pressures in Munda: Comparison between migrants to tea gardens in lower Assam and Sedents. *(In) Tea garden labourers of North-East India (Eds.)* by S. Karotemprel and B. Datta Roy. Shillong, Vendrame Institute: 310-21.

3000. **Basu, Debasis** : 1996 : Selection intensity in the Sonowal Kacharis of Assam. *Jr. Hum. Ecology,* 7(3), July: 223-24.

3001. —————— : *Report of tour among Sonowal Kachari and Kaibartas of Dibrugarh.* Shillong, *An. S.I.* (Unpub., about nutrition, etc.).

3002. —————— : Gene differentiation at the ABO locus in the caste populations of North-East India. Shillong, *An. S.I. (In) Golden Jubilee Seminar,* 13-14 Sept. 1996 *(Mimeo.).*

3003. **Basu, Debasis** *and* **Anita Verma** : 1993 : A note on sitting height and weight of Kalita boys. *An International Conference on Human Genetics & Family Welfare,* held on 11-12 December, organised by Poona Medical College, Pune *(Mimeo.).*

3004. **Basu, Mahadeb Prasad** : 1990 : *An Anthropological study of bodily height of Indian population.* Calcutta, Punthi Pustak : 29, 82, 111, 125, 127, 131, 135, 154, 157, 175, 228, 255, 265, 269, 274, 295-97, 337 (Assam).

3005. **Basu, Provash Ch.** : 1929 : The Anthropometry of the Bhuyan of Mayurbhanj. *Jour. of Asiatic Soc. of Beng. (N.S.),* 25: 157-63.

3006. **Basu Roy Choudhury, J., Atrayee Bhowmik** *and* **P. Das** : 1976 : Economic co-relates of tribal fertility in Eastern India. *Bull. Cul. Research Inst.,* XII (1-2): 83-7.

3007. **Basu, R.N.** *and* **M.N. Basu** : 1941-42 : Physical Anthropology of the Bhuyans of Mayurbhanj. *Sc. & Cul.* (Cal.), 7: 571-72.

3008. **Batabyal, J.N.** *and* **J.M.G. Wilson** : 1958 : Sickle cell anaemia in Assam. *Jour. Ind. Med. Ass.* (Cal.), 30(1), January, 1: 8-11.

3009. **Begum, Eleza** : 1980 : *Birth weight among the Assamese new born.* Unpub. M.Sc. Dissert. Anth. Deptt., Dib. Univ.

3010. **Begum, G.** : 1996 : Health among the Assamese Muslims of Kamrup district, Assam. *Bull. Deptt. of Anth., Dib. Univ.,* 24: 87-94.

3011. **Begum, Gulrukh** : 1996 : Health status of the school children of Guwahati city. *(In) Communities of North-East India: An anthropological perspective. (Eds.)* by Farida Ahmed Das and Indira Barua. Delhi, Mittal Pubn.: 128-43.

3012. **Begum, N.A.**: 1976 : *A comparison between the two emigrant population; the Sema Naga and the Nepalee of Udaipur, Assam, in respect of Anthropometry, Somatoscopy and some other genetic traits.* Unpub. M.Sc. Dissert. Anth. Deptt., Dib. Univ.

3013. **Begum, Saleha** : 1983 : *A study of ear-lobe types cerumen type* *and colour blindness among the Deuris of Kolowlowa gaon.* Unpub. M.Sc. Dissert. Anth. Deptt., Dib. Univ.

3014. **Benkmann, H.G.** *and* **H.W. Goedde** : 1975 : Esterase D. polymorphism in Assam by Cellulose Acetate Electrophuresis. *Humangenetik,* 27: 343-45.

3015. **Bhagabati, A.C.** : 1962 : Investigations on the finger prints of the Khamyangs. *Jr. Univ. of Gau.*, 13(2).

3016. ———— : 1963 : Somatometric characters of the Khamyangs. *Jr. Univ. of Gau.*, 14 (2).

3017. ———— : 1964 : The palm prints of the Khyamyangs. *Jr. Univ. of Gau.*, 15 (2).

3018. **Bhasin, M.K.; H. Walter** *and* **H. Danker-Hopfe** : 1992 : *The distribution of genetical, morphological and behavioural traits among the people of Indian Region (Bangladesh, Bhutan, India, Maldives, Nepal, Pakistan, Sri Lanka).* Delhi, Kamla Raj Enterprises.

3019. ———— : 1994 : *People of India: An investigation of biological variability in ecological, ethno-economic and linguistic groups.* Delhi, Kamla Raj Enterprises.

3020. **Bhasin, Veena** : 1994 : *People, health and disease: The Indian Scenario.* Delhi, Kamla Raj Enterprises, 267p.

3021. **Bhatia, H.M.** *and* **V.R. Rao** : 1986 : *Genetic atlas of the Indian tribes.* Bombay, Institute of Immunohaematology (Indian Council of Medical Research).

3022. **Bhatnagar, D.P.** *and* **P. Singhal** : 1993 : A comparative study of athletes and volleyball players from rural areas of Assam and Madhya Pradesh. *(In) Modern Perspectives in Physical Education and Sports Sciences (Eds.)* by L.S. Sidhu et al. New Delhi, Harnam Pub.: 117-24.

3023. **Bhattacharjee, Anerbha** : 1983 : *A study of finger and palm prints of the Bengali Brahmin of Dibrugarh town.* Unpub. M.Sc. Dissert. Anth. Deptt., Dib. Univ.

3024. **Bhattacharjee, P.N.** : 1975 : Blood group of the Austro-Asiatic and Tibeto-Burman speaking people in Eastern India: A review. *Indian Soc. Hum. Genet., 2nd Ann. Conf.*, Calcutta.

3025. **Bhattacharjee, R.P.** : 1991 : Demographic profile of North-East (1991): A brief analysis. *Seminar on Pattern and problems of population growth in India with special reference to North-East India*, held on 4 October by Population Education Club, Women College, Shillong *(Mimeo.).*

3026. **Bhattacharjee, R.P.** : 1994 : Demographic profile of North-East (1991):. *(In) Demographic profile of North-East India. (Eds.)* by Sanu Mukherjee, Fatima Imdad Hussain, Parjit Chakravorty and Gurudas. New Delhi, Omsons Pub.: 8-27.

3027. **Bhattacharya, D.K.** : 1971 : Variation of C line termination in palmar dermatoglyphics: The three co-ordinate as a possible method of population discrimination. *The Anth.,* 18 (1-2).

3028. **Bhattacharyya, U.S.** : 1991 : Drug trafficking in North-Eastern States: A Profile. *Paper presented in a Seminar on Youth and Psychotropic drug abuse in North-East India* held on 3-4 May, 1991 organised by N.E.I.A.R. & Dir. of Social Welfare, Shillong.

3029. **Bhowmik, D.C.** : 1980 : Growth Studies in North-East India: A bio-cultural approach. *Jr. NEICSSR,* IV (1), April: 15-6.

3030. **Bhowmik, D.C.; Faizul Haq** *and* **Arabinda Basu.** : 1988 : *All India Anthropometric Survey: North Zone (Basic Anthropometric Data) Vol. I: Assam.* Calcutta, Anth. S.I., 150p. (Ahom, Brahmin, Jogi, Kachari, Kaibarta, Kalita, Koch, Lalung, Mech, Miri, Muslim, Rajbanshi).

3031. **Bhuyan, Bandana** : 1994 : Feeding practices and growth pattern of children in some tribal communities of Assam. *Bull. Deptt., Anth. Gau. Univ.,* VIII: 34-8.

3032. **Bhuyan, Banti** : 1981 : *Distribution of ABO blood groups, cerumen types and earlobe types among the Mishings of Kamalabari area Majuli.* Unpub. M.Sc. Dissert, Anth. Deptt. Dib. Univ.

3033. **Bhuyan, Jogen** : 1994 : Child health care in Assam. *A.T.*, April 8: 4(3-8), 6(3-4).

3034. **Biswas, Giban** : 1984 : Population and family planning (A case of some villages in Cachar). *Proceedings of a Seminar on Pattern and Problems of Population in North-East India: A multidimensional study,* organised by NEICSSR, Shillong on 7-8 December.

3035. ———— : 1986 : Population and Family Planning: A case study of some villages in Cachar. *(In) Pattern and Problems of population in North-East India. (Ed.)* by B. Datta Ray. New Delhi, Uppal Pub.: 389-406.

3036. **Boissya, C.L.** *and* **R. Majumder** : 1980 : Some folklore claims from the Brahmaputra valley (Assam). *Ethnomed* (W. Germany), VI (1-4): 139-45.

3037. **Boissya, C.L., R. Majumder** *and* **A.K. Majumder** : 1981 : Some medicinal plants from Darrang district of Assam. *Anthropos* (W. Germany), 76: 220-22.

3038. **Boissya, S., C.L. Boissya** *and* **R. Majumder** : 1983 : Economic aspects of some medicinal plants available in Nowgong district of Assam, India. *Anthropos*, 78: 241-45.

3039. **Bora, Anee** : 1972 : *A Study of finger and palm prints among the Mikir (female)*. Unpub. M.Sc. Dissert., Anth. Deptt., Dib. Univ.

3040. **Borah, Hemi** : 1983 : *Child rearing practices in a tea garden community of the South Jalan Nagar T.E. Dibrugarh*. Unpub. M.Sc. Dissert., Anth. Deptt., Dib. Univ.

3041. **Bora, Malaya Madhuri** : 1994 : *A study of the health habits and sanitary practices of the housewives of cattle farmers in Kamrup District.* Unpub. Ph.D. Thesis, Assam Agricultural Univ., Jorhat.

3042. **Bora, Nomal Ch.** : 1991 : Prevalence of Neurological disorder in an Urban population in North Eastern Region of India. *Proceedings of World congress of Tropical Neurological* held in Limoges (Near Paris city) of France, on 8 October *(Mimeo).*

3043. **Borgohain, H.** : 1974 : *A study on finger and palm prints of Turung.* Unpub. M.Sc. Dissert., Anth. Deptt., Dib. Univ.

3044. **Borgohain, Hiren** : 1982 : An investigation on the finger patterns of the Turungs. *Jr. NEICSSR,* VI (I), April: 29-34.

3045. ———— : 1984 : A note on ridge counts of finger patterns of the Turung of Assam. *Jr. NEICSSR,* VIII (I), April: 35-7.

3046. ———— : 1985 : Palmar dermatoglyphics of the Turung male. *Jr. NEICSSR,* IX (II), October: 30-5 (Turungs are in Sibsagar district of Assam).

3047. **Borooah, Guna Lata** : n.d. : *Population Geography of Assam.* New Delhi, Mittal Pub.

3048. **Boruah, Tultul** : 1992 : Health behaviour of the migrant Mundas in an Assam tea plantation: Some preliminary appraisals. *Bull. Deptt. Anth., Dib. Univ.,* 18-19 (1989-90): 137-50.

3049. **Bose, Ashish, Tilplut Nongbri** *and* **Nikhilesh Kumar** *(Eds)* : 1990 : *Tribal demography and development in East India.* New Delhi, B.R. Pub.

3050. **Brahma, Birendra Kr.** : 1994 : *Ethno-Botany of the Boros.* Unpub. Ph.D. Thesis, Botany Deptt., Gau. Univ.

3051. **British Research Association** : 1939 : Blood groups among primitive people. *Nature,* 144: 714.

3052. **Bulletin** : 1973 : A cross-sectional study of growth in height and weight of an endogamous caste of Assam. *Bull. Deptt. of Anth.*, II, December; 24-31.

3053. **Buragohain, R.** : 1980 : *A study on the finger and palm prints of the Kachari of Lepetkata*, Unpub. M.Sc. Dissert., Anth. Deptt., Dib. Univ.

3054. **Buragohain, Satyendra Nath** *et al* : 1971 : A study of some genetic traits in two caste groups of Assam. *Jr. Assam Sc. Soc.*, 12.

3055. —— *et al*: 1971 : Taste sensitivity to phenylthiourea in two caste groups of Assam. *MII*, 51 (3): 252.

3056. **Buzarbarua, P.M.** : 1982 : A short note on fertility among the Santal women of Nagrijuli area, Kamrup district, Assam. *North-East Quarterly*, 1.

3057. ———— : 1984 : *Effects of environment and migration on the physical and genetic characters of the Mundas and the Santals of Assam.* Unpub. Ph.D. Thesis, Anth. Deptt., Dib. Univ.

3058. ———— : Effect of migration and environment on physical features of the Santal of Nagrijuli. *(In) The Tribes of North-East India. (Ed.)* by S. Karotemprel. Calcutta, Firma KLM: 391-97 (Goalpara dist.).

3059. ———— : Effects of birth orders and mothers age on reproductive wastage of the Mishings of Dishangmukh of Sibsagar, Assam. *Ind. Jr. Phy. Anth.*, X: 155-58.

3060. ———— : 1989 : A general study among the two immigrant populations of Assam. *Jr. NEICSSR*, XIII (II), October: 24-7.

3061. ———— : Effects of migration and environment on anthropometric characters of Munda population of Assam: A preliminary observation. *MII*, 69 (3), Sept.: 292-304.

3062. ———— : 1991 : ABO blood groups among the Mishings of Dishangmukh area, Sibsagar district, Assam. *Jr. NEICSSR*, XV (2), October: 51-4.

3063. **Buzarbaruah, P.M.** *and* **M.N. Phookan** : 1982 : Variation in respect of anthropometric characters between two immigrant groups of Assam. *Bull. Deptt. of Anth., Dib. Univ.*, IX (1980): 90-100.

3064. **Buzarbaruah, P.M.** *and* **M.N. Phookan** : 1984 : Effect of birth order and mother's age on reproductive wastage of the Mishings of Disangmukh of Sibsagar, Assam. *Indian Jr. Phy. Anth. & Hum. Gen.*, X (2-3), Aug.-Dec.: 155-58.

3065. ———— : 1985 : A study on some morphological traits of

the two immigrant population of Assam.. *(In) Anthropological perspectives on North-East India. (Ed.)* by B.M. Das, Dib. Univ., Deptt. of Anth., (It is also *Bull. Deptt. of Anth., Dib. Univ.*, Vol. X, 1981): 61-6.

3066. **Buzarbaruah, P.M.** *and* **M.N. Phookan** : 1986 : Birth order, mother's age and reproductive wastage among the Mishings of Disangmukh of Sibsagar, Assam. *Ind. Jr. Phy. Anth. & Hum. Gen.*, XII(1), Jan.-April: 43-50.

3067. ———— : 1992 : A study on some morphological traits of the two immigrant populations of Assam. *Bull. Deptt. of Anth., Dib. Univ.*, X(1985): 61-6.

3068. **Buzarbarua, P.M.** *and* **S.H.M. Rizvi** : 1996 : The Garias of Assam : A bio-demographic study. *(In) People of North-East India: Anthropological Perspectives. (Ed.)* by Sarthak Sengupta. New Delhi, Gyan Publishing House: 62-72.

3069. **Campbell, A.** : 1839 : A note on the Meches together with a small vocabulary of the language. *Jr. Royal Asiatic Soc. Beng. (N.S.),* 8: 623-31.

3070. ———— : 1984 : Some aspects of physical anthropology of the Tribes of North-East India. *(In) The Tribes of North-East India. (Ed.)* by S. Karotemprel. Calcutta. Firma KLM: 39-57.

3071. ———— : 1985 : *People of Assam: Their Ethnic Compositions* (A Text book of Foundation Course). Gau. Univ.

3072. ———— : Microevolutionary trend in North-East Indian Tribes: An overview.. *(In) Genetic Micro-differentiation in Human and other Animal Populations. (Eds.)* by Y.R. Ahuja and James V. Neel. Delhi, Indian Anthropological Association, Deptt. of Anth.: 94-106 (Boro: 96-100, Rabha, Kachari, etc.: 102-06).

3073. ———— : 1987 : *The Peoples of Assam.* Delhi, Gyan Pub. House, 98p.

3074. ———— : A note on marriage area among rural Assamese people. *Bull. Deptt. Anth., Dib. Univ.*, XI-XII (1982-83): 21-4.

3075. ———— : 1990 : Trend of variation with respect to certain Anthropometric traits in two populations of North-East India. *(In) Human Variation in India: Proceedings of the Seminar on Physical Anthropology, 27 June-2 July, 1977. (Ed.)* by K.S. Singh Calcutta, Anth. S.I.: 189-94 (Rabha, Kachari, Rajbanshi etc.).

3076. **Campbell, A.** : 1990 : Health and sanitation versus culture: An Appraisal of Tea Labour in Assam. *(In) Cultural and*

Environmental Dimensions on Health. New Delhi, Inter India Pub.: 31-45. *(Ed.)* by Uddhadeb Choudhuri.

3077. **Campbell, A.** : 1991 : Biological contact in Brahmaputra valley. *A.T.*, July 21: 4(3-6), 7(6) (Rabha, Hajong, Koch, Chutiya, Ahom-Chutiya, Rajbanshi, etc.).

3078. ——————— : Haemoglobinopathy: An overview. *Bull. Deptt. of Anth., Dib. Univ.*, 16-17 (1987-88): 8-23.

3079. ——————— : 1992 : Physical Anthropology and development in North-East India. *(In) Anthropology of Development. (Ed.)* by R. Malhotra. New Delhi, Mittal Pub.: 168-79.

3080. ——————— : A Glance on some aspects of biological contact in North-East India. *Bull. Deptt. of Anth. Dib. Univ.*, 18-19(1989-90): 1-9 (Assam).

3081. ——————— : Physical anthropological research in North-East India : A historical perspective. *(In) Science, Culture and Development. (Eds.)* by N.K. Behura and K.C. Tripathy. Bhubaneswar, Paragon Publisher: 197-209.

3082. ——————— : 1993 : Physical Anthropology of the tribes of North-East India. *(In) New Perspectives in Anthropology. (Ed.)* by P.K. Seth and S. Seth. New Delhi, M.D. Pub.: 159-92 (Assam and other states of North-East India).

3083. ——————— : Frontiers of Genetic Research among the tribals of India. *South Asian Anthropologist* (Ranchi), 14(1-2), March-Sept.: 75-91 (Assam etc.).

3084. ——————— : 1994 : Ethnic elements in North-East India. *Bull. Deptt. of Anth., Dib. Univ.*, 22: 1-12 (Assamese, Tai Phake, Khamyang, Turung, Aiton, Brahmin, Kalita, Kaibarta, etc.).

3085. ——————— : Frontiers of Genetic Research Among Tribals of India. *(In) Tribal Health in India. (Ed.)* by Salil Basu. Delhi, Manak. Pub.: 196-224 (Kachari, Karbi, Sonowal etc.).

3086. ——————— : 1996 : Trends of studying Physical Anthropology of the people of the Brahmaputra valley : An overview. *(In) Communities of North-East India : An Anthropological Perspective (Eds)* by Farida Ahmed Das *and* Indira Barua. Delhi, Mittal Pub.: 49-54.

3087. **Census of India** : 1903 : *Census of India 1901: Summary of measurements; Mongoloid type, Eastern Himalaya, Chittagong Hill Tracts and Assam, in order of orbito-nasal index.* Calcutta, Supdt. of Govt. Printing (Vol. I, India, Ethnographic Appendices): 34-5.

3088. **Chakraborty, Ajita** *and* **D.C. Bag** : 1989 : Genesis of the Koro epidemic in West Bengal and Assam: Implication of Turtle Cults. *Human Sc.*, 38(2), June: 142-49.

3089. **Chakraborty, Anjana** : 1995 : *Fertility control in Assam.* Unpub. Ph.D. Thesis, Deptt. of Obs. & Gyn., Gau. Med. College, Gau. Univ.

3090. **Chakraborty, M.R.** : 1964 : Study of Haematological factors, blood groups, anthropometric characters of some of the tribal and caste groups of South India and North-East India. *Proc. IXth Congress of Inter. Soci. Blood Transfusion*, Mexico, 1962.

3091. ————— : 1989 : n.d. : *Blood groups and diseases in India.* New Delhi, Pub. by TSR Naik.

3092. **Chakraborty M.R.; B.N. Mukherjee; B.M. Das; H. Walter** *and* **K.C. Malhotra** : n.d. : *Gene differentiation among ten endogamous population groups of Assam, India.*

3093. **Chakravorty, M.R.** *and* **D.P. Mukherjee**: 1961 : Dermatoglyphic study of tribes and castes of Assam. *Sc. & Cul.*, 27 (12): 584-85.

3094. **Chakravorty, Purabi** : 1972 : *PTC tastes among the Mikirs of Assam.* Unpub. M.Sc. Dissert. Anth. Deptt., Dib. Univ.

3095. **Chakraborty, S.** : 1972 : *Distribution of ABO blood groups among the Mikirs.* Unpub. M.Sc. Dissert. Anth. Deptt., Dib. Univ.

3096. **Chakravorty, S.K.** : 1976 : Selection potential among Bengalee Muslims of Cachar. *Paper presented at 3rd Annual Conference of the Indian Anth. Soc.*, Santiniketan (Abstract Pub. in *Jr. Ind. Anth. Soc.*, XI (2), May: 177).

3097. ————— : 1977 : ABO blood group distribution among the Mikir of Assam. *Bull. Deptt. of Anth., Dib. Univ.*, 5: 14-8 (1976).

3098. ————— : 1982 : *Microevolutionary dynamics in a hybrid population: The Man.* Unpub. Ph.D. Thesis Gau. Univ.

3099. ————— : 1990 : Blood group systems in North-East India. *(In) Human variation in India. (Ed.)* by K.S. Singh. Calcutta, Anth. S.I.: 199-209.

3100. **Chatterjee, J.B.** : 1967 : Assamese and Nepalese instances of *HbE. Bull. Cal. School of Tropical Med. Sc.*, 28: 4.

3101. **Chaudhuri, B.** : 1990 : *Cultural and environmental dimensions on health.* New Delhi, Inter India Pubn., 470p.

3102. ————— **(Ed.)** : *Cultural and environmental Dimensions on Health.* New Delhi, Inter-India Pub., 470p.

3103. **Chaudhuri, S.; M.R. Chakravorti; B. Mukherjee; S.N. Sen; J. Ghosh** *and* **A. Maitra** : 1962 : A study of haematological factors, blood groups, anthropometric measurements and some genetical aspects of some of the tribal and caste groups of India. *Proc. 9th Cong. Int. Soc. Blood Transfusion* (Mexico): 196 (Toto, a small tribe at the Bengal-Assam border).

3104. **Chaudhuri, Tusharkanti** : n.d. : *Demographic trends in Assam. 1921-71*. New Delhi, Mittal Pub.

3105. **Chetry, H.B.** *and* **S. Sengupta** : 1993 : A note on hand clasping, arm-folding, handedness and dominant eye among the Dibongiya Deori of Assam. *Bull. Deptt. of Anth., Dib. Univ.*, 20-21 (1991-92): 68-73.

3106. **Choudhury, Anwaruddin** : 1989 : *Primates of Assam: Their distribution, habitat and status.* Unpub. Ph.D. Thesis, Gau. Univ.

3107. **Choudhury, A.S.** : 1972 : *Finger and palm prints of the Duania.* Unpub. M.Sc. Dissert., Anth. Deptt., Gau. Univ.

3108. **Chaudhury, B.** : 1978 : *A cross-sectional study of growth of some somatometric characters of Rabha boys of Kamrup district, Assam.* Unpub. Ph.D. Thesis Anth. Deptt., Gau. Univ.

3109. **Choudhury, Bapukan** : 1975 : Tongue rolling and earlobe attachment of Duanias of Assam. *Jr. Assam Sc. Soc.*, XVIII (1), June: 10-4.

3110. ———— : 1978 : *A cross-sectional study of growth of some somatometric characters of Rabha boys of Kamrup district, Assam.* Unpub. Ph.D. Thesis., Anth. Deptt., Gau. Univ.

3111. ———— : Age changes in some somatometric characters in adult Rabhas of Kamrup district, Assam. *Proc. Int. Cong. Anth. Ethno. Sc.* (Delhi).

3112. ———— : 1984 : Impact of culture on growth: A case study among the Rabhas of Kamrup, Assam.. *(In) The Tribes of North-East India. (Ed.)* by S. Karotemprel. Calcutta, Firma KLM: 398-413.

3113. ———— : 1985 : Changes of some somatometric characters in adult Rabhas of Kamrup District, Assam, due to ageing. *(In) Anthropological Perspectives on North-East India. (Ed.)* by B.M. Das. Dib. Univ., Deptt. of Anth., (It is also *Bull. Deptt. of Anth., Dib. Univ.*, X, 1981): 87-93.

3114. **Choudhury, Bapukan; Gulrukh Begum** *and* **Tiluttoma Barua**: 1992 : Growth patterns of school children of Guwahati city. *Bull. Deptt. of Anth., Gau. Univ.*, VI, March: 74-86.

3115. **Choudhury, Bapukan** *and* **Sarat Ch. Bhuyan** : 1994 : Growth and nutritional status of Kalita children of Kamrup district, Assam. *Bull. Deptt., Anth., Gau. Univ.*, VIII : 65-86.

3116. **Choudhury, D.R.** : 1962 : Palmar dermatoglyphics of the Rajbanshis of Midnapur, West Bengal. *The Anthropologist*, IX (1-2): 31-8.

3117. **Chowdhury, Arabinda N.** : 1994 : Medico-cultural cognition of Koro epidemic: An ethnographic study. *(In) Frontiers of Anthropology: Biology, Culture and Human Development in retrospect and Prospect. (Eds.)* by Ajit K. Danda, Amitabha Basu, Arabinda Basu. Calcutta, Ind. Anth. Soc.: 155-70.

3118. **Chowdhury, A.T.** : 1982 : *Demographic Trends in Assam.* Delhi, Mittal Pub.

3119. **Chutia, Aparajita** : 1977 : *A comparative study of menarcheal and menopausal age of the Chutiya and the Kachari women of Dibrugarh.* Unpub. M.Sc. Dissert. Anth. Deptt., Dib. Univ.

3120. **Danker-Hopfe H., B.M. Das; H. Walter, P.B. Das** *and* **Renuka Das** : 1988 : Anthropological studies in Assam, India, 6. Differentiation processes among Assamese population. *Anthrop. Anz.*, 46: 159-84.

3121. **Das, A.K.** : 1996 : Growth pattern of school children in two communities of Dibrugarh. *(In) Communities of North-East India: An Anthropological Perspective. (Eds.)* by Farida Ahmed Das and Indira Barua. Delhi, Mittal Pubn.: 90-100.

3122. ———————— : A study on growth among the Assamese and Rajasthani boys. *(In) People of North-East India : Anthropological Perspectives. (Ed.)* by Sarthak Sengupta. New Delhi, Gyan Publishing House: 30-61.

3123. **Das, Arun Kr.** : 1974 : A note on ridge counts of finger patterns of the Sonowal Kacharis of Assam. *(In) Contemporary Anthropological Research in North-East India. (Ed.)* by B.M. Das (This is also *Bull. Anth. Deptt. of Dib. Univ.*, Vol. III, 1974): 63-6.

3124. ———————— : 1976 : A note on the variation of earlobe attachment. *Bull. Deptt. Anth., Dib. Univ.*, IV (1975): 25-7 (Ahom).

3125. ———————— : 1977 : A note on the growth pattern of stature, body weight and chest circumference of Assamese school boys. *Bull. Deptt. of Anth., Dib. Univ.*, V (1976): 19-24.

3126. ———————— : 1978 : A study of growth of height, weight and chest circumference of Assamese and Rajasthani boys. *(In) Cultural and Biological adaptability of man with special reference to North-East India. (Ed.)* by A.C. Bhagabati. (This is also Bull. Anth. Deptt., Dib. Univ., VI): 176-80.

3127. **Das, Arun Kr.** : 1983 : *Growth and body built of the Assamese and Rajasthani boys aged six to seventeen years: A comparative study.* Unpub. Ph.D. Thesis, Anth. Deptt. Dib. Univ.

3128. ————— : 1992 : Growth pattern of Rajasthani boys of Dibrugarh, Assam. *Bull. Anth. Deptt., Dib. Univ.*, 18-19 (1989-90): 51-88.

3129. **Das, A.K., M.N. Dutta** *and* **S. Sengupta** : 1986 : Anomalous colour vision among the Ahom of Dibrugarh, Assam. *Bull. Anth. Deptt., Dib. Univ.*, 15(1990): 151-56.

3130. **Das, A.K.** *and* **S.K. Banerjee** : 1972 : Finger prints of the Ahoms of Assam. *Bull. Anth. Deptt., Dib. Univ.*, Vol. 1: 23-7.

3131. ————— : 1973 : Palm prints of the Ahom. *Bull. Anth. Deptt., Dib. Univ.*, Vol. II: 50-4.

3132. **Das, A.K.** *and* **T.C. Sharma** : 1958 : Traditional Methods of Treatment of Leprosy Among Mikir. *Adivasi*, 3: 25-33.

3133. **Das, B.K.** : n.d. : *Sanitation in Guwahati: Status, Planning and Prospect.* Unpub. Article.

3134. **Das, B.M.** : 1959 : Finger prints of the Hajong. *MII*, 39 (1): 20-7.

3135. ————— : Whorl on head hair of the Rajbanshis and the Kacharis. *Jour. Assam Sc. Soc.*, III: 58-60.

3136. ————— : Whorl on head hair of Rajbanshis and Kacharis. *Proc. Ind. Sc. Cong., 46th Session (Abstract).*

3137. ————— : A short note on the relation between stature and sitting height of some Bodo tribes of Assam. *Jour. Gau. Univ. (Sc.)*, X(2): 133-37.

3138. ————— : Relative lengths of the first and second toes of the Rabha foot. *Jour. Gau. Univ.*, X(2).

3139. ————— : *Somatic variability among some population of South Goalpara, Assam.* Unpub. D.Phil. Thesis, Gau. Univ.

3140. **Das, B.M.** : 1960 : Physical affinity of the Kachari. *Jour. Gau. Univ. (Sc.)* XI (2): 61-81.

3141. ————— : 1962 : Physical affinity of the Rajbanshi. *Bull. Deptt. of Tribal Culture & Folklore Research (Gau. Univ.)*, 1(2): 23-9.

3142. **Das, B.M.** : 1962 : Investigations on the finger prints of the Khamyang. *Jour. Gau. Univ. (Sc.),* XIII (2).

3143. —————— : Finger prints of the Kacharis. *Acta Criminologiae et Medicinae Legalis Japonica,* Vol. 28 (24).

3144. —————— : 1963 : Investigations on the finger prints of the Khamyang. *Jour. Gau. Univ. (Sc.),* XIV (2).

3145. —————— : Somatometric characters of the Khamyang. *Jour. Gau. Univ. (Sc.),* XIV (2).

3146. —————— : Finger prints of the Bodo population of Assam. *Jour. Gau. Univ.,* XIV (2): 77-9.

3147. —————— : 1964 : Somatic variability among some populations of South Goalpara, Assam. *Proc. of National Institute of Science, India,* 30B (5-6): 315-38 (Boro).

3148. —————— : *Ethnic affinities of the Rabha.* Gau. Univ., 149p.

3149. —————— : 1965-66 : On the palm prints of Rajbanshi. *Jour. Univ. of Gau. (Sc.),* 16-17: 33-41.

3150. —————— : 1966 : On the palm prints of the Hajong. *MII,* 46(3), July: 248-55.

3151. —————— : 1967 : On the palm prints of the Rajbanshi. *Proc. Ind. Sc. Cong., 54th Session* (Abstract).

3152. —————— : Age at menarche of Kalita girls in Assam. *MII,* 47(2) April: 113-17.

3153. —————— : 1978 : Fertility and mortality differentiation among the Shyam people of two villages in Sibsagar district. *Proceedings of Genetic Demography in India, Anth. S.I.,* Calcutta.

3154. —————— : 1985 : Fertility and mortality differentiation among the Khamyang and the Turung population of Jorhat district. *Jour. Assam Sc. Soc. and Proceedings of the Institute of Advanced Study in Sc. and Technology* (Gauhati), 28 (1), Sept.: 14-9.

3155. —————— : 1989 : Fertility and mortality differentiation among the Shyam people of two villages in Sibsagar district. *(In) Genetical Demography of Indian Population. (Ed.)* by K.S. Singh. Calcutta, Anth. S.I.: 12-8.

3156. —————— : 1994 : Natural increase of population among Deuri of Assam. *(In) Demographic Profile of North-East India. (Eds.)* by Sanu Mukherjee et al., New Delhi, Omsons Pubs.: 96-102.

3157. —————— : 1996 : Deori health condition of urban and rural people. *Paper for TRI, Guwahati Seminar on Nutrition, Health and Growth, etc.*

3158. **Das, B.M.** : 1996 : Body build and menarcheal age in rural Assamese women. *(In) People of North-East India: Anthropological Perspectives. (Ed.)* by Sarthak Sengupta. New Delhi, Gyan Publishing House: 81-90.

3159. **Das, Bandana**: 1974 : *A note on the dermatoglyphic study of Turung and Khamyang of Sarupathar.* Unpub. M.Sc. Dissert., Anth. Deptt., Dib. Univ.

3160. **Das, Bharat** : 1972 : *An analysis of some finger and palm prints of the Mikir (male).* Unpub. M.Sc. Dissert., Anth. Deptt., Dib. Univ.

3161. **Das, Bhuban Mohan** : 1955 : A study of the somatoscopic characters of the Rabhas. *Jour. of the Univ. of Gauhati*, Vol. 6: 139-49.

3162. ———— : 1956 : The study of whorl on head hair of the Pati Rava. *Jour. Gau. Univ.*, Vol. 7: 19.

3163. ———— : Physical character of the Rabhas of Assam. *Forty-third Indian Science Congress,* Agra, January.

3164. ———— : Physical character of the Rabhas of Assam. *MII*, 36 (2), April-June: 92-9.

3165. ———— : 1958 : Finger prints of the Pati Rabha. *Proc. of 45th Session of Ind. Sc. Cong. (Abstract).*

3166. ———— : Blood Groups of Rabhas. *Proc. of Ind. Sc. Cong., 45th Session (Abstract).*

3167. ———— : Blood groups of the Rabhas. *MII,* 38(3), July-Sept.: 213-15.

3168. ———— : Demographic study of a Rabha village. *Vanyajati,* VI(2), April: 74-9.

3169. ———— : Note on child mortality among the Rabha. *Jour. Gau. Univ. (Sc.),* IX (2).

3170. ———— : A note on leprosy among the Mikirs. *Jour. Gau. Univ.,* IX.

3171. **Das, Bhubanmohan** : 1974 : *Prathamik Abaybik Nritatta.* Gauhati, Gau. Univ. (*in Assamese*).

3172. ———— : 1967 : A note on the variation of earlobe attachment. *Acta Genet.*, Basel, 17: 154 (Kachari, Rabha, Rajbanshi, etc.).

3173. **Das, Bhubanmohan** : 1967 : Somatic variability in South

Goalpara, Assam. *Acta Geneticae Med. et. Gemmel.*, 16(2): 178-89.

3174. ———— : 1968 : A comparative study of the relative lengths of human first and second toes. *MII*, 48(3), July: 258-63.

3175. ———— : Physical affinities of the Rajbanshis. *Bull. Deptt. of Tribal Culture and Folklore Research.* Gau. Univ.

3176. ———— : Book Review: *Ethnic affinities of the Rabha.* Gauhati University, 1964, x, 149p., *East. Anth.*, 2(1), Jan.-April: 130-31.

3177. ———— : 1969-71 : A study on some aspect of growth of the Assamese boys. *Jour. Gau. Univ. (Sc.)*, 20-22: 51-65.

3178. ———— : 1969 : A short note on the relation between stature and sitting height of some Bodo tribes of Assam. *Proc. Ind. Sc. Cong., 56th Session (Abstract).*

3179. ———— : 1970 : *Project on physical anthropology of the Castes of Assam.* Anth. Deptt., Gau. Univ.

3180. ———— : Variation in cross section of head hair among three caste populations of Assam. Proc. *Indian Sc. Cong., 57th Session (Abstract).*

3181. ———— : *Anthropometry of the tribal groups of Assam, India. (Ed.)* by Henry Field. Miami, Florida (USA), Field Research Projects, Coconut Grove *(Study No. 41)*, 25p.

3182. ———— : 1971 : A study on some aspects of growth of Assamese boys. *Proc. of Annual Meeting of Assam Sc. Society.*

3183. ———— : Caste and head hair. *MII*, 51(S.C. Roy Centenary).

3184. ———— : 1972 : Medullary structure of head hair in some Caucasoid and Mongoloid populations of Assam, India. *Z. Morph. Anthrop.*, 63(1): 102-09.

3185. ———— : 1973 : Caste and head hair. *Indian Anth.*, 3(2): 135-38.

3186. ———— : Distances Anthropometriques Entre Quatre Castes de I' Assam, Inde. *L' Anthropologie,* Tome 77, no. 5-6: 637-43 (in German).

3187. ———— : Height, weight and chest circumference of the Baishya children. *Jour. Assam Sc. Soc.*, 16(1): 34-42.

3188. ———— : 1974 : A study of cross-sections of head hair from some Caucasoid and Mongoloid populations of Assam, India. *Z. Morph. Anthrop.*, 65(3): 324-28.

3189. **Das, Bhubanmohan** : 1974 : A cross sectional study of growth in height and weight of an endogamous caste of Assam. *Bull. Deptt. of Anth., Gau. Univ.* III, Dec.: 24-40.

3190. ———————— : Physical anthropology in North-East India, a short review. *(In) Contemporary Anthropological Research in North-East India. (Ed.)* by B.M. Das. Dibrugarh, Dib. Univ.: 1-15. (This is also *Bull. Anth. Deptt., Dib. Univ.* Vol. III, 1974).

3191. ———————— : 1975 : Cerumen types in some populations of North-East India. *The Anth.,* XIII (1-2), March-Sept.: 36-40.

3192. ———————— : 1976 : Distance between Austro-Asiatic and Tibeto-Burman people in respect of certain physical traits. *Bull. Anth. Deptt., Dib. Univ.,* IV (1975): 35-43 (Rabha, Kachari, Bodo, Hajong, etc.).

3193. ———————— : 1977 : Inheritance of cerumen type and its importance in population studies. *MII,* 57(4), Oct.-Dec.: 305-12 (Koch etc.).

3194. ———————— : Trend of variation in respect of certain anthropometric traits in two populations of North-East India. *Proceedings of a Seminar on Human Variation in India,* organised by Anth. S.I., Calcutta.

3195. ———————— : Variation among four Assamese castes in respect of finger patterns. *Abstract. Ind. Jour. of Phy. Anth. & Hum. Gen.* (Lucknow).

3196. ———————— : 1978 : Cerumen types in some populations of North-East India. *The Anth.,* XVI (1-2): 1-5.

3197. ———————— : 1979 : On some aspects of variation and ongoing human evolution. *Presidential Address, Section of Anth. & Arch., 66th Ind. Sc. Cong. Association, Hyderabad.*

3198. ———————— : On some aspects of variation and ongoing human evolution. *MII,* 59(1), Jan.-March: 1-25 (Rabha, Mikir).

3199. ———————— : Physical variation in three Assamese castes. *Anthropologischer Anzeiger,* 37(3): 204-10.

3200. ———————— : 1981 : *Micro-evolution.* New Delhi, Concept Pub. Comp. (Boro, Chutia, Rabha, Kachari, Rajbanshi, etc.).

3201. ———————— : 1982 : *Speech on Ethnic elements in North-East India,* Lecture delivered in the Institute of Anthropology, Univ. of Rome, November (Under Indo-Italian Cultural Exchange Programme).

3202. **Das, Bhubanmohan** : 1982-83 : Ethnic elements in North-East India. *Rivista di Anthropologia* (Rome), LXII.

3203. **Das, Bhubanmohan** : 1983 : A cursory glance on the problems and prospects of Physical Anthropological Research in North-East India. *(In) Souvenir: Anthropological Society of North-East India. (Eds.)* by H.C. Sharma and B. Choudhury. Anth. Deptt., Gau. Univ.: 41-5.

3204. ———————— : Micro-evolutionary trend in North-East Indian tribes: An overview. *Proceedings of an International Symposium on Genetic Micro differentiation in Human and other animal populations,* held at Hyderabad in December, 1983.

3205. **Das, B.M.** *and* **A.C. Bhagabati** : 1962 : Investigation on the finger prints of the Khamyang. *Jour. Univ. of Gau. (Sc.),* XIII(2): 75-8.

3206. ———————— ; 1963 : Somatometric characters of the Khamyang. *Jour. of Gau. Univ. (Sc),* XIV(2): 49-54.

3207. ———————— : Investigations on the finger prints of the Khamyang. *Jour. of Gau. Univ.,* XIV.

3208. ———————— : 1964 : Investigation on the palm prints of the Khamyang. *Jour. of Gau. Univ. (Sc),* XV(2): 80-7.

3209. **Das, B.M.; A.C. Patowary; S. Patowary** *and* **R. Das** : 1979 : On some clinical aspects of haemoglobin E. *Jour. As. Sc. Soc.,* XXIIA: 6-9.

3210. **Das, B.M.; Anee Deka** *and* **Ranjan Deka** : 1978 : Ear lobe types in some population of North-East India. *Ind. Jour. Phy. Anth. & Hum. Gen.* IV(2), Dec.: 151-55.

3211. **Das, B.M.** *and* **Bonoshree Devi** : 1967 : Interspaces between toes of urban and rural population of Assam. *Jour. Assam So. Soc.,* IX.

3212. ———————— : 1985 : Weight, crown-heel length and head circumference of new born Assamese babies. *(In) Children in North-East India. (Ed.)* by B.M. Das. Calcutta, Anth. Surv. India: 1-13.

3213. **Das, B.M.** *and* **B.C. Lahkar** : 1990 : Culture change in a disturbed physical environment: A microlevel case study. *Jour. Human Ecology,* 1(1), Jan.: 39-42.

3214. **Das, B.M.; G. Flatz; M.R. Chakraborty** *and* **H. Delbruck** : 1971 : High prevalence of haemoglobin E in two populations in Assam. *Humangenetik* (Germany), XII: 264-66 (Khasi-Bhoi and Ahom).

3215. **Das, B.M.; G. Flatz; M.R. Chakraborty** *and* **H. Delbruck** : 1972 : Genetic survey in the population of Assam, I. ABO blood groups, glucose-6-phosphate dehydrogenase and Haemoglobin type. *Human Heredity,* 22(4): 323-30.

3216. **Das, B.M.; H. Walter; K. Gilbert; P. Lindenberg; K.C. Malhotra; B.N. Mukherjee; R. Deka** *and* **R. Chakraborty**: 1987: Genetic variation of five blood group polymorphisms in ten populations of Assam, India. *International Jour. of Anth.,* 2(4): 325-40.

3217. **Das, B.M.; H.W. Geodde; H.G. Benkmann; S. Singh; M.R. Chakraborty; H. Delbruck** *and* **G. Flatz** : 1972 : Genetic survey in the population of Assam, II. serum protein and erythroeyte enzyme polymorphism. *Human Heredity,* 22(4): 331-37.

3218. **Das, B.M.; Irshad Ali** *and* **Renuka Das** : 1985 : Some aspects of child rearing practices among the rural Assamese Hindu. *(In) Ibid*: 30-6.

3219. **Das, B.M.** *and* **Kanti Bhusan Pakrasi** : 1955 : Blood groups. *Science and Culture* (Calcutta), XIX, Sept.: 1-2.

3220. —————— : 1956 : A study of the distribution of hair on the digits (Hand) from Assam. *East. Anth.,* IX (3-4): 196-201.

3221. **Das, B.M.** *and* **M.N. Phookan** : 1959 : A short note on blood groups from Gauhati. *Jour. Gau. Univ. (Sc).* X (2): 139-40.

3222. **Das, B.M.** *and* **M.S. Das** : 1969 : Anthropometry of the Kaibarta of Assam. *MII,* 49(1), Jan.-March: 49-57.

3223. **Das, B.M.** *and* **P.B. Das** : 1967 : Age at menarche of Kalita girls in Assam. *MII,* 47(2): 113-17.

3224. —————— : 1969 : *Physical characters of the Brahmin of Kamrup, Assam.* (Unpublished).

3225. —————— : 1971 : A study on some aspects of growth of the Assamese boys. *Proc. Annual Meeting of Assam Sc. Soc.*

3226. —————— : 1972 : Physical characters of the Muslim of Kamrup, Assam. *Proc. Ind. Sc. Cong., 59th session (Abstract).*

3227. —————— : A study of growth of the head in Assamese boys. *Bull. Deptt. of Anth., Gau Univ.,* I, December: 88-96.

3228. **Das, B.M.; P.B. Das** *and* **R. Das** : 1973 : Genetic distances in respect of ABO blood groups among four castes of Assam, India. *Human Genetik,* XX; 179-81.

3229. —————— : 1978 : Population and region wise variation in the distribution of ABO blood groups in Assam. *India Abs. No. 0051, vol. 1, Xth ICAES,* New Delhi.

3230. **Das, B.M.; P.B. Das** *and* **R. Das** : 1980 : *Study No. 10: Population and region-wise variation in the distribution of ABO* *blood groups in Assam, India.* Gau. Univ., Anth. Deptt., (*Mimeo.* UGC Scheme).

3231. **Das, B.M.; P.B. Das** *and* **R. Das** : 1980 : *Study No. 1: The Lalung: Their physical features and biosocial profile.* Gau. Univ., Deptt. of Anth., 19p. (*Mimeo.*, UGC sponsored scheme).

3232. ———————— : *Study No. 2: A comparative study of physical anthropology of five Mongoloid populations of Assam.* Gau. Univ. Anth. Deptt, 32p (*Mimeo.*, UGC sponsored scheme).

3233. ———————— : *Study No. 3: Physical anthropology of Brahmins of Assam.* Gau. Univ., Deptt. of Anth., 23p. (*Mimeo.*, UGC sponsored scheme).

3234. ———————— : *Study No. 4: Biological variation in the Kalita, a caste of Assam.* Gau. Univ., Anth. Deptt., 31p. (*Mimeo.*, UGC sponsored scheme).

3235. ———————— : *Study No. 5: Variation in physical characteristics in the Kaibartas of Assam.* Gau. Univ., Anth. Deptt., 35p. (*Mimeo.*, UGC scheme).

3336. ———————— : *Study No. 6: The Assamese Muslims: Their physical features.* Gau., Univ. Anth. Deptt., 44p. (*Mimeo.*, UGC scheme).

3237. ———————— : *Study No. 7: A comparative study of physical anthropology of four Assamese castes: Jogi, Hira, Kumar and Kaibarta.* Gau. Univ., Anth. Deptt., 31p. (*Mimeo.*, UGC scheme).

3238. ———————— : *Study No. 8: Biosocial profile of five Mongoloid populations of Assam.* Gau. Univ., Anth. Deptt., 47p. (*Mimeo.*, UGC scheme).

3239. ———————— : *Study No. 9: The Assamese Hindus and Muslims: Their biosocial profile.* Gau. Univ. Anth. Deptt., 46p. (*Mimeo.*, UGC scheme).

3240. **Das, B.M.; P.B. Das; R. Das; H. Walter** *and* **H. Danker-Hopfe** : 1985 : Anthropological studies in Assam, India, Observations on five Mongoloid populations. *Anthropologischer Anzeiger*, 43: 193-204.

3241. ———————— : Anthropological studies in Assam, India, Observations on Muslims. *Anthrop. Anz.*, Jg. 43(4): 299-310.

3242. ———————— : 1986 : Anthropological studies in Assam, India, Observations on three Brahmin groups. *Anthrop. Anz.*, 44(1): 35-43.

3243. ———————— : Anthropological studies in Assam, India, Observations on the Kalitas. *Anthrop. Anz.*, 44(2): 105-15.

3244. **Das, B.M.; P.B. Das; R. Das; H. Walter** *and* **H. Danker-Hopfe** : 1986 : Anthropological studies in Assam, India, Observations on four caste groups (Jogi, Hiras, Kumars, Kaibartas). *Anthrop. Anz.*, 44(2): 239-48.

3245. ——————— : 1989 : Anthropological studies in Assam, India, Socio-biological observations of Assamese population. *Anthrop. Anz.*, 47(2): 129-43.

3246. **Das, B.M., P.B. Das, R. Das** *and* **S. Sengupta** : 1980 : Descriptive physical anthropology of the Kayastha caste of Kamrup, Assam. *Bull. Anth. Deptt., Dib. Univ.* IX: 101-11.

3247. ——————— : 1982 : Descriptive physical anthropology of the Kayastha caste of Kamrup, Assam. Bull. Anth. Deptt., Dib. Univ. IX(1980): 101-11.

3248. **Das, B.M.** *and* **P.B. Uzir** : 1959 : Relative lengths of the first and second toes of the Rabha foot. *Jour. Gau. Univ. (Sc),* X(2): 153-58.

3249. ——————— : 1960 : Interspaces in the Rabha foot. *Jour. Gau. Univ.*, XI(2): 83-5.

3250. **Das, B.M.** *and* **R. Das** : 1981 : Intra and inter tribal variation in palmar flexion crease: A population study. *Ind. Jour. Phy. Anth. & Hum. Gen.*, VII(3): 173-78.

3251. **Das, B.M.; R. Das** *and* **P.B. Das** : 1979 : Taste sensitivity for phenylthiourea of seven Assamese population groups of Kamrup, Assam. *Proceedings of the 66th Annual Session of Ind. Sc. Cong. Asson., Calcutta (Abstract).*

3252. **Das, B.M.; R. Das** *and* **R. Deka** : 1979 : A note on population variation in respect of haemoglobin percentages. *Jour. Assam Sc. Soc.*, 22(A): 62-3.

3253. **Das, B.M.** *and* **R. Deka** : 1976 : Cultural factors in fertility regulation. *Procdg. of a Seminar on Social change in North-East India,* organised by the Deptt. of Anth., Dib. Univ., March 26-27.

3254. ——————— : 1980 : Haemolgobin E in North-East India: A review. *Ind. Jour. Phy. Anth. & Hum. Gen.*, VI (1), June: 55-62.

3255. ——————— : 1982 : Cultural factors in fertility regulation. *Ind. Anth.*, 12(2), Dec.: 181-85.

3256. ——————— : 1985 : Haemoglobinopathies in the population of North-East India. *Indian Anth.*, XV(1), June: 21-32.

3257. **Das, B.M.** *and* **R. Deka** : 1985 : Population study in Assam : ABO blood groups, haemoglobin E and G-6-PD deficiency. *Anthropologischer Anzeiger*, 43(1): 81-6.

3258. **Das, B.M., R. Deka** *and* **G. Flatz** : 1975 : Predominance of the haemoglobin E gene in Mongoloid population of Assam, India. *Humangenetik, (Human Heredity)*. XXX: 187-91.

3259. ———————— : 1982 : Glucose-6- phosphate dehydrogenase deficiency in five populations of Assam, India. *Indian Anth.*, XII(1): 73-5.

3260. **Das, B.M.; R. Deka** *and* **Renuka Das** : 1980 : Haemoglobin E in six populations of Assam. *Jour. Ind. Anth. Soc.*, XV(2-3), July-Nov.: 153-56.

3261. ———————— : 1982 : ABO Blood Groups and Rh-factor in six populations of Assam. *Bull. Anth. Sur. India,* XXIX(1-2), Jan.-June (1980): 1-3.

3262. ———————— : 1980 : ABO blood group and Rh-factor in six populations of Assam. *Bull. Anth. S.I.*, 29(1-2): 1-3 (Garo, Rabha, Kachari, Bodo, Mikir, Lalung, Rajbanshi).

3263. **Das, B.M.** *and* **Renuka Das** : 1965 : An anthropometric study of the Kalita. *MII* 45(2), April-June: 170-76.

3264. ———————— : Finger prints of the Kalita. *MII,* 45 (3): 247-50.

3265. ———————— : Palm prints of the Kalita. *MII,* 45(4): 301-5.

3266. ———————— : 1966 : Ridge count of finger prints of the Kalita. *Jour. As. Sc. Soc.,* IX: 32-4.

3267. ———————— : 1967 : A study of the Hira foot. *MII,* 47(2): 139-48.

3268. ———————— : 1968 : Whorl on head hair of the Kalita and some other populations of India. *Jour. As. Sc. Soc.* (1967), X: 26-8.

3269. ———————— : Interspaces between toes of an urban and rural populations of Assam. *Jour. As. Sc. Soc.,* X(1967): 34-8.

3270. ———————— : A study of Mikir foot. *Proc. Ind. Sc. Cong., 55th Session (Abstract).*

3271. **Das, B.M.** *and* **Renuka Das** : 1968 : A study on the Mikir foot. *Jour. Gau. Univ. (Sc.)* XVI-XVIII(2): 42-53.

3272. ———————— : 1971 : Medullary structure of head hair in some

Caucasoid and Mongoloid populations in Assam. *Z. Morph. Anth.*, 63(1): 102-09.

3273. **Das, B.M.** *and* **Renuka Das** : 1972 : A note on the ridge counts of finger pattern of the Khamyang, Mongoloid population of Assam. *Bull. Deptt. of Anth., Dib. Univ.*, 1: 50-3.

3274. ——————— : 1973 : Ethnic position of the Kalita in relation to some other castes of Assam. *Bull. Deptt. of Anth., Dib. Univ.*, II: 35-8.

3275. ——————— : 1974 : A study of cross section of head hair from some Caucasoid and Mongoloid populations of Assam, India. *Z. Morph. Anth.*, 65(3): 324-28.

3276. **Das, B.M.** *and* **S. Sengupta** : 1980 : Age at menarche among rural Assamese women. *Miscellaneous Paper, Study No. 10.* (*Mimeo.*, UGC scheme). Anth. Deptt., Gau. Univ.

3277. ——————— : 1984 : Age at menarche among rural Assamese women. *Jour. Assam Sc. Soc.*, XXVII(1): 6-13.

3278. **Das, B.M.** *and* **Sarthak Sengupta** : 1985 : Variation in palmar C line termination polymorphism among some endogamous groups of Assam. *Anthropologie,* XXIII (2): 97-100.

3279. **Das, B.M.** *and* **T.C. Sharma** : 1958 : Traditional methods of treatment of leprosy among Mikirs. *The Adivasi* (Orissa), 3(1): 25-33.

3280. **Das, B.M.** *and* **U. Deka** : 1959 : Physical characters of the Suris of Assam. *Proc. Ind. Sc. Cong., 46th Session (Abstract).*

3281. ——————— : 1960 : Physical characters of the Suri of Assam. *Jour. Gau. Univ. (Sc),* XI (2): 87-98.

3282. **Das, B.M.** *and* **U. Deka Mahapatra** : 1958 : Finger prints of the Suris. *Jour., Gau. Univ. (Sc.)* IX (2): 121-26.

3283. ——————— : 1958 : A note of the leprosy among the Mikirs. *Jour. Gau. Univ. (Sc).* IX.

3284. **Das Chaudhuri, A.B.** : 1991 : Primate studies in India: A Review. *MII,* Spl. Issue, 71(1), March: 241-77 (Assam etc.).

3285. **Das, Chuman** : 1993 : AIDS: Unending nightmare. *A.T., Sunday Reading.* Dec. 12: I(1-8) (Assam etc.).

3286. **Das, D.** : 1974 : *A study on certain genetic traits among the Khamyangs and the Ahoms.* Unpub. M.Sc. Dissert., Anth. Deptt., Dib. Univ.

3287. **Das, D.** : 1981 : *Folk Medicines from Assam.* Shillong, Meghalaya Govt. Press (Chief Conservator, Conservatory & Forest Deptt.).

3288. **Das, D.D.** : 1979 : *Inter-group variability in respect of certain dermatoglyphic characters.* Unpub. Ph.D. Thesis, Anth. Deptt., Dib. Univ.

3289. **Das, D. Dutta** : 1982-83 : Ridge counts of finger pattern of the Ahom: A Mongoloid population of Assam. *Bull. Deptt. of Anth., Dib. Univ.*, XI-XII(1987): 25-8.

3290. ——— : 1986 : Genetics of epidermal thickness and radral cushioning factors among the three caste groups of Assam. *Bull. Deptt. of Anth., Dib. Univ.*, 15 (1990): 104-88.

3291. **Das, Deepanjana Dutta** : 1996 : Main line index and transversality among three Mongoloid populations of Assam. *(In) Communities of North-East India: An Anthropological Perspective. (Eds.)* by Farida Ahmed Das and Indira Barua. Delhi, Mittal Pubn.: 101-04.

3292. **Das, F.A.** : 1972 : Distribution of ABO blood groups among the Assamese Muslim. *Bull. Deptt. of Anth., Dib. Univ.*, I: 14-7.

3293. **Das, Farida Ahmed** : 1974 : A comparison of the Assamese Muslims with the Assamese Hindu and the Muslims of some other states of India in respect of ABO blood groups. *(In) Contemporary Anthropological Research in North-East India. (Ed.)* by B.M. Das (*Bull. Anth. Deptt., Dib. Univ.*, Vol. III), 79-81.

3294. ——— : 1976 : Distribution of middle phalangeal hair among the Assamese Muslim. *Bull. Deptt. of Anth., Dib. Univ.*, IV(1975): 21-4.

3295. ——— : 1977 : The Rh blood group among the Muslims of Assam. *Bull. Deptt. of Anth., Dib. Univ.*, V(1976): 25-6.

3296. ——— : *A study of the genetic composition of the Assamese Muslims of Dibrugarh, Assam.* Unpub. Ph.D. Thesis, Anth. Deptt., Dib Univ.

3297. ——— : 1978 : Somatometric traits of the Assamese Muslims in relation to Assamese Hindu castes. *(In) Cultural and Biological Adaptability of Man with special reference to North-East India. (Eds.)* by A.C. Bhagabati and R.K. Kar. *Bull. Deptt. of Anth., Dib. Univ.*, Vol. 6, 1977: 170-75.

3298. ——— : 1979 : Position of Assamese Muslims in relation to Bihari Muslims in respect of Anthropometric Characters. *Ind. Jour. Phy. Anth & Hum. Gen.*, 5(1), June: 65-70.

3299. **Das, Farida Ahmed** : 1980 : Biological affinity of the Hindus and Muslims of Assam in respect of somatometric traits, ABO blood groups and finger pattern. *Jour. Ind. Anth. Society*, 15(2-3), July-Nov.: 179-85.

3300. **Das, Farida Ahmed** : 1981 : A note on the ear-lobe types among the Muslims of Assam. *Bull. Anth. Deptt., Dib. Univ.*, VII-VIII (1978-79): 49-51.

3301. ———— : 1982 : Biological relationship among the Muslims of Assam in respect of somatometry, ABO blood groups and finger pattern. *Bull. Deptt. Anth., Dib. Univ.*, IX(1980): 112-18.

3302. ———— : 1984-85 : Taste threshold for phenyltiourea among the Assamese Muslims. *Bull. Deptt. Anth., Dib. Univ.*, 13-14: 104-10.

3303. ———— : 1992 : Trend of menarcheal age in the Kaibarta girls of Dibrugarh, Upper Assam. *Bull. Deptt. Anth., Dib. Univ.*, 18-19 (1989-90): 113-19.

3304. ———— : 1996 : Micro-differences at biological level among the Muslim communities of Dibrugarh (Assam).. *(In) Communities of North-East India: An Anthropological Perspective. (Eds.)* by Farida Ahmed Das and Indira Barua. Delhi, Mittal Pubn.: 75-82.

3305. **Das, Farida Ahmed** *and* **Anjali Borah** : 1995 : Blood groups and colour blindness among the Tai Phake. *Bull. Deptt. Anth., Dib. Univ.*, 23: 103-08.

3306. **Das, Farida Ahmed** *and* **Dipika Mohan** : 1993 : A dermatoglyphic study of the Deoris of Dibrugarh district, Assam. *Bull. Deptt. Anth., Dib. Univ.*, 20-21(1991-92): 84-93.

3307. **Das, Farida Ahmed** *and* **S. Sengupta** : 1979 : Distribution of ABO blood groups among three castes of Dibrugarh, Upper Assam. *Jour. Assam Sc. Soc.* 22B: 68-72.

3308. **Das, Hiralal** : 1987 : *Age changes in some somatometric characters of the Hajongs of Meghalaya.* Unpub. Ph.D. Thesis, Anth. Deptt., Gau. Univ.

3309. **Das, Hiralal** *and* **M.N. Phookan** : 1981 : Relation between stature and sitting height of the Hajong of Tikrikilla of Garo Hills, Meghalaya: An appraisal. *Bull. Anth. Deptt., Dib. Univ.*, 7-8, 1978-79: 72-77.

3310. **Das, Hiralal** *and* **P.B. Das** : 1978-79 : A study of some genetic traits among Caibartas of Kachar, Assam. *Bull. Deptt. Anth., Gau. Univ.* 4: 65-70.

3311. **Das, Hiralal** *and* **P.B. Das** : 1981 : A study of some genetic traits among the Kaibartas of Cachar, Assam. *Bull. Deptt. of Anth., Dib. Univ.*, VII-VIII (1978-79): 24-8.

3312. **Das, Indira** : 1978 : *Blood group among the Bodo-Kachari, Kokrajhar.* Unpub. M.Sc. dissertation, Anth. Deptt., Dib. Univ.

3313. **Das, M.** : 1967 : *Physical Affinity of the Kaibarta of Assam.* Unpub. M.Sc. Dissertation. Anth. Deptt., Gau. Univ.

3314. **Das, P.B.** : 1966 : A study of the middle phalangeal hair among some castes of Kamrup, Assam. *Jour. Assam Sc. Soc.,* IX: 35-9.

3315. ———— : 1967 : *A study of growth of somatometric characteristics of a selected caste of Assam.* Ph.D. Thesis, Anth. Deptt., Gau. Univ.

3316. ———— : Relation between stature and sitting height of Kalita children. *Jour. Assam Sc. Soc.,* X : 29-33.

3317. ———— : 1970 : Relative lengths of the first and second toes of different populations of Assam. *MII,* 50(2), April-June: 141-48.

3318. ———— : 1971 : *Growth studies of the Kalita children (Assam). (Ed.)* by Henry Field. Miami, Florida (USA), Field Research Projects, Coconut Grove *(Study No. 57),* 50p.

3319. ———— : Taste threshold for phenylthiourea among the Kaibarta of Assam. *Proceedings of S.C. Roy Century.*

3320. ———— : 1973 : Height, weight and chest circumference of Baishya children. *Jour. of the Assam Sc. Soc.,* XVI(1), June: 34-42.

3321. ———— : A cross-sectional study of growth in height and weight of an endogamous caste of Assam. *Bull. Deptt. of Anth., Gau. Univ.,* II, December: 24-31.

3322. ———— : Growth of study of Head dimensions of Baishya children. *Jour. Indian Anth. Society,* 8(2), Oct.: 5a.

3323. ———— : 1974 : A comparative study of growth in respect of height, weight and chest circumference of rural Assamese boys. *(In) Contemporary Anthropological Research in North-East India. (Ed.)* by B.M. Das *(Bull. Deptt. of Anth., Dib. Univ.,* Vol. III, 1974). Dib. Univ., Deptt. of Anth.: 43-55.

3324. ———— : A study of growth of head dimensions of Baishya children. *Bull. of the Deptt. of Anth., Gau. Univ.,* III, December: 52-7.

3325. **Das, P.B.** *et al* : 1975 : Distribution of ABO blood groups of some population of Assam. *Bull. Deptt. Anth., Gau. Univ.,* IV: 74-9.

3326. **Das, P.B.** : 1976 : A study of fertility performance among three rural populations of Kamrup, Assam. *Bull. Deptt. of Anth., Gau. Univ.,* 5: 75-81.

3327. ——————— : 1979 : Physical Anthropology in North-East India: A review of progress.. *(In) Eastern Himalayas (Eds)* by T.C. Sharma and D.N. Majumdar. New Delhi, Cosmo Pubs.: 86-101.

3328. ——————— : 1983-1986 : Variation in age at menarche of Assamese girls. *Gau. Univ. Jour. (Sc),* 29(2): 1-8.

3329. **Das, P.B.** *and* **A.K. Ghosh** : 1970 : A study of ABO blood groups taste threshold for P.T.C. and ear lobe attachment among the Kumar of Assam. *Jour. Assam Sc. Soc.,* 13: 14-8.

3330. **Das, P.B.** *and* **B. Bhattacharjee** : 1973 : Frequency of colour blindness in five groups of Assam. *MII,* 53(4), Oct.-Dec.: 363-67.

3331. ——————— : 1986 : Birth weight of the Assamese and Bengali new born babies of Gauhati, Assam. *Bull. Deptt. of Anth., Dib. Univ.,* XV (1990): 157-62.

3332. **Das, P.B.** *and* **B. Choudhury** : 1982 : A mixed longitudinal study of growth in height and weight of Assamese children from 1-7 years. *Bull. Anth. Surv. of India,* XXXI (3-4): 37-42.

3333. **Das, P.B.** *and* **B. Choudhury** : 1985 : A mixed longitudinal study on growth in height and weight of Assamese children from 1 to 7 years. *(In) Children in North-East India. (Ed.)* by B.M. Das. Calcutta, *Anth. Surv. of India:* 37-42.

3334. ——————— : 1992 : A mixed longitudinal study of growth of Assamese children from 8 to 16 years. *Bull. Deptt. of Anth., Gau. Univ.,* VI, March: 62-9.

3335. **Das, P.B.** *and* **B.M. Das** : 1967 : Age at menarche of Kalita girls in Assam. *MII,* 47(2): 113-17.

3336. ——————— : 1973 : Incidence of child mortality in a Kachari village. *Science and Culture,* IX(1), Jan.: 127-29.

3337. **Das, P.B., D.K. Duarah** *and* **B. Choudhury** : 1984 : The blood groups (ABO and MN) of the Brahmins of Kamrup, Assam. *Jour. NEICSSR,* VIII(2): 6-11.

3338. **Das, P.B.** *and* **J. Hazarika** : 1975 : Height and weight of Post-Graduate students of Gauhati University. *Jour. of Assam Sc. Soc.* XVIII(1), June: 24-8.

3339. **Das, P.B.** *and* **N.N. Sengupta** : 1972 : Finger dermatoglyphics of the Kumar of Assam. *Jour. Assam Sc. Soc.*, XV (1), June: 36-43.

3340. **Das, P.B., R. Das** *and* **B.M. Das** : 1979 : Taste sensitivity for phenylthiourea of seven Assamese population groups of Kamrup, Assam. *Proceedings of 66th Annual Session of Indian Sc. Cong.*, Pt. III, Sec. VIII, *Abst.* No. 30: 11.

3341. **Das, P.B.** *and* **S.N. Buragohain** : 1969 : Taste threshold for P.T.C. of Vaishyas and Keota.

3342. ―――――― : 1971 : Taste sensitivity to phenylthiourea in two caste groups of Assam. *MII,* 51(3), July-Sept.: 252-56.

3343. **Das, P.B.; S.N. Buragohain** *and* **B.K. Goswami** : 1969 : A study of genetic traits in two caste groups of Assam. *Jour. Assam Sc. Soc.*, XII: 23-9.

3344. **Das, P.B.** *and* **T.C. Sharma** : 1967 : Age at menarche of Kalita girls in Assam. *Jour. Assam Sc. Soc.*, 10.

3345. ―――――― : 1968 : Physical characters of the Lalung of Assam. *Jour. Assam Sc. Soc.*, XI: 51-8.

3346. ―――――― : Physical characters of the Lalung of Assam. *Jour. Assam Sc. Soc.*, XI: 36-50.

3347. ―――――― : 1970 : The earlobe attachment among some Indian populations. *Jour. Anth. Society of Nippon*, 78: 157.

3348. **Das, P.B.** *and* **Usha Deka** : 1975 : Studies of hand clasping, arm-folding and dominant eye among some endogamous groups of Assam. *Jour. Ind. Anth. Soc.*, X(2): 195-99.

3349. **Das, R.C.** : 1974 : Social aspect of leprosy. *(In) Contemporary Anthropological Research in North-Eastern India. (Ed.)* by B.M. Das *(Bull. Deptt. Anth., Dib. Univ.* Vol. III): 122-26 (Mikir).

3350. **Das, Rekha** : 1992 : *A study of differential fertility and child mortality among two Assamese caste groups of Mirza area in Kamrup District.* Unpub. Ph.D. Thesis, Anth. Deptt., Gau. Univ.

3351. ―――――― : 1993 : Education and fertility. *Bull. Deptt. of Anth., Gau. Univ.*, VII: 46-9 (Brahmin and Koch, Assam).

3352. **Das, Rekha** : 1994 : Inter birth spacing, pregnancy wastage and knowledge, attitude and practice of family planning methods among some Koch women of South Kamrup, Assam. *Bull. Anth. Deptt., Gau. Univ.*, VIII: 57-64.

3353. **Das, Rekha** : 1995 : Variation in fertility of two populations of Kamrup, Assam. *Bull. Deptt. Anth., Dib. Univ.*, 23: 139-49.

3354. ―――――― : 1996 : Child mortality and morbidity among two groups of south Kamrup (Assam). *(In) Communities of North-East India: An anthropological perspective. (Eds.)* by Farida Ahmed Das and Indira Barua. Delhi, Mittal Pubn.: 171-78.

3355. **Das, Renuka** : 1964 : A note on the ear lobe of the Kalita. *Jour. of Assam Sc. Soc.,* VII: 91.

3356. ——————— : Finger prints of some Kalita girls. *Jour. of Assam Sc. Soc.,* VII: 91.

3357. ————— : 1971 : *A study on some morphological characters of human foot with special reference to their heredity and growth.* Unpub. Ph.D. Thesis, Anth. Deptt. Calcutta Univ.

3358. ————— : 1972 : *A study on some morphological characters of the human foot with special reference to heredity and growth. (Ed.)* by Henry Field, Miami, Florida (USA) Field Research Projects, Coconut Grove *(Study No. 75).*

3359. ————— : 1974 : A preliminary note on a twin study on interspaces of foot. *(In) Contemporary Anthropological Research in North-East India. (Ed.)* by B.M. Das. Dibrugarh, Dib. Univ.: 56-9 *(Bull. Anth. Deptt., Dib. Univ.,* Vol. III).

3360. ——————— : Frequency of colour blindness among the three Assamese castes of Upper Assam. *(In) Contemporary Anth. Res. in NEI. (Ed.)* by B.M. Das., Dib. Univ.: 90.

3361. ————— : 1977 : Variation in interspaces of foot in certain populations of North-East India. *MII,* 57(3), July-Sept.: 263-68.

3362. ————— : 1980 : Taste sensitivity to PTC of some Caucasoid and Mongoloid populations of Assam. *Gauhati University Journal (Sc.),* 29: 9-14.

3363. ————— : 1981 : Cerumen types in four Mongoloid populations of North-East India. *Bull. Deptt. of Anth., Dib. Univ.,* Vol. 7-8 (1978-79): 52-5.

3364. ————— : 1982 : Variation in morphological character of human foot. *Bull. Deptt. of Anth., Dib. Univ.,* IX (1980): 119-35.

3365. ————— : 1985 : A study on variation of palmar flexion crease among three Assamese castes. *Ind. Jour. of Phy., Anth. and Human Genetics,* II(3), Aug.-Dec.: 175-77.

3366. ————— : 1986 : Biological contact: Somatoscopic traits. *Man and Life,* 12(3-4), July-Dec.: 211-13.

3367. ————— : 1991 : Population variation in palmar flexion creases. *(In) Dermatoglyphics Today. (Eds.)* by B. Mohan Reddy, S.B. Roy and B.N. Sarkar, Calcutta, Indian Institute of Biosocial

Research & Development, Anth. Surv. of India, Indian Stat. Inst.: 439-42.

3368. **Das, Renuka** : 1992 : A note on pregnancy wastage among some populations of Assam. *Bull. Deptt. of Anth., Gau. Univ.*, VI. March: 71-3.

3369. **Das, Renuka** *et al* : 1973 : Genetic distance in respect of ABO blood groups among four castes of Assam, India. *Humangenetik*, 20: 179-81.

3370. **Das, Renuka** *and* **B.M. Das** : 1965 : An anthropometric study of the Kalita. *MII*, 45(2): 170-76.

3371. ―――――― : Finger prints of the Kalita. *MII*, 45(3), July-Sept.: 247-50.

3372. ―――――― : Palm prints of the Kalita. *MII*, 45(4), Oct.-Dec.: 301-05.

3373. ―――――― : Ridge counts of the finger patterns of the Kalita. *Jour. Assam Sc. Soc.*, IX: 1-3.

3374. ―――――― : 1967 : A study of the Hira foot. *MII*, 47(2), April-June: 139-48.

3375. ―――――― : 1992 : A note on caste variation at bio-social level. *Presented in a National Seminar on Anthropology and Community*, Anth. Deptt., Dib. Univ., Nov. *(Mimeo.)*.

3376. ―――――― : 1993 : A note on caste variation at bio-social level. *Bull. Deptt. Anth., Gau. Univ.*, VII: 39-45 (Brahmin, Kalita, Kaibarta of Assam).

3377. **Das, Renuka, S. Pattowary, A.C. Patowary** *and* **B.M. Das** : 1971 : On some aspect of the body-build of the Assamese girls. *Jour. Assam Sc. Soc.*, XIV(2), Dec.: 124-28.

3378. **Das, S.R., D.P. Mukherjee** *and* **P.N. Bhattacharjee** : 1967 : Survey of the blood groups and PTC Taste among the Rajbanshi caste of West Bengal (ABO, MNS, Rh, Duffy and Diego). *Acta Genet. Stat. Med.*, 17: 433-45.

3379. **Das, S.R.** *and* **P.N. Bhattacharjee** : 1963 : Blood groups (A_1A_2BO), ABH secretion, sickle-cell, P.T.C. taste and colour blindness in Rajbanshi of Midnapore, West Bengal. *Bull. Anth. Surv. of India*, 12: 1-6.

3380. **Das, Sanghamitra** : 1993 : A note on palmar flexion creases in schizophrenia. *Bull. Deptt. of Anth., Dib. Univ.*, Vol. 20-21 (1991-1992): 121-25 (Dibrugarh, Assam).

3381. **Das, Susanta Krishna** : 1980 : Immigration and demographic transformation of Assam, (1891-1981): *EPW*, May 10.

3382. **Das, Uma** : 1994 : *A study of infant mortality in Kamrup district in Assam since Independence.* Unpub. Ph.D. Thesis, Anth. Deptt., Gau Univ.

3383. **Das, Upangshu** : 1972 : *PTC test threshold distribution among the Mikir.* Unpub. M.Sc. Dissert., Anth. Deptt., Dib. Univ.

3384. ————— : 1977 : PTC taste sensitivity among the Mikir of Assam. *Bull. Deptt. of Anth., Dib. Univ.,* V(1976): 71-3.

3385. **Datta, Amarendra Nath** : 1994 : *Some aspects of eco-biology of golden langur presbytis goei (Khajuria) of Assam.* Unpub. Ph.D. Thesis, Zoo. Deptt., Gau. Univ.

3386. **Datta, Birendranath** : 1936 : Note on the presence of light coloured eye iris amongst the population of North-Eastern India. *Indian Science Congress, 23rd Session, Indore, January.*

3387. ————— : 1938 : Note on the presence of light coloured eye iris amongst the population of North-Eastern India. *MII*, 18: 1-8.

3388. **Datta, D.K.** : 1974 : *A study on the foot of Khamyang and Turung.* Unpub. M.Sc. Dissert. Anth. Deptt., Dib. Univ.

3389. **Deb, A.K.** : 1979 : *Comparison between the Hill and Plain Mikirs of Assam in respect of certain anthropogenetic traits and their ethnic position.* Unpub. Ph.D. Thesis, Anth. Deptt., Dib Univ.

3390. ————— : 1985 : Affinity of the Karbis of Assam in respect of PTC taste sensitivity. *Ind. Jour. of Phy. Anth. and Hum. Genetics,* XI: 81-4.

3391. ————— : Anthropometric variation among the Hill and Plain Karbis of Assam and their ethnic position. *(In) Anthropological Perspectives on North-East India (Bull. Deptt. of Anth. Dib. Univ.,* Vol. X, 1981). Deptt. of Anth., Dib. Univ.: 123-34.

3392. **Deka, Akashi** : 1994 : Dermatoglyphics of the Bodos and the Karbis: A comparative study. *Bull. Deptt. of Anth., Dib. Univ.,* Vol. XXII: 46-53.

3393. **Deka, Anee** : 1973 : An investigation on the finger prints of the Mikirs. *Bull. Deptt. of Anth., Dib. Univ.,* II.

3394. **Deka, L., R. Majumder** *and* **A.M. Dutta** : 1983 : Some

Ayurvedic important plants from district Kamrup (Assam). *Science of Life* (Coimbatore), III: 108-15.

3395. **Deka Mahapatra, U.** : 1970 : Study of fertility in a tribe of North-East India. *Jr. Soc. Res.*, 13: 74-82.

3396. **Deka, M.U.** *and* **P.B. Das** : n.p. : *Studies of hand clasping, arm folding and dominant eye among some endogamous groups of Assam* (unpublished).

3397. **Deka Mahapatra, Usha** *and* **Priyabala Das** : 1968 : Taste threshold for phenylthiocarbamide in some endogamous groups of Assam. *The Anthropologist*, XV(1-2), March-Sept.: 25-32.

3398. ———— : 1973 : Ear lobe variation in various populations of Assam. *MII*, 53(3), July-Sept.: 256-61.

3399. **Deka, R.** : 1978 : *Report on Serogenetic Survey among Garo and Hajong.* Report submitted to An. S.I., Shillong (*Mimeo.*).

3400. ———— : 1984 : A genetic survey in four Mongoloid populations of the Garo Hills. *(In) Garo Hills Land and the People. (Ed.)* by L.S. Gassah. Omson Pub., Gauhati.

3401. **Deka, Ranjan** : 1974 : Frequency of colour blindness among the three Assamese castes of Upper Assam. *(In) Contemporary Anthropological Research in North-East India. (Ed.)* by B.M. Das. Dib. Univ.: 60-2 (*Bull. Anth. Deptt., Dib. Univ.*, III).

3402. ———— : 1975 : *Fertility and Haemoglobin Genotypes: A population study in Upper Assam*. Unpub. Ph.D. Thesis/ Anth. Deptt., Dib Univ.

3403. ———— : Age at menarche and haemoglobin genotypes among the Kachari woman of Assam. Paper presented at the *2nd Annual Conference of Indian Society of Human Genetics*. Calcutta (*Mimeo.*).

3404. ———— : Predominance of the haemoglobin E genes in a Mongoloid population in Assam (Co-Author). *Humangenetik*, XXX.

3405. ———— : 1976 : Age at menarche and haemoglobin "E" among the Kachari women of Upper Assam. *MII*, 56(4), Oct.-Dec.: 349-54.

3406. ———— : 1977 : Menarcheal age among the Kachari women of Upper Assam. *Bull. Deptt. of Anth., Dib. Univ.*, Vol. V(1976): (1-6).

3407. **Deka, Ranjan** : 1977 : Selection potential among the Sonowal

Kachari of Upper Assam. *Seminar on Human Variation in India*, held on 27 June-2 July, 1977 by Anth. Surv. of India, Calcutta.

3408. **Deka, Ranjan** : 1980 : Selection potential among the Sonowal Kachari of Upper Assam. *Bull. Deptt. of Anth., Dib. Univ.* Vol. IX: 136-40.

3409. ———— : 1981 : Fertility and haemoglobin genotypes: A population study in Upper Assam (India). *Human Genetics*, 59: 172-74.

3410. ———— : Cerumen types in four Mongoloid population groups of North-East India. *Bull. Deptt. Anth.*, Dib. Univ., VII-VIII (1978-79): 52-5.

3411. ———— : 1982 : A_1 A_2 BO and Rh blood groups among the Mikir of Assam. *Indian Jour. of Phy. Anth. & Hum. Gen.*, 8(2-3), Aug.-Dec.: 151-54.

3412. ———— : Selection potential among the Sonowal Kachari of Upper Assam. *Bull. Deptt. of Anth., Dib. Univ.*, IX(1980): 136-40.

3413. ———— : 1982 : The other backward classes movement in Assam. *(In) Tribal Movements in India*, Vol. I. *(Ed.)* by K.S. Singh. New Delhi, Manohar Publications: 295-305.

3414. ———— : 1990 : Haemoglobin polymorphism in India and South-East Asia. *(In) Human Variations in India* by Director General. Calcutta, Anthropological Survey of India: 10-7 (Assam).

3415. **Deka, Ranjan** *and* **Anee Bora** : 1973 : An investigation on the finger prints of the Mikirs. *Bull. Deptt. of Anth., Dib. Univ.*, II: 55-60.

3416. **Deka, Ranjan, A.P. Reddy, B.N. Mukherjee, B.M. Das, S. Banerjee, M. Roy, B. Dey, K.C. Malhotra** *and* **H. Walter** : 1988 : Haemoglobin E distribution in ten endogamous population groups of Assam, India. *Hum. Heredity,* 38(5), Sept.-Oct.: 261-66.

3417. **Deka, Ranjan, B.C. Gogoi, J. Hundrieser** *and* **G. Flatz** : 1987: Haemoglobinopathies in North-East India. *Haemoglobin*, XI: 531-38.

3418. **Deka, Ranjan** *and* **Renuka Das** : 1980 : Haemoglobin E in six populations of Assam. *Jour. Ind. Anth. Soc.*, XV: 153.

3419. **Deka Sharma, Chandana** : 1995 : *A Study of surface water and settlement pollution for a few entrap water sources in and around Guwahati city.* Unpub. Ph.D. Thesis, Geog. Deptt., Gau. Univ.

3420. **Deka, U. and P.B. Das** : 1975 : Studies of hand clasping, arm folding and dominant eye among some endogamous groups of Assam. *Jour. Ind. Anth. Soc.*, X(2): 195-99.

3421. ———— : 1976 : Tongue rolling: A genetic trait in some populations of Assam (*Abstract*). *Proceedings of Indian Science Congress.*

3422. **Deka, U.** *and* **P. Patojoshi** : 1977 : Fertility and pregnancy wastage. *(In) Cultural and Biological Adaptability of Man with special reference to North-East India. (Ed.)* by A. C. Bhagabati. Dibrugarh, Anth. Deptt., Dib Univ.: 193-99.

3423. **Dev, A.K.** : 1985 : Affinity of the Karbis of Assam in respect of PTC taste sensitivity. *Ind. Jour.. Phy. Anth. & Hum. Gen.*, XI(1-2): 81-4.

3424. **Dev, Anil Kr.** : 1980 : *Comparison between the hill and plain Mikirs of Assam in respect of certain anthropogenetic traits and their ethnic position.* Unpub. Ph.D. Thesis, Anth. Deptt., Dib. Univ.

3425. **Devi, B.** : 1980 : Economic status and body dimensions of new born baby. *Jour. Assam Sc. Soc.*, 25(1).

3426. ———— : 1981 : *A study of some aspects of body dimension of new born babies and pertinent mothers.* Unpub. Ph.D. Thesis, Anth. Deptt., Gau. Univ.

3427. **Devi, B.** *and* **B.M. Das** : 1967 : Interspace between toes of an urban and rural populations of Assam. *Jour. Assam Sc. Soc.*, Vol. X.

3428. **Devi, Bonoshree** *and* **Bhuban M. Das** : 1969 : Anthropometric characters of foot of a rural and an urban population of Assam *MII*, 49(1), Jan.-March: 41-8.

3429. **Devi, Ng. Shreela** *and* **T. Shyamacharan Singh** : 1990 : Gene differentiation at two Loci between the Muslims of Manipur and Assam. *Jour. Ind. Anth. Soc.*, 25(1), March: 35-8 (The Muslims of Manipur and Assam, *Sunni* sect of Islamism).

3430. **Devi, S.** : 1978 : *Finger and palm prints of Bodo-Kachari*. Unpub. M.Sc. Dissert. Anth. Deptt., Dib. Univ.

3431. **Dey, Kripasindhu** : n.d. : *Measurement of women fertility in Assam*. Unpub. Ph.D. Thesis, Anth. Deptt., Gau. Univ.

3432. **Director General. (Ed.)** : 1990 : *Human Variations in India*. Calcutta, Anthropological Survey of India, 393p.

3433. **Duarah, Dwijendra Kr.** : 1978 : The blood groups (ABO & MN) of the Brahmins of Kamrup, Assam (Co-author). *Jour. Assam Sc. Soc.*, Vol. 21.

3434. **Duara, Hitendra** : 1995 : *The food and feeding habits of three Indian Major Crops from the Brahmaputra drainages of Assam.* Unpub. Ph.D. Thesis, Gau. Univ.

3435. **Dunlop, K.J.** *and* **U.K. Majumdar** : 1952 : The occurrence of sickle-cell anaemia among a group of tea garden labourers in Upper Assam. *Ind. Med. Gaz.*, 87: 387-91.

3436. **Dutta, B.C.** : 1990 : Somatoscopic variation in North-East India. *(In) Human variations in India: Proceedings of the Seminar on Physical Anthropology 27 June—2 July 1977. (Ed.)* by Director General. Calcutta, Anth. Surv. of India: 195-98.

3437. **Dutta Chaudhuri, S.S.** : 1994 : Cephalic capacity: A study of 7 ethnic groups of North-East India. *Vanyajati*, XLII (2), April: 22-5 (Brahmin, Kalita, Kaibarta etc.).

3438. ———————— : 1973 : Distances anthropometriques entre quarte castes de I'Assam Inde. *L' Anthropologie*, 77(5-6): 637-43 (i.e. Anthropometric distances among four castes of Assam, in French).

3439. ———————— : Incidence of child mortality in a Kachari village. *Sc. and Cul.*, IV(1): 127-29.

3440. ———————— : 1974 : A study on some aspects of growth of the Assamese boys. *Jour. Gau. Univ. (Sc)*, XX-XXII (1969-71): 51-65.

3441. ———————— : 1977 : Variation among four Assamese castes in respect of finger prints. *Proc. Seminar of Phy. Anth. & Hum. Gen.* (Lucknow).

3442. ———————— : 1982 : Child mortality among rural Assamese. *Bull. Anth. Sur. India*, 31: 14-29.

3443. ———————— : 1985 : Child mortality among rural Assamese. *(In) Ibid*: 14-29.

3444. ———————— : 1992 : A note on some aspects of fertility among eleven Assamese populations of the Brahmaputra valley. *Bull. Deptt. Anth., Gau. Univ.* VI, March: 53-60.

3445. **Dutta, D.** : 1978 : *Intergroup variability in respect of certain dermatoglyphic characters.* Unpub. Ph.D. Thesis, Dib. Univ.

3446. **Dutta, D.; R. Phookan** *and* **P.D. Das** : 1982 : The Koro epidemic in lower Assam. *Ind. Jour. of Psychiatrics* (Delhi), 24: 370-74.

3447. **Dutta, Deepanjana** : 1977 : A note on the finger prints of the Miris of Assam. *Bull Deptt. of Anth. Dib. Univ.*, 5(1976): 53-6.

3448. **Dutta, Deepanjana D.** : 1995 : Genetics of epidermal thickness and cushioning factors among the three Mongoloid populations of Assam. *Bull. Deptt. Anth., Dib. Univ.* 23: 96-102.

3449. **Dutta, Dilip** : 1974 : *A study of foot of Khamiyangs and Turungs.* M.Sc. Dissertation (Unpub.), Anth. Deptt., Dib. Univ.

3450. **Dutta, Dipsikha** : 1977 : *A preliminary study on fertility and family planning of Kachari and Ahom women of Dibrugarh.* Unpub. M.Sc. Dissert., Anth. Deptt., Dib. Univ.

3451. **Dutta, M.N.** : 1977 : *A study on some anthropometric traits among the Brahmin and Kaibarta of Dibrugarh (Upper Assam).* Unpub. M.Sc. Dissert., Anth. Deptt., Dib. Univ.

3452. ———— : 1979 : Ear lobe attachment among the Ahom of Dibrugarh, Upper Assam. *Current Anth.*, 20(2): 339.

3453. ———— : Distribution of ABO blood groups among the Ahom and its relations with other tribe and caste populations of N.E. India (*Abstract*). *Indian Sc. Cong., 66th Session*, Pt. III, 6.

3454. ———— : 1980 : Note sur les tourbillons du vertex Chez les Ahom at D'autres population de L'Assam. *L'Anthropologie (Paris)*, 84(3): 474-75. (in French).

3455. ———— : 1981 : Ear lobe attachment and ABO blood groups among the Savara of Dibrugarh. *Bull. Deptt. of Anth., Dib. Univ.*, X: 116-22(1985). *Nissa* tribe of Assam Tea Garden.

3456. ———— : 1982-83 : Finger prints among the Ahoms of Dibrugarh. *Bull. Deptt. of Anth., Dib. Univ.*, 11-12 (1987): 50.

3457. ———— : 1986 : Anthropometric characters of scheduled caste population of Upper Assam. *Vanyajati*, 34(1), Jan.: 3-6.

3458. ———— : 1991 : An investigation on the finger-prints of the Savara of Dibrugarh. *Bull. Deptt. of Anth., Dib. Univ.*, 16-17(1987-88): 131-36.

3459. ———— : 1992 : Ear lobe attachment and colour blindness among the Kaibarta: A scheduled caste of Assam. *Vanyajati*, XL(4), Oct.: 8-10.

3460. ———— : A note on some genetic traits among the Konyak Naga of Sibsagar District, Assam. *Bull. Deptt. of Anth., Dib. Univ.*, 18-19 (1989-90): 107-12.

3461. **Dutta, M.N.** : 1993 : Ear lobe attachment and relative length of 1st and 2nd toes of the Tanti: A tea garden community of Assam. *Vanyajati*, XLI(4), Oct.: 28-30.

3462. ———— : Cerumen type and ear lobe attachment among the Assamese castes of Dibrugarh, Assam. *Bull. Deptt. of Anth., Dib. Univ.*, 20-21 (1991-92): 63-7.

3463. ———— : 1994 : ABO blood groups among the Khamyangs: A scheduled tribe of Assam. *Vanyajati*, XLII(1), Jan.: 12-4.

3464. **Dutta, M.N., J.L. Sharma** *and* **S. Sengupta** : 1994 : A note on main line index and transversality in three Mongoloid populations of North-East India. *Bull. Deptt. of Anth., Dib. Univ.*, 22: 131-35 (Ahom, Deuri etc.).

3465. **Dutta, M.N.** *and* **M.N. Phookan** : 1978-79 : A study of some genetic traits among the Ahom (male) populations of Dibrugarh, Assam. *Bull. Deptt. of Anth., Dib. Univ.*, 7-8: 29-33 (1981).

3466. **Dutta, M.N.** *and* **S. Sengupta** : 1984-85 : A study of palmar creases among the Ahom, Deuri and Savara population of Dibrugarh district, Assam. *Bull. Deptt. of Anth., Dib. Univ.* 13-14: 133-39 (1989).

3467. ———— : 1986 : A comparative anthropometric study of three endogamous castes of Dibrugarh, Assam. *Bull. Deptt. of Anth., Dib. Univ.*, 15(1990): 81-7.

3468. ———— : 1991 : Study on palmar flexion creases among the Sonowal Kachari of Assam. *Social Sciences* (Silchar), 4(1-2), June-Dec.: 255-59.

3469. **Dutta, M.N.** *and* **Sabeha Begum** : 1996 : A short note on the somatometric characters of the Tanti: A tea garden labour population of Assam. *Bull. Deptt. Anth., Dib. Univ.*, 24: 95-7.

3470. **Dutta, P., D.R. Bhattacharyya** *and* **L.P. Dutta** : 1989 : Incrimination of anopheles virus as a vector of malaria in Dibrugarh district, Assam. *Ind. Jour. Malar.*, 26: 149-52.

3471. **Dutta, P.C.** : 1995 : Effect of occupational difference in consumption pattern in Barak valley of Assam: A case study. *Jr. NEICSSR*, 19(2), Oct.: 8-14. (Consumption pattern according to five different occupational groups of households viz. cultivators).

3472. **Dutta, Renu** : 1976 : *A preliminary study of certain aspects of fertility performance of the Koch women of Nirmaligaon, Dibrugarh.* Unpub. M.Sc. Dissert. Anth. Deptt., Dib. Univ.

3473. **Dutta, S.K.** : 1976 : Cerebral Malaria is again taking a heavy toll of life in Assam. *Times of India*, Aug. 27: 4(7-8).

3474. **Dutta, Sukla** : 1972 : *Distribution of blood groups among the Mikirs.* Unpub. M.Sc. Dissert. Anth. Deptt., Dib. Univ.

3475. **Dutta, Tripti** : 1972 : *Study of somatometric and somatoscopic characteristic among the Mikirs of United North Cachar and Mikir Hills.* Unpub. M.Sc. Dissert. Anth. Deptt., Dib. Univ.

3476. **Flatz, G.** : 1971 : High prevalence of haemoglobin E in two populations in Assam. *Humangenetik*, 12: 264.

3477. ———— : 1976 : Haemoglobinopathies in the population, Assam, Vol. II. *(In) German Scholars on India: Contributions to Indian Studies. (Ed.)* by Cultural Deptt., Embassy FRG. New Delhi. Bombay, Nachiketa Pub.

3478. **Flatz, G.; M.R. Chakravartti; B.M. Das** *and* **H. Delbruck** : 1972: Genetic survey in the population of Assam. 1. ABO blood groups, glucose-6-phosphate dehydrogenase and haemoglobin types. *Human Heredity*, 22(4): 323-30.

3479. **Foll, C.V.** : 1961 : The age at menarche in Assam and Burma. *Archives of Disease in Childhood, Burma* (Rangoon), 36: 302-08.

3480. **Forsyth, E.P. Charles** : 1924 : Note on Tezpur, 1923. *(In) Handbook of Castes and Tribes employed on tea estates in North-East India (Comp)* by Tea District Labour Association. Calcutta, Printed by Catholic Orphan Press: 330-34.

3481. **Geddes, Arthur** : 1942 : The population of India, a variability of change as a regional demographic index. *Geog. Review*, 32: 562-73 (Physical Anth. includes Myanmar and Assam).

3482. **Gee, E.P.** : 1952 : Possible occurrence of the snub-nosed monkey (Rhinopithecus roxellanae) in Assam. *Jour. Bombay Natural Hist. Soc.*, 51: 264-65.

3483. ———— : 1955 : A new species of langur in Assam. *Jour. Bombay Nat. Hist. Soc.*, 53: 252-54.

3484. **Ghosh, Dipika** : 1971 : *A study of somatometric and somatoscopic characteristics of the Mikirs.* Unpub. M.Sc. Dissert. Anth. Deptt., Dib. Univ.

3485. **Giri, A.K., S. Datta, B. Gajra, A. Ray Chaudhury, G. Talukdar** *and* **A. Sharma** : 1982 : Some genetic markers in tribals of Eastern India. *Acta Anthropogenetica*, 6: 99-106.

3486. **Giri, A.K., S. Datta, G. Talukder** *and* **A. Sharma** : 1985 : Transfer of various tribals of Eastern India. *Human Heredity*, 35: 56-8.

3487. **Goedde, H.W.; H.G. Benkmann; S. Singh; B.M. Das; M.R. Chakravartti; H. Delbrueck** *and* **G. Flatz** : 1972 : Genetic survey in the population of Assam II. Serum/protein and erythrocyte enzyme polymorphisms. *Human Heredity*, 22: 331-37.

3488. **Gogoi, Banajyoti** : 1983 : *The distribution of ABO blood group system among the Deuri of Kolowlowa village of Dibrugarh.* Unpub. M.Sc. Dissert. Anth. Deptt., Dib. Univ.

3489. **Gogoi, Bharatee** : 1974 : *A study on somatoscopic and somatometric characteristics of the Savare females of Mancotta tea estate.* Unpub. M.Sc. Dissert., Anth. Deptt., Dib. Univ.

3490. **Gogoi, D.** : 1972 : Menarche and menopause among women of an Ahom village in Upper Assam. *Bull. Deptt., Anth., Dib. Univ.*, I: 18-22.

3491. **Gogoi, J.K.** : 1990 : Tribal demography in North-East India: Some preliminary observation. *(In) Tribal Demography and Development in North-East India. (Eds.)* by Ashish Bose, Tiplut Nangbri and Nikhelesh Kumar. Delhi, B.R. Pub.: 85-94.

3492. **Gogoi, J.K.** *and* **Napoleon Hazarika** : 1980 : Pattern of migration in Assam 1951-1971. *Paper presented at the Annual Conference of India Association for Study of Population* held at Calcutta, Dec. *(Mimeo.)*.

3493. **Gogoi, Kalpana** : 1983 : *A study on fertility performance and ABO blood group of the Ahom people of Bokel Maj Gaon of Dibrugarh and their ABO blood group incompatibility in respect of fertility.* Unpub. M.Sc. Dissert. Anth. Deptt., Dib. Univ.

3494. **Gogoi, Mina** : 1974 : *A study on the finger pattern of Khamyang.* Unpub. M.Sc. Dissert., Anth. Deptt., Dib. Univ.

3495. **Gogoi, P.; S. Boissya** *and* **C.L. Boissya** : 1979 : A few ethnogynaecological records from the state of Assam, India. Paper presented on the *First International Conference on Traditional Asian Medicine at the Australian National University, Canberra, Australia.*

3496. **Gopalan, C.** : 1971 : *Nutritional Atlas of India.* New Delhi, Indian Council of Medical Research.

3497. ——— : 1995 : Towards food and nutrition security. *EPW* (52), Dec. 30: A 134-A 141 (Assam and other states).

3498. **Goswami, Atul** : 1982 : Migration into Assam: 1901-1971: Demographic dimensions. *(In) India's North-East: A multifaceted view. (Ed.)* by Pankaj Thakur. Tinsukia, Prakash Pubg. House: 46-65.

3499. **Goswami, Basanta Kr.** *(Jt. auth.)* : 1969 : A study of some genetic traits in two caste groups of Assam. *Jour. Assam. Sc. Soc.*, XII.

3500. **Goswami, G.** : 1975 : *The Kacharis of Tengakhat: Their palm prints*. Unpub. M.Sc. Dissert., Anth. Deptt., Dib. Univ.

3501. **Goswami, Homeswar** : 1975 : Population growth in the Brahmaputra Valley 1881-1931, *Assam Economic Journal* (Gauhati), 1, March.

3502. ———— : 1977 : Fertility patterns in the Brahmaputra Valley Districts of Assam, 1881-1931. *Assam Economic Jr.*, 3(1), March: 21-41.

3503. **Goswami, P.** : 1969 : Vegetation and wildlife. *(In) The Land and People: Assam (Comp.)* by S. Barkataki. New Delhi, National Book Trust: 26-44.

3504. **Goswami, R. Barua** : 1973 : *A clinical study of birth weight and size of the new born babies in Assam*. Unpub. M.D. Thesis, Gau. Univ.

3505. **Goswami, U.** : 1965 : *Growth and development of child from birth to 5 years*. Unpub. Ph.D. Thesis, Gau. Univ.

3506. **Guha, Anima** : 1986 : Folk Medicine of the Boro-Kacharis: A Plain tribe of Assam. *(In) Tribal Health: Socio-cultural dimensions. (Ed.)* by Buddhadeb Chaudhuri. New Delhi, Inter-India Pub.: 191-200.

3507. ———— : Herbs in the disease treatment by the Boro-Kachari: A Plain tribe of Assam. *Jour. Ind. Anth. Soc.*, XXI(3), Nov.: 219-30

3508. ———— : 1990 : Health care among two rural populations of Assam: A comparative study. *(In) Cultural and Environmental Dimensions on Health. (Ed.)* by Buddhadeb Chaudhuri, New Delhi, Inter India Pub.: 207-48 (Boro-Kachari and Koch-Rajbanshi).

3509. **Guha, Anima** *and* **D.P. Mukherjee** : 1990 : Influence of cultural traditions and social movements on the genetic structure of the Boro-Kachari population. *Jour. Ind. Anth., Society,* XXV(1), March: 73-81.

3510. **Guha, B.S.** : 1938 : *The Racial Element in Indian Population.* Oxford, Oxford Univ. (London).

3511. ———— : 1954 : Nutrition, *The Assam Tribune,* August 15.

3512. **Guha, Seema** : 1978 : Despondency and madness. *Eco. & Pol. Weekly,* 13(46), Nov. 18: 1881-82.

3513. **Gupta, Pabitra** *and* **Pratap C. Dutta** : 1966 : *Anthropometry in India (1868-1961), Memoir No. 10, 1962.* Calcutta, Anth. Survey of India, 373p. (Ahom, Arleng/Mikir, Bodo/Kachari, Koch, Mising/Miri, etc.).

3514. **Gupta, S.S.** *and* **S.S. Gupta** : 1979 : Genetic distance among three Assamese castes of Upper Assam in respect to ABO blood groups and colour blindness. *Ind. Jour. of Phy. Anth. & Hum. Genet.,* V: 43-8.

3515. **Harlan, R.** : 1834 : Description of a species of Orang (Simla hoolock) from the North-Eastern province of British-East India, lately the Kingdom of Assam. *Trans. Amer. Phil. Soc.,* IV: 52-9.

3516. **Harrison, J. Park** : 1873 : On the artificial enlargement of the ear-lobe. *Jour. Anth. Inst.*: 190-99.

3517. **Hazarika, A.N.** *and* **Ziauddin Ahmed** : 1973 : Somatometric characteristics of the Ahom (Male). *Bull. Deptt. of Anth., Dib. Univ.,* II: 39-43.

3518. ———— : 1974 : A comparative study of growth of stature, girth of thorax and weight of Ahom and Kalita boys of Assam. *(In) Contemporary Anthropological Research in North-East India.. (Ed.)* by B.M. Das, Dibrugarh, Anth. Deptt., Dib. Univ.: 73-7 (This is also *Bull. Anth. Deptt.,* Vol. III, 1974).

3519. **Hazarika, A.N. Z. Ahmed** : 1978 : *A study of growth of head, face, trunk and limbs of the Ahom boys of Assam.* Unpub. Ph.D. Thesis, Anth. Deptt., Dib. Univ.

3520. **Hazarika, S.** : 1971 : *Study on some aspects of body build and figure of Gauhati University girl students and tea garden workers of Assam.* Unpub. M.Sc. Dissert. Anth. Deptt., Gau. Univ.

3521. **Hiernaux, J.** : 1980 : Human Biological variations in Asia with special reference to India. *(In) La Diversite Biologique humaine: Human Biological Diversity (Collection d'Anthropologie physique)* by J. Hiernaux. Paris, Masson Publications: 197-273.

3522. **Hindustan Times** : 1990 : Cancer on the rise in N-E. Feb. 14: 9(1-3).

3523. **Hundrieser, J.; R. Deka, B.C. Gogoi, T. Papp** *and* **G. Flatz** : 1988 : DNA haplotypes and frameworks associated with the beta-globin gene in the Kachari population of Assam (India). *Human Heredity,* 34(4), July-Aug.: 240-45.

3524. **Huq, F.** : 1970 : Earlobe attachment and eyebrows in nine population groups in Assam. *Proc. of a Seminar on Physical Anthropology and Allied Discipline*. Calcutta, Anth. Survey of India (Mimeo.).

3525. ———— : 1975 : Earlobe attachment in nine population groups in Assam region (Lakhimpur, Sibsagar and Nowgong districts).. *(In) Bio-Anthropological Research in India. (Ed.)* by H.K. Rakshit. Calcutta, Anth. Survey of India: 153-56.

3526. **ICMR** : 1988 : *Genetic Atlas of Indian Tribes*. Bombay, Indian Council of Medical Research.

3527. ———— : 1996 : *Nutrition Project* inaugurated in Assam Medical College, Dibrugarh on March 3, 1996 by Ind. Coun. Med. Res., New Delhi.

3528. **International Institute** : 1994 : *India (Introductory Report) National Family Health Survey, 1992-93*. Bombay, Int. Inst. for Pop. Sc.

3529. **Islam, Anowar** : 1990 : Letters to the Editor: Health-care in Assam. *A.T.*, July 7: 4(3-5).

3530. **Jain, S.K. (Ed.)** : 1981 : *Glimpses of Indian ethno-botany*. New Delhi, Oxford & IBH Pub.

3531. **Journal** : 1975 : Studies of hand clasping, arm folding and eye dominance. *Jour. Anth. Society*, 10(2), Oct.: 195-200.

3532. **Kar, R.K.** : 1986 : A Note on health and sanitation among the tea labour in Assam. *Vanyajati*, XXX (IV): 2.

3533. ———— : 1990 : Health and sanitation versus culture: An appraisal of tea labour in Assam. *(In) cultural and environmental dimensions on health. (Ed.)* by Buddhadeb Choudhuri. New Delhi, Inter India Pub.

3534. ———— : 1991 : Some aspects of health culture of a Plain tribe in Assam. *Procg. of 78th Conf. Ind. Sc. Cong.* held at Indore (*Mimeo.*).

3535. ———— : 1994 : Some aspects of health-culture of a Plain tribe in Assam. *Bull. Deptt. of Anth., Dib. Univ.*, 22: 29-45. (Mishings, Hill Miri, Chutia Miri, Adis, Abor, Assam, A.P., etc.)

3536. **Karna, M.N.** : 1989 : *Assessment of drug abuse, drug users and prevention services in GHY, Imphal, Dimapur and Shillong*. North-East Hill University, Sociology Deptt., Shillong (Mimeo.).

3537. **Karnick, C.R.; K.C. Tiwari; R. Majumder** *and* **S. Bhattacharjee**: 1981 : Newer ethno-botanical and folklore studies of some medicinal plants of Guwahati and surrounding areas. *Jour. Nagarjun* (Calcutta), XXIV(1): 240-45.

3538. **Kaur, Daisan** : 1981 : *A study on finger and palm prints of the Kaibarta of Dibrugarh district.* Unpub. M.Sc. Dissert. Anth. Deptt., Dib. Univ.

3539. **Khajuria, H.** : 1956 : A new langur (Primates: Colobidae) from Goalpara district, Assam. *Am. Mag. Nat. Hist. Ser.* 12(9): 88-9.

3540. ———— : 1966 : Some observations on the habits of the Assamese macaque. *Proc. 2nd All-India Cong. Zoo.* (Varanasi, 1962), 2: 284.

3541. **Khan, Sakiya:** : 1989 : Poverty and nutrition level of the rural population in Assam. *Proceedings of a Seminar on Perspective, Issue and Experiences of Rural Development in North-East India* held on 26-27 May, 1989 by *NEICSSR*, Shillong (*Mimeo.*).

3542. ———— : 1991 : Poverty and nutrition level of the rural population in Assam. *(In) Rural Development in North-East India: Perspective, Issues and Experiences. (Ed.)* by R.K. Samanta. New Delhi, Uppal Pub. House: 126-37.

3543. **Khatoniar, A.** : 1972 : *Demographic study of the Mikirs of Assam.* Unpub. M.Sc. Dissert. Anth. Deptt., Dib. Univ.

3544. **Kumar, G.D.** : 1973 : *Ethnic Affinities of the Rajbansis of North-Bengal. (Ed.)* by Henry Field. Miami, Florida, Field Research Projects, Coconut Grove (*Study No. 83*), 60p.

3545. ———— : 1975 : The ethno-genesis of the Rajbansi of North-Bengal. *(In) Bio-anthropological Research in India. (Ed.)* by H.K. Rakshit. Calcutta, Anth. Survey of India: 47:53.

3546. **Kumar, Nikhlesh** : 1988 : Health seeking behaviour. Deptt. of Soc., *NEHU*, Shillong.

3547. **Kurup, G.U.** : 1974 : Mammals of Assam and the Mammal Geography of India. *(In) Ecology and Biogeography in India (Eds)* by M.S. Mani and W.Junk. The Hague, B.V. Publishers: 585-613.

3548. **Lekharu, Anjalee** : 1972 : *A study of growth pattern among the Mikir girls of United Mikir Hills and North Cachar District, Assam.* Unpub. M.Sc. Dissert. Anth. Deptt., Dib. Univ.

3549. **Macfarlane, E.W.E.** : 1937 : Eastern Himalayan blood groups. *Man*, 37(158): 127-29.

3550. **Mahanta, K.C.** : 1993 : Over-exploitation of North Sub-

Himalayan vegetal resources, its impact on the Brahmaputra valley of Assam. *Jr. Hum. Eco.*, 4: 261-66.

3551. **Mahanta, K.C.** : 1995 : A study of ethno-medicines in Assam: A general perspective. *Jr. Hum. Eco.*, 6(2), April: 105-17.

3522. ——————— : Shamanism and treatment of disease in Assam. *Bull. Anth. Deptt., Dib. Univ.*, 23: 60-75.

3553. **Mahanta, Pramananda** : 1992 : Women, Family and Health Care. *(In) Status of women in Assam. (Ed.)* by S.L. Baruah. New Delhi, Omsons Pub.: 150-53.

3554. **Mahapatra, Usha Deka** *and* **Priyabala Das** : 1968 : Taste threshold for phenylthiocarbamide in some endogamous groups of Assam. *The Anthropologist*, XV(1-2), March-Sept.: 25-32.

3555. ——————— : 1973 : Ear lobe variation in various population of Assam. *Man in India*, 53(3), July-Sept.: 256-61.

3556. **Majumder, Partha P.; B. Uma Shankar; Amitabha Basu; C. Kailash Malhotra; Ranjan Gupta; Barun Mukhopadhyay; M. Vijayakumar** *and* **K. Subrata Roy** : 1990 : Anthropometric variation in India: A statistical appraisal. *Current Anthropology*, 31(1), Feb.: 94-103.

3557. **Majumder, R.** : 1980 : *Economic aspects of plants of Ayurvedic importance from the Brahmaputra valley (Assam)*. Ph.D. Thesis, Gauhati Univ., Guwahati. (Pub. by G.U. Pub.).

3558. **Majumder, R.; A.R. Nair** *and* **T.K. Talukdar** : 1986 : Some sastriya medicinal plants of greater Guwahati and sub-urban. *Paper submitted in a Seminar on Medicinal Plants* held at Guwahati in June, 1986.

3559. **Majumder, R.; A.R. Nair; K.C. Tiwari** *and* **T.K. Talukdar** : 1986 : Ethno-medico botanical aspect of dominant aquatic & marshy plants of Kamrup district (Assam), India. *Nigerian Jour. of Biological Sciences*, University of IFE, Nigeria (West Africa).

3560. **Majumder, R., B.N. Sharma, A.R. Nair** *and* **T.K. Talukdar**: 1986 : Ethno-medico botanical aspect of some medicinal plants of Kamrup district (Assam). Paper read in *Silver Jubilee Seminar of JNAMPG&H*, Pune.

3561. **Majumder, R.; K.C. Tiwari; S. Bhattacharjee** *and* **A.R. Nair**: 1978 : Some folklore medicines from Assam and Meghalaya. *Quarterly Jour. Crude Drugs Research* (Netherland), 16(4): 185-89.

3562. **Majumder, R.; K.C. Tiwari; S. Bhattacharjee** *and* **A.R. Nair**:

1979 : Other economic values of plants of Ayurvedic importance from Kamrup district. *Netherland Jour. Agricultural Science Wageningen* (Netherland).

3563. **Majumder, R.; N.K. Dutta; C.L. Boissya** *and* **A.K. Majumder**: 1982 : Economic aspects of some medicinal plants from Assam, India. *Paper read in the International Horticultural Congress* held at Hamburg (W. Germany).

3564. **Malhotra, K.C.; B. Vijay Bhanu; M.R. Singh** *and* **V.S. Shastree** : 1971 : Cleft chin as a population maker. *Science & Culture,* 37 (2): 96-8.

3565. **Medhi, Birinchi K.** : 1994 : Health culture in a Kaibarta village. *Bull. Anth. Deptt., Gau. Univ.,* VIII: 39-45.

3566. ————— : 1995 : Socio-cultural dimensions of health in a Scheduled Caste village. *(In) Core Problems of the Scheduled Castes of Assam. (Ed.)* by Bimal Kr. Hazarika. Guwahati, AIRTSC(TRI) : 38-48.

3567. **Medhi, D.K.** : 1990 : *Traditional medicine in modern times*: The place of herbal and geo-products in the life of the people of Assam. *Paper presented in the School of Public Health,* Deptt. of Community Health Development, Bio-Medical School, University of Hawaii, Honolulu, April 12, 1990.

3568. **Mitra, Durga Das** : 1939 : A study of diet and nutrition in North-Bengal, Upper Assam and Calcutta. *Indian Jour. Medical Research* (Delhi), 27: 441-51.

3569. **Mitra, P.N.** : 1935 : Blood groups and heredity (Assamese-Plains) *Indian Jour. of Med. Res.,* 22: 495-97.

3570. **Mittal, K.** : 1979 : Primitive medicine versus modern medicine among the Santals. *Jr. Social Research*, XXII: 49-54.

3571. **Mohan, Dipika Rani** : 1983 : *A study on the finger and palm prints of the Deuri people of Kolowlowa adarsa Deuri gaon of Dibrugarh.* Unpub. M.Sc. Dissert. Anth. Deptt., Dib. Univ.

3572. **Mohanty, A.K.; D.K. Behera; K. Sarkar** *and* **D.R. Mohanty** : 1991 : Dietary pattern of the expectant and nourishing mothers among the Plain Bhuiyan tribe. *Man in Asia*, IV (II), Dec.: 8-18.

3573. **Mukherjee, B.N.; K.C. Malhotra; M. Roy; S. Banerjee; H. Walter** *and* **R. Chakraborty** : 1989 : Genetic heterogeneity and population structure in Eastern India: Red cell enzyme variability in ten Assamese populations. *Zeitschrift fur Morphologie und Anthropologie,* 77: 287-96.

3574. **Mukherjee, D.P.** : 1963 : Colour blindness among four Mongoloid groups of India. *Proc. Ind. Sc. Cong., 50th Session (Abstract).*

3575. ——————— : 1963 : Variation in defective colour vision among some tribes of Assam. *Bull. Anth. Survey of India,* XII(1-2): 39-42.

3576. ——————— : 1964 : Manual mid-phalangeal hair among some Mongolian tribes of Assam. *Abst. Proc. Ind. Sc. Cong. 51st session*: 233-34 (*Abstract*).

3577. ——————— : 1965 : Anthropological observations on the print patterns among the Hill tribes of North-East India. *Z. Morph. Anthrop.,* 56: 217-31.

3578. ——————— : 1982 : Some Biological dimensions of tribal economy in India. *(In) Economies of the Tribes and their transformation. (Ed.)* by K.S. Singh. New Delhi, Concept Pub. Comp.: 21-7 (Sonowal Kachari etc.)

3579. ——————— : 1986 : Ethnic bearing of triradial number on palms with special reference to North-East India. *Bull. Deptt. of Anth., Dib. Univ.,* 15(1990): 1-11.

3580. **Mukherjee, D.P.** *and* **Anima Guha** : 1990 : Colour blindness, manual mid phalangeal hair and attached ear lobe among Boro-Kacharis. *Jour. Ind. Anth. Soc.,* 25(2), July: 153-63.

3581. **Mukherjee, D.P.** *and* **Sanjib K. Chakravarty** : 1976 : Aspects of genetical structure in Bengalee Muslims of Cachar. *Jour. Ind. Anth. Society,* XI (2) May: 175-76 (*Abstract*).

3582. ——————— : 1983 : Aspects of genetical structure of Bengalee Muslims of Cachar. *Bull. Anth. Survey of India,* 26: 49-56 (1977).

3583. **Mukherjee, R.P.** *and* **S.S. Saha** : 1974 : The golden langurs (Presbytis geei Khajuria, 1956) of Assam. *Primates,* 15: 327-40.

3580. **Mukhopadhyay, S.K.** : 1972 : *A study of growth among the Mikir boys.* Unpub. M.Sc. Dissert. Anth. Deptt., Dib. Univ.

3585. **Nag, Anil Kr.** : 1990 : Drug addiction main cause of AIDS in N-E region. *Am. Baz. Pat., Nov.* 11: 5(5-7) (Manipur, Assam).

3586. **Nag, Moni** : 1965 : Family type and fertility. *Paper contributed to the World Population Conference,* Belgrade, Yugoslavia, 30: 131-38. (New Delhi).

3587. **Nath, A.C.** : 1975 : *The Ahom and Kacharis of Tengakhat: A study on their foot.* Unpub. M.Sc. Dissert., Anth. Deptt., Dib. Univ.

3588. **Nath, A.C.** *and* **B. Das** : 1994 : The digital formula of human foot. *TUI: A quarterly research Magazine on Tribal Life and Culture,* II(3), June-Aug. (About Tiwa-Lalung).

3589. **Nath, A.C.** *and* **B. Devi Das** : 1995 : A note on earlobe attachment among the Kaibartas of Assam. *India Jour. Human Ecology,* VI(3): 219-20.

3590. **Nath, Ananda Ch.** : 1996 : A study on the variation of earlobe attachment among the Karbis of Karbi Anglong in Assam. *Vanyajati,* XLIV(1), Jan.: 16-22.

3591. **Nath, Dilip C.; K. Kamshalendra Singh; C. Kenneth Land** *and* **K. Pijush Talukdar** : 1993 : Age of marriage and length of the first birth interval in a traditional Indian Society: Life table and hazards: Model Analysis. *Human Bio.,* 65(5), Oct.: 783-97(Assam).

3592. **National Sample Survey** : 1971 : Caloric and protein content of food items consumed per diet per consumer unit in rural and urban areas of Assam and Bihar. *26th Round (258/1) National Sample Survey,* June 1970-July 1971 *(Mimeo.).*

3593. **Naz, M.** : 1980 : *Earlobe types among the Maria and Bihari Muslims of Dibrugarh and a note on the inheritance of earlobe type.* Unpub. M.Sc. Dissert. Anth. Deptt., Dib. Univ.

3594. **NEICSSR** : 1993 : *Seminar on Social Health, Amity and Development,* organised by NEICSSR, Shillong and Voluntary Health Association, Shillong on 24-25 March *(Mimeo.).*

3595. ———— : 1995 : *Seminar on Population Studies,* organised by NEICSSR, Shillong.

3596. **Pachal, T.K.** : 1970 : Construction of life table for Assam females, 1951-60. *Sankhya (B),* 32(1-2), June: 31-40.

3597. **Pakrasi, K.; K. Basu; T. Mallik; S. Chowdhury** *and* **M. Chakraborty** : 1986 : Mentally retarded children of Eastern India: A biosocial study. *Social Biology,* 33.

3598. **Pakrasi, Kanti B.** *and* **Bhuban M. Das** : 1956 : A study of the distribution of hair on the digits (Hands) from Assam. *Eastern Anth.,* IX (3-4), Double no., March-Aug. (1955-56): 196-201.

3599. **Pakrasi, Kanti B.** *and* **Malakar** : 1967 : The relationship between family type and fertility. *Milback Memorial Fund Quarterly,* XIV(4): 451-60.

3600. **Pakrasi, Kanti Bhusan** : 1953 : A study of the physical characters of the Arlengs (Mikirs). *Jour. Univ. of Gau. (Sc.),* 4: 29-42.

3601. **Pakrasi, Kanti Bhusan** : 1954 : On the study of the somatoscopic characters of the Arlengs (Mikirs). *Jour. Univ. of Gau. (Sc.),* 5: 135-40.

3602. ———— : 1955 : On further statistical study of Arleng (Mikir) somatology. *Jour. Univ. of Gau. (Sc.).* 6: 23-31.

3603. **Pal, A.** : 1964 : Observations on the dentition of the crania from Eastern India. *Bull. Deptt. of Anth.,* (Anth. Sur. of India), XIII (1-2): 9-18.

3604. **Pathak, Vijoylakshmi** : 1992 : Women and Health care. *(In) Status of Women in Assam. (Ed.)* by S.L. Baruah. New Delhi, Omson Pub.: 146-49.

3605. **Pattanayak, S; R.G. Roy; D. Phukan** *and* **B.N. Barkakaty** : 1979 : Chloroquine resistance in 'P. falciparum' in Assam state. *Ind. Jour. of Med. Res.,* 70, Dec., Supplementary Issue: 14-9.

3606. **Paul, Subhra** : 1984 : *A study on foot type among the Bengali Brahmin of Gangapara at Dibrugarh.* Unpub. M.Sc. Dissert., Anth. Deptt., Dib. Univ.

3607. **Pegu, S.** : 1974 : *A note on the anthropometric study on the Turungs and Khamyangs.* Unpub. M.Sc. Dissert. Anth. Deptt., Dib. Univ.

3608. **Pegu, S.S.** : 1980 : Diphu: A study in urban growth. *(In) Family, Marriage and Social Change on the Indian Fringe. (Eds.)* by S.M. Dubey, P.K. Bordoloi, B.N. Borthakur. New Delhi. Cosmo Pubs.: 196-206 (Karbi Anglong district H.Qs).

3609. **Phookan (Gogoi), Arundhati** *and* **Sarthak Sengupta** : 1995 : Finger Prints of the Boro Kacharis of Assam. *Jr. Hum. Eco.,* 6(4), Oct.: 297-98.

3610. **Phookan, M.N.** *and* **Aparajita Barua** : 1987 : Malaria, its effect on people according to age, sex and ecology : An appraisal. *Bull. Deptt. Anth., Dib. Univ.,* XI-XII (1982-83) : 129-38 (Khelua and Kakapather).

3611. **Phookan, M.N. and Hiralal Das** : 1973 : Somatometric characters of the Hajong of Tikrikilla, Garo Hills, Meghalaya. *Bull. Anth. Deptt., Dib. Univ.,* 2, Dec.: 13-23.

3612. **Phookan, M.N.** *and* **N.A. Begum** : 1977 : A comparative study in respect of some genetic traits of two populations of Udaipur, Assam. *Bull. Deptt. of Anth., Dib. Univ.,* V (1976): 57-61 (Sema Naga and Nepalee).

3613. **Phookan, M.N.** *and* **T. Shyamacharan Singh** : 1994 : Variation in gene frequencies for two Loci among Assamese Tai. *Current Anth.,* 35(2), April: 191-93.

3614. **Phookan, Manabendra Nath** : 1961 : Anthropometric characters of the Jharua Kachari of Assam. *Jour. Univ. of Gau. (Sc.)*, XII(2): 35-46.

3615. ———————— : 1962 : Anthropometric characters of the Sonowal Kachari of Assam. *Bull. Deptt. of Tribal Culture & Folklore Research, Gau. Univ.*: 98-112.

3616. ———————— : 1969 : Anthropometric characters of the Dimasa Kachari of Assam. *Jour. Assam Sc. Soc.*, XII: 23-9.

3617. ———————— : 1972 : Some non-metric visuals characters of the Dimasa Kachari of Assam. *Bull. Deptt., Anth. Gau. Univ.*, 1, December: 81-7.

3618. ———————— : 1974 : *The Kachari : A study of intra-tribal relations in respect of anthropometry, ABO blood groups and taste sensitivity.* Unpub. Ph.D. Thesis, Anth. Deptt., Dib Univ.

3619. ———————— : 1975 : Phenylthiourea test of the Kachari of Assam and their comparison with other Mongoloid tribes of North-East India. *(In) Contemporary Anthropological Research in North-East India. (Ed.)* by B.M. Das. Dibrugarh, Dib. Univ.: 82-5. (This is also *Bull. Anth. Deptt., Dib. Univ.*, Vol. III, 1974).

3620. ———————— : 1976 : Biological distances among some sub-divisions of the Kachari of Assam in respect of ABO blood groups and their position among other tribes of North-East India. *Bull. Anth. Deptt., Dib. Univ.*, IV (1975): 28-34 (Kachari, Rabha, Dimasa, Sonowal, etc.).

3621. ———————— : 1978 : Biological adaptation of the Kachari of Assam. *Bull. Deptt. of Anth., Dib. Univ.*, VI (1977). This is also a book entitled *Cultural and Biological Adaptability of Man with special reference to North-East India. (Eds.)* by A.C. Bhagabati and R.K. Kar. Dib., Dib. Univ.: 156-69.

3622. ———————— : 1979 : Taste threshold for PTC among Mishing of Gogamukh of Assam. *Proceedings of Ind. Sc. Cong., 66th session, Pt. III, Section VIII, Abstract no.* 27: 10.

3623. ———————— : 1993 : Ethnic affinities of the Kachari people with other populations of North-East India 1. Somatometric characters. *Bull. Deptt. of Anth., Dib. Univ.*, 20-21: 94-109.

3624. ———————— : 1994 : Ethnic affinities of the Kachari people with other populations of North-East India, 1. Somatometric characters. *Bull. Deptt. of Anth., Dib. Univ.*, XXII: 80-95.

3625. **Phukan, Minoti** *and* **Utpala Goswami** : 1985 : Child rearing practices of Assamese mothers of Jorhat town. *Jour. NEICSSR,* IX (2), Oct.: 43-9.

3626. **Prakash, A.; P.K. Mahapatra** *and* **V.K. Srivastava** : 1996 : Vector-incrimation in Tamulpur Primary Health Centre, district Nalbari, lower Assam during malaria outbreak, 1995. *Indian Jour. of Medical Research* (New Delhi), 103 (March): 146-49.

3627. **Purbanchal Prahari** : 1995 : *Jorhat men sabse jyada charma rogi (in H.). Pur. Pra.,* March 2: 7(3-5) (In 1994, 14% dry eczema, 10.22% Leucoderma, 9.49% Fungal infection, 7% Soriacici, 2.19% skin alergy, 2.19% other skin diseases).

3628. ——————— : *Rajyo men AIDS ke sirf teen rogi, jismen se do mar gaye (in H.). Pur. Pra.,* April 1: 1(2-3).

3629. ——————— : *Ek aur AIDS rogi chal basa (in H.). Pur. Pra.,* May 31: 1(8) (5 died in AIDS.).

3630. **Rahman Borborah, T.** : 1991 : Cancer research in Assam. *A.T.,* Jan. 29: 4(7-8).

3631. **Rajkhowa, M.** : 1992 : A study on somatometry and ABO blood groups of the Savaras of Mancotta, Dibrugarh. *Unpub. M.Sc. (Anth.) Dissertation,* Dib. Uni. (Santal, Oraon, Munda, Ho, Kharia, Gond, Savara etc.).

3632. **Rakshit, H.K.** : 1960 : Birth order, sibship size and sex ratio. *Eastern Anth.,* XIII (3): 95-104.

3633. **Rakshit (Guha), Sipra** : 1960 : A short note on the menarcheal age of Assamese girls. *Man in India,* 40(1), Jan.-March: 52-5.

3634. **Ramsay, G.C.** : 1924 : The district of Cachar. *(In) Handbook of Castes and Tribes employed on Tea. Estates in NEI (Comp)* by Tea District Labour Asc. Cal., Prin. by Catholic Orphan Press: 335-38 (Reprinted in 1989).

3635. **Rao, V. Raghavendra** : 1990 : Digital formula of hands and feet in Indian populations. *(In) Human variations in India: Proceedings of the Seminar on Physical Anthropology, 27th June-2nd July, 1977.* Calcutta, Anth. Survey of India: 51-9 (Hira, Kalita, Kaibarta, Vaishya, Brahmin, Mikir, Rabha, etc.).

3636. **Ray, Gautam Sankar** : 1946 : A study of the Physical characteristics of Rajbanshis. *Jour. Royal Asiatic Soc. of Bengal (Letters),* XII: 31-42.

3637. **Rizvi, S.H.M.** *and* **P.M. Buzar Barua** : 1993 : Inbreeding among Indian Muslim: A case study of Maria Muslims of Assam. *Anthropologie,* XXXI (3).

3638. **Roy, Anirban** : 1993 : Siliguri: Gateway to AIDS in North-East. *Shillong Times,* Sept. 8: 3(3-6).

3639. **Roy Choudhury, A.K.** : 1984 : The genetic composition of the people in Eastern India. *Jour. Ind. Anth. Soc.,* 19(1), March: 153-70.

3640. ———— : 1992 : Genetic relationships of the populations in eastern India. *Annals of Human Biology, 19(5),* Sept.-Oct.: 489-501 (Rajbanshi, Kachari, Kalita, Kaibarta, Karbi, Ahom, Chutiya, Sonowal, Rabha, etc.).

3641. **Roy Choudhury, Dibyendu** : 1957 : Rajbanshis: Anthropometric data. (Unpublished).

3642. ———— : 1961 : Middle phalangeal hair among Rajbanshis of Midnapur, West Bengal. *East. Anth.,* 14(2): 182-88.

3643. ———— : 1962 : Palmar dermatoglyphics of the Rajbanshis of Midnapur, West Bengal. *The Anth.,* IX(1-2): 31-8.

3644. ———— : 1963 : Anthropometry of the Rajbanshis of Midnapur, West Bengal. *Bull. Tribal Res. Inst.* (Chhindwara), 3(2): 36-47.

3645. ———— : 1968 : Finger ball patterns of Rajbanshis of Midnapur. *(In) Proceedings Volume of International Symposium on Dermatoglyphics. (Eds.)* by P.C. Biswas and A. Sharma. Delhi, Univ. of Delhi.

3646. **Roy Choudhury, Dibyendu; J. Basu; Atrayee Bhowmik** *and* **P. Das** : 1976 : Economic correlates of tribal fertility in Eastern India. *Bull. Cul. Res. Inst. (Cal.),* XII(1-2): 83-7 (Kachari, Mikir, Rabha etc.).

3647. **Roy, J.K.** *and* **S.K. Biswas** : 1964 : Proteins in the diets of some Indian tribes. *Science and Culture,* 30(3): 126-29.

3648. **Roy, R.C.** : 1935 : Anthropometric data on Hill Bhuiya. *(In) The Hill Bhuiya of Orissa* by S.C. Roy. Ranchi, *Man in India Office,* Appendix A, 321.

3649. **Sadashivaiah, K.** : 1979 : Trend in age at marriage : Family size and level of education among sterilised cohort in Assam and Kerala. *Jr. of Family Welfare,* 35(3), March: 46-56.

3650. **Saha, N. (Physical)** : 1990 : Distribution of Haemoglobin E in several Mongoloid populations of North-East India. *Hum. Bio.,* 62: 535-44.

3651. **Saha, N. (Physical), J.S.H. Tay, M.K. Das, K. Das, M. Roy, B. Dey, S. Banerjee** *and* **B.N. Mukherjee** : 1990 : The distribution of some serum protein and red cell enzyme polymorphisms in the Koch ethnic group of West Bengal, India. *Japanese Jour. of Human Genetics*, 35(3), Sept.: 253-57.

3652. **Saha, N. (Physical), S.H. Hong, H.A. Wong** *and* **J.S.H. Tay** : 1990 : Red cell glucose-6-phosphate dehydrogenase phenotypes in several Mongoloid population of Eastern India: Existence of a non-deficient fast variant in two Australasian tribes. *Human Biology*, 17(6): 529-32 (Bodo Kachari etc.).

3653. **Saikia, Anil** : 1989 : *A study of human mortality in Assam.* Unpub. Ph.D. Thesis, Anth. Deptt., Dib. Univ.

3654. **Sarkar, P.K.; N.G. Das** *and* **K.M. Rao** : 1981 : Mosqui to fauna in certain places of Dibrugarh district in Assam. *Ind. Jour. of Med. Res.*, 73, March: 331-34.

3655. **Sarma, Dimbeswar** : 1989 : A peep into Assam Museum. *A.T., (Sunday Reading)*, Feb. 12: I (1-8).

3656. **Sarma, Dinesh Ch.** : 1985 : A study of some genetic traits in two caste groups of Kamrup-Assam.. *(In) Anthropological perspectives on North-East India (Bull. Deptt. of Anth., Dib. Univ.*, Vol. X, 1981), Deptt. of Anth., Dib. Univ.: 77-86.

3657. **Sarma, Rumi** : 1992 : *A study of some demographic aspects of the Rabhas of Boko area, Kamrup District.* Unpub. Ph.D. Thesis, Gau. Univ.

3658. **Sarma, Sarada Kanta** : 1986 : Medical plants of Assam. *A.T.*, Oct. 26: 4(3-6).

3659. **Sarma, Siddhi N.** *and* **Abani K. Bhagabati** : 1989 : Impact of slope on population distribution and land use in the Boko thana area of Assam, a special analysis. *North-Eastern Geographer* (Gauhati Univ.), 21(1-2).

3660. **Seminar** : 1994 : *IVth International Congress on Ethnobiology*, sponsored by Int. Soc. of Ethnobiology, organised by Society of Ethnobotanists, inaugurated by Nat. Bot. Res. Inst., Lucknow on 22-23 Nov. at Guwahati.

3661. ———— : 1996 : *Seminar on Nutrition, Health and Growth, etc.* Guwahati, Directorate of Assam Inst. of Res. for Tribal & Sch. Caste (To be held).

3662. ———— : *Seminar on Demographic Profile of Assam*, organised by Cultural and Recreational Club of the Directorate of Census Operation, Assam, on the occasion of the Silver Jubilee Celebration of the Club on March 8, 1996. (*Mimeo.*).

3663. **Sengupta, K.W.** : 1939 : Genetic investigation in some N.E. Indian population. *Acta Anthropologenetis*, 4: 241-44.

3664. **Sengupta, N.N., A. Bhattacharyya** *and* **N.K. Das** : 1985 : Symmetrical and asymmetrical papillary patterns of the Kumar of Assam. *Vanyajati,* 33(3), July: 6-12.

3665. **Sengupta, Nipendra Nath** *and* **P.B. Das** : 1972 : Finger dermatoglyphics of the Kumar of Assam. *Jour. Assam. Sc. Soc.,* 15(1).

3666. **Sen Gupta, P.N.** : 1953 : The dietaries of the primitive tribes of India. *March of India,* VI (2): 60-6.

3667. **Sen Gupta, P.N.** *and* **R.K. Rao** : 1957 : Studies on the living conditions, dietary habits and nutritional status of Tripuri Rangkal and Riang Tribes of Tripura state. *Bull. Anth. Survey of India,* VI(1): 1-19.

3668. **Sengupta, Sarthak** : 1976 : A note on distribution of ABO blood groups among the Kaibartas of Upper Assam. *Jour. Ind. Anth. Soc.,* 14; 285-87.

3669. ——————— : 1977 : *A study on the ABO blood groups and colours blindness among the Assamese caste populations of Dibrugarh (Upper Assam).* Unpub. M.Sc. Dissert., Anth. Deptt., Dib. Univ.

3670. ——————— : 1978 : Biological variations among three endogamous castes of Assam. *Current Anth.,* 19: 660-61.

3671. ——————— : 1979 : A note on distribution of ABO blood groups among the Kaibartas of Upper Assam. *Jour. Ind. Anth. Soc.,* 14(3), Nov.: 285-87.

3672. ——————— : Genetic distances among Assamese castes in terms of ABO blood groups. *Current Anth.,* 20: 399-400.

3673. ——————— : 1980 : Genetic investigations in some North-East Indian populations. New Delhi, *Acta Anthropogenetica,* 4: 241-44.

3674. ——————— : The earlobe attachment among the Ahoms of Assam (India). *Proceedings of 67th Indian Sc. Cong. Asso.,* III (IX): 19.

3675. ——————— : 1981 : Note sur les variations de la ceceite aux colours chez trois castes endogamous le L'Assam. *L'Anthropologie* (Paris), 85: 328-31. (in French).

3676. ——————— : Earlobe type in three Mongoloid population of Assam. *Ind. Jour. Phy. Anth. & Hum. Gen.,* 7(2), Aug.: 113-18.

3677. **Sengupta, Sarthak** : 1982 : Variation in the termination of polymorphous C line in palmar dermatoglyphics of the Deuri Chutiyas of Assam. *Bull. Anth. Deptt., Dib. Univ.*, IX: 159-66 (1980).

3678. ——————— : Study of sexual maturation in Ahom girls. *Ind. Jour. Phy. Anth. & Hum. Gen.*, 8(1): 63-6.

3679. ——————— : Observation on earlobe attachment types among the Deoris. *Vanyajati*, 30(1), Jan.: 12-4.

3680. ——————— : ABO blood in the Brahmins of India with special reference to the Assamese Brahmins. *IJPA & HG*, 8(2-3), Aug.-Dec.: 143-49.

3681. ——————— : *Biological variations among the Koch populations of Assam*. Ph.D. Thesis, Anth. Deptt., Gau. Univ.

3682. —————— : 1983 : *A study of certain anthropological variables in the population of North-East India*. UGC Research Project under Gau. Univ. of Anth. Deptt.

3683. —————— : 1984 : Studies of the whorl in head hair in two Mongoloid population of Assam. *Vanyajati*, 32, Oct.: 20-2.

3684. —————— : 1985 : Note sur L'Age a la Puberte des filles Ahom der Haut Assam, Inde. *Bulletin of Memoires de la societe Anthropologie de Paris*, 14(1): 55-8 (*in French*).

3685. ——————— : Analyse de quelques characters Genetique chez les Kaibartas de L'Assam. *Bull. St. Mem. de* la eco d' *Anthropologie de Paris* t_2 series, 14(4): 247-52.

3686. —————— : 1987 : Taste sensitivity to phenylthiourea among the Ahom. *Jour. NEICSSR*, XI(2), Oct.: 40-3.

3687. ——————— : ABO blood groups among the Koch population of Brahmaputra valley, Assam. *The Anthropologie*, XXX(2): 171-73.

3688. ——————— : A note on main line terminations in palmar dermatoglyphics. *Vanyajati*, XXXV(4), 87-9.

3689. ——————— : A note on the ear lobe attachment of the Mishing of Assam. *Vanyajati*, XXXV(1), Oct.: 27-30.

3690. —————— : 1987 : Earlobe types in various populations of Assam, India. *The Anthropologie*, XXIII(3): 269-71.

3691. —————— : 1989 : Genetic distances among the Koch populations of Assam, India. *The Anthropologie*, XXVII: 39-43.

3692. ——————— : Variation in palmar-C line termination among the Koch population of Assam. *Jour. NEICSSR*, 13(1), April: 29-35.

3693. ———————— : A note on the relation between stature and sitting height of the Koch of Assam. *Social Science* (Silchar), 2(1), June: 88-93.

3694. ———————— : Taste sensitivity to PTC among the Koch population of Assam. *Social Sc.*, 2(2), Dec.: 112-17.

3695. —————— : 1990 : Etude Anthropologique des populations Koch du district de Goalpara. *Bulletin et Memoires de la Societe d' Anthropologie de Paris,* 2(2): 203-12.

3696. ———————— : Finger dermatoglyphics of the Koch population of Assam. *MII*, 70(4), Dec.: 390-400.

3697. —————— : 1991 : A physical anthropological profile of the Koch of Darrang district, Assam. *Ind. Jour. Phy. Anth. & Hum. Gen.*, 17(1): 65-72.

3698. —————— : 1992 : A morpho genetical study among the Koch population of Dibrugarh, Assam. *Bull. Deptt. Anth. Dib. Univ.*, 18-19 (1989-90): 39-50.

3699. —————— : 1993 : *Physical Anthropology of the Koch Population of India: A study from Assam.* New Delhi, Mittal Pub., 210p. (Ph.D. Thesis).

3700. —————— : 1994 : Anthropological studies among the Koch population of Goalpara district, Assam. *(In) Tribal Situation in North-East India. (Ed.)* by Sarthak Sengupta. New Delhi, Inter India Pubn.: 230-40.

3701. ———————— : The a-b ridge count in palmar dermatoglyphics of Deuri tribe of Assam, India. *Vanyajati*, XLII(3), July: 11-3.

3702. ———————— : Dermatoglyphics of the Koch population of Brahmaputra valley, Assam. *Bull. Deptt., Anth., Dib. Univ.*, XXII: 67-79.

3703. —————— : n.d. : Finger dermatoglyphics of the Deuri of Assam. *Vanyajati.*

3704. **Sengupta, Sarthak** : 1996 : Menarche and its trend in North-East India. *(In) Peoples of North-East India: Anthropological Perspectives. (Ed.)* by Sarthak Sengupta. New Delhi, Gyan Publishing House: 129-39.

3705. ———————— **(Ed.)** : *Peoples of North-East India: Anthropological Perspectives.* New Delhi, Gyan Publishing House.

3706. ———————— **(Ed.)** : *Studies in Anthropology.* New Delhi, Inter India Pubn.

3707. **Sengupta, Sarthak** *and* **B.M. Das** : n.d. : *An investigation on the finger patterns of the Jogis of Kamrup district*, Assam.

3708. **Sengupta, Sarthak** *and* **D. Sarmah** : 1993 : Palm prints of the Sonowal of Assam. *Bull. Deptt. of Anth., Dib. Univ.*, 20-21 (1991-92): 30-40.

3709. **Sengupta, Sarthak** *and* **F.A. Das** : 1981 : Isolation by distance and change in gene frequency: A case study among the Kaibarta of Assam. *Bull. Anth. Deptt., Dib. Univ.*, VII-VIII(1978-79): 46-8.

3710. **Sengupta, S.** *and* **G. Gogoi** : 1993 : Menarche and menopause among the Kaibarta women of Dibrugarh, Assam. *Jr. Assam Sc. Soc.*, 35 (2): 113-19.

3711. **Sengupta, Sarthak** *and* **Gitimallika Gogoi** : 1995 : Some demographic variables among the Kaibartas of Dibrugarh district, Assam: A preliminary appraisal. *Bull. Anth. Deptt., Dib. Univ.*, 23: 86-95.

3712. ———————— : Selection Intensity of Kaibartas of Assam. *Jr. Hum. Eco.*, 6(4), Oct.: 267-70.

3713. **Sengupta, Sarthak** *and* **Harka Bahadur Chetry** : 1992 : Tooth occlusion pattern among Dibongya Deori of Assam. *MII*, 72(4), Dec.: 497-99.

3714. ———————— : 1994 : Physical Anthropology of the Deoris of Assam.. *(In) Tribes of North-East India. (Ed.)* by Sarthak Sengupta. New Delhi, Gyan Pub. House: 172-84.

3715. ———————— : 1996 : A note on some Morphogenetic variables among the mishings of Assam. *Jour. Human Ecology*, 7(3), July: 215-18.

3716. **Sengupta, Sarthak** *and* **Jina Baruah** : 1996 : On neonatal twining in a hospital of Dibrugarh, Assam. *Jour. Human Ecology*, 7(3), July: 207-10.

3717. **Sengupta, Sarthak** *and* **Kanta Chakrabarty** : 1995 : Maternal age and birth order: A study on determinants of pre-natal reproductive wastages among the Ahoms of Assam. *Man and Life*, 21(3-4), July-Dec.: 147-54.

3718. **Sengupta, Sarthak** *and* **M.N. Dutta** : 1980 : ABO blood groups in the Kaibarta, Ahom and Wancho of N-E India. *Acta Anthropogenetica* (Delhi), 4(3-4): 245-46.

3719. ———————— : 1981 : Variation in anthropometric characters between two Assamese caste of Dibrugarh, Upper Assam. *Assam Sc. Soc.*, 24(1): 59-62.

3720. **Sengupta, Sarthak** *and* **M.N. Dutta** : 1985 : Ethnic affinities of the Ahom in respect of ABO blood groups. *Jour. NEICSSR,* IX(1), April: 52-5.

3721. ———————— : Palmar C line termination polymorphism among some Mongoloid populations of North-East India. *Vanyajati,* XXX(2), April: 3-8. (Deuri, Ahom etc.).

3722. ———————— : Les groups sanguins ABO des Ahoms de L'Assam, Inde. *Bulletin et Memoires de la societe d' Anthropologie de Paris,* XIV(4): 253-58.

3723. **Sengupta, Sarthak; M.N. Dutta** *and* **J.L. Sharma** : 1985 : Pattern of C line termination among Ahoms of Dibrugarh, Assam. *(In) Anthropological perspectives on North-East India (This is Bull. of Deptt. of Anth., Dib. Univ.,* Vol. X, 1981). Deptt. of Anth., Dib. Univ.: 50-4.

3724. **Sengupta, Sarthak** *and* **Mina Rajkhowa** : 1996 : Menarche and menopause among the Ahom women of Dibrugarh, Assam. *Jour. Human Ecology,* 7(3), July: 211-13.

3725. **Sengupta, Sarthak** *and* **Mondira Kalita** : 1996 : Selection intensity among the Sonowals of Assam. *(In) Peoples of North-East India: Anthropological Perspective. (Ed.)* by Sarthak Sengupta. New Delhi, Gyan Publishing House: 73-80.

3726. **Sengupta, Sarthak** *and* **P.M. Buzarbarua** : 1991 : Dermatoglyphics of the Boro-Kachari of Assam, India, *Bull. Deptt. of Anth., Dib. Univ.,* 16-17 (1987-88): 137-48.

3727. **Sengupta, Sarthak** *and* **Sabhuj Sengupta** : 1979 : Genetic distance among three Assamese castes of Upper Assam in respect of ABO blood groups and colour blindness. *Ind. Jour. Phy. Anth. & Hum. Gen.* 5(1), June: 43-8.

3728. **Sentinel** : 1995 : 16% HIV positive cases in NE. Jan. 24: 1(1-2).

3729. ———————— : Youth dies of AIDS in city. March 8: 1(3).

3730. ———————— : Editorial: Of mosquitoes and men. May 27: 4(1-2).

3731. ———————— : About a million people affected by the killer disease says VHAI Report "18 districts' of Assam in grip of malaria." June 4: 3(3-7) (Voluntary Health Ass. of India).

3732. ———————— : AIDS victims in city. June 18: 1(3-5). (Guwahati, AIDS).

3733. **Sentinel** : 1995 : Mother opens hospital. Sept. 17: 1(3-5) (Mother Teresa inaugurated S.E. Asia's largest rural hospital at Hojai constructed at Rs. 15 Crore).

3734. ———— : 1996 : Monthly update on HIV/AIDS in India. Feb. 8: 5(3-4).

3735. ———— : Yoga hospital set-up. June 25: 3(1-2) (Manav Kalyan Sanstha has established a Yoga Hospital with 5-bed indoor facilities in Kahilipara opposite DPI Office).

3736. ———— : Unabated migration has changed the demographic pattern of Assam : Influx posing threat to Nation. March 9: 1 (3-6).

3737. ———— : Editorial: Our Demographic scenario. March 10: 4 (1-2) (Assam, Muslim community).

3738. **Shah, L.** : 1975 : *The Ahoms of Tengakhat: Their palm prints.* Unpub. M.Sc. Dissert., Anth. Deptt., Dib. Univ.

3739. **Sharma, A.** : 1963 : Sui Metodi per il relevamento dei dermatoglif palmari, Un nuovo tempone, di lino, *A.T. Riv. de Anthrop.*, 50: 231-39 (in Germany).

3740. **Sharma, Jagadeswar Lall** *and* **Sarthak Sengupta** : 1987: Finger dermatoglyphics of the Rajasthani Jains of Dibrugarh, Assam. *Bull. Deptt. Anth., Dib. Univ.*, XI-XII (1982-83): 139-48.

3741. **Sharma, Jagadeswar Lall; Mohendra N. Dutta** *and* **Sarthak Sengupta** : 1993 : Pattern of C line termination among the Rajasthani Jains and Agrawals of Dibrugarh, Assam. *Bull. Deptt. of Anth., Dib. Univ.*, 20-21 (1991-92): 126-30.

3742. **Sharma, K.** : 1967 : *A study of finger and palm prints of the Brahmins of Jorhat, Assam.* Unpub. M.Sc. Dissert., Gau. Univ., Anth. Deptt.

3743. **Sharma, M.K.** : 1983 : A plan for health educational pyramid in Assam. *EPA Bull.*, VI(2), July: 13-21.

3744. **Sharma, P.K.** : 1965 : Vital capacity of men and women of different age groups : An observation at Gauhati, Assam. *Jr. Assam Sc. Soc.*, 8: 114-17.

3745. **Sharma, Rabin Ch.** : 1992 : *The determinants of rural fertility in Assam.* Unpub. Ph.D. Thesis, Dib. Univ.

3746. **Sharma, S.K.; S.K. Benara; D. Hazarika** *and* **K. Satyanarayana**: 1992 : The out-reach of iodised salt in North-East urban Assam. *Proceeding of XXVth Annual Meeting of*

Nutrition Society of India, held at National Inst. of Nut., Hyderabad on 18-19 Dec., 66 (*Abstract*).

3747. **Sharma, S.K.; P.K. Chelleng; R.K. Phukan** *and* **D. Hazarika**: 1994 : Out-reach of iodised salt in rural households of Assam. *Jour. Human Ecology* (Delhi), 5(3), July: 237-39.

3748. **Sharma, T.C.** : 1961 : Physical characters of the Miri. *Jour. Gau. Univ. (Sc.),* XII (2): 45-7 (about Mishing).

3749. ——————— : 1962 : Anthropometry of the Deuri. *Jour., Gau. Univ. (Sc.),* XIII(2): 79-84.

3750. ——————— : Finger prints of the Miri. *Bull. Deptt. of Tribal Culture & Folklore Research, Gau. Univ.,* I: 65-73.

3751. **Sharma, T.C.** *and* **B.M. Das** : 1961 : A report on ABO blood groups from Gauhati. *Jour. Assam. Sc. Soc.,* IV.

3752. **Sharma, T.C.** *and* **P.B. Das** : 1968 : Physical characters of the Lalung of Assam. *Assam Science Society,* XI.

3753. **Shillong Times** : 1995 : "171 HIV positive cases detected in Assam": Minister. April 1: 3(5-7).

3754. ——————— : Malaria toll rises to 100 in Assam. April 24: 3(3-4).

3755. **Singha, Jyotsna** : 1983 : *Child care and motherhood: A study among the Harijan in an industrial setting.* Unpub. M.Sc. Dissert. Anth. Deptt., Dib. Univ.

3756. **Singh, Indera P.** *and* **M.K. Bhasin** : 1979 : Ethnic-Geographic frequency distribution of dermatoglyphic traits in India: A review. *(In) Birth Defects: Original Article series,* Vol. XV(6): 347-87 (Rabha, Kachari, Kalita, Ahom, Miri, etc.).

3757. **Singh, K.S.; V. Bhalla** *and* **Vinod Kaul** : 1994 : *People of India, Vol. X: The Biological Variation in Indian Population.* Delhi, Oxford University Press for Anth. S.I., Calcutta, 758p.

3758. **Singh, L.; S. Sidhu** *and* **K.K. Deol** : 1980 : An estimation of reproductive performance in the women of Assam. *Proceedings of the 67th Indian Science Congress (Abstract No. 82), Sec. Anth. & Arc.*: 32.

3759. **Singh, T. Shyamacharan** : 1993 : A note on comparison of the Metei with the Tai and the Khasi in respect of ABO blood group locus. *Bull. Anth. Deptt., Dib., Univ.,* 20-21 (1991-92): 41-8.

3760. **Singh, T.S.** : 1990 : *A physical anthropological perspective of some Tai people of Assam.* Unpub. Ph.D. Thesis, Anth. Deptt. Dib. Univ.

3761. **Singh, T.S.** *and* **M.N. Phookan** : 1989 : Incidence of taste sensitivity to phenylthiourea in four Tai Buddhist communities of Assam. *Bull. Deptt. Anth. Dib. Univ.*, 13-14 (1984-85): 96-103.

3762. ———— : 1990 : A note on the variation of earlobe attachment among four Tai populations of Assam. *Bull. Deptt. of Anth., Dib. Univ.*, 15(1986): 63-9.

3763. ———— : A note on the frequency distribution of ABO and Rhesus blood groups in four Tai populations of Assam (India) and their position among the Mongoloids of this region. *Anthrop. Anz.*, 48(1): 29-35.

3764. ———— : A note on finger print dermatoglyphics of four Tai populations of Assam (India). *Paper presented at International conference on progress and trends in Dermatoglyphic Research* (Calcutta), Jan. 27-29, 1990.

3765. ———— : 1991 : Finger dermatoglyphics of the four Tai populations of Assam, India.. *(In) Dermatoglyphics Today. (Eds.)* by B. Mohan Reddy, S.B. Roy and B.N. Sarkar. Calcutta, Indian Inst. of Bio-social Res. & Development, Anth. Survey of India and Ind. Stat. Inst.: 381-87.

3766. ———— : 1993 : Stature and foot size in four Tai communities of Assam, India. *Anthropologischer Anzeiger*, 51(1): 349-55.

3767. **Sinha, S.M.** : 1955 : Maternity statistics from Gauhati. *MII*, 35(2), April-June: 101-09.

3768. **Sonowal, Barun** : 1981 : *A study of the Kaibartas of the village Shukanpukhuri, district Dibrugarh, Assam with special reference to food habit and nutrition.* Unpub. M.Sc. Dissert. Anth. Deptt., Dib. Univ.

3769. **Srivastava, R.P.** : 1969 : Finger prints, colour blindness and other features in the Miris of Assam. *MII*, 49(4), Oct.-Dec.: 398-403.

3770. **Srivastava, R.P.** : 1983 : Incidence of colour blindness in Assam and its variability among Indian populations. *Indian Anth.* (Delhi), XIII (II), Dec.: 51-62.

3771. ———— : 1995 : Biological affinities among four populations in Assam. *South Asian Anthropologist,* 16(1), March: 41-5 (Brahmin, Kayastha, Kalita, Ahom).

3772. **Srivastava, R.P.** *and* **D. Gogoi** : 1972 : Menarche and menopause among women of an Ahom village in Upper Assam. *Bull. Deptt. of Anth., Dib. Univ.*

3773. **Srivastava, R.P.** *and* **M. Goswami** : 1968 : Menarcheal age of Assamese girls. *The Anthropologist,* XV (1-2), March-Sept.: 57-60.

3774. **Srivastava, S.C.** : 1987 : *Demographic profile of North-East India.* Delhi, Mittal Pub., 343p.

3775. **Stonor, C.R.** : 1947 : Notes and Queries: Medicinal use of Pangolin scales in Assam. *MII,* XXVII (2), June: 184-85.

3776. **Tahsildar, Gangaram** : 1927 : *Collection of Assamese folk medicine.*

3777. **Tamuli, N.K.** : 1980 : *Variation in respect of Anthropometric measurements and genetic traits among the Santal and the Mundas of Assam.* Unpub. M.Sc. Dissert. Anth. Deptt., Dib. Univ.

3778. **Tiwari, K.C.; R. Majumder** *and* **S. Bhattacharjee** : 1979 : Folklore medicine from Assam and Arunachal Pradesh (District Tirap). *Quarterly Jour. Crude Drugs Research* (Netherland) 17: 61-7.

3779. ―――――― : 1982 : Folklore informations from Assam for family planning and birth control. *Quarterly Jour. Crude Drugs Research* (Netherland), 20(3): 133-37.

3780. **Trivedi, Onkar Dutta** : 1970 : *Standardisation of culture free test of mental ability for Assam.* Unpub. Ph.D. Thesis, Gau. Univ.

3781. **Turner, W.** : 1899 : Contributions to the craniometry of the people of the Indian Empire I. The Hill Tribes of the North-East Frontier and the people of Burma with three plates. *Trans. Roy. Soc. Edinb.,* 39, pt.3: 703-47.

3782. **Waddell, L.A.** : 1901 : The Tribes of the Brahmaputra Valley: A contribution on the physical types and affinities. *Jour. of the Asiatic Society of Bengal* (Calcutta), LXIX, Pt. III (1900): 1-127. (Reprinted in 1975 by Sanskaran Publications, Delhi, 127p).

3783. **Waheed, Padma** : 1992 : Letters to the Editor: AIDS in N-E Region. *A.T.,* Aug. 8: 4(3-4).

3784. **Walter, H.; B.N. Mukherjee; K. Gilbert; P. Lindenberg; A. Dannewite; K.C. Malhotra; B.M. Das** *and* **R. Deka** : 1986 : Investigations on the variability of haptoglobin transferring and Gc polymorphisms in Assam, India. *Human Heredity,* 36(6), Nov.-Dec.: 388-96.

3785. **Walter, H.; H. Matsumoto; T. Miyazaki; B.N. Mukherjee; K.C. Malhotra; B.M. Das; K. Gilbert** *and* **P. Lindenberg** : 1987 : Distribution of Gm and Km Allotypes among ten populations of Assam, India. *Am. Jour. Phy. Anth.*, 73(4), Aug.: 439-45.

3786. **Wilson, H. Ellis C.** : 1938 : A diet and physique survey in Assam, rural Bengal and Calcutta. *Ind. Jour. Med. Res.*, 26: 131-54.

3787. **Wilson, J.M.G.** : 1958 : Arterial blood pressure in plantation workers in North-East India. *Brit. Jour. Pmy. Soc. Med.*, 12(4); 204-81.

3788. **Wroughton, R.C.** : 1916 : The langurs of Assam. *Jour. Bombay Nat. Hist. Soc.* 24: 653-55.

PART-II (C)

FULL BIBLIOGRAPHY OF PRE-HISTORIC ARCHAEOLOGY

3789. **Ahmed, Kamaluddin** : 1981 : Islamic architecture in Assam. *Assam Information,* 33, April-July: 18-26.

3790. ———— : 1994 : *The Art and Architecture of Assam.* Guwahati, Spectrum Pub., 350p.

3791. **Ahmed, Sarharuddin** : 1991 : An assessment of the literary elements of the Sanskrit inscriptions of Medieval Assam *(In) Archaeology of North-Eastern India (Eds)* by J.P. Singh and G. Sengupta. New Delhi, Har Anand and Vikas Pub.: 244-51.

3792. **Ansari, Z.D.** *and* **M.K. Dhavalikar** : 1970 : Excavation at Ambari, Gauhati. *Jour. Univ. of Poona (Humanities Section),* 35: 78-87.

3793. **Ashraf, A.A.** : 1994 : Anthropo-Archaeological background of the Nishi material culture. *Bull. Anth. Deptt., Gau. Univ.,* VIII: 105-14 (Assam also).

3794. **Asom Sahitya Sabha** : n.d. : *Asamar chitrakala (in A.).* Jorhat, Asom Sahitya Sabha, 25p.

3795. **Assam Research Society** : 1984 : *A source book of Archaeology of Assam and other states of north-eastern India* (Reprinted from the Reports of the Archaeological Survey of India bearing on Assam and other states of North-Eastern India). Guwahati, Assam Research Society, 200p.

3796. **Assam Tribune** : 1970 : Ambari finds belong to 4th Century AD says Dr. Sankalia. Jan. 10.

3797. ———— : Archaeological finds discovered at Judges field. Jan. 23.

3798. ———— : Historical relics of 8th Century dug out in Manas. Nov. 19: 1.

3799. ———— : Evidence of Brahmaputra Valley Civilization. Nov. 30.

3800. ———— : Terracotta boat unearthed at Nabagraha cemetry. Dec. 14.

3801. ———— : Ambari antiquities bear testimony of two ancient cultural periods. Dec. 17 : 1.

3802. ———— : Stone icon of Nataraj found at Ambari. Feb. 19 : 1(8).

3803. ———— : 1971 : Ambari finds similar to those in Borneo. June 29.

3804. **Assam Tribune** : 1973 : Interesting finds: Excavated art, Marakdola in Kamrup. Feb. 14.

3805. ———————— : Interesting finds: Excavated art Marakdola in Kamrup. Feb. 17: 5(1-3).

3806. ———— : 1985 : Coins of Kachari rulers collected. Nov. 14: 1.

3807. ———— : 1986 : Prehistoric stone tools discovered. April 25: 1(3), 8(4) (At Boro Bhatarmari village near Kokrajhar town on the left bank of Gaurang river, tools are of neolithic period).

3808. ———— : 1987 : Ambari: An ancient artist's guild. March 15: 4(3-6), 5(2-3) (Guwahati-Archaeology).

3809. ———— : 1988 : Ambari Excavation. March 15: 1(2-4).

3810. ———————— : A rare archaeological find. April 17: 7(3-5) (Eradighalpani archaeological site near Howraghat, Assam).

3811. ———— : 1989 : Archaeologists look for lost city. June 16: 3(4-5).

3812. ———————— : New archaeological site discovered. June 18: 7(3) (Kalapahar, Guwahati).

3813. ———— : 1990 : Ambari excavation. Jan. 12: 5(4-5).

3814. ———————— : Ambari: An Indo-Roman and Indo-Chinese Training Station. Jan. 30: 3(4-5).

3815. ———— : 1991 : Plea to preserve historical monuments in Karbi Anglong. Jan. 24: 3(4-6).

3816. ———— : 1993 : Megalithic site discovered. April 21: 6(4-6). At Makri 15 Kms. away from Goalpara, Assam.

3817. ———————— : Coins minted with a fascinating intent. Oct. 8: 5(4-5) (Ahom, Kachari etc.).

3818. ———— : 1994 : Ancient relics found near Tihu. March 9: 5(3-5).

3819. **Badam, G.L.** : 1974 : Fossil elephant from the Brahmaputra valley of Assam, India. *Jr. Assam Sc. Soc.*, 17(1-2): 75-8.

3820. **Barman, Chandi Ch.** : 1990 : Letters to the Editor: Dirgheswari Sculptures. Jan. 20: 4(3).

3821. **Barman, Dilip Kr.** : 1995 : Madan Kamdev : Legend and Reality. *Sentinel, Sat. day Fare*, I(1-8), 2(3-8) (Ancient Kamrup's archaeological ruins).

3822. **Barpujari, H.K.** : 1988 : Thoughts on Ambari Excavation. *A.T.*, June 12: 4 (3-6), 6(4-5).

3823. **Barua, B.K.** : 1951 : Fine Arts *(In) A cultural History of Assam (Early Period)* Vol. I by B.K. Barua. Nowgong (Assam), Pub. by K.K. Barooah: 167-96 (Archaeology, Architecture, Sculpture, Iconography).

3824. **Barua, Khanindra Ch.** : 1969 : Letters to the Editor : Antiquities and Structures at Ambari. *A.T.*, April 21: 4.

3825. **Barua, K.L.** : 1939 : Pre-historic culture in Assam. *Jour. Assam Research Society*, 7(1): 6-18 and, 7(2): 35-41.

3826. **Bhattacharjee, Arun** : 1978 : *Icons and sculptures of early and medieval Assam*. Delhi, Inter India Pubs., 76p.

3827. **Bhattacharya, P.K.** : 1969 : The shape of the Ahom coin. *Indian Studies: Past & Present*, X(3), April-June: 275-77.

3828. **Bhattacharya, Jyotindra Mohan (Comp)** : 1989 : *Catalogues catalogorum of Assamese Manuscripts*. Calcutta, Asiatic-Society.

3829. **Bhattacharya, K.** : 1992 : Sibsagar: A sleeping town *(In) India Through Ages*, Vol. 3 (*Eds*) by T.R. Sareen and S.R. Bakshi. New Delhi, Anmol Pubs.: 344-45 (Sibsagar tank, Muktinath Temple, etc.).

3830. **Bhattacharyya, Manoranjan** : 1990 : Archaeology: Chaigaon me Chandra Soudagar ki ek aitihasik haveli. (*in H.*) *Pur. Pra. (Lok Bha.)*, Dec. 30: I(4-8).

3831. **Bhattacharyya, Nagen** : 1990 : Bell-Metal Industry of Assam: Its Past and Present. *Assam Information*, XXXXII, Sept.: 23-5.

3832. **Bhattacharyya, Padmanath** : 1909 : Notes on certain archaeological remains at Tezpur (Assam). *Jour. Proc. As. Soc. Bengal*, 5(1): 19-20.

3833. **Bhattacharyya, Satis Ch.** : 1987 : Bhomoraguri Rock Inscription. *A.T.*, April 19: 4(3-6) 5(2-4).

3834. **Bhuyan, G.N.** : 1972 : A survey of Assam sculpture. *Jour. Assam Research Society*, XXII: 48.

3835. ———— : 1974 : A survey of the Ahom sculptures. *Jour. Assam Res. Society*, 22: 40-8.

3836. ———— : 1989 : Letters to the Editor: Ambari sculpture. *A.T.*, May 5: 4(4-5).

3837. **Bloch, T.** : 1906-07 : Conservation in Assam. *Annual Report of Archaeological Survey of India* (Delhi): 17-28.

3838. **Block, T.** : 1905 : A crude figure of Saraswati was recovered from the ruins of the Tamreswarh temple, Sadiya. *Annual Report, Eastern Circle, 2.*

3839. **Borah, D.** : 1985 : Pottery Industry in Assam. *The Economic Times* (Cal.), August.

3840. **Bose, S.K.** : 1986 : Newly discovered silver-imitation Gupta coin. *North-East India History Association, no. 7.* Shillong, Hist. Deptt., NEHU: 61-4.

3841. ———— : 1987 : Symbols in Naranarayan's mudra and a case of Kyriem coin. *Ibid, no. 8.* Ibid: 92-111.

3842. ———— : 1989 : Rare coins throw fresh light on Dimacha rulers of Maibong. *Ibid, no. 10.* Ibid: 44-9.

3843. ———— : 1990 : Raghu Deva's coin in Nara Narayan's name. *Ibid, no.11.* Ibid: 20-2.

3844. **Botham, A.W.** : 1940 : *Catalogue of the Provincial coin cabinet Assam.* Allahabad, Govt. Pub., 525p.

3845. **Brown, J. Coggin** : 1914 : Grooved stone hammers from Assam and the distribution on similar forms in Eastern Asia. *Jour. Asiatic Soc. of Beng.*, X(4): 107-09.

3846. **Chakraborty, Satyabrata** : 1995 : A private trove of antiquities. *St.*, Nov. 19: 13 (1-6).

3847. **Chanda, Ramaprasad** : 1927 : Beginning of art in eastern India with special reference to sculptures in the Indian Museum, Calcutta. Calcutta, Govt. of India, Central Publication Branch. *Memoirs of Archaeological Survey of India, no. 30*: 1-54.

3848. **Chatterjee, S.K.** : 1955 : *The place of Assam in the history and civilization of India.* Gauhati, Gau. Univ.

3849. **Choudhury, Nishipada** : 1968 : Ring well: New theory. *Jour. Assam Res. Soc.*, 18: 59-63 (Archaeology).

3850. **Choudhury, Nishipada Deva** : 1985 : *Historical Archaeology of Central Assam: From Earliest time to 12th Century AD.* New Delhi, B.R. Pubg. Corp., 287p.

3851. **Choudhury, P.C.** : 1957 : *The History of the Civilization of the people of Assam.* Gauhati, Deptt. of Historical & Antiquarian Studies in Assam, 538p.

3852. ———— : 1967 : Archaeological finds in Narakasura Hills. *Jour. Assam Res. Soc.*, XIV.

3853. ———— : 1970 : The Gachtal stone inscription. *A.T.*, April 9: 4.

3854. ———— : Significance of the three stone inscriptions at the Assam State Museum, Gauhati. *Jour. Ind. History,* 48(1), April: 91-101.

3855. **Choudhury, P.C.** : 1977 : Historical materials in the Caratbari copper plate grant to Ratnapalavarmadeva. *Jour. Ind. History,* 55(1-2), April-Aug.: 61-9.

3856. ———— : 1977-78 : Historical significance of the stone inscription from Lanka (Nowgong), Assam. *Jour. Assam Res. Society,* 23: 57-63.

3857. ———— : 1978 : A hoard of silver coins from Haflong. *Jour. Assam Res. Soc.*, XXIV: 35.

3858. ———— : 1988 : *Assam Bengal Relations from the earliest times to the twelfth century A.D.* Guwahati, Spectrum Pub., 187p.

3859. **Choudhury, P.D.** : 1959 : The sculpture of Assam *(In) Souvenir on aspects of the heritage of Assam (Ed)* by K.N. Dutt. Gauhati, 22nd Session of Indian History Congress, December: 18-21.

3860. ———— : 1960 : Some ancient sites in Assam. *Jour. Assam Res. Soc.*, 14: 110-12.

3861. ———— : 1964 : *Archaeology in Assam: An Introduction.* Gauhati, Deptt. of Archaeology (Assam), DHAS, Govt. of Assam 60p. (Koch, Ahom).

3862. ———— : 1969 : Archaeological remains *(In) The Land and People: Assam* (Comp.) by S. Barkataki. New Delhi, NBT: 63-73.

3863. **Choudhury, P.D.** *and* **M.C. Das** : 1959 : Ancient treasures *of Assam*. Gauhati, DHAS, Govt. of Assam, 38p.

3864. **Choudhury, Pratap** : 1944 : Neolithic culture in Kamrup. *Jour. of Assam Res. Soc.*, 2(1-2): 41-7.

3865. **Choudhury, R.D.** : 1977 : A note on the temple ruins of Majgaon, Assam. *Jour. Ind. History,* 55(3), Dec.: 15-7.

3866. ———— : 1979 : The sculptures from Pingalesvar. *Proceedings of a Seminar on History and Culture of NEI*, History Deptt., NEHU in collaboration with UGC, 26-28 April 1979. (The site is 30 km. north of Guwahati across the Brahmaputra).

3867. ———— : 1985 : *Archaeology of the Brahmaputra valley of Assam*. Delhi.

3868. ———— : 1986 : Archaeological remains at Bhuvan Pahar. *Sentinel*, June 8.

3869. ———— : 1987 : *A surprise book of the Numismatic studies in North-East India*. Guwahati, Directorate of Museum, 152p.

3870. ———— : 1989 : Letters to the Editor : Ambari sculptures. *A.T.*, May 5: 4(3-4).

3871. **Choudhury, R.D.** : 1991 : On three hoards of cowriest from Assam *(In) Archaeology of North-Eastern India (Eds)* by Jai Prakash Singh and Gautam Sengupta. New Delhi, Har Anand & Vikas Pub.: 228-31.

3872. ———————— : Symphony in sculpture. *A.T., Sunday Reading,* March 17: 1(1-8).

3873. ———— : 1993 : Asomat Gabeshana: Tetia aru Atia. *Ajir Asom, Saradiya Sankha*: 250-53 (*in A.*, History, Archaeology).

3874. **Choudhury, Rabin Dev** : 1971 : 1893 shak: Prak Ahom jugar Brahmaputra upattakar puratatta. *Saptahik Neelachal,* Aghon 21, 1893 shak: 7(1-5), 10(1-5), 8(1-10) (*in A.*) September.

3875. ———— : 1974 : Pre-Ahom antiquities of the Brahmaputra valley. *North-Eastern Affairs,* 3(1), April-June: 15-8.

3876. **Choudhury, Rabin Dev** *and* **Dharmeswar Chutia** : 1968 : A note on the archaeological finds at the Narakasur hills. *Jour. Assam Res. Soc.*, 18: 23-38.

3877. **Choudhury, Sujit** : 1991 : Bhuvan Tirtha: A cult spot on the hill top *(In) Archaeology of North-Eastern India (Eds)* by J.P. Singh and G. Sengupta. New Delhi, Har Anand and Vikas Pub.: 160-66.

3878. **Choudhury, Vasant** *and* **Parimal Ray** : 1970 : Coin type of the Kings of Kachar. *Jour. Ancient Indian History (Cal. Univ.),* V(1-2): 208.

3879. ———————— : A unique gold coin-type of the Kachari kings. *Monthly Bulletin of the Asiatic Society,* V(9): 4-5.

3880. **Chutia, Dharmeswar** : 1968 : Some observations on symbols of the Navagraha temple at Gauhati. *Jour. Assam Res. Soc.*, 18: 98-106 (Archaeology).

3881. ———— : 1991 : A note on the Umachal Rock Inscription *(In) Archaeology of North-Eastern India (Eds)* by J.P. Singh and G. Sengupta. New Delhi, Har Anand and Vikas Pub. 232-43.

3882. **Coggin Brown, J.** : 1914 : Grooved stone hammer from Assam and the distribution of similar forms in Eastern India. *Jour. Asiatic. Soc. of Beng.*, X(4): 107-09.

3883. **Dalton, E.T.** : 1855 : Notes on Assam temple ruins. *Jour. Roy. As. Soc. Beng.*, 24: 1-24.

3884. **Dani, A.H.**: 1960 : *Prehistory and Proto History of Eastern India.* Calcutta, Firma K.L. Mukhopadhya, 248p.

3885. **Das Gupta, Hem Ch.** : 1913 : On two shouldered stone implements from Assam. *Jour. Roy. As. Soc. Beng. (N.S.)*, 9: 291-93.

3886. **Dasgupta, R.** : 1968 : Coins of Medieval Assam. *Jour. Assam Res. Soc.,* 18: 49-58.

3887. ———— : 1982 : *Art of Medieval Assam.* New Delhi, Cosmo Pub., 224-48p.

3888. ———— : 1991 : Some newly discovered Tai Ahom illustrated manuscripts *(In) Archaeology of North-Eastern India (Eds)* by J.P. Singh and G. Sengupta. New Delhi, Har Anand and Vikas Pub.: 300-03.

3889. **Das, Murari Charan** : 1986 : Coins of Assam. *A.T.*, Dec. 5: 4(3-6) 6(4-5).

3890. **Das, Renuka** *and* **B.M. Das** : 1996 : A note on caste variation at biosocial level *(In) Communities of North-East India: An Anthropological Perspective (Eds)* by Farida Ahmed Das and Indira Barua. Delhi, Mittal Pubn.: 83-9.

3891. **Das, Sarat Ch.** : 1898 : Notes on the Antiquity of Chittagong. *Jour. Roy. As. Soc. Beng., Pt.I* : 20 (Kachar, Assam etc. based on Tibetan Records).

3892. **Datta, Birendranath** : 1980 : Clay folk toys of Assam. *Jour. NEICSSR*, IV(1), April: 1-5.

3893. **Datta, Dilip Kr.** : 1976 : From Prehistory to History : A schematic view of culture in the tribal world of North-Eastern India. *Bull. Deptt. of Anth., Dib. Univ.*, 4(1975) : 16-20.

3894. ———— : 1984 : Ancient pottery in NE India & SE Asia. *A.T.*, Dec. 9: 4(3-6) 5(1-3).

3895. **Datta, Hemendra Nath** : 1988 : Archaeological aspects in our lives: The lessons, new generations should learn. *A.T., Sunday Reading*, Sept. 4: I(1-8).

3896. **Dhavalikar, M.K.** : 1972 : Archaeology of Gauhati. *Bull. Deccan College Res. Inst.*, 32(II): 137-49.

3897. ———— : 1979 : Boat burial of eastern India. *Paper read at the Seminar on the History and Culture of North-East India.* Shillong, History Deptt., NEHU in collaboration with UGC, 26-28 April, 1979.

3898. **Dutta, Jogesh Ch.** : 1891 : *Old Relics in Kamrup.*

3899. **Dutta, P.C.** : 1991 : Early man in North-East India *(In) Archaeology of North-East India (Eds.)* by J.P. Singh and G. Sengupta. New Delhi, Har Anand & Vikas Pub. House: 59-73.

3900. **Dutta, S.** : 1983 : A study on the Matak coins. *Jour. Ind. History,* 61(1-3), April-Dec.: 117-25.

3901. **Dutta, S.** : 1991 : A rare silver coin of Ramakanta Simha: An analysis *(In) Ibid*: 224-27.

3902. **Economic and Political Weekly** : 1969 : The Ambari Ruins. 4(18), May 3: 752-53.

3903. **Ede, Frank** : 1902 : The sacred caves of Cachar. *Jour. Roy. As. Soc. Beng.*, 71, Pt. 3: 36-7.

3904. **Fox, C.S.** : 1933 : *Letters to J.P. Mills of 7/7/33 and 4/10/33 on the minerals used in the manufacture of Assam celts (with J.P. Mills correspondence)*. Oxford, Pitt Rivers Museum Library.

3905. **Francis, Conyngham** : 1902 : *List of inscriptions in tombs or monuments in Assam. Shillong, Secretariat* Printing Office, 120.

3906. **Furer-Haimendorf, C.von** : 1939 : The Megalithic culture of Assam *(In) Forgotten Kingdoms in Sumatra* by F.M. Schuitger. Leyden, *Appendix*: 218f.

3907. ———————— : Die Megalithkulturen von Assam und ihre Bezie hungen zu Indonesien. *Actes du ze Congres International des Sciences Anthropologiques et Ethnologiques* (Copenhagen).

3908. **Gait, E.A.** : 1895 : Notes on some Ahom coins. *Jour. Roy. As. Soc. Beng.*, 64, Pt. I: 286-89.

3909. **Ganapatrika** : 1993 : Koch amaler mudra pawa gelo *(in B)*. Aug. 1: 1(5) (currency of Koch period).

3910. **Ghosh, B.K.** : 1977-78 : A note on the image and temple of Jainteswari. *Jour. Assam Research Society,* 23: 45-8.

3911. **Gogoi, Jiban** : 1987 : Letters to the Editor: Old Monuments in Assam. *A.T.*, March 5: 4(3-4).

3912. **Gogoi, Nityananda** : 1988 : New reading of Biswanath Rock inscriptions. *North-East India History Association, no. 9*. Shillong, Hist. Deptt., NEHU: 59-64.

3913. **Goswami, H.C.** : 1930 : *A Descriptive Catalogue of Assamese Manuscripts*. Calcutta University.

3914. **Goswami, M.C.** : 1972 : A report on an iron celt bar from N.C. Hills: Assam. *Bull. Deptt. of Anth.*, I, Dec.: 99-100.

3915. **Goswami, M.C.** *and* **A.C. Bhagabati** : 1959 : A preliminary report on a collection of Neolithic tool types from Western Assam. *MII*, 39(4), Oct.-Dec.: 312-24.

3916. **Goswami, M.C.** *and* **S.K. Roy** : 1963 : Further report on the investigations into the prehistoric archaeology of North Cachar Hills, Assam. *Jour. Univ. of Gau. (Sc.)* XIV(2): 45-7.

3917. **Goswami, M.C.** *and* **S.K. Roy** : 1972 : A report on selected potsherds from Ambari, Assam, India. *Bull. Deptt. of Anth.*, Gau. Univ., I, December: 22-7.

3918. ———— : 1976 : An introductory study of the pottery of Assam with special reference to Ambari excavation. *Bull. Anth. Deptt., Gau. Univ.* V: 1-19.

3919. **Goswami, M.C.** *and* **T.C. Sharma** : 1962 : A brief report on the investigation into the Prehistoric Archaeology of North Cachar Hills. *Jour. Univ. of Gau. (Sc.),* XIII(2): 63-6.

3920. ———— : 1966-67 : *Indian Archaeology 1966-67: A Review (First time in Assam tools resembling Palaeolithic choppers and scrapers).* New Delhi.

3921. ———— : 1978 : An Introductory study on pottery of Assam: With special reference to Ambari excavation. *Bull. Deptt. of Anth., Gau. Univ.*, IV: 1-9.

3922. ———— : 1981 : From history to Pre-History in Assam *(In) Cultural Contours of India*, Pt. II (*Ed*) by V.S. Srivastava. Calcutta, Abhinav Pubn.

3923. **Guha, Amalendu** : 1988 : Archaeology of North-East India: Some points *(In) National Seminar on the Archaeology of North-East India, Oct. 26-28, 1988, Papers and Abstracts (Ed)* by Jai Prakash Singh, Deptt. of History. Shillong, NEHU.

3924. ———— : 1991 : Archaeology of North-East India: Some points *(In) Archaeology of North-Eastern India (Eds)* by Jai Prakash Singh and G. Sengupta. New Delhi, Har Anand and Vikas Pub.: 1-4.

3925. **Hannay, S.F.** : 1848 : Notes on ancient temples and other remaining in the vicinity of Sadyah, Upper Assam. *Jr. Roy. As. Soc. Beng.*, 17, Pt. I: 459-72.

3926. **Hutton, J.H.** : 1923 : Carved Monoliths at Jamuguri in Assam. *Jour. Roy. Anth. Inst.*, 53: 150-59.

3927. ———— : 1924 : The occurrence of the blow-gun in Assam. *Man*, 24(77), July: 104-06.

3928. ———— : 1925 : Some carved stones in the Dayang Valley, Sibsagar. *Jour and Proceedings Asiatic Society of Bengal (N.S.)*, XX(1924), No. 5: 143-47.

3929. **Hutton, J.H.** : 1928 : Prehistory of Assam. *MII*, 8(4): 228-32.

3930. ———— : 1929 : Assam Megaliths. *Anthropos*, 3: 324-38.

3931. **Hutton, J.H.** *and* **J.P. Mills** : 1929 : Ancient Monoliths of North Cachar. *Jour. Proc. As. Soc. Beng.*, 25: 285-300.

3932. **Indian Archaeology** : 1974-75 : Explorations and excavations: Assam. *Indian Archaeology*, VII.

3933. **JASB** : 1910 : Coinage of Assam. *Jour. As. Soc.* Beng., IX: 619.

3934. **Joshi, R.V., S.N. Rajguru, R.S. Pappu, T.A. Singh, O.K. Singh, T.S. Singh, H.C. Sharma** *and* **D.K. Medhi** : 1979 : Indian Archaeology: A review, 1978-79. New Delhi.

3935. **Journal** : 1966 : *Banikanta Kakati Commemoration Volume*. Guahati, Jour. Kamrup Anusandhan Samiti.

3936. **Kamrupa Anusandhan** : 1988 : *A source book of the Archaeology of Assam and other states of North-Eastern India, vol. I.* Guwahati, Kamrup Anusandhan Samiti, 600p.

3937. **Kataki, S.** : 1942 : The discovery of three stone images at Gauhati. *Jr. Assam Research Society*, IX: 88-92.

3938. **Kauffmann, Hans E.** : 1955 : A megalithic tank at Mao, Assam. Actes du IVe Congress International des Sciences Anthropologiques et Ethnologiques, vol. 2. Vienna. *Verlang Adolf Holzhausens Nfg*: 190-91.

3939. **Lahiri, A.N.** : 1977 : Unique gold coins of Biradarpanarayana and Harishehandranarayana of Kachar. *67th session, Numismatic Society of India*, Shillong: 1-4.

3940. ———— : A comprehensive account of the Noteworthy features of the Hindu coins of North-Eastern India. *65th Session of the Numismatic Society of India*, Shillong, 26p.

3941. **Lahiri, Nayanjoti** : 1991 : Pre-Ahom Assam: *Studies in the inscriptions of Assam between the fifth and the thirteenth Century A.D.* New Delhi, 179p.

3942. **Lubbock, John** : 1867 : The stone tools of Assam. *Man*, 2(1): 126-28.

3943. ———— : The Stone Age: Stone tools in Upper Assam. *Athenaeeum* (London), No. 2069, June 22: 822.

3944. **Medhi, B.** : 1990 : Pre-history of Assam. *Asian Perspectives*, XXIX(1); 37-44 (University of Hawaii, Honolulu, USA).

3945. ———— : 1992 : *The potters and pottery of Nalbari district,*

Assam: A study in ethnohistory and ethnoarchaeology. Unpub. Ph.D. Thesis, Anth. Deptt., Gau. Univ.

3946. **Medhi, Dilip Kr.** : 1991 : A survey of Neolithic cultures of Assam and Meghalaya *(In) Archaeology of North-Eastern India (Ed)* by Jai Prakash Singh and Gautam Sengupta. New Delhi, Har Anand and Vikas Pubg. House: 131-36.

3947. **Medhi, D.K.** *and* **S.N. Rajguru** : 1977 : Discoveries in Assam. *Indian Archaeology: A Review 1977-78*. New Delhi.

3948. **Medlicott, H.B.** : 1875 : A short hatchet from Dibrugarh, Upper Assam. *Proc. Asiatic Soc. Beng.*, 159p.

3949. **Mills, J.P.** : 1929 : Assam Megaliths. *Antiquity*, 3: 324-38.

3950. ———— : 1930 : An ancient stone image in Assam. *Man*, 30(19); 34-5.

3951. ———— : 1933 : Assam as a field of Research. *Jour. Assam Res. Soc.*, 1(1): 3-6 (Archaeology).

3952. **Mills, J.P.** *and* **J.H. Hutton** : 1929 : Ancient Monoliths of North Cachar. *Jour. Asiatic Soc. Beng.*, 25: 285-300.

3953. **Momin, M.** : 1991 : Urbanisation in the Brahmaputra valley circa AD 600-1200 *(In) Archaeology of North-Eastern India (Eds)* by J.P. Singh and G. Sengupta. New Delhi, Har Anand and Vikas Pub.: 260-79.

3954. **Nath, Anjan Kr.** : 1980 : Boat worship in ancient India. *MII*, 60(1-2), June: 92-7 (Kamrup).

3955. **Nath, Rajmohan** : 1974 : Chutia jatir puratatta*(In) Smriti Grantha (Ed.)* by Paban Ch. Saikia. Sadou Asam Chutia Sanmilanar Astadash Adhibeshan, Sonali Jayanti: 10.

3956. **Nath, R.M.** : 1941 : Ruins of Na-Bhanga. *JARS*, VIII: 35-7.

3957. ———— : 1981 : *Antiquities of Cachar*. Silchar, 22p.

3958. **Neog, Maheswar** : 1961 : Illustrated manuscripts in Assam. *Assam Quarterly*. 1(2), April: 61-9.

3959. **North Eastern Hill University** : 1988 : Seminar on *Archaeological Studies of North-Eastern Region* organised by History Deptt., NEHU, Shillong on Oct. 26.

3960. **Pakrasi, K.B.** : 1956 : A study of some neolithic artifacts from Assam. *Jour. Univ. of Gau (Sc.)*, 7: 1-18.

3961. **Phukan, Biren** : 1982 : Paintings of Assam: A note *(In) India's North-East (Ed)* by Pankaj Thakur. Tinsukia, Prakash Pubg. House: 151-68.

3962. **Phukan, J.N.** : 1982 : *Proceedings and transactions of Seminar on 21-22 Feb., 1981.* Guwahati, Kamarupa Anusandhan Samiti: 50-2.

3963. ———— : 1985 : Date of the Sadiya Stone Pillar Inscriptions. NEIHA, 6: 85-90.

3964. ———— : 1986 : A trilingual copper plate charter of Laksmisinha *(In) Studies in the History of North-East India: Essays in honour of Professor H.K. Barpujari (Ed)* by J.B. Bhattacharjee. Shillong, NEHU Pubn.: 38-44.

3965. ———— : 1995 : King Sivasimha's religious affiliation as reflected in coins and inscriptions. *Jr. NEICSSR,* 19(1), April: 18-20.

3966. **Phukan, Partha Pratim** : 1986 : Letters to the Editor: Save the monuments. *A.T.*, April 10: 4(4-6).

3967. **Purbanchal Prahari** : 1990 : Agyanatavash vilupt ho rahi hai ye puratattik sampadayen. *Pur. Pra.*, April 4: 7(1-8) (Nowgong Dist. Archaeology, *in H.*).

3968. ———— : 1993 : Surya pahar par prapta murti Adinath Bhagavan ki. *Pur. Pra.*, March 2: 3(5-7) (Bijoynagar is nearby Goalpara where Surya pahar is situated, (*in H.*).

3969. ———— : 1996 : Prachinkal ke shilankit patthar meele (*in H.*). *Pur. Pra.*, Oct. 24: 7(2-4) (Some prehistoric tools are found under the earth of Pagaltek Shivalaya, 12 km. west side of Goalpara).

3970. **P.C.S.** : 1992 : Gauhati—The Temple Town of Assam *(In) India Through Ages, Vol. II (Ed)* by T.R. Sareen and S.R. Bakshi. Anmol Pub., New Delhi.

3971. **Raikar, Y.A.** : 1979 : Archaeology in North-Eastern India 300AD to 1200 : A broad survey. *Proceedings of a Seminar on History and Culture of NEI*, organised by His. Deptt., NEHU, Shillong in collaboration with UGC, 26-28 April.

3972. **Rajaguru, S.N.** : 1981 : Geo-climatic background of prehistoric Assam *(Appendix From History to Pre-History in Assam by H.D. Sankalia) (In) Cultural contours of India (Part-II (Ed)* by V.S. Srivastava. Delhi, Abhinav Pubn.

3973. **Rao, S.N.** : 1973 : The neolithic culture of Sarutaru, Assam. *Bull. Deptt. of Anth., Dib. Univ.*, II: 1-9.

3974. ———— : 1974 : A report on the excavation at Marakdola in Kamrup District, Assam *(In) Contemporary Anthropological*

Research in North-East India (Ed) by B.M. Das. Dibrugarh, Dib. Univ.: 132-35 (This is also Bull. Anth. Deptt., Dib. Univ., III).

3975. **Rao, S.N.** : 1974 : Excavation at Sarutaru: A Neolithic site in Assam. Paper submitted in a Seminar on Prehistory, Poona.

3976. ———— : 1977 : Excavation at Sarutaru, a Neolithic site in Assam. *Man and Environment*, I: 39-43.

3977. **Rhodes, N.G.** : 1994 : *The progress of research on coinage of Assam* (Dr. Surya Kr. Bhuyan Memorial lecture held on Oct. 24, inaugurated by Prof. H.K. Barpujari and presided by Dr. B.N. Shastri). Guwahati, Kamrupa Anusandhan Samiti and State Museum Directorate (*Mimeo.*).

3978. ———— : The coins of North-East India *(H.K. Barpujari Endowment Lecture delivered in the Deptt. of History, NEHU, Shillong on Oct. 27, 1994)*.

3979. **Rhodes, N.G.** *and* **M.B. Mitchiner** : 1987 : A series of forged coins from North-East India *(In) A source book of the Numismatic Studies in North-East India*. Guwahati: 113-15.

3980. **Roy, S.K.** : 1976 : An Introductory study of pottery of Assam with special reference to Ambari excavation. *Bull. Deptt. of Anth., Gau. Univ.*, V: 1-12.

3981. ———— : 1977 : *A study of ceramics from the Neolithic to the Medieval period of Assam*: An ethnoarchaeological approach. Unpub. Ph.D. Thesis, Anth. Deptt., Gau., Univ.

3982. ———— : 1979-80 : A note on some archaeological relics in and around Barpeta and Golaghat, Assam: An Appraisal. *Jour. Assam Research Society*, 25: 32-9.

3983. ———— : 1982 : A report on a neolithic celt from Na Tengani Gaon, Borpathar, Golaghat in Sibsagar district, Assam. *Bull. Anth. Deptt., Dib. Univ.*, IX(1980): 206-07.

3984. ———— : 1983 : Pottery and classical codes in Assam. *Bull. Deptt. of Anth., Dib. Univ.*, X: 30-49.

3985. **Saikia, P.C.** : 1982 : A preliminary study of some neolithic tools from Dibrugarh District, Assam. *Bull. Deptt. Anth., Dib. Univ.*, IX (1980): 167-78.

3986. **Sankalia, H.D.** : 1970 : From History to Pre-history in Assam. *Assam Information*, XX(II), Feb.: 27-9.

3987. ———— : From History to Pre-History of Assam, I and II. *A.T.*, Jan. 17: 4(3-8) and Jan. 18: 4(3-8).

3988. ———— : 1981 : From History to Pre-history in Assam. *(In)*

Cultural Contours of India: Dr. Satya Prakash Felicitation volume, Pt. II (Ed) by Vijai Shankar Srivastava. Jaipur, Abhinav Pubn.: 1-5.

3989. **Sankalia, H.D.** : 1986 : From History to Pre-history in Assam-I. *A.T.*, April 27: 4(3-6)7(1) (Assam: Ambari).

3990. ——————— : From History to Pre-History in Assam-II. *A.T.*, May 4 (*Sunday Reading*): 4(4-6)5(5-6).

3991. **Sarkar, Niranjan** : n.d. : Neolithic celts in Arunachal Pradesh and Assam. *Pine* (Shillong), I(III): 70-5 (year of Pubn. c. 1971).

3992. ——————— : 1982 : Neolithic celts and the associate myths from among the Dimasas. *MII*, 62(4), Dec.: 409-13.

3993. **Sarma, Dimbeswar** : 1989 : A peep into Assam Museum. *A.T., (Sunday Reading),* Feb. 12: I (1-8).

3994. **Sarma Kataki, Sarbeswar** : 1930 : Antiquities of Assam. *Ind. Hist. Quart.*, 6: 364-72.

3995. **Sarma, Mukunda Madhava** : 1981-1982 : On the Nagajari Khanikargaon fragmentary stone inscription. *Jour. Assam Research Society,* 26: 12-21.

3996. **Sarma, Pradip** : 1986 : Studies in the original source-materials on the history and culture of North-Eastern India: Archaeological source. *Jr. Assam. Res. Soc.,* 28(1984-85): 62-71.

3997. ——————— : 1988 : Studies in the Architecture of Assam: Problems and prospects. National Seminar on the Archaeology of NEI, Oct. 26-28, 1988, *Papers and Abstracts (Ed.)* by Jai Prakash Singh. Deptt. of History, NEHU, Shillong: 1-29 (*Mimeo.*).

3998. ——————— : 1991 : Studies in the architecture of Assam *(In) Archaeology of North-Eastern India (Eds)* by J.P. Singh and G. Sengupta. New Delhi, Har Anand and Vikas Pubg.: 137-59.

3999. ——————— : 1993 : On the Aryanisation of Brahmaputra valley: An archaeological approach. *Proceedings of a Seminar-cum-Workshop on the Cultural Heritage of the North-East India*, held on 25th Sept. 1993 at Gouri Sadan, Guwahati by Vivekananda Kendra Institute of Culture (*Mimeo.*).

4000. **Sarma, Pratap** : 1981-82 : Antiquity of the Kamakhya temple on the Nilachal. *Jour. Assam Res. Soc.*, 26: 46-52.

4001. **Sarma, P.C.** : 1988 : *Archaeology of Assam.* Delhi, Agam Kala Prakas.

4002. **Seminar** : 1988 : *Seminar on The Archaeology of North-East India,* organised by NEHU & NEC in NEHU Hist. Deptt., Shillong on 26-28 Oct.

4003. **Sengupta, Gautam** : 1984 : *Eastern Indian sculpture (c. 4th-7th cent. AD)*. Unpub. Ph.D. Thesis, Calcutta University.

4004. ———— : 1987 : Recent trends in the history of Art of Ancient Assam. *North-East India History Association, no. 8*. Shillong, Hist. Deptt., NEHU: 586-97.

4005. ———— : 1988 : An almost forgotten work on Assam. *Ibid, no. 9*. Ibid: 65-77.

4006. ———— : Brahmaputra valley sculpture: The formative period. *National Seminar on the Archaeology of NEI, Oct. 26-28, 1988, Papers and Abstracts (Ed)* by J.P. Singh. Deptt. of Hist., NEHU, Shillong: 1-16 (*Mimeo.*).

4007. ———— : 1990 : Studies in the early art of North-East India: An overview. *Proceedings of North-East India History Association, no. 11. Shillong*, Hist. Deptt. NEHU: 73-9.

4008. ———— : 1991 : Brahmaputra valley sculpture *(In) Archaeology of North-Eastern India (Eds)* by J.P. Singh and G. Sengupta. New Delhi, Har Anand and Vikas Pubg.

4009. ———— : 1995 : The art of Assam. *St.*, Literary, Oct. 20: 3(1-6) (Assam monuments).

4010. **Sengupta, Gautam** *and* **S. Chakrabarty** : 1989 : Gauhati Monuments: Rock types and sources. *Proceedings NEIHA, no. 10*. Shillong, Hist. Deptt., NEHU: 25-40.

4011. **Sentinel** : 1995 : 9th century coin found. Jan. 23: 1(3).

4012. ———— : 1996 : Findings of excavation by Archaeological Survey of India at Suryya Pahar, Goalpara: Vital traces of ancient civilization unearthed. June 26: 3(3-8) (Between 6-12th century, Kumar Bhaskar Burman, Hindu, Buddhist and Jain images, ponds, traces of buildings excavated since 9th March, 1993).

4013. **Sen, Sipra** *and* **T.C. Sharma** : 1968 : A note on terracotta objects from Ambari. *Jour. Assam Res. Soc.*, XVIII: 46-8.

4014. **Sharma, A.K.** : 1993 : *Emergence of early culture in North-East India*. New Delhi. 117p.

4015. **Sharma, H.C.** : 1969 : Ambari Excavation. *A.T.*, May 2.

4016. ———— : 1975 : A note on some selected potsherds from Belbari, Kamrup, Assam. *Jour. Assam Sc. Soc.*, XVIII(1), June: 82-4.

4017. **Sharma, H.C.; A.A. Ashraf** *and* **H.C. Mahanta** : 1994: Ceramic tradition in Brahmaputra valley, Assam: A case study from Ambari, Guwahati. *Bull. Dept. of Anth., Gau. Univ.*, VIII: 87-104.

4018. **Sharma, H.C.** *and* **D.C. Sharma** : 1991 : Pottery making by the Assamese potters *(In) Aspects of history and culture (Eds)* by R.D. Choudhury and B. Singh. New Delhi, Ramananda Vidya Bhawan: 275-88.

4019. **Sharma, M.M. (Ed)** : 1978 : *Inscriptions of ancient Assam*. Gau., Univ., Sanskrit Deptt., 100p.

4020. **Sharma, Tarun Ch.** : 1962 : Archaeology of Assam, I and II. *A.T.*

4021. ———— : 1963 : Excavations at Daojali Hading. *A.T.*

4022. **Sharma, T.C.** : 1966 : *Pre-historic Archaeology of Assam: A study of neolithic culture*. Unpub. Ph.D. Thesis, London Univ.

4023. ———— : Researches on the Pre-historic Archaeology of Assam. *Jour. Assam Sc. Soc. (Gau.)*, IX: 4-7.

4024. ———— : 1967 : A note on the Neolithic pottery of Assam. *Man*, II (N.S.), no. 1: 126-28.

4025. ———— : Assam in Pre-historic times. Kamarupa (Souvenir), *XII session, All India Sc. Teachers' Association*: 83-9.

4026. ———— : 1969 : Archaeology in Assam. *Paper presented in the IInd International Conf. of Asian Archaeology*, Colombo.

4027. ———— : 1970 : Archaeological Research in Assam. *A.T.*, Dec. 6.

4028. ———— : 1973 : Archaeological chronology of N-E India *(Reprint Paper no. 9339). IXth Int. Cong. Anth. Soc.*, Chicago.

4029. ———— : 1974 : Recent Archaeological discoveries in North-Eastern India. *Puratta: Bull. of Indian Archaeological Society*, no. VII: 17-9.

4030. ———— : Prehistory of Assam *(In) Indian Anthropology Today (Ed)* by D. Sen. Calcutta, Cal. Univ.: 63-70.

4031. **Sharma, T.C.** : 1974 : Prehistoric Archaeology in North-Eastern India: Its problems and prospects *(In) Contemporary Anthropological Research in North-East India (Ed)* by B.M. Das *(Bull. Anth. Deptt., Dib. Univ., III)*. Dibrugarh, Dib. Univ.: 147-55.

4032. ———— : 1976 : Archaeology of Assam. *North-Eastern Spectrum* (Gau.), I(I), July: 17-22.

4033. ———— : Pre-historic background of shifting cultivation *(In) Shifting Cultivation in North-East India*. Shillong, NEICSSR: 1-4.

4034. **Sharma, T.C.** : 1976 : The lower Palaeolithic of North-Eastern India *(In) Resume's des Communications, IXth Int. Cong. of Prehistoric and Protohistoric Sciences*, NICE, 130p.

4035. ———— : 1978 : On the significance of shouldered celts in the Prehistory of North-East India. *Paper presented in Xth Int. Sc. Cong., Anth. & Arch. Session*, New Delhi.

4036. ———— : North-East India through the ages. *Souvenir: Anthropological Student Forum*, Anth. Deptt., Gau. Univ.: 22.

4037. ———— : 1979 : Neolithic patterns of North-East India. Proc. *of a Seminar on The History and Culture of North-East India.* Deptt. of Hist., NEHU held on 26-28 April.

4038. ———— : Archaeology in Assam *(In) Ancient Ceylon* (*Colombo*) III: 277-95.

4039. ———— : 1980 : Excavation at Ambari: Its problems and prospects *(In) Proceedings of North-East India History Association, no. 10*. Shillong, Hist. Deptt., NEHU.

4040. ———— : Pre-historic Archaeology in North-East India: A Review of Progress *(In) Eastern Himalayas (Eds)* by T.C. Sharma and D.N. Majumdar. New Delhi, Cosmo Pubn.: 102-35.

4041. ———— : 1981 : A note on some pre-historic survivals in North-East India. *Bull. Deptt. of Anth.*, Dib. Univ., VII-VIII (1978-79): 1-7.

4042. ———— : 1982 : Assam through the ages *(In) India's North-East (Ed)* by Pankaj Thakur. Tinsukia, Prakash Pubg. House: 114-25.

4043. ———— : 1983 : North-East India in Pre-historic Times. *Proceedings of a Seminar on Electoral Politics in North-East India*, organised by NEICSSR, Shillong on Dec. 14-15.

4044. ———— : 1984 : North-East India in Pre-historic Times *(In) The Tribes of North-East India (Ed)* by S. Karotemprel. Calcutta, Firma KLM: 1-21.

4045. ———— : Neolithic Pattern of North-East India *(In) Madhu: Recent Research in Indian Archaeology and Art History (Ed)* by Nagaraja Rao. Delhi.

4046. ———— : 1986 : Recent advances in Pre-history and Archaeology of Northeast India. *Jour. Assam Research Society (Prof. Dibakar Goswami Commemoration volume)*. Guwahati, XXVIII, 1984-85 (1984): 1-28.

4047. ———— : 1987 : Recent advances in Pre-history and

Archaeology of North-East India. *Jour. Assam Res. Society*, 28(1984-85): 1-28.

4048. **Sharma, T.C.** : 1989 : Ambari: Sculptor's Studio of classical age. *A.T.*, (*Sunday Reading*), April 30: I (1-8).

4049. ———————— : Letters to the Editor: Ambari sculpture. *A.T.*, May 17: 4(3-5).

4050. ———————— : Excavation at Ambari (Guwahati): Its problems and prospects. *Proceedings NEIHA, no. 10*. Shillong, Hist. Deptt., NEHU: 21-4.

4051. ———————— : 1990 : On the Prehistoric background of Social and Political Institutions *(In) Social and Political Institutions of the Hill People of North-East India (Eds)* by Jayanta Sarkar and B. Datta Ray. Calcutta, Anth. Survey of India: 1-7.

4052. ———————— : Assam from pre-historic age to historic age. *Lecture delivered at Gauri Sadan, Guwahati, the 2nd Jwalti Ram Lahkar Memorial lecture on 23rd June, 1990*

4053. ———————— : 1991 : Prehistoric situation in North-East India *(In) Archaeology of North-Eastern India (Eds)* by J.P. Singh and G. Sengupta. New Delhi, Har Anand & Vikas Pub. House: 41-58.

4054. ———————— : n.d. : Research in the Pre-historic Archaeology of Assam. *Jour. Assam Res. Soc.*, IX(1).

4055. **Sharma, Tarun Ch.** *and* **M.C. Goswami** : 1962 : A brief report on the investigations into the Pre-historic Archaeology of North Cachar Hills, Assam. *Jour. Gau. Univ.*, 13(2).

4056. ———————— : 1963 : Further report on the investigations into the pre-historic archaeology of the North Cachar Hills, Assam. *Jour. Gau. Univ.*, XIV(2).

4057. ———————— : 1963 and 1967 : Archaeological explorations and excavations in Assam. *Indian Archaeology*, 1962-63, 1966-67.

4058. **Sharma, Tarun Ch.** *and* **M.C. Goswami** : 1967 : Assam in Pre-historic times. *Souvenir*. Pub. in connection with the Gau. session of the All India Sc. Teachers' Conference.

4059. **Sharma, T.C.** *and* **Gautam Sengupta** : 1990 : Ambari excavation (A note on recent sculpture find) *(In) A Comprehensive History of Assam, vol.I (Ed)* by H.K. Barpujari. Guwahati, Spectrum Pubn. (United Publisher).

4060. **Shillong Times** : 1989 : Ancient coins speaks of Assam-Cachar ties. July 18: 3(1-2).

4061. **Shillong Times** : 1992 : Neolithic sites discovered. Oct. 27: 3(7). (At Hamren in Karbi Anglong).

4062. ———— : 1993 : 18th century tanks explored. *Shg. T.*, Jan. 19: 3(8). (Dunaimukh, South West of Golaghat town, Upper Assam).

4063. **Singh, Jai Prakash** : 1980 : On the nature of Ahom money. *Lik Phan Tai*, II.

4064. ———— : 1984 : On a gold coin of Harshapala of Assam. *Jour. Oriental Institute,* 34(1-2), Sept.-Dec.: 97-102.

4065. ———— : 1988 : Jayantia coins and the Koch historical tradition: An examination. *Numismatics International Bulletin*, May.

4066. ———— : 1989 : *Monetary development in early Assam.* Jorhat.

4067. ———————— : Lauhitya in early inscriptions of Kamarupa. *NEIHA,* 10: 59-61.

4068. **Singh, J.P.** *and* **N. Ahmad (Eds)** : 1977 : *Coinage and economy of North-Eastern States of India.* Varanasi, N.S.I.

4069. **Singh, J.P.** *and* **G. Sengupta (Eds)** : 1991 : Archaeology of North-East India. Delhi, Har Anand & Vikas Pub., 216p.

4070. **Sircar, D.C.** : 1974 : On some early inscriptions of Assam. *Jour. Assam Res. Soc.,* 22: 1-11.

4071. ———— : 1977 : Money in Pre-Ahom Assam and its neighbourhood *(In) Coinage and Economy of North-Eastern States of India (Ed)* by J.P. Singh and N. Ahmad. Varanasi, N.S.I.

4072. **Sonowal, M.** : 1991 : A brief study of the Shakti Icons of Ambari excavations. *Proceedings of the Annual Conference of Kamrup Anusandhan Samiti*, held on 5th, 6th Sept., Guwahati.

4073. **Sonowal, Minarva** : 1992 : Mahishasuramardini and Chandanayika: An Iconographic study on two types of Shakti Icons of Ambari, Guwahati, Assam. *Bull. Deptt. of Anth., Gau. Univ.*, VI, March: 99-103.

4074. **Statesman** : 1992 : Remains of an ancient civilization. April 3: 12(1-5) (Archaeology of 11th Century in Cotton College Campus).

4075. **Telegraph** : 1995 : The portrayal of erotic images and stylistic carvings on stones. Oct. 20.

4076. **Thakuria, Ramcharan** : 1987 : Khuspuran silalipi: Brahmaputra aru Barak upatyakar sampriti setu. *Smriti Grantha, Asam Sahitya Sabha, Hailakandi Session*, 1987: 127.

4077. **Trivedi, Krishna Kant** : 1973 : Early history and ancient states of Saran district in the light of archaeological finds. *Prajna*, 18 (2), March: 161-68.

4078. **Vatsayan, Kapila** : 1981 : Some dance sculptures from Assam. *Quarterly Jour. of National Centre of Performing Arts*, 10(3), Sept.: 19-35.

4079. **Verma, Atul Kr.** : n.d. : Neolithic culture of Eastern India. *Heritage of Ancient India*. no. 16.

4080. **Westmacott, G.E.** : 1835 : Description of ancient temples and ruins at Chardwar in Assam. *Jour. Roy. As. Soc. Beng.*, IV: 185-95.

4081. **Worman, E.C.** : 1949 : The Neolithic problem in the Pre-history of India. *Jour. Washington Academy of Science*, 39(6): 181-201.

PART-II (D)

FULL BIBLIOGRAPHY OF LINGUISTICS

4082. **Ajir Asam** : 1994 : Editorial : Boror Roman Lipi *(in A.) Ajir Asam*, March 9 (33rd Boro Sahitya Sabha on 4-6 March in South Guwahati's Garchuk Ahom village's resolution).

4083. **Akash Bani** : 1996 : Discussion of Radio-talk on Asamiya Bhasha. Asamiya Jati Janagosthir Atmaprakashar Madhyam (*in Assamese*). *Dibrugarh, Akash Bani (AIR), 8 pm on Feb. 11, 1996.*

4084. **Amrita Bazar Patrika** : 1986 : Assam language policy: Tribals demand status quo. Aug. 5: 7(2-4).

4085. ———— : 1987 : Paper in Dimasa language. July 7: 3(1-2).

4086. ———— : 1990 : Bishnupriya language. Oct. 15: 5 (6).

4087. **Anthropological Survey of India** : 1981 : All India Linguistic Traits Survey *(A workshop Seminar on 21-22 Sept. 1981*, organised by Anth. S.I., Calcutta).

4088. **Asam Sahitya Sabha** : n.d. : *The evolution of Assamese script.* Jorhat, Asam Sahitya Sabha, 26p.

4089. ———— : n.d. : *Pratna-Asamiya Bhasar Ruptattic Bisleshan.* Jorhat, Asom Sahitya Sabha *(in A.).*

4090. ———— : *Assamese for all.* Jorhat, Asam Sahitya Sabha, 28p.

4091. **Assam Tribune** : 1973 : Call for united stand to defend Assamese language. Jan. 4.

4092. ———— : 1991 : Census: A new trend on "Mother Tongue". Jan. 4: 3(6-8) (Assamese 2nd language, Bengali for Bengalis before 1971).

4093. ———— : Tea tribes for Assamese as mothertongue. Feb. 10: 1(2-5), 6(4).

4094. ———— : 1991 : Plea to develop Bodo language. *A.T.*, March 19: 5(1-3).

4095. ———— : 1992 : Inclusion of Bodo language in 8th Schedule demanded. March 5: 1(1-3).

4096. ———— : 1993 : Plan for Tai language, culture institute. Nov. 11: 5(4-6).

4097. ———— : 1994 : Roman script for Bodo languages. March 7: 1(3-5).

4098. **Avery, J.** : 1887 : On the relationship of the Kachari and Garo languages of Assam. *Proceedings of the Am. Oriental Soc.*, Vol. VIII: 158.

4099. **Bandopadhyay, P.K.** : 1982 : The coming of the alphabet: A study of the script of some North-Eastern languages *(In) Linguistic situation in North-East India (Ed)* by Mrinal Miri. Shillong, NEICSSR: 38-43.

4100. **Barman, Sivnath** *and* **Prasanjit Choudhury** : 1986 : *Bastav Bibaran: Asamat Bangla Bhasar Prabartanar Oitihasik Utsha Sandhan (in A.).* Dibrugarh, Student Emporium.

4101. **Barua, B.K.** : 1935 : A note on the word Assam. *JARS*, II: 102-4.

4102. **Barua, Bimal Kanta** : 1974 : *Tai Bhasha*. Jorhat, Asom Sahitya Sabha.

4103. **Barua, Bhaben** : n.d. : *Language and the National Question in North-East Asia*. Gauhati, Bani Prakash.

4104. **Barua, Birinchi Kumar** : 1985 : *Asamiya Bhasa Aru Sanskriti (in A.).* Nalbari, Journal Emporium 5th edition.

4105. **Barua, Hem** : 1958 : Re-introduction of Assamese in NEFA *(In) The Outlook on NEFA (Comp)* by Parag Chaliha. Jorhat, Asam Sahitya Sabha: 37-42 (Assamese *lingua franca* of Arunachal people).

4106. **Barua, Nagendra Nath** : n.d. : *Dimasa Bhashar Bharal (in A.).* Gauhati, Asam Prakashan Pari.

4107. **Baruah, S.L.** : 1987 : Historiography in Assamese language in the nineteenth century and the British response to it *(In) Historiography in Modern Indian Languages (Ed)* by T.S. Banerjee. Calcutta: 1-18.

4108. **Beams, J.** : n.d. : On one Koch words in Mr. Deuarts article on the Palis of Dinajpur. *Indian Antiquary Bombay,* I: 371.

4109. : 1992 : The Boro language and literature. *A.T.*, March 3: 4(3-8) 6(3-6).

4110. **Bhattacharya, Pramod Ch.** : 1964 : *A descriptive analysis of the Boro language*. Unpub. Ph.D. Thesis, Gau. Univ.

4111. ———— : 1973-74 : Analogy in Assamese language. *Jour. of the Univ. of Gau.,* 24-25(1): 44-7.

4112. ———— : n.d. : *Descriptive analysis of Boro language*. Gau. Univ. Pub.

4113. ———— : 1982 : Sino-Tibetan Languages of North-East India: Social aspects *(In) Linguistic situation in North-East India (Ed)* by Mrinal Miri. Shillong, NEICSSR: 84-6.

4114. **Bhattacharya, P.C.** : 1977-78 : The languages and dialects of Cachar District in Assam. *Jour. Assam Res. Soc.,* 23: 12-5.

4115. **Bhuyan, D.C.** : 1969 : Assamese language and literature *(In) The land and people: Assam (Comp)* by S. Barkataki. New Delhi, NBT: 45-62.

4116. **Biswas, S.** : 1977-78 : Alternate of Assamese and Bengali. *Jour. Gau. Univ (Arts)*, 28-29: 198-205 (Grammar, Language).

4117. **Biswas, Sukumar** : 1996 : n.d. : *Morpho-Phonemic Analysis of the Assamese and Bengali verbals.* Guwahati, Anundoram Barooah Inst. of Lang. Art & Cul. Assam.

4118. **Bodo Text Book Committee** : 1974 : *How Roman script helps the Bodos* ? Kokrajhar, Bodo Sahitya Sabha (Nov. 27, 1974 typed copy).

4119. **Bora, Kamaleswar** : 1987 : Assamese as link language. *A.T.*, March 28: 4(3-6).

4120. **Brown, J.M.** : 1965 : *From ancient Thai to modern dialects.* Bangkok, Social Sc. Association Press of Thailand, 179p.

4121. **Brown, N.** : 1837 : Alphabets of the Tai language. *Jr. Roy. As. Soc. Beng.*, 6: 17-21.

4122. ________ : Comparison of Indo-Chinese language. *Jr. As. Soc. Beng.*, 6: 1023-1038.

4123. ________ : 1893 : *Grammatical notes on the Assamese language.* 3rd edition revised by P.H. Moore. Nowgong, Assam, American Baptist Missionary Union [1st edition, 1848, Sibsagar, American Baptist Mission Press].

4124. **Brown, W.B.** : 1895 : *An outline grammar of the Deuri-Chutiya language spoken in Upper Assam.* Shillong, Govt. Pubn.

4125. ________ **(Ed.)** ________ : *An outline Grammar of Deuri-Chutiya language spoken in Upper Assam.* Govt. Pubn.

4126. **Burabhakat, Kantiram** : 1927 : *Collection of Assamese Proverbs.*

4127. **Burling, Robin** : 1959 : Proto-Bodo. *Language (Bultimore)*: 11-60.

4128. **Burling, Robin** *and* **P.C. Bhattacharya** : 1956 : Lexico-Statistic dating of Boro-Garo linguistic separation. *Jr. Univ. of Gauhati*, 7: 67-73.

4129. **Campbell, A.** : 1839 : A note on the Meches together with a small vocabulary of the language. *Jr. Royal Asiatic Soc. Beng. (N.S.)*, 8: 623-31.

4130. **Campbell, George** : n.d. : Further languages from Tipperah and Cachar *(In) Specimen of language* by G. Campbell: 204-17, 254-69, 220-35.

4131. **Campbell, George** : n.d. : List of words and phrases showing Shan and Cacharee dialects of Assam *(In) Specimens of Languages* by G. Campbell: 168-86.

4132. **Chaliha, D.** : n.d. : *Origin and growth of Assamese language and literature.* Gauhati, Pub. by author.

4133. **Chamberlain, J. R.** : 1975 : A new look at the History and classification of the Tai languages *(In) Studies in Tai Linguistics in honour of William J. Gedney (Eds)* by J.G. Harris *and* J.R. Chamberlain. Bangkok, Central Institute of English Language: 58.

4134. **Chatterjee, S.K.** : 1962 : *Language and literature of Modern India.* Calcutta, Prakash Bhawan.

4135. **Chatterjee, Suniti Kr.** : 1955 : Tribal language *(In) The Adivasis* by Publication Division, Delhi, Ministry of Information & Broadcasting, Pub. Div.: 70-8.

4136. **Choudhury, Runima** : 1994 : *Assamese Verbs : A Study in the structural paradigm.* Guwahati, Anundoram Barooah Inst. of Lang. Art & Cul. Assam.

4137. **Cutter, H.B.C.** : 1840 : *Vocabulary and phrases in English and Assamese.* American Baptist Mission Press, 251 p.

4138. **Das, Naren** : 1994 : Letters to the Editor: Boror Roman Lipi *(in A.) Ajir Asam,* March 12: 2(3-8).

4139. **Das, Prabin Ch.** : n.d. : *Asamiya Bhasa Aru Sahityar Katha (in A.).* Guwahati, Bani Prakash.

4140. **Datta Baruah, P.N.** : 1975 : Negative formation in Assamiya and Oriya, *Indian Linguistics,* 36(2), June: 144-51.

4141. **Datta, Birendranath** : 1971 : The Dialects of Goalpara *(In) Assam Academic Review (Ed)* by B. Barua. vol. I, no. I.

4142. ———— : 1980 : Assamese Folk Toys. *Illustrated Weekly of India,* 101(22), June : 16.

4143. **Datta, S.P.** : 1969 : Rabha speech: A preliminary study *(In) District Handbook of West Bengal: Jalpaiguri; Census of India 1961, Appendix-V (Comp)* by B.Roy. Calcutta, Govt. Printing Press: 113-38.

4144. **Devi, Bhamati** : 1992 : *A contrastive study of Assamese and Hindi verbs.* Unpub. Ph.D. Thesis, Gau. Univ.

4145. **Dhekial Phukan, Anandaram** : 1856 : *A few remarks on the Assamese language and on Vernacular Education in Assam.* Sibsagar, American Baptist Mission Press (*Reprinted* by Maheswar Neog in 1977 from Jorhat).

4146. **Dundas, W.C.M.** : 1908 : *An outline grammar and dictionary of the Kachari-Diamasa language based on Mani Charan Barman's Kachari grammar*. Shillong, Eastern Bengal and Assam Secretariat Press.

4147. **Dutta Barua, P.N.** : 1992 : *Assamese Phonetic Reader*. Mysore, Central Inst. Ind. Lang.

4148. ———— : 1996 : *Pictorial Glossary in Assamese*. Mysore, CIIL.

4149. **Dutta Baruah, P.N.; T.K. Goswamy; Bhamati Devi and B. Mahapatra** : 1994 : *Asamiya Bhasha Mukul-II*. Mysore, CIIL (*in A.*).

4150. **Dutta Baruah, Phanindra Narayan** : 1993 : *Comparative analysis of the Morphological aspect of Assamese and Oriya*. Delhi, Mittal Pubs.

4151. **Endle, S.** : 1884 : *Outline grammar of the Kachari (Bara) language as spoken in the District Darrang, Assam; with illustrative sentences, notes, reading lessons, and a short vocabulary*. Shillong, Assam Secretariat Press, 99p.

4152. **Forbes, C.J.F.S.** : 1878 : On Tibeto-Burman languages. *Jour. of Royal Asiatic Society of Great Britain and Ireland* (New Series), vol. 10: 210-27.

4153. **Gogoi, Lila** : 1967 : The origin and development of Assamese script. *Proceedings of a Seminar of Gau. Univ., sponsored by UGC*.

4154. ———— : 1981 : *Ruput/Roopoot (It is a Tai-Ahom word meaning Record for Reconstruction, A critical study of Assamese Buranji literature*. Ph.D. Thesis, Dib. Univ.

4155. **Gohain, A.K.** : 1992 : The Tai and Tai language in North-East India *(In) Dibrugarh University Silver Jubilee Commemoration volume (Eds)* by U. Mishra and P.K. Baruah. Dib. Univ., Pub. by the Registrar.

4156. **Gohain, Hiren** : 1994 : Roman Lipi aru Boro Sahitya *(in A.) Ajir Asam*, March 9.

4157. **Goswami, H.C.** : 1930 : *A descriptive catalogue of Assamese manuscripts*. Calcutta University.

4158. **Goswami, Hemchandra** *and* **Padmanath Gohain Boroah** : 1907: A note on Assamese language and literature; Appendix *(In) Pandit Hemchandra Goswami Rachanaboli (Ed)* by Benudhar Sarma. Jorhat, Asam Sahitya Sabha.

4159. **Goswami, P.D.** : 1982 : Loan words in North-Eastern India *(In)*

Linguistic Situation in North-East India (Ed) by Mrinal Miri. Shillong, NEICSSR: 69-73.

4160. **Goswami, S.N.** : 1968 : Assamese phonetics: A historical study. *Jour. Assam Res. Soc.,* 18: 68-75.

4161. ———— : 1971 : The case-suffixes in Assamese. *Indian Linguistics,* 32(2), April-June: 139-47.

4162. **Goswami, U.C.** : 1970 : *Kamrupi: A dialect of Assamese*: 10-5.

4163. **Goswami, Upendranath** : 1970-72 : The language of North-Bengal and Western Assam. *Jour. Gau. Univ (Arts),* 21-23(1): 62-70.

4164. ———— : 1976 : A historical note on the negative particle in Assamiya. *Indian Linguistics,* 37(2), June: 143-45 (Language).

4165. ———— : 1977-78 : A script for the tribal language of Assam. *Jour. Gau. Univ. (Art),* 28-29: 195-97.

4166. ———— : 1993 : *An Introduction to the Deuri Language.* Guwahati, Anundoram Borooah Inst. of Lang. Art & Cult. Assam.

4167. **Grierson, George A. (Ed.)** : 1903 : *Linguistic Survey of India, vol. III, Tribe to Burman Family, Pt. 2, Specimens of the Bodo, Naga and Kachin Groups.* Calcutta, Office of the Supdt. of Govt. Printing.

4168. ———— **(Ed.)**——— : *Linguistic Survey of India, Vol. 5 Indo-Aryan Family, East Group, Part I: Specimens of the Bengali and Assamese languages.* Calcutta, Supdt. Govt. Printing, India.

4169. ———— **(Ed.)** : 1909 : *Linguistic Survey of India, Vol. 3,* Part-I. Calcutta, Supdt. Govt. Printing, 641p.

4170. ———— **(Ed.)** : 1966 : *Linguistic Survey of India, Vol. I.* Delhi, Motilal Banarasi Dass (*Reprinted*).

4171. ———— : 1971 : The History of the Tai and their languages *(In) The Tai Khamtis (Comp)* by Lila Gogai. Chowkham (NEFA), Chowkhamoon Gohain (Namsoon): 31-40, 183-85 (*Reprinted*).

4172. ———— : 1987 : *Languages of North-Eastern India,* Vol. I. Delhi, Gian Pubg. House (*Reprinted*) (Ahom: 81, Miri: 296, Lalung: 31, Dimasa: 322, Rabha : 357).

4173. ———— : *Ibid. Vol. II.* Ibid (*Reprinted*).

4174. **Gurdon, P.R.T. (Comp)** : 1903 : *Some Assamese Proverbs* (2nd edition). Shillong, Assam Secretariat Printing Office, (1st Pub. in 1896 from Shillong).

4175. **Hagjer, Nirupama** : 1972 : *Dimasa Bhasha Siksha (in A.).* Jorhat, Asom Sahitya Sabha.

4176. **Hazarika, Bisweswar** : 1968 : Negative formation in Assamese. *Indian Linguistics,* 29(1): 34-9.

4177. ——————— : Ibid. *Jour. Assam Research Society,* 18: 35-40 (Grammar, language).

4178. **Hodson, Brian Houghton** : 1847 : *Essay on the Koch, Bodo and Dhimal tribes (Part-I. Vocabulary, Part-II. Grammar, Part-III. Location Numbers, creed, customs, condition, physical and moral characteristics of the people).* Calcutta, J. Thomas, Baptist Mission Press, 200p. (*Reprinted* by Hodgson, Miscellaneous Essays. London, 1880: 1-160p.).

4179. ————— : 1849 : On the Aborigines of North-Eastern India, and Comparative Vocabularies of the Tibetan, Bodo and Garo Languages. *Jour. Asiatic Society of Bengal,* Vol. 18, Part-I: 451-60 (*Reprinted* by Hodgson, Miscellaneous Essays, vol. 2: 1-10).

4180. ————— : 1857 : Comparative vocabulary of the several dialects of the Kirantee language. *Jour. Asiatic Soc. of Beng.,* Vol. 26: 350-71.

4181. **Hutton, J.H.** : 1932 : Linguistic Pre-History *(In) Census of India 1931, Vol. I, India, Part-I,* Report. Delhi, Manager of Publications: 357-69.

4182. **Itagi, N.H.; B.D. Jayaram** *and* **V. Vani** : 1986 : *Communication Potential in the Tribal Population of Assam and Madhya Pradesh.* Mysore, CIIL.

4183. **Jeyapaul, V.Y.** : 1987 : *Karbi Grammar.* Mysore, Central Institute for Indian Language.

4184. **Kakati, B.** : 1951 : Certain Austic-Sanskrit word Correspondence *(In) A Cultural History of Assam (Early Period) vol. I* by B.K. Barua. Nowgong (Assam), Pub. by K.K. Barooah: 208-10.

4185. ——————— : Place and Personal names in the early land grants of Assam *(In) A Cultural History of Assam (Early Period), Vol. I* by B.K. Barua. Nowgong (Assam), Pub. by K.K. Barooah: 202-08.

4186. ————— : 1962 : *Assamese: Its formation and development: A Scientific treatise on the History and Philosophy of Assamese language.* Gauhati, Lawyers Book Stall (2nd edition, 1st pub. in 1941).

4187. **Kakati, Banikanta** : 1938-39 : Austric Sub-Stratum in the Assamese language. *New Indian Antiquary,* vol. I: 259-64.

4188. **Kataki, S.** : 1936 : *Ancient Assamese scripts.* Gauhati.

4189. **Katre, Sumanta Manges** : 1961 : Introduction to Modern Indian Linguistics (with special reference to Indo-Aryan and Assamese). *Gau. Univ., Prativa Devi Memorial Lecture,* 57p.

4190. **Kay, Sardoka Perrin** : 1904 : *An English-Mikir vocabulary with Assamese equivalents to which have been added a few Mikir phrases.* Shillong, Eastern Bengal & Assam Secretariat Printing Office, 189p.

4191. **Koch, J.** : 1986 : An analytical study in Koch (Rabha) language. *Amai-Ju: Souvenir, 4th Annual Conference of Koch Student Union,* Kokrajhar Dist., 42p.

4192. **Konwar, Arpana** : 1992 : *Karbi people and their language: A critical study.* Unpub. Ph.D. Thesis, Gau. Univ.

4193. **Kumar, Braj Bihari** : 1977 : *Hindi Bodo Dictionary.* Kohima, Nagaland Bhasa Parishad, 64p.

4194. ———— : 1978 : *Boro Vyakaran Kee Ruprekha.* Kohima, Nagaland Bhasa Parishad, 16p. *(in H.).*

4195. ———— : *Hindi Mirie (Mishing) dictionary.* Kohima, Nagaland Bhasa Parishad, 64p.

4196. **Kumar, Braj Bihari** *and* **Hariprasad Gorkha Roy** : 1974 : *Hindi Karbi (Mikir) Dictionary [Hindi Karbi (Mikir) Kosh].* Kohima, Nagaland Bhasa Parisad, 60p.

4197. **Lahiri, Srabana** : 1995 : Professor Satyendranath Sarma: Lord of the language. *Sentinel Sunday,* Feb. 26: I, (1-8) (Assamese language).

4198. **Leyden, J.** : 1908 : On the languages and literature of the Indo-Chinese nations. *Asiatic Researches,* vol. 10: 158-289.

4199. **Lyall, Charles J.** : 1903 : A Grammar and Specimen of the Mikir language. *Indian Antiquary,* 32: 101-11, 205-12.

4200. **Mahanta, Rap Ch.** : n.d. : *Asamiya Vyakaranar Ruprekha (in A.).* Delhi, NBT.

4201. **Mahanta, Rohini Kr.** : 1975-76 : The category of cash in Assamese: A phonological study. *Jour. Univ. Gau. (Arts),* 26-27 (1): 79-94.

4202. **Mahapatra, Bijoy Prasad** : 1971 : Bhuyan dialect. *Bull. Anth. Survey of India,* XVII(2), April (1968): 185-208.

4203. **Majumdar, D.N.** : 1973 : Size-shape categories in the languages of North-East India, an exploration of the Sapier-whorl Hypothesis. *Bull. Anth. Deptt., Gau. Univ.,* vol. II: 41-61.

4204. ———— : 1974 : Affect of bilingualism on Song Koch phonemic structure. *Bull. Anth. Deptt., Gau. Univ.,* III, December: 58-67.

4205. **Malik, Syed Abdul** : 1961 : *Asamiya Musalmanar gharua bhasha*. Asam Sahitya Sabha Patrika, 17(2): 51-2 *(in A.)*.

4206. **Man in India** : 1938 : Notices of Books: Assamese Grammar and Origin of the Assamese Language with an introduction containing a short History of Assamese Literature by Kaliram Medhi, 1936, pp. 539. XVIII (I), Jan.-March: 80.

4207. **Maral, Bhagaban Ch.** : 1986 : *Semantic of Assamese*. Unpub. Ph.D. Thesis, Gau., Univ.

4208. **Medhi, Kaliram** : 1936 : *Assamese Grammar and Origin of the Assamese Language with an Introduction containing a short History of Assamese Literature*. Gauhati.

4209. **Miri, Mrinal (Ed)** : 1982 : *Linguistic situation in North-East India*. Shillong, NEICSSR, 102p.

4210. **Mishra, Partha Sarathy** : 1967 : *Dimasa : Language and Society. ICSSR Project*, Haflong Govt. College.

4211. ———— : 1979 : Dimasa: The language and the Society: A study of linguistic acculturation. *ICSSR Research Abstract Quarterly*, VIII(3).

4212. ———— : 1983 : Who speaks what language to whom and when. *Jour. NEICSSR*, 7(2), Oct.: 31-4 (Dimasa of N.C.Hill).

4213. **Mitra, A.** : 1964 : *Census of India 1961, Vol. I, India, Pt. II-C (ii): Language Tables*. Delhi, Manager of Pubn., 534p. (Tibeto-Burman Sub-Family, Assam-Burmese Branch, Bodo Group) Bodo, Kachari, Mech, Lalung, Dimasa, Koch, Rabha, Deori, Mikir, etc.).

4214. **Mitra, Debashish** : 1996 : Newsletter (Assam) chucking culture. *Statesman*, Sept. 16: 9(1-2) (Bodo, Rabha, Missing script).

4215. **Nag, Amit Kr.** : 1367BS: Prachin Cacharer Bangla Bhasa O Sahitya. *Sambhar (in B.*, Silchar) : 25-7.

4216. **Nath, D.** : 1986 : The Mishing language movement in Assam. *Proceedings of a Seminar on question of Nationality, Ethnicity and Cultural Identity in the context of North-East India*, 5-6 Dec. organised by NEICSSR, Shillong.

4217. ———— : 1990 : The Mishing language movements in Assam *(In) Nationality, Ethnicity and Cultural Identity in North-East India (Ed)* by B. Pakem. New Delhi, Omsons Pubs.: 165-72.

4218. **Neighboor, R.E.** : 1878 : *A vocabulary in English and Mikir with sentences illustrating the use of words*. Calcutta, G.H. Rouse, Baptist Mission Press, 84p.

4219. **Neog, D.** : 1964 : *The origin and growth of the Assamiya language*. Xuwani Prakas (Besoty Pubn.), 200p.

4220. **Neog, Maheswar** : 1972 : Prakrits and Assamese. *Jour. Ganganath Jha Kendriya Sanskrit Vidyapeetha,* 28(1-2), Jan.-April: 407-28.

4221. **Neog, Maheswar; Rajanikanta Dev Sharma** *and* **Nabakanta Barua** : 1977 : *Adhunik Asamiya Abhidhan.* Guwahati, Asam Prakashan Parisad *(in A.).*

4222. **Nicholl, C.F.** : 1885 : *Manual of the Bengali language including an Assamese Grammar.* London, Crosby Lockwood & Sons.

4223. **Nigam, R.C.** : 1964 : An introductory note on classification *(In) Census of India 1961, Vol. I, India, Pt. II-C (ii): Language Tables* by A. Mitra. Delhi, Manager of Pubn.

4224. **Padun, Nahendra** : 1970 : Mishing Bhasa *(In) Mising Sanskritir Alekhya (Ed)* by Bhrigumoni Kagyung. Birubari, Gauhati, 236p.

4225. **Pathak, Jiban Ch.** : 1993 : *Descriptive analysis of the dialect of Darrang district.* Unpub. Ph.D. Thesis, Gau., Univ.

4226. **Pathak, Ramesh** : 1986 : *Studies in Assamese vocabulary.* Unpub. Ph.D. Thesis, Gau. Univ.

4227. ———— : 1992 : *Names of Places in Assam.* Proceedings of a workshop on North-East Language. Shillong, NEHU, June 4.

4228. **Paul, Gemini** : 1956 : Origin of certain tribal names pertaining to Assam. *Vanyajati,* IV(4), Oct.: 147-53.

4229. **Peal, S.E.** : 1879 : A peculiarity of the river names in Assam and some of the adjoining countries. *Jour. Asia. Soc. Beng.,* I(4).

4230. **Phukan, Amrit** : 1977 : Sadani : The Tea Garden language of Assam. *North-Eastern Spectrum,* 1(8-10): 35.

4231. **Phukan, Anandaram Dhekial** : 1854 : *The case of Assamese language.* Nowgong.

4232. **Phukan, Dambaru Deodhai** : n.d. : *Phung-su.* (in Tai Ahom language). Patsaku (Sibsagar, Assam), Unpub. Tai-Ahom Language Mss.

4233. **Phukan, Dipti** : 1991 : *An analysis of the Assamese verb system: A historical study.* Unpub. Ph.D. Thesis, Dib. Univ.

4234. **Phukan, J.N.** : 1964 : Basic aspects of the Tai (Ahom language). *Jour. Gau. Univ. (Arts),* 15(1): 73-81.

4235. ———— : 1980 : Sources of the History of Assam in Ahom language. *(In Sources of the History of India, Vol. III (Ed)* by Nihar Ranjan Ray. Simla, Institute of Historical Studies: 101-18.

4236. **Phukan, Mukunda Deodhai** : n.d. : Phe-lung phe-ban *(In Tai-*

Ahom language). Patsaku (Sibsagar, Assam), Unpub. Tai-Ahom language Mss.

4237. **Prabhakar, M.S.** : 1974 : The politics of a script : Demand for acceptance of Roman script for Bodo language. *EPW*, IX(51), Dec. 21: 2097-102.

4238. **Prasad, Bal Ram; G. Devi Prasada Sastry** *and* **P.T. Abraham**: 1991 : *Mishing Grammar*. Mysore, CIIL (Rev. edition).

4239. **Rabha Hakasam, Upen (Ed)** : 1995 : Seminar on *Rabha Bhasa Sahitya, Atit, Bartaman Aru Bhavisyat*, held on 27 February, organised by Bebak Rabha Kraurang Runchum (Nikhil Rabha Sahitya Sabha), Tenth Annual Conference at Tamreswar Kshetra, Khairabari, Darrang District (As per this Seminar there was no ancient history and no record of Rabha language prior to 1632).

4240. **Rabha, T.K.** : 1974 : Some problems in teaching Assamese as a second language. *Jour. of Lal Bahadur Shastri National Academy of Administration*, 19(1), Spring: 65-7.

4241. **Rajkhowa, Benudhar** : 1913 : *Notes on the Sylhette dialect.* Maulavi Bazar (Sylhet), Pub. by the author.

4242. **Rajkowar, J.B.** : 1971 : Traces of early History of North-Eastern India in Kachari Dimacha and Tipra languages. *Pine*, I (I): 39-45.

4243. **Research Deptt.** : 1994 : *Seminar on Socio-Linguistic aspects of NEI*, organised by Research Deptt., Itanagar, Arunachal Pradesh (*Mimeo.*).

4244. **Robinson, William** : 1849 : Notes on the languages spoken by the various tribes inhabiting the valley of Assam and its mountain confines. *Jour. of Asiatic Society of Bengal*, vol. 18, part-I: 183-237.

4245. **Saha, R.M.** : 1981 : *Bangla bhasar sange tulana prasange Koch-Rabha bhasa (in Bengali).* Bilasipara, Pub. by the author.

4246. **Samaiprabaha** : 1994 : Editorial: Boro Bhasa O Roman Lipi. (*in Beng.*) *Samaiprabaha*, March 10: 4 (1-2).

4247. **Samuel, John** : 1993 : Language and nationality in North-East India. *EPW*, XXVIII (3-4), Jan. 16-23: 91-2 (Assam etc.).

4248. **Sarma, Binod** : 1990 : Dr. Chatterji on Assamese language and literature. *A.T., (Sunday Reading),* Sept. 23: I(1-8).

4249. **Sarma, Mukunda Madhava** : 1978 : *Inscriptions of ancient Assam.* Gau. Univ., 329p.

4250. **Sarma, Nabin Chandra** : 1986 : Study of a few Assamese proverbs. *Folklore*, 27(3), March: 71-7.

4251. **Seminar** : 1985 : UGC Seminar on *The Problems of Development of the Tibeto-Burman languages of N.E. India* was held at Bilasipara College, Dhubri District of Assam on September 23-29, 1985.

4252. **Sentinel** : 1995 : Right sound, wrong letters. Dec. 19: 4 (1-2) (Assamese word *sha, shah, sa* speech sound of *gamosa, sadar, Manalisa, chemonia chora,* etc.).

4253. **Shafer, Robert** : 1964 : Foreign loans in Assamese, *Jour. Univ. of Gau.,* 15(1): 33-4 (Language).

4254. **Sharma and Choudhury** : n.d. : *Asamiya Bhasatatta (in A.).* Guwahati, Bani Prakash.

4255. **Sharma, Harendra Nath** : n.d. : *Asamiya Bachan-Bhangi (in A.).* Guwahati, Bani Prakash.

4256. **Sharma, Nabin Ch.** : 1986 : Study of a few Assamese proverbs. *Folklore,* 27 (4), April : 71-7.

4257. **Shillong Times** : 1984 : Editorial: Bodo as associate language. May 12: 2(1-2).

4258. **Shree Krishan (Ed.)** : 1990 : *Linguistic Traits Across Language Boundaries: A Report on All India Linguistic Traits Survey.* Calcutta, Anthropological Survey of India.

4259. **Singh, K.S.** *and* **S. Manoharan** : 1993 : *People of India, National Series, Vol. IX, Languages and Scripts.* Delhi, Oxford University Press for Anthropological Survey of India, Calcutta.

4260. **Skrefsrud, L.** : 1889 : *A short grammar of the Mech of Boro language.* Assam, Ebenezer Santhal Mission Press.

4261. **Soppitt, C.A.** : 1885 : *A short account of the Kachcha (Empeo) tribe in the North Cachar Hills with an outline grammar, vocabulary and illustrative sentences.* Shillong, Assam Secretariat Press, 47p (*Reprinted* with an Introduction by E.C. Stuart Baker in 1901).

4262. **Sten, Konow** : 1902 : Notes on the languages spoken between the Assam Valley and Tibet. *Jour. of Royal Asiatic Society of Great Britain and Ireland*: 127-37.

4263. **Taid, T.** : 1978 : A note tribal languages as media of instruction. *Souvenir of All India Tribal Conference & National Seminar on Tribal Welfare* (Gau.): 29-31.

4264. **Taid, Tabu** : 1982 : A short note on Mishing phonology *(In) Linguistic Situation in North-East India (Ed)* by Mrinal Miri, Shillong, NEICSSR: 87-95.

4265. **Talukdar, B.N.** : 1982 : Language problems in the North-East Region *(In) Linguistic situation in North-East India (Ed)* by Mrinal Miri. Shillong, NEICSSR: 49-51.

4266. **Talukdar, Jitendra Kr.** : 1976 : Matak Sabdar Utpatti aru tatparjya. *Asam Bani.* Aug. 20 *(in A.).*

4267. ———— : 1981 : Matak shabdar utpatti aru tatparja *(In) Mayamara Satra Samaj: Bhasan aru Pravandha (Ed)* by Sushil Kr. Gogoi. Chabua (Assam), Mayamara Kala Kristi Anusandhan Aru Prachar Samity: 67-86 *(in A.).*

4268. **Talukdar, Kailash Ch.** : 1993 : *The Mishing people and their spoken language: A critical study.* Unpub. Ph.D. Thesis, Gau. Univ.

4269. **Teran, Lenkam** *and* **R.B. Terang** : 1967 : *A grammar in Karbi language.* Gauhati, Pub. by the authors.

4270. **Terang, R.B.** : 1974 : *Karbi Lamtaam (Karbi-Assamese-English Dictionary).* Calcutta.

4271. **Tiwari, Dharmadev** : 1978 : *Bodo Hindi Self Teacher.* Kohima, Nagaland Bhasha Parishad, 74p.

4272. ———— : 1990 : Asamiya aur Bhojpuri ke varna-vinyas *(in Hindi) Pur. Pra. (Lohit Bharati),* Dec. 23: I (1-4).

4273. **Tunga, S.S.** : 1996 : *Bengali and other related dialects of South Assam.* Delhi, Mittal Pubn.

4274. **Tunga, Sudhangsu S.** : 1977 : *Bengali and other dialects of the district of Cachar : A comparative and descriptive study.* Unpub. D.Litt. Thesis, Cal. Univ.

4275. ———— : 1982 : Sociology of language : North-Eastern case *(In) Linguistic Situation in North-East India (Ed)* by Mrinal Miri. Shillong, NEICSSR: 74-9.

4276. ———— : 1994 : *Bengali and other related dialects of Assam.* Delhi, Mittal Pubn., 385p.

4277. **Uwari, D.R.** : 1980 : *Bodo Language through English and Assamese.* Gauhati, Pub. by the author, 108p.

4278. **Walker, G.D.** : 1925 : *A Dictionary of the Mikir language.* Shillong, Assam Govt. Press. 462p.

4279. **Wesari, D.R.** : 1980 : *Bodo language through English and Assamese.* Mysore, Central Institute of Indian Language, 108p.

4280. **Wolfenden, S.N.** : 1929 : *Outlines of Tibeto-Burman Linguistic Morphology with Special Reference to the Prefixes, Infixes and suffixes of Classical Tibetan and the languages of the Kachin, Bodo, Naga, Kuki, Chin and Burma Groups.* London, Royal Asiatic Society, 216p. (Royal Asiatic Society, Prize Publication Fund, vol. 12).

PART-II (E)

FULL BIBLIOGRAPHY OF THE GENERAL SUBJECT

4281. **Allen, B.C.** : 1905 : *Assam District Gazetteers, Vol. III, Goalpara.* Calcutta, City Press, 145p.

4282. ———————— : *Ibid, Vol. V,* Darrang. *Ibid,* 291p.

4283. ———————— : *Ibid, Vol. IV,* Kamrup. *Ibid,* 283p.

4284. ———————— : *Ibid, Vol. VIII,* Lakhimpur. *Ibid,* 287p.

4285. ———— : 1906 : *Ibid, Vol. VII,* Sibsagar. *Ibid,* 323p.

4286. ———————— : *Ibid, Vol. VI,* Cachar. *Ibid,.* 281p.

4287. **Allen, B.C.; E.A. Gait; C.G.H. Allen** *and* **H.F. Howard**: 1979: *Gazetteer of Bengal and North-East India.* Delhi, Mittal Pubn.: 16-133, 439-56, 512-604 (*Reprinted,* 1st Pub. in c. 1908 by Horace Hart Printer to the University, Oxford).

4288. **Balfour, Edward** : 1976 : *Encyclopaedia Asiatica,* vol. I. New Delhi, Cosmo Pubn. (*Reprint* of 1858): 189-91.

4289. **Bordoloi, B.N.** : 1972 : *District Handbook: United Mikir and North Cachar Hills.* Shillong, Tribal Research Institute, 136p.

4290. **Census of India** : 1932 : *Census of India 1931, Assam, Vol. 3, Pt. I.* Shillong, Assam Govt. Press: 209-24 (The depressed and backward classes of Assam).

4291. **Choudhury, N.K.** : 1981 : *Census of India 1971, Series III, Pt. IX, Census Atlas, Assam.* Delhi, Controller of Pubn., 257p.

4292. ———— : 1981 : *Ibid, Series-III, Assam, District Census Handbook: Lakhimpur District.* Gauhati, Directorate of Census Operation Assam, 313p.

4293. ———— : 1982 : *Ibid: Goalpara* District, *Ibid,* 236p.

4294. ———— : 1983 : *Ibid: Cachar District. Ibid,* 324p.

4295. **Datta, D.** : 1969 : *Cachar District Records.* Silchar (Assam), D. Datta, 216p.

4296. **Dev Sharma, Rajanikanta** : 1987 : *Asamiya Biswakosh, Ist part.* Guwahati, Asom Prakashan Parishad *(in A.).*

4297. **Directorate** : 1993 : *Statistical Hand Book: Assam.* Guwahati, Directorate of Economics & Statistics, 518p.

4298. **Dutta, N.C.** : 1991 : *Census of India 1991, Assam, Series-4, Provisional Population Total (Paper-I of 1991).* Guwahati, Census Operation, 27p.

4299. ———————— : Social study projects of Assam Census. *A.T.,* Feb. 9: 4(3-6). [Titaguri (Jonagaon), Khara, Katanipara, Nasatra, Batasipur, Kumargaon, Japisajia].

4300. **Encyclopaedia** : 1977 : *The New Encyclopaedia Britanica (Macropaedia) 15th edition, vol. 2 and (Micropaedia), 15th edition, vol. I.* Chicago (USA), Encyclopaedia Britanica Inc.

4301. **Fisher, T.** : 1840 Memoir of Sylhet Kachar and the adjacent district. *Jour. Asiatic Society of Beng., IX*: 13-6.

4302. **Friel, R.** : 1914 : *Assam District Gazetteers: Cachar.* Assam Secretariat Press, Shillong.

4303. ——————— : *Ibid: Cachar, Supplement to Vol. I.* Shillong, Assam Secretariet Press.

4304. ——————— : *Ibid: Kamrup, Supplement to Vol. IV. Ibid.*

4305. ——————— : *Ibid: Goalpara, Supplement to Vol. III. Ibid.*

4306. ———— : 1915 : *Ibid: Darrang, Supplement to Vol. V. Ibid.*

4307. ——————— : *Ibid: Nowgong, Supplement to Vol. VI. Ibid.*

4308. ——————— : *Ibid: Sibsagar, Supplement to Vol. VII. Ibid.*

4309. ——————— : *Ibid: Sylhet, Supplement to Vol. II. Ibid.*

4310. ———— : 1916 : *Ibid: Lakhimpur, Supplement to Vol. VIII. Ibid.*

4311. **Gait, E.A.** : 1892 : *Census of India 1891 Vol. I: Assam—Census Report.* Shillong, Assam Secretariat Printing Office : 212-17, 224-27.

4312. ———— : 1926 : *History of Assam.* Calcutta, Thacker & Spink, 366p. (*Reprinted* in 1963 from Calcutta by Thacker Spink which revised and enlarged by B.K. Barua and H.V. S. Murthy (3rd *Revised* edition), 449p and again *Reprinted* in 1981 from Gauhati by LBS Pubn.).

4313. **Gazetteer** : 1908 : *Provincial Gazetteers of India: Eastern Bengal and Assam.* Oxford, Horace Hart Printer to the University: 439-456, 513-604.

4314. ———— : 1996 : *The Encyclopaedic District Gazetteers of India* (Tribes, History, Geography etc.) Gyan Publishing House, New Delhi.

4315. **Hastings, James (Ed)** : 1908 : *Encyclopaedia of Religion and Ethics,* Vol. I Edinburg, T & T Clark (*Reprinted* in 1921 from London), in 1973 from New York), 530p.

4316. **Holland, David T.** : 1988 : *Encyclopaedia Americana, Vol. I.* Danburg, Grolier incorporated (8th edition).

4317. **Hunter, W.W.** : 1879 : *A Statistical Account of Assam, Vol. I and II.* London, Trubner & Co. (*Reprint* of *Imperial Gazetteer* Vol.

IV and *Reprinted* by Vol. VI by B.R. Pubg. Corn., Delhi in 1975), 490p. (Goalpara dist., Cachar, Mikirs, etc).

4318. **Hunter, W.W.** : 1974 : *A Statistical Account of Bengal, Vol. X: Districts of Darjiling and Jalpaiguri, the state Kuch Behar (Reprinted).* Delhi, D.K. Pubg. House, 459p.

4319. ―――――― : 1975 : *A Statistical Account of Assam, Vol. I & II.* Delhi, B.R. Pubg. Corn. (*Reprint* of 1879).

4320. **Hutton, J.H.** : 1986 : *Census of India 1931 with complete Survey of Tribal Life and Systems, vol. I-III (with an Introduction by K.S. Singh).* New Delhi, Gyan Pubg. House, 1516p (*Reprinted*).

4321. **Mackenzie, Alexander** : 1989 : *The North-East Frontier of India (Introduction by B.K. Roy Burman).* Delhi, Mittal Pubn.: 1-8, 73-6 (*Reprinted* in 1979, 1981, 1989; 1st pub. in 1884 *History of the Relations of Government with the Hill Tribes of the North-East Frontier of Bengal*) [Sadiya, Moamariahs of Muttuck].

4322. **Martin, M.** : 1976 : *The History, Antiquities, Topography and Statistics of Eastern India, Vol. V: Rangpur and Assam.* Delhi, Cosmo Pubn. (1st Indian *Reprint*): 351-714.

4323. **Mathew, K.M. (Ed)** : 1994 : *Manorama Year Book 1994.* Kerala, Manorama Pub. House.

4324. **M'Cosh, J.** : 1837 : *Topography of Assam.* Calcutta, Bengal Military Orphan Press (G.H. Huttmann). *Reprinted* in 1975 by Sanskaran Prakashak, 166p.

4325. **Mills, A.J. Moffatt** : 1980 : *Report on Assam.* Delhi, Gian Pubn. (*Reprint* of 1853): 2, 3, 64, 50, 51, 52.

4326. **Mulla, M.K.U.** : 1966 : *The New Province of Bengal and Assam* 1905-11. Ph.D. Thesis, Univ. of London (1965-66).

4327. **Newall, D.J.F.** : 1984 : *The Highlands of India, Vol. I.* New Delhi, Logos Press (Section IX, Assam etc.: 116-29).

4328. **North Eastern Council** : 1992 : *Basic Statistics of North-Eastern Region 1992.* Shillong, North Eastern Council Secretariat, 279p.

4329. **Pakyntein, E.H.** : 1964 : *Census of India 1961, Assam, District Census Hand Book: Kamrup.* Govt. of Assam, 544p.

4330. ―――――――― : *Ibid: Darrang.* Ibid, 477p.

4331. ―――――――― : *Ibid: Lakhimpur.* Ibid, 554p.

4332. ―――――――― : *Ibid: Cachar.* Ibid, 528p.

4333. ―――――― : 1965 : *Ibid: Nowgong.* Ibid.

4334. ―――――――― : *Ibid: United Mikir & North Cachar Hills.* Ibid, 376p.

4335. **Pakyntein, E.H.** : 1965 : *Ibid: Goalpara.* Ibid, 574p.

4336. ——————— : *Ibid: Sibsagar.* Ibid.

4337. ——————— : *Census of India 1961, Vol. III, Assam, Pt. VI, Village Survey Monographs No. 16: A Monograph on Phonjangre (Baithalangso P.S.; United Mikir & North Cachar Hills District).* Delhi, Manager of Pubn., 63p.

4338. ——————— : *Ibid No. 1: Titaguri (Jonagaon, Bodo Kachari village, Assam), Kokrajhar P.S., Goalpara district. Delhi,* Ibid, 75p.

4339. ——————— : *Ibid No. 2: Fulertal (Cachar).* Ibid.

4340. ——————— : 1967 : *Ibid No. 3: Gunjong (North Cachar).* Ibid.

4341. **Pataskar Commission** : 1965-66 : *Report of the Commission on the Hill Areas of Assam.* New Delhi, Ministry of Home Affairs, GOI.

4342. **Publication Division** : 1969 : *State of Our Union : Assam.* New Delhi, Pubn. Division.

4343. **Saikia, A.K.** : 1971 : *Census of India 1971: A Portrait of Population, Assam.* Delhi, Director of Census Operation, 143p.

4344. **Stevens, E.** : 1836 : A description of Assam: Extent and boundaries of its three principal divisions with notices of the States and tribes, bordering on the north and south. *Chinese Repository,* Vol. V; 49-55, 97-104.

4345. **Vaghaiwalla, R.B.** : 1952 : *Ibid: Nowgong.* Ibid.

4346. ——————— : *Ibid: United Mikir and North Cachar Hills.* Ibid.

4347. ——————— : 1953 : *Census of India 1951, Assam, District Census Handbook : Sibsagar.* Shillong, Assam Govt. Press, 381p.

4348. ——————— : *Ibid: Darrang.* Ibid.

4349. ——————— : *Ibid: Goalpara.* Ibid, 478p.

4350. ——————— : *Ibid: Kamrup.* Ibid, 480p.

4351. ——————— : *Ibid: Lakhimpur.* Ibid, 391p.

4352. ——————— : *Ibid: Cachar.* Ibid, 348p.

4353. ——————— : *Census of India (Assam, Manipur, Tripura) 1951, Pt. I-A-Report, Vol. XII.* Shillong, Assam Govt. Press, 431p.

4354. ——————— : *Ibid, Pt. I-B.* Ibid, 225p.

4355. ——————— : *Ibid, Pt. II-A.* Ibid, 189p.

4356. **Vaghaiwalla, R.B.** : 1953 : *Ibid, Pt. II-B.* Ibid, 306p.

4357. ———— : 1954 : *Census of India 1951, paper-I, Language.* New Delhi, Govt of India Press.

4358. **Vansittart, H. (Tr)** : 1792 : A Description of Assam by Md. Cazim (translated from the Persian). *Asiatic Researches,* II, XI.

PART-III
(APPENDICES)

APPENDIX-A

GLOSSARY OF WORDS AND SHORT NOTES

Acculturation = Cultural process of human society which is in course of time modified and changed.

Acharya = Teacher/A spiritual guide.

Adhikari = Religious head of *Vaisnava Satra* or monastery.

Agarwal = Trading caste of the Marwari. Many of them are Jains by religion. It is said that, they are the descendants from a *Nag.* (snake).

Ahom = Shan tribe. They were *Animists* and followed *Taoism*. Afterwards, they had converted to *Hinduism*.

Aksaya-banti = An earthen lamp kept burning. It is generally seen in *Satras* Sri Sri Madhavdev first lighted *aksaya-banti* at Barpeta *Satra* and which still exists.

Animism = A religious belief in spiritual beings or souls *(anima)* on objects of the nature.

Ankiya-Nut = A type of drama initiated by Srimanta Sankardev.

Anuloma = The status of the groom is socially higher in caste group, than that of the bride, is known as *anuloma* which is seen in hypergamous marriages of a low caste woman marrying high caste man.

Arora = A trading caste of Punjab.

Athpariya = An officer who keeps vigil at *Satra* in the eight stages of a day and night.

Avunculate = Social relationship in between mother's brother and sister's children.

Ayyar/Aiyar = An honorific title of Tamil Brahmin.

Baidya/Vaidya = Physician caste of Bengal. They claim to be descended from Aswini Kumar, the physician of heaven.

Bailung = An Ahom priest mainly engaged in astrological calculations.

Bania = They are called *Mahajan* or *Vaish*. It is a term for Marwari trading castes of North-India. *Agarwal, Maheshwari* and *Khandelwal* are all *Bania*.

Barbarua = Chief Secretary to the Ahom king. He commanded 14,000 *Paiks*. He was one of the five members of the Council Ministers of Ahom Administration.

Bargit = Devotional songs in classical tunes specially composed by Srimanta Sankardev and Madhavdev.

Bargohain = One of the three cabinet ministers of Ahom administration. He administered the tract from the south of the Dikhow river to Kaliabar. He commanded 80,000 *Paiks*.

Barmedhi = An officer who looked after the religious affairs of one or more villages under the supervision of the *Rajmedhis*.

Barpatra Gohain = One of the three cabinet ministers of Ahom kingdom.

Barphukan = A viceroy of lower or western Assam of Ahom administration.

Barsatola = Head of the Satolas or officers, appointed by the *Adhikaris* of some *Satras* for collecting a tenth part of the production of land from their disciples.

Barsenapati = Commander-in-Chief; the title of the ruler of the *Matak* administration.

Barua = An officer of *Khel* (a social unit of a clan).

Barui = *Pan* (betel-leaf) grower's caste of Bengal.

Bauri = Paddy field labourer caste of Bengal and Bihar.

Bayan = Officer-in-Charge of instrumental music.

Bhagavati = An officer who is engaged in reading and explaining the **Bhagavata** (sacred books).

Bhakat = A devotee of the *Satra*.

Bhandari/ Bharali Barua = Storekeeper of Ahom administration.

Bhangi = Sweeper and scavenger caste.

Bhaona = A dramatic performance of *Vaisnavite* religion.

Bharali = Provision-keeper of a *Satra*.

Bhitarual Phukan = Commander-in-Charge of royal palace and its boundary.

Bhuiya = A Kolarian tribe of Chotanagpur and Bengal.

Bihu = National festival of the Assamese.

Bil = A small lake/pond.

Bilateral relation = Kinship relation equally with the line of father and mother.

Bora = Junior most officer of Ahom kingdom who commanded 20 *Paiks.*

Brachycephalic = Anthropometric expression of broad head form with a cephalic-index varies from 80 to 85 cm.

Brahmin = The general name for all high status, priestly class member.

Brittiyal Baniya = An exterior caste of Assam.

Buragohain = A chief of the three ministers of the Ahom cabinet. He governed the track from the north of the Dikhow river to Sadiya and commanded 80,000 *Paiks.* He was senior most member of Ahom kingdom.

Buranji = Chronicle.

Caste = It is a closed social division which is characterised by endogamy, a specific title, a traditional occupation and a hierarchical position determined by respective ritual status.

Chadar = A single cloth wrap round the body.

Chamaeprosopy = A broad face.

Charua Muslim = Muslim of river island or bank.

Chamua = An Ahom subject of high status than the *Paiks.*

Changmai = A cook of Ahom *Khel.*

Charit-Puthi = A biographical book of Vaisnava saints.

Chekani = A bamboo stick.

Cheleng = A thin cloth wrapped round the body or shoulders.

Choladhara Phukan = Royal chamberlain.

Clan = It is an exogamous group. Members of a group of families having a common ancestor or ancestress.

Cross-Cousin Marriage = It is a marriage between the children of brothers and sisters. It is of two types : one is Mother's Brother's Daughter (MBD) and the other is Father's Sister's Daughter (FSD).

Culture = It is a learned behavioural pattern of human beings.

Cymotrichy = Wavy hair.

Dambaru = Small drum for music.

Damodariya = Followers of *Damodardev* who established the *Brahmana-Samhati.*

Dangaria = A title applied to the three cabinet ministers of the Ahom kingdom : the *Buragohain, Bargohain* and *Barpatra Gohain.* Now, this word is applied for a respected middle aged person.

Dao = A knife of a different shape.

Deka Barbarua = The heir-presumptive to the office of the *Barbarua.*

Dekadhikar/Deka Adhikar = Vice-Adhikar of *Vaisnava Satra* or monastery.

Deka Phukan = A Commander of 6,000 youths (Deka). There were two *Deka Phukans* : one at Rangpur and another at Gauhati (Guwahati).

Deodhai = An Ahom priest who worships deities of Ahom pantheon in orthodox form.

Deori/Deori Chutiya = A priest; a priestly caste of the *Chutiyas.*

Dhekial Phukan = An officer commanded 6,000 **Paiks.**

Dhuti/Dhoti = Man's lower garment.

Dihingia Phukan = A military officer of Dihing. There were two of them : one at Rangpur and another at Gauhati. They are also called *Deka Phukan.* Each of them commanded 6,000 men.

Dolichocephalic = Anthropometric expression of long or narrow headform with a cephalic index varies from 70 to 75 cm.

Dolmen = It is a stone structure where three or more vertical slabs or rocks covered horizontally with a flat slab of stone.

Durbar = Conference.

Endogamy = It is a marriage custom where a marriage is performed with a person within his own caste, clan and village.

Epicanthic fold = The corner of the opening portion of the eye is known as *canthus.* This *canthus* is of two varieties : inner and outer. Sometimes it is seen among certain people that a fold of skin covers the inner portion of the *canthus.* This fold is called the *epicanthic fold.* It is also called *Mongolian fold* as it is seen mostly among the *Mongols.*

Ethnos = A group of people, linked by both nationality and race.

Euryprosopy = A broad face.

Exogamy = It is a marriage custom where a marriage is performed with a person who belongs to outside his own caste group, clan and village.

Family = The household members of bilateral kinship group which is characterised by conjugal, parcutal, filial and sibling relationship.

Ga-dhan = Bride price.

Gam = In the hills, each clan of Mishing have a chief who is known as *Gam.* The *Gam* is generally the most powerful man of his locality. The headman of each village of Mishing area is also called *gam.* This gamship now seems to lost.

Gamocha = Towel.

Gaon-bura = Village headman.

Gayan-bayan = Officer in Charge of music and singing performances on different occasions in front of the public.

Genna = It means forbidden or prohibited, puja, prayer ceremony.

Ghat = Bank of river.

Gosain = Spiritual guide. Head of *Satra.* In old days, only Brahmin Satradhikars were allowed to be *Gosains* but now, all *Satradhikaries* either Brahmin or non-Brahmins are called *Gosain.*

Gotra = An exogamous group, descended from a common ancestor, inside the endogamous caste.

Guru = Spiritual teacher.

Guru-griha = House of a *Guru.*

Hari = A scavenger caste of eastern India.

Hatimur = A unit of retainers of thousand men alloted to the *Buragohain, Bargohain* and *Barpatra Gohain.*

Hira = A sub-caste of *Chandal.*

Hundi = An indigenous bill of exchange.

Hypergamy = Marriage of a low caste woman with a high caste man.

Hypogamy = Marriage of a high caste woman with a low caste man.

Jaliya Kaibarta = A fishing caste.

Jangphai = Amber.

Japi = Bamboo made hat for the Assamese field cultivators etc.

Jhum cultivation = This is a kind of natural cultivation practised by the hill tribes in the hilly areas. The jungle in the hills is cleared by the people and burnt. The burnt ashes serve as the only manure. The seeds are sown, broadcast there by the people. In this field, they cultivate for a year or two or so and thereafter they leave that field for a considerable period to gather fertility in soil after a new growth of jungle on them. This is also known as '*shifting cultivation*'.

Jubaraj = Prince.

Jugi = A caste of rearer of silkworms and weavers of silk in Assam.

Kachari = A Hinduised tribe of Assam.

Kaibarta = Fishing caste. They are also known as *Dom* and *Nadial.* But they now consider this appellation as derogatory. As per *Purana,* a

Kaibarta was born of a *Kshatriya* father and a *Vaishya* mother. Tezpur rock inscription of Harjar Varman (c.820-836 AD) focused light on *Kaibarta*. Thus, it seems that, they are one of the early inhabitants of Assam.

Kalita = Cultivating caste.

Karbi Plateau = Karbi tableland lies on the south bank of Brahmaputra and east of Meghalaya plateau and is detached from Meghalaya plateau by the Kopili Gorge and Diyung, Lumding, Lankajan, etc. rivers. On the south-eastern side, it is separated from Naga hills by Dhansiri river and its other streams. This range's highest elevations are at Chengheheson peak (1,359 metres) and Dambukso (1,361 metres) in the central part. This plateau has Dhansiri, Kalang and Kopili river and other tributaries.

Kewat = Fishing and cultivating caste.

Khania = Double cloth.

Khanikar = Decorator or painter. Also, maker of images.

Khataniar = Representative of an *Adhikar* or *Mahanta*.

Khel = A social unit or division of a clan in a part of a village.

Kirtana = Act of chanting prayers to God.

Kirtan-ghar = Prayer-hall to pray God.

Lalbegi = Scavenging caste, partly Hindu and partly Muslim.

Lao-pani = Rice-beer.

Leiotrichy = A straight hair. It is found among the *Mongoloid* people.

Leptoprosopy = A narrow face.

Leucoderms = White skin coloured people.

Levirate = Marriage of a widow with her deceased-husband's brother. It is of two types : one is *Senior Levirate* and another one is *Junior Levirate*. Marriage of a woman with her deceased-husband's younger brother is called *junior levirate* and with the elder brother is called *senior levirate*.

Lineage = It is an exogamous unilateral kinship group which traces descent from known common ancestor.

Mahanta = Religious head of *Satra*. He is either *Brahmin* or *non-Brahmin*. Generally, they are *Sudra* caste group.

Mahapurusha = Srimanta Sankardev is called as *Mahapurusha*; for this, his religion is also called *Mahapurushiya Dharma*.

Mahishya = A Bengali caste, sprung from a *Brahmin* father and a *Kshatriya* mother or *Kshatriya* father and a *Vaishya* mother and ranking with *Kayastha*.

Mali = A caste of domestic and market gardeners.

Manikut = Shrine where the sacred scriptures are installed.

Manusanghita = It suggested a code of conduct, law and creeds of about third century BC.

Mauza = A fiscal unit of land.

Medhi/Raj Medhi = An appointed person by the *Satra* to look after the religious affairs of the disciples in a village.

Megalith = It is a large parallel stone structure in the memory of a death or an important event.

Meghalaya Plateau = The tableland with steep edges faces the Sylhet plain of Bangladesh to the south and the Brahmaputra valley to the north. The plateau rises slowly towards north till reached the central part where *Tura-Kylas Range* and *Shillong Range*. Tura Kylas range's highest elevations are at *Nokrek* (1,412 metres) in Garo Hills and Shillong Peak (1,961 metres) in Khasi Hills. The western and eastern part of the tableland are Garo and Jaintia Hills merge with Brahmaputra plain through hills and hillocks.

Mekhela = Lower garment of the Assamese women.

Melanoderms = Black skin coloured people.

Menhir = This is a stone structure of an elongated and vertical slab of stone raised as a monument.

Mesocephalic = Anthropometric expression of medium headform with a cephalic index varies from 75 to 80 cm.

Moiety = It means one of the two equal parts of a society which has two unilineal sibs. When a tribe is socially divided into only two groups for its social activities, each group is called a moiety. Moieties regulate marriages but, sometimes they are hostile to one another. This hostility is connected with the belief in the difference of the physical and mental characters and in the claim of the superiority of these.

Monogamy = Marriage with an individual which is restricted to one spouse (matrimony) only.

Morung = It is a dormitory for the young unmarried boys. There is a separate dormitory for young unmarried girls. The *morung* act as a recreation club. The trophies were displayed in the past in the morungs. Many of them learnt to sing, weave, cane and bamboo work and discipline from *morungs.*

Na-Assamiya = New Assamese.

Pamua Muslim = The former Muslim.

Nadiyal = Boatman and fishermen's caste.

Nama-prasanga = Devotional prayers, recitations and religious discussions.

Namasudra = Caste of cultivator or boatmen.

Namghar = A prayer hall.

Naobaicha-Phukan = Officer-in-Charge of the navy, commanded 6,000 *Paiks.*

Naosalia-Phukan = Officer-in-Charge of the royal dockyard, commanded 7,000 men.

Nascent Family = A family with issueless couple, having the potentiality to bear children in future.

Neolocal = In this type after marriage, the newly married couple, live separately, rather than staying in either of the parents house. They prefer to stay in a new house of their own.

Nirmali = A flower with blessings of a deity.

Nuclear Family = A family with a husband, his wife and their unmarried offsprings.

Oja Pali = Choric dance, illustrating scriptural stories.

O.B.C. = Other backward classes. It is classified by the government to give preference in various ways. Bishnupriya Manipuries are now O.B.C. in Assam(March 1996).

Pachani = Informant of orders of *Satras*. He also collects *tithes* and contributions from the disciples.

Pan = Betel leaf/plant.

Panchayat = A council to govern a caste, a market, or a locality.

Pargana = A revenue division, introduced by the **Mughals** and continued by the *Ahoms* (after occupied Kamrup) with little modification. An officer was allotted for each Pargàna whom they called Choudhury in Ahom administration.

Patni = Caste of fishermen and basket-makers.

Patramantris = A council of five ministers of *Ahom* kingdom with *Buragohain*, *Bargohain*, *Barpatra gohain*, *Barbarua* and *Barphukan*.

Patriliny = It means descent through the father's line only.

Patrilocal = It is a rule of post-marital residence in the locality of the father-in-law.

Patronymy = A custom of giving the children the surname of their father's lineal group.

Patta = A lease deed about land.

Phratry = Phratry is a social group based on kinship, which consists of two or more related clans between which exists a special bond of unity as against clans joint in other phratries within the tribe. It is a brotherhood of each tribe who are individualised by a name, separate dialect, supreme government and possession of a territory as their own.

Pike = Soldier of Ahom kingdom.

Polyandry = It is a form of marriage with a marital union of a woman with two or more men. It is of two types : one is *fraternal* or *adelphic* and *non-fraternal*. In *fraternal* polyandry the husbands are brothers of the actual married husband. All the brothers have their sex-right over a woman whom a brother brought home as a bride. In *non-fraternal* polyandry the husbands are not brothers of the actual married husband.

Polygamy = It is a form of marriage with a marital union of an individual with a number of spouses (matrimonies).

Polygyny = It is a form of marriage with a marital union of a man with two or more women. It is of two types : *Sororal* and *non-sororal* polygyny. In sororal polygyny the wives are sisters of the actual married wife. In non-sororal polygyny the wives are not sisters of the actual married wife.

Polytheism = It is a religious belief which prescribes the worship of multiple Gods.

Poona Pact = It is an agreement in between the caste Hindu and Congress Organisation. It signed on 24th September, 1932 at *Pune* and popularly known as *Poona Pact.* According to this pact, the untouchable lower class people got reservations in all elected bodies and in services. Before this, on 17th August, 1932, there was a communal announcement that a separate electorate for the Scheduled Castes. At this, Hindu leaders of India were displeased. For that, it was modified by the *Poona Pact.*

Pratiloma = The status of the bride is higher than that of the groom, is known as *pratiloma* which is found in hypogamous marriages against the grain (literaly : 'against the heir').

Puja = Worship of god.

Rabha = A tribe of *Garo* and *Kachari* affinities.

Raij-mel = A conference of people.

Rajbansi = A tribe (caste) formed from the *Koch* (tribe).

Rajkhowa = Governor of specific areas having power over men under their command.

Rajmantri = A premier minister.

Rajmedhi = An officer appointed to look after the religious affairs of villages. He collects *guru-kar* (spiritual teacher-tax, tithe) and supervises his juniors like *Barmedhi, Satola, Pachani* etc.

Rarhi = Brahmin caste of Bengal.

Riha = Breast-cloth of the Assamese women.

Rupit Land = Cultivable land.

Sadiakhowa Gohain = A frontier governor of Sadiya.

Saha = Trading caste of Bengal.

Sanatani = The orthodox Hindu party, opposed to the *Arya Samaj.*

Sandhya-Gayatri = A sacred verse of *Rig Veda.*

Santal = A Kolarian tribe of Chota Nagpur, Bihar and Bengal.

Saran = Initiation

Satola/Sajtola = An officer appointed by the religious head of a Vaisnava *Satra* to collect *guru-kar* (tithe).

Satra = **Vaisnavite** monastery.

Satradhikar/Satradhikari = Religious head of a Satra.

Saumar = A division of ancient Assam which had present districts of Dibrugarh, Lakhimpur and Sibsagar.

Scheduled Caste/Tribe = Castes/Tribes classified by government as requiring economic help and therefore given preference in various ways.

Shraddha = Hindu ceremony which is performed in honour and benefit of the soul of a dead-one by the family members of the deceased, at fixed intervals.

Sib = A common unilateral ancestry is called a *Sib*. A common male ancestry is called *gens* and a common female ancestry is called *clan.*

Siblings = It is a relationship between the offspring of one and the parent.

Sororate = A marital alliance with sisters of a married woman. Sisters of a married woman are regarded as wives of a man whom their sister has actually married. It is a marriage with wife's sisters.

Stature = Physical height of human beings.

Subarna Banik = Trading caste of Bengal.

Sutradhar = Carpenter caste of Bengal.

Sutradhara = Prompter of drama. He is to organise dances and dramas and producer of *Ankiya Nut*.

Swargadeo = God of heaven. This was the title of the *Ahom* kings.

Taboo = It defines a forbidden act.

Tamuli-Phukan = Officer-in-Charge of the royal garden.

Terrace cultivation = It is practised on hill-slopes. Gradual low embankments of stones or earth are built to make the fields in different patches on the gradual slopes. The terraces thus formed and are irrigated by artificially constructed channels.

Than = Sacred place.

Thia-Mekhela = Petticoat type garment used by the Assamese women.

Totem = It is a figure of an object of a kinship unit who have a special mystical relationship with it and sometimes the name of that group is expressed in terms of their totem object. The totem may be animal, plant, object or heavenly body.

Tribe = It is a group of families bearing a common name, speaking a common dialect, occupying or professing to occupy a common territory and observing the rule of endogamy.

Ulotrichy = Woolly hair.

Vamsawali = Geneological table.

Vamsha = Race/family.

Varna = A division of Hindu castes in four groups—*Brahmins* (Priest), *Kshatriyas* (Warriors), *Vaishyas* (traders) and *Sudras* (servants). Now there are many subcastes and this *varna* classification is not always relevant.

Wet cultivation = In this type, cultivation is made in a wet cultivated agricultural field situated at the foot of the valley where it has plenty of water and is divided into small fields. Its soil is made thick as a paste by driving cattle therein. Water is let in by artificial channels to submerge the tiny fields and to drain out the water as required.

Xanthoderms = Yellow coloured skin.

Yati = A Jain holy man.

Zu = Rice-beer.

APPENDIX—B

Scheduled Castes and Scheduled Tribes of Assam According to Order (Amendment) Act, 1976 (No. 108 of 1976, dated the 18th September, 1976)

Scheduled Castes

Bansphor

Bhuimali, Mali

Brittial Bania, Bania

Dhupi, Dhobi

Dugla, Dholi

Hira

Jalkeot

Jhalo, Malo, Jhalo-Malo

Kaibartta, Jaliya

Lalbegi

Mahara

Mehtar, Bhangi

Muchi, Rishi

Namasudra

Patni

Sutradhar

Scheduled Tribes

I. In the autonomous districts :

1. Chakma
2. Dimasa, Kachari
3. Garo
4. Hajong
5. Hmar
6. Khasi, Jaintia, Synteng, Pnar, War, Bhei, Lyngam
7. Any Kuki Tribes including :

i. Biate, Biete

ii. Changsan

iii. Chongloi

iv. Doungel

v. Gamalhou

vi. Gangte

vii. Hanneng

viii. Haokip, Haupit

ix. Haolai
x. Hengna
xi. Hongsungh
xii. Hrangkhwal, Rangkhol
xiii. Jongbe
xiv. Khawchung
xv. Khawathlang, Khothalong
xvi. Khelma
xvii. Kholhou
xviii. Kipgen
xix. Kuki
xx. Lengthang
xxi. Lhangum
xxii. Lhoujem
xxiii. Lhouvum
xxiv. Lupheng
xxv. Mangjel
xxvi. Misao
xxvii. Riang
xxviii. Sairhem
xxix. Selnam
xxx. Singson
xxxi. Sitlhou
xxxii. Sukte
xxxiii. Thado
xxxiv. Thangngen
xxxv. Uibuh
xxxvi. Vaiphei

8. Lakher
9. Man (Tai speaking)
10. Any Mizo (Lushai) tribes
11. Mikir
12. Any Naga tribes
13. Pawi
14. Synteng.

II. In the State of Asssam excluding the autonomous districts :

1. Barmans in Cachar
2. Boro, Borokachari
3. Deori
4. Hojai
5. Kachari, Sonwal
6. Lalung
7. Mech
8. Miri
9. Rabha

Source : Census of India 1981 : List of Scheduled Castes and Scheduled Tribes—P. Padmanabha (1981 : 5-7).

1. *All the earlier autonomous districts became different States of North-East India. The Centre has included the *Koch-Rajbangshis* in the list of Scheduled Tribes of Assam, excluding those in the autonomous districts. An extra ordinary gazette notification was issued to this effect by the Union Welfare Ministry on January 28, 1996. Process is going on to give soon the status of Scheduled Tribe to *Tea Garden Labourer, Ex-Tea Garden Labour, Tai-Ahom, Motok, Maran, Chutiya, Hajong,* etc. people of Assam.

APPENDIX—C

Tea Garden Labourers in Assam

1. Arya
2. Asur
3. Bhumij
4. Baiga
5. Baijars
6. Basor
7. Balder
8. Bharaik
9. Bhil
10. Bhokta
11. Birhor
12. Bowri
13. Chamar
14. Charo
15. Chik Barik
16. Dandari
17. Dhanwar
18. Dusad
19. Gor
20. Gonda
21. Ghansi
22. Ghatowar/Ghatour
23. Gorai
24. Kandhal
25. Kalahandi/Kalihandi
26. Karmali
27. Kashan
28. Kawar
29. Kharia
30. Kharwar
31. Khodal
32. Khond
33. Khonyor
34. Kohar
35. Kol
36. Kondpan
37. Korwa
38. Kotwal
39. Koya
40. Koiri
41. Kurmi
42. Lahar/Lahara
43. Mahara
44. Munda
45. Mura
46. Mahli/Mohli

47. Majwar
48. Malpaharia
49. Manki
50. Mirdhar
51. Mahato
52. Nonia/Nunia
53. Nagasia
54. Nagbansi
55. Oraon
56. Panika
57. Pana
58. Parja
59. Rajwar
60. Santhal
61. Saora, Savara
62. Turi
63. Tantripal, Tanti, Tantri.
64. Tause.

APPENDIX—D

SCHEDULED CASTES OF BRAHMAPUTRA AND BARAK VALLEY

In Assam the following castes were entered in the list of Scheduled Castes adopted on the basis of the *Poona agreement* and the constitution orders 1950 (a) Part (ii) Assam.

Assam Valley	*Surma Valley*
1. Namasudra	1. Bhuimali or Mali
2. Hira	2. Dhubi
3. Kaiborta	3. Dholi
4. Bania	4. Jhalo or Malo
5. Mehtor	5. Mahara
6. Lalbegi	6. Sutradhar
7. Bansphor	7. Muchi
	8. Patni
	9. Namasudra
	10. Jalia (Jal Keot)
	11. Lalbegi
	12. Mehtor
	13. Bansphor

Source : *A Glimpse of the Scheduled Castes and their Socio-Economic Development in Assam by Bhakta Das : 26.*

APPENDIX—E

CHRONOLOGY OF AHOM KINGS

Name of Kings	*Reign*	
	Commenced	*Ended*
Sukapha	1228	1268
Suteupha	1268	1281
Subinpha	1281	1293
Sukhangpha	1293	1332
Sukhrangpha	1332	1364
Sutupha	1364	1376
interregnum	1376	1380
Tyackhamti	1380	1389
interregnum	1389	1397
Sudangpha	1397	1407
Sujangpha	1407	1422
Suphakpha	1422	1439
Susenpha	1439	1488
Suhenpha	1488	1493
Supimpha	1493	1497
Suhungmung or the Dihingia Raja	1497	1539
Suklenmung or Garhgaya Raja	1539	1552
Sukhampha or Khora Raja	1552	1603
Susengpha or Burha Raja or Pratap Singh	1603	1641
Surampha or Bhaga Raja	1641	1644
Sutyinpha or Nariya Raja	1644	1648

Sutyinpha or Jayadhvaj Singh	1648	1663
Supungmung or Chakradhvaj Singh	1663	1669
Sunyatpha or Udayaditya Singh	1669	1673
Suklampha or Ramdhvai	1673	1675
Suhung 1675	1675	
Gobar	1675	1675
Sujinpha	1675	1677
Sudaipha	1677	1679
Sulikpha or Lora Raja	1679	1681
Supatpha or Gadadhar Singh	1681	1691
Sukhrungpha or Rudra Singh	1696	1714
Sutanpha or Sib Singh	1714	1744
Sunenpha or Pamata Singh	1744	1751
Surampha or Rajesvar Singh	1751	1769
Sunyeopha or Lakshmi Singh	1769	1780
Suhitpangpha or Ganrinath Singh	1780	1794
Suklingpha or Kamalesvar Singh	1795	1810
Sudinpha or Chandrakant Singh	1810	1818
Purandar Singh	1818	1819
Jogesvar Singh	1819	—
Burmese Rule	1819	1824
British Conquest	1824	—
Purandar Singh Rule in Upper Assam	1832	1838

Source : Edward Gait's *History of Assam* (1981 reprint) : 364.

THE KOCH DYNASTY

Name of the Kings	*Reign*	
	Commenced	*Ended*
Bishwa Singha	1515	1540
Nara-Narayan	1540	1587

Lakshmi Narain	1587	1627
Bir-Narain	1627	1632
Pran Narain	1632	1665
Moda Narain	1665	1678
Basudev Narain	1678	1682
Mahindra Narain	1682	1693
Rupa Narain	1704	1714
Upendra Narain	1714	1763
Debendra Narain	1763	1765
Dhairyya Narain	1765	1770
Rajendra Narain	1770	1772

THE EASTERN KOCH DYNASTY

Raghu Deva	1580	1603
Parikshit Narain	1603	1616
Chandra Narain alias Bijit Narain (Bijni)	1616	1640
Jay Narain	1640	1662
Mahendra Narain (Darrang)	—	—

THE MUHAMMEDAN RULERS OF KAMRUP

Makram Khan	1612	1614
Mir Sufi	1614	1616
Sheik Kamal	1616	1632
Abdus Sala	1632	1638
Nurullah	1638	1656
Mir Lutfullah	1656	1658

Source : *R.M. Nath's Background of Assamese Culture (1948)* : 2-3.

APPENDIX—F

LIST OF PERIODICALS AND NEWSPAPERS USED AS SOURCE MATERIALS

1. *Academic Review* (Guwahati).
2. *Acta Anthropogenetica* (Delhi).
3. *Acta Anthropogenetis* (Basel).
4. *Acta Criminologiae of Medicine Legalis Japonica* (Tokyo).
5. *Acta Ethnographica.*
6. *Acta Geneticae Med. et Gemmel* (Rome).
7. *Acta Genet. Stat. Med.* (Basel).
8. *Actes du ze Congress International des science Anthropologiques et Ethnologiques* (Copenhagen).
9. *Adivasi* (Orissa).
10. *Agradut (in A.,* Guwahati, Daily).
11. *Ajir Asom (in A.,* Guwahati, Daily).
12. *Ajkal (in B.,* Calcutta, Daily).
13. *Akashvani* (Dibrugarh, Calcutta, Guwahati).
14. *A.E.S.*
15. *All India Congress Committee Economic Review.*
16. *Amar Pratinidhi (in A.,* Guwahati).
17. *American Anthropologist* (Washington).
18. *Amrita Bazar Patrika* (Calcutta, Daily).
19. *Ancient Ceylon* (Colombo).
20. *American Jr. of Phy. Anth.* (Philadelphia).
21. *Annals of Human Biology* (London).
22. *Anthropos* (W. Germany).
23. *Anthropologie* (Prague).

24. *Anthropologischer Anzeiger* (Stuttgart).

25. *(The) Anthropologist* (Delhi).

26. *Antiquity.*

27. *Archive fur Religious Wissenschaft.*

28. *Achives of Disease in Childhood* (Rangoon).

29. *Art in Industry.*

30. *Arunachal News* (Itanagar).

31. *Arunodoi* (Calcutta, Gauhati).

32. *Asie Francaise* (Paris).

33. *Assam Academy* Review (Guwahati).

34. *Asom Bani* (in A., Guwahati, Daily).

35. *Asia Major* (London, Leipzing).

36. *Asian Perspectives* (Honolulu, U.S.A.).

37. *Asian Studies* (Calcutta).

38. *Asiatic Researches* (Calcutta).

39. *Assam Information* (Guwahati).

40. *Asam Jagriti* (in A., Guwahati).

41. *Assam Quarterly* (Gauhati).

42. *Assam Research Society* (Guwahati).

43. *Assam Review* (Gauhati).

44. *Assam Sahitya Sabha Patrika* (Jorhat) *(in A.).*

45. *Assam Tribune* (Guwahati, Daily).

46. *Athenaeeum* (London).

47. *Bandana (in A.,* Guwahati).

48. *Birth Defects : Original Article Series* (Delhi).

49. *British Jr. Pmy. Soc. Med.*

50. *Bull. Academy of Folklore.*

51. *Bull. Anth. Survey of India* (Calcutta).

52. *Bull. Assam Inst. of Res. for Tribals & Sch. Castes* (TRI, Guwahati).

53. *Bull. Bot. Survey of India* (Calcutta).

54. *Bull. Cal. School of Tropical Medical Science* (Calcutta).

55. *Bull. Cul. Res. Inst. Tribal Welfare* (Calcutta).

56. *Bull. Deccan College Res. Inst.* (Poone).
57. *Bull. de la Societe de Geography* (Germany).
58. *Bull. Deptt. of Anth. Dibrugarh University* (Dibrugarh).
59. *Bull. Deptt. of Anth. Gauhati University* (Guwahati).
60. *Bull. Deptt. of Tribal Culture & Folklore Research, Gau. Uni.* (Guwahati).
61. *Bull. Institute of Traditional Cultures* (Madras).
62. *Bull. Inter. Committee for Urgent Anth. & Eth. Research* (Vienna, Austria).
63. *Bull. of Memoires de la societe Anthropologie de Paris* (Paris).
64. *Bull. St. Mem. de la eco. d'Anthropologie de Paris* (Paris).
65. *Bull. Tribal Research Institute* (Guwahati).
66. *Calcutta Review* (Calcutta).
67. *Campak Jyoti (in A.,* Guwahati).
68. *Chetana (in A.,* Guwahati).
69. *Current Anthropology* (Chicago).
70. *Dainik Asom (in A.,* Guwahati, Daily).
71. *Desh (in B.,* Calcutta, Weekly).
72. *Eastern Anth.* (Lucknow).
73. *Economic and Political Weekly* (Bombay, Mumbai).
74. *Economic Times* (Calcutta).
75. *Educational Review* (Madras).
76. *Ethnologica* (Leipzing).
77. *Ethnomed.* (W. Germany).
78. *Ethnos* (Stockholm).
79. *Folklore* (Calcutta).
80. *Folklore* (London).
81. *Forschungen und Fortschritte* (Berlin).
82. *Gana Chabuk (in B.,* Calcutta).
83. *Geographical Journal* (London).
84. *Geographical Review* (New York).
85. *Geographical Review of India* (Calcutta).
86. *Hemoglobin.*

87. *Heritage of Ancient India.*

88. *Hidyotiolok-Gilolo-gishe* (Middlesex).

89. *Highlander : The Bull. of the CR & SM* (Kohima, Delhi).

90. *Himalaya : Man and Nature* (Delhi).

91. *Hindustan Times* (Delhi, Daily).

92. *Human Biology* (Michigan).

93. *Human Genetik* (Germany).

94. *Human Heredity* (Basal).

95. *Human Science* (Calcutta).

96. *Illustrierte Volkerkunde* (Stuttgart).

97. *Illustrated Weekly of India* (Bombay).

98. *Indian Anthropologist* (Delhi).

99. *Indian Antiquary* (Bombay).

100. *Indian Archaeology : A Review* (Delhi).

101. *Indian Culture.*

102. *ICSSR Research Abstract Quarterly* (Delhi).

103. *Indian Economic & Social History Review.*

104. *Indian Educational Review.*

105. *Indian Folklore* (Calcutta).

106. *Indian Foreign 'Review.*

107. *Indian Geographical Journal* (Madras).

108. *Indian History Congress* (Calcutta).

109. *Indian History Quarterly* (Calcutta).

110. *Indian Jr. Humatol. Blood Transf.*

111. *Indian Jr. of Malarial.*

112. *Indian Jr. of Medical Research (Delhi).*

113. *Indian Jr. of Padiatrics (New Delhi).*

114. *Indian Jr. of Physical Anth. & Human Gen.* (Lucknow).

115. *Ind. Jr. of Politics.*

116. *Ind. Jr. of Psychiatrics* (Delhi).

117. *Ind. Jr. of Social Work* (Bombay).

118. *Ind. Linguistics* (Poone).

119. *Ind. Med. Gaz.* (Delhi).
120. *Ind. Missiological Review* (Madras).
121. *Ind. Sc. Congress* (Calcutta).
122. *Ind. Soc. Hum. Genetics* (Calcutta).
123. *I.S.* (Calcutta).
124. *Indian Studies : Past & Present* (Calcutta).
125. *India Today* (Delhi).
126. *Interdiscipline.*
127. *International Jr. of Anth.*
128. *Iowa*
129. *Janajati (in A.,* Guwahati).
130. *Janasikhya.*
131. *Japanese Jr. of Human Genetics* (Tokyo).
132. *Jhankar* (Guwahati).
133. *Jr. Ancient Indian History* (Calcutta University).
134. *Jr. Anthropological Institute.*
135. *Jr. Anth. Soc. of Bombay.*
136. *Jr. Asiatic Soc. of Bengal* (Calcutta).
137. *Jr. Assam Research Society* (Guwahati).
138. *Jr. Assam Science Society* (Guwahati).
139. *Jr. Assam Phy. India.*
140. *Jr. Bihar & Orissa Research Society.*
141. *Jr. Biosocial Science* (Cambridge).
142. *Jr. Bombay Branch of the Royal Asiatic Society.*
143. *Jr. Bombay Nat. Hist. Soc.*
144. *Jr. Buddhist Text Society* (Calcutta).
145. *Jr. Historical Research* (Dibrugarh University).
146. *Jr. Human Ecology* (Delhi).
147. *Jr. Indian Archipelago and Eastern Asia* (Singapore).
148. *Jr. Indian Art & Industry.*
149. *Jr. Indian Anth. Soc.* (Calcutta).
150. *Jr. Inst. of Great Britain & Ireland* (London).

151. *Jr. Indian History.*

152. *Jr. Ind. Med. Asson.* (Calcutta).

153. *Jr. Music Academy* (Madras).

154. *Jr. North Eastern Council* (Shillong).

155. *Jr. Nagarjun* (Calcutta).

156. *Jr. North East Indian Council of Social Science Research* (Shillong).

157. *Jr. Procg. Asiatic Society of Bengal* (Calcutta).

158. *Jr. & Procg. of the Asiatic Society of Bengal, N.S.* (Calcutta).

159. *Jr. Royal Anth. Inst.* (London).

160. *Jr. Royal Asiatic Soc. of Bengal* (Calcutta).

161. *Jr. Royal Asiatic Soc. of Great Britain & Ireland* (London).

162. *Jr. Royal Asiatic Soc. of Bengal, Letters* (Calcutta).

163. *Jr. Royal Society of Arts* (London).

164. *Jr. Social Research* (Ranchi).

165. *Jr. Siam Society* (Bangkok).

166. *Jr. University of Poona, Humanities Section* (Poone).

167. *Jr. University of Gau. Uni., Science/Arts* (Guwahati).

168. *Jr. Washington Academy of Science* (Washington).

169. *Khada.*

170. *L'anthropologie* (Paris).

170a. *Lik Phan Tai* (Jr. Tai Hist. & Cul. Soc. of Assam).

171. *Lokayata* (Karimganj).

172. *Mainstream* (Delhi).

173. *Man* (London).

174. *Man in Asia* (Ranchi).

175. *Man and Environment.*

176. *Man in India* (Ranchi).

177. *March of India* (Delhi).

178. *Man and Life* (Calcutta).

179. *Man and Nature* (Calcutta).

180. *Marg* (Delhi).

181. *Manushi* (Calicot Univ., Kerala).

182. *Marxist.*
183. *Memoirs of Archaeological Survey of India* (Delhi).
184. *Mezdunarodnyj Kongress Anthropologiceskikhi i Ethnographceskikh Nauk* (Moscow).
185. *Milback Memorial Fund Quarterly* (New York).
186. *Missye Katolickie* (Krakau).
187. *Mitteilungen der Anthropologischen Gesellschaft in Wien* (Horn).
188. *Modern Review* (Calcutta).
189. *Monthly Bull. of the Asiatic Society* (Calcutta).
190. *Murong* (Dibrugarh).
191. *Nagarjun* (Calcutta).
192. *Nature* (London).
193. *New Age.*
194. *NEFA Information* (Shillong).
195. *New Indian Antiquary* (Bombay).
196. *Newsfront* (Guwahati).
197. *News Star* (Guwahati).
198. *Netherland Jr. Agricultural Science Wageninger* (Netherland).
199. *Nigerian Jr. of Biological Sciences, University of IFE* (Nigeria).
200. *Nilachal* (Guwahati).
201. *North Eastern Affairs* (Shillong).
202. *North Eastern Economic Review* (Guwahati).
203. *North Eastern Geographer* (Gauhati University).
204. *North East India Historical Association* (History Deptt., NEHU, Shillong).
205. *North East Politics* (Guwahati).
206. *North Eastern Research Bull.*, Dibrugarh University (Dibrugarh).
207. *NEHU Jr. of Social Science & Humanities* (Shillong).
208. *North Eastern Specturm* (Guwahati).
209. *North East Times* (Guwahati, Daily).
210. *North East Quarterly* (Gauhati University).
211. *Nouvelles Annaies des Voyages* (Paris).
212. *Numismaties International Bull.* (London).

213. *Patsaku* (Sibsagar).

214. *Pine* (Shillong).

215. *Prakash (in A.,* Guwahati).

216. *Prantik.*

217. *Primates.*

218. *Proceedings of the American Oriental Society* (New Haven, Conn.)

219. *Proceedings of the Institute of Advanced Study in Science & Technology* (Guwahati).

220. *Proceedings of National Institute of Science, India* (Calcutta).

221. *Proceedings of NEIHA (History Deptt.,* NEHU, Shillong).

222. *Puratta : Bull. Indian Archaeological Society.*

223. *Purbanchal Prahari (in H.,* Guwahati, Daily).

224. *Quarterly Jr. Crude Drugs Research* (Netherland).

225. *Ramdhenu (in A.,* Guwahati).

226. *Rasan (in A.,* Guwahati).

227. *Resarun* (Itanagar).

228. *Revue des Etudes Islamiques* (Paris).

229. *Ringsang : A Jr. All Assam Tiwa Yuba Chatra Sanmilan* (in A., Jorhat).

230. *Ringchang (in A.,* Jorhat).

231. *Rivista di Anthropologia* (Rome).

232. *Royal Asiatic Society* (Calcutta).

233. *Royal Commission in Opium.*

234. *Sadin (in A.,* Guwahati, Weekly).

235. *Samai Prabaha (in B.,* Guwahati, Daily).

236. *Samatat* (Calcutta).

237. *Sambar (in B.,* Silchar).

238. *Sangeet Natak* (Delhi).

239. *Sankhya : B* (Calcutta).

240. *Santap* (Guwahati).

241. *Saptahik Janambhumi (in A.,* Jorhat, Weekly).

242. *Saptahik Nilachal (in A.,* Guwahati, Weekly).

243. *Satsari* (Guwahati).

244. *Science and Culture* (Calcutta).
245. *Science of Life* (Coimbatore).
246. *Sentinel* (Guwahati, Daily).
247. *Shillong Times* (Shillong, Daily).
248. *Social Action*.
249. *Social Biology* (Oklahoma).
250. *Social Research* (Shillong).
251. *(Jr.) Social Research* (Ranchi).
252. *Social Sciences* (Silchar).
253. *Social Welfare*.
254. *Sociologus* (Berlin).
255. *South Western Jr. of Anth.* (Albuquerque, New Mexico).
256. *Statesman* (Calcutta, Daily).
257. *Stranyi narody Vestaka* (Moscow).
258. *Thinker* (Kohima).
259. *Trans. Amen. Phil Soc.* (Philadelphia).
260. *Trans. Roy. Soc.* (Edinburg).
261. *Tribal Mirror* (Silchar).
262. *T. Riv. de Anthrop.* (Germany).
263. *Triveni Quarterly* (Madras).
264. *United Asia* (Bombay).
265. *Vanyajati* (Delhi).
266. *Wiener Beitrage zur Kulturgeschichte und Linguistik* (Berlin).
267. *Yoginitantra* (Delhi).
268. *Zeitschrift fur Ethnologic* (Stuttgurt).
269. *Zeitschrift fur Morphologie und Anthropologie* (Stuttgurt).

Index

Author Index